P9-AQR-015

LB
1050.455
.R53
1990

156789

DATE DUE			

Lenoir Rhyne College

Reading to Learn in the Content Areas

Reading to Learn in the Content Areas

Judy S. Richardson
VIRGINIA COMMONWEALTH UNIVERSITY

Raymond F. Morgan
OLD DOMINION UNIVERSITY

Lenoir Rhyne College

WADSWORTH PUBLISHING COMPANY

Belmont, California

A Division of Wadsworth, Inc.

CARL A. RUDISILL LIBRARY
LENOIR RHYNE COLLEGE

LB
1050.455
.R53
1990
15-6789
Sept. 1992

Education Editor: Suzanna Brabant
Editorial Assistant: Andrea Varni
Production Editor: Harold Humphrey
Managing Designer: Donna Davis
Print Buyer: Karen Hunt
Text and Cover Designer: Al Burkhardt
Copy Editor: Stephanie Prescott
Illustrator and Art Editor: Mary Burkhardt
Compositor: Graphic Typesetting Service
Signing Representative: Bob Podstepny

© 1990 by Wadsworth, Inc. All rights reserved. No part of
this book may be reproduced, stored in a retrieval system,
or transcribed, in any form or by any means, electronic,
mechanical, photocopying, recording, or otherwise,
without the prior written permission of the publisher,
Wadsworth Publishing Company, Belmont, California
94002, a division of Wadsworth, Inc.

Printed in the United States of America   19

1 2 3 4 5 6 7 8 9 10——94 93 92 91 90

Library of Congress Cataloging in Publication Data
Richardson, Judy S., 1945–
    Reading to learn in the content areas / Judy S.
Richardson, Raymond F. Morgan.
        p.   cm.
        Bibliography: p.
        Includes index.
        ISBN 0-534-11748-1
        1. Content area reading—United States.   I. Morgan,
        Raymond F.   II. Title.
LB1050.455.R53   1990
428.4'0712—dc20   89-35655
                                                   CIP

Contents

Chapter 12   At-Risk Readers   426

Appendices

Preface

Who Should Read This Book?

This textbook is about using reading to learn in content areas. This book is for anyone who wants to know how to excite students to learn by using reading and the other language arts as tools for acquiring that knowledge. We are not writing about learning to read; that is for other authors, other courses. This book is for readers who have never studied about reading, as well as for those who have studied reading methodology but not how to apply that information to subject area learning.

Why Did We Write This Book?

We love to read to learn about new things and to augment our knowledge. We always have, which is why we have been teachers and college professors for twenty plus years each. We believe in what we teach. We have a sense of humor, realizing that all serious learning must be put in perspective. We have ideas about how to share the joy of reading, thinking, and learning with students of all ages. We have ideas to share with you.

These are changing times; these are troubling times for educators. Education in America is being scrutinized and found wanting. Our students are losing out because they are unable to think critically. Their reading seems to be superficial. Our preparation of teachers has been criticized. Some say teachers learn too much content, not enough methodology. Some say just the opposite. Some of our teachers have learned to teach content rather than to teach students the content.

We think we have some solutions to these problems. We believe that if teachers learn to follow a simple instructional framework and to use activities that demonstrate how reading is a tool for learning, many of our classroom problems can be alleviated.

Special Features of This Textbook

1. Reader involvement is important in this textbook. We practice what we preach. We believe that readers need to be prepared to read, need

some assistance to understand, and need to be guided to reflect on their reading. So we ask readers to engage in all three stages as they read each chapter of this textbook. We are also reader-friendly: We introduce new terms with explanation and example; we maintain informality to keep our readers comfortable and interested.

2. We take a balanced approach, providing a realistic and practical treatment of reading and methodology issues, theory, research, and historical perspective. We emphasize the effect of the past on the present; we keep the baby and pour in new bath water.

3. We write to teachers of primary through secondary levels. We look at reading in the classroom as a natural tool for learning, no matter what grade level or content area. We provide examples that show how an activity can work at different levels and in different contents.

4. We select one instructional framework, one which reflects current thought but is uniquely ours: PAR. We explain it, compare it, and stick to it throughout the book. Readers will appreciate this consistency and our constant reference to the framework.

5. We include several unique chapters. Chapter Two discusses the role of affect in reading to learn—a topic crucial to learning but so often neglected. Because comprehension is the crux of reading to learn, we devote three chapters to this area. Chapter Seven features the role of critical thinking and reading. Chapter Eleven applies PAR to the design of appropriate tests for classroom use. Chapter Twelve presents ways to help the at-risk reader in the content classroom. These chapters cover information on the cutting edge of content area instruction.

6. Our organization is considerate of our readers. You can expect to find a graphic overview at the beginning and end of each chapter; you will anticipate the cartoon which starts each chapter. There will always be objectives, a purpose for reading, a one-minute summary (for the streamlined reader), and beginning as well as ending activities. The references will be presented at the end of each chapter so that readers will see them immediately.

7. Visual literacy is featured in this textbook. We use plenty of visuals because visual literacy is the first literacy. One important visual is the chart on pages 536–537, which identifies specific activities for different content areas and grade levels.

8. Our perspective is that of reading and the other language arts working together. Just as we listen and discuss to learn, so do we read and write to learn. We integrate the communicative arts. When an activity is presented, we explore with the reader how that activity facilitates/encourages discussion, reading, and writing. We present information on writing to learn, an exciting area of current study. But we do this in several chapters, not one specific chapter, because our message is integration, not separation of the language arts. A separate chapter on writing might lead readers to think of it separately.

9. Ours is a strategy-based approach. When readers learn about a new activity, they should understand that activity as a strategic means to aid learning. We present the activity as a way to enhance instruction and help teachers see how this activity can be both an instructional strategy and a learner strategy.

Organization of This Book

The first two chapters are foundational. Chapter One discusses research and principles of content area instruction. In it you will discover our philosophy of teaching. Also, a capsule view of the PAR framework for instruction and how it works in two very different types of classrooms is given. Chapter Two explains how to provide for an affective focus for reading to learn.

Chapters Three and Four are the *Preparation* chapters. In them we show why and how to determine and build reader background. Chapters Five and Six are the *Assistance* chapters. In them we show why and how to provide purposeful reading and develop comprehension. Chapter Seven is a *Reflection* chapter because it focuses on why and how to help readers think critically about their reading.

Chapters Eight and Nine, on study skills, and Ten, on vocabulary, teach very important reading and thinking skills. We show how these skills can be used at all phases of the PAR framework.

Chapters Eleven and Twelve are specialized chapters pertaining to the difficult challenges of developing classroom tests and working with students who are at risk of failure.

Instructor's Manual

The *Instructor's Manual* is the most useful one available for this type of textbook. In addition to summarizing each chapter's main points, theories, and strategies, and providing test questions, the *IM* is designed to help instructors teach the class. With it, instructors will be able to: assign group activities for their classes; assign individual activities to students for homework; guide their students in analyzing content area reading material; give multiple choice, fill-in-the-blank, and essay tests; give out assignment sheets to their classes; and display the authors' Graphic Overviews and Vocabulary Inventories for each chapter.

Section I contains Preparation, Assistance, and Reflection activities; teaching tips on how to use the activities; and other resources that may be used in class, such as quotes, suggestions for further reading; book lists; graphic organizers; and vocabulary inventories for each chapter.

Section II provides specific suggestions for teaching each chapter in the text.

In Section III the authors provide a study guide which instructors may use with their classes. It is designed to guide students in analyzing printed matter, such as a chapter in a content area textbook. Questions and answers are provided along with reading aids to help students analyze content area material.

Section IV is a resource list of supplementary aids which teachers may use in teaching content area reading. A list of such things as videotapes which explore content area reading topics, computer programs, films, books, professional and community organizations is provided.

Acknowledgements

We extend our thanks to our colleagues who encouraged us and aided and abetted us in this endeavor, particularly John Oehler and Alan McLeod of Virginia Commonwealth University. A special thanks to Rich Vacca, who unselfishly gave encouragement. We thank Kathryn Davis, who read the manuscript and made helpful suggestions. Thank you to Cynthia Murray, who typed portions of the original draft. We appreciate the comments of our students of the spring semester 1989, who used the textbook in its raw form and provided useful suggestions.

Our writing was a more pleasant experience because of the support and kind assistance of our editor, Suzanna Brabant, and our production editor, Hal Humphrey.

We acknowledge gratefully the contributions of the reviewers, who gave us such excellent suggestions throughout the writing of this textbook: Lois A. Bader, Michigan State University; Timothy Blair, Texas A&M University; Larry Browning, Baylor University; Jim Duggins, San Francisco State University; Lois Exendine, Oklahoma Christian College; Pat Gallagher, San Francisco State University; Doris Jakubek, Central Washington University; Bruce Lloyd, Western Michigan University; Daniel L. Pearce, Northeastern Illinois University; and Katherine Weisendanger, Alfred University.

To my husband, Terry, who has always loved me, no matter how impossible I have been to live with, and to my three sons—Kevin, Darren, and Andrew—who have kept me grounded in reality when I tended to wander too far into the ivory tower.

Judy S. Richardson

To my wife Sue and sons Jon and Chris, who have made the difference in my life.

Raymond F. Morgan

1

Content Reading Instruction: A Principled View and a Framework for Instruction

The teacher, particularly the teacher dedicated to liberal education, must constantly try to look toward the goal of human completeness and back at the natures of his students here and now, ever seeking to understand the former and to assess the capacities of the latter to approach it."

Allan Bloom,
The Closing of the American Mind

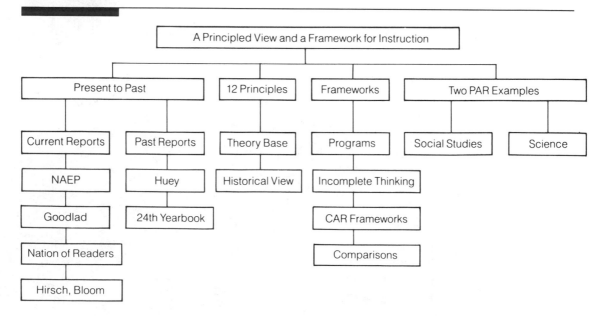

1. Write down three associations you have with the word *reading*. Be ready to share these with your classmates.

2. Below are five recommendations from the report entitled *Becoming a Nation of Readers*. Check those with which you agree. Be ready to explain your choices. After you have read this chapter, you will be asked to reconsider your selections.

   _____ Teachers should devote more time to comprehension instruction.

   _____ Children should spend more time in independent reading.

   _____ Children should spend more time writing.

   _____ Textbooks should contain more adequate explanations of important concepts.

   _____ Schools should cultivate an ethos that supports reading.

3. Below is a list of terms used in this chapter. Some of them may be familiar to you in a general context, but in this chapter they may be used in a different way than you are used to. Rate your knowledge by placing a + in front of those you are sure that you know, a √ in front of those you have some knowledge about, and a 0 in front of those you don't know. Be ready to locate and pay special attention to their meanings when they are presented in the chapter:

   _____ culturally illiterate   _____ assumptive teaching

   _____ real reading   _____ neuropsychology

   _____ overlap factor   _____ program

   _____ visual literacy   _____ two-finger thinking

   _____ primary   _____ framework

   _____ fading

Objectives:

As you read this chapter, focus your attention on the following objectives. You will:

1. become familiar with several recent reports about schooling and how these reports relate information about reading, thinking, and learning to content teaching.

2. become familiar with past recommendations about reading instruction and their relevance for current application in content classrooms.

3. become acquainted with twelve principles for content reading instruction and understand the importance of each.

4. be able to describe the reading framework PAR.

5. be able to apply PAR to two classroom examples.

The Born Loser. Reprinted with permission of United Media Syndicate.

| **Purpose:** | The winning combination for a content teacher is knowing why and knowing how to help students read to learn. In this chapter you will discover what others value as the important "whys" of reading to learn and two examples of "how" teachers might implement reading to learn in their classrooms. |

From Past to Present: A Principled View

Current Reports about Literacy in the Schools

Education in the United States has received a great deal of attention in the past few years. Miklos (1982) provided a synopsis of the National Assessment of Educational Progress (NAEP) data through 1981 which indicates that elementary students are doing well in the reading basics but that older students show declining inferential comprehension skills. The consensus of several NAEP reports published in the mid to late 1980s is that while schools are performing well in teaching the fundamentals of language arts, they lack success in teaching advanced reading and expressive skills. *The Reading Report Card: Progress Toward Excellence in Our Schools* (1985) describes trends in reading achievement over a fourteen-year period for students at ages nine, thirteen and seventeen, using data from four national assessments over a decade. Although young readers seem to be achieving better in this decade than in the last, students also seem to have the most difficulty with higher levels of comprehension. *The Writing Report Card: Writing Achievement in American Schools* (1987) indicates that students today, as measured in fourth, eighth, and eleventh grades, can write to communicate only at a minimal level and have difficulty using critical thinking and organizational skills to express themselves.

By sampling the population at ages twenty-one to twenty-five, Kirsch and Jungeblut (1986) in *Literacy: Profiles of America's Young Adults,* have unveiled a portrait of young adults who can read simple material with facility but cannot understand complex material nearly so well. They conclude that, although the United States may not have a major *illiteracy* problem, we do have a *literacy* problem. *Learning To Be Literate in America* (1987), which summarizes several NAEP surveys, cautions that schools need to help students learn to learn. All of these reports, published within a few years of each other, indicate that students experience difficulty with higher-level reading and writing skills such as critical thinking, drawing inferences, and applying what is read.

Goodlad, in *A Place Called School* (1984), comments on the "sameness and emotional flatness" (p. 100) in American classrooms. He observed students completing exercise after exercise without active involvement. He saw little opportunity for students to use knowledge in an active thinking environment. In his best seller *Cultural Literacy* (1987), Hirsch describes the problem of persons who can "read" but don't understand. He attributes this problem to students' general lack of exposure to "essential" knowledge. Such students, Bloom writes, are culturally illiterate: "To put the matter at its baldest, we live in a thought-world, and the thinking has gone very bad indeed" (p. 17). Bloom further asserts that "our students have lost the practice of and the taste for reading" (p. 62).

In *Becoming a Nation of Readers*, Anderson et al. (1984), after reviewing a large amount of the professional literature on reading, have drawn several conclusions and have recommended ways to improve the reading performance of our students. The authors think that literacy education in the United States needs more emphasis, particularly in the area of reading for meaning. You were asked to consider five of their recommendations at the beginning of this chapter.

Students in the schools are not the only ones who need more effective education, according to recent reports. In *A Nation Prepared* (Branscomb, 1986), better training of prospective and practicing teachers is recommended. According to this report, teachers need to acquire a broader background in the content areas and the liberal arts, and they also need instruction in methodology. The consensus is that teachers need more exposure to information which will enable them to attain—and then teach—higher levels of literacy.

Summarizing the Reports

The implications of current resources are disturbing but relevant to content area teachers as they plan their instruction. It would seem that our students are *not* learning what content teachers would like them to learn. Current reports indicate that our students

1. Are unable to express themselves effectively, in either oral or written form
2. Are unable to make inferences from their reading

3. Are unable to think critically about what they read
4. Cannot process complex written material with facility
5. Do not recognize a large body of content knowledge which experts consider essential for informed readers
6. Do not prefer reading as a way to learn

But content teachers depend on written materials as a primary instructional source. They expect that students in their classes will be able to process that material with facility, inferring and reading critically. They assume that students will be able to express their understanding of the material orally and on tests. They expect that students possess a certain amount of knowledge and have a desire to read to learn. The mismatch between what research reports indicate about our students' literacy profile and what most content teachers assume creates a grave instructional dilemma. In this chapter, we will lay the foundation for solving this dilemma.

Previous Reports about Literacy: The Overlap Factor

Does Anyone Here Hear Huey?

Professional concern with the problem of underprepared readers is not new. Although the preceding reports were all written within the last few decades, their findings are less startling when we realize that others have written about these problems and offered suggestions over a span of many years. For example, here are twenty tenets advocated by Edmund Burke Huey in 1908:

1. The home is the natural place for learning to read.
2. Oral language development should be of primary importance in the early elementary school years, with reading and writing being of secondary importance.
3. Reading should always be accomplished with a purpose in mind that is known by the student.
4. Elementary schools should stop making a fetish of beginning reading instruction.
5. Little reading should go on in the early school years.
6. Work done in phonics should be entirely separate from reading.
7. Reading should not be an "exercise," done as a formal process or end in itself. Rather it should be meaningful, with intrinsic interest and value.
8. Word pronouncing should always be secondary to getting whole-sentence meanings from the very first of reading instruction.
9. Silent reading should be stressed over oral reading.
10. Until speech habits are well formed, oral language development should be stressed over reading activities.

11. Grammar and other analytical study of language should not be taught in the elementary school.
12. Children should learn to read "real literature," i.e., books, papers, records, letters, children's own experiences or thoughts. These should be read as the need arises in a child's life.
13. Children from the first of reading instruction should be taught to read as fast as the nature of the reading materials and their purpose will allow. Speed drills should be practices in getting information efficiently and effectively.
14. Reading matter should be sufficiently interesting to challenge children and thereby discipline their minds for lifelong learning.
15. Children should be taught to group essential meanings, select and gather books for their own purposes, ignore the irrelevant, and contemplate the value of what is read.
16. Study skills such as library skills and note taking should be taught as early as possible in the elementary grades.
17. In high school, adolescents should be given free rein to read widely on subjects of interest. This is preferable to "intensive analytical study of a few texts and authors."
18. In both elementary school and high school, literature of merit should be chosen which transmits the culture and mirrors the values of society. Reading materials, then, will act to train students in what is best and most ideal about adult society.
19. *Real* reading (as described in 1–18 above) should increase rather than decrease in importance among school studies.
20. We should read the classics for the same reason we read in the sciences: for information, for control of nature, and for disciplining the mind.

If readers did not know that Huey's *The Psychology and Pedagogy of Reading* was published in 1908, would they think that these tenets were "modern" in origin? Robinson (1977) claims that Huey's book was recently reprinted because the ideas that Huey discussed are as relevant, or more so, today than they were in 1908. The premises held by both Bloom and Hirsch are very similar to Huey's tenets 17, 18, 19, and 20. Tenets 1 and 2 are almost identical to the first several recommendations in *Becoming a Nation of Readers*. Huey's stress on oral language reminds teachers of the current literature, which stresses the importance of an integrated language arts curriculum, with commensurate attention being given to listening and speaking. Tenets 7, 8, 14, and 15 seem to support the recommendations made in the NAEP studies.

Findings from 1925

In a similar vein, the objectives of *The Twenty-Fourth Yearbook of the National Society for the Study of Education* (1925) were to enable the reader to (1) react intelligently to the world and appreciate it, (2) develop strong reasons to read and a permanent interest in reading, and (3) form attitudes, skills, and habits for the many different reading activities which readers will encounter. To the best of our knowledge, these objectives are still viable for teachers in content area subjects today; they still drive the research and writing of professionals in the reading field. Robinson (1977) calls this contribution of information from the past to current literature the *overlap factor.* Herber (1987) also refers to the concept of overlap in the use of past reports to influence current knowledge. By considering the past as well as the present, content teachers can find much that is relevant to help them plan the best instruction for their students.

Twelve Principles for Content Reading Instruction

We believe that teachers who, because of professional study, are able to articulate their beliefs about teaching are in a good position to improve their instruction. Like all learners, teachers will alter their approaches if they see a need to do so. We, the authors of this textbook, have altered our instruction based on the articulation of our beliefs. In doing so, we have relied on twelve principles which reflect our beliefs in the writing of this book. By sharing these twelve principles with teachers and demonstrating how they are related to content area teaching, we hope to influence teachers to consider instructional changes in their own classrooms.

These principles are grounded in theory. As Wassermann (1987) notes, "the word *theory* has a bad reputation among educational practitioners" (p. 462). Many teachers think that theory has nothing to do with the classroom, perhaps because theory has been presented to them in isolation from the application. But we think that when teachers ask for "what works," they are also asking for the reasons why a particular technique works so that they can replicate it in optimal circumstances. We believe that teachers want more than "a bag of tricks." They know that superimposing an activity on students in the wrong circumstances can be a teaching disaster. Teachers want theory that makes sense because it explains why some activities work well at a particular time in the instruction.

Just as there is really "nothing new under the sun," the principles we present are not necessarily new. They are distinct expressions of what we believe, based on our own study and the study of others. As we present each principle, we recognize the "overlap" factor by introducing some of the history underlying the principle as well as recent insights. We will return to these principles throughout the textbook.

1. The communicative arts work in concert and cannot be separated from education in content subjects.

The traditional communicative arts (sometimes called language arts) are listening, speaking, reading, and writing. In natural circumstances listening and speaking are almost inseparable. Someone talks, someone listens, response and interaction occur. Writers express thoughts as a result of listening, speaking, reading. Readers read writers' thoughts. Kellogg (1972) says that the communicative arts are blocks which build on each other. From a base of experience a child begins to listen, then speak. Lubarsky (1987) notes that much research indicates talking is pivotal in enriching the other language arts. Huey, in tenets 2, 5, 6, and 10, seems to have agreed that listening and speaking are the foundation for reading and writing. One cannot use one communicative art without also using another. This integration occurs with greater facility as children practice each literacy.

Yet, school environments are often artificial rather than natural in their application of informative communication. Usually, teachers talk and students listen so much that little response and interaction can take place. Gagne (1965) noted that learners remember about 10 percent of what they read, 20 percent of what they hear, 30 percent of what they see, and 70 percent of what they say. Who *says* the most in schools? Teachers! We could assume, then, that teachers themselves may be learning the most in their classrooms. It is our premise that students can learn more if they spend more time practicing all of the language arts.

As Kane, a social studies teacher, has expressed it, "Education is premised upon language. . . . You cannot separate language from education. Language not only conveys, it shapes. If you increase or refine the ability of a human being to use language, you literally affect his mind. You cannot deal with any subject on any level without language. Indeed, how you use language affects the subject matter" (1984). In short, listening, speaking, reading, and writing are integral to learning; they are tools for thinking and learning. They enable learning by providing a form in which signals can be transmitted to and from the brain. They are demonstrations of learning. Thus, the communicative arts are *essential* to teaching content area subjects, and teachers will want to encourage students' use of all the communicative arts as effective thinking and learning tools. As we present activities, we will often identify how they facilitate the use of language to enhance content learning. We will discuss the role of writing, in particular, in many chapters of this textbook.

2. Literacy includes not only the traditional communicative arts but also visual literacy.

Sometimes communication occurs most easily through nonverbal, visual literacy. For instance, a picture of a pie divided into pieces may convey the concept of fractions more effectively than a page of expla-

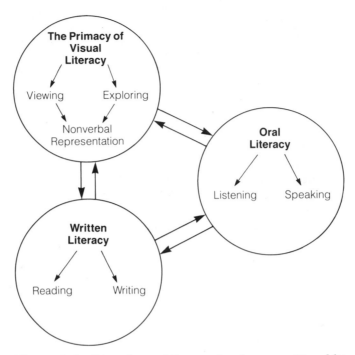

Figure 1.1. Stage three of literacy development: Visual literacy and its interactive relationship with the oral and written languages.
From Sinatra, R., *Visual Literacy Connections to Thinking, Reading and Writing*, 1986. Courtesy of Charles C. Thomas, Publisher, Springfield, Illinois.

nation. Sinatra (1986) calls visual literacy the first and most pervasive literacy. Sinatra's model of literacy development indicates the interactive relationship of visual literacy with the oral and written literacies (see Figure 1.1).

Visual literacy, which conveys emotion through such means as illustration, art, and music, precedes listening and builds experiences necessary to thinking and learning. Visual literacy is impressionistic and action-oriented; the scribbles which young children call writing are a manifestation of visual literacy. Teachers discover that when they make use of visual aids such as graphs and pictures, they ensure a concomitant and reinforcing approach for many and an alternative for the learner who excels in visual but not traditional literacy. Because visual literacy has implications for the affective aspects of instruction, it will be discussed further in chapter 2. In addition, several activities presented in this book capitalize on visual literacy.

3. **The content of a subject should dominate the instructional focus, and the communicative arts should permeate the instruction.**

Subject matter and language are inextricably bound. But the main concern for the subject teacher is teaching the content. Nila Banton Smith (1965) reminds readers that the term "primer" did not originally mean "first book to read," as it does today, but referred to the contents of a book as being *primary*, or foremost. Today, the content of a subject is still primary for the teacher, as it should be. But using the communicative arts as a major learning tool creates a very positive combination for enhancing critical thinking and learning. For example, Feathers and Smith (1987) report an observational study of content instruction in elementary and secondary classrooms. Although content predominated instruction at both levels, content was presented differently in the different grades. Secondary teachers transmitted content predominately through lectures or text reading. Elementary teachers infused content with more of the communicative arts. The latter method was seen to be more effective.

4. Reading for meaning is a highly individualized process influenced by the reader's personal store of experiences and knowledge.

Even though many may share the same experience, read the same book, or hear the same lecture, the thinking and learning which occurs from individual to individual will be different because of what each brings to the experience. Persons relate to a common body of knowledge in different ways because of what they already know—or don't know. For example, converting to the metric system will probably be more difficult for those learners who were taught measurements in terms of inches, feet, and miles instead of centimeters, meters, and kilometers. Readers who are not familiar with Tennyson's poem, "The Charge of the Light Brigade" would probably think that the phrase *Charge of the Right Frigate* is a strange choice of words for a headline accompanying an article on naval buildup; they would not see the headline as a play on words. If learners cannot find relevance in a subject, they are likely to ignore it. Teachers, then, must become aware of what previous knowledge and experiences their students possess about a particular concept in content subjects. They can use this information to generate assisted reading which is directed, meaningful, and highly personalized.

5. The most effective thinking and learning occurs when critical reading is encouraged.

The act of reading should provoke thought. Real reading is an active, thinking-related process. As soon as readers can pay more attention to the meaning of words than to the recognition of them, they can begin to think and learn about the material itself rather than about reading the material. One of the messages of the reports mentioned earlier in this chapter is that students lack critical thinking skills. It is not that students are incapable of critical thinking; they just have not had the practice. By using the tools of literacy and being immersed in a thinking climate, students can practice. Raths and Wasserman (1986) believe that teachers who provide students with extensive practice in thinking will train thinkers. Readers must be challenged to think critically about what they read. Where only "lower-order" exercises are provided, thinking deficits will occur (Wassermann, 1987).

The concern for teaching critical reading is not new. Robinson (1977) cites Keagy, a key reading figure in the late 1700s who emphasized that thinking during reading is the crucial element in the act of reading. Following Keagy in the late 1800s, Horace Mann and others advocated a thinking approach to reading instruction. This emphasis has been fairly consistent in the literature, with proponents such as Nila Banton Smith, Russell Stauffer, and, more recently, Frank Smith. Most authorities agree, and have for a long time, that critical reading leads to effective thinking and learning. The problem seems to be "that most teachers do not teach these skills" (Beyer, 1984). We speculate that teachers feel constrained by an overload of prescribed curriculum goals which seem to stress lower-level reading comprehension. Hence students are being taught to be regurgitators of information rather than thinkers, reasoners, and problem solvers. Chapter 7 of this textbook not only defines critical thinking, it also provides concrete examples of ways to teach critical thinking in all content area subjects.

5a. Literal reading is a necessary first step toward critical reading.

This subprinciple is included so that readers of this textbook do not mistake the authors' emphasis on critical reading as a disregard for factual reading. A reader must already understand material at a factual level and be able to interpret what is read before critical reading can occur. It is probably because teachers realize the necessity of literal reading that so much classroom time is spent on literal recall of reading material, to the detriment of higher-level thinking and reading comprehension.

Piaget (1952) observed that children need to form concrete associations before they form concepts. Descriptions of comprehension levels include a literal or factual level which precedes the critical level. Our principle 3 assumes a store of experience *and* knowledge that a reader must have before reading for learning and thinking can begin. Persons cannot think about nothing; there must be a base for thinking and learning. However, we do think that too much emphasis is placed on knowing facts and not enough on knowing when and how to use them to learn. Teachers need to design content lessons in which the facts have a place in the larger scheme of thinking and learning.

6. Meaningful reading about content subjects is a lifetime experience which should start early and continue throughout life.

Learning content material is part of most school curricula from first grade on. Some schools even introduce science, math, and social studies material in kindergarten. *The Weekly Reader*, that ubiquitous early grades newspaper, contains content material. Because most children are still learning to read in the early grades, reading to learn may not be employed as often as visualizing, listening, and speaking to learn. However, as a result of current study on how literacy emerges, reading and writing to learn are being advocated with more frequency for children in early grades.

There is really nothing new about this principle. Just as Huey stressed "real reading" (tenet 19), so Bloom (1987) wishes that the classics were introduced much earlier in children's lives. Hirsch (1987) says that "the single most effective step would be to shift the reading materials used in kindergarten through eighth grade to a much stronger base in factual information and traditional lore" (p. 140). Teachers need only peruse their curriculum guides to see objectives for content instruction at every grade level. No matter what the communicative arts medium, we must begin early to teach thinking and learning in content area subjects.

By the same reasoning, learning about content subjects continues far past high school. The need to think about and apply content information faces learners daily as they listen to and watch the television, read the newspaper, and write to communicate. The basic difference in this learning is that the learner can structure the environment and choose what to learn and what to avoid. The adults whom teachers meet daily will attest that they continue to enjoy and learn about topics which interested them most in school. The topics that remain interesting are most often those which were best understood and with which the adults were most successful. And so the cycle continues. Teachers want students to learn their content subjects, and students are stimulated to learn more when they are successful in their learning. We develop lifelong learners by introducing them to reading for learning's sake at an early age.

7. Reading should be a pleasurable experience.

Reading in content subjects should be satisfying. Reading for thinking and learning will most likely not even happen if the reader does not perceive reading to learn as a pleasurable experience. People avoid doing what is not interesting or rewarding in some personal way. Students avoid reading in content subjects if they find it uninteresting and unrewarding. The authors believe that there should be a natural flow between students' attitudes and reading habits. Sinatra (1986, p. 142) expresses it this way: "The climate should be based on a meaningful need to know in which the learning of the 'three Rs' is bound to the learning of the natural and artistic world and in which eagerness to know forms the emotional basis of the classroom learning atmosphere." Huey, too, believed that interest generates reading rewards (see tenet 17). Students, like everyone else, want to satisfy a need for feeling good. When left to their own devices, children will often select content trade books to read just as readily as fiction. We have noted that younger children are even more likely to read for information than are older ones. If teachers can help by providing a beneficial reading environment in content subjects, learning will improve. Because we think and feel that this principle is so important, we have devoted an entire chapter to the affective dimension of reading in the content areas.

8. Content area reading requires the interaction of the reader, the text, the teacher, and the environment.

Successful reading depends on numerous factors. The reader's store of knowledge and experience will certainly contribute, as well as the reader's attitude toward reading. The appeal of the reading material and the enthusiasm of the teachers also play a role. Novak and Gowin (1984) describe this interaction in the following way: "It is the teacher's obligation to set the agenda and decide what knowledge might be considered and in what sequence. . . . The learner must choose to learn; learning is a responsibility that cannot be shared. The curriculum comprises the knowledge, skills, and values of the educative process (p. 6)."

A text which is optimal for one student or set of students will not be optimal for another. While there are some factors which make a text very readable, that does not mean that all readers would be equally willing and able to read it. For more specific information on this principle, the reader is referred to chapters 2 and 5.

9. Reading begets reading.

Pleasurable feelings about reading will lead to successful reading, and to more reading. After listing "twelve easy ways to make learning to read difficult," Frank Smith (1973) provides one difficult way to make reading easy: provide students with a lot of reading. The more students observe teachers and parents reading, the more they will want to try it. The more students hear parents and teachers read to them, the more they will want to try it. In his introduction to *The Princess Bride*, William Goldman tells how he hated to read until the age of ten. Then, while recuperating from pneumonia, his father read him *The Princess Bride*. As a result, Goldman became a voracious reader.

Young children are fond of saying "monkeys always look." While teachers do not necessarily want monkeys in their classrooms, they'd like to have students who imitate good reading habits. This cannot happen simply because teachers tell, or even implore, students to read. However, it will happen through modeling. For instance, one of the authors observed secondary students' behavior in school libraries. When teachers took students to the library to read, but then sat down to grade papers, students did not read but talked. When teachers talked to each other, students did not read but talked. When teachers also read, students read. Modeling can also take place when teachers share a newspaper article on the content subject or a book they've read that relates to the topic at hand. Modeling is a form of visual literacy. When teachers model reading visually, they are using one communicative art to promote another. The double whammy really works!

Good readers tend to read because it gives them pleasure and because they do it well; consequently they get practice in reading and thus get better at it. Poor readers tend to avoid reading because it is not easy, pleasurable, or satisfying. In a series of questionnaires administered over a four-year period to incoming college students, one of the authors found a consistent correlation between those who chose not to read and those who perceived that they had poor reading and study habits. Teachers need to provide many opportunities for successful reading in their content classrooms.

10. Ultimately, reading efficiently and effectively is the student's responsibility. Initially, however, it is the teacher's responsibility to instruct students in how to read efficiently and effectively. Between the two roles, a transition is necessary.

Dependent readers wait for the teacher to tell them what the word is, what the right answer is, and what to do next. Such readers are crippled. When they need to function independently, they will not know how. Teachers who abandon the textbook because it seems too hard for their students do their students no favor. Teachers who give students all the answers or hand out the notes already organized in the teacher's style have bypassed opportunities for the students to learn how to find answers or to take notes. Kane, the high school social studies teacher quoted earlier, is concerned that high school is a place where students avoid responsibility. He thinks that schools perpetuate an environment where students are excused from learning. (His essay is included in the Appendices.) There is an old saying which applies here: Give a man a fish and you feed him one meal; teach a man to fish and he can feed himself forever.

Herber and Nelson-Herber (1987) agree that many students are dependent learners but stress that they do not have to remain so. However, "students should not be expected to become independent learners independently" (p. 584). It is not fair to expect that students can use communicative arts to think and learn without the benefit of instruction. No matter what the grade level or content subject, teachers can assist students in the transfer to responsibility when they balance the students' level of proficiency and the content to be studied. "Fading" is a term currently in use to describe this change from dependence to independence (Moore et al., 1986). Singer and Donlan (1985) have called it "phasing out the teacher and phasing in the student." Early elementary level children can become responsible just as high schoolers can. However, before they can be responsible for their own thinking and learning, students need to be taught a system which makes sense and which they can readily apply by themselves. PAR, explained at the end of this chapter and used as the basis for this textbook, is such a system. PAR enables the teacher to show students how to become responsible learners. First, the teacher models PAR and then gradually weans students to independent use of PAR. The two examples described at the end of this chapter illustrate such independent learning.

11. Assumptive teaching can be a detriment to content area teachers.

Herber (1978) has used the term "assumptive teaching" to describe what teachers do when they unconsciously take for granted that students know something that the students really don't know. Teachers do make assumptions about students. They may assume that students will appreciate poetry and enjoy mathematics. They may assume that students understand what war is. Teachers often assume that students know how to read, will use reading to learn, and have the motivation and interest to do so. They may picture all students as having plenty of reading resources and supportive home environments. Unfortunately, these assumptions are not always true.

Some assumptive teaching is necessary. Teachers cannot "start all over again" every year in a content subject. They may need to assume that a particular skill or concept was covered the year before. And yet, if a teacher assumes too much about a student's knowledge or frame of mind, that "teacher often behaves as though the persons being taught already know what is being taught" (Herber, 1978). Finding the point of familiarity with a concept and guiding the students forward is crucial. Content area teachers should be very clear about what they are assuming their students already know. Further, they should be sure that their assumptions are fair. By learning to consistently determine and build student background, teachers will be able to avoid unfair assumptive teaching.

12. The study of content area reading can be enhanced by studies made by professionals in related fields.

The influence in reading of psychologists such as Edward Thorndike, David Ausubel, and Frank Smith has helped reading professionals understand how students learn and apply learning strategies to reading. Similarly, linguists such as Leonard Bloomfield, C.C. Fries, and Noam Chomsky have enriched the study of reading by calling attention to factors about language to which readers must attend. Developmental psychologists such as Jean Piaget, Lawrence Kohlberg, Eric Erikson, and Robert Havighurst have been enormously influential in informing teachers about the chronological and mental ages at which children can be taught certain moral, social, and intellectual constructs. To date, a predominant influence has been from the differential psychologists, who advocate that learning equals changes in behavior. The influence of developmental psychologists and linguists has placed more emphasis on changes in the meaning of experience.

Given recent research and findings about the brain, we should also begin to look for educational implications which can inform teachers about not only change in behavior and the meaning of experience but also the role of the brain in learning. Chall and Mirsky, editors of *Education and the Brain*, predicted that the 1980s would "bring a fruitful collaboration between neuroscientists and educators" (p. 376). Neuropsychology may offer teachers much insight about teaching reading in content subjects. If the influence is anything like that of the psycholinguists during the 1970s, the teaching of reading will be powerfully redirected throughout the 1990s. Neuropsychology as it applies to affective teaching will be discussed in chapter 2.

Throughout this textbook, we will share our study of related fields as we think the information enhances content reading instruction. For example, we have drawn upon studies of critical thinking and applied them to the teaching of content reading. We have also discussed studies which integrate knowledge about the writing process and teaching in the content areas. Where applicable, we offer information about neuropsychology and content reading instruction.

A Framework for Content Reading Instruction

Programs for Learning

Hart (1983) believes that humans acquire and activate "programs" to learn. He defines a program as "a fairly fixed sequence of steps to achieve some goal" (p. 6). Programs are used consistently as a reliable way for a person to accomplish an objective. A person usually follows a sequence of steps in starting a car; another person might reorder the steps but still performs the same actions to start the car. Using a word processing program is another example. Although WordPerfect and Bank Street Writer are different programs and offer different levels of word processing, the basic features and steps for use are similar: both programs will allow the user to record data, revise data, and save and print the product.

Any program becomes fairly automatic with practice. As the steps are learned and applied with facility, concentration on the final goal becomes most important. After a person learns to start a car, for example, the act of starting it is relegated to a position of lesser importance than driving to a destination. After a person learns the word processing program, writing the material is what becomes important, not the steps to facilitate the writing. Knowing the program allows a shift to accomplishing the goal in the most efficient manner.

Similarly, school children acquire programs which aid their learning. For example, a learner may acquire a program to identify the characteristics of a story. Once the program is learned and applied to the reading of new stories, the learner can focus on the theme, plot, and characters in stories. Knowing these characteristics facilitates the learner's appreciation of the story. To help students realize the steps they should follow to learn the content information, teachers can use activities as instructional tools. By consistently using specific steps that are relayed by the activities, students learn a strategy which can be used independently of the teacher. A fixed sequence of steps is applied to achieve the goal: students learning content material. When teachers use activities which demonstrate an effective instructional program, students acquire strategies for learning.

Incomplete Thinking

Optimal programs include enough steps to accomplish the goal. "Two-finger thinking," as explained by de Bono (1976), is often unsatisfactory. For example, if one has a lot of time and needs only to type a few pages, then perhaps two-finger typing will do. However, the purpose of typing is usually to save time, so it is preferable to take the time initially to learn to type well and thereby save time later. Two-finger thinking is also incomplete; the learner is missing steps crucial to achieving the learning goal. Many readers may be victims of such incomplete thinking if they try to use an incomplete program: just turning pages is a way of seeing material, but it is not necessarily a way of comprehending.

Similarly, teachers who have learned to rely only on the teacher's manual for their instructional resources are victims of incomplete thinking. Houseman (1987) experienced great difficulty in trying to teach social studies to fourth graders until she completed a content reading course and discovered new ideas. What Houseman learned enabled her to expand her program for teaching social studies. She reports a very positive change in her own and her students' receptiveness to social studies after using her newfound knowledge.

Complete Thinking: Frameworks

Defining a Framework

A framework is the arrangement of the basic parts of something. It is an organized plan condensed to a series of steps, usually represented by key words. A framework represents a program because it suggests how to do something. Because a framework is a model for completing a task, it must be complete. All pertinent steps must be identified. Hence, a framework for instruction should be an aid to thinking and learning and a way to activate student programs for learning. An instructional framework which identifies successful components of a content lesson would facilitate a relationship between reading, thinking, and learning.

Characteristics of a Framework

Frameworks for content reading instruction are becoming increasingly popular (Herber, 1978; Singer and Donlan, 1985; Vaughan and Estes, 1986). We propose that this is so because these frameworks represent programs which are complete and flexible as well as easily implemented by teachers. They are explanations or "how-to's" of the instructional process; they guide the learning process. The most popular content reading frameworks include the same three basic assumptions: (1) the learner must be ready to learn, and the teacher must prepare the learner; (2) the learner must be guided through the learning, so the teacher must develop comprehension; (3) the learner should review what was learned, so the teacher must provide a comprehension check. If these basic steps are repeated in the instructional sequence consistently, the learner begins to use them independently of the teacher, in a self-instructional manner.

It does not matter what key words are used in a framework, as long as they stimulate recall of the program represented by the framework. Table 1.1 shows a comparison of four content area reading (CAR) frameworks, including ours: Preparation, Assistance, Reflection (PAR). Herber's instructional framework (IF) is considered to be the first CAR framework. Singer and Donlan's modification of the directed reading activity (DRA) for content instruction has components similar to ARC (anticipation, realization, contemplation) and to PAR. All four frameworks have similar steps. Rosenshine and Stevens (1984) also found these same basic steps in the instructional sequences they studied.

PAR—A Framework for Instruction

PAR, which stands for Preparation, Assistance, and Reflection, is a framework for content reading instruction. Within the Preparation step, teachers need to determine and build students' background. Within the Assistance step, teachers provide purposeful, directed reading experiences. Within the Reflection step, teachers use the material which was read to provide extension, enrichment, and critical thinking opportunities. Only at this step can teachers determine whether students have comprehended the material. After teachers have consistently modeled the PAR steps, students will begin to adopt the steps as they read on

TABLE 1.1 *A Comparison of Content Area Reading (CAR) Frameworks*

IF	DRA	ARC	PAR
Herber 1978	Singer & Donlan 1985	Vaughan & Estes 1986	Richardson & Morgan 1990

Preparation
  Motivate
  Provide background
  Develop purposes, anticipation
  Provide direction
  Develop language
Guidance
  Develop reading guides
  Develop reasoning guides
	Determine background
	
	Build background
		Anticipation	Preparation
			  Determine background
			  Build background

	Prequestion and read
	
	Review actively
		Realization	Assistance
			  Read purposefully
			  Develop comprehension

Independence	Provide extension	Contemplation	Reflection
			  Provide extension, critical thinking
			  Determine comprehension

their own. Each step will be discussed in greater depth, with suggested activities and examples, in the other chapters of this book. Later in this chapter are two examples of content lesson units that apply a PAR framework.

Special Features of PAR

PAR is a new acronym, but it represents the basic sequence of steps included in other content instructional frameworks. The acronym PAR was coined to develop a deliberate association with the golf term *par*, which means to complete a hole of golf taking only an allotted number of strokes but not exceeding the limit. Golfers usually feel very pleased that they've played a good game if they achieve par for the course. By achieving par, they have reduced their *handicap*. We want teachers to be satisfied with their instruction for *their* courses in the same way. In the words of one teacher we know, "The purpose of PAR is to cut down on your students' handicaps!"

PAR includes three basic steps which are applicable in any content area and at any grade level. It illustrates the instructional steps that a

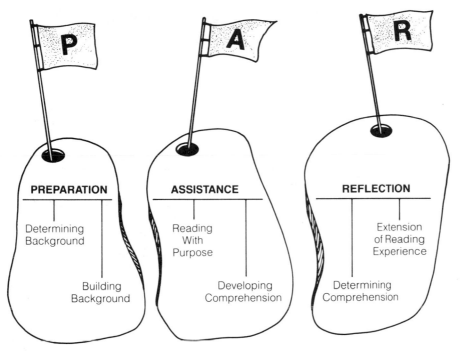

Figure 1.2.
Developed by Dawn Bubb and Walter Richards.

teacher and a learner can follow to ensure maximum thinking and learning from the reading experience. PAR works for both narrative and expository material. The basic terms—Preparation, Assistance, Reflection—are already part of the professional language of teachers. But the terms are combined in a new way to create an acronym that we hope will form a special association for content teachers. Just as achieving par is an aspiration of many golfers, we hope that PAR will inspire teachers to successfully follow the three steps of Preparation, Assistance, and Reflection that promote solid instruction and learning.

PAR in Action: Two Examples

Following are two demonstrations of how PAR might be applied by teachers at two grade levels and in two different content areas. These are "big picture" examples that show how teachers might use PAR in their content instruction. The specific activities worked for the teachers who selected them; others might work better for you. The rationale and directions for constructing these activities will be found in succeeding chapters.

Example 1: PAR for a Tenth-Grade Social Studies Teacher

A tenth-grade social studies teacher wanted to introduce some value thinking on the topic of capital punishment. Fortunately, an abundance of material is available on this topic. This teacher preferred to rely on a short, charged reading rather than a textbook entry. He selected a letter written in February 1968 by Caryl Chessman, a San Quentin death row inmate, to California's governor, Edmund Brown.

Chessman's letter is challenging material, stylistically sophisticated and enriched with vocabulary usually beyond the reading experiences of tenth-grade students. The teacher considered the material carefully for its appropriateness by using a checklist (see chapter 3). The teacher decided that, although the letter would be hard for his students to read, as measured by a readability formula, it would nevertheless be very useful for his and his students' purposes.

How would this teacher instruct using this material? What is important to teach? Keeping the content subject foremost is a content teacher's job. So the teacher studied the selected letter carefully to see what major concepts he wanted to teach. He saw that the letter is very well written and so might serve as a model for writing persuasive letters. He saw that Chessman's rich vocabulary might serve as a model for teaching word meanings and associations. He saw that he could teach a history lesson as well, since this letter was written in 1968 and might illustrate that the more things change, the more they stay the same. Chessman's references to the interdependence of the three branches of government in making decisions about capital punishment could also help the teacher to explain the system of government in the United States. A lesson on social systems in the United States was also possible.

However, the teacher probably could not teach all of this to his students unless he used this material for far longer than he originally intended. He considered what he knew about his students. They would read challenging material thoughtfully and eagerly if they enjoyed it and saw a need for the lesson. But he had noticed that they seemed vague about how their government is organized into three branches. Value thinking about capital punishment was his primary reason for using this letter. He decided on the following major goals:

1. To present the topic of capital punishment by providing one very compelling viewpoint and provoking discussion
2. To introduce how the U.S. government is divided into three branches and how that organizational system allows for laws about capital punishment to be made and changed

Because of space limitations, we cannot provide the teacher's lesson, complete with dialogue. What can be shown is how the reading activities this teacher selected enhanced the lesson.

The first step in PAR is Preparation, which includes determining students' background and building on this background. This teacher had already determined some background as he considered what he knew about his students' knowledge of government and their reading habits. Next, he determined and built background using PreP (Langer, 1982, p. 154), which will be explained in chapter 3. Part one of PreP is "Initial Associations" with concepts. He asked his students to tell him all of the facts they knew about capital punishment and the associations the term brought to mind. He was pleasantly surprised to discover that his students already knew a great deal, as the list he compiled illustrates.

Execution	Fried
Pain	Appeal
Murder	Protest
Jail	Death row
Crime	Mecklenburg boys
Controversial	Briley brothers
Electric chair	Stay of execution

Part two of PreP calls for reflecting on the initial associations, so he asked what made them think of a particular response. In part three of PreP, which covers reformulation of knowledge, students were asked whether they had gained any new ideas about capital punishment. By using these steps, he helped the students to build their own background of information.

By considering their responses, the teacher could see that his students had at least a partial understanding of the information presented in the Chessman letter. Since the only word association they gave which related at all to the administrative structure was "appeal," he was reassured that his goal of teaching about the administrative structure was important for this lesson. Using some of the responses his students gave and relying on vocabulary in Chessman's letter which illustrated his goals, he then designed a "graphic organizer" (described in chapter 4), which is a visual means of providing further background for the reading assignment. He presented it to the class and explained the three major categories it covers. He did not define unknown words but asked his students to notice how those words were used in the letter. Activity 1.1 illustrates this teacher's graphic organizer for this lesson.

The second step in PAR is Assistance. To assist his students' reading, the teacher first explained that Chessman was a death row prisoner when he wrote his letter about capital punishment to Governor Brown. He said that when he read the letter, he was emotionally swayed and found himself reacting to capital punishment in a new way. He hoped that the letter would have an impact on them too. To establish a purpose for reading, he suggested that, as they read, they refer to the list

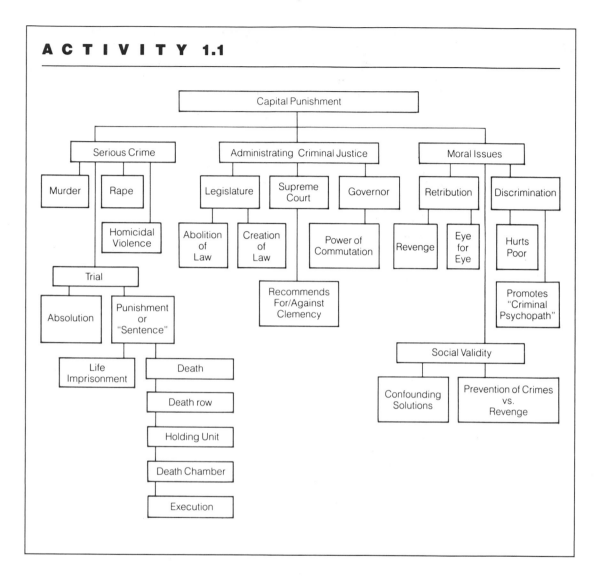

A C T I V I T Y 1.1

of terms they had generated earlier and compare it to terms Chessman used. He also encouraged them to refer often to the graphic organizer as they read what Chessman wrote about the three branches of government. He made sure that copies of their terms and the organizer were available.

When students finished reading, the teacher developed comprehension with a discussion in which they compared their list of terms to Chessman's terms. They then made a second, expanded list of terms about capital punishment. He asked them to explain why they thought

A C T I V I T Y 1.2

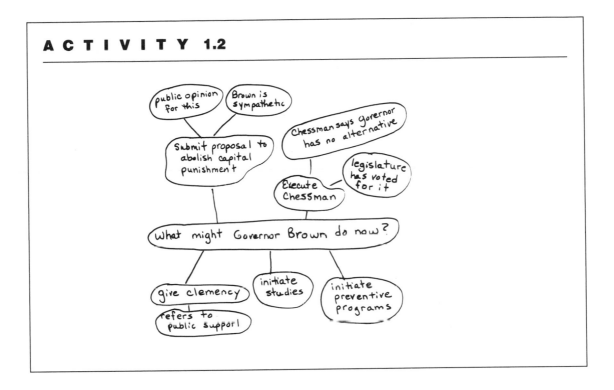

he had constructed the graphic organizer as he did. To further develop their comprehension, he "mapped" their responses to this question: What might Governor Brown do now? The map is found in Activity 1.2. (For more information about mapping, see chapter 6.)

The third step in PAR is Reflection. To enrich and extend their thinking, the teacher asked students to form small groups and map responses to these questions: How are decisions made about capital punishment? Is capital punishment justified? He asked students to be on the lookout during the next week for any information on capital punishment and on the administrative procedures related to it. He also invited a judge to talk to the class. As a critical thinking activity, he used the critical thinking paradigm explained in chapter 7 of this textbook. Students were encouraged to draw on all of the resources they had collected as well as their maps, Chessman's letter, and the talk given by the judge.

As a last Reflection activity, the teacher determined his students' comprehension. If they could demonstrate what they had learned, he would know that he could continue to the next topic. He chose a non-traditional test format. (For more information about designing tests, see chapter 11). Capitalizing on his activities, he presented the same graphic organizer, but with some gaps. (See Activity 1.3.)

A C T I V I T Y   1.3

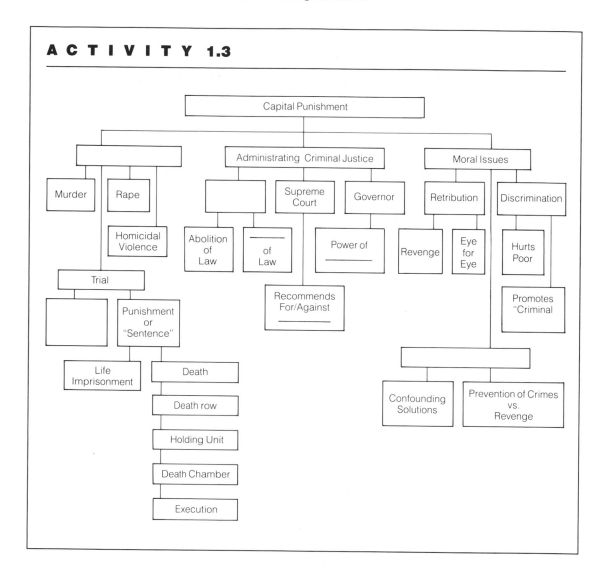

He asked students to fill in the gaps and explain their choices. Then he asked them to answer a question they had previously mapped: How are decisions made about capital punishment? They were to write an essay in which they included at least three ways decisions are made. Students could use their maps as references. Each paragraph was to include one way and supporting information for that way. In a fourth paragraph they were to argue two points of view about capital punishment.

Example 2: PAR in a Primary Science Lesson

A primary teacher wished to set up an aquarium in her classroom so the children could observe goldfish and begin to realize how an ecosystem operates. She wanted the children to help select the type of goldfish for the aquarium and to learn how to take care of them. To accomplish this, she preferred to use written material as the source of information, rather than presenting them with her own knowledge, because she believed that her students needed to practice reading for the purpose of learning and would find discovery more interesting than lecture.

To find the appropriate materials, she consulted the school media specialist, who suggested several informational books written for young audiences. By selecting several books, the teacher prepared her readers because they were able to browse in books that matched their reading and interest levels to gather ideas before any instruction began. The teacher placed all of the books on classroom shelves, and she selected *All About Goldfish* (Cooper, 1976) to read aloud to her class. She decided on Cooper's book because it provides a lot of information about goldfish and is divided into short sections, each of which she could read in a time frame which matched her students' attention span. By using the checklist discussed in chapter 3, she was satisfied that *All About Goldfish* was a suitable resource.

Next, she formulated her goals and objectives. The following were her overall goals:

1. Children will learn about an ecosystem.
2. By reading about goldfish, children will make informed choices about providing the best environment for them.

Her objectives were as follows:

1. Children will select from many kinds of goldfish the kind they want to raise.
2. Children will identify the materials needed to equip the aquarium.
3. Children will learn what goldfish need to live and will monitor their goldfish for several months.

The first step in PAR is Preparation. To determine what the children already knew, the teacher asked them to tell her about goldfish. As they answered, she wrote their responses on the board. They said:

They are gold.	Sometimes they die.
They swim.	They have to live in water.
They are good pets.	They have fins.

The teacher was satisfied that her class already had some knowledge and even firsthand experience with goldfish, so she did not have

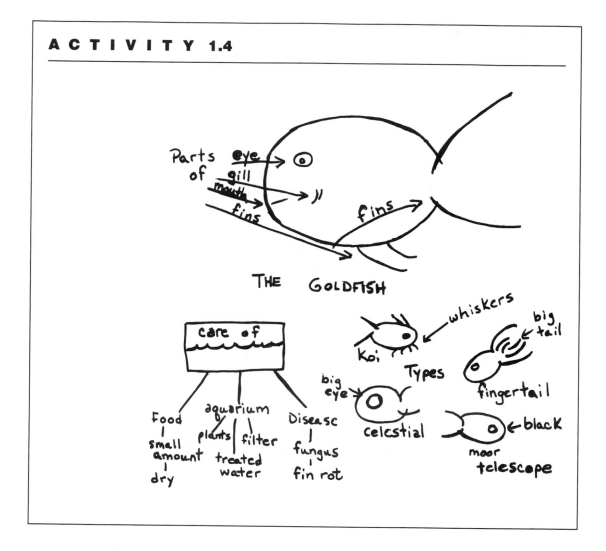

to "start from scratch" in her instruction. She began to build background by using their responses in the construction of a graphic organizer. Activity 1.4 illustrates her graphic organizer, which is very different from the one shown for tenth graders but which is suitable for primary children.

When she showed the graphic organizer to the children, she used their list of sentences as a base for her explanation. "You said that goldfish are gold, but there are fish in the goldfish family of a different color. You said that goldfish have fins; different goldfish have differently shaped fins."

Next, she guided students' listening behavior as she assisted them in their learning. (Chapter 12 describes such listening guidelines.) She told the children to listen carefully for all of the new information they heard about goldfish as she read one section of *All About Goldfish* to them. Such a statement sets a purpose for listening. After reading to them, she asked them to tell her the new information they heard. She wrote their responses on the board. Then she read the list, told them to listen again, and reread the section of the book. The children then revised their list. Such an activity develops comprehension. Now the students were ready to decide what type of goldfish to purchase. They selected Black Moor Telescopes! They planned what would go in the aquarium and prepared it twenty-four hours in advance so the environment would be right for the goldfish.

For Reflection, this teacher encouraged her students to leaf through the many books on goldfish and add to their knowledge. They collected information, writing it down or asking another student or the teacher to record facts. The children used their recordings to organize and write a group report entitled "An Ecosystem for Fish." The teacher guided their writing by encouraging students to plan, draft, and revise their report. This teacher did not determine comprehension by testing. Her best evidence of their learning came when they discovered that their fish had white spots on their fins. They researched this problem to find out about fin rot and its treatment. When they cured their fish, the teacher knew that they had learned.

Even though many primary children have not yet learned to read with proficiency, PAR is applicable when reading is viewed in a total communicative arts perspective. The teacher may be the main reader, but for the students, listening, discussion and comprehension will take the place of actual reading. Even at the high-school level, reading should not be isolated from the other communicative arts. Listening activities are often a welcome change for all students.

What's Next? The Organization of This Textbook

The themes underlying the twelve principles presented in this chapter will surface in every chapter. Chapters 1 and 2 are foundation chapters; they present the basic theory and rationale for the approach used in this text. In chapter 2, principles 7, 9, and 12 guide the discussion; the focus is on reading and affect because, without a positive attitude about reading, thinking and learning are hard to achieve. In chapter 3, principle 8 guides the discussion about ways to match students and reading material.

Chapters 3 through 7 are methodology chapters. Each of these chapters highlights a step in PAR. Applications for teachers are provided as well as examples from several content areas and grade levels. Chapters 8 through 12 are application chapters. Specific strategies and activities are provided. The principles are an integral part of the discussion in all of these chapters.

In each of our chapters, we employ the PAR steps by asking our readers to *Prepare* themselves to read and then to *Assist* as well as *Reflect* on their comprehension. To aid you in applying information, we recommend that you now select a subject textbook, one you are either currently using or may use in the future as you teach students. The book you select will be a resource for completing some of the assignments given at the end of each chapter. Upon completion of this textbook, you should be able to pick up a textbook in a selected subject area and analyze it for its suitability for learners, its affective qualities, its attention to PAR, its study skills and vocabulary aids, and its attention to at-risk learners. In addition, you should be able to construct activities which help teach content through a reading-to-learn approach.

One-Minute Summary

In this chapter we have introduced you to some major reports and recommendations, both current and past, which demonstrate the importance of a reading-to-learn approach in content classrooms. We have summarized our beliefs about reading to learn and have laid our foundation for this textbook in the form of twelve principles for content reading instruction. By explaining the concept of programs and incomplete thinking, we have demonstrated the need for an instructional framework in content reading instruction. We have explained our framework, PAR, and have provided two examples, one from secondary social studies and one from primary science, to assist our readers in their understanding of how PAR works. Finally, we have discussed how our twelve principles and the PAR framework will be applied throughout this textbook as well as how the textbook is organized.

End-of-Chapter Activities

Preparing the Reader

1. How did the authors prepare you to read this chapter? Did we give you an opportunity to determine your background knowledge? If so, how?

2. Did we build your background in any way before you began the actual chapter? If so, how?

Assisting Comprehension

1. Study the following graphic organizer and, without looking back at the beginning of the chapter, fill in the blanks with correct words that

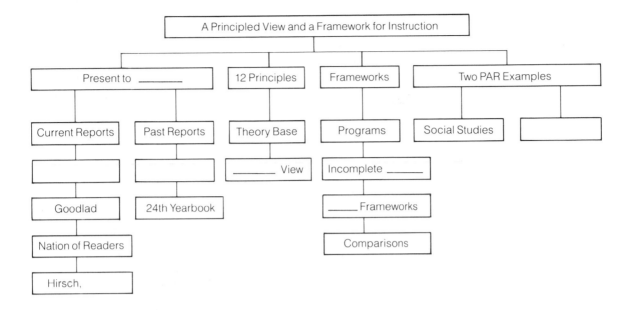

convey key concepts taught in this chapter. You may scan back through the chapter text. What does each term mean, and what is its relationship to reading, thinking, learning?

2. After reading this chapter, would you revise your opinions about the statements from the recommendations of *Becoming a Nation of Readers*?

3. Return to the terms presented at the beginning of this chapter. Has your understanding of these terms altered? In what ways?

Reflecting on Your Reading

1. Of the principles we presented, with which do you agree and why? Are there some with which you do not agree? Why?

2. As you read about the two example PAR lessons, could you see any of these principles in action? Which ones?

3. If you'd like to read a book about one content teacher's struggles to teach his content, please try Eliot Wigginton's *Sometimes a Shining Moment*. It's enjoyable and inspiring and informative!

4. If you'd like to see how reading can inspire a child, read the preface for Goldman's "good parts version" of *The Princess Bride*.

5. For some more challenging reading about students' literacy problems, read Hirsch's *Cultural Literacy*—a bit easier—or Bloom's *The Closing of the American Mind*—a bit harder.

6. *Emergent Literacy* by Teale and Sulzby is a good book for teachers who want to know more about children's early writing and reading patterns.

References

Anderson, R.; Hiebert, E.; Scott, J.; & Wilkinson, I. (1984). *Becoming a nation of readers*. Washington, D.C.: The National Institute of Education.

Ausubel, D. (1963). *The psychology of meaningful learning*. New York: Grune & Stratton.

Beyer, B. (1984). Improving thinking skills—defining the problem. *Phi Delta Kappan, 65*, (7) 486–490.

Bloom, A. (1987). *The closing of the American mind*. New York: Simon & Schuster.

Branscomb, L., et al. (1986). *A nation prepared*. New York: Carnegie Forum on Education and the Economy.

Chall, J. & Mirsky, A. (Eds.). (1978). *Education and the brain*. Chicago: University of Chicago Press.

de Bono, E. (1976). *Teaching thinking*. London: Temple Smith.

Feathers, K. & Smith, F. (1987). Meeting the reading demands of the real world: Literacy-based content instruction. *Journal of Reading, 30*, (6) 506–511.

Gagne, R. (1965). *The conditions of learning*. New York: Holt, Rinehart & Winston.

Goldman, W. (1973). Preface. In Morgenstern, J. *The Princess Bride*, New York: Ballantine Books.

Goodlad, J. (1984). *A place called school*. New York: McGraw-Hill.

Hart, L. (1983). Programs, patterns and downshifting in learning to read. *The Reading Teacher, 37*, 5–11.

Herber, H. (1978). *Teaching reading in the content areas*. Englewood Cliffs, NJ: Prentice-Hall.

Herber, H. (1987). Foreward. In Alverman, D., Moore, D. & Conley, M. (Eds.). *Research within reach / Secondary school reading*. Newark, DE: International Reading Association.

Herber, H. & Nelson-Herber, J. (1987). Developing independent readers. *Journal of Reading, 30*, (7) 584–588.

Hirsch, E. D. (1987). *Cultural literacy*. New York: Houghton Mifflin.

Houseman, M. (1987). Textbook-related methods in social studies. *The Reading Teacher, 40*, 820–822.

Huey, E. (1908). *The psychology and pedagogy of reading*. New York: MacMillan; Cambridge, Mass.: MIT Press, 1968.

Kane, B. (1984). Remarks Made at the Regional Meeting on Reading Across the Curriculum, Reading to Learn in Virginia, Capital Consortium.

Kellogg, R. (1972). Listening. In Lamb, P. (Ed.), *Guiding children's language learning*. Dubuque, IA: William C. Brown.

Kirsch, I. & Jungeblut, A. (1986). *Literacy: Profiles of America's young adults*. Princeton, NJ: National Assessment of Educational Progress.

Langer, J. (1981). From theory to practice: A prereading plan. *Journal of Reading, 25*, 152–156.

Learning to be literate (1987). Princeton, NJ: National Assessment of Educational Progress and the Educational Testing Service.

Lubarsky, N. (1987). A glance at the past, a glimpse of the future. *Journal of Reading, 30*, (6) 520–529.

Miklos, J. (1982). A look at reading achievement in the United States. *Journal of Reading, 25,* (8) 760–762.

Moore, D., Moore, S.A., Cunningham, P. & Cunningham, J. (1986). *Developing readers and writers in the content areas.* New York: Longman.

Novak, J. & Gowin, B. (1984). *Learning how to learn.* New York: Cambridge University Press.

Piaget, J. (1952). *The language and thought of the child.* London: Routledge & Kegan Paul.

Raths, L., Wassermann, S., Jones, A. & Rothstein, A. (1986). *Teaching for thinking: Theories, strategies and activities for the classroom.* New York: Teachers College Press.

The reading report card: Progress toward excellence in our schools: Trends in reading instruction over four national assessments, 1971–1984 (1985). Princeton, NJ: National Assessment of Educational Progress and Educational Testing Service.

Robinson, H. A., (Ed.). (1977). *Reading and writing instruction in the United States: Historical trends.* Newark, DE: International Reading Association.

Rosenshine, B. and Stevens, R. (1984). Classroom instruction in reading. In Pearson, P.D., (Ed.). *Handbook of reading research.* New York: Longman.

Sinatra, R. (1986). *Visual literacy connections to thinking, reading and writing.* Springfield, IL: Charles C. Thomas.

Singer, H. & Donlan, D. (1985). *Reading and learning from text.* Hillsdale, NJ: Erlbaum.

Smith, F. (1973). *Psycholinguistics and reading.* New York: Holt, Rinehart & Winston.

Smith, N. B. (1965). *American reading instruction.* Newark, DE: International Reading Association.

Stauffer, R. (1969). *Teaching reading as a thinking process.* New York: Harper & Row.

Thorndike, E. L. (1917). Reading and reasoning. *Journal of Educational Psychology, 8,* 323–332.

Twenty-fourth yearbook of the national society of the study for education (1925). Bloomington, IL: Public School Publishing Company.

Vaughan, J. and Estes, T. (1986). *Reading and reasoning beyond the primary grades.* Boston: MA: Allyn and Bacon.

Wassermann, S. (1987). Teaching for thinking: Louis E. Raths revisited. *Phi Delta Kappan, 68,* (6) 460–466.

The writing report card: Writing achievement in American schools (1987). Princeton, NJ: The National Assessment of Educational Progress and the Educational Testing Center.

2 Impact of Affect on Reading

Attitude is altitude."

Jesse Jackson

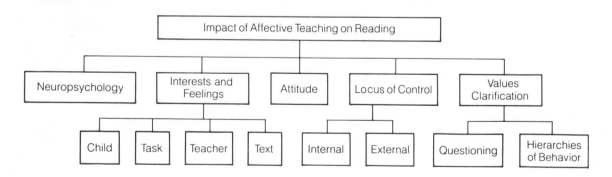

1. One of the authors was admonishing his three-year-old not to play with an older child who was being particularly hard on the younger child. The toddler was told not to play with such a "bad boy." The three-year-old's retort was, "No, he's a good boy. He just does bad things to me." This statement dramatically illustrates an important point adults need to keep in mind: Good children do bad things, but we must not equate the things they do with the spirit within. This point is especially important to teachers. When children behave poorly in classrooms, there are reasons. We need to discover why some students are discipline problems and others are not.

   This chapter is devoted to affective teaching and its importance for teaching in every classroom. Affective teaching is that which brings about an emotional response or change in the learner. The following questions are designed to test your "affective quotient" (AQ as opposed to IQ) and to help you discover how much you know about this important area of teaching.

   (1) What is your definition of affective teaching?

   (2) How can teaching to the affective domain influence comprehension and achievement?

   (3) What is locus of control? What role does it play in teaching?

   (4) Why is it important to clarify and extend students' values?

   (5) How can students' actions be tied to the way they feel? How can students' actions be tied to brain function?

2. Below is a list of terms used in this chapter. Some of them may be familiar to you in a general context, but in this chapter they may be used in a different way than you are used to. Rate your knowledge by placing a + in front of those you are sure that you know, a √ in front of those you have some knowledge about, and a 0 in front of those you don't know. Be ready to locate and pay special attention to their meanings when they are presented in the chapter.

   _____ affective   _____ locus of control
   _____ attitude   _____ internal movitation
   _____ neuropsychology   _____ aesthetics
   _____ triune brain   _____ prior knowledge
   _____ downshifting   _____ positive reinforcement

3. Three jokes:

   Knock-knock
   Who's there?
   Ammonia.

"Soon as you learn to read, Joey, the whole world's against you."

Dennis the Menace. Used with permission of Hank Ketcham and © by North America Syndicate.

Ammonia who?
Ammonia little boy and I can't reach the door bell.

A man comes into a service station with a frog on his head. The service station attendant asks, "What in the world is that?" "It started as a little lump on my foot," replied the frog.

A degenerate, down-on-his-luck golfer begs a philanthropist to lend him money for his wife's operation.

"If you don't lend me money," he said, "my wife will die. They won't take my check at the hospital. You've got to help me."

"No, I won't do it. If I lend you money, you'll just spend it on golf," replied the philanthropist emphatically.

"Oh, don't worry about that," said the man, "I've got money for golf."

Although we are the first to admit that these jokes are not the funniest in the world, we are willing to bet that you felt a little more lighthearted and spirited after reading them. Similarly, your *feelings* about reading are important, so much so that we are devoting this chapter to the affective area of teaching.

Objectives: As you read this chapter, focus your attention on the following objectives. You will:

1. be able to define what is meant by the affective domain.
2. understand why affect is important to reading.
3. understand what part neuropsychology plays in affective teaching.
4. understand how to improve student attitude through reading.
5. be able to incorporate affective strategies into the content area curriculum.
6. better understand the construct of locus of control and its importance for content area instruction.
7. be able to incorporate values clarification exercises in a content area classroom.
8. be able to use questions which stress the affective domain of learning.

Purpose: The affective area of teaching in any content area is very important to learning. Yet, it is often overlooked in the daily rush toward better grades and higher achievement scores on standardized tests.

Affect As a Teaching Tool

Any response to a stimulus which evokes feelings or emotions is said to be a part of the affective domain of learning. Students in kindergarten through twelfth grade "dwell" in the affective domain, i.e., feelings, emotions, and strong attitudes are very much a part of almost every waking hour. Conversely, teachers "dwell" mainly in the cognitive domain, where student achievement is perceived to be the single most important *raison d'être* of schooling. It is our contention that because of this perceptual mismatch, teachers and students often don't "meet" intellectually in the classroom. Put another way, their needs are so different—teachers driven to impart knowledge, students to discover the range of emotions inherent in each new day—that real communication sometimes does not occur in classrooms where the focus of instruction is content.

Two principles noted in chapter 1 need to be reemphasized here. Principle 7 stated that reading should be a pleasurable experience. In this chapter and throughout the book, we will be describing strategies that students will enjoy and find pleasure in. When reading is pleasurable, students will tend to read more, as principle 9 (reading begets reading) states. These two principles, then, speak to the importance of the affective domain of teaching.

Why Affect Is Important to Reading

Of course, the importance of affect has been known by educators for a long time, even before the term "affect" was widely used. In 1886, Emerson White wrote:

> It seems important to note in this connection that the development of the intellectual faculties is conditioned upon the corresponding development of the sensibility and the will. The activity of the mind in knowing depends, among other things, on the acuteness and energy of the senses, the intensity of the emotions and desires, and the energy and constancy of the will. (p. 92)

Over five decades ago Adler (1931) wrote of the importance of self-concept and the negative effects of children who can learn but won't (p. 159). More recently Dechant (1970) concluded that

> learning may be motivated not so much by what the teacher does or by the after-the-learning events such as rewards and punishments, as by what the learner wants, is interested in, or by what he feels will enhance his self-esteem and personal worth. The motivating condition begins within and is more psychological than physiological. (p. 537)

As was noted in chapter 1, many reports have indicated that our students are not reading well. Glasser (1986), in his book *Control Theory in the Classroom*, states that over half of all students are making little or no effort to learn, mainly because they don't believe that school provides any satisfaction. In a spirited repudiation of stimulus/response theory, Glasser maintains that human behavior is generated by what goes on inside the person. In an interview (Gough, 1987), Glasser spoke eloquently of the importance of affect:

> Except for those who live in deepest poverty, the psychological needs—love, power, freedom, and fun—take precedence over the survival needs, which most of us are able to satisfy. All our lives, we search for ways to satisfy our needs for love, belonging, caring, sharing, and cooperation. If a student feels no sense of belonging in school, no sense of being involved in caring and concern, that child will pay little attention to academic subjects. (p. 657)

Neuropsychology and Affect

Researchers are beginning to understand the importance of feelings and emotions in language development. Sinatra (1986) has theorized that feelings, like language, are linked to brain activity. Debunking the simplistic "left brain-right brain" literature, Sinatra cites a wealth of new research to show that most learning tasks require both left hemisphere processing and right hemisphere processing. He cites Restak's (1982; 1984) research indicating that cooperation rather than competition between the two brain hemispheres is the prevailing mode in most learning. Moreover, Sinatra proposes the importance of the two subcortical brains in the emotional and motivational aspects of learning. He states that "since the neural pathways between the cortex and the reticular and limbic systems function all the time without our conscious awareness, educators must realize that curriculum content cannot be approached solely by intellectual reasoning. The systems regulating feeling, emotions, and attentiveness are tied to the very learning of information (p. 143)." He further states that the teacher's attitude toward the reason for learning information, and toward the learners themselves, may be a more important factor in how well something is learned than the content itself. In making learning interesting and challenging, teachers are, in reality, activating brain subsystems responsible for alertness and emotional tone (p. 143). Sinatra criticizes dull worksheet drills as decoding exercises that negate students' eagerness to learn. Berry (1969) agrees that motivation, attention, and memory all operate in an interlocking fashion to enhance learning.

Sinatra's work is compatible with the triune brain theory as described by MacLean (1978). This model clarifies how the brain works in general and precisely why affect is so important in reading. The middle section of the brain—called by MacLean the "old mammalian brain"—is the seat of the limbic system. Sometimes called the "emotional mind" (Clark, 1983), it contributes significantly to the learning process. Students who feel positive and happy about a learning experience will be better able to process and retain information. Students who are uncertain and unhappy in a learning situation, either at school or at home, will become, in a real sense, emotionally unable to attend to a task for any length of time. Medical researchers know that, through the release of limbic system neurotransmitters, cells of the cortex are either helped or hindered in their functioning. The limbic system actually secretes different chemicals when one is experiencing a negative emotional event, thereby impeding learning and retention. Research has also shown that brain functioning has significantly increased when novelty is present (Restak, 1979) and when subjects experience feelings of pleasure and joy (Sagan, 1977). Conversely, researchers have found that removing touch and movement has resulted in increases in violent behavior (Penfield, 1975). All of this gives credence to how important attitudes, feelings, emotions, and motivation are to thinking, reading, and learning.

For example, a small boy fell into Lake Michigan's 32-degree water in the dead of winter. When rescued after twenty minutes, no heartbeat or pulse were detectable. And yet, a year later, he had recovered almost fully. How can this be? The explanation scientists think most likely is that a biological phenomenon called "mammalian diving reflex" enables humans to live without breathing for long periods of time (Richmond Times-Dispatch, Jan. 13, 1985).

If a human is in a life-threatening situation, with no time for reflection, an instinctive action is called for. The reptilian brain "kicks in" at the message of panic from the old mammalian brain and overrides reason. This scenario probably applies to Jimmy Tontlewicz, the boy whose story is told above. When his body was finally recovered, the prognosis was very grim. However, Jimmy is now functioning at much the same level as other children of his age. Doctors speculate that his brain "shut his body down" to minimal performance in order to save his life. Jimmy did not will his brain to do this; the brain reacted automatically. Hart (1983) describes this process, in which messages are sent from the old mammalian to the reptilian brain, as *downshifting*. Another term to describe this reaction might be *overdrive*.

How does this information about the triune brain apply to reading and thinking about content material? Consider the student who has not read an assignment and is confronted with a pop quiz. The old mammalian brain may be activated; a sense of frustration, even panic, may occur. Since the new mammalian brain (neocortex) has little information to contribute, and since hormones associated with anxiety are being generated by the old mammalian brain, the message gets routed or rerouted from the new mammalian brain to the reptilian brain: Shut down and save me! When students say "my mind went blank," they have provided an apt description of what literally happened. Or, how about the teacher who is struggling to find a way to present content material but cannot seem to get it across to her students? She is using the chapter information, but it just isn't working. She becomes more and more frustrated and less and less effective. A sort of downshifting may be occurring.

In further focusing on the brain and how students learn, Hart (1975) proposes that the following are important in teaching:

1. Making learning immediately important to students in order for them to make sense of the situation
2. Giving students opportunities to talk about what they are learning to allow heightening of brain activity
3. Providing a free environment where students can move around and talk about the projects they are doing

4. Allowing students time to build elaborate "programs" of thinking for storage and memory retrieval by the brain
5. Limiting threats and pressures which cause the neocortex (newest and highest level of the brain alluded to above) not to function well
6. Stressing intuitive learning as much as step-by-step logic to allow creative thinking to emerge

A Model of Affective Comprehension

McDermott (1978) suggests that a child's progress in reading is less influenced by the nature of the reading activity than by the personal relationship the child has developed with the teacher. The argument is that children respond most often to the feelings the teacher displays when asking them to complete an assignment than to the activity itself. Implied in McDermott's theory is that reading is as much a social event or transaction as it is an intellectual one. Building on McDermott's and Dechant's work, Meeks (1987) has proposed a model of "affective metacognition," postulating that affect and metacognition (students thinking about what they do and do not know) are so interwoven that they cannot be artificially separated. Figure 2.1 represents the four key elements of the model and subsystems inherent to each element. Following is a brief description of each of the components of the model:

Figure 2.1.

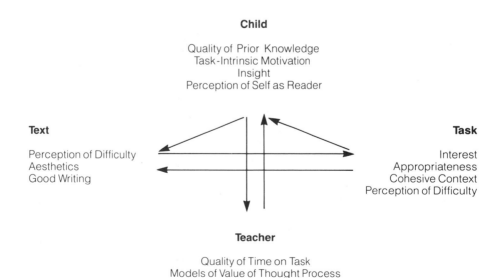

Child

Quality of Prior Knowledge
Task-Intrinsic Motivation
Insight
Perception of Self as Reader

Text

Perception of Difficulty
Aesthetics
Good Writing

Task

Interest
Appropriateness
Cohesive Context
Perception of Difficulty

Teacher

Quality of Time on Task
Models of Value of Thought Process
Fosters "Inquisitive Curiosity"

The Child

Quality of prior knowledge. The learner's prior knowledge can be clear and factual or unclear and represent false knowledge.

Task-intrinsic motivation. This refers to a child's readiness to perform an activity as a goal in itself.

Insight. This is reflective awareness that comes through cooperative interchange between students.

Perception of self as a reader. This perception is important for children because they must see themselves as generators of information, not passive receptors of knowledge.

The Teacher

Quality of time on task. Teachers must develop caring relationships with children in completing the task.

Modeling value of thought processes. Teachers must value thinking and discussion as tools to develop the thought processes of children.

Fostering curiosity. Teachers must believe inquisitiveness and curiosity are most important in the learning process.

The Text

Perception of difficulty. Students cannot perceive the book in a negative way, as being too difficult to comprehend.

Aesthetics. The text must be appropriate for the audience, with a pleasing format.

Good writing. The subject must come alive through the author's use of good writing.

The Task

Interest. The task must be interesting to the student.

Appropriateness. The task must be appropriate to the intellectual, psychological, social, and moral development of the student.

Cohesive context. The student must perceive that the task assigned makes sense in relation to what is read.

Perception of difficulty. Students cannot perceive the task in a negative way, as being too difficult to perform.

In this model, Meeks sees the processes of thought and its expression in class discussion and group process as legitimate and important ends in their own right; thought emerges as a social process and material is internalized only after it has been expressed socially. According to this interactive model, teachers who are stressing affect show that they value inquiry, sharing, and curiosity about learning. This model is important for content area teachers because it illustrates that more has to be emphasized in a lesson plan than any one of the four elements of the model—the text, for instance—can emphasize if it is isolated. To adequately stress the affective domain, the teacher must assess how these four variables are operating at any one time in the content lesson. Is the teacher modeling reasoning and thinking strategies during the lesson? Do students have enough background knowledge of the subject? Is the text "user friendly," i.e., readable and enjoyable? Is the task reasonable, or is it too difficult? Students probably will not be successful and will not enjoy what they are doing unless the teacher pays close attention to the four concepts of teaching described in the model. According to Meeks, overemphasis on any one element in a lesson will weaken learning and retention. We will discuss these four areas in more depth in chapters 3 and 4.

Improving Attitude Through Reading

One factor that has been found to be positively correlated with both teacher effectiveness and attitudinal change in students is teacher enthusiasm (Rosenshine and Furst, 1971; Gage, 1979; Hamachek, 1975; Rosenshine, 1968; Streeter, 1986). According to Collins (1976), teacher enthusiasm affects vocal delivery, eyes, gestures, body movements, facial expressions, word selection, acceptance of ideas and feelings, and overall energy. The following teacher attitude survey, Teacher Inventory of Attitude—Creating a Reading Environment with Feeling, will help teachers assess whether they are enthusiastic and positive about reading in their classroom. The TIA-CREWF can be used by any K-12 teacher for self-assessment.

Besides assessing how well we teach and model affect, we should also assess students so that we can determine positive and negative attitudes toward subject matter.

The Mikulecky Behavioral Reading Attitude Measure (1979), for older students, and Campbell's Reading Attitude Inventory, for kindergarten-aged students (1986) are reprinted below. These questionnaires were designed to cover a broad range of affective interest and developmental stages.

Promoting Positive Attitudes Toward Content Area Reading

Table 2.1 represents a model for the development of a curriculum of the affect. Adapted from a Ford Foundation Report (1970), it describes steps a teacher should consider in trying to bring a more affective approach into the curriculum.

Research by Heathington and Alexander (1984) indicates that while teachers see attitudes as important, they spend little time trying to

S U R V E Y

Teacher Inventory of Attitude—Creating a Reading Environment with Feeling

Directions: Please read each of the following questions and then circle *often, sometimes, seldom* or *never* after each question.

1. Do you have patience with those who are having difficulty reading?	often	sometimes	seldom	never
2. When you finish explaining the reading assignment, do your students want to find out more about the assignment?	often	sometimes	seldom	never
3. Do your students ever get so interested in your reading assignment that they talk about the assignment after it is completed?	often	sometimes	seldom	never
4. Do you ask thought-provoking questions about the reading assignments?	often	sometimes	seldom	never
5. Do you discuss with your students concepts they might look for before reading their assignment?	often	sometimes	seldom	never
6. Do you make difficult material seem easier to read?	often	sometimes	seldom	never
7. Do you give students aid in finding resource books for assignments?	often	sometimes	seldom	never
8. Do you give reading assignments from materials that are not too difficult for students to understand?	often	sometimes	seldom	never
9. Do you explain or define the new concepts in reading assignments?	often	sometimes	seldom	never
10. Do you tell students when they have done a creditable job on a reading assignment?	often	sometimes	seldom	never
11. Do you give reading assignments of appropriate length?	often	sometimes	seldom	never

change poor attitudes of students. The keys for promoting positive attitudes in all classes are caring, empathy, feeling, high expectations, sensitivity, vulnerability, honesty, firmness and support, respect, humanness. A number of activities for promoting favorable attitudes toward

12. When students are reading silently, do you monitor the classroom to make certain the environment is conducive to quiet study?	often	sometimes	seldom	never
13. Do you talk to students about the value of reading well in today's society?	often	sometimes	seldom	never
14. Do you let students decide how much reading is needed to complete assignments?	often	sometimes	seldom	never
15. After an assignment, do you ask students what they would like to read for further study?	often	sometimes	seldom	never
16. Do you know how interested your students are in reading?	often	sometimes	seldom	never
17. Are you interested in reading in your daily life?	often	sometimes	seldom	never
18. Do you read books for pleasure?	often	sometimes	seldom	never
19. Are you flexible in your reading, i.e., do you read at different rates for different purposes?	often	sometimes	seldom	never
20. Do you find yourself exhibiting more enthusiasm than normal when discussing a certain book?	often	sometimes	seldom	never

All 20 items should be answered "often" or "sometimes."
Scoring key:

15–20	"often" or "sometimes" responses			Very effective.
12–14	" " " "			Reasonably effective; fair in the affective areas.
8–11	" " " "			O.K. Need some improvement.
0– 7	" " " "			Poor. Do some rethinking!

Adapted from a questionnaire developed by James Laffey in Laffey, J. and Morgan, R. (1983). *Successful Interactions In Reading and Language: A Practical Handbook For Subject Matter Teachers.* Harrisonburg, VA: Feygan.

reading have been described by Readance and Baldwin (1979), Cooter and Alexander (1984), and Rieck (1977). To change student attitude in general, these researchers note that the teacher should

accept students as they are

assume students want to learn

Mikulecky Behavioral Reading Attitude Measure

On the following pages are 20 descriptions. You are to respond by indicating how much these descriptions are either unlike you or like you. For "very unlike" you, circle the number 1. For "very like" you, circle the number 5. If you fall somewhere between, circle the appropriate number. *Example:*

You receive a book for a Christmas present. You start the book, but decide to stop half-way through.

Very   1   2   3   4   5   Very
Unlike Me   Like Me

1. You walk into the office of a doctor or dentist and notice that there are magazines set out.

   Very   1   2   3   4   5   Very
   Unlike Me   Like Me

2. People have made jokes about your reading in unusual circumstances or situations.

   Very   1   2   3   4   5   Very
   Unlike Me   Like Me

3. You are in a shopping center you've been to several times when someone asks where books and magazines are sold. You are able to tell the person.

   Very   1   2   3   4   5   Very
   Unlike Me   Like Me

4. You feel very uncomfortable because emergencies have kept you away from reading for a couple of days.

   Very   1   2   3   4   5   Very
   Unlike Me   Like Me

5. You are waiting for a friend in an airport or supermarket and find yourself leafing through the magazines and paperback books.

   Very   1   2   3   4   5   Very
   Unlike Me   Like Me

6. If a group of acquaintances would laugh at you for always being buried in a book, you'd know it's true and wouldn't mind much at all.

   Very   1   2   3   4   5   Very
   Unlike Me   Like Me

7. You are tired of waiting for the dentist, so you start to page through a magazine.

   Very   1   2   3   4   5   Very
   Unlike Me   Like Me

8. People who are regular readers often ask your opinion about new books.

   Very   1   2   3   4   5   Very
   Unlike Me   Like Me

9. One of your first impulses is to "look it up" whenever there is something you don't know or whenever you are going to start something new.

   Very   1   2   3   4   5   Very
   Unlike Me   Like Me

10. Even though you are a very busy person, there is somehow always time for reading.

        Very   1   2   3   4   5   Very

      Unlike Me   Like Me

11. You've finally got some time alone in your favorite chair on a Sunday afternoon. You see something to read and decide to spend a few minutes reading just because you feel like it.

        Very   1   2   3   4   5   Very

      Unlike Me   Like Me

12. You tend to disbelieve and be a little disgusted by people who repeatedly say they don't have time to read.

        Very   1   2   3   4   5   Very

      Unlike Me   Like Me

13. You find yourself giving special books to friends or relatives as gifts.

        Very   1   2   3   4   5   Very

      Unlike Me   Like Me

14. At Christmas time, you look in the display window of a bookstore and find yourself interested in some books and uninterested in others.

        Very   1   2   3   4   5   Very

      Unlike Me   Like Me

15. Sometimes you find yourself so excited by a book you try to get friends to read it.

        Very   1   2   3   4   5   Very

      Unlike Me   Like Me

16. You've just finished reading a story and settle back for a moment to sort of enjoy and remember what you've just read.

        Very   1   2   3   4   5   Very

      Unlike Me   Like Me

17. You *choose* to read non-required books and articles fairly regularly (a few times a week).

        Very   1   2   3   4   5   Very

      Unlike Me   Like Me

18. Your friends would not be at all surprised to see you buying or borrowing a book.

        Very   1   2   3   4   5   Very

      Unlike Me   Like Me

19. You have just gotten comfortably settled in a new city. Among the things you plan to do are check out the library and book stores.

        Very   1   2   3   4   5   Very

      Unlike Me   Like Me

20. You've just heard about a good book but haven't been able to find it. Even though you're tired, you look for it in one more book store.

        Very   1   2   3   4   5   Very

      Unlike Me   Like Me

Reprinted with permission of Larry Mikulecky.

The data regarding the construction, validation, and interpretation of this test are contained in the dissertation by the same title completed at the University of Wisconsin, 1977.

S U R V E Y

Campbell Reading Attitude Inventory

1. How do you feel when your teacher reads a story out loud?

2. How do you feel when someone gives you a book for a present?

3. How do you feel about reading books for fun at home?

4. How do you feel when you are asked to read out loud to your group?

5. How do you feel when you are asked to read out loud to the teacher?

6. How do you feel when you come to a new word while reading?

7. How do you feel when it is time to do your worksheet?

8. How do you feel about going to school?

9. How do you feel about how well you can read?

10. How do you think your friends feel about reading?

11. How do you think your teacher feels when you read?

12. How do you think your friends feel when you read out loud?

13. How do you feel about the reading group you are in?

14. How do you think you'll feel about reading when you're bigger?

simply expect considerable achievement
praise whenever appropriate
be critical in a constructive manner
be honest with students
accentuate the positive, i.e., build on strengths
talk *with* students, not *at* students
have a sense of humor
learn some interesting characteristics of each student
trust students and exude warmth
be enthusiastic

To change student attitude about reading, the teacher should

actively listen to student comments and discussions
make reading fun and rewarding
make the task in reading clear
encourage students to read on their own
make reading assignments shorter for poor readers
have frequent group and sharing experiences to benefit especially
the poor readers
speak well of reading and share the works he or she is reading
use the PAR system described in this text

Teachers need to remember that they are very important in the lives of their students. A teacher should never give up on any student, no matter how negative the behavior that is being displayed. Many famous people did poorly in school, including Albert Einstein, Woodrow Wilson, Thomas Edison, George Bernard Shaw, Pablo Picasso, William Butler Yeats, Henry Ford, even Benjamin Franklin. If we emphasize the positive, each of us might someday play a central role in helping a future genius realize his or her potential. Most important of all, the teacher must value, and we mean truly value, the notions of inquiry, problem solving, and reasoning. By keeping an open mind and letting students take part in open-ended discussions, the teacher will be making a statement about the true art of teaching that cannot be ignored or misinterpreted by even our most limited students. In chapters 5 and 6, the importance of open-ended discussions in critical reading and comprehension is described, and suggestions for fostering such discussions are provided.

Any discussion of attitudinal teaching would be incomplete if teacher discouragement—sometimes called "burnout"—were not mentioned. Dreikurs, Grunwald, and Pepper (1971) described succinctly the discouragement a teacher faces when teaching students who can but won't learn. The progression from frustration to discouragement and finally to burnout is as much a fact of life today as it was almost two decades ago. More recently, Wigginton, in *Sometimes A Shining Moment* (1986), has documented through teacher questionnaires the depths of discour-

TABLE 2.1   *A Model for Developing a Curriculum of Affect (Adapted from the Ford Foundation's Report, 1970)*

I.   Teachers first identify the learning group:
  A. On-grade level readers
  B. Readers working below grade level
  C. Very poor readers
  D. A combination

II. Shared concerns that may be identified within the group:
  A. The need for feeling secure
  B. The desire to achieve and succeed—a drive to win
  C. A seeking for recognition, appreciation and praise
  D. A sense of belonging and being needed
  E. The desire to know something new or more about the old

III. How to discover underlying factors relating to the feelings and concerns of pupils: (Why are they aggressive, insecure, rebellious, fearful, anxious, possessive, over-ambitious, glory-seeking, power-hungry, hostile?)
  A. Use conferences and informal conversations
  B. Make systematic observation of pupil at work and play
  C. Keep anecdotal records
  D. Administer informal inventories, checklists and questionnaires
  E. Make contacts with parents and community wherever possible

IV. Appropriate organizing ideas for humanistic teaching:
  A. The way we see ourselves in relation to other people, things and events
  B. How people behave when placed in various group structures and organizational patterns
    1. A pupil may behave favorably in one classroom and poorly in another
    2. When given the leadership role, the rebellious student may exhibit a new sense of responsibility and agreeableness
    3. One's expectations depend on previous experience (favorable and unfavorable)

V.   Some acceptable vehicles for delivering content relating to the learner's reality—his experiences, his feelings
  A. Content may be traditional subject area (English, Math, Science, Social Studies)
  B. Out-of-school experiences which the learner shares—background should be considered and utilized in teaching pupils
  C. Create classroom situations, incidents, episodes, problems to be worked through

agement teachers, especially career teachers with much experience, can encounter. To combat these real feelings of frustration at not getting through to problem children, teachers need to develop the following three attributes:

VI. Learning skills needed by students in order to achieve desired outcomes:
   A. Basic skills or tools: reading, writing, speaking, listening, computation, are most significant.
   B. Skill in learning "how to learn" must be developed.
   C. Self-awareness and others—awareness skills are vital to personal growth and development.
      1. Makes decisions and chooses among feelings that have been tested.
      2. Compares his feelings and responses to others.
      3. Analyzes responses and their consequences.
      4. Tests alternatives and options open to him for action or decision-making.

VII. Teaching procedures that are most appropriate:
   A. Children learn through a study of inductive and deductive reasoning, concrete examples, direct confrontation, structured practice and well-spaced review.
   B. Cross-age teaching gives older children the responsibility for teaching younger pupils.
   C. Open discussion allows children to see the positive, as well as the negative characteristics of each other.
   D. Frequent interaction should be developed to support the pupils emotionally by strengthening feelings of self-worth.
   E. Well-chosen stories and articles for silent reading should carry direct or implied messages of courage, self-confidence, sensitivity to the need of others, etc.

VIII. Evaluation of an Affective Curriculum:
   A. Do pupils seem to enjoy what they are doing in reading, in sharing, in working with others each day?
   B. Has behavior changed for the better?
      1. What was it like before?
      2. What is it like now?
   C. Have affective (feeling, attitudinal and beliefs) activities kept pace with the teaching of cognitive (knowing, thinking, and doing skills)?
   D. Are students gradually becoming less shy and withdrawn?
   E. Do they express their beliefs without fear of rejection or deprecation?
   F. Do they seem to feel good about themselves?
   G. Are they willing to risk failure, but determined to try something worthwhile?

---

flexibility—keeping a positive attitude by ignoring all negative thoughts and by being open and receptive

willingness—being willing to try new ways of reaching problem students without sacrificing tried and true methods

ability—working and struggling to be the best teacher one can be in order to inspire students

Teachers must remember that they can and do exert a significant influence on children. By being flexible, willing, and able, they can influence even the hard-to-reach child. In chapter 12 we discuss strategies for reaching these at-risk students.

Teachers must also be aware that they may not have the same degree of success with every student. But there is always the possibility that with the next teaching experience, the reluctant student will experience an attitudinal change. Teachers must balance the real and the ideal in their affective role.

Applications of Locus of Control to Affective Teaching of Reading

Defining Locus of Control

The locus of control construct is said to have begun with Rotter's social learning theory (1966), which suggested that individuals attributed their successes and failures to different sources. People with an "internal" locus of control accept responsibility for the consequences of their behavior. They also perceive the relationship between their conduct and the outcomes. However, those with an "external" locus of control blame fate, chance, other individuals, or task difficulty for their successes and failures (Chandler, 1975). The concept of locus of control is a promising diagnostic tool for affective teaching because it assists teachers in understanding and predicting affective behaviors in the classroom.

Several studies have specifically tested locus of control and reading achievement (Drummond, Smith and Pinette, 1975; Culver and Morgan, 1977). Although more research needs to be done in the area, these studies support the notion that internally controlled students make the greatest gains in reading achievement.

Throughout two decades of research, investigators have found internally controlled individuals to be more cognitively active in search and learning activities (Lefcourt, Gronnerud and MacDonald, 1972). In contrast, Coleman and others (1969) found that the largest deficiency in ghetto children was in their acceptance of their inability to control their environment. Coleman concluded that passivity caused these children to accept control by others as their fate; often this perceived control became a reality.

Locus of Control: Practical Applications

Greer (1972, p. 338) offers numerous ideas and techniques to promote the goal of affective development in the reading class and proposes this description for developing the affective curriculum:

1. Learning experiences are selected to provide a balance between skills and affective development.
2. Activities, materials, environment, and teaching strategies required for affective growth are systematically planned and incorporated into the reading program throughout the year.
3. Activities are structured (a) to create a context for feeling in increasingly greater depth, (b) to expand the store of emotions available, (c) to stimulate analysis of emotions and values, and (d) to provide for sharing of the entire affective process.

Quandt (1977) calls for more affective content through the development of a separate affective curriculum or through the incorporation of affective content into the existing curriculum. According to Quandt, the teacher begins with activities to develop self-awareness, then builds toward responsibility in relation to other people and things. He describes specific activities that can be incorporated into the curriculum to help children deal with emotions, attitudes, and values. Some of the activities include discussions of attitudes of characters in stories, language experience charts expressing students' emotions and attitudes, listening activities, values-clarification activities, dramatizations, puppetry, music, art, and creative writing. Quandt maintains that these activities can be built into any curriculum readily, without any sacrifice of skills or of needed cognitive components.

Morgan and Culver (1978) propose certain guidelines for teachers to remember when selecting activities that reinforce internal behaviors. They are summarized in Table 2.2 and contrasted with activities that reinforce externally controlled behaviors. First, teachers need to minimize anxiety over possible failure by building patterns of success for each student in the class. This can be accomplished in several ways. To begin with, teachers need to develop a realistic reward system of praise for work completed. A system of reward can be made simpler if the teacher uses a contractual type of arrangement that specifies a sequence of graduated tasks, each of which is attainable. The teacher should stress the concept of mastery of the task in grading students, thereby eliminating arbitrary grading, which serves as a source of agitation for those students who are external in their thinking. Also the teacher may deemphasize the concept of time and thus lessen compulsiveness by allowing students unlimited time to complete and master certain tasks. In addition, teachers should aid school guidance staff

TABLE 2.2

Reinforcing "Externally Controlled" Behaviors	Reinforcing "Internally Controlled" Behaviors
1. Arbitrary grading	1. Using concept of mastery in grading
2. Setting time limits for tasks, which makes students constantly aware of time (compulsiveness)	2. Allowing unlimited time to complete and master a task
3. Building anxiety over possible failure	3. Building patterns of success
4. Neglecting to offer rewards for efforts	4. Rewarding student in a controlled manner for effort (praise)
5. No graduated sequencing in learning tasks	5. Developing graduated sequences for the learning tasks
6. Fostering the student's unrealistic goals	6. Counseling student toward realistic life goals (with support from administration)

in counseling students toward realistic life goals, since externally controlled persons often have unrealistic aspirations.

Teachers can also attempt strategies that foster self-direction and internal motivation in the learning process. For instance, teachers can let students make a set of rules of conduct for the class and start their own class or group traditions to reinforce the importance of both the group and the individuals in the group. Such an activity relies on the use of listening and speaking and can be implemented even in the early grades. Another excellent activity for older students is the "internal-external" journal. Students keep a record of recent events that have happened to them. In the journal they can explain whether the events were orchestrated and controlled by someone other than themselves and, if so, whether these externally controlled events frustrated them. As a variant on the journal idea, students can make a "blame list" to identify whether positive and negative events that happen to them are their own fault or the fault of others. These activities rely on the use of writing, thus integrating another communicative art into affective education.

One of the most important classroom strategies for helping students develop an internal locus of control is to have them practice decision making whenever possible. Study guides and worksheets can be constructed in such a manner that individuals and groups are asked to reason and react to hypothetical situations where decisions need to be made. Group consensus in decision making about a possible conclusion to a story can be a powerful way to teach self-awareness and self-worth and to teach about relationships with others. The Directed Reading Thinking Activity (Stauffer, 1969) is another excellent strategy for teaching group decision making through hypothesizing the outcome of a story. This activity, explained in chapter 5, enables students to believe in themselves by feeling that what they have to say and predict has dignity and worth.

Classroom teachers who use affective strategies, such as those based on locus of control, to teach the cognitive skills of reading will be considerably more successful than those who omit such strategies from their reading program.

Values Clarification in Content Classrooms

Clarification of values is designed to assist children in forming and solidifying values. The purpose of values clarification is not to teach a set of values but to provide activities that will aid children in forming or identifying their own values. Harsain and Simon (1973) listed the following as skills students need to analyze the values they hold:

1. Seeking alternatives among choices
2. Judging possible consequences before choosing
3. Making independent choices
4. Being aware of one's preferences and values
5. Being willing to publicly affirm one's choices
6. Acting consistently with one's choices and preferences
7. Repeating the acts consistently until they become a patterned way of life

For students in middle childhood and young adolescence, values can often be clarified in a game-like situation. For example, questions are posed that reveal values and prejudices and that require the examination of beliefs. Jones, Garrison, and Morgan (1985) give these examples:

The Provocative Question: What are the best reasons for lying? Under what conditions would you take sides with your mother or father in an argument? What would the world be like without firemen?

What Would You Do If: Your friends want you to join them in a protest march against unfair trade imbalance and your father works for Toyota? Your teacher holds the class after school until someone tells who stole the class trip money and you think you know?

Value Continuum: Place yourself on the scale between these two extremes:

Hard-nosed Mac: We should annihilate those "commies" for the way they've treated us. Never trust them. The cold war should get more frigid.

Silly-Putty Sid: The Russians have the right to be different from us. We need to peacefully coexist and take the initiative to sign more disarmament

Double the defense budget in order to better ready for communist aggression throughout the world.

treaties with them. After all, we have more in common, especially economically, with them than it might first appear.

Values clarification for the content area of science at the primary level can be taught by an activity such as the following:

What would you do if: (In science) You learned that all the right whales are being killed for their blubber? You know that people need the blubber, but you also know all the whales will die.

Questions are raised with students to explain why and to reflect on their values. Studies by Kirschenbaum (1974) reveal that children practicing values clarification have shown an increased awareness of their personal control over their own lives. They behave more self-reliantly, improving their ability to make decisions. Some students have been able, according to this research, to reduce their use of drugs. This approach to helping children practice moral decision making has promise in all subject areas.

Affective Domain Questioning

Values, then, furnish *linkage* between emotions, attitudes, and thoughts or knowledge (Jones, Garrison, and Morgan, 1985). When students studying the problems faced by Richard Nixon as President of the United States are asked to consider their feelings about these problems, implicit or explicit, they are connecting knowledge and feelings. In a scheme developed by Krathwohl, Bloom, and Masia (1964), the investigators attempted to order and relate the different kinds of affective behavior. They made use of the concept of internalization—the process of incorporating something into one's behavior as one's own. Internalization can be described not only from the external to the internal, but also from the simple to the complex and from the concrete to the abstract. The scheme is reproduced in part here:

1.0 Receiving (attending)
    1.1 Awareness—the person is aware of the feelings of others whose activities may be of little interest to him.
    1.2 Willingness to Receive—the person listens to others with respect.
    1.3 Controlled or Selected Attention—someone being alert toward human values and judgments of life as they are recorded in history.
2.0 Responding
    2.1 Acquiescence in Responding—someone obeying job regulations.

    2.2 Willingness to Respond—the person practices the rules of safety on the job.

    2.3 Satisfaction in Response—the person enjoys participation in activities and plays according to the rules.

3.0 Valuing

    3.1 Acceptance of a Value—the person accepts the importance of social goals in a free society.

    3.2 Preference for a Value—the person assumes an active role in clarifying the social goals in a free society.

    3.3 Commitment—the person is loyal to the social goals of a free society.

4.0 Organizing

    4.1 Conceptualization of a Value—the person judges the responsibility of society for conserving natural resources.

    4.2 Organization of a Value System—the person develops a plan for conserving natural resources.

5.0 Characterization of a Value or Value Complex

    5.1 Generalized Set—the person faces facts and conclusions that can be logically drawn with consistent values orientation.

    5.2 Characterization—the person develops a philosophy of life.

Practical Applications: Questioning in the Affective Domain

The extent to which teachers stress affective teaching depends, of course, on the objective of the lesson, but certainly teachers can try to elicit emotional responses during selected lessons in all content area subjects. For example, following Krathwohl's taxonomy, teachers can do the following:

1. *Receiving.* Questions can be formulated to determine whether students are actively involved, whether they are receiving from the text, lecture, etc. Teachers can ask students to explain what they are thinking about a subject at any time during the lesson. Through these techniques, teachers can assess the degree of student involvement.

2. *Responding.* Students should be called upon periodically by teachers to respond to emotions and feelings inherent in a given lesson. Teachers might say, "Tell us how you feel now after you have answered that question." Students need to feel good about their responses to questions.

3. *Valuing.* This is usually the highest level of attainment reached in the classroom situation. Here students show that they appreciate and value reading. Teachers can ask students why they value a certain literature selection, a chapter in social studies ("because it

teaches me about other cultures"), or a particular application to a mathematics problem. Teachers stress valuing anytime they ask students why they enjoyed a reading selection.

4. *Organizing.* At this level students conceptualize their values over a period of time, internalizing the concept valued and making it a part of their belief structure. Teachers can emphasize this affective level by asking students to write about their beliefs regarding particular national, state, or local issues. Anytime a teacher asks, "What do you believe?" she is helping in the creation of a value system.

5. *Characterization.* This level represents a continuation of level four in that the student recognizes that a value has been internalized. At this level, the student is committed to the value. Teachers can determine whether students are on this level by asking if students strongly believe in a certain concept.

The GATOR (Gaining Acceptance Toward Reading) system can assist teachers in asking more affective questions. To help gain student acceptance toward reading, the teacher announces that all questions asked about a lesson, either by the teacher or students, have to be based on "feelings," as do all the responses. The entire lesson is taught with questions such as

How did that make you feel?
Why is this lesson important to you?
How did you feel about the main character? Why would you have done or not done what the main character did?
Why is this chapter important?
Tell us why you like what you just read.

GATOR can also be played as a game—the feelings game—where students in small group discussion are allowed to discuss only emotion-laden questions. In this manner, the teacher will be stressing what we call "meta-affection," the act of thinking about how one feels directly after a reading. No matter what variation is used, the most important aspect of GATOR is that no factual comprehension questions can be asked by anyone, students or teachers. There are no "What happened here?" or "What happened there?" questions. We recommend GATOR as an excellent affective teaching strategy, one that will not "snap back" on you!

The following are affective questions teachers and students generated during a brainstorming session after reading *Goodbye, Grandma* by Ray Bradbury.

If you knew that a close relative of yours were about to die, would you treat him or her differently?
Do you think Grandma was ready for death?
How do you think Grandma felt about the beginning and ending of her life?

What if you were given three years to live; how would you do things differently?

There is humor in this story. How do you feel about having humor in a story about death?

Do you feel Grandma is like anyone you know?

What lasting feeling were you left with at the end of the story?

During what parts of this story did you have a warm, happy feeling? Read these parts aloud to the class.

How do you think it will feel to be old?

Do we treat people differently who are dying? Should we?

Using expository material in a junior-high-school lesson about seasons and climate from an earth science textbook, a teacher could ask the following affective questions:

How do you feel about today's weather?

Can weather affect your mood and how you feel? Give examples.

How do you feel about the seasons?

If the sun did not tilt on its axis, would there still be seasons?

What if there were never any change of seasons? Describe your feelings.

Remember to Relax

Here we wish to insert a final reminder to relax in your teaching. Good results can only come from a relaxed, friendly classroom environment where students, though respectful, feel that they can discuss and make comments without fear of reprisal. When teachers feel physically drained and perhaps a little irritable, we recommend relaxation exercises and visual exercises. For instance, one can imagine oneself on a train going through a long and deep tunnel. One can visualize the word "deep" on one side of the tunnel and the word "relax" on the other side. Students can be taken through such relaxation drills when they are particularly nervous and jittery.

The letters in the word *RELAX* suggest five behaviors that teachers need to practice to ensure this relaxed type of teaching: Reflection, Enthusiam, Laughter (at least, smile), Anticipation, and X-citement. If teachers reflect good behaviors, show enthusiasm, laugh with their students every now and then, and, in general, build an exciting classroom environment, certainly the affective domain of teaching will be enhanced.

One-Minute Summary

There is probably no area so misunderstood and neglected as the area of affect in teaching. In this chapter we have maintained that students rarely, if ever, achieve without having certain concomitant feelings, including a positive attitude and strong emotions of belonging and caring for other students, the subject, and the teacher. Teachers in every content area must be aware of the importance of the smile, the gesture, the kind remark. They should try to structure positive experiences as an integral part of daily instruction. In addition, teachers need to plan how to deliver a lesson so students enjoy what they are learning and see purpose in the material to be studied. The classroom atmosphere should be warm and supportive so that students feel good about both what they know and how much they can learn. Students need to explore values and take part in discovery types of learning activities which lead to a more internal locus of control. Most important of all, to bring about lasting achievement, teachers must pay attention to both the cognitive and affective domains of learning.

End-of-Chapter Activities

Preparing the Reader

1. Did the authors of the text prepare you adequately for reading this chapter?

2. Name some other ways they could have prepared you for reading the chapter.

Assisting Comprehension

1. Describe more ways you might be motivated to change your classroom environment to better incorporate the affective domain in your teaching.

2. Study the graphic overview introduced at the beginning of the chapter and see if you can put the listed terms into the overview so that they make sense to you. If asked by the instructor, be prepared to justify your answers in a small group or to a whole class.

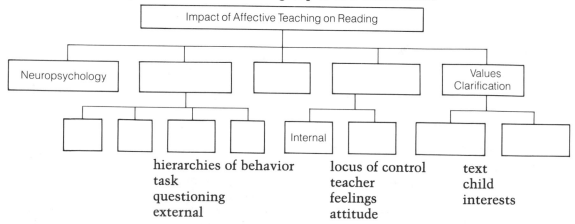

hierarchies of behavior
task
questioning
external

locus of control
teacher
feelings
attitude

text
child
interests

Reflecting on Your Reading

1. A case has been presented that no curriculum can be concerned solely with the cognitive domain of learning and that thinking and learning skills are actually interwoven with feelings, motivation, and attention. After reading this chapter, can you study the following diagram and write down your thoughts about how thinking through both domains of learning can be emphasized?

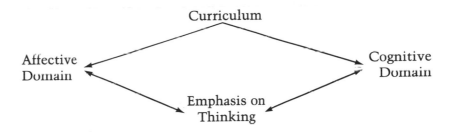

2. What do you feel was the single most important point made in this chapter? Think about how you would like to expand on this point.

References

Adler, A. (1931). *What life should mean to you.* New York: Capricorn.

Berry, M. (1969). *Language disorders of children: The bases and diagnoses.* New York: Appleton-Century-Croft.

Chandler, T. A. (1975). Locus of control: A proposal for change. *Psychology in Schools, 12,* 334–339.

Clark, B. (1983). *Growing up gifted: Developing the potential of children at home and at school.* 2nd Ed. Columbus, OH: Charles Merrill.

Coleman, J. C. and others. (1969). *Equality of educational opportunity.* Washington, DC: Superintendent of Documents.

Collins, M. L. (1977). The effects of training for enthusiasm on the enthusiasm displayed by pre-service elementary teachers (Doctoral dissertation, Syracuse University). *Dissertation Abstracts International.*

Cooter, R. B. & Alexander, J. E. (1984). Interest and attitude: Affective connections for gifted and talented readers. *Reading World, 24,* 97–102.

Culver, V. I., and Morgan, R. F. (1977). The relationship of locus of control to reading achievement. Unpublished manuscript, Norfolk, VA: Old Dominion University.

Dechant, E. (1970). *Improving the teaching of reading.* Englewood Cliffs, NJ: Prentice-Hall.

Dreikurs, R., Grunwald, B., and Pepper, F. (1971). *Maintaining sanity in the classroom: Illustrated teaching techniques.* New York: Harper & Row.

Drummond, R. J., Smith, R. K., and Pinette, C. A. (1975). Internal-external control construct and performance in an individualized community college reading course. *Reading Improvement, 12,* 34–38.

Gage, N. L. (1979). The generality of dimensions of teaching. In Peterson, P. I. & Walberg, H. J. (Eds.). *Research on teaching.* Berkeley, CA: McCutchan, 264–288.

Ginsberg, H. (1986). Research on personality and cognition: implications for instruction. Address to the Eastern Educational Research Association, Miami, FL.

Glasser, W. (1986). *Control theory in the classroom.* New York: Harper & Row.

Goodacre, E. J. (1968). Teachers and their pupils' home background. *Slough,* NFER.

Gough, P. B. (1987). The key to improving schools: An interview with William Glasser. *Phi Delta Kappan,* May, 656–662.

Grady, M. L. (1971). An assessment of teachers' attitudes toward disadvantaged children. *The Journal of Negro Education, Spring,* 146–151.

Greer, M. (1972). Affective growth through reading. *The Reading Teacher, 25,* 336–341.

Hamachek, D. E. (1975). *Behavior dynamics in teaching, learning and growth.* Boston: Allyn & Bacon.

Harsain, M. and Simon, S. B. (1973). In Simon, S. B. and Kirschenbaum, H. (Eds). *Readings in value clarification.* Minneapolis, MN: Winston.

Hart, L. (1975). *How the brain works.* New York: Basic Books.

Hart, L. (1983). Programs, patterns and downshifting in learning to read. *The Reading Teacher, 37,* 5–11.

Heathington, B. and Alexander, J. (1984). Do classroom teachers emphasize attitudes toward reading? *The Reading Teacher, 37,* (6) 484–488.

Jones, F. R., Garrison, K. C. and Morgan, R. F. (1985). *The psychology of human development.* New York: Harper & Row.

Kirschenbaum, H. (1974). Recent research in values clarification. *National Humanistic Education Center Monograph.*

Klausmeier, H., Ghatala, E. and Frayer, D. (1974). *Conceptual learning and development: A cognitive view.* New York: Academic Press.

Krathwohl, D., Bloom, B. & Masia, B. (1964). *Taxonomy of educational objectives: Handbook II: Affective domain.* New York: McKay.

Laffey, J. L. and Morgan, R. (1980). Sociocultural bases. In Lamb, P. and Arnold, R. (Eds.). *Teaching reading, foundations and strategies.* Belmont, CA: Wadsworth.

Lefcourt, H. M., Gronnerud, P. and MacDonald, P. (1972). Cognitive activity and hypotheses formation during a double entendre word association test as a function of locus of control and field dependence. Unpublished educational document, Ontario Mental Health Foundation, Toronto, Ontario.

MacLean, P. (1978). A mind of three minds: Educating the triune brain. In Chall, J. and Mirsley, A. (Eds.). *Education and the brain.* Chicago: University of Chicago Press.

McDermott, R. P. (1978). Some reasons for focusing on classrooms in reading research. *Reading: disciplined inquiry in process and practice.* Clemson, SC: 27th Yearbook of the National Reading Conference.

Meeks, J. (1987). Toward defining affective metacognition. A paper delivered to the International Reading Association, Anaheim, CA, May.

Meeks, J. and Morgan, R. (1982). Reading teachers' affective awareness concerning teaching the culturally different student. *ADSIG Journal of the Affective Interest Group of the International Reading Association, 4*(1).

Mikulecky, L., Shanklin and Caverly. (1979). Mikulecky behavioral reading attitude measure. From *Adult reading habits, attitudes and motivations: A cross-sectional study*. Bloomington, IN: School of Education, Indiana University.

A model for developing a curriculum of affect. (1970). Ford Foundation Report.

Morgan, R. and Culver, V. (1978). Locus of control and reading achievement: Applications for the classroom. *Journal of Reading, 21*(5), February.

Penfield, W. (1975). *The mystery of the mind: A critical study of consciousness and the human brain*. Princeton, NJ: Princeton University Press.

Quandt, I. (1977). *Teaching reading: A human process*. Chicago: Rand McNally.

Rajpal, P. L. (1972). Teacher judgments of minority children. *Integrated Education, Nov.-Dec.*, 33–36.

Readance, J. E. and Baldwin, R. S. (1979). Independence in critical reading: An instructional strategy. *Educational Considerations, 6*, 15–16.

Restak, R. (1979). *The brain: The last frontier*. Garden City, NY: Doubleday.

Restak, R. (1982). The brain. *The Wilson Quarterly, 6*, 89–115.

Restak, R. (1984). *The brain*. New York: Bantam Books.

Rieck, B. J. (1977). How content teachers telegraph messages against reading. *Journal of Reading, 20*, 646–648.

Rosenshine, B. (1968). Objectivity measured behavioral predictors of effectiveness in explaining. In N. L. Gage, et al. (Eds.). *Explorations of teacher's effectiveness in explaining*. Technical Report No. 4. Stanford, CA: Stanford Center for Reading and Development in Teaching, 36–45.

Rosenshine, B. and Furst, N. (1971). Research on teacher performance criteria. In Smith, O. (Ed.). *Research in teacher education: A symposium*. Englewood Cliffs, NJ: Prentice-Hall.

Rosenthal, R. (1968). Self-fulfilling prophesy. *Psychology Today, II*, September, 44–52.

Rosenthal, R. and Jacobson, L. (1968). *Pygmalion in the Classroom*. New York: Holt, Rinehart & Winston.

Rotter, J. B. (1966). Generalized expectancies for internal versus external control of reinforcement. *Psychological Monographs: General and Applied, 80*(1).

Sagan, C. (1977). *The dragons of eden*. New York: Random House.

Saracho, O. N. (1986). Development of a pre-school reading attitude scale. *Child Study Journal, 16*(2), 113–124.

Sinatra, R. (1986). *Visual literacy connection to thinking, reading and writing*. Springfield, IL: Charles C. Thomas.

Stauffer, R. G. (1969). *Directing reading maturity as a cognitive process*. New York: Harper & Row.

Streeter, B. (1986). The effects of training experienced teachers in enthusiasm on students' attitudes toward reading. *Reading Psychology, 7*(4), 249–259.

White, E. E. (1886). *The elements of pedagogy*. New York: American Book Company.

Wigginton, E. (1986). *Sometimes a shining moment*. New York: Anchor Press.

3 Determining the Reader's Background for Content Material

Material is not inherently meaningful: it is endowed with meaning by a reacting individual, and experiences or previous reaction, is a necessary condition."

James Stroud,
Psychology in Education

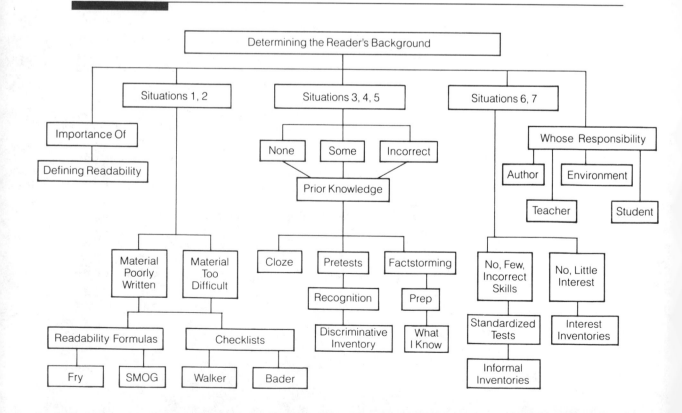

Preparing the Reader Activities:

1. Have you read any material lately with which you just didn't "connect?" Perhaps you tried to read a software documentation guide or a technical report? Describe your experience: How did you react? How did you cope with this strange material? What did you do to ensure your reading success?

2. You will be better prepared to read this chapter by reviewing principle 8 in chapter 1: The act of reading requires the interaction of the reader, the text, the teacher, and the environment.

3. While reviewing in chapter 1, take a look at Huey's tenets 14 and 15 once again. Consider how these tenets might be relevant to a chapter on determining a reader's background.

4. Below is a list of terms used in this chapter. Some of them may be familiar to you in a general context, but in this chapter they may be used in a different way than you are used to. Rate your knowledge by placing a + in front of those you are sure that you know, a √ in front of those you have some knowledge about, and a 0 in front of those you don't know. Be ready to locate and pay special attention to their meanings when they are presented in the chapter.

_____ readability	_____ cloze
_____ inconsiderate text	_____ maze
_____ readability formulas	_____ prior knowledge
_____ Fry graph	_____ schema/schemata
_____ SMOG	_____ factstorming
_____ rule of thumb	_____ cognitive dissonance

Objectives:

As you read this chapter, focus your attention on the following objectives. You will:

1. define the term *readability*.

2. be able to make judgements about the readability of textbook material.

3. become acquainted with seven situations which may cause readability problems and be able to use this information to determine if a readability problem exists for students.

4. become acquainted with several activities which help determine a reader's background.

5. understand the responsibility of the author, teacher, environment, and student in determining the reader's background for reading content material.

Peanuts. Reprinted with permission of UFS, Inc./United Media.

Purpose: By realizing what students do and don't already know about the material they are to read, teachers can plan content lessons which are relevant and successful. In this chapter you will discover which situations can cause difficulties in reading content material and find ways to determine if these situations affect your students. Read to find out what the concept of readability implies and how you can ensure a successful connection between readers and content material.

Why Is Determining Background So Important?

Peppermint Patty's question in the cartoon—"Is it an interesting book?"—reflects the hesitancy many readers experience when they encounter new reading material. Most of us would like to feel comfortable with what we're about to read. We don't want someone else to be in charge of our feelings and future experiences so completely that "they" know and we have to find out. So good readers usually attempt a little exploration of what they're about to read before they read it. Probably the first step in a good reader's exploration is to wonder, as Peppermint Patty did, if this material will be interesting. Good readers will next try to determine how much they already know about this material, how much they like this topic, and why they ought to read it anyhow. Only after they have made this assessment of the material will they be willing to persevere with the reading. Often this assessment is almost automatic and unconscious for proficient readers. However, most students need the teacher's guidance in determining their background until they reach such a stage of proficiency. When someone, such as a teacher, tells students, by words or actions, "just read," or "that's for me to know and you to find out," students are cheated out of a very productive way to improve comprehension.

Suppose you were assigned to read the following excerpt on the pathology of viral hepatitis? Unless you were already highly interested and knowledgeable about the topic, you might feel a little apprehensive. We ask you to read the passage now, but we tell you in advance that this is an experiment; you're not expected to learn this material. Our objective is rather that you grade it according to the criteria which follow the passage.

A READER'S IMPRESSIONS

Pathology of Viral Hepatitis

Chapter 68, "Disorders of the Liver," in Luckmann, J. & Sorensen, K. (1980). *Medical Surgical Nursing—A Psychophysiological Approach.* New York: D. B. Saunders Company.

The physical signs and symptoms that the person with hepatitis experiences are reflections of cellular damage in the liver. The hepatocyte has alterations in function resulting from damage caused by the virus and the resultant inflammatory response. The endoplasmic reticulum is the first organelle to undergo change. Since this organelle is responsible for protein and steroid synthesis, glucuronide conjugation, and detoxification, functions that depend on these processes will be altered. The degree of impairment depends on the amount of hepatocellular damage. The mitochondria sustain damage later than the endoplasmic reticulum. The Kupffer cells increase in size and number. The vascular and ductule tissues experience inflammatory changes. In most cases of uncomplicated hepatitis the reticulum framework is not in danger, and excellent healing of the hepatocytes occurs in three to four months.

Rate this reading material:

The language and vocabulary are clear to me:

A   B   C   D   F

The concepts are well developed:

A   B   C   D   F

The paragraph is organized:

A   B   C   D   F

The paragraph is well written:

A   B   C   D   F

The paragraph is interesting to me:

A   B   C   D   F

How did you rate this material? You might want to share reactions with your classmates. Forty-one teachers who were asked to rate this material gave varied ratings. Compare their impressions to yours:

Rate this reading material:

The language and vocabulary are clear to me:

A	B	C	D	F
2	0	7	16	16

The concepts are well developed:

A	B	C	D	F
2	3	19	8	9

The paragraph is organized:

A	B	C	D	F
6	12	14	3	6

The paragraph is well written:

A	B	C	D	F
2	9	14	12	4

The paragraph is interesting to me:

A	B	C	D	F
1	1	3	10	26

The paragraph can be perceived very differently, depending on the individual, as you can see. Although all forty-one teachers read the same material, the experiences each brought to the material, the interaction each personally had with the material, and the skill of each reader greatly influenced their reactions. These forty-one teachers represent a fairly homogeneous group: they have a common profession and a recognized level of competence. Therefore, we might expect their reactions to the passage to be fairly similar. The challenge of the classroom, on the other hand, is the heterogeneity of the students. The experiences, personal interactions and reading skills of students will most likely be more varied than those of our forty-one teachers.

Singer and Bean (1988) note that "when a heterogeneous group of students progresses through the grades, we can expect its range of reading achievement (in reading age equivalents) to increase from four years at grade one to twelve years at grade twelve" (p. 162). To find out the range of reading in a heterogeneous class, Singer and Bean advise multiplying the median age of the class by two-thirds. Thus, the range in a third-grade class (with a median age of eight) would be about five years, while in a tenth-grade class (median age of fifteen) the range would be about ten years. This indication of variation, while not an absolute measure, does demonstrate how the *same* reading material can generate very different reading reactions from students.

It is crucial, then, that teachers carefully study their students' reading needs as well as the materials they use as teaching tools. By determining in advance as much as one can about what the readers will encounter on the page and what they bring to the page, a teacher can help students think and read more effectively. If teachers and readers ignore this step, a crucial part of preparation for reading is neglected. Then readers may play guessing games with the teacher, as Peppermint Patty and her teacher did.

What Is Readability?

We prefer an encompassing definition for the often-used term *readability*. One such definition is suggested by Harris and Hodges in *A Dictionary of Reading*. They equate the term with "ease of understanding or comprehension because of style of writing" (1981, p. 262). We feel that it is important to add, as their definition does, "as well as many other variables including those inherent to the material *and* the reader." Dreyer (1984) has written that "the goal of readability research is to match reader and text." Simply stated, readability is that match. Professional judgement is essential in determining readability; no score or formula can do more than help teachers to understand problems which might occur between the reader and the material. Too many factors are involved for teachers to settle for simple solutions. However, there are some basic situations which often exist. Teachers who realize what these situations are, and why they can cause readability problems, will use this information to determine whether a problem exists for their students. The successful connection between the reader and the material ensures readability.

Text-Related Situations Which Affect Readability

The first two of the situations which affect readability are text related; that is, they pertain more to the material to be read than to the reader. In these situations, all readers probably face similar problems with the material. What follows are descriptions of these two situations and of activities which will help teachers determine if these situations exist in their materials.

Situation One: The Material May Be Poorly Written

How many readers have abandoned or postponed the mastery of a new software program because its documentation was so poorly written? Whole sections of explicit instructions to the reader may have been forgotten by the author of the manual. How many parents have become exasperated with the poorly written instructions for assembly of a toy? Similarly, some content material, particularly that found in textbooks, may be poorly written and therefore place unnecessary stress on a reader.

If such is the case, and teachers must use this less-than-desirable material, then they must determine how difficult the material is and what makes it so poorly written.

Anderson and Armbruster (1984) have examined several content textbooks which they have classified as poorly written primarily because the text material seemed to have no logical structure. Such texts may list facts or provide lengthy descriptions of events without reference to the underlying concepts which those descriptions are meant to support. Students are ill equipped to ferret out the theme or concept from such "wandering" exposition. This poorly written material is recognizable because of its loose organization, its lack of a discernible style, its incorrect syntax, or its incoherent passages. Armbruster and Anderson (1981) have assigned the label "inconsiderate discourse" to such material. Another type of poorly written textbook is one in which its authors have tried to simplify content to an impossible degree. Former Secretary of Education Terrell Bell (Toch, 1984) expressed a concern about these textbooks, calling them "dumbed down."

Situation Two: The Material May Be Too Difficult for Its Intended Readers

Even if material is generally well written, it may be beyond the ability of the audience for whom it is intended. The excerpt from "Pathology of Viral Hepatitis" is a good example. This paragraph is well written in that it does describe the condition fairly clearly for someone who has appropriate background. A practicing nurse or doctor would probably feel comfortable reading the passage. However, the paragraph is taken from a text for first- and second-year nursing students, who would be expected to read at about the thirteenth or fourteenth levels—freshman or sophomore in college. But when a readability formula was used to determine the difficulty of the text from which this paragraph was taken, the score placed this material at about seventeenth grade level. Of course, factors other than those used to measure a readability level must be considered, but many of those factors were included in the checklist used by the forty-one teachers to rate this material. It appears that the material is difficult for the intended audience.

Hill and Erwin (1984) found that more than half of the textbooks they studied were at least a level above their target grade. Social studies texts seemed to be the worst offenders. Some texts for middle-school students were found to be at college level! Derby (1987) suggests that, while vocational texts are becoming less difficult for students to read, there is still a problem with material being too difficult for the target audience. Although publishers of content materials have become more sensitive to producing materials which are content rich *and* readable by the intended audience, many materials which teachers are using today are too difficult for their students.

How Can Teachers Determine if Situations One or Two Apply to Their Students?

There are several ways of measuring readability, some preferable to others. Teachers need to consider how much time they can spend determining readability and how much they need to know about the difficulty of the material before they can teach effective lessons. Applying some of the following measures to determine reading difficulty will provide teachers with this necessary insight.

Readability Formulas

Readability formulas have commonly been used as a major resource for determining the difficulty of material. Fry, a noted expert on readability, quotes Farr as estimating that "over 40 percent of the state and local school districts in the United States use readability formulas as one criterion in textbook selection" (1987, p. 339). Fry believes that "the reason educators use readability formulas is that if you match the learner's ability to the difficulty of the material, you can cut down on oral reading errors and increase silent reading comprehension" (1987, p. 334). For content teachers, this reasoning is especially important because comprehension of the content material is very important. Readability formulas are effective measures to help make this match.

Formulas most often report information about difficulty by reading-level scores. For instance, a readability formula applied to "Pathology of Viral Hepatitis" reflected seventeenth-grade level. The assumption that it is possible to place a material at a certain grade level of difficulty underlies most readability formulas. The use of a formula to determine reading level can be very helpful for decisions about content material when a prediction of difficulty is necessary. Such would be the case when a textbook adoption committee considers several texts but has no students on whom to "try out" the material. Or, when a teacher wants to identify in advance of use several materials that students can read independently in the library, a formula may be useful and efficient. A readability formula gives a bit of information which predicts the difficulty of a material. It is a fairly quick measure and is independent of student interaction. But we cannot rely on the grade level obtained as an exact measure; it is only a predictor.

How do readability formulas work? Klare (1974–75) reviewed the development and uses of readability formulas from 1960 to the mid-1970s and explained their basic components. Over several years, reading researchers have developed and statistically validated many readability formulas. Some have been cumbersome in that they necessitate checking long lists of words. Both the Dale-Chall (1948) and the Spache (1953) measure "word familiarity"—that is, whether students should be expected to know a word within a given passage—by relying on a lengthy word list. Some formulas necessitate several computational steps (Bormouth, 1969). Such formulas have required analysis of several factors relating to readability but, essentially, two measurements are used in the majority of formulas: one of sentence difficulty and one of word difficulty. The assumption is that the longer the sentence and the longer the word, the harder the material will be. Usually, this assumption holds true. Sometimes, however, it is questionable. For instance, in William Faulkner's *The Sound and the Fury*, several sentences are as much as one and a half pages long! Most readers would agree that the length of such sentences makes for challenging material. Yet, could one say that because Hemingway's style leans to short sentences, his material is easy to read? In either case, one will read to understand style and theme; sentence length will be of little import.

The syntactical structure of a sentence probably deserves more attention than it receives in readability formulas (Hunt, 1965; Richardson, 1975). For example, sentences in the active voice may be easier to understand than those in the passive voice. Readability formulas do not measure with such sensitivity. However, teachers would probably agree that first graders do need to read material with shorter sentences than sixth graders can read. But teachers also recognize that first graders can accommodate some variety in sentence patterns. So, longer sentences may be a fairly accurate measure of difficult material, if taken with "a grain of salt."

Just as short sentences seem to be easier to read, the assumption that short words are easier on a reader also seems generally true. First graders do recognize a lot of one-syllable words with facility. Yet, wouldn't *elephant* be an easier word for young readers than *the? Elephant* may be longer than *the*, but it's a lot easier to see a picture of an elephant than a *the!* Since seeing the word in one's mind facilitates comprehension, the longer word is easier in this case. Few readers wish to encounter too many long words all at once, but they also would be very bored by too many short ones. Given these qualifiers, the way most readability formulas measure a material makes sense.

To further illustrate the point, read these two sentences:

The children played on the playground with the elephant.
We reneged all prior briefs.

The first sentence would measure as more difficult on a readability formula, but would it be?

Many formulas are available for teachers to use in determining text difficulty. Klare (1974–75) describes several. A few formulas have remained popular over several years because they are easy to apply and seem reliable. In this text, we will present the Fry readability graph, the Fry short form, and the SMOG. These formulas give teachers a choice according to their purposes for the measure; they are simple to calculate and are accepted favorably by teachers. Hill and Erwin (1984) found that most teachers in their study preferred the Fry formula to others. Each formula is presented below with a set of directions. Readers will find the Raygor graph in the appendix.

The Fry Readability Graph. The Fry graph was originally developed by Edward Fry in the 1960s for African teachers who taught English as a second language. In 1977 Fry revised his graph to include explanations, directions, and an extension to the seventeenth-grade level. The Fry graph and its version for use with short selections are plausible

Figure 3.1. The Fry readability graph.
From *Journal of Reading 21*, 242–252.

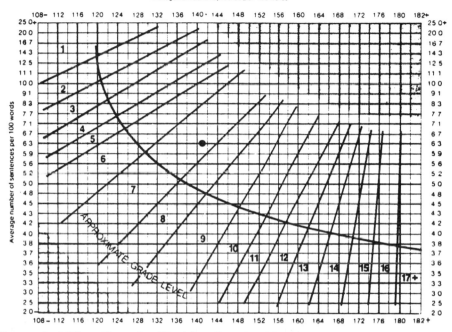

Expanded Directions for Working Readability Graph

1. Randomly select three (3) sample passages and count out exactly 100 words each, beginning with the beginning of a sentence. Do count proper nouns, initializations, and numerals.
2. Count the number of sentences in the hundred words, estimating length of the fraction of the last sentence to the nearest one-tenth.
3. Count the total number of syllables in the 100-word passage. If you don't have a hand counter available, an easy way is to simply put a mark about every syllable over one in each word, then when you get to the end of the passage, count the number of marks and add 100. Small calculators can also be used as counters by pushing numeral 1, then push the + sign for each word or syllable when counting.
4. Enter graph with *average* sentence length and *average* number of syllables; plot dot where the two lines intersect. Area where dot is plotted will give you the approximate grade level.
5. If a great deal of variability is found in syllable count or sentence count, putting more samples into the average is desirable.
6. A word is defined as a group of symbols with a space on either side; thus *Joe, IRA, 1945,* and *&* are each one word.
7. A syllable is defined as a phonetic syllable. Generally, there are as many syllables as vowel sounds. For example, *stopped* is one syllable and *wanted* is two syllables. When counting syllables for numerals and initializations, count one syllable for each symbol. For example, *1945* is four syllables, *IRA* is three syllables, and *&* is one syllable.

ways to measure the difficulty of material on which the teacher will provide instruction.

To use this graph, teachers select at least three 100-word passages from different parts of the selected material. (See direction 1 in Figure 3.1.) For each 100-word passage, they make two counts: the number of syllables, and the number of sentences (directions 2 and 3). The three counts of syllables are added, then averaged; the three counts of sentences are added, then averaged (direction 4). The teacher then locates the average for the number of syllables across the top of the graph and the average for the number of sentences along the side of the graph. The point at which these two averages intersect is the readability score. The point will fall within a fan-like, numbered segment on the graph; this number corresponds to the grade-level score. Teachers should note that Fry says to count all words, including proper nouns, initializations, and numerals (direction 1) and that he defines *word* as well as *syllable* (directions 6 & 7). If a point falls in a gray area, it is an unreliable score and should be recalculated using additional 100-word passages. The Fry worksheet (Figure 3.2) is designed to help the reader remember and apply the directions during readability calculations.

Using the Fry Graph for Short Selections. The Fry graph can be used with selections of less than 100 words if some conversions are made (Forgan and Mangrum, 1985). This technique will be useful to teachers of primary grades where material is partly visual and partly verbal, or for teachers using newspaper or magazine articles to supplement instruction. It can also help teachers to measure the difficulty of word problems in math or of essay questions on tests. The material should contain fewer than 100 words; if the material contains at least 100 words, then the Fry graph can be applied. With this shortened version, a teacher should

1. Count the total number of words.
2. Round *down* to the nearest ten.
3. Refer to the conversion chart (Figure 3.3), and identify the conversion number corresponding to the rounded number.

Figure 3.2. Fry worksheet.

	1st 100 Words	2nd 100 Words	3rd 100 Words	Average
Page #				
# Syllables				
# Sentences				

Plot the averages found on the Fry Graph.

4. Count the number of syllables and sentences in the rounded-down number of words (see steps 1 and 2).
5. Multiply the number of syllables by the number on the conversion chart; multiply the number of sentences by the number on the conversion chart.
6. Plot the final numbers on the regular Fry graph.

In addition to the conversion chart itself, Figure 3.3 includes an example given by Forgan and Mangrum.

The SMOG. McLaughlin (1969) named his readability formula SMOG as a tribute to another formula—the FOG—and after his birthplace, London, where "smog first appeared" (p. 611)! Some have said

Figure 3.3. Conversion chart for Fry's graph for selections with fewer than 100 words.

From *Teaching Content Area Reading Skills,* Third Edition, by Harry W. Forgan and Charles T. Mangrum II, copyright © 1985. Merrill Publishing Co., Columbus, Oh. Used with permission.

If the number of words in the selection is:	*Multiply the number of syllables and sentences by:*
30	3.3
40	2.5
50	2.0
60	1.67
70	1.43
80	1.25
90	1.1

Refer to Fry's graph to find the grade level band that indicates the readability level. The following essay questions demonstrate these directions.

Essay Questions

Syllables

1. To what extent do you believe it is possible for people of different races, religions, or political beliefs to live together in harmony? What suggestions can you make to help people become more tolerant?   *19* *22* *14* *3*
2. It is often said that communism develops fastest in those countries where people do not have the basic necessities of life. Why do you think this might be possible?   *18* *17* *4*

60 words   Total *97*

Counting the words, you will find a total of 62. Rounding down to the nearest ten, you will use 60 words in our sample. There are 97 syllables and 3.8 sentences in the 60 words. Both numbers are then multiplied by 1.67 to convert them to a scale of 100 words. Thus, we have 162 syllables and 6.3 sentences, indicating readability at the eleventh-grade level.

60 Nearest ten (# of words used in determining readability)
97 Number of syllables × *1.67* = *16.2*
3.8 Number of sentences × *1.67* = *6.3*
11th Estimate of readability

that SMOG stands for the Simple Measure of Gobbledygook! Although its name is very lighthearted, this formula is a serious solution to the problem of measuring the readability of material which students may have to read on their own.

The SMOG formula is very easy to use. However, the teacher needs to use a calculator which computes square roots or have a table of square roots handy. To use the SMOG formula, follow these steps:

1. Count three sets of ten sentences (a total of thirty sentences).
2. Count all words of three or more syllables.
3. From this number, determine the nearest perfect square root.
4. Add 3 to this square root.
5. The final number is the readability level.

Figure 3.4 lists some perfect square roots in case a calculator with a square root function is not handy.

Differences between the Fry Readability Graph and the SMOG. Differences between the Fry graph and the SMOG are important to note. Since each formula is based on a different premise, the readability scores must be read differently. The Fry formula measures the readability of material used in an instructional setting. Since the difficult words and sentences will be explained by the teacher, the score is based on students understanding 65 to 75 percent of the material at a given grade level. The SMOG formula is intended to measure the readability of material that a teacher will not be teaching. Perhaps it is material that the teacher has suggested a student use independently. Since the teacher will not be explaining the difficult words and sentences, the score is based on students understanding 90 to 100 percent of the material. If a Fry and a SMOG were calculated on the same material, the Fry score would probably be lower. The chart in Table 3.1 illustrates the basic differences between the two popular measures of readability.

Computer-based Readability Formulas. Computer-based readability formulas are available for teacher use. Most are programs which use popular formulas and allow the teacher to type in text. The program then calculates readability scores and displays them for the teacher. By using a computer program, a teacher can easily use such formulas as the Dale-Chall, which is highly regarded but cumbersome because a long list of words must be checked. Some programs will calculate and compare up to ten different readability formula measures. Others cal-

Figure 3.4. Square root chart.

$\sqrt{1} = 1$	$\sqrt{16} = 4$	$\sqrt{42} = 6.5$	$\sqrt{81} = 9$
$\sqrt{2} = 1.4$	$\sqrt{20} = 4.5$	$\sqrt{49} = 7$	$\sqrt{90} = 9.5$
$\sqrt{4} = 2$	$\sqrt{25} = 5$	$\sqrt{56} = 7.5$	$\sqrt{100} = 10$
$\sqrt{9} = 3$	$\sqrt{30} = 5.5$	$\sqrt{64} = 8$	$\sqrt{121} = 11$
$\sqrt{12} = 3.5$	$\sqrt{36} = 6$	$\sqrt{72} = 8.5$	$\sqrt{144} = 12$

TABLE 3.1   *A Comparison of the Fry Graph and the SMOG Readability Formula*

Readability Measure	Provides readability score for	Teacher will be assisting instruction?	Student is expected to comprehend	Readability score may be	Apply this formula when
Fry	instructional reading settings	Yes	65–75% of material	lower*	teacher will instruct the group using the material being measured
SMOG	independent reading settings	No	90–100% of material	higher*	student will be reading the measured material on own, as in report-writing, homework, etc.

*as measured on the same passage

culate just one measure. For a busy teacher who has several calculations to make, computer programs can be very helpful. However, if only a few calculations are to be made, typing into a computer probably takes more time than performing calculations by hand. A descriptive list of computer readability programs is provided in the appendix.

Rule of Thumb. A very quick and reader-centered way to determine readability is to teach students how to use a "rule of thumb" (Veatch, 1968). Younger students are told to select the book they want to read and to open to a middle page. If they spot an unknown word while reading that page, they press a thumb on the table. For each hard word, they press down another finger. If, when they have finished the page, they have pressed down five or more fingers, the book may be too hard. Three or fewer fingers indicates a more reasonable challenge. No fingers means the book is very easy. Of course, students should read the book even if it appears to be too easy or too hard, if they wish to. Older students can determine readability by using two hands and closing their fingers into fists. One fist closed indicates that the book is just right, two fists closed may indicate difficulty, and only one or two fingers in a fist indicates easy material. These activities are not very scientific, but they do ask the reader to be responsible for determining difficulty. This involvement promotes independence.

Some Cautions about Readability Formulas

In recent literature, professionals have warned teachers to be aware of the limitations of readability formulas. Walker (1985) even titles an article "Requiem for Readability" to emphasize the limitations. Readability formulas are simply not precise determiners of the difficulty of material. We have already mentioned three reasons why not. First, a readability formula gives a grade-level score, which is not a very specific measure of difficulty because grade level can be so ambiguous. Cadenhead (1987) describes this ambiguity as the "metaphor of reading level" and claims that it is a major problem of readability formulas. What does seventeenth-grade level mean when applied to "Pathology of Viral Hepatitis" without a consideration of a reader's interests, background, and knowledge? In 1981, the delegate assembly of the International Reading Association passed a resolution calling for caution in using grade equivalents. A grade-level readability score gives teachers a start in their considerations of text difficulty, not a complete picture.

Second, although the lengths of sentences and words are convenient and credible indicators of readability and fit neatly into a formula, these measures are not comprehensive. Dreyer (1984), for one, suggests several other textual factors to consider, including word frequency, clarity of writing, and concept density. It would be difficult to "compute" such factors in a simple readability formula.

Third, measures of word and sentence length are sometimes not the most accurate indicators of difficulty, as our references to Faulkner and Hemingway, *elephant* and *the*, and the two sentences demonstrated. To further illustrate our point, we refer readers to noted author E. B. White's essay "Calculating Machine." This essay recounts White's reaction when he received a "Reading-Ease Calculator" developed by General Motors and based on the Flesch Reading Ease Formula. According to White, "Communication by the written word is a subtler (and more beautiful) thing than Dr. Flesch and General Motors imagine" (p. 166). His point—that it is dangerous to reduce language to such simplistic evaluation—is well taken.

A fourth factor to consider is reliability and consistency. The fewer sections of material measured, the less consistent and reliable the resulting score is likely to be. Even three sections may be too few. This is why the Fry Short Formula should be used *only* when the material contains less than 100 words and the teacher cannot judge readability efficiently by relying on checklists and professional judgement. If three or fewer sections are measured, the teacher should be careful about accepting the results.

If content teachers are cautious when using formulas, they will find them helpful. Evidence from many studies indicates that a writer's language, especially as measured through vocabulary, is an important factor in simplifying reading. A readability formula can predict the match between the student and the writer and is, as Klare states, "more likely to be actually used" (1974, p. 71) than other predictors, such as tests constructed by teachers.

Use of a Checklist

A more comprehensive way to determine whether material is poorly written or too difficult for a group of readers is to evaluate factors such as those Dreyer suggests: word frequency, clarity, and concept density.

The teacher can apply a formula first, to provide a quick overview and to indicate what else to search for; then the teacher can use a checklist as a more thorough guide. Such a combination allows for "readability and relevance" (Danielson, p. 185).

Walker (1985) developed the following simple checklist and rating system. The items included on this list and the points per item should depend on teacher judgment.

Interest level 1–3 _____
Appropriate vocabulary 1–2 _____
Sentence length controlled 1–3 _____
Suitable for use with study strategy 1–3 _____
Locational skills suitability 1–2 _____
Organizational patterns used 1–2 _____
Graphics suited to extending skills 1–2 _____
Vocabulary load (new) under 10% (depends on material) 1–5 _____
Suited to research skills usage 1–2 _____
Adjunct print aids for comprehension 1–3 _____
Emphasis on higher-level comprehension 1–3

Rating: 26–30, Excellent; 21–25, Good; 15–20, Fair; Below 15, Poor.

In using the rating system, teachers assign the higher numbers to the more desirable traits. For example, if the passage appears to be very interesting, then a rating of 3 would be given. The term "sentence length controlled" refers to passages with no marked variation between very short and very long sentences. Passages "suitable for use with a study strategy" would lend themselves to study techniques such as those described in chapters 8 and 9. If information can be easily located in the passage, then "locational skills suitability" would rate a 2. If aids like margin notes to the reader are available, then "adjunct print aids" would rate a 3.

Bader Textbook Analysis Chart. One fairly brief checklist to help teachers consider readability carefully and efficiently is Bader's textbook analysis chart (1987). The chart separates areas of concern in determining the readability of material and lists specific items for teachers to evaluate and comment on. The user is encouraged to summarize the textbook's strengths and weaknesses after completing the checklist and then to decide what this summary indicates for teaching the material presented (see Figure 3.5). Charts completed by teachers of music and history are included in the appendix.

The Bader analysis encourages teachers to consider several factors that contribute to readability. For example, under Linguistic Factors, the items cover word difficulty more carefully than a word-length measure in a formula can do. The Writing Style category covers sentence length, but in a more direct and sensible manner than a formula could.

Figure 3.5. Text book analysis chart.

+	√	–
Excellent/	Average/	Poor/
Evident	Somewhat	Not
Throughout	Evident	Evident

Book Title _____

Publisher _____

Grade Level _____

LINGUISTIC FACTORS:

Content Area _____

Checklist   *Comments*

_____	_____	_____	Generally appropriate to intended grade level(s) according to _____ formula	_____
_____	_____	_____	Linguistic patterns suitable to most populations and fit intended level(s)	_____
_____	_____	_____	Vocabulary choice and control suitable	_____
_____	_____	_____	New vocabulary highlighted, italicized, in boldface or underlined	_____
_____	_____	_____	New vocabulary, defined in context	_____
_____	_____	_____	New vocabulary defined in margin guides, glossary, beginning or end of chapter	_____

CONCEPTUAL FACTORS:

_____	_____	_____	Conceptual level generally appropriate to intended grade level(s)	_____
_____	_____	_____	Concepts presented deductively	_____
_____	_____	_____	Concepts presented inductively	_____
_____	_____	_____	Major ideas are highlighted, italicized, in boldface type or underlined	_____
_____	_____	_____	Appropriate assumptions made regarding prior level of concepts	_____
_____	_____	_____	Sufficient development of new concepts through examples, illustrations, analogies, redundancy	_____
_____	_____	_____	No evidence of sexual, racial, economic, cultural, or political bias	_____

ORGANIZATIONAL FACTORS:

_____	_____	_____	Units, chapters, table of contents, index present clear, logical development of subject	_____
_____	_____	_____	Chapters of instructional segments contain headings and sub-headings that aid comprehension of subject	_____
_____	_____	_____	Introductory, definitional, illustrative, summary paragraphs/sections used as necessary	_____
_____	_____	_____	Topic sentences of paragraphs clearly identifiable or easily inferred	_____
_____	_____	_____	Each chapter/section/unit contains a well-written summary and/or overview	_____

WRITING STYLE:

_____	_____	_____	Ideas are expressed clearly and directly	_____
_____	_____	_____	Word choice is appropriate	_____
_____	_____	_____	Tone and manner of expression are appealing to intended readers	_____
_____	_____	_____	Mechanics are correct	_____

+ Excellent/ Evident Throughout	√ Average/ Somewhat Evident	− Poor/ Not Evident	*Checklist*	*Comments*
_____	_____	_____	Questions/tasks appropriate to conceptual development of intended age/grade level(s)	_____
_____	_____	_____	Questions/tasks span levels of reasoning: literal, interpretive, critical, values clarification, problem-solving	_____
_____	_____	_____	Questions/tasks can be used as reading guides	_____
_____	_____	_____	Suitable supplementary readings suggested	_____

TEACHING AIDS:

_____	_____	_____	Clear, convenient to use	_____
_____	_____	_____	Helpful ideas for conceptual development	_____
_____	_____	_____	Alternative instructional suggestions given for poor readers, slow learning students, advanced students	_____
_____	_____	_____	Contains objectives, management plans, evaluation guidelines, tests of satisfactory quality	_____
_____	_____	_____	Supplementary aids available	_____

BINDING/PRINTING/FORMAT/ILLUSTRATIONS:

_____	_____	_____	Size of book is appropriate	_____
_____	_____	_____	Cover, binding, and paper are appropriate	_____
_____	_____	_____	Type-face is appropriate	_____
_____	_____	_____	Format is appropriate	_____
_____	_____		Pictures, charts, graphs are appealing	_____
_____	_____	_____	Illustrations aid comprehension of text	_____
_____	_____	_____	Illustrations are free of sexual, social, cultural bias	_____

SUMMARY:

_____	_____	_____	Totals	_____

The strengths are:

The weaknesses are:

As a teacher, I will need to:

Original TEXT ANALYSIS CHART by: Dr. Lois Bader, Michigan State University
Used with permission of Lois Bader.

Under Conceptual Factors and Organizational Factors, there are items which many authors have identified as crucial in determining text difficulty. In addition, the teacher is asked to think about Learning Aids for the students, because such aids will make otherwise difficult material easier to handle. The Teaching Aids category also gives teachers direction in how to guide reading of otherwise difficult material. As Sinatra (1986) points out, visual aids often make difficult material readable. Features such as typography, format, illustrations, and book appearance can enhance meaning in a text. Bader includes these items in her last category.

Cautions about Checklists. The use of checklists to determine whether material is poorly written or difficult must be qualified, just as the use of readability formulas should be. No one checklist can cover all factors important to teachers. Checklists must be general; only teachers can make them specific by adding their own items according to their own needs for the instructional material. Most checklists will cover instructional design, but not instructional content (Moore and Murphy, 1987). However, with such tools as those contained in this chapter and with a knowledge of why determining the difficulty factors of reading material is important, we believe that teachers can proceed wisely.

Reader-Based Situations Which Affect Readability: Situations Three, Four, and Five

While situations one and two deal with determining text difficulty, situations three, four, and five deal with reader difficulties. They are reader-based—the possible problems they pose reside inherently in the reader and only secondarily in the text, which may be well written and have most of the characteristics which one could hope for in a readable text. However, the text is only one part of the interaction necessary for successful reading. As principle 8 in chapter one states: The act of reading requires the interaction of the reader, the text, the teacher, and the environment. Drum (1985) found that fourth-grade science and social studies texts which were equal in vocabulary frequency, syntactic complexity, and overall structure were not equally easy for the fourth graders in her study to read. Prior knowledge seemed to play a significant part in making the social studies texts easier for these students.

Situation Three: Readers May Have No Prior Knowledge

The following dialogue illustrates how difficult it is to understand material when one has no prior background:

"Do I deserve a mulligan?" asked Bob.

"No, but don't take a drop," said Al. "Use a hand-mashie, then fly the bogey high to the carpet and maybe you'll get a gimme within the leather."

"You're right," said Bob, "I'll cover the flag for a birdie and at least get a ginsberg if I'm not stymied." [From *Critical Reading Thinking Skills for the College Student* by Raymond F. Morgan, Jane W. Meeks, Andrea Schollaert, and Joanne Paul (1986), Kendall/Hunt Publishing Company.]

If one is not a golfer, reading this dialogue just to pronounce the words is easier than answering the following questions:

1. Does Bob deserve a mulligan?
   a) yes b) no c) maybe
2. What does Al think Bob should do?
   a) catch a gimme b) take a drop c) use a hand-mashie d) fly a kite
3. What does Bob decide to do?
   a) cover the flag b) take a drop c) birdie-up
4. How can Bob get a birdie?
   a) getting stymied b) getting a ginsburg c) by covering the flag
5. If Bob is not stymied, what will he get?
   a) a hickie b) a birdie c) a mulligan d) a ginsberg

The words and sentences are short, so one would expect that a readability formula would yield a low grade-level score for readability. The syntax is a redeeming feature of the story; a reader could answer the questions by relying on syntax and familiar words in the passage. Yet most readers, no matter what their age or background, have great difficulty understanding the dialogue. In fact, many readers select the correct responses but cannot explain why! The problem lies in the readers' lack of prior knowledge. What is a mulligan? What is a birdie? Readers may try to create meaning for these words by calling on their store of information, but they don't really know the answers if they don't know golf! (For correct answers, see the Preparing the Reader section of chapter 5.)

Principle Four, in chapter one, addresses this type of reader-based situation: Reading for meaning is a highly individualized process that is influenced by the reader's personal store of experiences and knowledge. Thus, textbook authors may write well but produce material which is difficult for some students because of their lack of background in the subject. Children reading about coral reefs, for example, may have difficulty simply because they have never heard about or seen one. It is up to the teacher to determine if this is the case. Ausubel (1978), a noted educational psychologist, has stressed that what the learner already knows is the most important factor for future learning. Dechant (1970) expressed a similar view when he said, "Without the proper experience, the reader cannot respond with the proper meaning to the author's words" (p. 555). The situation will be dire if a reader has no background in the subject being taught. It is crucial that the teacher not assume that students know more than they do. Determining reader background is essential.

Situation Four: Readers May Have Some Prior Knowledge

Ideally, more readers will have some knowledge than no knowledge. Perhaps students know very little about the specific content to be read but do understand a related concept. For instance, fourth graders may not know much about the Pilgrims, but they may know what it's like to be uprooted and have to relocate to a strange place. These students, then, would have some background the teacher could use in introducing the reading.

In chapter 1, we emphasized the importance of the reader's previous experience and knowledge. Schema theory explains this correlation by proposing that prior knowledge and the correct application of that knowledge leads a reader to comprehension. Recently, the term "schema" has been prominent in the professional literature, but advocates of the importance of prior knowledge span several decades: Bartlett, 1932; Ausubel, 1960 and 1978; Piaget, 1963; Bransford and Johnson, 1973; Anderson and Pearson, 1984. Rumelhart (1981) stresses that schemata, which may be likened to diagrams or drawings stored in the brain, are fundamental to all processing of information. Often the diagrams are incomplete, but they become a fuller picture as more information is found to complete them. (Chapter 4 includes more information about schema theory.)

As we noted in chapter 1, Hart stresses the importance of building programs for learning which include as much information as possible. Proficient readers will try to determine before they read new material what they do and don't know about the subject. Teachers will have to help their students by making this determination with them and for them.

Situation Five: Readers May Have Incorrect Knowledge

A teacher wrote this "telegram" to illustrate how incorrect knowledge can influence one's reading:

> Won trip for two . . . stop . . . St. Matthew's Island . . . stop . . . pack small bag . . . stop . . . meet at airport . . . stop . . . 9 am tomorrow. (by Grace Hamlin)

If readers "know" that islands are tropical, have a warm climate, are surrounded by beaches where lots of sunbathing and swimming are enjoyed, they will pack a suitcase with sunglasses, shorts, bathing suits, and suntan lotion. However, St. Matthew's Island is off the coast of Alaska, where the average temperature is 37 degrees. Incorrect knowledge in this case will impede comprehension. Similarly, if readers "know" that the dinosaurs were destroyed by other animals, they will have difficulty reading and understanding a theory which proposes that dinosaurs were destroyed by a giant meteor. Maria and MacGinitie (1987) discuss the difference between having correct, if insufficient, prior knowledge and having incorrect prior knowledge. They conclude that students are less likely to overcome a problem of incorrect knowledge because the new information conflicts with their prior "knowledge." In this situation, determining students' background is very important because material will be most "unreadable" to students who refute the material.

Some Methods for Determining the Background of Readers

In each of the preceding reader-based situations, readers will be confounded by their reading. If they have to build a base of understanding from scratch, their reading will be tedious and they may lose interest and stamina quickly. If their "mind diagram" is incomplete, readers will also read laboriously and perhaps leave the material with still-incomplete pictures. If they must reorient their thinking because they have incorrect information, their need to hold on to the familiar may win over their need for correct information. Unless the teacher determines such problems in advance and then delivers strategies which can build students' background accordingly, reading comprehension may be in jeopardy. Following are some ways to determine if these three situations exist for students.

The Cloze Procedure. The term *closure* is derived from an old Teutonic word meaning "to mutilate" or "to cut up;" *cloze* is a shortened variant of closure. In the cloze procedure, a passage is clozed (cut up) so that it can be closed (filled in) by the student. The premise is that readers will rely on prior knowledge and use of context as they close the cut-up passage. This technique relies heavily on the Gestalt concept of perceiving the whole of things. Ebbinghaus, in the late 1800s, used a modified form of closure when he conducted his verbal learning and retention studies (described in chapter 9).

Taylor designed the cloze procedure, as we now use it, in 1953. His purpose was to determine readability of material. In its strict form, cloze is constructed by selecting a passage of 250 words or more and deleting words at regular intervals of every fifth, tenth, or Nth (any predetermined) word. The beginning and ending sentences remain intact. Blanks replace the deleted words, but no clues other than the context of the material are provided to the readers, who must refill those blanks. Only the exact word which was deleted should be counted as a correct answer. Research (Bormouth, 1969) has indicated that the exact word score is the most valid. When synonyms are accepted, the scoring criteria change and the cloze must be modified, usually for instructional rather than readability purposes. Although scoring seems stringent, the criteria for achieving an instructional level of readability are quite relaxed to compensate. A score of only 40 to 60 percent correct is acceptable.

In a review of the research, Jongsma (1980) found that the cloze procedure is useful at any grade level if the pattern of deletions is sensitive to the students' familiarity with language. We recommend that, generally, every tenth word be deleted for primary students and every fifth word be deleted for older students (fourth grade and above). By using cloze, a teacher can find out if students have prior knowledge about upcoming material and if they can adapt to the author's style. If students complete the cloze with ease, they will achieve an independent-level score, indicating that they can read the material on their own. If they can adapt when instruction about the material is provided by the teacher, they will achieve an instructional-level score. A frustration-level score indicates that the material will be extremely difficult for readers to understand even with instruction.

Here is a basic set of directions for constructing a cloze:

1. Select a passage of about 250–300 words.
2. Leave the first and last sentences intact to help the readers use context clues.
3. Delete *consistently* every Nth word, (fifth, tenth, or other) starting with the Nth word in the second sentence and continuing until the next-to-last sentence.
4. Make a key of the exact words that fill the blanks.
5. Write directions for your students. These directions should stress the purpose for this activity—to determine background, not to test them—and explain that they are to fill each blank with a word they think the author might have used.
6. Decide on the scoring criteria you will use. An easy way, if you have fifty blanks, is to double the number of correct responses. Or use this formula (Holdzkom, 1987):

$$\text{Percent Correct} = \frac{\text{Words correct}}{\text{Total \# Blanks}} \times 100$$

7. Using these scores to determine the independent, instructional, and frustrational levels, make a chart such as the following to categorize your students:

Independent Material Easy Scores Above 60%	Instructional Material Suitable Scores Between 40 and 60%	Frustration Material Too Hard Scores Below 40%
(list students)	(list students)	(list students)

Activity 3.1, which follows, is a cloze constructed by an eighth-grade science teacher.

A cloze procedure can reveal what students already know about a subject and can indicate if the material is appropriate. The better that students do, probably the more they know about the topic. If most students fall in the frustrational level, the material is inappropriate.

TABLE 3.2 *Readability Formulas Compared to Cloze/Maze*

Characteristics	Readability Formulas	Cloze/Maze
Estimated match of reader to material	Yes	Yes
Match derived by	Applying a formula to a text, i.e., a count of words and syllables	Deleting words in a consistent pattern and having students replace exact words
Materials needed	Text and teacher	Text, teacher, and student
Application situations (1 through 5, described earlier)	1 and 2: material too difficult or poorly written	3, 4, and 5: estimate of prior knowledge desired

Ashby-Davis (1985) cautions that a cloze is not like the usual reading students do. One's speed of reading, eye movements, and use of context are likely to be different while reading a cloze. Therefore, although a cloze may be a helpful indicator of the particular background a student has in a topic, it should not be relied on to tell a teacher about a student's general reading skills.

Maze. A predeterminer similar to cloze but easier for students to respond to is a maze (Guthrie, 1974), which is especially useful for determining students' prior knowledge and understanding of a subject. With a maze, one may use a passage of 100 to 120 words selected from a representative part of the textbook. Every fifth or tenth word is deleted by the teacher, but then three choices are given to the students: the correct word, a grammatically similar but incorrect word, and a "distractor," which is a grammatically different and incorrect word. Since the maze is easier for students to complete, the scoring criteria are more stringent, as the example illustrates. Although a maze is a bit harder to construct than the cloze because three choices must be provided, many teachers prefer it. Activity 3.2 shows how a maze for elementary social studies material would look and be scored.

Readability Formulas Compared to Cloze and Maze. Readability formulas, cloze, and maze are all useful for determining background. They help find the match between reader and text. However, they are used in different circumstances. Table 3.2 illustrates these distinctions.

Pretests of Knowledge. Pretests of knowledge are quick, sensible ways to measure background knowledge. Teachers construct these tests for students to take before they begin reading. These tests are not graded; the teacher and students use them to see what students already know

A C T I V I T Y 3.1

Cloze for Determining Background

Determining the individual levels of the students I teach is very important. Therefore, to determine background, I selected a passage from the text approximately 275 words long and have the students perform the cloze test on this passage.

Energy, Reactions, and Catalysts

Energy is either gained or lost during a chemical change. In some reactions, _____1_____ as burning, energy is _____2_____ . In other reactions, energy _____3_____ be added for a _____4_____ change to occur. If _____5_____ is released, the reaction _____6_____ called exothermic. If energy _____7_____ be added during a _____8_____ , the reaction is called _____9_____ .

The burning of magnesium _____10_____ an exothermic reaction. Though _____11_____ heat is needed to _____12_____ the reaction, the heat _____13_____ off when magnesium bonds _____14_____ oxygen is more than _____15_____ to keep the reaction _____16_____ .

The reaction between ammonium _____17_____ and barium hydroxide is _____18_____ exothermic reaction. Energy is _____19_____ as the two solids _____20_____ . The temperature of the _____21_____ flask decreases. In fact, _____22_____ may form on the _____23_____ of the flask. A _____24_____ amount of energy is _____25_____ up as the products _____26_____ . However, much more energy _____27_____ absorbed to keep the _____28_____ going. Thus, the reaction _____29_____ endothermic.

The time it _____30_____ for a reaction to _____31_____ can vary greatly. The _____32_____ change that occurs when _____33_____ tarnishes may take place _____34_____ a few months. The _____35_____ of silver chloride from _____36_____ nitrate and sodium chloride _____37_____ takes place in an _____38_____ . In some cases, a _____39_____ may be too slow _____40_____ be of use.

Recall _____41_____ Activity on page 240 _____42_____ the decomposition of hydrogen _____43_____ . Since the decomposition of _____44_____ dilute solution of hydrogen _____45_____ is a slow process, _____46_____ dioxide is added. The _____47_____ speeds the reaction so _____48_____ oxygen is formed faster.

(continued)

and what they should learn. Pretests can be developed in any number of ways.

Recognition Pretests. Holmes and Roser (1987) recommend the recognition technique as an informal pretest. Teachers can use the subheadings in a chapter as stems for a multiple choice format. Alterna-

---

A C T I V I T Y 3.1 *Continued*

___49___ , the MNO$_2$ is unchanged. ___50___ this case, MNO$_2$ acts as a catalyst. A catalyst changes the speed of a reaction without being permanently changed itself.

Answers:

1. such	14. with	27. is	40. to
2. released	15. enough	28. reaction	41. the
3. must	16. going	29. is	42. involving
4. chemical	17. thiocyanate	30. takes	43. peroxide
5. energy	18. an	31. occur	44. a
6. is	19. absorbed	32. chemical	45. peroxide
7. must	20. react	33. silver	46. manganese
8. reaction	21. reaction	34. over	47. MNO$_2$
9. endothermic	22. ice	35. formation	48. the
10. is	23. outside	36. silver	49. However
11. some	24. small	37. solutions	50. In
12. start	25. given	38. instant	
13. given	26. form	39. reaction	

Independent Material Easy Scores Above 60%	Instructional Material Suitable Scores Between 40 and 60%	Frustrational Material Too Hard Scores Below 40%
Dawn (missed 16 = 68%) Charles (missed 15 = 70%) Elsie (missed 18 = 64%)	Walter (missed 20 = 60%) Chuck (missed 28 = 44%) Frances (missed 22 = 56%) Cyndi (missed 24 = 48%)	John (missed 32 = 36%) Bill (missed 34 = 32%)

Activity developed by Carole Baughan. Source of cloze material is *Focus on Physical Science* by Heimler & Price (1981). Charles E. Merrill. Reprinted by permission of the publisher.

tives are derived from chapter content. The recognition pretest in Activity 3.3 was developed by a teacher to determine background for a middle school science chapter.

A Discriminative Self-Inventory. A discriminative self-inventory (Dale, O'Rourke, and Bamman, 1971) will help the teacher and students

ACTIVITY 3.2

A Maze Prepared on an Excerpt from "The Battle of Sempach"

The Swiss knew that the enemy army was made up mostly of knights in armor, on horseback. Knights usually fought only { one / a / get } way—they galloped straight

{ backwards / walk / ahead } in a charge, with { her / their / sword } long lances held straight { in / hurry. They / out }

would try to { smash / wander / enemy } into the Swiss and { straight / scatter / avoid } them.

But the Swiss { were / that / had } learned that the horses { would / will / night } not be able to

{ conquer / get / Swiss } past the wall of { horses / curly / pike } points. The charge would { come / go / but } to a stop in

{ side / front / with } of the square, with { knights / kings / gallop } and horses all jammed { fight / apart, / together } hardly able

to move. { Then / Charge / Before } those Swiss armed with { brief / long / wall } swords and axes would

{ up / wander / rush } out of the square { to / for / fight } hack and chop at { won / the / that } helpless knights. This

was how the Swiss had won their other battles.

Key:	one	smash	would	come	together	rush
	ahead	scatter	get	front	Then	to
	their	had	pike	knights	long	the
	out					

Independent Material Easy Scores 90% and Above (list students)	Instructional Material Suitable 70–90% (list students)	Frustrational Material Too Hard Below 70% (list students)

Pp 110–111, *Stories of Freedom*, 1988, Childcraft Annual, World Book, Inc.

A C T I V I T Y 3.3

Recognition (Science: Sources of Energy)

1. Energy can come in which of the following forms:
   a. electrical
   b. light
   c. magnetic
   d. heat
   e. chemical
   f. kinetic
   g. listening
2. Which of the following statements have the same meaning as the law of the conservation of energy? (Energy cannot be created or destroyed, but can be transformed.)
   a. energy can be changed from one form to another
   b. energy can be made from matter alone
   c. energy can be used up
   d. resources used to transform energy can be used up
3. Sources used in producing energy today include:
   a. fossil fuels (coal, gas, oil, water power, geothermal power)
   b. ocean tidal power
   c. nuclear power
   d. solar power
   e. lunar power

Source: Holmes, Betty C. and Nancy L. Roser. "Five Ways to Assess Readers' Prior Knowledge," *The Reading Teacher, 40,* March, 1987. Developed for the classroom display by Holly Corbett.

know which words in the text they do and don't know. The teacher identifies and lists the important words with a symbol system, such as checks for older students or faces for younger students. Students then react to each word. The self-inventory in Activity 3.4 was developed by a teacher to determine background for reading a middle school art text. The self-inventory in Activity 3.5 was developed by a teacher to determine background for reading a third-grade health text.

Activity 3.6 was developed by a teacher who uses attention-getting symbols to capture students' interest in completing the activity.

Factstorming. Factstorming types of activities are very useful in determining reader background. They are simple to conduct because a whole class can participate at once and the activity proceeds from a single, generative question. Factstorming is similar to brainstorming

A C T I V I T Y 3.4

Self-Inventory

Below are listed terms from Chapter 5. You are not expected to know all the terms listed, nor will you be graded on your answers. Place a + beside the ones you know well; place a √ beside the ones you know something about; place a 0 beside the ones you don't know.

_____ lintels	_____ hypostyle hall
_____ secular	_____ stylization
_____ Stonehenge	_____ descriptive perspective
_____ low relief	_____ Great Sphinx
_____ pyramids	_____ registers (*not cash registers*)
_____ Pharaohs	_____ ziggurats
_____ mastabas	_____ cave paintings
_____ Tutankhamen	_____ Mesopotamia

Developed by Joan Phipps.

A C T I V I T Y 3.5

Self-Inventory

Use the following symbols to tell how well you know these words. Remember: you won't be graded and you aren't supposed to know all the words.

I know it!   So-so   I don't know it.

_____ 1. FATS	_____ 7. MINERALS
_____ 2. CAR-BO-HY-DRATES	_____ 8. PROTEIN
_____ 3. OXYGEN	_____ 9. CARBON
_____ 4. WATER	_____ 10. HYDROGEN
_____ 5. VITAMINS	_____ 11. FOOD
_____ 6. AMINO ACIDS	_____ 12. MARROW

Developed by Kathy Feltus.

A C T I V I T Y 3.6

Self-Inventory

The following words will be used in the selection you are about to read. In order to give me an idea of your vocabulary background, please check the appropriate category for each word. REMEMBER: This is not a test, and it will *not* be graded.

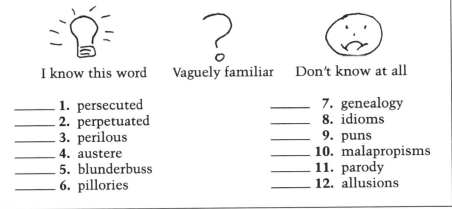

I know this word   Vaguely familiar   Don't know at all

_____ 1. persecuted   _____ 7. genealogy
_____ 2. perpetuated   _____ 8. idioms
_____ 3. perilous   _____ 9. puns
_____ 4. austere   _____ 10. malapropisms
_____ 5. blunderbuss   _____ 11. parody
_____ 6. pillories   _____ 12. allusions

Developed by Rebecca McSweeney.

but focuses on facts and associations pertinent to the topic, whereas brainstorming focuses on problem solving. The teacher asks students to tell anything they can think of about the topic to be read; for instance: "Tell anything you know about capital punishment." Responses are written on the chalkboard or a transparency and discussed as they are entered. An example of factstorming is given in chapter 1.

PreP: A sophisticated version of factstorming is PreP, a prereading plan (Langer, 1981). PreP has three phases: (1) initial associations with the concept during factstorming; (2) reflections on the initial concept when students are asked to explain why they thought of a particular response, thus building an awareness of their prior knowledge and associations; (3) re-formation of knowledge when new ideas learned during the first two phases are articulated. An example of PreP for fourth-grade mathematics is given in Activity 3.7.

What-I-Know Sheets. What-I-Know sheets (Heller, 1986) offer another structured approach to factstorming. The typical sheet is similar to the example given here, with columns labeled "What I Already Know," "What I Know Now," and "What I Don't Know." Students also

A C T I V I T Y 3.7

PreP (Prereading Plan)

The prereading plan will be used to estimate the level of background knowledge a fourth-grade class brings to the study of fractions. The plan will stimulate discussion and develop awareness of fractions in a class of six to twelve students. These students should be familiar with four of the major concepts to be developed in this unit; therefore, by listening and observing students, the teacher can tell whether the students have much, some, or little knowledge about fractions.

Phase 1: *Initial associations with the concept*
> Teacher: Tell me anything that comes to mind when you hear the word "fractions."

As each student relates ideas that come to mind, the teacher writes the responses on the chalkboard. Students activate prior knowledge through the associations.

Phase 2: *Reflections on initial associations*
> Teacher: What made you think of "numerator"? (or denominator, parts, equal parts, pies, regions, number lines, dividing, multiplying, sharing, whole, etc.).

This phase helps students develop awareness of their networks of association and to interact with other ideas and change their own ideas about fractions.

Phase 3: *Re-formation of knowledge*
> Teacher: Based on our discussion, and before we study the chapter, have you any new ideas about fractions?

This allows students to verbalize associations, to probe their memories, and to refine responses.

Developed by Nancy Campbell.

fill in the topic, the purpose for reading, and the answer to the purpose question. Before reading, students will factstorm on what they already know about this topic. After reading, they will list what they have learned and what else they should learn. Some teachers have modified the third column from "What I Don't Know" to "What I *Still* Don't Know" to help students realize that this is a category for what they didn't learn by reading but still need to learn. Activity 3.8 shows a What-I-Know sheet completed by a primary science class.

A C T I V I T Y 3.8

What-I-Know Sheet

Topic: Marine Life
Purpose for Activity: Learn More about Sea Shells

What I Already Know	What I Know Now	What I Still Don't Know
Some of them are round	Some shells have points	What do shells come from
Some of them are smooth	They look different	
They come in different sizes	They have different names	
Some are in water		
Some are pretty		

Developed by Marcie Mansfield.

The example in Activity 3.9 shows how a teacher makes clear the *before reading* and *after reading* sections of a What-I-Know sheet and helps readers clarify their own background knowledge.

Situation Six: Readers May Possess No, Some, or Incorrect Knowledge of Reading and Study Skills

The following two situations, like situations three, four, and five, are reader-based. The problems they pose originate primarily in the reader and only secondarily in the text. In situation six, readers may not possess reading and study skills, but the author of the material could not predict this. For instance, if a text includes graphs to present material and the students reading that text do not have the skill to read graphs correctly, a readability problem exists. It is also possible that students will have in mind one definition for a word, perhaps a general meaning, but the text is using that word in a very specific, content-oriented way. *Bank* is such a word: Does it mean the slope of a river side? a place where money is kept? to count on something? Realizing that words have multiple meanings and are dependent on context and content is a reading skill which some readers do not possess fully, and some do not possess at all. When students assure the teacher that they "studied,"

A C T I V I T Y 3.9

What-I-Know Sheet

Before Reading		After Reading	
What I already know:	What I would like to know:	What I know now:	What I still need to know:

Adapted by Paula Mitchell.

but in fact their definition of study is to read over the material for the first time, they have incorrect knowledge of a study skill.

Many studies conducted in the past few years indicate that some children, particularly those tested in grades three through nine, do not understand the difference between a major idea and supporting ideas; they have difficulty distinguishing a main idea from its details (Garner *et al.*, 1986; Meyer, Brandt and Bluth, 1980; Williams, Taylor and Ganger, 1981). It is important for teachers to realize what reading and study skills their students need to use in understanding a content lesson. It is important that teachers know whether their students have those skills.

Some Methods for Determining the Reading and Study Skills Levels of Students

Because comprehension, vocabulary, and study skills for content reading are addressed in other chapters of this book, they will not be discussed in depth here. However, teachers should be aware that they need to determine how reading skills affect the match between the reader and content material. They should also realize that if the problems they discover are severe, a reading specialist needs to be called on for help. Content and regular classroom teachers should not be expected to diagnose and remediate severe reading difficulties. Nor should the regular teacher be responsible for special testing to determine such difficulties. If the teacher suspects that situation six exists, the following options may be helpful. But the best option is to depend on the school reading specialist.

Standardized Tests. Sometimes the results of standardized achievement tests, those given to students to determine the general progress of a school system, can be used by classroom teachers. If the test results report subscores for areas of reading achievement like word knowledge and comprehension, they will provide at least an indicator of students' levels of achievement. Teachers who suspect that their students have no, few, or incorrect reading and study skills might start their process of determining students' background by reviewing these already-available scores. If a teacher discerns a pattern—the vocabulary scores for a majority of the class are below grade level, for example—it is a clear indicator for adapted instruction. The key here is discerning a pattern or trend within the class. Rather than using standardized tests as a measure of a student's individual achievement, teachers will find that standardized tests provide an overview of the performance they can expect from the whole class. Group standardized tests are designed to compare groups, not to diagnose individuals. Standardized tests are discussed further in chapter 11.

Already Constructed Informal Inventories. A content teacher who decides to test students' reading and study skills needs adequate time to administer, score, and interpret the results. Although creating informal measures is time-consuming, the effort can be useful over a long period of time and reveal much information to teachers. Informal ways to measure students' general study skills will be discussed in chapter 8. Informal ways to measure reading skills are best constructed with help from a reading specialist. Unfortunately, very few already-constructed informal or standardized tests of reading and study skills are available for teachers. Textbook authors are becoming more sensitive to the need for such measures, however, and are beginning to include inventories of study skills, such as proficiency in using textbook aids, in their textbooks.

The Content Inventories (McWilliams and Rakes, 1979) is a collection of group inventories already constructed for English, social studies, and science at grades seven to twelve. Students read selected passages and answer questions which the teacher scores. In addition, several study skills tests are provided. Although *The Content Inventories* covers only the secondary grade levels and the subjects listed, it provides a model teachers may use to construct a similar set of informal tests.

The Wiebe-Cox Mathematical Reading Inventory is another model for an informal test of reading skills specific to a content area. For

---

A C T I V I T Y 3.10

Sample Items from Wiebe-Cox Inventory

Part 1: Circle the word I say:

once   ones   won   no   none

Part 2: Which picture tells about the word?

Minute

Part 3: Which word tells about the underlined word?:

<u>pair</u>

    part of   quail   paid   two   three

Part 4: Which word fills in the blank best?:

A triangle is a _____ .

    numeral   multiply   shape   shame   measure

From J. Cox and J. H. Wiebe, "Measuring reading vocabulary and concepts in mathematics in the primary grades,"*The Reading Teacher*, January 1984. Reprinted with permission of Juanita Cox and the International Reading Association.

example, words important to math computations as well as word problems are included in this inventory. Cox and Wiebe (1984), in a recent article, explain the inventory and include the complete battery of tests. Activity 3.10 provides a sample of items in the inventory.

Teacher-Constructed Textbook Inventories. At the beginning of a school year, content teachers might use a textbook inventory as a class activity to help them learn about their students' proficiency in using textbooks. The following inventories were designed by teachers to help them make that assessment. The Textbook Treasure Hunt (Bryant, 1984), Activity 3.11, is used with an English textbook. An elementary social studies teacher devised Activity 3.12 for her students to complete to demonstrate their knowledge of the parts of a chapter. Similarly, a middle school mathematics teacher devised an inventory of students' knowledge of their math book, from which the following excerpt is taken:

Do You Know Your Math Book?

1. Who are the authors of your book? Who are the publishers?
2. How many chapters are in your book?

3. How many pages are there in the whole book?
4. What is the title of chapter 15?
5. What is the title of chapter 10, section 3?
6. On what page will you find the definition of "complex plane" and on what page did you find this definition?
7. By using the glossary, check each word that is a mathematical tool:
_____ calculator _____ product _____ remainder _____ abacus _____ center

Developed by Dana Walker.

Situation Seven: Readers May Have No, Little, or Misdirected Interest or Negative Attitudes

Even the most proficient reader will experience difficulty in understanding and thinking about a subject he or she is not interested in. Remember that a majority (twenty-six) of the forty-one teachers who graded the "Pathology of Viral Hepatitis" paragraph rated it an F for interest! Yet these were good readers. We might speculate, and probably correctly, that their lack of interest in this subject negatively influenced their reading. If teachers recognize this situation among their students, they can use many activities to stimulate greater interest, better attitudes, and more appreciation for the subject. But if a teacher simply assumes that students are interested in and positive toward the subject, it is likely that the teacher will be disappointed and the students will not understand the reading. This situation may be seen as a form of "cognitive dissonance," which *A Dictionary of Reading* (1981) defines as "a perceived inconsistency between one's attitudes and one's behavior" (p. 54). In short, students' reading proficiency may conflict with their lack of interest to create a conflict which blocks learning.

We are reminded of an old story, told by one of our reading professors, about the little boy who goes to the library and asks for a book about penguins. The librarian is so excited that this small child is requesting information that she selects a large volume on penguins and offers it to him. The child takes the book, almost staggering under its weight, and trudges home. The next day he returns it. "How did you like that book about penguins?" the librarian eagerly asks him. "To tell you the truth," the boy replies, "this book was more about penguins than I care to know." A similar situation occurs when teachers misinterpret a little interest as a lot and do not match the reader with a suitable text; that mismatch may lead to misdirected interest. Chapter 2 covers this situation in depth and offers the teacher several means to determine students' interest and attitudes as well as activities to stimulate interest and attitudes.

CARL A. RUDISILL LIBRARY
LENOIR RHYNE COLLEGE

A C T I V I T Y 3.11

Textbook Treasure Hunt

There are many hidden treasures in your grammar book. After you have completed the path below, you will have discovered some interesting facts! Write your answers and the page number(s) on which you found the information on a clean sheet of notebook paper.

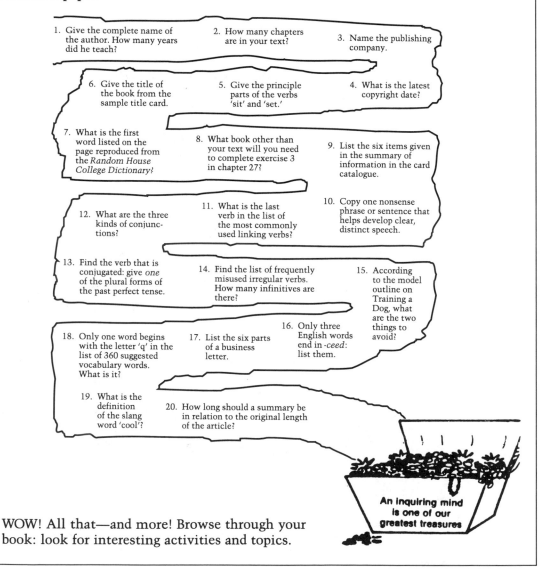

1. Give the complete name of the author. How many years did he teach?

2. How many chapters are in your text?

3. Name the publishing company.

4. What is the latest copyright date?

5. Give the principle parts of the verbs 'sit' and 'set.'

6. Give the title of the book from the sample title card.

7. What is the first word listed on the page reproduced from the *Random House College Dictionary?*

8. What book other than your text will you need to complete exercise 3 in chapter 27?

9. List the six items given in the summary of information in the card catalogue.

10. Copy one nonsense phrase or sentence that helps develop clear, distinct speech.

11. What is the last verb in the list of the most commonly used linking verbs?

12. What are the three kinds of conjunctions?

13. Find the verb that is conjugated: give *one* of the plural forms of the past perfect tense.

14. Find the list of frequently misused irregular verbs. How many infinitives are there?

15. According to the model outline on Training a Dog, what are the two things to avoid?

16. Only three English words end in *-ceed*: list them.

17. List the six parts of a business letter.

18. Only one word begins with the letter 'q' in the list of 360 suggested vocabulary words. What is it?

19. What is the definition of the slang word 'cool'?

20. How long should a summary be in relation to the original length of the article?

An inquiring mind is one of our greatest treasures

WOW! All that—and more! Browse through your book: look for interesting activities and topics.

A C T I V I T Y 3.11 *continued*

Textbook Treasure Hunt answers

---

	page
1. John E. Warriner: 32 years	ii
2. 30	xvi
3. Harcourt Brace Jovanovich	i
4. 1982	ii
5. sit: sit, sitting, sat, (have) sat	171
set: set, setting, set, (have) set	
6. *The Complete Book of Sports Medicine*	573
7. funky	593
8. dictionary	622
9. call number, author, title, subject, cross references, publisher	574
10. The big black bug bit the big black bear.	692
11. could have been	18
12. coordinating, correlative, subordinating	31
13. we (or you or they) had flown	163
14. 27	156
15. coddling, overfeeding	684
16. exceed, proceed, succeed	649
17. heading, inside address, salutation, body, closing, signature	447
18. quaint	642
19. having a dispassionate or detached attitude	433
20. 1/4 to 1/3	378

The above activity uses the Third Course of *Warriner's English Grammar and Composition* New York, N.Y.: Harcourt Brace Jovanovich, 1982.

From JoAnne Bryant, "Open to Suggestion" section, *Journal of Reading,* March 1984. Reprinted with permission of the International Reading Association.

Who Is Responsible for Determining the Reader's Background?

Of course, all parties involved have a responsibility. The interaction between textbook, author, reader, teacher, and environment is crucial. The particular responsibilities of each are summarized below.

The Author's Responsibility

Some authors are inconsiderate of their readers, as Armbruster and Anderson demonstrate in their research comparing passages written on a single topic (1981). Authors should always keep their readers in mind as they write. If a passage includes many concepts, its organization

---

A C T I V I T Y 3.12

Reading Text Chapter Sheet—Chapter 3

Book Title   Indians of Virginia
Chapter Title   Virginia Indian Tribes
Number of Pages in Chapter   7 pages
List Major Indian Groups of the Eastern Woodland Indians
    1. Eastern Woodland Indians
    2. Algonquian Indians
    3. Iroquoian Indians
    4. Siouan Indians

How many maps are in the chapter?   3
How many pictures are in this chapter? 5

Developed by Meg McKenzie.

should be very clear to readers and teachers. This clarity enables teachers to develop instructional activities which aid the learning of those important concepts. Authors should include important terms in the material, but if the author suspects that these terms are new to the reader, then meaning and pronunciation keys should be provided.

In his preface to Allan Bloom's *The Closing of the American Mind*, Saul Bellow, a noted novelist, admits that "it is never easy to take the mental measure of your readers." He says further that "a piece of writing is like an offering" (p. 15). Although textbook writers cannot know the individual literacy levels of prospective readers, nor their interests and attitudes, they can be sensitive to the general needs of a group of readers. Authors should take into account what readers should be expected to know and what they will need an author's help to learn. In this way, authors fulfill their responsibility to be considerate of readers.

The Teacher's Responsibility

Teachers play a very important role in determining the readers' background, as this whole chapter has conveyed. Hittleman (1978) encourages teachers to think of readability as "ever changing. . . . We should never eliminate the reader and the act of reading from our concept of readability" (p. 121). Shanker (1984) discusses the importance of evaluating textbooks and lays the responsibility for doing so on the teacher. He calls for training in education courses to enable teachers to evaluate textbooks.

The Role of "Environment"

Teachers can determine a great deal about readability, but they also need help from other educational leaders. For example Speigel and Wright (1983), reporting on a study of biology teachers' impressions of the readability of text material they use, comment that teachers were aware of many readability factors. Teachers, they write, should be encouraged to apply this good, intuitive understanding in their selection of text materials. Such encouragement must come from administrators and textbook selection committees, to name a few "environmental resources."

The environment might also include the ambiance within a classroom as well as the encouragement from home and community. Such factors do enhance the readability of material by providing the encouragement necessary. Noisy, disorganized classrooms do not provide a good climate for reading, and too little encouragement from one's surroundings will tend to dampen one's reading match with the best of materials.

The Role of the Student

The ultimate consumer of the content material is the student. Students need to move toward independence in determining their own background for reading as soon as possible in their reading careers. Students must begin to ask the questions about their reading material by applying the situations we have presented in this chapter to their material: Is this material too difficult for me? Is it poorly written? What do I already know about this topic? How interested am I? What are the conditions I should find to make my reading easier? Questions like these will not even occur to many students until teachers model their importance by helping students understand why they should be asked.

Many college textbooks on reading and study skills do encourage students to ask such questions. But we believe that, by then, it may be too late. Not all students attend college, and not all of those who do will take a reading and study skills course. If background for reading is discussed only in college textbooks, many students may be denied the opportunity to take a responsible role. Isn't a student's responsibility for determining background important throughout his or her school years? A first grader is very capable of determining the difficulty of a book by using the "rule of thumb." A fifth grader can ask, "What do I know about fractions already?" A tenth grader can assess whether poetry causes him difficulty. Students might be encouraged by teachers to learn and apply a simple readability formula to their textbooks. They should learn to use the resulting score as a guide to stimulate thinking about the situations we have described. Perhaps students and teacher could construct a simple checklist of readability factors which students could then use on their own.

Ultimately, the "buck stops" with the students. But what a terrible burden to place on students as readers of content material if authors, teachers, and the environment offer them little help as they try to assume responsibility for their own reading.

One-Minute Summary

In this chapter we have explained the concept of readability and its importance for successful instruction in content areas. We have presented seven situations and their impact on readability. These situations involve material that is poorly written or too difficult for readers; readers with no, some, or incorrect prior knowledge; readers with no, few, or incorrect skills; and readers with no or little interest in the content. We have shown how, through a series of activities, you can find out if any of these situations apply to your students. Finally, we have discussed how ensuring readability of content material rests not only with the student, but also with the textbook author, the teacher, and various environmental resources.

End-of-Chapter Activities

Preparing the Reader

1. Of the four activities presented under the heading of *Preparing the Reader Activities* at the start of this chapter, which ones were most helpful to you? Did you determine your own background of knowledge for reading this chapter?

Assisting Comprehension

1. Study the following graphic organizer and, without looking back at the beginning of the chapter, fill in the blanks with correct words that convey key concepts taught in this chapter. You may scan back through the chapter text.

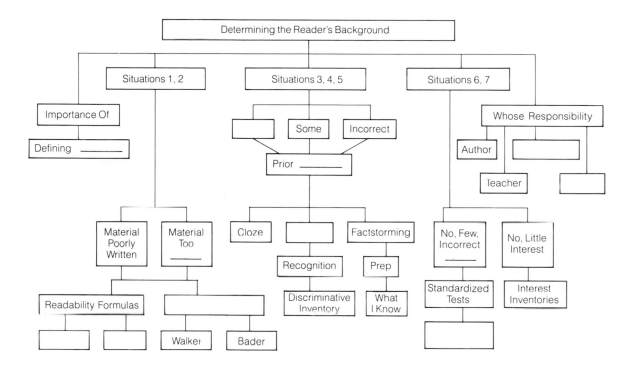

2. Practice with the Fry graph and the SMOG. (Only by doing do learners really learn!) Select passages to rate, and then follow the formula procedures to obtain a Fry and a SMOG rating. Are the ratings the same? Do they follow the expectations suggested on the chart? What do you think about these ratings? Are they accurate and informative?

3. Now apply the Bader analysis to the same textbook from which you selected the passages. After filling in the analysis items, summarize strengths and weaknesses and see what you can determine about teacher responsibilities. Check the appendix for examples of how other teachers responded.

Reflecting on Your Reading

1. Select a chapter from a content textbook. Use the following questions to guide you as you determine what aids your text offers the teacher:

What textbook aids are included in my chapter to help the teacher determine students' background? Is there mention of the match between reader and text? Is there a cloze or an inventory provided?

Are these aids suitable for my students?

Are these aids sufficient for determining background?

As a teacher, should I construct some aids to determine background? If so, what will I construct?

2. Some teachers do not use any reading material to teach their content subject. They argue that their students can't or won't read it anyhow. So they lecture, explain, and provide notes. What is your reaction to their solution and why?

3. If you'd like to read a reaction to readability formulas by a most distinguished author, read E. B. White's "Calculating Machine" in *The Second Tree from the Corner*, available from Harper & Row.

4. For information about two other readability formulas, try these articles:

Baldwin, R. S. & Kaufman, R. (1979). A concurrent validity study of the Raygor readability estimate. *Journal of Reading, 23,* 148–153.

Anderson, J. (1983). Lix and rix: Variations on a little-known readability index. *Journal of Reading, 26,* 490–496.

5. To see how one teacher has analyzed a textbook chapter by applying the PAR framework, look in the appendix. Following the analysis of each step in PAR, this teacher constructed a set of activities to fill in the gaps in the chapter.

References

Anderson, R. & Pearson, P.D. (1984). A schema-theoretic view of basic processes in reading. In P.D. Pearson (Ed.), *Handbook of reading research.* New York: Longman.

Anderson, T. & Armbruster, B. (1984). Content area textbooks. In R.C. Anderson, J. Osborn, & R.J. Tierney (Eds.), *Learning to read in American schools: Basal readers and content texts.* (pp. 193–226). Hillsdale, NJ: Erlbaum.

Armbruster, B. & Anderson, T. (1981). *Content area textbooks.* (Reading Education Report Number 23.) Urbana: University of Illinois Center for the Study of Reading.

Ashby-Davis, C. (1985). Cloze and comprehension: A qualitative analysis and critique. *Journal of Reading, 28,* 585–593.

Ausubel, D. (1960). The use of advance organizers in learning and retention of meaningful verbal material. *Journal of Educational Psychology, 51,* 267–272.

Ausubel, D. (1978). *Educational psychology: A cognitive view* (2nd ed.). New York: Holt, Rinehart & Winston.

Bader, L. (1987). Textbook analysis chart. *Reading, writing, speaking, listening and critical thinking in content area subjects.* Unpublished manuscript, Michigan State University.

Bartlett, F.C. (1932). *Remembering.* Cambridge, MA: Cambridge University Press.

Bellow, S. (1987). Preface. In Allan Bloom, *The closing of the American mind* (p. 15). New York: Simon & Schuster.

Bormouth, J.R. (1969). Development of a readability analysis. Final Report, Project No. 7–0052, Contract No. OEC–3–7–070052–0326. USOE, Bureau of Research, U.S. Department of Health, Education and Welfare.

Bormouth, J.R. (1975). Literacy in the classroom. In W.D. Page (Ed.), *Help for the reading teacher: New directions in research.* Urbana, IL: National Conference on Research in English and ERIC/RCS Clearinghouse, 60–90.

Bransford, J. & Johnson, M. (1973). Considerations of some problems of comprehension. In W. Chase (Ed.) *Visual information processing.* New York, N.Y.: Academic Press.

Bryant, J.A.R. (1984). Textbook treasure hunt. *Journal of Reading, Vol. 27,* 547–548, March 84.

Cadenhead, K. (1987). Reading level: A metaphor that shapes practice. *Phi Delta Kappan, 68,* 436–441.

College Board. (1986). *Degrees of Reading Power.* New York: College Board.

Cox, J. & Wiebe, J. (1984). Measuring reading vocabulary and concepts in mathematics in the primary grades. *Reading Teacher, 37,* 402–410.

Dale, E. & Chall, J. (1948). A formula for predicting readability. *Educational Research Bulletin, 27,* 11–20; 37–54.

Dale, E., O'Rourke, J. & Bamman, H. (1971). *Techniques of teaching vocabulary.* Palo Alto, CA: Field Educational Publications.

Danielson, K.E. (1987). Readability formulas: A necessary evil? *Reading Horizons, 27,* 178–188.

Dechant, E. (1970). *Improving the teaching of reading.* Englewood Cliffs, NJ: Prentice-Hall.

Derby, T. (1987). Reading instruction and course-related materials for vocational high school students. *Journal of Reading, 30,* 308–316.

Dreyer, L.G. (1984). Readability and responsibility. *Journal of Reading, 27,* 334–338.

Drum, P.A. (1985). Retention of text information by grade, ability, and study. *Discourse Processes, 8,* 21–51.

Forgan, H.W. & Mangrum, C.T. (1985). *Teaching content area reading skills.* Columbus, OH: Charles E. Merrill Publishing Company.

Fry, E. (1968). The readability graph validated at primary levels. *The Reading Teacher, 3,* 534–538.

Fry, E. (1977). Fry's readability graph: Clarifications, validity, and extension to level 17. *Journal of Reading, 21,* 242–252.

Fry, E. (1987). The varied uses of readability measurement today. *Journal of Reading, 30,* 338–343.

Garner, R., Alexander, P., Slater, W., Hare, V.C., Smith, J. & Reis, R. (1986, April). Children's knowledge of structural properties of text. Paper presented at the meeting of the American Educational Research Association, San Francisco, CA.

Guthrie, J. (1974). The maze technique to assess, monitor reading comprehension. *Reading Teacher, 28,* 161–168.

Harris, T., & Hodges, R. (1981). *A dictionary of reading.* Newark, DE: International Reading Association.

Heller, M. (1986). How do you know what you know? Metacognitive modeling in the content areas. *Journal of Reading, 29,* 415–422.

Hill, W. & Erwin, R. (1984). The readability of content textbooks used in middle and junior high schools. *Reading Psychology, 5,* 105–117.

Hittleman, D. (1978). Readability, readability formulas, and cloze: Selecting instructional materials. *Journal of Reading, 22,* 117–122.

Holdzkom, D. (1987). Readability. In D. Alvermann, D. Moore & M. Conley (Eds.), *Research within reach/Secondary school reading,* (p. 80–92). Newark, DE: International Reading Association.

Holmes, B. & Roser, N. (1987). Five ways to assess readers' prior knowledge. *Reading Teacher, 40,* 646–649.

Hunt, K. (1965). *Grammatical structures written at three grade levels.* Champaign, IL: National Council of Teachers of English.

Jongsma, E. (1980). *Cloze instruction research: A second look.* Newark, DE: International Reading Association.

Klare, G. (1974–75). Assessing readability. *Reading Research Quarterly, 10,* 62–102.

Langer, J.A. (1981). From theory to practice: A prereading plan. *Journal of Reading, 25,* 152–156.

McLaughlin, H. (1969). SMOG grading—a new readability formula. *Journal of Reading, 12,* 639–646.

McWilliams, L. & Rakes, T. (1979). *The Content Inventories.* Dubuque, IA: Kendall/Hunt.

Maria, K. & MacGinitie, W. (1987). Learning from texts that refute the reader's prior knowledge. *Reading Research and Instruction, 26,* 222–238.

Meyer, B.J.F., Brandt, M.D. & Bluth, G.J. (1980). Use of top-level structure in text; key for reading comprehension of ninth grade students. *Reading Research Quarterly, 16,* 72–103.

Moore, D. & Murphy, A. (1987). Selection of materials. In D. Alvermann, D. Moore, & M. Conley (Eds.). *Research within reach/Secondary school reading* (pp. 94–108). Newark, DE: International Reading Association.

Piaget, J. (1963). *The origin of intelligence in children.* New York: Norton.

Resolutions passed by the Delegate Assembly. (1981, April) *Reading Research Quarterly, 16,* 615.

Richardson, J. (1975). A study of the syntactic competence of adult beginning readers. Doctoral dissertation, University of North Carolina at Chapel Hill.

Rumelhart, D. (1981). Schemata: The building blocks of cognition. In J. Guthrie (Ed.), *Comprehension and teaching: Research review.* Newark, DE: International Reading Association.

Shanker, A. (1984, September 5). Where we stand—who should evaluate the textbooks? *Education Week.*

Sinatra, R. (1986). *Visual literacy connections to thinking, reading and writing.* Springfield, IL: Charles C. Thomas.

Singer, H. & Bean, T. (1988). Three models for helping teachers to help students learn from text. In S.J. Samuels & P. David Pearson (Eds.), *Changing school reading programs* (pp. 161–183). Newark, DE: International Reading Association.

Spache, G. (1953). A new readability formula for primary grade reading materials. *Elementary School Journal, 53,* 410–413.

Speigel, D.L. & Wright, J. (1983). Biology teachers' use of readability concepts when selecting texts for students. *Journal of Reading, 27,* 28–34.

Taylor, W. (1953). Cloze procedure: A new tool for measuring readability. *Journalism Quarterly, 30*, 415–433.

Toch, T. (1984, March 7). Bell calls on education to push publishers for better materials. *Education Week*, 11.

Veatch, J. (1968). *How to teach reading with children's books.* New York: Citation Press.

Walker, J. (1985). Requiem for readability. *Reading Today, 3*, 13.

White, E.B. (1951). Calculating machine. In *The second tree from the corner*, 165–167. New York: Harper & Row.

Williams, J.R., Taylor, M.B. & Ganger, S. (1981). Text variations at the level of the individual sentence and the comprehension of simple expository paragraphs. *Journal of Educational Psychology, 73*, 851–865.

4 Building the Reader's Background for Content Material

> If I had to reduce all of educational psychology to just one principle, I would say this: the most important single factor influencing learning is what the learner already knows. Ascertain this and teach him accordingly."
>
> David Ausubel,
> *Educational Psychology*

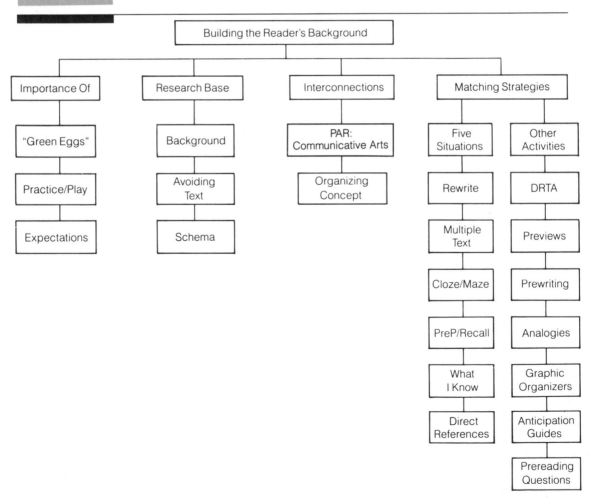

1. Read the following headline and decide what the newspaper article which would accompany it is probably about: "A Generation after Bullet Shattered King's Vision, Leaderless Peers Reign" (*Richmond Times-Dispatch*, January 17, 1988).
Did you interpret "King's vision" as: a) An eye problem b) A monarch's dilemma c)The dream of an American hero?
How did you interpret "leaderless peers reign"?

2. You will be better prepared to read this chapter by reviewing principle 4 in chapter 1: Reading for meaning is a highly individualized process influenced by the readers' personal store of experiences and knowledge.

3. Below are some phrases, terms, and persons' names introduced in chapters 1 and 3. Check yourself now to determine if you remember what each means and its relationship to preparation for reading. If you can explain the term or phrase, place a + beside it; if you're familiar with the term or phrase, but not able to explain it fully, place a √ beside it; if you're unsure or draw a blank, place a 0 beside it:

   _____ Schema   _____ Prior knowledge

   _____ Ausubel   _____ R.C. Anderson

4. Following are four statements. Read and consider each one. If you agree with the statement, place a + beside it; if you disagree, place a − beside it. Be ready to explain your reasoning.

   _____ The more you know, the more you learn.

   _____ Hindsight is always better than foresight.

   _____ An ounce of prevention is worth a pound of cure.

   _____ Readiness is a term associated with beginning reading instruction.

   As you read this chapter, each of these statements will be discussed in context. Compare your responses with those in the chapter.

5. Below is a list of terms used in this chapter. Some of them may be familiar to you in a general context, but in this chapter they may be used in a different way than you are used to. Rate your knowledge by placing a + in front of those you are sure that you know, a √ in front of those you have some knowledge about, and a 0 in front of those you don't know. B ready to locate and pay special attention to their meanings when they are presented in the chapter:

   _____ readiness   _____ organizing concept

   _____ chunking   _____ page to eye to brain

B.C. Reprinted with permission of Johnny Hart and Creators Syndicate, Inc.

Objectives:

As you read this chapter, focus your attention on the following objectives. You will:

1. be able to explain the importance of building background before assigning reading in content material.
2. be able to identify pertinent research which supports the concept of building background.
3. understand how building background facilitates the development of good communicative arts skills.
4. be able to match activities which can build background to five of the situations presented in chapter 3.
5. see how activities presented in chapter 3 can be used not only to determine but also to build background.
6. learn about several new activities to build background.

Purpose:

In chapter 3 you discovered ways to determine if the match between students and content reading material is satisfactory. What do you do after you find out that your students and the content material you teach from are not perfectly matched? In this chapter, we'll present several ways to provide a better match.

The Importance of Building Background

Green Eggs and Ham by Dr. Seuss is a favorite children's story. What a lot of time Sam I Am spends arguing with his friend about trying this delectable concoction! The friend assumes that he won't like green eggs and ham, probably because green is not a color usually associated with eggs unless they're rotten! His background—limited to the color rather than the taste of green eggs—interferes. Poor Sam I Am! His only strategy is to nag. Finally the friend does try the dish, and he likes it! He vows to eat it in any number of creative ways in the future. The ending of this delightful story is happy, and the nagging dialogue is fun for young readers.

In real life, convincing someone to try anything as seemingly revolting as green eggs and ham will require more than nagging. Teachers may often feel like Sam I Am nagging students to read the content material because it's really interesting if only they would try it. Unfortunately, sometimes students' backgrounds are as limited as that of Sam I Am's reluctant friend. An unpleasant experience with any aspect of reading or with a subject can cause students to be just as stubborn about reading an assignment as about eating green eggs and ham. A teacher who assigns and nags doesn't have much impact. However, both research and practice confirm that strategies which build reader background do work. Such strategies entice students to try the reading and give them the connection point to understand what they read. To illustrate, a group of young students who had just completed a background-building activity remarked that it was fun and they wished that more teachers would "try this stuff." In this chapter, several strategies which convince readers to try a reading material will be discussed.

William Bosher, a school division superintendent has noted (1987) that the process of reading in content areas is much like a basketball game. Actually *playing* the game really takes up the smallest amount of time; the greatest amount of time is spent in workouts, strategy sessions, and practice, all of which are intended to ensure success in the game itself. After the game, more time is spent analyzing what actually occurred on the court and then the preparation for the next game begins. So it is with reading. A proficient reader spends time getting ready to read by determining and building background. Instead of plunging into the reading, this reader will prepare. Good comprehension is a natural result, just as playing a game successfully is the natural result of hard work in practice. Teachers who are aware of this phenomenon and aid students in the preparation stage of reading are like good coaches. Students who realize that preparation for reading is like court practice will reap benefits in higher achievement and better grades.

Preparation is the basis for comprehension. If we're not prepared or expectant, our understanding will suffer. In the "B.C." cartoon at the beginning of this chapter, the angel food cake our heroine is mixing up will certainly suffer from her failure to understand what "separate" means. Her cake will most likely be wasted. She may have to bake another one after she finds out what to do with those eggs. Likewise, a reader who expects to read about a monarch's poor eyesight will be very confused by the article following the "King's Vision" headline. The reader will either abandon the reading in confusion, spend time rereading after rethinking expectations, or read words without comprehension. In any case, time is wasted because the reader's expectations do not provide adequate preparation. Without building background before reading, readers have no support for understanding what they read. Thus, this chapter is really about comprehension, because building background is the foundation for reading, thinking, and learning.

What Research Has to Say about Building Background

The More You Know, the More You Learn

Two groups of college students were asked to read two passages about weddings. The groups were carefully matched, except for nationality: One group was American, the other was from India. The passages were carefully controlled, with consideration of many of the readability factors discussed in chapter 3, except that one passage was about an Indian wedding and the other was about an American wedding. After testing the students' comprehension of the passages, the researchers (Steffenson, Joag-Des, and Anderson, 1979) found that the Indian students received higher comprehension scores on the passage about Indian weddings and the American students received higher scores on the passage about American weddings. The culture-specific results are not surprising because the more we know about something, the more we will understand about it. One who has grown up in a certain culture knows about the traditional ceremonies of that culture and can easily read and understand material written about them. But one who has little experience in a culture cannot be expected to read and understand much about it until he learns some background.

Avoiding the Textbook Is a Poor Answer to Diverse Student Backgrounds

Teachers seem to be ambiguous about their use of textbooks (Hinchman, 1987). Students may be learning that it is not necessary to really read the text at all because teachers will tell them what they need to know. Some findings indicate that teachers do not rely on their textbooks for much of their instruction because they realize that there is a mismatch between the text and the students. Davey (1988) found that several teachers use the textbook only as a supplement to their instruction, not as a base for it. The teachers in this study indicated that they avoided textbooks because of differences among their students and a lack of time to cover the whole text.

We suspect that what Davey found is true in many classrooms. Teachers think that they cannot use a text because all of their students do not have the same IQ, reading ability, or background knowledge. They think that it will take too much time to cover all of the text material, particularly if their students are heterogeneously grouped. When teachers use such reasoning, they have at least applied the first step in determining reader background. They are aware that they face a situation such as those described in chapter 3 and that the situation thwarts the match between students and text. But, as we demonstrated in chapter 3, this awareness is only a start.

Teachers do students a definite disservice to decide at this point to avoid or skim the text material. Such messages to students are powerful deterrents to future reading for knowledge. First, important information in the text may be overlooked by the teacher and missed entirely by the students when teachers avoid the text material. So students miss an opportunity to learn. Second, as our principle 9—Reading begets reading—implies, students need to read and see teachers valuing reading material if they are going to become informed and avid readers themselves. The less practice students receive in reading to learn, the weaker their reading will be. The more students receive the message that they can skip this material and just listen to the teacher, the more ambivalent they will be about reading to learn. Last, and most crucial, when teachers avoid the text material, they may be contributing to the literacy problem Kirsch and Jungeblut (1986) describe in their NAEP report. Students who have the basic skills to read but don't read much are ill equipped to live in a literate America. By avoiding text material because of students' diverse backgrounds, teachers really contribute to the very problem that their profession is supposed to be solving.

If, before assigning reading material, teachers take the time to build background, all of the students in the classroom will have one common experience to aid their reading. Students will also begin to see the role that their personal store of experience and knowledge plays in reading for meaning. By building background, teachers ultimately give students the tools to become responsible and independent readers. This time spent up front enhances comprehension so greatly that using the text is much less time-consuming. In other words, *an ounce of prevention is worth a pound of cure.*

More about Schema

Principle 12 in chapter 1 stated that the study of content area reading can be enhanced by the study of many related professions. This principle applies as we see how discoveries about the importance of prior knowledge on learning have influenced reading professionals.

For several years, psychologists have studied the impact of past knowledge on present understanding. Ausubel, who was quoted at the beginning of this chapter, has been a chief advocate of the "conceptual starting place" (1968) of meaningful learning. Lange (1902) noted, at the turn of the century, that "we see and hear not only with the eye and ear, but quite as much with the help of our present knowledge, with the apperceiving content of the mind" (p. 21). More recently, Frank Smith (1971) has compared the reading activity which occurs between the page and the eye, and between the eye and the brain. He concluded that the eye-to-brain connection is far more complex than the mere intake of information. Learning occurs by a process of planning and building information in the brain. Just seeing words (page-to-eye) or even saying words (page-to-eye-to-mouth) is fairly superficial. Connecting the intent of the words to what is already stored in one's "mind diagram" (eye-to-brain) is real reading. So what learners already know helps them to read more effectively.

Gestalt psychologists probably introduced the term *schema* in the 1930s (Anderson and Pearson, 1984). Bartlett (1932) used the term to explain how information that has been learned is stored in the brain and, with repeated use, becomes part of a system of integrated knowledge. Anderson and Pearson speculate that the term became popular because Piaget used it extensively. Piaget (1952) believed that children form a mental image of previous experiences, which in turn contributes to new experiences. Miller (1956) discussed the relationship of short-term to long-term memory in a similar way. A learner "chunks" knowledge in an organized fashion by connecting a new "chunk" to what is already known. Only by so doing can a learner move the new chunk from short-term memory to long-term memory. Prior knowledge, schema, or chunks are essential to new learning. According to psychologists Combs and Snygg (1959), learning takes place when the "perceptual field" is organized in a pattern. This perceptual field, which they define as a "more or less fluid organization of meanings existing for every individual at any instant" (p. 20), is the basis for a person's reactions to any new event.

To summarize, psychologists have stressed that learning new information depends on relating the new to something already known. A schema is a picture in one's mind of that already-known information. Learning is much harder if we have no background—no schema—to relate the new information to.

Anderson (1985) is credited with introducing schema theory to the field of reading, although the concept, if not the term, had been applied in reading research previously. When Chall (1947) tested sixth and eighth graders on their knowledge of tuberculosis and then tested their reading of a passage on the same topic, she found that those who made the highest knowledge scores also made the highest reading comprehension scores. She concluded that previous knowledge heavily influences reading. Rumelhart (1980) has also written extensively about how learners comprehend by building "blocks of cognition" as they fill in a partially completed schema during reading. Hirsch (1987) writes that schemata are essential to literacy in two major ways: Information is stored so that it can be retrieved, and it is organized so efficiently that it can be used quickly by a reader.

Reading professionals have defined schema as "a conceptual system for understanding something" (Harris and Hodges, 1981). Pearson and Spiro (1982) describe schema in this way:

> What is a schema? It's the little pictures or associations you conjure up in your head when you hear or read a word or sentence. You can have a schema for an object (chair, boat, fan), an abstract idea or feeling (love, hate, hope), an action (dancing, swimming, buying) or an event (election, garage sale, concert). It's like a concept but broader. For example, you see the word *tree* and you conjure up the concept of a tree—trunk, branches, leaves, and so on. Your schema for a tree includes all this, plus anything else you associate with trees—walks down country lanes, Christmas trees, birds' nests, and so on (pp. 46–47).

Content teachers will find schema theory useful as they prepare their students to read an assignment. For instance, suppose that fifth graders in a rural community are about to study ballet in their music class. The teacher is sensitive to her students' misconceptions about ballet. She has determined that their schema for ballet includes such incorrect prior knowledge as: "Ballet is sissy; It's something girls do, not strong men; It's boring." If the teacher ignores this schema, incorrect as it is, the students will likely reject any new information about ballet and hold fast to their already-formulated picture of ballet. Instead, a fifth grade music teacher we know used the children's schema as a base for expanding knowledge. The music teacher used an anticipation guide, explained later in this chapter. By presenting the statements shown in Activity 4.1, she got students to verbalize their prior knowledge. Then she presented new experiences and information by showing a videotape of *The Nutcracker Suite.* The reader should note that these students reformulated their knowledge after discovering new information—they changed their opinions for all four statements! A different schema was created.

If learners cannot find relevance in a reading selection, they are likely to ignore it. As we pointed out earlier, the newspaper headline "Charge of the Right Frigate" may simply seem to be a strange introduction to a story about a naval buildup for readers who are not familiar with Tennyson's poem "The Charge of the Light Brigade." These readers are likely to skip this article. Teachers, then, must become aware of their students' knowledge and experiences of a particular concept to be taught in the content subject. Discovering these schemata can help the teacher generate assisted reading which is directed, meaningful, and highly personal.

A C T I V I T Y 4.1

The Anticipation of Ballet

Before we begin our lesson today, read each of the following statements carefully and circle agree or disagree to show what you think. Be ready to discuss your opinions with the class. Do not talk with anyone else *yet* about your answers. Remember . . . this is *your opinion* and it will not be graded!

Agree	Disagree	**1.** Ballet is only for girls.
Agree	Disagree	**2.** Ballet music is always slow and soft.
Agree	Disagree	**3.** Ballet dancers are strong, muscular, and in very good physical condition.
Agree	Disagree	**4.** The Soviet Union is one country that has produced many very good ballet dancers.

Developed by Todd Barnes.

A Rose by Any Other Name Would Smell as Sweet

What constitutes building background? Although many teachers associate *readiness* with instruction for beginning readers, Thorndike (1932) proposed the term in his "Law of Readiness" to mean a developmental stage at which new learning occurs. In its broadest sense, then, readiness means being ready to receive information; reading readiness means being prepared for the material that is to be read. A young student does achieve readiness for beginning reading instruction, but all readers must achieve a state of readiness for any reading to be done. If a reader does not understand what separating eggs means, as it applies to baking a cake, that reader is not ready to bake that cake. If a reader does not know what the phrase "leaderless peers reign" means, readiness for reading that article has not yet been attained. Building background is readiness instruction. It means building the knowledge upon which learning is based. Therefore, we would want to add "not only" to the statement presented at the beginning of this chapter: Readiness is a term associated *not only* with beginning reading instruction.

Chall (1983) calls the background that readers possess "world knowledge" which is "essential to the development of reading and writing skills" (p. 8). If readers have little world knowledge, they will have limited understanding. A misinterpretation of the Martin Luther King headline is a good example of how a lack of world knowledge can interfere with reading. We think that the best way to acquire world knowledge is through the thinking and learning which should occur in content classrooms every day. Acquiring world knowledge is a form of building *background*, which either equals or is closely associated with *readiness*. Readiness depends upon applying *prior knowledge*, which depends on activating *schemata*. All of these terms relate to the P in PAR, Preparation. These terms are roses called by other names. Good comprehension demands that readers stop to smell these roses. In the case of preparation, then, *hindsight is not better than foresight*. Foresight is crucial.

The Interconnectedness of PAR Activities

Throughout this text, activities are presented as examples of how content teachers can implement PAR in their classrooms. An activity is selected to complement a PAR step. In this chapter, activities are presented for their value in promoting Preparation, particularly building background. The most popular activities will promote development and practice of all of the communicative arts: listening, speaking, and writing as well as reading. Furthermore, an activity might be useful at every step of PAR, depending on its application. As each activity is discussed, its possibilities for interconnections will be pointed out.

The Organizing Concept

The versatility of activities presented in this text will be appreciated by teachers who realize that activities are not neatly categorized but reflect the principle of the *organizing concept* (Phelps, 1984). As Phelps states, the organizing concept is surprisingly simple: Teachers decide what they want students to learn and define content objectives for reading. At this point, an organizing concept has been formulated. Once the "what" of the lesson is stated, then the reading-thinking-learning strategies which promote that "what" best can be selected. The strategies become the "how." Often, one strategy will work for an entire content lesson. Sometimes, several strategies work better. Phelps gives the following example of an organizing concept statement for high-school biology:

> Plants can reproduce themselves in two ways, by vegetative propagation and by sexual reproduction. (p. 267)

For this organizing concept, perhaps a What-I-Know sheet could be used for all of PAR: each column would represent one PAR step. Phelps suggests the following statement for high school geometry:

> The area of a circle is computed by multiplying *pi* times the square of the radius. (p. 267)

For this organizing concept, perhaps a graphic organizer would be a good preparation activity, followed by other activities for assisting comprehension and reflection.

Matching Situations to Building-Background Activities

In chapter 3 we described several situations which cause a mismatch between reader and text and several ways to determine the mismatch. In this section, we present activities to overcome the mismatch in situations one through five.

Situations One and Two

In situation one, the material may be poorly written. The Martin Luther King headline we quoted at the beginning of this chapter may fall in this category. In situation two, the material may be too difficult for a given group of readers. The recipe in the "B.C." cartoon must fall in this category. In either case, what are solutions to the problem?

Rewriting

The obvious solution is to find easier and better-written material on the topic in question. This is sometimes easier said than done. Perhaps another newspaper article about Martin Luther King will be available which contains all of the pertinent information a social studies teacher needs to teach this content. Perhaps there is another recipe for angel food cake with careful descriptions of each ingredient and each step. Often, however, such material is not available. Often the text provided to the teacher is all there is. So, a teacher has used a checklist or formula and determined that situation one or two exists but is limited to that material anyhow. In such a case, rewriting is one solution. Siedow and Hasselbring (1984) found that when eighth-grade social studies material was rewritten to a lower readability level, the comprehension of poor readers improved. In another study (Beck, McKeown, Omanson & Pople, 1984) the researchers found that revising third-grade material significantly improved the children's comprehension. In both studies the authors caution that rewriting must be done carefully and is time-consuming. It is a technique which works but takes time.

Rewriting, when used to prepare students and then introduce them to the original material, can be a very successful technique. By using rewritten material as an introduction to the original text, teachers can simplify writing styles and make clearer those concepts which students may have difficulty understanding. However, by returning to the original material, teachers will still be using required materials, and students will receive the message that the text material is important.

Many teachers may feel that they have tampered with an author's material when they rewrite it. English teachers especially become very nervous about rewriting material of established authors unless they realize that the original will also be used.

The revision of Virginia Woolf's essay "The Angel in the House" (Activity 4.2) illustrates the value of rewriting. One of the authors rewrote this essay as a desperate move. The author was teaching a freshman college English class and assigned this required essay to stimulate the students' own writing. The students interpreted Woolf's metaphoric angel literally and thought that she had a ghost looking over her shoulder. They also could not understand why Woolf would mention buying an expensive cat in this essay. Their backgrounds apparently did not include the metaphors or experiences which Woolf selected, and they did not know how to relate to the allusions in the essay. The author chose to rewrite the essay because it was required reading for the course: no other could be substituted for it, even though it was clearly too difficult for the readers. Students read the rewrite first, as an introduction, and then they read the original essay and compared the two versions. The results were very satisfactory. Students understood clearly the concepts Woolf was conveying, and, as an unexpected bonus, they realized how much better written was Woolf's essay than the teacher's! As a preparation strategy, rewriting was very successful.

Rewriting can reduce a readability level, according to a readability formula, sometimes to a significant degree. As the example illustrates, the level of Woolf's essay was found to be ninth-grade level but the rewrite was seventh-grade level (according to the Fry graph). Sometimes a revision will not reduce readability level at all but will clarify difficult material. This was the case with the third-grade study reported earlier (Beck et al.) where researchers found that revision did improve comprehension. The goal should be to present necessary material in a readable form, as a prelude to the original.

Rewriting, like so many other activities, can be used at every step of PAR. The organizing concept and particular purpose for its use will determine the way that rewriting is used. For instance, if a rewrite is used in place of the original material, then it is no longer being used for preparing the reader; in that case, rewriting assists comprehension. One of the authors once rewrote portions of the Georgia Juvenile Court Code because the code was measured at fourteenth-grade level and was too hard for the students to understand in its legal form. The rewrite, to seventh-grade level, enabled students to read with attention to the main points. Rewriting might also be used as a reflective reading technique. A teacher might ask students to think about the material and try to rewrite that material for younger students. In this way, students gain writing practice and demonstrate their learning. Thus, an integration of the communicative arts is taking place. Rewriting can also be

A C T I V I T Y   4.2

A Rewrite of "The Angel in the House" (excerpt)

I was asked to speak to you about women as professionals and tell you about what has happened to me. This is difficult because my experiences in my job as a writer may not be that outstanding. There have been many famous women writers before me who have learned and shown me the best way to succeed at writing. Because of their reputations, families today accept women who become writers. They know that they won't have to pay a lot of money for writing equipment or courses!

My story is this. I wrote regularly everyday, then submitted an article to a newspaper. The article was accepted, I got paid; I became a journalist. However, I did not act like a struggling writer who spends her hard-earned money on household needs; I bought a Persian cat.

My article was a book review. I had trouble writing it and other reviews because something nagged at me. I felt that because I am a woman, I should be "feminine": have sympathy, be charming, unselfish, keep the family peaceful, sacrifice, and be very pure. When I began to write, this is what women were supposed to be like, and every family taught its girls to be this way. So when I started to write criticisms of a famous man's novel, all of the things I had learned about being a woman got in the way of my writing critically instead of writing just nice things. This problem was like a ghost whispering in my ear. I called this problem ghost The Angel in the House because it was always there, in my "house" telling me to be nice rather than truthful.

I got rid of this problem. I realized that being nice is not always the most important thing. Also, I had inherited some money, so I felt I didn't have to do what others expected of me in order to earn a living! I had to get rid of this obsession with being feminine rather than being truthful in order to write clearly. I killed my problem ghost before it could kill my true thoughts and reactions. This is really hard to do because "feminine" ideas creep up on you before you realize that what you're writing is not a true criticism but something you were raised to believe. It took a long time to realize what was my idea and what was society's idea about what I should write.

Readabilities according to Fry formula:
Original passage = 9th grade
Rewrite passage = 7th grade

a useful tool for the at-risk reader, who needs to learn the same content as classmates but has difficulty reading at the same level.

Rewriting takes time. For one rewrite of a fifteen-page social studies selection, one of the authors spent four hours. The Woolf rewrite consumed two hours. Since a teacher's time is precious, teachers will want to weigh their options carefully. In some situations, rewriting is the best option.

Craig (1977) describes the rewriting procedure and suggests several steps for rewriting. Although a teacher would not use all of these steps, applying a majority of them will ensure a more effective rewrite:

1. Read the passage; record the main ideas in your own words.
2. Identify the main ideas which are especially important for the students to know.
3. List the difficult words, especially those which represent difficult concepts. Try not to use more than five of these per hundred words in your rewrite.
4. Using a high-frequency word list, begin to rewrite. Try to use an "easy" word in place of one of the identified difficult words whenever possible.
5. Follow some of these guidelines:
   Avoid polysyllabic words
   Use easily pronounceable words
   Use common nouns
   Underline proper nouns and specialized vocabulary, which you can preteach
   Limit sentence length, perhaps to five to ten words
   Use terms familiar to students
   Turn written numerals (five) into numbers (5)
   Use simple sentence construction and present tense
6. Now check the passage readability of the original and your rewrite to decide if the rewrite is on a simpler level.

Multiple-Text Strategy

If the teacher can locate other material which covers the same content as the text, then using several materials at varied reading levels is a viable solution. By enlisting the help of a media specialist, the teacher may discover several trade books which treat the topic to be studied. Then the teacher should study the books to determine that they will match the reading levels and backgrounds of students. This can be done through the checklists and formulas described in chapter 3. The right book for the right student can then be assigned as a preparation for the content text which will be introduced later. In chapter 1, a multiple-text approach was used by the primary teacher introducing a unit on goldfish. That teacher selected several trade books about fish and made them available to the children before starting the unit. The teacher prepared the children by encouraging them to browse and discover what they knew and might be learning about goldfish.

A multiple-text strategy is versatile because different reading levels within a classroom can be accommodated when many books are used. The list of books can be expanded over the years with the help of the media specialist and through resources such as book reviews in professional journals. However, the multiple-text strategy requires additional time. Teachers must know thoroughly the content of the required material and then read each new book which might be included on the multiple-text list. In addition, most teachers will want to apply readability checks to each book for assurance of a good reading match.

If trade books are presented as a background builder before the required text is introduced, then their use represents a preparation strategy. However, if the teacher substitutes multiple texts for the original textbook, then the strategy can be classified as one to assist comprehension. Such an approach is helpful to at-risk readers. Another popular way to use multiple texts is in a reflection activity. To enrich students' knowledge, teachers often give students a list of books from which to do independent reading. One second-grade teacher has prepared a set of suggestions for using trade books about dinosaurs. Some suggestions prepare, some assist, and some help young readers reflect. A sampling of this teacher's suggestions can be found in the appendix.

An algebra teacher who worked with gifted students wanted to prepare a list of books which her gifted ninth graders could read for assigned independent projects. She studied five books recently purchased by the school librarian. Using the SMOG, she determined a reading level for each book. As a result of this exercise, she identified three books by Isaac Asimov as being most suitable to her students' needs (see Activity 4.3). She also decided that she should become more involved in the selection process so that her library would stock trade books useful for her multiple-text approach.

Situations Three, Four, and Five

Situations three, four, and five are concerned with readers' varying levels of prior knowledge about the material they are to read. Several of the solutions given in chapter 3 to determine if a lack of prior knowledge is the problem can also be used to build background. These strategies, which encompass both of the preparation steps (determining background and building background) are cloze and maze procedures, free recall and PreP, and What-I-Know sheets. Also useful as strategies for these situations are direct references to misconceptions and unstructured discussions. Each of these strategies is discussed in relation to its role in building background.

A C T I V I T Y 4.3

Multiple Text

Books and Authors	Sample 1 of Polysyllabic Words	Sample 2 of Polysyllabic Words	Sample 3 of Polysyllabic Words	Total	Nearest Perfect Square	Square Root + 3	Reading Level
1. *Playing with Infinity* by Rózsa Péter	39	38	28	105	100	10 + 3	13
2. *A History of* π by Petr Beckman	33	37	47	117	100	10 + 3	13
3. *Realm of Measure* by Isaac Asimov	19	15	20	54	49	7 + 3	10
4. *Realm of Algebra* by Isaac Asimov	20	22	23	65	64	8 + 3	11
5. *Quick and Easy Math* by Isaac Asimov	13	19	13	45	36	6 + 3	9

Developed by Frances Reid.

The Cloze Technique

When used for instructional rather than readability purposes, possible cloze constructions are increased. Instead of reflecting exact replacement of vocabulary, scores can reflect replacement with synonyms. For instance, Beil's cloze, adapted from his article "The Emperor's New Cloze," uses a synonym key and much higher scoring criteria (see Figure 4.1). The reader will notice that this excerpt from the article also provides information about the many uses of cloze.

To construct the instructional cloze, the teacher will still leave beginning and ending sentences intact, but deletions can serve different instructional purposes. For example, the teacher may delete all of the nouns and then ask students to predict what part of speech the words to replace deleted words must be. This cloze activity builds an awareness of nouns that helps readers to be proficient readers of their grammar book. An instructional cloze can also include clues. For example,

Figure 4.1 A cloze exercise.

Adapted from Beil, Drake. "The Emperor's New Cloze." *Journal of Reading:* Apr. 77, pp. 601–604. Reprinted with permission of Drake Beil and the International Reading Association.

Because no major publishing company has a cloze closet of its own, the catch is you have to make your own. There is a bundle to be made in new _____ 1) , and there is no reason to wait for handy _____ 2) or attractive boxes.

Now for the first step in _____ 3) your new wardrobe, start with the next book you _____ 4) to use in class. Select the *three* most meaningful _____ 5) of 100–200 words each. Almost any source can be _____ 6) : try classic literature, fantasy fiction (the clozed Hobbit is _____ 7) treat!), Greek myths, or sci-fi and choose which passages _____ 8) reflect the import and content of the story.

Some _____ 9) in making new cloze is common. Basically, you uniformly _____ 10) one word in every ten (some folks say every f _____ 11) or every seventh word) throughout the passages and make _____ 12) gaps ten spaces long. On some materials you may _____ 13) to provide clues or cues to the cloze units, _____ 14) blanks can have the same number of spaces as _____ 15) missing words. Initial or ending consonants can also be _____ 16) —as long as these aids help meet your need.

F_____ 17) research or diagnostic purposes, keep the blanks and the _____ 18) of the deletions internally consistent; for teaching grammar, vocabulary, _____ 19) syntax, vary them as suits your purpose. Researchers often _____ 20) the first and last sentences intact, but if the _____ 21) chosen are interesting and meaningful enough, they will provide _____ 22) the clues necessary for completion. *Good luck on furnishing your cloze closet!*

(continued)

Cloze Key

1. cloze	**7.** a	**13.** want	**19.** or
2. kits	**8.** most	**14.** and	**20.** leave
3. designing	**9.** variety	**15.** the	**21.** passages
4. intend	**10.** delete	**16.** supplied	**22.** all
5. passages	**11.** fifth	**17.** for	
6. used	**12.** the	**18.** structure	

Scoring by Synonym Replacement
Independent level: 91% or 20 correct
   no more than 2 wrong

Instructional level: 75–90% or 16–19 correct
3–6 wrong

Frustrational level: less than 75% or 15 or less correct

the first letter of a word or all of its consonants may be left in. The number of letters in the word can also be indicated, or a list of words from which to select can be provided. Whatever the design, the instructional cloze can be used to help teachers determine what their students already know and, by discussion of the choices made, build their knowledge of the clozed material. Discussion should also whet the readers' appetites for the reading material which follows, thus giving students a purpose for reading and assisting their comprehension of the material.

Since discussing the students' choices is an obvious part of the activity, cloze for preparation also fosters listening and speaking opportunities. Although writing is limited to single word entries, some writing is occurring as well. Some teachers find cloze useful as a technique to determine comprehension, perhaps as an alternative to a traditional test. Such an activity, the interactive cloze procedure, will be explained in chapter 10.

Maze

Maze was previously described as a technique for determining students' prior knowledge, but, like cloze, maze builds background as it determines it. Because three choices are given, students who lack prior knowledge have some material to react to. This interaction promotes the use of partial associations. In fact, many teachers prefer maze to cloze for building background because it is less threatening to students and promotes discussion successfully. From the maze, students can move right into reading the whole material, practicing use of context clues.

PreP and Free Recall

When factstorming is followed by discussion of why the particular facts were mentioned, or when the steps of reflection and re-formation of knowledge are applied in PreP, then background building is occurring. These steps encourage the reader to use whatever prior knowledge is available by listening carefully to the opinions of others. Misperceptions can be corrected in a nonthreatening way, with whole group discussion as a supportive environment for expression. Listening, speaking, and reading are all taking place in a PreP activity.

Free recall (Holmes and Roser, 1987) is a similar strategy. The teacher presents a situation and asks students to respond with ideas. The ideas give the teacher a picture of students' prior knowledge and a chance to begin the building process necessary. Holmes and Roser give this example of free recall: "Imagine that in this story is written everything there is to know about snakes. What do you think it will say?" (p. 647). They caution that free recall may work best with older students who have better organized knowledge than do younger students. We believe that younger students will benefit from the activity when it is used as a background builder rather than as a determiner.

What-I-Know Sheets

When students fill in the column labeled "What I already know," they are building their background as well as giving the teacher information about their prior knowledge. If students are encouraged to add to their own list after listening to and learning from class discussion, they are building background by using other students' knowledge. Reading to find out what else can be learned ("what I now know") and what wasn't learned ("what I still don't know—and hope to find out") will encourage development of comprehension and reflective thinking also. The class discussion and recording of associations integrate the communicative arts.

Direct References and Simple Discussions

These strategies, although not mentioned in chapter 3, are also ways to solve the problems identified in situations three, four, and five. Maria and MacGinitie (1987) conducted a study in which they asked students in fifth and sixth grades to read two types of materials. The first made specific reference to the misconceptions that the researchers had identified during a pretest and contrasted these misconceptions with correct information. The second was written with the correct information but no direct refutation of predetermined misconceptions. The researchers found that student recall was significantly better on the text which confronted the misconceptions.

In a research study, it makes sense to construct materials which will fit the particular questions being asked. In a classroom, teachers will not have enough time to alter text materials so that misperceptions can be countered. Yet, because making direct references to misconceptions appears to be such a good strategy for overcoming incorrect prior knowledge, teachers will want to incorporate it into lessons which build the background correctly. If some rewriting of portions of text can be done, the rewrite might include a specific confrontation. Another possibility is to use a simple discussion as a building-background activity. In such a discussion, the teacher who has determined that a misconception exists in students' prior knowledge can confront it with a written or oral statement. The misinformation can be compared with the correct information which will be read in the text. In this way, background can be built and the misperception cleared up. If students were assigned to write brief statements comparing a prior misconception to a revised understanding of the content, they would be integrating writing with reading at the reflective step of PAR.

Situations Six and Seven

As we explained in chapter 3, these situations are reader-based, not text-based. Building background in these two situations involves improving reading skills and attitudes about reading, which is discussed in several other chapters of this book.

Other Strategies Which Build Background

DRTA

The Directed Reading-Thinking Activity (DRTA) as advocated by Stauffer (1969) is a good example of the interconnectedness of reading-thinking-learning strategies. There are three basic steps in the DRTA: predicting, reading, proving. Predicting involves asking readers to use what they already know and can learn from a quick preview of the reading material to predict what the material will be about; this is preparation. Predicting prepares the reader for comprehension; it is an extremely important step in the DRTA, but it cannot stand alone. Because students are encouraged to predict aloud, and to justify predictions, a lively listening and speaking opportunity is available. The DRTA can also be used in the assisting and reflecting steps of PAR and will be discussed in this context in chapter 5.

Previewing

Previewing is an excellent strategy that is often associated with the DRTA (Valeri-Gold, 1987) because it encourages the reader in the same way that the prediction step of the DRTA does. Previewing usually includes these steps:

1. Determining the length of the reading material and judging how much time should be spent reading it
2. Reading the title and thinking about the associations it calls forth
3. Reading each subheading and forming a question or expectation about what could be learned from the material under this subheading
4. Looking at the illustrations, graphs, charts, or other visuals accompanying the material and trying to figure out how they will enhance the material
5. Reading the introduction and summary
6. Reviewing any pre- or post-questions

Previewing will help the reader depend on past learning to develop expectations. For instance, a reader will know at what pace he or she can read material of this sort. That prior knowledge, combined with the new information gained by the preview, will allow the reader to reserve enough time to read this material. In addition to its use by students, teachers use this previewing strategy to develop the recognition pretest discussed in chapter 3. In chapter 8, we discuss this important strategy in relation to study skills.

Written Previews

Graves, Prenn, and Cooke (1985) suggest that teachers write brief previews of material to be read by students. These previews, which are especially valuable for difficult material, provide a reference point for the material and offer students a way to organize the new information. The preview should be fairly short and is usually read aloud to the class before silent reading of the material is done. Students enjoy previews and demonstrate improved comprehension when they have been exposed to them. Teachers can use the information gained from their own previewing of the material to write a preview. In writing previews, a teacher can follow these steps:

1. Select a situation which students will know about and which connects to the topic. Describe the situation and pose a question which will lead to the topic.
2. If the material demands background knowledge students will not have, write a brief section including this information.
3. Provide a synopsis of the material.
4. Provide directions for reading the material which will facilitate comprehension.

A C T I V I T Y 4.4

Preview of "Counting Squares"

Have you ever built objects with plastic blocks? Before you began, did you have a plan for what your building would look like? It's important to make sure that you have the right number of blocks for the object you want to build. Otherwise, you might end up with a strange-looking building. Suppose you had a job and had to order the correct number of blocks to build a very large building. If you didn't order enough, you would have to order more later, which would waste time. If you ordered too many, you would be wasting money. Either way, your boss would be angry. What could you do to be sure that you were ordering the right number?

In this passage, you will read about Ahmose, a chief builder for an ancient Egyptian king. Ahmose had to order the right number of stone blocks for the king's home. If he made a mistake, the king would be angry. So he devised a counting table to help him figure correctly. This counting table was a lot like the multiplication table.

As you read this passage, see how a counting table and a multiplication table are alike. Discover how a multiplication table is more useful.

Based on pages 120–123 of *Mathemagic,* the 1978 *Childcraft Annual.*

After a teacher reads the first few sentences of the preview, time should be allotted for discussing the questions posed in the first part of the preview. When the teacher has read the remainder of the preview, students should read the material right away. "Counting Squares" (Activity 4.4) is an example of a preview.

Prewriting

Carnes (1988) describes a strategy for teaching content reading by having students write books. One of the stages in this activity is prewriting, when students are planning standards for the books they will write. Carnes' students studied many textbooks to become acquainted with book parts, structure, and style. Then they chose topics and brainstormed for information which might be included under those topics. This information became a rough outline. They scanned possible resources and compiled a reference list. This process is not unlike the ones we have used consistently in writing this textbook. A good portion of the authors' time has been spent at the preparation stage. Probably

40 percent of the total composition time has been devoted to prewriting, which has included a lot of reading and outlining in preparation for writing.

Prewriting might occur as preparation for reading content material. Such a technique might be particularly helpful at the beginning of a school year before textbooks are distributed. Students could be encouraged to decide how their text might be organized and to write possible topics and subheadings for an anticipated table of contents. By placing themselves in the position of authorship, students can experience the crucial prewriting step and become aware of their own background for reading. In addition, a prewriting activity can integrate the communicative arts.

Analogies

When a high-school junior resisted reading a history chapter which explained the circumstances leading to the American Revolution, his parent (a reading specialist, of course!) tried the preparation strategy described below:

> "Suppose," the parent suggested," that your parents decided to go to Europe for six months, leaving you on your own at home. You would have the car and access to money; you would be able to make all of your own decisions. What would your reaction be?" As you may imagine, this high-school junior thought this would be an excellent arrangement. "However," the parent continued, "we would arrive home again and take charge once more. We would want our car back, and you would have to ask for permission to use it. You would begin to receive an allowance again. You would have to ask permission to do the things you'd been doing freely. Now, how would you feel?" As you can imagine, this junior did not like the turn of events. "Would you still love us?" the parent inquired, assuming, of course, that teenagers *do* love their parents even though they have funny ways of showing it!
>
> "Well, yes," the junior reluctantly agreed. "But I'd be insulted, and family life wouldn't be the same."
>
> "Exactly," agreed the parent. "That's the way it was with the British and their American colony. The British had to attend to problems in Europe and in their own government. They let the American colonists have free rein for a while. Then they turned their attention back to the Americans. But the Americans didn't appreciate the intervention after this period of time. Many of them still 'loved' the British, but they resented the renewed control deeply. While you're reading this chapter, you might want to keep in mind your own reactions to this hypothetical situation and compare those feelings to the reactions of the colonists."

Much later in the month, this junior grudgingly reported to his parent that the chapter had turned out to be "pretty easy to read" because he understood the circumstances better than with most of the chapters in the book. This on-the-spot analogy was simple enough to construct.

The teacher/parent understood several characteristics of sixteen-year-olds and applied them to building an analogy which would "hook" the content material to the reader. The informal analogy was a simple preparation strategy. It worked because the reading took on new meaning for the student. His comprehension was enhanced, enough so that he admitted it to a parent!

Analogies present comparisons between known and unknown concepts. The comparison that the superintendent made between practicing for a basketball game and preparing to read relates a familiar concept for students to a less familiar one. Analogies are like previews in that both begin with a connection point to the reader's background. However, analogies carry out a comparison, whereas previews focus more directly on the material to be read. Analogies are excellent tools for content reading teachers because they are simple to create and so relevant for students. They can be presented in oral or written form, as an informal introduction to content material. They also promote listening and speaking, and if students are encouraged to write their own analogies after reading material, then analogies become useful reflection and writing activities as well. A third-grade teacher developed the following lesson in building background with an analogy as its base (Activity 4.5).

Graphic Organizers

Like previews and analogies, graphic organizers help the reader prepare for reading by organizing the important concepts. Graphic organizers do what their name implies: organize information graphically. The graphic organizer is a hierarchical overview which demonstrates how the important concepts, as represented by the vocabulary in a reading selection, fit together. In a way, it is the teacher's depiction of the schema of the material. A graphic organizer is effective because a teacher can prepare readers with a concise, comprehensive, and compact visual aid. Thus, the teacher can capitalize on the visual literacy of the learner. Note that at the beginning of each chapter, we present a graphic organizer to help readers see the relationship between the concepts and the key words and phrases in the chapter. This organizer is a visual representation of the content in each chapter.

Structured overview is another term for graphic organizer. We note two differences between structured overviews and graphic organizers. While some associate structured overviews with a hierarchical diagram of words, we associate graphic organizer also with a pictorial representation. The diagram in chapter 1 for secondary social studies students is what some would label a structured overview. The diagram for primary students in chapter 1 contains an illustration as well as terms presented in an order; it might be more appropriately called a graphic

---

A C T I V I T Y   4.5

Analogy

Goal: To enable students to "connect" new knowledge with existing knowledge.

Directions: Read the following paragraphs as a primer for small-group discussion comparing cars with bodies.

Materials: Paper
Pencils

Your body is very similar to a car in the way that it acts. You may have been told to "rev up your engine" one time. When a car revs up, it begins to go.

A car needs many different substances to keep it running well. It might need oil for the parts and air for the filters, as you would need oil for your joints or air for your lungs.

Actually, there are many other things that a car and your body have in common. A car needs gasoline to make it go. What do you need? (food)

Now divide the students into small groups and let them list on paper the ways that cars and bodies are similar. Some suggestions that you will be looking for are:

Fats/oil
Protein/gasoline
Carbohydrates/spark plugs
Vitamins/fuel additives, super power gasoline
Minerals/paint, rustproofers
Air/air conditioning
muscles/wheels
heart/engine

Return to the class group in fifteen or twenty minutes and share the group information. Write the analogies on the board. Ask for comments or changes.

Developed by Kathy Feltus.

---

organizer than a structured overview. Second, structured overviews are generally equated with the preparation stage of content reading while graphic organizers are often useful at all PAR stages. For the preparatory portions of the chapters in this textbook, we call the diagrams "graphic organizers" because they precede the chapter but are sometimes pictorial rather than hierarchical diagrams.

Earle and Barron (1973) comment that the research on prior knowledge supports the use of overviews or organizers. This finding makes sense because graphic organizers are designed to show relationships. When readers understand the relationships of concepts in a reading selection, they can begin to connect the new relationships to their previous knowledge. A graphic organizer is grounded in this theory.

Teachers usually find graphic organizers challenging to prepare but very much worth the effort. To construct one, a teacher should follow these steps:

1. Write an organizing concept and then identify all supporting concepts in the material.
2. List all key terms from the material which reflect the identified concepts.
3. Connect the terms to show the relationships between the concepts.
4. Construct a diagram based on these connections, and use it to introduce the reading material.

It will not be necessary to use every word which might be new to readers in developing the graphic organizer. Some new words may not contribute to the diagram. It is useful to include words known to the students when these words reflect the diagram because the familiarity will aid understanding. We have found that when graphic organizers are pictorial, students enjoy and remember them better.

Teachers should explain to the students why they prepared the graphic organizer as they did, noting the relationships. This presentation should include a discussion to which students can contribute what they know about the terms as well as what they predict they will be learning, based on the chart. Students should also have the organizer available for reference while they are reading, so that they can occasionally check back to see the relationships as they encounter the terms. After reading, the students can use the graphic organizer as an aid for refocusing and reflecting on the learning. It can even be used as a check of comprehension, which is how we have used it at the end of chapters in this textbook. Thus, the graphic organizer is an activity which can be useful for all of the PAR steps and which promotes integration of the communicative arts.

Activities 4.6 through 4.9, which follow, are examples of graphic organizers prepared by teachers in several different content areas. The polygon and research process organizers follow a traditional format, much like the organizers which precede many chapters in this book. The organizer on nonfiction writing is pictorial, and the organizer for primary science students uses circles, rectangles, and arrows to show relationships.

A C T I V I T Y 4.6

Geometry Overview (Key)

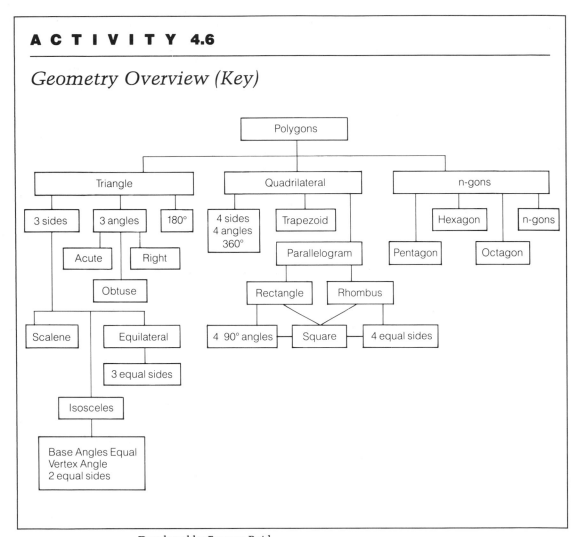

Developed by Frances Reid.

Anticipation Guides

Anticipation guides, also called reaction or prediction guides, prepare readers by asking them to *react* to a series of statements which are related to the content of the material. In reacting to these statements, students *anticipate* or *predict* what the content will be. Hence, the three different labels for this activity. An anticipation guide is used at the beginning of this chapter when readers are asked whether they agree or disagree with four statements and why. Each statement is reintro-

A C T I V I T Y   4.7

Structured Overview

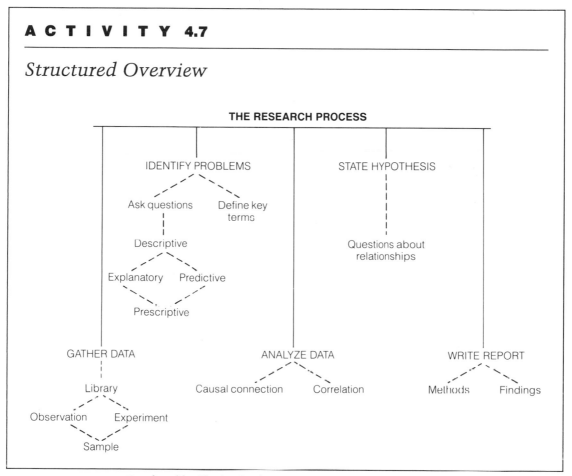

THE RESEARCH PROCESS

IDENTIFY PROBLEMS

Ask questions   Define key terms

Descriptive

Explanatory   Predictive

Prescriptive

STATE HYPOTHESIS

Questions about relationships

GATHER DATA

Library

Observation   Experiment

Sample

ANALYZE DATA

Causal connection   Correlation

WRITE REPORT

Methods   Findings

Developed by Charles Sicola.

duced later in the chapter, in a discussion intended to focus the reader's comprehension.

Erickson (1987) and her coauthors cite three reasons for the value of anticipation guides: 1) Students will need to connect what they already know with new information and will realize that they do already know something that will help them comprehend better; 2) Students tend to become interested and participate in lively discussion, which motivates reading; 3) Reading and writing instruction are easily integrated when anticipation guides are used. Anticipation guides, then, involve students in discussion and reading and can also include writing if students are asked to respond in writing to the statements. Many teachers also have students refer to the guide as they are reading, which enhances

A C T I V I T Y   4.8

Developed by Rebecca McSweeney.

comprehension. If students return to the guide after reading, to clarify or rethink previous positions, then the guide is applied throughout PAR. Conley (1985) argues that such guides are also excellent tools for developing critical thinking and promoting cross-cultural understanding. For all of these reasons, anticipation guides are truly eclectic and very well received by both teachers and students.

Making an anticipation guide takes some thought, but it becomes easier with practice. The process has been described in several textbooks, including those of Herber (1978) and Readance, Bean, and Bald-

---

A C T I V I T Y   4.9

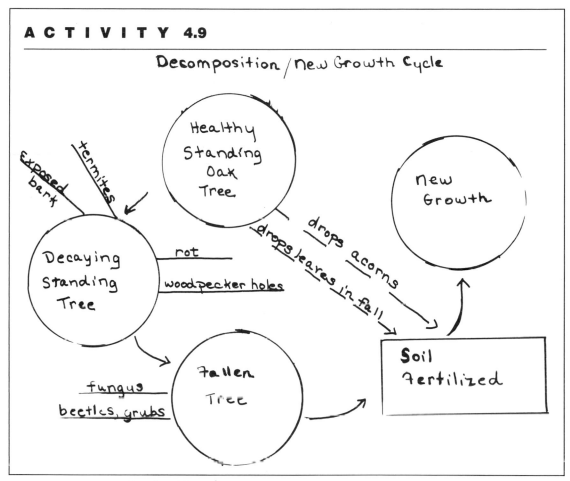

Decomposition / New Growth Cycle

Developed by Kathryn Davis.

win (1981). The following are the basic steps for constructing an anticipation guide:

1. Read the content passage and identify the major concepts.
2. Decide which concepts are most important to stimulate student background and beliefs.
3. Write three to five statements based on the concepts. The statements should reflect the students' background and be thought-provoking. We have found that general statements, rather than statements related specifically to the content, work best. Famous quotations and idioms are successful.
4. Display the guide on the chalkboard, on an overhead projector, or on ditto sheets. Give clear directions. (These will vary depending

on the age group and variations in the guide.) Leave space for responses.

5. Conduct class discussion with the statements as the basis. Students must support their responses; "yes" and "no" are not acceptable answers. Students should argue from their past experiences and explain their decisions. (After guides have been used a few times, small groups can conduct discussion simultaneously or individuals can complete guides independently and then reconvene.)

6. It is best to return to the anticipation guide after the material has been read. In this way, students can compare their first responses to their new information.

An anticipation guide that was used with fifth-grade music students appeared earlier in this chapter. Activities 4.10 through 4.13, which follow, include examples of anticipation guides constructed by primary and intermediate teachers of science and social studies as well as a middle school art teacher.

One secondary teacher was so enchanted with anticipation guides that she wrote a tribute in the form of an acrostic (see Figure 4.2).

There is no "right" way to make an activity. Activities which reflect sound instructional principles and research are developed every day by enterprising teachers. In fact, we have discovered just how creative teachers can be when they like an activity and understand its benefits.

A C T I V I T Y 4.10

Anticipation/Prediction Guide: Social Studies

Directions: Read these statements to yourself as I read them aloud. If you agree with a statement, be ready to explain why. We will check all statements we agree with in the prereading column. Then we will read to see if we should change our minds.

Prereading   *Postreading*

_____ (1) Pioneers traveled west in search of adventure and   _____
                     a new and better life.
_____ (2) You can be a pioneer.   _____
_____ (3) A community is a place where people live and   _____
                     work closely together.
_____ (4) More Americans live in the East.   _____
_____ (5) There are only four necessities of life.   _____
_____ (6) Much of the desert earth is rich.   _____

Developed by Helen Lipscomb.

A C T I V I T Y 4.11

Anticipation/Prediction Guide: Social Studies

Directions: Read the statements below carefully. Put a ✓ beside "agree" or "disagree" to show what you think. Be ready to defend your answer.

| Prereading | | | Postreading | |
Agree	Disagree	Statements	Agree	Disagree
———	———	It is easy to adjust when you move from one place to another.	———	———
———	———	Hard work and faith bring success.	———	———
———	———	There is a price to pay for everything you do.	———	———
———	———	People who do not obey the law should be put in jail.	———	———
———	———	Make the best of what you have, or it will do you no good.	———	———

Developed by Dianna Gordon.

A C T I V I T Y 4.12

Anticipation/Prediction Guide: Science

Directions: Put a check beside every sentence you think is true.

——— There are many different kinds of animals.
——— Animals need some kind of covering.
——— Some animals cannot move.
——— All animals need food.
——— All animals get food the same way.

Note: I would read each statement orally and let the children respond individually on their papers. Upon completion, we would discuss (as a class) our responses, and why we responded as we did.

Developed by Elizabeth Proffitt from *Health Science* "Animals" 1st grade.

A C T I V I T Y 4.13

Anticipation/Prediction Guide: Art

Directions: Read the statements below **before** and **after** you read Chapter 5. Put a check next to each statement to show your opinion. This is not a test.

Before Reading			*After Reading*	
Agree	*Disagree*		*Agree*	*Disagree*
_____	_____	The cave paintings in France and Spain are the earliest records man will ever have.	_____	_____
_____	_____	Early architects were concerned with religion, rituals and self preservation.	_____	_____
_____	_____	The largest and greatest pyramid was built for Cheops and covered thirteen acres.	_____	_____
_____	_____	The pyramids were built to honor the gods and as places of worship.	_____	_____
_____	_____	Egyptians used descriptive perspective in which the important figures are shown larger than the less important ones.	_____	_____

Developed by Joan Phipps.

A
Necessary
Tool to use for
Instruction in teaching
Critical thinking and for getting students
Involved in
Predicting
Activities
That
Integrate the use
Of all of the communicative arts to comprehend
New material. The

Goal is to
Ultimately produce
Independent thinkers who use
Discussion and reading to
Enhance comprehension.

Figure 4.2. Anticipation Guide.
Developed by Linda R. Cobb.

One English teacher modified and merged factstorming and anticipation guide format. He wrote three statements relevant to the short story "An Occurrence at Owl Creek Bridge." When he presented these to his class, he asked them to respond with the thoughts which came to mind as they reacted to the statements. He listed their responses beside each statement and then asked for a consensus (see Activity 4.14).

Preguiding Questions

Questions can be used to develop student background. Preguiding questions are particularly useful when students have already read and reflected on much text material and will be required in the forthcoming chapter

---

A C T I V I T Y 4.14

Modified Anticipation/Prediction Guide

think scared worry over-react nervous cry How can we solve the problem?	confusion life flashes before eyes mad religion happy past thoughts	1. During a crisis, the mind works very rapidly.
pressure tired dentist, doctor, etc. illness death work school	practice, games accident pressure (extreme) movies family guys gals	2. Great stress can be provoked by everyday kinds of experiences.
escape pain family friends guilty or innocent	life/death future thoughts past thoughts Help! life is flashing before my eyes	3. The human mind undergoes many psychological reactions when a person is about to be hanged.

Developed by Robert Witherow.

A C T I V I T Y 4.15

Preguiding Questions

1. What two ways can energy be transported?

2. What are the five general properties of waves?

3. We know that sound is transmitted through waves. Sound bends around corners, as evidenced by the fact that we can hear around corners. Light casts sharp shadows; we can not see around corners. Based on this knowledge about the behavior of light, would you classify light as a wave or particle? Explain your answer.

4. A beam of light strikes a smooth surface as pictured below; the angle of incidence (i) is found to be equal to the angle of reflection (r). Can a model of light based on waves be used to explain this behavior?

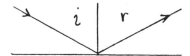

Developed by Tom Fleming.

to relate new information to the known. A chemistry teacher devised a set of questions which related both to previous study about waves and to new information about light. He placed the questions in the middle of the page, with a prereading column on the left and a postreading column on the right. Before the assigned reading, students wrote group responses to the questions in the prereading column, using their previous knowledge and predictions. After reading, they responded with the correct answer in the postreading column and compared their educated guess to the facts. Group interaction promoted communication, and the activity spanned all PAR steps (see Activity 4.15).

One-Minute Summary

In this chapter we have argued for the importance of building background before assigning reading materials. We have presented research and practical examples that illustrate why preparation is important. We have described several activities, and we have included versions developed by teachers. We have related these activities to five of the situations presented in chapter 3 which can cause readability problems. Some of the activities demonstrated in chapter 3 were represented in this chapter to illustrate how an activity can be useful for more than one PAR step. Some new activities were also presented in this chapter. Our purpose has been to demonstrate how these activities promote reading, writing, speaking, and listening and can span all steps of PAR. We have tried to emphasize that the *way* a teacher uses an activity is more important than rigorous adherence to prescribed steps. Finally, we have included variations of activities that demonstrate the creativity of the teachers who constructed them.

End-of-Chapter Activities

Preparing the Reader

1. How does the quotation we selected to introduce this chapter relate to this chapter's theme?

2. Which readability situation applies best to the "B.C." cartoon?

Assisting Comprehension

1. Study the following organizer and, without looking back at the beginning of the chapter, fill in the blanks with correct words that convey key concepts taught in this chapter. You may scan back through the chapter text.

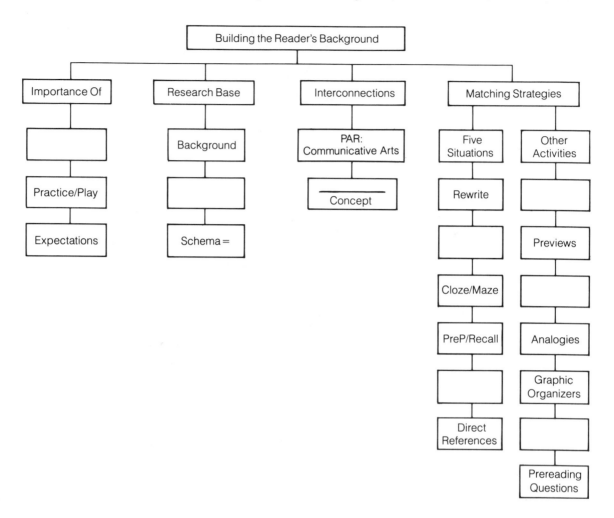

2. Look back at the anticipation guide from the start of this chapter. Did you find where each statement was discussed in this chapter? Have you changed your responses since beginning your reading?

3. To help you see the many possibilities of cloze for building background, you might want to read Gove's article "Using the Cloze Procedure in a First-Grade Classroom." You will find this in *The Reading Teacher*, October 1975, pages 36–38.

Reflecting on Your Reading

1. Select a chapter from a content area textbook. Using the following questions as a guide, reflect on what your text offers to help you as a teacher to build your students' backgrounds for reading the text:

What aids are provided in my text chapter to help the teacher build background? Is there any chapter preview or summary which could be used to build background? Are any statements given which could be used in an anticipation guide, such as those identifying objectives? Is there a graphic organizer?

Are these aids suitable for my students?

Are these aids sufficient for my students?

As a teacher, should I construct some aids to help me build student background? If so, what will I construct?

2. To extend your reading about prior knowledge, we recommend that you read chapter 2, "The Discovery of the Schema" in *Cultural Literacy* by Hirsch. This is an informative, historically based discussion peppered with several interesting stories and experiments which illustrate the importance of readers' backgrounds in achieving literacy.

References

Anderson, R. C. (1985). The role of the reader's schema in comprehension, learning and memory. In H. Singer and R.B. Ruddell (Eds.), *Theoretical models and processes of reading* (3rd ed.)(372–384). Newark, DE: International Reading Association.

Anderson, R. C. & Pearson, P. D. (1984). A schema-theoretic view of basic processes in reading comprehension. In P. D. Pearson (Ed.), *Handbook of reading research* (255–291). New York: Longman.

Ausubel, D. (1968). *Educational psychology: A cognitive view.* New York: Holt, Rinehart & Winston.

Bartlett, F. C. (1932). *Remembering.* Cambridge, MA: Cambridge University Press.

Beck, I. L., McKeown, M., Omanson, R. C. & Pople, M. (1984). Improving comprehensibility of stories: The effects of revisions that improve coherence. *Reading Research Quarterly, XIX,* 263–277.

Beil, D. (1977). The emperor's new cloze. *Journal of Reading, 20,* 601–604.

Bosher, William (1987). Remarks made during Superintendents' Teleconference on Reading To Learn, Virginia State Department of Education, December.

Carnes, E. J. (1988). Teaching content area reading through nonfiction book writing. *Journal of Reading, 31,* 354–360.

Chall, J. (1947). The influence of previous knowledge on reading ability. *Educational Research Bulletin, 26,* 225–230.

Chall, J. (1983). *Stages of reading development.* New York: McGraw-Hill.

Combs, A. W. & Snygg, D. (1959). *Individual behavior.* New York: Harper & Row.

Conley, M. (1985). Promoting cross-cultural understanding through content area reading strategies. *Journal of Reading, 28,* 600-605.

Craig, L. (1977). If it's difficult to read, rewrite it! *The Reading Teacher, 21,* 212–214.

Davey, B. (1988). How do classroom teachers use their textbooks? *Journal of Reading, 31,* 340–345.

Earle, R. & Barron, R. F. (1973). An approach for teaching vocabulary in content subjects, in H. L. Herber and R. F. Barron (Eds.), *Research in reading in the* content areas: Second year report (84–100) Syracuse, NY: Syracuse University Reading and Language Arts Center.

Erickson, B., Huber, M., Bea, T., Smith, C. & McKenzie, V. (1987). Increasing critical reading in junior high classes. *Journal of Reading, 30,* 430–439.

Graves, D., Prenn, M. & Cooke, C. (1985). The coming attraction: Previewing short stories. *Journal of Reading, 28,* 594–598.

Harris, T. & Hodges, R. (1981). *A dictionary of reading.* Newark, DE: International Reading Association.

Herber, H. (1978). *Teaching reading in content areas.* Englewood Cliffs, NJ: Prentice-Hall.

Hinchman, K. (1987). The textbook and three content-area teachers. *Reading Research and Instruction, 26,* 247–263.

Hirsch, E. D. (1987). *Cultural literacy.* New York: Houghton Mifflin.

Holmes, B. C. & Roser, N. (1987). Five ways to assist readers' prior knowledge. *The Reading Teacher, 40,* 646–649.

Kirsch, I. & Jungeblut, A. (1986). *Literacy: Profiles of America's young adults.* Princeton, NJ: National Assessment of Educational Progress.

Lange, K. (1902). Apperception, In de Garma, C. (Ed.), A monograph on psychology and pedagogy. Boston, MA: Heath.

Maria, K. & MacGinitie, W. (1987). Learning from texts that refute the readers' prior knowledge. *Reading Research and Instruction, 26,* 222–238.

Miller, G. (1956). The magical number seven, plus or minus two. *Psychological Review, 63,* 81–97.

Pearson, P. D. & Spiro, R. (1982, May). The new buzz word in reading is schema. *Instructor,* pp. 46–48.

Phelps, S. (1984). A first step in content area reading instruction. *Reading World, 23,* 265–269.

Piaget, J. (1952). *The language and thought of the child.* London: Routledge & Kegan Paul.

Readance, J., Bean, T. & Baldwin, S. (1981). *Content area reading: An integrated approach.* Dubuque, IA: Kendall/Hunt.

Rumelhart, D. E. (1980). Schemata: The building blocks of cognition. In R. J. Spiro, B. C. Bruce & W. F. Brewer (Eds.), *Theoretical issues in reading comprehension,* (33–58). Hillsdale, NJ: Erlbaum.

Siedow, M. D. & Hasselbring (1984). Adaptability of text readability to increase comprehension of reading disability students. *Reading Improvement, 21,* 276–279.

Smith, F. (1971). *Understanding reading.* New York: Holt, Rinehart & Winston.

Stauffer, R. G. (1969). *Directing reading maturity as a cognitive process.* New York: Harper & Row.

Steffenson, M. S., Joag-Des, C. & Anderson, R. C. (1979). A cross-cultural perspective on reading comprehension. *Reading Research Quarterly, 15,* 10–29.

Thorndike, E. L. (1932). *Educational psychology.* Columbia University, New York: Teachers College Press.

Valeri-Gold, M. (1987). Previewing: A directed reading-thinking activity. *Reading Horizons, 27,* 123–126.

5 Assisting Reading by Setting Purposes

By teaching us how to read, they had taught us how to get away."

Robert O'Brien,
Mrs. Frisby and the Rats of NIMH

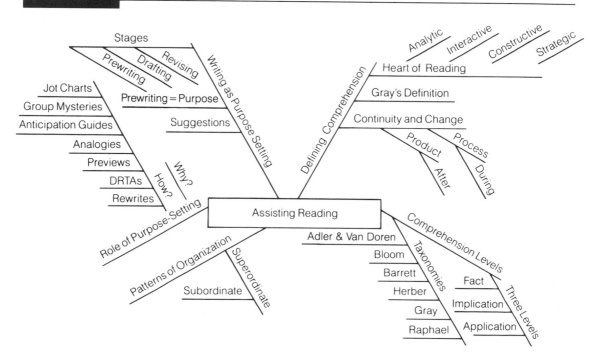

1. What is your definition of reading comprehension? Try this activity to write your own definition:

    For two minutes, write anything that comes to your mind about reading comprehension; now, stop and study what you wrote. You should see a line of thought or a particular idea emerging. Identify or write a single sentence expressing that thought or idea.

    Now, write again for two minutes about reading comprehension, using that sentence as your focus. Stop and study what you wrote, identifying the line of thought you have generated. Identify or write a single sentence which expresses that line of thought.

    Write again for two minutes, using this second sentence. After your third "loop" of writing, study this last "loop" and culminate by writing your definition.

    Be ready to share this definition with others in your class.

    [This activity is called "looping" by Cowan and Cowan (1980). Try it with your students to help them determine their own background for a topic.]

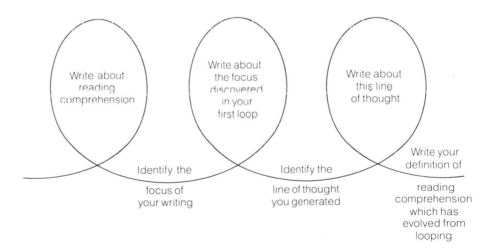

2. Remember the golfers' dialogue presented in chapter 3? It is incomprehensible if one does not know esoteric golf terminology. Although the questions following the dialogue could be answered just by using the syntax of the language, not much comprehension will occur until a translation is provided. Here is the dialogue again, with an accompanying translation:

    "Do I deserve a mulligan?" asked Bob.

Shoe. Reprinted with permission of Tribune Media Services.

Bob asks if he deserves a second shot without a penalty.

"No, but don't take a drop," said Al. "Use a hand-mashie, then fly the ball high to the carpet and maybe you'll get a gimme within the leather."

Al says no, but warns not to drop the ball (without penalty). Al tells Bob to kick the ball out of trouble with his foot (hand-mashie) and then hit the ball with a high trajectory to the green (where golfers putt). If Bob gets it within eighteen inches of the cup (leather), he can pick up his ball, counting himself one stroke (gimme).

"You're right," said Bob. "I'll cover the flag for a birdie and at least get a ginsberg if I'm not stymied."

Bob agrees to hit the ball close to the hole so he has a chance for a birdie (one under par). If he gets on the green, he can lay up his putt to the hole (ginsberg). In older days golfers did not mark their balls, so you might get stymied by another ball, i.e., have to shoot around the ball. Bob is being facetious here. One cannot get stymied on the green in modern golf.

Now, here are the questions again:

Does Bob deserve a mulligan? a) yes b) no c) maybe

What does Al think Bob should do? a) catch a gimme b) take a drop c) use a hand-mashie d) fly a kite

What does Bob decide to do? a) cover the flag b) take a drop c) birdie-up

How can Bob get a birdie? a) getting stymied b) getting a ginsberg c) by covering the flag

If Bob is not stymied, what will he get? a) a hickie b) a birdie c) a mulligan d) a ginsberg

Compare the answers you gave in chapter 3 to the ones you can now give. Is there a difference? What does this exercise tell you about the role of assistance in enhancing comprehension?

3. By reviewing several principles presented in chapter 1, you will be better prepared to read this chapter:

The communicative arts work in concert and cannot be separated from education in content subjects.

Literacy includes not only the traditional communicative arts but also visual literacy.

The most effective thinking and learning occurs when critical reading is encouraged.

Meaningful reading about content subjects is a lifetime experience which should start early and continue throughout life.

The study of content reading can be enhanced by studies made by professionals in related fields.

4. Below is a list of terms used in this chapter. Some of them may be familiar to you in a general context, but in this chapter they may be used in a different way than you are used to. Rate your knowledge by placing a + in front of those you are sure that you know, a √ in front of those you have some knowledge about, and a 0 in front of those you don't know. Be ready to locate and pay special attention to their meanings when they are presented in the chapter:

_____ constructive

_____ taxonomy

_____ inside-outside factors

_____ street-smart

_____ discourse

_____ superordination

_____ subordination

_____ informative communication

Objectives: As you read this chapter, focus your attention on the following objectives. You will:

1. be able to define reading, using both past and present definitions given in the professional literature.

2. understand the difference between process and product as related to reading comprehension.

3. identify three levels of comprehension which will help teachers assist students in comprehension.

4. identify several patterns of organization which are often used in content materials.

5. understand why it is important to set reading purposes and describe several activities which help set purposes.

6. see the role of writing in helping readers set purposes.

Purpose:

In chapter 4 you discovered ways to prepare your students to read in your content. The reason to prepare them is so they will read with greater understanding. The next step in the PAR framework is to assist reading by developing goals. A reader's goals provide purpose, which enhances comprehension. In this chapter, we will present the following activities that promote purposeful reading: looping; cubing; DRTA; group mystery clue game; jot charts; and prewriting. Read to find out why and how to provide purposeful reading in content materials.

What Is Reading Comprehension?

As a student in an eleventh-grade history class, one of the authors had a lesson in what reading comprehension is *not*. The author remembers—painfully—reading each assigned chapter for homework, trying to memorize as much of the content as possible on the first reading because the history teacher always employed the same "instructional strategy." The day after this assigned reading, we would be told to close our books. The teacher opened his copy and, rocking on his toes, called out the name of a student, then a question from his teacher's manual. He also had the answers, of course. More than once, we didn't have the answers because we could not remember. This lapse on our part caused our embarrassed silence and his consternation, a zero marked in his grading book, and another question. And so on. No one in that class liked history that year. Most of us just stopped reading the assigned chapters. What was the point?

One parent tells the inspiring story of her daughter who had always received C's and D's in science, but in seventh grade brought home A's all year. Her mother asked her what the secret was. Her daughter explained, "This teacher makes me think and it's *fun*! I finally understand what science is about."

Comprehension as the Heart of Reading

The Analogy Explored

Comprehension is the heart of reading. This analogy works well when one considers the intricate relationship that the human heart enjoys within the body. The heart seems to beat automatically, but unless conditions are favorable, the beating, and life itself, stops. The heart depends on the atria and ventricles for a supply of blood so necessary to life. When veins become clogged, blood cannot be recycled efficiently; the relationship is jeopardized.

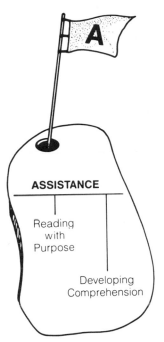

ASSISTANCE

Reading with Purpose

Developing Comprehension

Figure 5.1. Developed by Dawn Bubb and Walter Richards.

Reading may not "beat" automatically either. If readers are not prepared, they may have "clogged" comprehension. The reading heart is more likely to function efficiently when sustained by sensitive teachers, sound instructional practice, well-written texts, a supportive environment, and student interaction with the content. In eleventh-grade history class one year, several reading hearts slowed down or stopped beating. In seventh-grade science class one year, a reading heart beat to capacity.

In the children's novel *Mrs. Frisby and the Rats of NIMH,* the scientists conducted experiments to teach rats to read. Because the rats had been fed a superdrug to make them smart, the scientists anticipated that the rats would learn some letter-sound and word-picture relationships. They did not expect that the rats would actually ever *understand* what they read. They underestimated the heart of reading. These rats *wanted* to escape their lab. Their goal was vital; they were willing to work at learning to read so they could use this new skill to learn how to escape.

The rats used all of their communication skills to learn to read and then to escape. They studied pictures presented to them, they listened to clues to the meaning of the pictures, and they consulted with each other about what they were learning—the connections between letters and sounds, pictures and words. And then they read! Later, in their new home, they even began to keep a written record of their progress.

The story of the rats of NIMH demonstrates how the communicative arts, including visual literacy, work together to produce critical thinking and how meaningful reading can become a lifelong process. It also exemplifies the importance of assisted comprehension, which consists of sound, clear purposes to read and the opportunity to develop understanding. When the act of reading merges with thinking, comprehension results. The relationship is integral and cannot be separated *if* the conditions for learning are optimal. In this novel, the rats had a great desire to escape NIMH and plenty of opportunities for practice as well as plenty of clues in their environment. With such a rich supply, their reading hearts beat very efficiently. The natural result was comprehension and escape. The scientists, to their misfortune, did not recognize the role of purpose in their experiment.

Gray's Definition of Reading Comprehension

William Gray (1941; republished in 1984) proposed that there are three views about reading. The first is held by those who argue that the process of recognizing written symbols can be separated from understanding these symbols. This must have been what the scientists at NIMH supposed reading to be. According to proponents of this view, once one recognizes the symbols, comprehension occurs on its own (unless the subjects are rats, who cannot be expected to comprehend). This view was popularized by methods of teaching reading that rely on such approaches as synthetic phonics and linguistics, which are based on instruction in the relationship between sound and symbols, separate from comprehension. The expectation is that, once pronunciation is mastered, the "ah-ha" of comprehension will occur automatically. The content reading teacher who applies this theory would expect that, because students turn pages and pronounce words, they should learn the content. To us, separating recognition and comprehension is as difficult as separating the heart from the major vessels which supply it. Only the very motivated will succeed through such instruction. Gray did not support this view.

Secondly, Gray describes "a much broader concept of reading" which "assumes that it [reading] involves not only the fluent, accurate recognition of words but also the fusion of the specific meaning represented into a chain of related ideas (p. 17)." This concept was popular in Gray's era and is still a respected view.

Gray's third view—his own definition—is even more compelling; it "assumes that the reader not only apprehends the author's meaning but also reflects on the significance of the ideas presented, evaluates them critically, and makes application of them in the solution of problems (p. 18)." Gray prefers this last view as his definition of comprehension but he cautions that some professionals would criticize such a view because "it includes much that psychologists and educators have commonly called thinking (p. 18)." The argument of the professionals Gray alludes to seems to us to deny the integral relationship demanded by the reading heart. How can comprehension occur without thinking? How can reading occur without comprehension? The scientists at NIMH may have had a separatist view of reading, but the rats would surely agree with us. Apparently the owl in the "Shoe" comic strip that opened this chapter, puzzled by the meaning of those letters on his eye chart, agrees as well. In chapter 7 we will discuss further the impact of Gray's definition and of our principle 11: The study of content area reading can be enhanced by studies made by professionals in related fields.

The *Reading Report Card* Definition

In *The Reading Report Card* (1985), reading is described as analytic, interactive, constructive, and strategic. This definition implies that apprehension and reflection are requisites of comprehension, as does Gray's third concept of reading. A reader must analyze, or think about, the significance of the content; this analysis must be active and interdependent; some positive result will occur which produces a strategy to aid the reader in future reading. The active, integrated thinking which leads to a conclusion as a result of reading *is* comprehension.

Historical and Research Perspective

Continuity: Definitions of Comprehension from 1908 to the Present

Comprehension is one of the most researched and discussed areas in the study of reading. Because reading comprehension is related to so many fields of study, such as linguistics, psychology, neurology, and sociology, many professionals have made significant contributions to our understanding of reading comprehension. The interest has burgeoned within the last twenty years, as more professionals have agreed that it is very difficult to separate reading comprehension from discoveries about language and learning.

Although historically the study of reading comprehension has reflected different schools of thought during certain decades, such as the view of the 1950s and 1960s that separated the acts of reading and comprehension, the changes in definition have probably served to provide more continuity than disjunction. Huey (1908) and then Thorndike (1917) defined reading as a thinking process, implying that comprehension is more than recognizing letters and words; it includes thinking about what those symbols mean. Sixty years later, Hillerich (1979) drew the same conclusion when he identified reading comprehension as "nothing more than thinking as applied to reading (p. 3)."

A little earlier, Frank Smith (1971), drawing from his study of communication systems, argued for a definition of comprehension as "the reduction of uncertainty (pp. 17-19)." Smith explained that, as readers gain information by reading, they rely on what they know to "reduce the number of alternative possibilities (p. 17)." For instance, for some time after the rats of NIMH read the directions for unlatching their cages, the words were only pronounceable units. But by watching the scientists perform particular actions each time they took a rat from a cage, the rats began to use what they knew about the actions. They hypothesized that the words were some sort of direction. When they realized that a particular set of actions matched a set of words, they comprehended. The process they followed is not unlike that described by Pearson and Johnson (1978), who created a picture definition of reading comprehension as the building of bridges between the new and the known. The continuity among these definitions, which span seventy years, is apparent. How does the definition you wrote as you "looped" compare with these?

Change: Process versus Product

While the way many have defined comprehension has not changed substantially, the way we study comprehension has changed, as Pearson (1985) has indicated. New interest in how to teach reading comprehension has been generated because we recognize that comprehension is not a passive, receptive, or text-based process but an active, constructive, reader-based process. In the past, reading researchers studied the results of reading comprehension to help them explain how comprehension occurs. They listed and described measurable results of comprehension. They expected that, after reading, readers would be able to answer questions of varying difficulty, organize information, and explain its implications. The answers, which demonstrate whether the reader *has* learned the content, are the *products* of comprehension.

The *process* of learning, in contrast, refers to the mental activity that goes on *as* the reader is reading and thinking about the material. While this mental activity is occurring, the reader is seeking assistance to understand the material. The reader will want to be sorting facts from implications, identifying the organization of the material, and using picture clues and text aids to help with this understanding. The teacher's role is to employ teaching strategies which assist this understanding, such as those which integrate listening, speaking, reading, and writing.

The study of comprehension today is related to this emphasis on what occurs as the reader reads to learn. It is process-oriented. By discovering what readers do as they read, we can design strategies for assistance which enhance their learning.

Using Process and Product Together

Most reading professionals today acknowledge that, although certain "products" can be expected as a result of reading comprehension, these are not in themselves the act of comprehending, nor is it necessary that all behaviors occur before comprehension can occur. Cooper (1986) explains that "to comprehend the written word, the reader must be able to 1) understand how an author has structured or organized the ideas and information presented in a text, and 2) relate the ideas and information from text to ideas or information stored in his or her mind" (p. 4). Cooper is describing a process one uses while reading. The reader is actively searching for a pattern of organization and actively relating what he reads to what he already knows.

If a teacher asks a question whose answer relies on the organi zational pattern (such as "what was the effect of this action?"), then the student can produce an answer which shows he processed the information. It is up to teachers to demonstrate to students *how* to process text so students can then demonstrate the product—what they have learned. The act leads to the result.

This distinction is the foundation for a discussion of reading process versus product. An instructional dilemma would result if a teacher were limited to either the process or the product strategies. As long as teachers recognize that a product results from understanding but that understanding cannot be measured before some assistance is provided, then the roles of process and product can be used effectively in content reading instruction. By studying the products of comprehension and by listening to readers describe the strategies they use to apprehend meaning, reading professionals are developing instructional practices which assist readers most effectively. The diagram in Figure 5.2 shows the integral relationship between process and product in reading comprehension.

A tape (Goodman and Burke, 1972) of a child reading a story and reflecting on his reading illustrates this relationship. The story is about an oxygen failure on a spaceship. A canary is kept on board to help

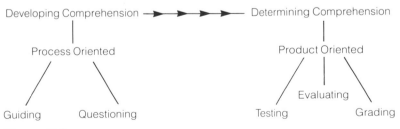

Figure 5.2

warn of such an oxygen failure. The child reads aloud but consistently skips the word "oxygen" because he says he doesn't know it. Yet, at the end of the story, while trying to retell the events to the teacher, he comments that they should have put an oxygen mask on the canary. After this comment, he says with excitement: "Oxygen! That was the word I couldn't get!" This child was thinking as he read, trying to put together the clues. He was assisting his own reading by processing what he thought of as "unknown data." When he reached the stage of retelling the story, he realized that he did know; he had put the clues together. If the teacher had interpreted his failure to pronounce the word while he was reading as a final product, she would have thought he did not know the word. In fact, all along he was still processing the information. Ultimately, this processing led to a correct product. As this experience illustrates, we must give our students every chance to process information, thus discovering meaning as they read, before we measure their understanding. For that reason, this chapter includes background information about the comprehension process and many strategies which facilitate its development.

What Recent Studies on Reading Comprehension Indicate

Some recent studies have had a powerful influence on views of reading comprehension. Brooks, Fusco, and Grennon (1983) recommend that educators use the studies of Piaget and Epstein to gain a greater understanding of the cognitive development of children. When teachers examine their own teaching and questioning styles in relationship to the cognitive development of learners, they will be able to match their questioning to children's current abilities and to the content in question. Olshavsky (1975) and Golinkoff (1976) have been able to describe the behavior of good and poor readers in terms of their abilities to use comprehension strategies. For example, good readers will be able to pause and demonstrate their comprehension by retelling and analyzing what they have read and by using certain strategies consistently. However, poor readers seem to lose track of their reading and to have no particular strategies for comprehending.

Williams, Taylor, and Ganger (1981) have found that a typical instructional task of "finding the main idea" can be very difficult for students through the middle-grade levels, particularly when the text is vague. Brown and Day (1983) found that the ability to construct main idea statements develops later than other summarization skills. Although summarizing is difficult for many poor comprehenders, Hare and Borchardt (1984) trained students to summarize effectively by demonstrating how to use many parts of a text. And, according to a study by Meyer, Brandt, and Bluth (1980), children tested at both the third-grade and ninth-grade levels have been deficient in their knowledge of superordination and subordination of information. All four of these studies indicate that comprehension is influenced by how a text is organized and by how much teachers help students to understand the organization of text. Another recent study (Hargis, Terhaar-Yonkers, Williams, and Reed, 1988) emphasizes the importance of repetition and practice for reading mastery, especially in the case of learning-disabled and mildly handicapped students. Garner (1985), by reviewing several studies, provides evidence that specific instructional assistance can guide students from a stage of strategic deficiency to a stage of strategic efficiency.

The sobering news from Garner's review and the studies mentioned above is that teachers may have been assuming that students automatically comprehend what they read. Comprehension is not that easy. The good news is that, with careful and directed instruction, students can acquire effective strategies for reading comprehension.

Conditions That Facilitate Reading Comprehension

Remember the analogy from chapter 4 that compares reading to a basketball game? Coaching and practice before the basketball game strongly influence the playing of the game. During the actual game, the coach can provide guidance but relies mainly on the preparation which has already taken place. Similarly, adequate preparation is the single most important factor in facilitating reading comprehension. It is so important, in fact, that we have discussed preparation strategies in several chapters of this textbook.

Inside-Outside Factors

Pearson and Johnson (1978) propose that reading comprehension is heavily influenced by factors within and beyond the teacher's control. They describe "inside factors" as those which are inherent to the individual reader. The teacher should understand these factors, but cannot control them. For instance, as we discussed in chapter 2, readers' attitudes about their reading ability and their interest in the content are powerful factors in learning. The teacher can influence these factors but cannot control them.

"Outside factors," which the classroom teacher can control more realistically, also affect comprehension. For example, Pearson and Johnson list the "elements on the page," referring to the readability of the material, as a significant outside factor, one we discussed in depth in chapter 3. Although teachers can influence some conditions readily in the school setting, they can't control the climate in students' homes. However, they can make suggestions to students and parents; in chapters 8 and 9 we provide some such suggestions.

Kohl (1973) suggests that teachers also be aware of the sociological factors which affect comprehension. For example, many times teachers do not give enough credit to students who are "street smart." Street-smart students can comprehend if instruction is assisted in terms they readily understand. Translating information into concrete examples will help these students. For instance, likening the power structure in governments to the way clubs or gangs are formed might facilitate understanding of government.

Teachers have often asked the authors why it is that students today do not seem able to comprehend as well as these teachers did when they were in school. The answer is complicated but probably is related to the very different set of inside-outside factors at play in students' lives today. By paying attention to these factors, teachers can help provide a good climate for comprehension. In chapter 12, we discuss how these factors influence the at-risk student.

Categorizing Comprehension Levels and Skills

Cubing: An Exercise for All Levels

Please read the following paragraphs:

> The wild African elephant faces extinction in the near future. Only 20,000 elephants of the 165,000 that were counted in Kenya fifteen years ago are still alive; 50,000 elephants in Tanzania have been killed within the last ten years. In Uganda, 90 percent of the elephants have been killed by poachers.
>
> Why is this destruction occurring? Because poachers are killing elephants for their ivory tusks. The ivory is made into jewelry which is sold all over the world. Would people buy this jewelry if they knew that elephants were a dying race? (facts from The African Wildlife Association, 1988)

Now, show your comprehension of what you read through the following exercise. Take no more than one minute to respond to each of the following tasks:

1. Describe it: What is the issue?
2. Compare it: Does this issue remind you of any similar example of animal extinction?
3. Associate it: What does it make you think of? Is there an incident you recall, or a feeling you get?
4. Analyze it: Are there two sides to this issue?
5. Apply it: What might be done to solve this problem?
6. Argue for or against it: Take a stand. What are your opinions and the reasons for your stand?

You have just participated in an exercise called "cubing," originated by Cowan and Cowan (1980). They developed this exercise to stimulate writing, especially when writers have a "block" and can't think of what to write. They encourage the writer to imagine a cube, put one of the six tasks on each of the six sides, and consider each one for no more than five minutes. Such an exercise forces a writer to look at a subject from a number of perspectives, so all six sides should be considered—and quickly. The six cubing tasks are similar to generally accepted levels of reading comprehension. (They parallel Bloom's comprehension steps shown in Table 5.1.) In 1986, Vaughan and Estes applied cubing to reading comprehension. Cubing can be used to provide purposeful reading and to develop reading comprehension.

When a teacher actually constructs a cube and uses it as a visual prop for students, they can gain a rapid understanding about the reading material. It is simple to make a cube: Cover a square tissue box with construction paper, and label each side. Activity 5.1, which follows, is the result of a cubing exercise completed by third graders who were reading about triangles.

One high school teacher, concerned that her students would not be receptive to using a "prop", adapted a "flat cube." Instead of using a

---

A C T I V I T Y 5.1

Cubing about triangles

1. Describe it: "It looks like a teepee or a rocket."
2. Compare it: "It is not round like a circle."
3. Associate it (the teacher asked, "What does it make you think of?"): "A fingernail, an arrowhead, a piece of pizza."
4. Analyze it (the teacher asked, "Tell how it is made."): "Three lines, three points, three sharp ends, three flat sides tied together."
5. Apply it (the teacher asked, "How can it be used?"): "As a trowel, as a weapon, to rake stuff up."
6. Argue for or against it (the teacher asked, "Why is it important?"): "We need it so we can dig a hole."

Developed by Debbie Prout.

cube, she drew a diagram which included the cubing steps. Students wrote notes in the flat cube. Activity 5.2 is a flat cube for high school social studies.

Fact, Implication, Application

Comprehension occurs at different levels. We asked you to cube as a way of illustrating several levels of comprehension. To simplify, there are three basic levels of comprehension. First, one must understand the *facts*. After one has a basic understanding, one can see the *implications* of a topic. At the third level, one can *apply* what was understood to other topics. This hierarchy is similar to the concept in principle 5a: *Literal reading is a necessary first step toward critical thinking.* These three levels—fact, implication, application—are those that classroom content teachers will employ when assisting their students' instruction. They represent a way to facilitate comprehension, not to simplify or isolate information. Understanding must be connected to be effective. Teachers will want their students to read the material carefully for a literal understanding of the facts, to see the connection between the facts and the entire subject, and to apply what they have learned to other situations. Gardner and Smith (1987) suggest that one such application is to take another's perspective on the material. The cubing activity demands that readers take another perspective.

Consider the following as an example of these three basic levels of comprehension. To understand the significance of the Alamo in this country's history, students would have to comprehend the following: 1) At the fact level, what the Alamo is, where it is located, and what happened there; 2) At the implication level, why the Alamo is considered to be an important battle when it involved so few people; and 3) At the application level, how the phrase "Remember the Alamo" might incite fervor and inspiration in soldiers going to battle.

Taxonomies: Roses by Other Names

Mature comprehension demands that readers grasp the facts before they can interpret and apply them. Usually, the literal level must precede the implication level, which must precede the application level. This hierarchical relationship is called a taxonomy. Adler and Van Doren, in the best-seller *How To Read a Book* (1952; 1972), present one of the first taxonomies developed for reading comprehension. Their taxonomy includes four levels. Their highest level, syntopical, requires the sophisticated reaction and involvement of readers. Another well-known taxonomy of comprehension is Bloom's (1956). Bloom studied comprehension from a cognitive perspective, not specifically within reading situations. His taxonomy is a comprehensive, albeit complicated, model

A C T I V I T Y 5.2

World War I Cubing Example

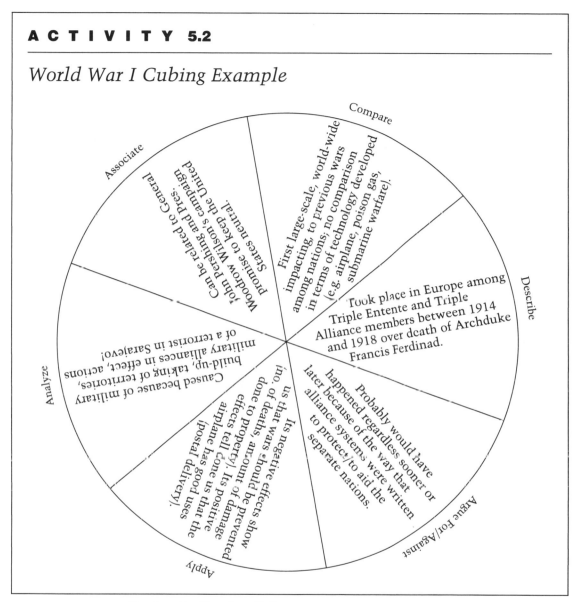

Developed by Mary Jane McKay.

from which many reading professionals have drawn. Bloom's six levels of comprehension are somewhat analogous to the cubing tasks presented earlier. Barrett (1972), drawing on Bloom's taxonomy, developed a hierarchy which includes four levels, the highest being appreciation, which has to do with a reader's emotional response to reading.

Many reading professionals who have developed taxonomic views of reading present three major levels which, when described, are fairly similar. Gray's taxonomy (1960) may be the simplest and friendliest of the taxonomies. He said that one needs first to read the lines and then to read between the lines; next, one can read beyond the lines. Herber (1978) described these levels: literal, interpretive, and applied. Raphael (1984; 1986) has recently proposed a taxonomy which has four levels and uses terminology which even young readers can appreciate. She refers to "right there" information, "think and search" information, "on my own" information, and "author and you" information. Raphael's terms allow readers to understand the type of comprehension required of them as well as how to activate their comprehension search.

Table 5.1 compares each of the taxonomies described here so that the reader can see the basic similarities and the nuances of each. Teachers will want to select the terminology they prefer: the rose still smells the same!

The Importance of the Organization of Material

All writing is organized. All writing follows patterns. Reading professionals have discovered some especially helpful applications about patterns of organization. Good writing will contain a major (superordinate) pattern and supporting (subordinate) relationships. Although as many as seventeen patterns of organization have been identified in good writing, some basic patterns predominate in the kind of writing found in textbooks. The study and identification of patterns of organization in written material is called *discourse analysis.*

At any level, a reader will need to understand the superordinate and subordinate relationships within the text and to identify the significant patterns of organization in the material. Once the overall pattern of organization has been discovered, the main ideas and significant

TABLE 5.1   *Comparison of Comprehension Taxonomies*

Bloom	Barrett	Adler and Van Doren	Gray	Herber	Raphael
Knowledge Comprehension Application Analysis Synthesis Evaluation	Literal Inference Evaluation Appreciation	Elementary Inspectional Analytical Syntopical	Reading the Lines Reading Between the Lines Reading Beyond the Lines	Literal Interpretive Applied	Right There Think & Search Author & You On My Own

supporting details can be determined. This ability takes practice and requires the teacher's assistance, as recent research has indicated. Henk and Helfeldt (1987) explain that even capable readers need assistance in applying the sequence patterns used in directions. When readers learn to search for the organizational patterns and the relationship between superordinate and subordinate information, they have taken the first steps toward independence in reading.

We have combined lists identifying several basic patterns (Kolzow and Lehmann, 1982; Vacca and Vacca, 1989) to target the following seven patterns that are often recognizable in content textbooks:

1. **Simple listing** or enumeration of facts or events, which is a random ordering of items. The superordinate information would be the topic or event, with the facts or traits which follow being the subordinate or supporting information. Some words which suggest this pattern are *also, another, several, next, then.*

   Example: "We presented several principles in chapter 1. For the most part, each can be considered independently of another. The first one stresses the relationship of the communicative arts to content reading instruction. Another states that reading should be a pleasurable experience."

2. **Sequential listing,** a chronological sequence of items. The order of presentation is important with sequential listing. The superordinate information would be the topic or event, with the facts or traits then presented as ordered being the subordinate information. Some words which suggest this pattern are *first, second, next, before, during, finally.*

   Example: "Gray's taxonomy may be the simplest and friendliest of the taxonomics. He said that one needs first to read the lines and then to read between the lines; then one can read beyond the lines."

3. **Analysis,** which takes an important idea (superordinate information) and investigates the relationships of the parts of that idea (subordinate information) to the whole. Some words which suggest this pattern are *consider, analyze, investigate, the first part suggests, this element means.*

   Example: "Consider how the child concluded that the word he had been unable to pronounce was oxygen. The first portion of his behavior, when he skipped the word, indicated that he did not know the word at all. Yet he was able to recognize it when he had a context for it during the recall stage. This means that he was processing information all along."

4. **Cause-effect,** which takes an event or effect as the superordinate information and presents discourse in terms of the causes (subordinate information) for that event. The effect is shown as a result

of causes. Some words which suggest this pattern are *because, hence, therefore, as a result, this led to.*

   Example: "When teachers prepare students to read content material, they help students understand better. Teachers will see, as a result of such preparation, that students are more interested, pay more attention, and comprehend better."

5. **Compare-contrast,** which is for the purpose of showing similarities and differences about facts, events, or authors. The comparison/contrast would be the superordinate information while the specific likeness and differences would be the subordinate information. Some words which suggest this pattern are *in contrast, in the same way, on the other hand, either/or, similarly.*

   Example: "A checklist is similar to a readability formula because both are measures of the match between the reader and the text. On the other hand, a checklist provides more qualitative information."

6. **Definition,** which provides an explanation of a concept or topic (superordinate information) by using synonyms to describe it (subordinate information). Some words which suggest this pattern are *described as, synonymous with, is, equal to.*

   Example: "Reading can be described as analytic, interactive, constructive and strategic. The active integrated thinking which leads to a conclusion as a result of reading is comprehension."

7. **Example,** which provides a similar situation (subordinate information) to explain a topic or concept (superordinate information). Some words which suggest this pattern are *likened to, analogous with, is like.*

   Example: "Reading is like a game of basketball. To play one's best game, lots of preparation and practice are necessary. In reading, this is analogous to preparing by determining and building background for the material to be read."

Often, a mixture of these patterns will occur even in one section of text. A writer may analyze by using a compare-contrast pattern. Definition is often presented by example. A pattern or pattern combination is usually easily discernable in well-written material.

   Some patterns seem to be used often in particular content subjects. The chart in Table 5.2 suggests some possible matchings. It is only a guide. Teachers will need to consider the grade level they teach and the specific materials they use because different patterns may dominate at different grade levels and in different subjects.

   When patterns of organization are identified, the possibilities for developing comprehension are greatly enhanced. Just by looking in the table of contents of a textbook, for example, the teacher can help students determine patterns of organization. Groups can also study para-

TABLE 5.2   *Some Patterns of Organization Used in Different Content Textbooks*

Science	Math	Social Studies	English	Health
Sequence	Sequence	Cause-effect	Cause-effect	Compare-contrast
Cause-effect	Listing	Listing	Compare-contrast	Listing
Definition	Analysis	Example	Example	Definition
	Definition	Analysis		

graphs to identify particular patterns. Study guides can then be devised using identified patterns. Chapters 7 and 8 explain how to construct such activities, and in chapter 6, pattern guides as an aid to developing comprehension are explained. In this chapter, several purpose-setting activities which capitalize on organizational patterns are presented.

Assisting by Setting Purposes for Reading

The Role of Purpose Setting

In optimal reading circumstances, readers will realize what they already know about a topic and have the background to continue studying it. However, their *need* to actually read about the topic is contingent on their purpose for reading. Having a purpose is basic motivation in accomplishing any task; if one has no particular reason to do something, it probably won't get done. Thus, setting meaningful purposes for students to read content material is crucial to their comprehension. Telling students to read chapter 14 or pages 20–50 is usually not very inspiring. Students *might* read that text; they might not. If they do, and the teacher has provided no more purpose than this, students have had very little assistance in knowing why they're reading. Whether or not they discover the organizational pattern and the major ideas will be pretty much a hit-or-miss proposition. The best reason, then, to assist reading by setting purposes is to make sure that the reading gets completed and understood. How many teachers would argue that this is not a goal of their instruction?

Doesn't Every Teacher Set Purpose?

Durkin (1984) found that elementary teachers instructing from reading materials rarely provided purpose-setting questions for their students. Such a finding is very disturbing, especially since the teachers' manuals did include purpose-setting guidance. Apparently many elementary teachers ignore this part of the manual. Perhaps secondary teachers are guilty of the same behavior. We speculate that, if the teachers who have purpose-setting suggestions available do not use them, then teachers using content materials, which often do not include purpose-setting guidance, probably neglect purpose setting also.

Setting Purposes through Informative Communication

Allen, Brown, and Yatvin (1986) use the term "informative communication" to mean: "Through listening, speaking, reading, and writing, children acquire knowledge of the world and learn to use that knowledge productively in their own lives" (p. 204). Just as students read to learn, they listen to learn, speak to learn, and write to learn. In every case, students should have a reason to listen, speak, read, or write to learn. Communication informs learners when they are "set" for the information. As each of the activities in the following section is presented, their possibilities for listening, speaking, and writing as well as for reading will be highlighted.

Setting Purpose by Relying on Preparation Activities

The stage is already set for a teacher to provide purposes when activities and strategies similar to those described in chapters 3 and 4 have been used to determine and build background. In this section, we will show how some of those activities can be extended for use as purpose setters.

Rewrites and Multiple Texts. Rewrites and the use of multiple texts were explained as ways to prepare readers for more difficult reading material. After presenting the rewrite, the teacher can suggest that students read the original material while keeping the rewrite handy. Readers should decide the following while reading:

Does the rewrite contain the same information that the original does?
How is the rewrite different?
Why did the teacher provide a rewrite first?

The teacher might ask readers to see if the same organizational pattern was followed in the rewrite and the original. Some specific purposes for reading related to the rewrite have thus aided the readers as they confront the harder material. Working in small groups, students can speculate about what they will discover when comparing rewrites to originals and can write down their expectations. Purpose setting is then provided in an environment of informative communication.

In using the multiple-text approach, the teacher might ask students to contrast organizational patterns as well as the depth and breadth of information in each text. The readers will be actively involved in a comparison, which ensures a purpose for reading.

Cloze, Maze, PreP, Factstorming, What I Know, and Recognition.
Use of a cloze or maze can be extended to purpose setting by encouraging readers to compare what they inserted as a choice with what they discover as they are reading. With PreP, the purpose for reading might be to check what the group said against what is included in the text. One second-grade social studies teacher explains how she used a factstorming activity to provide reading purpose:

> The students were curious as to why I taped a huge piece of chart paper to the chalk board, so I immediately had their attention. As I wrote the terms *town, city, suburb, farming community* on the paper, the students immediately began reading them aloud and guessing what we would be doing.
>
> First I asked for a volunteer to read *town.* Then I asked my class to tell me all they knew about towns. I recorded their responses. I did the same thing for each term. Then I told them we'd check their answers by reading our books. Then I had the students follow along as I read the text out loud to them. We discussed the terms and pictures. (Byrd, 1987. Used with permission.)

With What-I-Know sheets, readers could be reading with the intention of completing the second column, "What I Know Now," as well as comparing with the "What I Already Know" column. In the same way, the recognition activity is useful in providing a checkpoint between what readers expected would be true and what they find to be true as they read. The listening, speaking, and writing connections are already built into these activities.

DRTAs. The directed reading-thinking activity is so versatile that it is difficult to categorize it under any one PAR step. In chapter 4, we briefly described the DRTA steps and suggested possibilities for helping to prepare readers. The following examples of DRTAs illustrate their use in setting purposes.

Figures 5.3 and 5.4 outline the DRTA steps that might be applied to fiction and nonfiction material, respectively. Note that step 2 in the fiction DRTA requests that readers read to find out if predictions they made were accurate. Step 4 in the nonfiction DRTA requests that readers read to find the answers to questions they have generated. These steps focus on purposeful reading; they are the foundation for a successful DRTA.

The predicting steps of the DRTA build purpose for reading. When readers are asked what they think might happen next and then read to verify their prediction, they are being encouraged to read purposefully. Readers become very excited about this predictive involvement in their own reading. Often they share their predictions orally before the individual reading occurs. This activity incorporates listening and speaking. If students are asked to write down what they predict during various portions of the reading and then review those written predictions at the end of the DRTA, writing has been used as a way to set purpose within the DRTA.

1. **Previewing**
   Preread: Title
   Pictures
   Subtitles
   Introduction (if story is long enough)

   Close book and make hypotheses: What do you think will happen?

   Why do you think that? (What gives you the clue?)

2. **Verifying**
   Read: To find whether or not predictions were right

3. **Reflecting on Reading**
   Developing comprehension by: Checking on individual and group hypotheses
   Staying with or redefining hypotheses

Figure 5.3 DRTA, fiction.

The following dialogue (Activity 5.3), transcribed from a seventh-grade social studies teacher's DRTA lesson on the caste system in India, is another good example of the purpose-setting value of a DRTA. Teachers can see from this transcript how all of PAR is used in a DRTA. The purpose-setting statements are italicized.

1. **Previewing**
   Study: Title
   Introduction
   Subtitles
   Pictures
   Charts
   Maps
   Graphs
   Summary or conclusion
   Questions

2. **Decision Making**
   What is known after previewing?
   What do we need to learn?

3. **Writing**
   Writing specific questions students need to learn

4. **Reading**
   Finding the answers to students' written questions

Figure 5.4 DRTA, nonfiction.

A C T I V I T Y 5.3

DRTA Transcript, Seventh-Grade Social Studies

Material Used: "A Coward"

Objective: Students will describe the role of persons or groups in India's society.

Teacher: We have been learning about the caste system in India and how parents arrange their children's marriages. Today we are going to read another story about the caste system and marriages in India. What is the title of this story?

Students: "A Coward."

Teacher: What do you think that has to do with marriage?

Student: He must be afraid to get married.

Teacher: Read the first paragraph and see if you get any clues.

Teacher: Was he afraid to get married?

Student: No, SHE's the coward!

Teacher: What do you think will happen?

Student: Maybe he will talk to her parents. He's in a higher caste, so they should like that. He doesn't care about his parents, so he will marry her anyway.

Teacher: Read the next part and see if he does talk to her parents.

Teacher: Did he ask her parents?

Student: No, she asked them. So she's gotten braver, but she got into more trouble.

Teacher: How?

Student: They made her quit college.

Teacher: Do you think Keshav will still talk to her parents?

Student: He might. When she doesn't come back to college, he might come to see what is wrong.

Teacher: Do you think Prema's parents will let her marry Keshav if they meet him?

Student: Probably not. They don't want to be disgraced.

Teacher: What do you think will happen next?

Student: I think that Reshav will come to talk to the parents. If they say no, they could run away to another town. If he can talk Prema into leaving her parents.

Teacher: Read the next section to see if that happens.

(continued)

Teacher: Did Reshav come to talk to Prema's parents?

Student: No, her father is going to talk to Reshav. He's afraid that she might kill herself. She's weird!

Teacher: How do you think the meeting with Reshav will go?

Student: They will probably start to like him. He goes to college, so he must be smart. They will probably let him marry her because her father doesn't want her to kill herself.

Teacher: Read the next section and see what happens.

Teacher: Did Keshav meet her parents?

Student: No, the two fathers met and Keshav's father got really mad.

Teacher: What about Keshav?

Student: He wants to marry Prema in secret, but he's afraid of his father. Maybe he's going to wait until his father dies, and then marry her.

Teacher: Finish the story and see if they do get married.

Teacher: What happened?

Student: Gosh! *He* was the coward! He's going to feel rotten when he finds out what she did. He might even kill himself. Then the parents would really feel bad.

Developed by Faye Freeman.

The next example, this one for a middle-grade English class, shows how a teacher used a DRTA to provide for purposeful reading of poetry.

The value of DRTAs is reflected in the many ways they can be used. Their value for providing reading purposes while integrating all of the communicative arts should be apparent. DRTA lessons also help teachers to model the reading process at its best: What readers do as they read is predict and speculate, read to confirm, stop and carry on a mental discussion of what they are understanding. DRTAs provide a vehicle for figuring out the content as the reading occurs; they emphasize reading as a process rather than a measurement of comprehension. In this way, DRTAs demonstrate the correct reading process. DRTAs also build readers' self-concepts: When readers see that what they predict helps them to understand better, that everyone's speculations are important whether or not they are proven to be what the author concluded, they feel more confident about their reading. At the elementary level, teachers can encourage readers to become reading detectives who have a chance to play a game of detection. As a result, they are motivated to read, and they are in charge of their own reading. We cannot stress enough the pervasive benefits of using DRTAs to teach content subjects.

A C T I V I T Y 5.4

DRTA Transcript: Middle Grades English

Goal: The goal of this activity will be to direct students' reading with a purpose and also develop their comprehension. I will teach "Acquainted with the Night" using the DRTA.

Activity: DRTA (directed reading to develop comprehension)

Teacher: Look at the poem by Robert Frost. What do you think the title means? Look first at the word "acquainted." What does that word mean?

Student: To know.

Student: To be familiar with.

Teacher: Those are good answers. Now what do you think the title means?

Student: To know the night?

Teacher: Good. How many times is that word used in the poem?

Student: Three.

Teacher: Why do you think it is used so many times?

Student: It's important to the meaning.

Student: He wants the reader to know why he knows the night.

Teacher: How many of you think you know or understand the night? (A few students raise hands.)

Teacher: What do you know about the night?

Student: It's dark.

Student: Stars come out, and the moon shines.

Student: That's when we sleep.

Student: Crime occurs then.

Teacher: To find out what Robert Frost knew about the night, read the first stanza. Remember that a stanza in a poem is like a paragraph. [Students read.]

Teacher: How is the poet "acquainted" with the night?

Student: He is walking at night.

Teacher: What is the weather?

Student: It's raining sometimes.

Teacher: How far does he walk?

Student: He walks past the "furthest city light."

Teacher: Why do you think he walks so far?

(continued)

Students: Exercise . . . Feels like it . . . Wants to think . . . Enjoys it . . .

Teacher: Read the next stanza and see if you have correctly predicted why he walks. [Students read.]

Teacher: Why do you think he walks?

Student: He's depressed, sad. He probably wants to be alone.

Teacher: Which line says that? Read it please.

Student: "I have looked down the saddest city lane."

Teacher: You read that well. Whom does he see while he walks?

Student: A watchman.

Teacher: Why do you think he "drops his eyes, unwilling to explain?"

Student: Watchman wonders why he's there—it's his job—but the walker looks away because he doesn't want to or know how to explain.

Teacher: Do you ever look away when you don't want to answer?

Students: Yes. When the teacher is asking for answers . . . When my parents want to know where I've been . . . When my friend wants to know something I don't want to tell her . . .

Teacher: In the next stanza you are going to read what he hears. Read the next stanza and continue reading until you get through the first line of the next stanza. [Students read.]

Teacher: What does he hear?

Student: A cry.

Teacher: What does he do?

Student: He stops.

Teacher: Was the crying for him?

Student: No.

Teacher: Read to us the line that says that, please.

Student: "But not to call me back or say good-bye."

Teacher: If you are walking and you hear cries, would you stop to see what was wrong?

Students: Yes . . . Maybe . . . Depends on the situation.

Teacher: How would you feel when you found out that the cries were not for you?

Students: Sad . . . Relieved . . . Lonely . . . Happy . . . Empty . . .

Teacher: These are probably the feelings that the poet felt too. In the next four lines you will read some unusual words. What do you think "unearthly" means?

Student: Doesn't belong to earth.

Teacher: Luminary?

(continued)

Student: Bright light.

Teacher: Proclaimed?

Student: Designated, told, pointed out.

Teacher: Read the rest of the poem. What does the walker decide? [Students read.]

Teacher: What is the luminary clock?

Student: The moon.

Teacher: What do you think Frost meant by "neither wrong nor right?"

Student: He probably meant no decision was made . . . decided not to commit suicide . . . decided to stop walking . . . the time was sort of in between something. [Discuss all reasoning.]

Teacher: Why are the first and last lines the same?

Students: I don't know . . . Maybe the poet wanted it that way . . . Maybe he wanted to show us that the walks continue . . . Maybe his troubles go on and on . . .

Teacher: Why do the sentences get longer?

Student: The walks get longer.

Teacher: You have done really well interpreting the meaning of this poem. It wasn't too hard, was it? Now I am going to read this poem to you. Note the fact that I do not pause at the end of every line, only at the places where there are punctuation marks. When you read poetry out loud, always read to punctuation marks, so it won't sound sing-songy and will make better sense. [Reads poem.] How many of you think you understand what Frost was saying in this poem? [Hands go up.] Who will volunteer to tell us the meaning of this poem?

Student: Frost knows the night because that is the time he walks and figures out his problems. He walks alone and talks to no one, and he stops when he comes to some conclusion.

Teacher: You expressed that well. To appreciate and understand poetry, you need to read each poem to yourself first and then perhaps again out loud. Few poems can be completely understood after the first reading.

Developed by Frances Lively.

Previewing, Previews, Prewriting. The first steps in previewing and previews encourage students to call upon past associations, thus preparing them to read. The later steps in these strategies use background building to create a purpose. With prewriting, the writing that students do in anticipation of the reading can then be used to check what's in the material.

Analogies, Graphic Organizers, Anticipation Guides. When students are encouraged, as they read, to refer back to the activity which was used to help build their backgrounds, they have a purpose for reading. For example, students might be challenged to find as many analogies as they can to other subjects. As a means of helping them understand new words, they might check the graphic organizer. They might jot down information under anticipation guide statements which will either support or change their opinions about the statements.

In Activity 5.5, an anticipation guide developed by a middle-school mathematics teacher includes a purpose-setting statement. Whereas in most anticipation guides there will be no "right" answers, in this anticipation guide, the teacher does expect correct answers, but not necessarily *before* reading occurs.

Other Activities Which Provide Purpose

Purpose Statements. The simplest purpose-setting activity is providing a statement which gives a reason for reading. The statements underlined in the social studies DRTA transcript (Activity 5.3) do this;

A C T I V I T Y 5.5

Anticipation Guide for Purpose Setting: Fractions

Read each of the statements below, and put a check in the appropriate blank space to indicate whether you agree or disagree with the statement. *After reading the text, you will see if your answers are correct.*

Agree Disagree

_____ _____ When dividing fractions, you take the reciprocal of the first number, then multiply.

_____ _____ For every decimal name there is a fraction name, and vice versa.

_____ _____ Sometimes you can use a shortcut for multiplying fractions.

_____ _____ You always need to get an exact answer when multiplying fractions.

_____ _____ To multiply fractions, you take the reciprocal of the second number.

Developed by Dawn Bubb.

if they were given out of the DRTA context, they would be simple statements. Sometimes simplest is best. The teacher must decide what the circumstances dictate and the time allows.

Mystery Clue Game. Whenever an activity can capitalize on the organizational pattern of the material, it will offer maximum assistance to readers. One of our favorite purpose-setting activities, the group mystery clue game, is designed to help readers understand sequence. It works very well when it is important for students to understand a sequence of events. The idea for this activity came from *Turn-Ons* (Smuin, 1978), but we have adapted it to fit content materials.

1. To construct a mystery clue game, the teacher first studies the sequence of events in the material and writes clear, specific clue cards to each event. More than one card may be made for each clue.
2. The teacher divides the class into small groups and gives each group member at least one clue card.
3. No student may show the card to another in the group, but the card can be read aloud or paraphrased so that all group members know what is on each card. In this way, students who are poorer readers will still be encouraged to try to read and to share in the group process.
4. Each group of students must use the clues the teacher gives them to solve the mystery. For example, they must find the murderer, the weapon, the time and place of murder, the motive, and the victim. Or they must find the equation which will solve this problem, or the formula which will make a chemical.
5. A time limit is usually given.
6. A group scribe reports the group's solution to the whole class.
7. Students are instructed to read the material to find out which group was closest to solving the mystery.

This cooperative activity promotes oral language as well as reading. Another bonus of this activity is that, when the teacher wishes students to concentrate in their reading on inferences and applications, the factual level has already been addressed, in advance of reading. This activity works equally well in several content areas. For instance, science teachers can write clues to solving an experiment, mathematics teachers can write clues to solving a formula, and social studies teachers can write clues for historical events. Activities 5.6 and 5.7, which follow, show how a twelfth-grade English teacher used the mystery clue game to provide a purpose for reading *Beowulf* and how a middle-grade social studies teacher used the game to provide a purpose for reading about the Sumerians.

Jot Charts. Another good purpose-setting activity which can demonstrate organizational patterns for readers is the jot chart (Vacca & Vacca, 1989). Enumeration or description, as well as cause-effect and

A C T I V I T Y   5.6

Mystery Clue Game: Beowulf

Directions: The class will be divided into groups of four to six people, depending on class size. Each person in the class will be given a clue card which is like no one else's. The task of the group is to solve the murder mystery by identifying:

1. the murderer
2. the murder weapon
3. the time of the murder
4. the place where the murder occurred
5. the motive
6. the victim

Clues to be communicated *orally* by *paraphrasing* given clues. Students may not show their clue cards to other group members. They will have approximately 10 minutes to discuss clues in their groups before coming back to the entire group to discuss findings.

The clues are:

1. Grendel's heart was filled with fury and hate.
2. The heroes lived happily in the mead hall, wanting nothing, until a wicked fiend appeared.
3. Grendel was an outcast of society, a descendant of Cain.
4. Grendel attacked the mead hall and killed thirty warriors.
5. Hrothgar, king of the Danes, closed his mead hall and kept it closed for twelve years.
6. Songs of Grendel and Hrothgar's mead hall were carried to other countries.
7. Beowulf, prince of the Geats, heard of the problem in Denmark.
8. Beowulf gathered together fourteen of his best men and prepared to sail to Denmark.
9. Beowulf and his men traveled over the seas a day and a night before reaching Denmark.
10. Beowulf asks Hrothgar's permission to fight Grendel.
11. Beowulf says he will face Grendel in hand-to-hand combat.
12. Beowulf will use no weapon, other than his own strength, in the fight with Grendel.
13. Beowulf and his men spend the night in the mead hall.
14. Grendel entered the mead hall after all Beowulf's men had gone to sleep.
15. Beowulf, awake, watched Grendel to see what he would do.

(continued)

16. Grendel ate one of Beowulf's men, then reached for Beowulf.
17. Beowulf caught Grendel's forearm and threw all his weight on it.
18. Beowulf was the strongest man Grendel had ever faced.
19. Beowulf had the strength of thirty men.
20. Grendel tried to get away from Beowulf, but he couldn't.
21. The fight between Beowulf and Grendel was so fierce that it shook the mead hall.
22. Grendel wailed in pain.
23. Beowulf's men held their swords ready to attack Grendel if Beowulf needed their help.
24. Grendel bore a charmed life; he could not be harmed by any weapon.
25. Grendel pulled away from Beowulf; Beowulf would not let go of Grendel's arm.
26. Grendel crawled home.
27. Hrothgar hangs Grendel's arm over the inside door of the mead hall.

Developed by Vicki Ford.

compare-contrast patterns, are effectively presented with a jot chart. The teacher uses the information in the reading to create a chart, leaving several blank spaces. Students fill in the chart's blank spaces as they read. Since students are writing important information, the jot chart gives them practice in writing, and, by the time the reading is finished, has helped them develop a study guide.

Readers will find several jot charts in this text. The appendix includes a jot chart designed to help identify PAR steps provided in a content textbooks. A jot chart to provide purposeful reading and to help students compare and contrast several short stories is presented in chapter 6. Activity 5.8 on page 186 is an example of a simple jot chart to help students read about the differences between dinosaurs that practiced parental care in their nesting behavior and those that did not.

Writing as Purpose Setting

The Stages of Writing. Researchers generally agree that the writing process includes three stages. In the *prewriting* stage, writers prepare by identifying what they already know about the topic, selecting ideas to write about, and establishing a purpose for their writing. This stage, which might include getting rough thoughts on paper, focusing on one

A C T I V I T Y 5.7

Mystery Clue Game: The Sumerians

Directions for the Teacher: Divide the class into small groups giving each student a clue slip. Explain to the students that they must share their clues with their group members without actually showing their clue slip. They are to work with their group to try and solve the mystery questions. Put these mystery questions on the board or overhead projector. Give the students a time limit to come up with their guesses. After that time has been allowed, ask students to share their responses with the entire class. Next they need to read the assignment to see if their predictions were accurate. These clues were developed from the "Background" information section in the teacher's edition and from the section the students will read, chapter one, section 4, "A Line of Conquerors." The teacher should number the clues and mix up the numbers when passing out clues to the students.

1. The Sumerians were constantly threatened with warfare.
2. The first conquerors of Sumer were from the city of Akkad.
3. There were no natural boundaries separating the different cities.
4. The Akkadian Empire lasted from 2400 to 2050 B.C.
5. Sargon of Akkad established an empire around 2300 B.C.
6. The southern Akkadians became the Babylonians.
7. The northwestern Akkadians became the Assyrians.
8. Sargon's empire lasted for about 200 years.
9. About 1800 B.C. Hammurabi conquered and reunited Mesopotamia.
10. Hammurabi developed a code of laws.
11. Babylon is a key city in the Babylonian empire.
12. Hammurabi's law code dealt with subjects like human rights.
13. Hammurabi's code included the "eye for an eye" law.
14. The Assyrian Empire arose after the collapse of Hammurabi's empire.
15. Assyrians lived in the shadow of the Babylonians and of other warlike people to the north of them.
16. These warriors used chariots, carts drawn by horses.
17. The Assyrians also learned to use chariots and horses.
18. The Assyrians organized armies using chariots, cavalry and bowmen.

(continued)

19. The Assyrians used battering rams, heavy beams for breaking down city walls.
20. In 701 B.C., the Assyrian king Sennacherib stormed Palestine, a part of the Fertile Crescent.
21. Sennacherib, the Assyrian king, captured 46 cities.
22. Sennacherib, the Assyrian king, destroyed Babylon in 689 B.C.
23. After destroying Babylon, Sennacherib had canals dug and flooded the city to try and turn it into a meadow.
24. In time the mighty empire of the Assyrians was also overthrown.
25. Free of the Assyrians, Babylon again became the center of Mesopotamian culture.
26. In about 539 B.C. Babylon was conquered by the Persians.
27. The Persians did not adopt the culture of Sumer as had the other conquerors.
28. The Persians developed a system of writing based on their own language.
29. The Mesopotamians invented the wheel and the plow.
30. The Mesopotamians farmed the land and built cities.
31. The Mesopotamians developed mathematics.
32. The Mesopotamians developed laws and recorded them.

Questions for the game:
1. Who are the conquerors?
2. Where did they come from?
3. Why did they do it?
4. What did they accomplish?
5. How did they do it?

Developed by Debra Sims Fleisher.

idea, or deciding on a certain approach to the topic, is very much like determining and building background and then setting purpose for reading. In the *drafting* stage, writers create a draft by writing to get the ideas down and to carry out their purposes. During this stage, writers are thinking, changing direction, organizing, and reorganizing. They are writing towards a finished product but, at this stage, are not focusing on functional writing concerns. In the *revision* stage, writers reflect on what they have written and rewrite. This step can include major reorganization of the material, additions and deletions, and editorial changes. Only at this third stage do writers pay a lot of attention to the format of the writing. Up to this point, they are more concerned with writing to get down the content. Writing at the first and second stages is a way

A C T I V I T Y 5.8

Jot Chart: Nesting Behavior of Dinosaurs

Dinosaur Species	Description	Method of Birth	Embryo Development at Hatching	Parental Feeding of Newborn	Parental Protection of Newborn
Orodromeus makelai	• Walked on 2 legs • 8 feet high • Embryos 8"–9"	• Hatched from eggs	• Bones developed • Able to walk	• Probably did *not* bring food to nest	• Probably did *not* protect
Maiasaura peeblesorum (duck bills)	• Walked on 2 legs • 30 feet high • Embryos 1"	• Hatched from eggs	• Bones *not* developed • Unable to walk	• Probably did bring food to nest	• Probably did protect

of thinking. The last stage of writing is the culmination of that thinking in a product to be shared with a particular audience.

The prewriting stage offers valuable opportunities for teachers to set purposes for reading. Therefore, in this chapter, we feature some prewriting activities which include purpose setting. In chapter 12, we propose writing stages similar to these to aid the at-risk student.

Prewriting in Content Subjects. Prewriting is seldom used in content classrooms, although its possibilities for assisting reading comprehension are powerful. Pearce and Davison (1988) conducted a study to see how often junior-high-school mathematics teachers used writing activities with their students. They found that writing was seldom used to assist thinking and learning, prewriting least of all. In a follow-up study, Davison and Pearce (1988) looked at five mathematics textbook series to determine if these texts included suggestions for writing activities. Not surprisingly, they found few suggestions, and almost none were suggestions for prewriting. Teachers in various content areas confirm that they can find few suggestions in their textbooks for using writing as a purpose-setting activity. Because teachers rely on teachers' manuals and textbooks for the majority of their instruction, they may, then, be missing a rich source of purpose setting through writing activities.

Suggestions for Content Teachers to Encourage Prewriting. The prewriting stage of writing calls for writers to determine what the topic of writing will be and what they know about that topic. Writers may have to build background through activities discussed earlier in this chapter, such as looping or cubing, to find out what they know. Several other activities discussed in this chapter also provide a writing connection: responses to anticipation guides, jot charts, the notations accompanying factstorms and PrePs, and What-I-Know sheets are all forms of prewriting. Whenever students have gathered content information, they can use that information to write. Applying the "data given," as such content information is sometimes called, to a writing situation, enhances student learning. The following additional suggestions may also help content teachers introduce prewriting into their classrooms.

1. Have students predict and write down the definition of a new word in the chapter.
2. Have students write what they think a visual aid is illustrating or could have to do with the topic.
3. Have students write how the new topic might fit with the previous topics studied.
4. For mathematics, students could write out what they think a particular symbol might mean, what the possible steps for solving a problem could be, or why a particular unit of study is presented at a particular place in the text.
5. For science, students could write what they anticipate to be the steps in an experiment, what a formula will produce, what the composition of a substance is, or why certain conditions facilitate certain results.
6. For social studies, students could write about problems people might face when they move from one place to another or after they have settled in a new place (Pearce, 1987).
7. For English, students could write why they think a particular punctuation rule might be necessary: what would happen if we didn't use commas in our writing?

It is important to make sure that students understand clearly what the writing assignment is, that it is not to be graded, and that it will be useful in guiding their reading.

To direct her students in their writing, a primary science teacher used an activity based on the stages of writing. Her plan is shown in Activity 5.9.

From Dependence to Independence in Purpose Setting

Although teachers must help readers set purposes initially, readers must begin to set their own purposes for reading as soon as possible. Hawkes and Schell (1987) caution that teacher-set reasons to read may encourage dependence and a passive approach to reading. Self-set reasons to read promote reading that is active and ultimately independent. To

A C T I V I T Y 5.9

Student Writing: Stages in the Writing Process

I. Prewriting:

The teacher will show the book, *Desert Voices*, written by Byrd Baylor and Peter Parnall, to the class, and she will mention that these authors have worked together on three Caldecott Honor Books. (It may be necessary to refresh their minds about the annual Caldecott and Newbery Awards.)

"Byrd Baylor, who writes the words of the book, lives in the Southwest. I don't know which *particular* state in the southwestern portion of the United States. The title of this book has the word *desert* in it, and she has written another book called *The Desert Is Theirs*. If she lives in the Southwest and likes to write about deserts, could you guess a state where she *might* live?" (The students will remember, hopefully, that Arizona has desert land.)

"Peter Parnall illustrates the book. He lives on a farm in Maine with his wife and two children."

"If the title of the book is *Desert Voices*, who might be speaking? Who are the voices in the desert?" (Wait for responses.) "Byrd Baylor has written the words for ten desert creatures as they tell us what it is like for the desert to be their home. I will read you what the jackrabbit and the rattlesnake have to say." (Teacher reads aloud.)

A. *Brainstorming:*

The teacher will divide the class into small groups of four or five students. She lists on the chalkboard the names of the other creatures who "speak" in *Desert Voices*: pack rat, spadefood toad, cactus wren, desert tortoise, buzzard, lizard, coyote. (The tenth voice is entitled "Desert Person.")

B. *The assignment:*

"Each group must select one of these creatures or any other desert animal or plant that has been mentioned in our unit. Each group member should jot down on a piece of paper any ideas he has about this creature's feelings relating to living in the desert. You may want to think about the appearance of this creature or thing. Does it have any body parts or habitat specifically suited to the desert's environment? After you jot down your ideas, place your paper in the center of the table and choose another member's paper. Add some of your ideas to his paper. After you have written something on every other group member's page, your group as a

(continued)

whole should compile the *best* list of ideas. Then we will begin to write our individual drafts."

II. Writing

III. Rewriting:

Students may work in pairs to edit and proofread each other's work. The child's partner would be from another "creature's" group.

IV. Postwriting:

Oral presentations
Room displays
Compilation of compositions dealing with the same "voice" into book form

Note: Naturally this project would continue for several days. Even the group brainstorming might require more than one day, especially if some reference work were necessary.

Developed by Kathryn Davis. The stages of writing and the description of brainstorming are adapted from Vacca and Vacca (1989), pages 227–279.

wean readers from dependence, teachers could use many of the activities mentioned here until students are familiar with them and understand what purpose setting involves. Then teachers could have readers create their own versions of these activities for the next group of readers. Eventually, as a result of these steps, readers will be setting their own purposes.

One-Minute Summary

In this chapter, we have presented the background for comprehension instruction in content areas. Definitions of comprehension from 1908 to 1985 show how professionals' views of reading have changed little, although the emphasis has shifted from the *product* to the *process* of comprehension. Through an analogy, we have illustrated one of these definitions of comprehension. We have also shown what recent studies of comprehension indicate for reading-to-learn instruction. We have compared several taxonomies of comprehension, focusing on a three-level taxonomy for teachers to use. We have stressed the role of the organization of material in content-reading instruction. We have focused on comprehension in this chapter to enhance the reader's background for reading the next chapters, which feature ways to assist readers and help them reflect. Finally, we have discussed the role of purpose setting in assisting reading instruction. We reintroduced several activities to show how the same activities can be used to set purposes as well as establish background. We illustrated the DRTA's use as an activity which spans all PAR steps. We also introduced some new activities: the group mystery clue game, jot charts, looping, and cubing.

End-of-Chapter Activities

Preparing the Reader

1. Most readers understand the golfer's dialogue when they read it with an accompanying translation rather than with no assistance. Why would this be?

2. Compare your looped definition of comprehension to the definitions given in this chapter. How is yours similar or different? Would you change your definition now?

Assisting Comprehension

1. Study the following map, and without looking at the beginning of the chapter, fill in this map with categories and supporting details which make sense. You may look back through the chapter for clues.

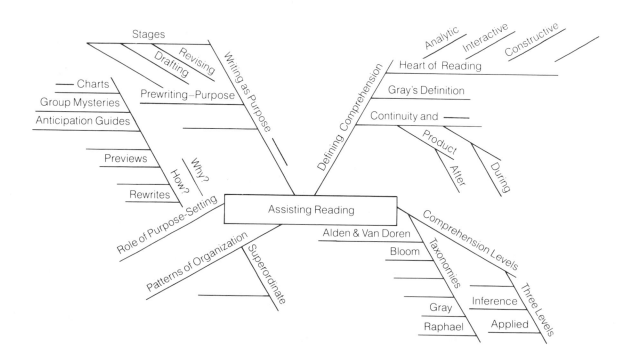

2. How do principles 1, 2, 5, 6, and 11 apply specifically to the content of this chapter? Find the places in this chapter where those principles are reviewed and then put an answer to this question in your own words. Think of a personal example to illustrate each principle in relation to this chapter's content.

Reflecting on Your Reading

1. You might want to extend your own learning about comprehension and double your pleasure with some leisure reading at the same time. Try reading *Mrs. Frisby and the Rats of NIMH* by Robert O'Brien.

2. Select a chapter from a content area textbook. Using the following questions to guide you, discover what your text offers to help you provide purposeful reading opportunities to your students:

What aids are provided to help the teacher and the students read with purpose? (Such as: statements of purpose or objectives for reading a portion of the chapter; motivational statement; rationale, preview, introductory statement, analogy, etc.; division of reading by segments within the chapter, which helps the reader focus on one section at a time . . .)

Are these aids sufficient, adequate, and easily understood? Why or why not?

What new activities might you want to design to supplement this chapter, as you provide for purposeful reading?

References

Adler, M. & Van Doren, C. (1972). *How to read a book.* New York: Simon & Schuster.

Allen, R., Brown, K. & Yatvin, J. (1986). *Learning language through communication: A functional approach.* Belmont, CA.: Wadsworth.

Barrett, T. (1972). A taxonomy of reading comprehension. *Reading 360 Monograph.* Lexington, MA.: Ginn.

Bloom, B.C. (1956). *Taxonomy of educational objectives: Cognitive domain.* New York: David McKay.

Brooks, M., Fusco, E. & Grennon, J. (1983). Cognitive levels matching. *Educational Leadership, 40,* 4–8.

Brown, A. & Day, J. (1983). Macrorules for summarizing texts: The development of expertise. *Journal of Verbal Learning and Verbal Behavior, 22,* 1–5.

Byrd, H. (1987). Paper submitted for partial fulfillment of course requirements. Virginia Commonwealth University, Richmond, VA.

Cooper, J.D. (1986). *Improving reading comprehension.* New York: Houghton Mifflin.

Cowan, G. & Cowan, E. (1980). *Writing.* New York: Wiley.

Davison, D. & Pearce, D. (1988). Using writing activities to reinforce mathematics instruction. *Arithmetic Teacher, 35,* 42–45.

Durkin, D. (1984). Is there a match between what elementary teachers do and what basal reader manuals recommend? *The Reading Teacher, 37,* 734–744.

Gardner, M.K. & Smith, M.M. (1987). Does perspective-taking ability contribute to reading comprehension? *Journal of Reading, 30,* 333–336.

Garner, R. (1985). Strategies for reading and studying expository text. Unpublished paper: University of Maryland.

Golinkoff, R. (1976). A comparison of reading comprehension processes in good and poor comprehenders. *Reading Research Quarterly, 11,* 623–659.

Goodman, Y. M. & Burke, C. L. (1972). *Reading miscue inventory kit: Procedure for diagnosis and correction.* New York: Macmillan.

Gray, W. (1941; 1984). *Reading.* Newark, DE: International Reading Association.

Gray, W. (1960). The major aspects of reading. In H. Robinson (Ed.), *Development of Reading Abilities.* Supplementary Educational Monographs #90. Chicago: University of Chicago Press.

Hare, V.C. & Borchardt, K.M. (1984). Direct instruction of summarization skills. *Reading Research Quarterly, 20,* 62–78.

Hargis, C.H., Terhaar-Yonkers, M., Williams, P.C., & Reed, M.T. (1988). Repetition requirements for word recognition. *Journal of Reading, 31,* 320–327.

Hawkes, K.S. & Schell, L.M. (1987). Teacher-set prereading purposes and comprehension. *Reading Horizons, 27,* 164–169.

Henk, W.A. & Helfeldt, J.P. (1987). How to develop independence in following written directions. *Journal of Reading, 30,* 602–607.

Herber, H. (1978). *Teaching reading in the content areas.* Englewood Cliffs, NJ: Prentice-Hall.

Hillerich, R.L. (1979). Reading comprehension. *Reporting on Reading, 5,* 1–3.

Huey, E. (1908). *The psychology and pedagogy of reading,* New York: Macmillan.

Kohl, H. (1973). *Reading, how to.* New York: Bantam Books.

Kolzow, L.V. & Lehmann, J. (1982). *College reading strategies for success.* Englewood Cliffs, NJ: Prentice-Hall.

Meyer, B.J.F., Brandt, D.M. & Bluth, G.J. (1980). Use of top-level structure in text: Key for reading comprehension of ninth grade students. *Reading Research Quarterly, 16,* 72–103.

O'Brien, R. (1971). *Mrs. Frisby and the rats of NIMH.* New York: Atheneum.

Olshavsky, J. (1975). Reading as problem solving: An investigation of strategies. *Reading Research Quarterly, 12,* 654–674.

Pearce, D. (1987). Group writing activities: A useful strategy for content teachers. *Middle School Journal, 18,* 24–25.

Pearce, D., & Davison, D. (1988). Teacher use of writing in the junior high mathematics classroom. *School Science and Mathematics, 88,* 6–15.

Pearson, P.D. (1985). Changing the face of reading comprehension. *The Reading Teacher, 38,* 724–738.

Pearson, P.D. & Johnson, D. (1978). *Teaching reading comprehension.* New York: Holt, Rinehart & Winston.

Raphael, T. (1984). Teaching learners about sources of information for answering comprehension questions. *Journal of Reading, 27,* 303–311.

Raphael, T. (1986). Teaching question answer relationships, revisited. *The Reading Teacher, 39,* 516–522.

The reading report card. (1985). (Report #15-R-01). National Assessment of Educational Progress. Princeton, NJ: Educational Testing Service.

Thorndike, E.L. (1917). Reading and reasoning. *Journal of Educational Psychology, 8,* 323–332.

Smith, F. (1971). *Understanding reading.* New York: Holt, Rinehart & Winston.

Smuin, S. (1978). *Turn-ons.* Belmont, CA.: Fearon Pitman.

Vacca, R. & Vacca, J. (1989). *Content area reading.* Glenview, IL: Scott, Foreman.

Vaughan, J. & Estes, T. (1986). *Reading and reasoning beyond the primary grades.* Newton, MA.: Allyn and Bacon.

Williams, J., Taylor, M.B. & Ganger, B. (1981). Text variations at the level of the individual sentence and the comprehension of simple expository paragraphs. *Journal of Educational Psychology, 73,* 851–865.

6 Assisting the Reader: Developing Comprehension

There are four kinds of readers.

The first is like the hourglass, and their reading being as sand, it runs in and it runs out, and leaves not a vestige behind.

A second is like the sponge, which imbibes everything, and returns it in nearly the same state, only a little dirtier.

A third is like a jelly-bag, allowing all that is pure to press away, and retaining only the refuse and dregs.

And the fourth is like the slaves in the diamond mines of Golcanda, who, casting aside all that is worthless, retain only pure gems."

Samuel Taylor Coleridge

"Teach a child what to think and you make him your slave. Teach a child how to think and you make all knowledge his slave."

Henry A. Taitt

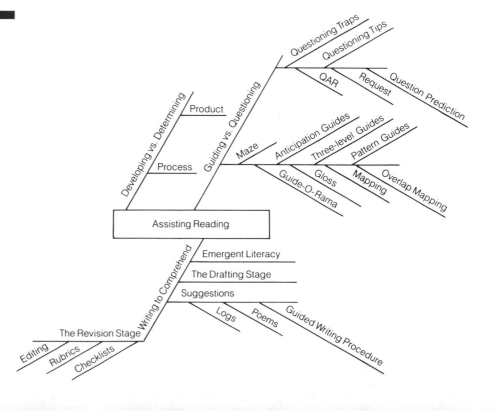

1. What constitutes a good question? Determine your response by searching your own background to describe three qualities of a good question. Now write a question you could pose to your students which would help develop their comprehension of a topic in your subject area.

2. How can teachers assist their students to develop comprehension in a subject area without asking any questions? Can you think of some ways you have used or that teachers have used while instructing you?

3. Below is a list of terms used in this chapter. Some of them may be familiar to you in a general context, but in this chapter they may be used in a different way than you are used to. Rate your knowledge by placing a + in front of those you are sure that you know, a √ in front of those you have some knowledge about, and a 0 in front of those you don't know. Be ready to locate and pay special attention to their meanings when they are presented in the chapter:

   _____ Developing vs. determining
   _____ Guiding vs. questioning
   _____ Metacognition
   _____ Comprehension monitoring
   _____ Writing rubric
   _____ Writing checklist

Objectives:

As you read this chapter, focus your attention on the following objectives. You will:

1. understand the relationship of process to product in reading comprehension.

2. learn how to guide readers to comprehend material without relying on questioning as the only instructional strategy.

3. know the steps for constructing several new comprehension activities.

4. be able to cite several traps about and tips for questioning.

5. learn several suggestions for writing activities which assist reading comprehension.

Purpose:

In chapter 5 you discovered ways to set purposes for your students as they read content material. By setting purposes, you give your students real and relevant reasons to read. You also need to instruct

Sally Forth. Reprinted with permission of NAS, Inc./King Features Syndicate.

students to achieve their best learning. In this chapter, we will present you with these activities to develop effective reading comprehension: three-level guides; pattern guides; guide-o-rama; marginal gloss; mapping; overlapping mapping; QAR; question prediction; writing to learn; guided writing procedure; and learning logs.

Developing Versus Determining Comprehension

The eleventh-grade history class described at the beginning of chapter 5 exemplifies what unfortunately happens in many content class-rooms: Teachers determine rather than develop their students' comprehension. Some teachers ask questions but do not discuss and explain answers to those questions. They require a product of comprehension from their students—the answers to questions—but they do not help students understand how to arrive at those answers. When a product of comprehension is expected before a process has been applied, students end up guessing what the teacher will ask rather than attempting to understand material. Students' purposes for reading are distorted. Students' comprehension is distorted. Some students will develop comprehension anyhow, but most find it difficult to learn by osmosis!

Nessel (1987) comments that question-and-answer sessions which do not develop understanding "amount to a thinly disguised test, not a true exchange of ideas" (p. 443). When question-and-answer sessions become drills, teachers will not be able to determine whether the question was misunderstood or poorly phrased or whether the student had difficulty constructing a response. The use of pop quizzes is an example of this problem. Pop quizzes are usually given to "check" if students really did the assignment. The problem is that a quiz is usually meant to determine comprehension, not to develop it. Unless teachers use pop quizzes for instruction rather than for grading, they will defeat their own purposes and send an incorrect message to students: It's not important to *understand* the material, just to recount it! The activities presented in this chapter can assist in developing comprehension while allowing the teacher to monitor students' responsible behavior in completing their work. Pop quizzes, as well as many other methods of determining comprehension, are discussed in chapter 11.

The primary use of text material is to assist comprehension of content. As such, the text should be used to *guide* students to learn information. Hinchman (1987) cautions, "If textbooks are at all important to teachers, their importance lies in their use as a means to an end: the gaining of course information" (p. 261). Developing comprehension is the *means* to the end. Determining comprehension might be considered the *end*, at least of the formal instruction.

Developing Comprehension with Guiding Activities

Guiding Versus Questioning

Questioning can be a fine means for developing comprehension. Questions which are constructed to draw from students their predictions and impressions of material, to facilitate discussion, and to provide a forum for further understanding are excellent tools for developing comprehension. The goal is understanding, not grading. Questioning is not the only way to develop comprehension, though. Often teachers can accomplish the same results by *guiding* their students to understand material, using carefully constructed exercises which do not include any questioning. Alvermann (1987) contends that "one of the simplest things teachers can do to limit the amount of teacher talk and increase the amount of student talk is to stop asking questions" (p. 11). Counselors practice such a philosophy when they avoid too many questions or suggestions and guide their clients with attentive listening.

Why Use Guiding Activities?

Students are bombarded with questions throughout their school years. Often they associate a question with a right-or-wrong response and think that a grade must be attached to any answer they give. Questions which develop comprehension do not fall into this evaluation category, but students may not realize that, given their prior experiences. By inserting guiding activities into the content curriculum, teachers can dispel negative associations with questioning and cultivate the best comprehension from students. Guiding activities may also offer assistance to the teacher who is "in a rut," who may need to break away from old questioning habits by trying a fresh approach. Guiding activities can follow very closely the three basic levels of comprehension and the organizational pattern of materials, making their construction fairly simple and very sensible.

Some Activities Revisited

Almost every activity introduced in this textbook has possible applications for almost every PAR step. To demonstrate, we reintroduce as guiding activities two activities we presented earlier. We hope that teachers will keep in mind that their application of the theory underlying PAR will dictate how they use an activity. Once objectives are formulated, the use of an activity naturally follows.

Maze

Guthrie, Burnham, Caplan, and Siefert (1974) review the maze procedure for various instructional applications. They point out that, while maze is a good measure of students' abilities to read difficult passages, it becomes an even better tool to help teachers monitor students' comprehension. When a maze is used for instruction, teachers can find out if students did understand what was read by studying the choices students make. Discussion of the logic underlying those choices will facilitate comprehension. According to Guthrie et al., several problems arise with questioning that do not with maze. For instance:

Did the child understand the question?
Did the child understand the passage?
Did the child relate the question to the correct portion of text?
Was the question consistent in quality with other questions which have been asked?
Did the child's answer reflect his real understanding of the content?

One of the authors once had the pleasure of observing a middle-school social studies teacher helping her students comprehend the Bill of Rights by using a maze activity. She had created a maze for the Bill of Rights and was asking her students to justify their choices and then check the original document. She commented that students enjoyed the interactive approach and seemed to learn much more about the content of the Bill of Rights than had her previous classes.

Maze will facilitate informative communication by employing listening, speaking, and reading skills. Although not much writing will occur, the attention given to suitable word choices can include a discussion of why the author chose particular words; thus, students gain insight about writing as a process.

Anticipation Guides

Anticipation guides have already been explained and illustrated as exemplary ways to prepare readers and set purpose by presenting statements to which students react. No questioning is involved. Students are often intrigued that their own opinions are requested and that there is no "preset" right response. The statements guide the students to consider their background and their knowledge of a topic. When anticipation guides are employed throughout the entire content reading lesson, students will be asked to compare their responses before the reading to their impressions after reading. These impressions then become the basis for a discussion of the differences between the content of their responses and the content of the reading; this discussion assists readers in their comprehension of the material. Listening, speaking, and reading are integral to this activity. If teachers request a written reaction to the statements, then writing completes the communicative arts circle.

Other Guiding Activities

Three-Level Guides

Three-level guides (Herber, 1978) connect and integrate the three levels of comprehension with a series of statements to which students react. Because three-level guides demonstrate the hierarchical interaction of the levels of comprehension and call for student reaction to a series of statements, they are a comprehensive activity for assisting comprehension. One elementary teacher we have worked with remarked that she would never again teach *Weekly Reader* articles without a three-level guide! Of course, if this teacher used this—or any other—activity that much with the same type of reading material, students would become bored very quickly. But, when used occasionally to help readers see the interconnectedness of literal, inferential, and applied learning, the three-level guide is an excellent activity.

Although three-level guides need follow no exact sequence or specific requirements, certain guidelines are helpful in their construction. The following are based on suggestions from Herber (1978) and Vacca and Vacca (1989) and our own trial-and-error experiences:

1. First, determine what the organizing concept should be. (Remember Phelps's organizing concept introduced in chapter 4?) If the organizing concept requires students to understand a major content concept and details which support it, then a three-level guide is a good activity to construct.
2. Next, determine the content objectives: What specifically do you want the students to know about this material? This specific con-

tent should be the major ideas, the implications or the interpretation that you want students to learn.

3. Take these content ideas and create a series of statements from them. (Some teachers find it easier to write the main ideas as questions, then rephrase them as statements, until they are comfortable with the generation of statements. Other teachers like to insert a mental "The author means. . ." in front of each statement to ensure that the statements match the interpretation level.) An ideal number of statements is about five or six. Edit them for clarity. You have designed the second level of your guide.

4. By studying these statements and referring to the passage, identify the major facts which support the major ideas you have made into level-two statements. Write these major facts down, either as paraphrases or as exact replications. (Some teachers like to insert a mental "The author says. . ." in front of these statements to ensure that the statements match the literal level.) You might have about two literal statements to support each major inference. These statements are level one of the guide.

5. Now you are ready to design the third level. Statements in this level should apply to the major ideas but should also capitalize on students' previous knowledge. These statements often look like those developed for an anticipation guide; the difference is that the statements constructed for a three-level guide are directly connected to the passage content. (Some teachers like to insert a mental "We can use. . ." in front of these statements to ensure that the statements match the applied level.) Probably four or more of these statements will round out the guide.

6. Last, devise your directions and decide if you want to add some distractors, particularly at levels one and two. Both of these tasks will depend very much on your students' ages, abilities, and appreciation of the content. Make sure that directions are complete and clear. If distractors are added, make sure that your students are ready for them.

We have found that, when introducing three-level guides for the first several times, teachers should use them as a whole class activity. All students should have their own copy or be able to view the guide on a chalkboard or overhead projector. In this way, the new activity is experienced by all students at once. Discussion is promoted in a nonthreatening environment, and students become acclimated to the new activity. Since the value of three-level guides lies in understanding at three levels and in articulating that understanding, oral communication is a very important part of the activity. Students begin to realize how interdependent are the facts, implications, and applications to the understanding of a topic by discussing reactions with each other. A teacher's basic problem will be to cut off conversation at an appropriate time. What a wonderful problem to have!

After some experience with guides, students can use them in small groups or independently with homework assignments. Distractors seem to us to be a desirable addition at this point if students are sophisticated enough to be discerning. If distractors are employed right away, they can give a hidden message to students that there really are right and wrong responses to these statements. Used later, they can give the message that it is important to be a discriminating reader.

Like anticipation guides, three-level guides offer plentiful writing opportunities. Since the statements require students to connect their former knowledge with new information, particularly at the third level, teachers can ask students to write explanations of why they responded in a certain way to a statement. To encourage reflection, teachers might ask students to write their own statements for each level.

Three-level guides are not necessarily easy to construct. Teachers need to practice making and using them. It might be wise to ask a teacher who is familiar with guides to look at yours before you try it in a class. Once you have tried three-level guides, you'll receive student feedback about your construction efforts. Since the assistance three-level guides provide to readers is immediately discernible, you will probably be as enthusiastic about them as most teachers.

Because three-level guides are so popular with teachers, we had a difficult time selecting from the many examples developed by teachers we know. We selected four, shown in Activities 6.1–6.4, which demonstrate variety in the use of directions, distractors, and considerations for age and content.

Pattern Guides

Pattern guides are a natural extension of three-level guides. Again, they are advocated by both Herber (1978) and Vacca and Vacca (1989). Teachers can use pattern guides when the material to be read follows a certain predominate pattern of organization. By using this pattern for the literal level, the teacher can assist students in understanding how the material is organized as well as what basic factual information is included.

Pattern guides will be most useful in helping students to see a consistently used pattern in the text material or to recognize an unusual pattern that may cause them to stumble because they have grown accustomed to another style. Whereas three-level guides really must be presented as a whole, pattern guides can be presented just at the one level at which the pattern is featured. To construct them, the teacher locates the pattern, decides on the major ideas to be stressed, and designs the pattern-oriented level. Activity 6.5 shows a three-level guide for secondary social studies which also contains a guide for the compare-contrast pattern.

A C T I V I T Y 6.1

A Three-Level Guide for Math

I. Below are 8 sentences. Read each one and check the ones that you think say what your author says on pages 1–3. If you have trouble, read the section referred to in parentheses.

_____ Statements made in mathematics have to be true or false. (Page 1, paragraph 1)

_____ Statements made in mathematics have to be true. (P. 1, par. 1)

_____ It is possible to make false statements true by using negation. (P. 3)

_____ A value can have more than one expression. (P. 1, par. 2)

_____ A value is defined as a numerical expression. (P. 1, par. 2)

_____ Equations indicate that a numerical expression either equals or does not equal a specified value. (P. 2)

_____ Equations have to contain 2 expressions of equal value. (P. 2)

_____ Conjunctions and disjunctions are statements using *and* or *but* or *or* to link numerical expressions about a value. (P. 2)

II. Place the following number sentences under the correct column. Sentences might be used more than once or not at all! Portions of sentences can be used in some columns.

$$4 + 3 \neq 7 \qquad\qquad 6 + 1 = 8$$
$$2 + 2 = 4 \text{ or } 2/2 = 4 \qquad \text{Divide } 9 \text{ by } 3.$$
$$4 + 1 \text{ and } 3 + 2 \text{ and } 5 = 5 \qquad \text{It is not true that } 6 + 1 = 8.$$

Numerical Expression Statement Value Equation Conjunction Disjunction Negation

III. Consider each assertion below. Check it if you agree with it. Star it if you think it can be supported by information on pages 1–4 and tell why.

_____ Statements are more than assertions.

_____ Values can be expressed in different ways but still be the same values.

_____ Symbols often convey meaning more efficiently than words.

_____ It is important to think carefully about what a statement means.

Developed from information on pages 1–4 of Chapter 1, "Mathematical Statements and Proofs," of *Modern School Mathematics*, Houghton Mifflin, 1971.

A C T I V I T Y 6.2

Three-Level Guide for Latter Part of Chapter Three: "Survey of the Stars"

I. *Directions:* Check the items you believe say what the authors said. Sometimes the exact words will be used; other times other words may be used.

_____ **1.** It takes four hydrogen nuclei to convert into one helium nucleus.

_____ **2.** The helium nucleus formed by fusion contains less mass than the four hydrogen nuclei which created it.

_____ **3.** A star that is far away will not appear as bright as a similar star that is closer.

_____ **4.** More massive stars look brighter than other stars at the same distance.

_____ **5.** Fusion takes place faster in stars with more mass than the sun.

_____ **6.** Stars that have less mass than the sun will live longer than the sun.

_____ **7.** The mass of a star determines how long it will live.

_____ **8.** Stars with more mass than the sun will become giants, supergiants, and supernovae.

_____ **9.** A black hole can occur when the mass that remains after a supernova is at least 5 times greater than that of the sun.

_____ **10.** Some astronomers believe small black holes were caused by explosions in space.

II. *Directions:* Put a check on the line beside any of the statements below which you think are reasonable interpretations of the authors' meaning.

_____ **1.** Large amounts of energy can be created when a particular mass becomes smaller through fusion.

_____ **2.** The brightness of a star can be determined by its distance and mass.

_____ **3.** More massive stars live longer than smaller ones.

_____ **4.** Some stars are going to explode.

_____ **5.** There may be several reasons for the existence of black holes in space.

(continued)

_____ **III.** *Directions:* Using information you have read or already knew, place a check in the blank beside any statements below with which you and the author would agree.

_____ **1.** Bigger is not always better.
_____ **2.** Mergers don't always produce more than there was to begin with.
_____ **3.** All living things go through the same life stages and meet the same end.
_____ **4.** It is impossible to be moved by an invisible force.

Developed by Holly Corbett.

Pattern guides can employ statements; such guidance is preferable to questioning when we want to lead students to recognize a pattern of organization. The cause-effect pattern guide presented in chapter 8 for middle-school social studies students is a good example. Many workbook exercises are also based on a pattern guide. The example in Activity 6.6 shows how an intermediate social studies teacher constructed a pattern guide.

Guide-O-Ramas and Marginal Glosses

Another guide which assists readers but does not necessarily rely on questioning is the "guide-o-rama" (Cunningham and Shablack, 1975), which signals the reader to note certain information in a reading passage. The teacher creates directions for these reading passages and encourages the students to use the directions as they are reading. For instance, if the teacher can see that the word *perverse* is used in an unusual way, he might right this: "For page 13, second paragraph, third line, the word *perverse* is used a little differently from what you'd expect. Pay attention to the meaning." When a teacher prepares several directions such as these and gives them to readers to refer to while reading, they have a panoramic view of the reading, hence the name guide-o-rama.

A marginal gloss (Singer and Donlan, 1985) can often be found in content textbooks. Glosses are the comments that authors make to their readers as "asides" or marginal notations. The comments are intended to help the reader understand the passage content; thus they assist the reader in developing comprehension. Teachers can make their own marginal glosses if their texts do not include them or if they are dissatisfied with those already included. A guide-o-rama can be designed as a gloss also. The point of these activities is similar; they both are

A Guide to Reading
"The Angel in the House"

I. *Directions:* Check the items you believe say what the author says. Sometimes the exact words will be used; other times other words may be used. Be able to locate the statement in the essay to support your response.

_____ **1.** Ms. Woolf's profession is literature.

_____ **2.** Other women have paved the way to making her career easier.

_____ **3.** Ms. Woolf sold an article and bought a Persian cat.

_____ **4.** Ms. Woolf had difficulty writing because of the Angel in the House.

_____ **5.** No one has yet adequately described what *woman* is.

_____ **6.** Her imagination left her when she thought her passions were unconventional.

_____ **7.** Ms. Woolf describes two experiences she has had in her professional life.

_____ **8.** For the first time, women are able to ask questions and decide on answers.

II. *Directions:* Put a check on the lines beside any statements which are reasonable interpretations of the author's meaning.

_____ **1.** Women often have to overcome cultural expectations in order to succeed in a challenging career.

_____ **2.** When one is successful, one will often succumb to frivolity.

_____ **3.** Writing fully and honestly, especially when you are a woman, is very difficult to do.

_____ **4.** Although being a female journalist leaves a woman prey to many phantoms, other professions may be much worse.

_____ **5.** Women are often censored for the same things a man could do and be accepted for.

III. *Directions:* To apply what you read means to take information and ideas from what you have read and connect them to what you know. Place a check beside any statements which are supported in II and by your previous experiences.

_____ **1.** Everyone has a ghost in his or her closet.

_____ **2.** Knowing oneself is a lifetime endeavor.

_____ **3.** Some problems never have solutions.

_____ **4.** Winning the battle does not mean the war is won.

_____ **5.** What appears simple is often complex.

ACTIVITY 6.4

Three-Level Guide to Pattern Guide-Sheet

I. *Directions:* Place a check (✓) before the statements that are correct based on the information in the guide sheet.

_____ 1. The first step in making this skirt is gathering the upper edge of the front between large ●'s.

_____ 2. Pockets are sewn in place after the skirt front is sewn to the back.

_____ 3. The zipper is placed in the center back seam.

_____ 4. The zipper is applied after the waistband is sewn to the skirt.

_____ 5. The waistband is interfaced before it is sewn to the skirt.

_____ 6. Seams that will be inside the waistband (when it is finished) are trimmed.

_____ 7. The pictures show that the center back seam and the side seams are pressed open.

_____ 8. A narrow hem is used to finish the lower edge of the skirt.

II. *Directions:* Place a check (✓) before each statement that you think is reasonable based on the information in the guide sheet. Be prepared to support your answer with statements from the guide sheet.

_____ 1. Sewing a skirt begins with sewing on the skirt front.

_____ 2. To save confusion and error, complete one step before going to another.

_____ 3. Finish completely (by removing basting, trimming, and pressing) one line of sewing before crossing it with another.

_____ 4. Trimming and clipping may be needed to keep a seam from being too bulky.

_____ 5. Pressing is an important part of sewing.

III. *Directions:* To apply what you read means to take information from what you have read and connect it to what you know. Place a check (✓) before any statements which are supported by statements in II and by previous experiences or study. Be sure that you have a reason for your answers.

_____ 1. A stitch in proper sequence (order) saves time.

_____ 2. The order in which something is done does make a difference.

_____ 3. If it's worth doing, it's worth doing well.

_____ 4. A picture is worth a thousand words.

_____ 5. A little time well used is better than much time ill used.

Developed by Ava Brendle.

ACTIVITY 6.5

Change and Continuity in the Lives of American Women

Three-Level Guide

I. Which statements are facts in this essay? Check them.
1. Women today live to be about seventy-five.
2. After 1850, immigrant families took farm girls' places in factories.
3. American women in the work force are usually considered as temporary workers.
4. Although many factors have influenced women's lives, three stand out as the most important: industrialization, contraception, and economic instability.
5. In the colonial period, a woman's obligations to her children and her household tasks often conflicted with one another.

II. Which statements are major ideas of this essay? Check them.
1. Tradition in the manner of gender roles is very strong.
2. The patterns of women's lives have shifted dramatically during the past two centuries.
3. More women are entering the career field every day.
4. Women are having fewer children today than in the 1800s.
5. The definition of the role of a woman has not changed.

III. With which statements would you and the author agree? Check them.
1. You've come a long way baby.
2. Physical changes occur more easily and faster than mental changes.
3. A woman should be barefoot, pregnant, and in the kitchen.
4. It takes a lot to get a little.
5. A woman's place is in the home.

Thesis: Women's positions in society have changed dramatically since 1800, yet society has not been as willing to accept the change as quickly as it has occurred.

Compare and Contrast

Subject	Today's Women	Yesterday's Women
1. Children	2 or fewer	More than 7
2. Life expectancy	75 years	55 years
3. Independence	Before marriage	After widowed
4. Work force	In and out of home	In home
5. Education	Advanced education	Only men

A C T I V I T Y 6.6

Pattern Guide: Communities Everywhere Have Needs

Thesis: Communities everywhere have needs. Some communities are alike and some are different.

Directions:

1. Read each sentence.
2. Decide if the sentence tells how communities are alike or how they are different.
3. Place an *A* beside the sentence if it shows how communities are *alike*.
4. Place a *D* beside the sentence if it shows how communities are *different*.

When everyone is finished we will discuss our answers.

_____ 1. Communities everywhere have a need to communicate.
_____ 2. The people of China speak many different dialects.
_____ 3. The people of Africa speak many different dialects. One language spoken is Swahili.
_____ 4. People everywhere live and work together.
_____ 5. People everywhere need food and shelter.
_____ 6. The people of China use chopsticks when eating.
_____ 7. The people of Quebec speak French.
_____ 8. The people in Canada enjoy going to concerts just like the people in America.
_____ 9. The people of Africa enjoy listening to and watching a story teller.
_____ 10. The people in Daktar enjoy watching television.
_____ 11. An abacus is used for counting in China.
_____ 12. People everywhere need transportation.
_____ 13. People everywhere need to communicate in writing.
_____ 14. The Chinese language has characters instead of letters.
_____ 15. Rice is an important grain in China.

Developed by Vicki Douglas.

like having the teacher go home with the students and look over their shoulders as they are reading to guide their reading attention. Singer and Donlan suggest that teachers make marginal glosses by:

1. Folding a ditto master against the margin of a text.
2. Identifying the book page at the top of the master and line numbers beside teacher directives.
3. Writing on the ditto master the marginal notes.
4. Duplicating and giving students copies of these notes to match to text pages and lines as they read.

With either of these activities, we suggest that the teacher select either very difficult portions of text to gloss or beginning portions, when the reading may be tougher. Making guide-o-ramas or glosses for use throughout a text would be very time-consuming. However, for providing assistance in developing comprehension with challenging reading, they are worth the time.

Mapping

Mapping (Pearson and Johnson, 1978; Heimlich and Hittleman, 1986) has become a popular activity for helping readers develop comprehension. Mapping is not really a new activity, nor is it only a reading activity. Novak and Gowin (1984) identify concept mapping as a good general learning strategy. (Concept mapping is explained in Chapter 10.) You may also have heard the terms *mind mapping, webbing,* or *semantic webbing* used to describe mapping. Because maps encourage students to use prior knowledge and interactive learning, reading educators recognize their value for assisting reader comprehension. Mapping can be useful to teach vocabulary, to introduce outlining and taking notes, and to use as a study aid. If mapping is used to introduce a topic before any reading has taken place, it is an excellent activity for preparing the reader. It can also be used to aid reading reflection, especially when it becomes a study aid. (We have discussed mapping for several of these uses in other chapters.)

The primary purpose of mapping is to demonstrate the relationship of major and supporting ideas visually by having the readers react and create responses. It is a guiding rather than a questioning activity, although the teacher may ask questions to stimulate responses which are then mapped. The following are suggestions for developing a map (based on Santeusanio, 1983):

1. Identify the main idea of your content passage. (Sometimes, just the topic or a question may stimulate map generation.) Write it anywhere on the page, leaving room for other information to be written around it.
2. Circle the main idea.
3. Identify secondary categories, which may be chapter subheadings.

4. Connect the secondary categories to the main idea.
5. Find supporting details.
6. Connect supporting details to the idea or category they support.
7. Connect all notes to other notes in a way that makes sense.
8. Remember—mapping a whole chapter may be too time-consuming. Mapping is recommended for portions of a chapter that a teacher identifies as very important.

Maps force students to pay attention as they read, reread, and study; they demonstrate the hierarchical pattern of comprehension. Since one usually starts with the applied or inferential level and works back to the supporting literal information, students can see the important connections between the levels. Muth (1987) reports that mapping, because it is a hierarchical strategy, has been found to be a highly successful aid to understanding expository text. Since a map is a diagram of information, it is a visual learning aid. Often, especially for younger readers, drawings added to the map will stimulate learning. Such visual reinforcement capitalizes on visual literacy and right-brain functions. The social studies teacher described in chapter one used mapping extensively in his instruction about capital punishment. Activity 6.7 shows how a high school English teacher mapped Act II of *Macbeth*. Activity 6.8 shows how a middle-grades science teacher mapped the detection of black holes. Once the teacher has mapped several times with students, students will become proficient at making their own maps.

Overlapping Mapping. Mapping can be a useful aid for the comparing and contrasting of concepts. We call this "overlapping mapping" because first one map is created, then another. The two maps are overlapped, preferably on overhead transparencies to demonstrate similarities and differences. One of the authors created an overlapping map to assist college freshmen in their understanding of the metaphor in the essay "Pedestrian Students and High-Flying Squirrels." In this essay, Liane Elbison Norman laments the fact that her journalism students are not risk takers, that they are too careful in their actions. She wishes that they were more like squirrels, who take leaps like acrobats. The author followed Pearson and Johnson's (1978) suggestion that vocabulary maps should show the relationship between examples of the word used in the material, properties of the word, and concepts associated with the word. The author drew two maps, in different colors, to show those relationships between the words *squirrels* and *students*. At the bottom of the maps, the author wrote Norman's examples of students as pedestrians and squirrels as acrobats. The properties or descriptions Norman used were listed to the right of the circled words. The concepts that Norman implied—students are passive while squirrels are active— were written at the top of the maps. When the maps, in two different colors, were overlaid, the comparison became clear to the students.

A C T I V I T Y   6.7

Macbeth, Act II

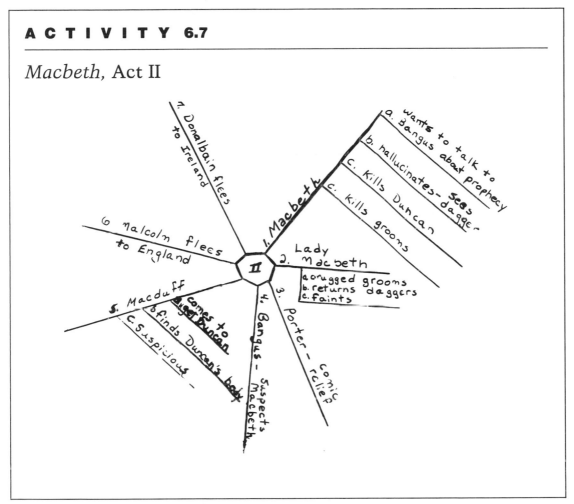

Developed by Vicki Ford.

The mapping of "Pedestrian Students and High-Flying Squirrels" is shown in Activity 6.9. Following that, Activity 6.10 demonstrates how mapped comparisons may be used to teach vocabulary in foreign languages, in this case, Latin.

The integration of all of the communicative arts is apparent when mapping is used. Class discussion must take place for the map to be developed. This requires students to listen to each other and speak on the topic. Reading is the source of the information mapped, and writing can be incorporated if the teacher asks students to use the map as a frame of reference for writing about the topic. For instance, students could be assigned to write a three-paragraph essay about the detection of black holes, using three statements generated from the map. The

A C T I V I T Y 6.8

Map of Black Holes

Central node: **Detection of Black Holes**

- masses of gas much larger than a dying star
- powerful explosions in space = small amounts of matter = small black holes
- other ideas of origin
- Constellation Cygnus - verified
- invisible star
- A visible star is being twirled
- gravity great enough to be created by more than 5X sun's mass
- unseen star probably a black hole
- Behavior of visible star
  - gravity pulls matter into hole
  - movements indicate invisible partner
- Matter pulled into hole becomes hot
- gives off X-Ray
- X-Ray comes from area where one star is visible and one invisible
- invisible star must have more than 5X the mass of the sun
- Requirements for invisible star to be a black hole
  - pair must be close enough to earth for invisible star to be seen by telescope if it were an ordinary dwarf

Developed by Holly Corbett.

A C T I V I T Y 6.9

Mapping Metaphors: Pedestrian and Squirrel

details under a statement provide paragraph support. A science teacher who wants students to write reports about planets could have students map the information on a planet from an encyclopedia. Next students might refer to primary resources to find out more about each portion of the map. Then the map could be transformed into the table of contents for a report on a planet (see Activity 6.11).

Questioning for Comprehension

Beware of Questioning Traps

The traditional method of developing comprehension is questioning. Durkin (1979) found that teachers use questioning more than any other comprehension technique. When it works, it works very well. Ques-

A C T I V I T Y 6.10

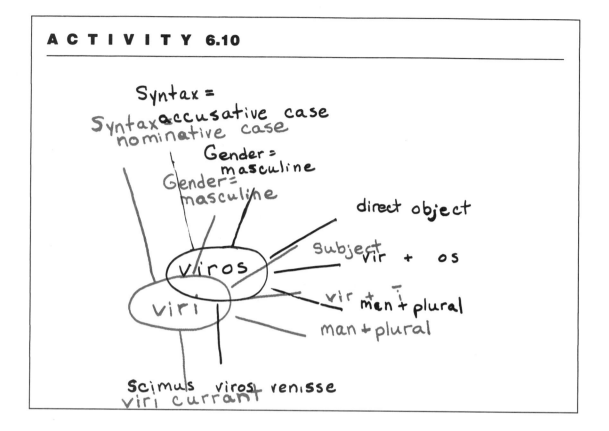

tions can help teachers to know if students are understanding text and can guide readers to consider many aspects of material. Questions are excellent probes.

However, often questioning does not work very well because teachers have fallen into some common "traps." As we pointed out earlier in this chapter, a major reason that questioning is not successful is that teachers confuse *determining* comprehension with *developing* comprehension when they question. For example, when the teacher requires students to close their books and recite information before they have had a chance to assimilate that information, teachers are really testing rather than assisting.

A second trap is that teachers' questions focus extensively on literal comprehension. This is the conclusion of several reading professionals who have learned a good deal about teachers' questioning habits through classroom observation. For example, Gusak (1967) reported in his study that, in second grade, 78 percent of the questions asked were literal; in fourth grade, 65 percent were still literal; in sixth grade, 58 percent were literal. Durkin (1979), observing at the upper elementary

A C T I V I T Y 6.11

A Map Becomes a Table of Contents

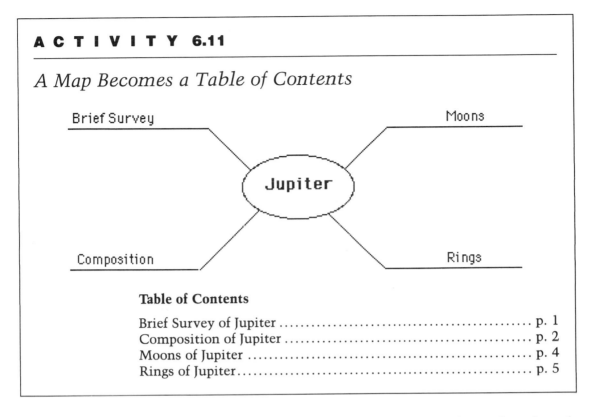

Table of Contents

level, found that most questions that teachers asked were literal, with only one correct response expected. Durkin (1981) then studied teachers' manuals for basal reading instruction and discovered that low-level literal questions with one correct response were the major instructional strategy provided for teachers. Reutzel and Daines (1987) have reached the same conclusions after a study of seven major basal readers. With little practice in answering higher-level questions, students are ill equipped to think critically. Elementary students are trapped into expecting only literal questions; secondary students will remain in the trap because the literal question has been their previous experience. However, research also shows that when instructional strategies are altered so that the focus is on inferences and main ideas, students respond with improved recall and greater understanding (Hansen, 1981; Hansen and Pearson, 1983; Raphael, 1984).

In addition, teachers sometimes misjudge the difficulty of questions they are asking or fail to match the questions to the students' ability. Generally questions are simpler when students are able to recognize and locate answers in the text rather than closing books and trying to recall the same information. Easier questions also include those asked during reading or shortly after reading, questions which have only one or two parts, oral questions rather than written questions, and those that allow students to choose an answer from among several alternatives. We are not suggesting that all questions should be asked in the simplest manner; we are cautioning that many times teachers have not considered the difficulty of their questions and their students' ability to answer them.

Another trap teachers often fall into when questioning is that of focusing more on the question asked and the expected response than on the student's actual response. As Dillon (1983) remarks, we should "stress the nature of questions rather than their frequency and pace, and the type of student response rather than the type of teacher question" (p. 8). Students' answers can tell a lot about their understanding of the topic. We need to listen for answers which let us know how well we are assisting the development of comprehension.

Tips for Constructing Good Questions

We have learned much about how to question from the extensive studies of reading comprehension conducted over the past few decades. Although much of this research has been conducted with elementary students, the implications are relevant for secondary instruction as well. Students who have not received a firm foundation in reading comprehension in elementary school will not be well equipped in secondary schools. To help the teachers construct good questions, we have tried to summarize what we consider the most important research considerations in the following tips:

1. Simplify your questions! Although teachers want to challenge their students, they should challenge within a range that allows students to succeed. Consider using guidelines such as these:

   Identify the purpose of the question. (Will it measure fact, implications, or applied levels of comprehension? a particular organizational pattern? a superordinate or subordinate idea?) Is this purpose justified? Does it contribute to a balance of comprehension levels within the lesson?

   Identify the type of response demanded by the question (recognition, recall, production, or generation of a new idea from the information). Is this response justified for the age and ability of the group? Have you provided an example of what you want? If you wish students to produce a modern dialogue for a character in *Hamlet,* can you give them an example first?

   Might the question elicit more than one reasonable response? If this is a possibility, will you be able to accept different responses and use them to assist instruction?

Does this question contain several parts? Will these parts be clear to the students and can they remember all of the parts as they respond?

Write the question clearly and concisely. Then decide whether to pose it orally or in writing to the students.

2. Share with students the reasons for your questions. Let them know the process you use to develop questions and the process you would use in answering them. This knowledge helps them to realize what type of questions are important to you in this area (Pearson, 1985). It also helps them to think about how they should be thinking when they respond and what you are thinking when you question. This process—thinking about thinking—is called *metacognition* (Babbs and Moe, 1983). Helping students think about your reasoning and about their own reading processes will eventually produce independent readers.

3. Encourage students to ask questions about your questions and to ask their own questions. Goodlad (1984) suggests that students will thrive when they can participate in classroom questioning more directly than they do in most classrooms today. Beyer (1984) says that teacher-dominated questioning inhibits student independence and limits thinking. "Instruction that leads to systematic question-asking by students would be more appropriate, but such an approach is rare indeed" (Beyer, p. 489).

4. Provide plenty of practice in answering questions at different levels of comprehension. Check yourself occasionally to make sure that you are not leaning on the literal level too heavily. Training and practice result in learning the material (Brown, Campione, and Day, 1981; Paris, Cross and Lipson, 1984) and in learning how to understand material in sophisticated ways. Wasserman (1987) argues that students' depth and breadth of understanding improves when they are asked challenging questions. Also, students who learn to take another's perspective may become better readers as a result (Gardner and Smith, 1987). But students must have opportunities for practice to master this ability.

5. Allow discussions which give students practice in asking and answering questions (Perez and Strickland, 1987; Alvermann, 1987a). In chapter 7, many suggestions are given for generating student discussions to facilitate critical thinking.

6. Ask students the types of questions you know they are able to answer; try not to expect too much too soon, but do expect as much as students can do. For example, Afflerbach (1987) reviews some of the recent research indicating that students can identify main idea statements earlier than they can make such statements. If students seem consistently unable to answer a certain type of com-

prehension question, even after you have followed these suggestions, we suggest that you review the most current findings in reading for clues.

Activities Which Promote Good Questioning

QAR

The question-answer relationship (QAR) has been studied and applied by Raphael (1984; 1986). QAR was introduced earlier as a taxonomy with four levels: right there; think and search; the author and you (presented in a 1988 International Reading Association publication as the writer and me); on my own. When QAR is introduced to and practiced with students for as little as eight weeks, reading comprehension improves greatly. Teachers should introduce QAR with a visual aid to show the QAR relationship. Figure 6.1 shows one teacher's illustrated introduction to QAR.

After introducing QAR, teachers should demonstrate with a short passage to show how QAR is applied. To model the use of QAR, teachers should provide, label, and answer at least one question at each QAR level. Teachers would move gradually to having students answer questions and identifying the QAR for themselves. Throughout the year of content instruction, the teacher should refer to QAR. These steps will saturate the students with a way of thinking about questions and answers which will help them read with better comprehension. Activity 6.12 demonstrates this procedure as a sixth-grade mathematics teacher used it.

Because QAR is a straightforward procedure, easily implemented, quickly beneficial to students, and useful at any grade and in any content area, we hope that many content teachers will start using it in their instruction. It fosters listening, speaking and reading, and, if students write their own QARs, it also extends writing opportunities.

Question Prediction

Using organizational patterns to practice good, independent questioning strategies is the intent of this procedure. Finley and Seaton (1987) propose a seven-step procedure to cultivate reading comprehension:

1. The teacher presents and explains common patterns of organization.
2. The teacher lists common groups (unlabeled) of key words which signal the patterns, such as "first . . . second . . . next" to signal sequence. Then the teacher asks students to scan some paragraphs to find such signal words.
3. The teacher gives students selected topic sentences and asks students to identify the probable pattern from the clue words in the topic sentences.

Q A R

I.   Where is the answer ?

Right there !

words are right
there in the text.

 In the text

II. Where is the answer ?

Think and search !

words are in the text but not
spelled out for you. Think about
what the author is saying.

hmm !
gotta think
about this.

III. Where is the answer?

what I
Know

You and the author !

think about what you have
learned and what is in
the text.

what the
author says

IV. Where is the answer?

On your own !

answer is in your head !

Figure 6.1
Developed by Rebecca McSweeney.

A C T I V I T Y 6.12

QAR Procedure Applied to Mathematics

The picture:

QAR

Question-Answer Relationship

INTRODUCE

The steps:

| Show completed QAR | Have class answer a QAR | Have class develop a QAR |

Apply QAR to problem in text

The example:

WORD PROBLEMS?

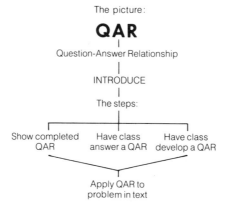

Step I

In the text
RIGHT THERE
word for word

Step II

THINK AND SEARCH
The answer is in the
text, BUT the words
used in the question
and the words used in
the text *may not be*
the same.

NO PROBLEM!!!

Step III

YOU AND THE AUTHOR
The information in the text
got you thinking. NOW, think
about the question, and use
what you already know to
answer the question.

Step IV

ON YOUR OWN
How can you use what
you learned for the next
word problem?

Laura set a goal to run five miles a day. On Friday she ran one mile
before breakfast. Then she went to school. In P.E. class she ran two
miles around the school track. After dinner that night, Laura and her
dad won first place in the "Run for Your Life" event at the county
fair. Laura went home that night tired, but satisfied.

1. QUESTION: What was Laura's goal?
   ANSWER: <u>to run 5 miles a day</u>
   QAR: <u>RIGHT THERE</u>
2. QUESTION: How far did Laura run before dinner??
   ANSWER: <u>3 miles</u>
   QAR: <u>THINK AND SEARCH</u>

(continued)

3. QUESTION: What was the length of the "Run for Your Life" event?
   ANSWER: <u>the race was at least 2 miles long</u>
   QAR: <u>YOU AND THE AUTHOR</u>
4. QUESTION: What benefits can result from running 5 miles a day?
   ANSWER: <u>You will be a healthier person.</u>
   QAR: <u>ON YOUR OWN</u>

Bill needed to lose some weight. He decided to eat only apples for three days. He should have listened to his mom. On the third day he didn't feel very well.

1. QUESTION: What did Bill need to do?
   ANSWER: _____
   QAR: <u>RIGHT THERE</u>
2. QUESTION: What did Bill's mother tell him?
   ANSWER: _____
   QAR: <u>THINK AND SEARCH</u>
3. QUESTION: Why did Bill get sick?
   ANSWER: _____
   QAR: <u>YOU AND THE AUTHOR</u>
4. QUESTION: How many apples would it take to make you sick?
   ANSWER: _____
   QAR: <u>ON YOUR OWN</u>

Using problem number 6 on page 45 of your *Addison-Wesley Mathematics* book, answer these questions.

1. QUESTION: How much did the uncut stone weigh?
   ANSWER: _____
   QAR: _____
2. QUESTION: How big were the largest and smallest diamonds?
   ANSWER: _____
   QAR: _____
3. QUESTION: How many carats were lost during the cutting process?
   ANSWER: _____
   QAR: _____
4. QUESTION: What is the biggest diamond in the world?
   ANSWER: _____
   QAR: _____

Developed by Mary Frances Siewert.

4. The teacher prepares clozed paragraphs from the content area. The content-specific information is what should be deleted; topic and key pattern words should not be deleted. Students are asked to underline the key words and predict the pattern.

5. The teacher asks students to read several text paragraphs and state the main ideas of each paragraph. Then the teacher has students combine the paragraphs' main ideas into an overall main idea.

6. The teacher asks students to translate the main idea statement into a possible question the teacher might ask, particularly on a test.

7. The teacher cautions that students will find several patterns within a text reading, but when students can find the main idea and make questions of it, they will become good pattern detectors.

Question prediction ultimately aids students in becoming aware that questions are not confined to literal comprehension. Students become more secure about answering questions because they understand how questions might be formulated and used on teachers' tests and on standardized tests.

ReQuest and Text Lookbacks

Students should be encouraged to ask informed questions. Manzo's ReQuest procedure (1969) encourages students to think carefully before and during their reading by formulating questions based on the text. Since Manzo had remedial readers and small groups in mind when he designed ReQuest, we have chosen to explain this procedure in depth in chapters 9 and 12. The reader may want to look ahead to find out more about it.

So many times students think that they must recall information rather than look back to answer questions. Text lookbacks (Garner, Hare, Alexander, Haynes, and Winograd 1984) show readers how to answer questions by referring back to key information. Again, because remedial readers were the original audience for this technique, we refer our readers to chapter 12 for further explanation. Text lookbacks are also discussed in chapter 9.

The Role of Writing as Assisted Comprehension

Emergent Literacy

Students can become writers at a younger age than was previously thought. Recent research on writing has indicated that very young children create forms of reading and writing which they can explain to adults (Teale and Sulzby, 1986). This writing includes pictures, which Vygotsky (1978) describes as gestures to represent the child's thought.

Children in the early grades are capable of writing reports about content subjects (Calkins, 1986); although these reports may contain inventive spellings and pictures which one might not expect to find in an older student's report, they reflect learning through language. Teachers are now encouraged to recognize this early reading and writing and to foster children's use of all of the communicative arts as early as possible in content subjects.

In Figures 6.2 and 6.3, which follow, a first grader writes about his trip to a science museum and about his "pet dinosaur." Both demonstrate learning about science through writing. The teacher made comments about the content of the writing, not about the invented spellings.

The Drafting Stage of Writing

In chapter 5, we discussed the stages of writing, including prewriting. We suggested ways for incorporating prewriting in content instruction. Now the second stage of writing, drafting, is emphasized. The drafting stage of writing is much like the assisted step in reading. Process is emphasized, and writers begin to realize what they have to say and what they understand about a topic. The flow of thought is represented in the draft as it is in the discussion of the reader.

Writing as a Means of Developing Comprehension

Many fiction writers confess that they didn't know what a particular fictional character was going to do until they started writing. Their preparation gave them direction for writing but not exact knowledge of how the writing would turn out. Only by creating did they discover. Similarly, we have learned more about what we know as we have written this book. We have *discovered* ways to express the information we have to share with readers; we did not *know* all that we would write before we drafted this text. In a similar way, readers will learn as they read. Since both reading and writing can assist comprehension, it seems logical to use both in tandem when assisting readers.

Unfortunately, writing is not used very often as an activity to help students understand content material (Pearce and Bader, 1984; Bader and Pearce, 1983). Teachers like Miss K, in *Ralph S. Mouse* (Beverly Cleary, 1982), are rare. Miss K would turn anything into a writing project. For example, when she and the class discover that Ralph the mouse has come to school with Ryan, she inspires the students to write about mice and, later, to write rejoinders to a newspaper article which included misinformation about their projects. Most teachers, in contrast, seem to use writing activities which are mainly product-oriented and graded. This use would seem to fit the editing or reflection stage rather than the assisting stage. However, as research has shown, writing can be a powerful tool to assist comprehension. According to Jacobs (1987),

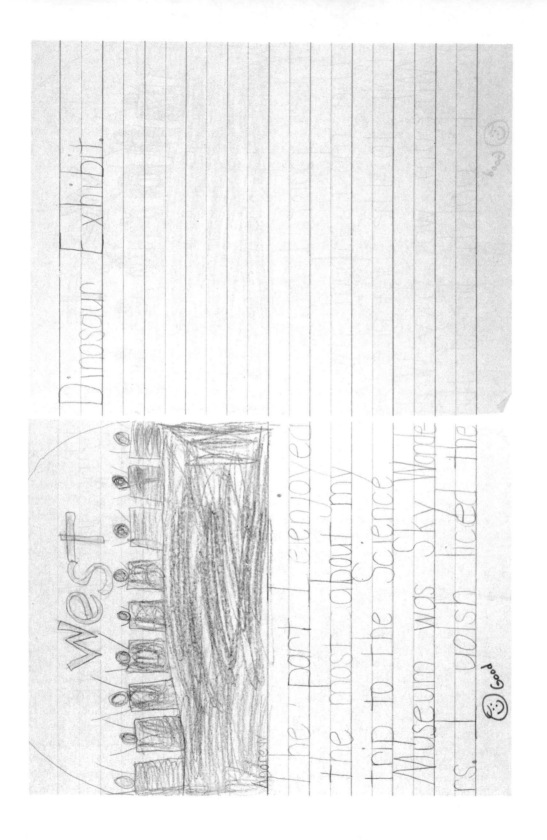

Dinosaur Exhibit.

West

he part I enjoyed
the most about my
trip to the Science
Museum was Sky Wone
rs. I wish liced the

😀 Good

😀 Good

Figure 6.2

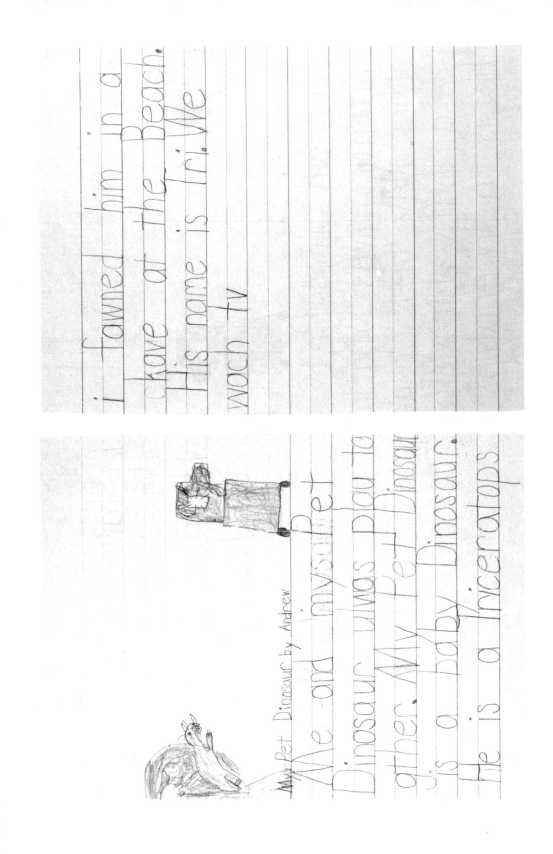

My Pet Dinosaur by Andrew

Me and my pet
Dinosaur Dinos Day to
gther. My Pet Dinosaur
is a Baby Dinosaur.
He is a Triceratops

i fowned him in a
cave at the Beach.
His name is Tri. We
woch tv

Figure 6.3

T A B L E 6.1   *The Whole Picture of Writing*

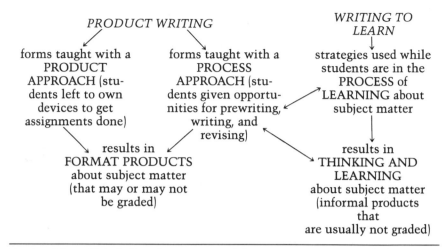

Reprinted from *Plain Talk* with permission of the Virginia Department of Education.

"Writing . . . is the ordering of thought. It is the formation of an idea, or a cluster of ideas, from a child's experiences and imagination. It is a conscious shaping of the materials selected by the writer to be included in the composition. In selecting what to put in and leave out, the child is using those elements of writing craftsmanship that he or she can manage" (p. 38).

Self's (1987) diagram (see Table 6.1) shows the relationship between the process of writing and the products of writing. Much process-oriented writing results in a formal product. The best products will be generated when students are given opportunities for prewriting, writing, and revising. Not all writing does lead to a formal product, but all writing can lead to writing as a means to learning.

Suggestions for Writing to Assist Comprehension

Gebhard (1983) suggests four principles for developing writing activities which assist in comprehension. First, students need an audience other than the teacher. Peers are a fine resource because they can provide supportive comments and suggestions. Often, students become much more active and committed to the writing when the audience is someone other than the teacher. Using peers as an audience conveys the message that the process of writing is more important than the final product, which is the case when writing is an activity to assist comprehension. Writing for peers may alleviate the teacher's need to "grade" the writing at all. If the teacher does decide to grade, then the peer revision and editing will mean that the teacher will see a more "polished" product. Correction will take second place to content. Second, the writing tasks should be "consequential." Just because the teacher will grade a piece of writing does not mean the student is motivated. Students need to be able to write about topics that interest them. The *Foxfire* books illustrate this principle of consequential writing very well. Eliot Wigginton (1986) inspired his English students in Raburn Gap, Georgia, to write about the crafts and habits of their own community. This assignment itself was much more inspiring to them than receiving a grade. The audience was their fellow students and their community. The result of their writing is the *Foxfire* books. Third, writing assignments should be varied. No one wants to do the same old thing again and again. Copying definitions gets pretty old pretty fast. Fourth, writing activities should connect prior knowledge to new information, providing students with a creative challenge.

According to Self (1987), using writing to teach content material fulfills the following purposes:

1. Focusing students' attention
2. Engaging students actively
3. Arousing students' curiosity
4. Helping students discover disparate elements in the material
5. Helping students make connections between the material and themselves
6. Helping students "make their own meaning" from the material
7. Helping students think out loud
8. Helping students find out what they do and do not know
9. Helping teachers diagnose the students' successes and problems
10. Preparing students to discuss material

Davison and Pearce (1988), by modifying Applebee's (1981) classification system, divide writing activities into five types:

1. Direct use of language (copying and transcribing information, such as copying from the board or glossary);

2. Linguistic translation (translation of symbols, words, etc. such as writing the meaning of a formula);

3. Summarizing/interpreting (paraphrasing, making notes about material, such as explaining in one's own words or keeping a journal);

4. Applied use of language (a new idea is applied to the information in written form, such as writing possible test questions);

5. Creative use of language (using writing to explore and convey related information, such as writing a report). (pp. 10–11)

Davison and Pearce found that the copying tasks were those predominately used by the junior high school mathematics teachers in their study. Creative activities were seldom used, group writing opportunities were scarce, and the audience for the writing was usually the teacher. In practice, then, teachers do not seem to be following the suggestions that Gebhard has made, probably because they do not realize how helpful writing activities can be to assist students' comprehension. Yet, the possibilities are great. Here are a few ideas for content teachers:

1. Have students write out the steps they would follow in solving a math problem or completing an experiment. Ask them to speculate on what would happen if they altered one step.

2. Bachman (1989) suggests "Top it off!" for practice in writing about mathematics problems. For instance, in this intermediate level example, students would be given a numerical or algebraic problem. Students must, in small groups, write two questions about the problem. The questions must reflect student knowledge of the vocabulary and the correct operations:

   The following example is missing directions which tell you what to do. You are to write 2 different questions pertaining to the example:

24 and 36	or	$7^2 + 90 \div 3$

   1. *(What is the sum of 24 and 36?)*
   2. *(What is the name of the sign which will precede the sum?)*

   1. *What are the operations involved in the expression?*
   2. *Simplify the expression.*

3. Ask students to rewrite an historic event by altering one cause or one effect. Then have them compare the way it really happened to their invented way.

4. Ask students to take the perspective of an author and, through the author's words, explain word choice or style or plot choices.

5. Have students write modified "biopoems," poems whose subject is the writer himself or herself. Gere (1985, p. 222) provides the following pattern for writing biopoems:

   Line 1: First name
   Line 2: Four traits that describe the author
   Line 3: Relative ("brother," "sister," "daughter," etc.) of
   Line 4: Lover of _____ (list three things or people)
   Line 5: Who feels _____ (three items)
   Line 6: Who needs _____ (three items)
   Line 7: Who fears _____ (three items)
   Line 8: Who gives _____ (three items)
   Line 9: Who would like to see _____ (three items)
   Line 10: Resident of _____
   Line 11: Last name

A biopoem can also be adapted to different subject matter, as the following example of an elementary social studies teacher shows. In this modified version, the subject is the state of Virginia. Thus, the first line is not the name of the author but the name of the state. The second line lists three descriptive words about Virginia, and the third line adds to this list. In this version, the poem is condensed to contain only seven lines. Our biopoem is a biography of the state of Virginia.

Virginia
Coastal, warm, fertile
Land, missionary, adventure
Planter, slave, farmer
First, tobacco, General Assembly
Smith, Rolfe, Pocahontas
Southern Colony

Written by M. J. Weatherford. Used with permission.

6. Encourage students to write information they discover on a jot chart, then to use the jotted information to write essays. The jot chart developed by a secondary English teacher will guide her students as they write comparative essays about three short stories (see Activity 6.13). The jot chart developed by a secondary home economics teacher will guide her students as they write their own interpretation of the directions from a pattern (see Activity 6.14).

7. Cinquains, discussed in chapter 10 as a way to learn content vocabulary, are an excellent and readily implemented writing activity.

8. As a way to demonstrate understanding of newly learned vocabulary, the teacher can guide writing using a "What I Learned" activity (Miller, 1989):

   a)   List several fact words (the teacher sets the number) learned about a content subject.

   b)   Write a sentence about one of those words. (sentence 1)

   c)   Underline a noun or pronoun in sentence one and write a second sentence explaining it.

   d)   Underline the most important noun in the second sentence and write a third sentence explaining that noun.

   e)   Repeat steps a–d; use all of your words.

   Melvin Harris, a seventh grader, started his "What I Learned" writing activity this way:

   control group;ok group

   "[1]I have learned that a science experiment sometimes has a <u>control group</u>.[2] The control group does not receive any testing, treatment, or all of the things an <u>experimental group</u> receives."

A C T I V I T Y 6.13

Plot Jot Chart—Short Story

Directions: As each story is read, fill in the information about plot development. The events are listed on the board. They are not in the correct order.

	"The Monkey's Paw" p. 2	"The Most Dangerous Game" p. 11	"Sixteen" p. 27
Position			
Narrative Hook			
Rising Action			
Climax			
Falling Action			
Resolution			

Developed by Linda Cobb.

9. Request that students write regularly in a journal, under headings such as "The two new ideas I learned this week in science and how I can apply them to my life"; "How I felt about my progress in math class this week." These entries can be read by other students or by the teacher but should be valued for their introspective qualities and not graded. Glaze (1987) suggests several such assignments, which are featured in chapter 12. Walpole (1987) has discovered a

---

A C T I V I T Y   6.14

Reading the Guide Sheet

Skim the front of the Guide Sheet. List 6 major headings. List 3 facts about each major point. Find vocabulary words and write them in the last column.

Major Points	3 Facts	Vocabulary Words
Select pattern pieces	The # of pieces given. What the pieces are going to look like. The letter is to tell you what it stands for.	
Cutting and marking	What to do before you cut. What to do after cutting. Shows you some more special cutting notes.	pre-shrink press
Cutting layouts	Shows sizes. Tell you what pieces to use. Shows you the inches and cm.	nap dots
The pattern	Tells what the symbols mean. How to adjust pattern. Tells you what a normal seam allowance is.	grain line notches cutting line seam line seam allowance selvage
The jumper	Shows sizes. Shows inches and cm. Shows the pieces used.	nap selvage
Short overalls	Shows the pieces used. Shows inches and cm. Show sizes.	nap selvage

Developed by Frances Lila Mait.

strategy using learning logs, a currently used term for journal entries, which can replace the pop quiz:

CLASS LOGS: I first heard about class logs during a summer spent with the Northern Virginia Writing Project. The class log is a notebook maintained by a different student each day; the student simply takes his notes for the day in the class log instead of in his own notebook. Though there are many uses for the class log, its primary use is a reference for students who are absent. Never again will I have to listen to someone ask, "Did we do anything in here yesterday?" The class log is my proof. Since people generally take unusually good notes when writing in the log (because they feel their notes are 'on display'), absent students find the log convenient to learn from; this saves both them and me hours of individual catch-up sessions after school.

As a side benefit, the log often builds class spirit. I encourage students to take notes on everything going on, as long as the academics aren't slighted ("Oh, yay—it's snowing!!!! OK, back to radicals . . . math is the 'root' of civilization . . . boo!"). Students delight in finding themselves quoted, and will flip through the log looking for gossip or doodles, as well as for explanations of new material. When this kind of spirit erupts in a class, I find that it rather surprisingly contributes to the educational value of the log. Students don't just read the funny comments; they also find themselves noticing note-taking styles, and they begin competing informally to be the clearest and the best at taking notes. This increases their awareness of the importance of note-taking in general. Of course, some classes will maintain their log simply because I tell them they must and therefore never really benefit from it as they could. But the classes that make it into a gossipy game also end up creating an extremely valuable learning tool (pp. 56–57).

Guided Writing Procedure

We have shown how several of the activities and strategies we have presented in the past several chapters can incorporate writing and promote reading to learn. The guided writing procedure (Smith and Bean, 1980) is a strategy which specifically uses writing to enhance comprehension. Smith and Bean give seven steps for its implementation, to be completed in two days. On the first day, the teacher should

activate students' prior knowledge to facilitate prewriting,
have students factstorm and categorize their facts,
have students write two paragraphs using this organized list, and
have students read about the topic.

On the second day, the teacher should

have students check their drafts for functional writing concerns,
assign rewriting based on functional needs and revision to incorporate the information from the reading, and
give a quiz.

Activity 6.15 is an example of a modified guided writing procedure as one middle-school English teacher used it for helping her students write limericks.

ACTIVITY 6.15

Guided Writing for Limericks

Strategy: The purpose of this activity is to extend the students' abilities to compose a poem. They will achieve this purpose in a guided writing exercise. I have students write poetry because they will understand poetry better after they have become poets. The exercise will begin with clustering and from there the students will be guided through their first and final drafts. Because this is a guided exercise, I will first determine the students' background, build on that background, direct the study, and finally determine their comprehension. The final extension of this activity is publishing these poems.

First Step: prewriting (determining background)

The teacher writes the word *limerick* on the board and then draws a circle around it. He/She then asks the students to think about the characteristics of that word. As they give him/her the answers, the teacher writes them on extended lines from the main word. Then the teacher directs them to look at the limericks on page 449.

Second step: prewriting (building background)

The limericks are read and studied for rhyme scheme and rhythm. The characteristics are listed as further subtopics of the main topic limericks.

Third step: guiding the first draft (developing comprehension)

1. Tell the students that instead of writing limericks, they will be writing pigericks.
2. Pigericks are like limericks, except they are always about pigs. They are short, have lines that rhyme, and contain a definite rhythm. Furthermore, they are humorous.
3. Pass out handouts on pigericks and show Arnold Lobel's book titled *The Book of Pigericks*. Go over the poems noticing the similarities between limericks and pigericks.
4. On the board or overhead, begin a line for a pigerick. Have the students continue brainstorming the remainder of the poem.
5. Assign the writing of a pigerick. Monitor.

Fourth step: revising (reflection)

6. Have students exchange their poems and share suggestions.

(continued)

7. Students then revise and rewrite onto large index cards. Next, they illustrate.
8. Post the finished products on the bulletin board.

Clustering

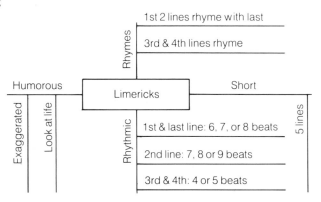

Students' Limericks:

There was a giant pig named Moe Cork
Who acted on a stage in New York
Said he, "Of we three
I am the greatest of thee"
Because my head is made of more pork.

There once was a piggy named Lance,
Who wanted to do nothing but dance.
He danced every day,
In a very awkward way.
But that was okay for dancing Lance.

Developed by Frances Lively.

The Revision Stage of Writing for Assisted Comprehension

At the revision stage, writers are concerned not only about the content of the writing but also about the form. After the writing is revised, an audience will read it and react in a formal way. During revision, writers are still learning to express what they understand about the information, but they are also learning to be considerate of their audience by putting the writing in a consistent, organized format. It is during revision that writers should be concerned with correct spelling, grammar, and organization. Often, teachers confuse the revision stage with the drafting stage and expect students to produce writing which meets format considerations before or while they are writing to express content. This is a difficult chore for the most polished writers.

Teachers sometimes question whether they should accept writing from students when it contains grammatical errors, misspellings, and other errors. "Surely seventh graders can write better than this!" they admonish. However, teachers must allow students to start where they are and to focus on one stage at a time.

Errors are a normal part of learning, and they will occur in student writing. The amount and types of writing practice students have had will determine their level of sophistication. If the pressures to focus on errors is eliminated during the prewriting and drafting stages, when content should be the focus, then attention to errors can be greater during the revision stage. If students have had these prewriting and drafting opportunities, their revised writing will reflect both improved content and improved form.

Teachers can assist students in their writing activities by making their expectations for the final product clear. When the students' writing is evaluated—after prewriting, drafting, and revision—students should understand what will be evaluated. Of course, the content of the writing is most important. But "content" is a vague criterion. To clarify expectations and grading criteria for students, Pearce (1983) suggests that teachers use a checklist or a rubric. A rubric is an expectation guide that lists the qualities of the papers—from the strongest to the weakest. A rubric aids the students, who can refer to it as they revise, and the teacher, who can refer to it during grading. Similarly, checklists are also useful because they list the features the teacher expects in the writing. Teachers can use a checklist to quickly rate the features in a written assignment, and students can check their papers against this list during revision. Figure 6.4 and Figure 6.5, which follow, are examples of a grading rubric and a checklist of writing quality.

Figure 6.4. A rubric for grading.

Paper topic: 1960s approaches to civil rights in the U.S.

High quality papers contain:
An overview of civil rights or their lack during the 1960s, with 3 specific examples.
A statement defining civil disobedience, with 3 examples of how it was used and Martin Luther King's role.
At least one other approach to civil rights, with specific examples, and a comparison of this approach with King's civil disobedience that illustrates differences or similarities in at least 2 ways.
Good organization, well developed arguments, few mechanical errors (sentence fragments, grammatical errors, spelling errors).

Medium quality papers contain:
An overview of Black civil rights during the 1960s, with 2 specific examples.
A statement defining civil disobedience, with 2 examples of its use and Martin Luther King's involvement.
One other approach to civil rights, with examples, and a comparison of it with King's civil disobedience by their differences.
Good organization, few mechanical errors, moderately developed arguments.

Lower quality papers contain:
A general statement defining civil disobedience with reference to Martin Luther King's involvement and at least 1 example.
One other approach to civil rights and how it differed from civil disobedience.
Fair organization, some mechanical errors.

Lowest quality papers contain:
A general statement on who Martin Luther King was or a general statement on civil disobedience.
A general statement that not all Blacks agreed with civil disobedience.
A list of points, poor organization, many mechanical errors.

From D. L. Pearce, "Guidelines for the use and evaluation of writing in content classrooms," *Journal of Reading*, December 1983. Reprinted with permission of D. L. Pearce and the International Reading Association.

The Role of Communicative Arts in Assisted Reading

We believe, as we shared in principle 1, that *the communicative arts work in concert and cannot be separated from education in content subjects.* "Writers, speakers, readers, and listeners all engage in reciprocal processes aimed at creating understanding through shared responsibilities of communication" (Alvermann, 1987b, p. 112). We have shown how it is possible to integrate communicative arts in the content areas through adapting the activities we have presented.

Figure 6.5. A general checklist of writing quality.

	Poor	Fair	Good	Outstanding	Superior
1. Definition of topic					
2. Exploration of topic (covered main points)					
3. Evidence to support generalizations					
4. Understanding beyond that of class and text					
5. Logical development of ideas					
6. Writing clarity					
7. Personal interpretation or reaction					
8. Summation of findings					
9. Correct spelling, diction, and grammatical usage					

Comments:

From D. L. Pearce, "Guidelines for the use and evaluation of writing in content classrooms," *Journal of Reading*, December 1983. Reprinted with permission of D. L. Pearce and the International Reading Association.

One-Minute Summary

What Can Teachers Do to Assist Comprehension?

Teachers must understand how to develop reading comprehension before testing it. By guiding readers and questioning carefully, they will achieve success in this endeavor. Writing to learn is often a good way to assist readers in their comprehension. We summarize what we have covered in this chapter by offering this "formula" for success:

Use PAR

By keeping the PAR steps in mind as they teach, teachers will find that students begin to understand and enjoy the content reading. The rewards are almost immediate as students perk up and get involved in their own learning. Assisting comprehension will not work without preparation; reflection will not work without assistance. PAR works when all steps are used in tandem.

Model

By demonstrating what they do to understand material as they read, teachers help students to learn. Teachers should "talk along" with their students. They need to demonstrate how they would go about learning what they are asking their students to comprehend.

Provide a Stimulating Environment

By offering a class where learning is enjoyable and active, teachers can encourage effective content reading. When students get to discuss and write, they are no longer passive learners. Relevance is clear.

Direct Students to Independence

Adult educators write about lifelong learners. The ultimate goal of content reading is surely to produce lifelong learners. Adults prefer to learn independently. Although they may study in formal courses, they identify their own areas of concentration and structure their learning accordingly. By introducing new activities, allowing plenty of practice, and then directing students to apply the strategies learned from those activities as they read on their own, teachers show students how to become independent learners. This independence goes a long way toward ensuring that students will still be learning about your subject long after they have graduated.

End-of-Chapter Activities

Preparing the Reader

1. How did chapter 5 prepare you to read this chapter? Did you have the foundation for understanding the points we made and the reasons for introducing guiding activities in your classroom?

2. How many of the terms did you recognize in advance? How many can you explain now?

Assisting Comprehension

1. Study the following map and, without looking at the beginning of the chapter, fill in this map with categories and supporting details which will make sense. You may look back through the chapter for clues.

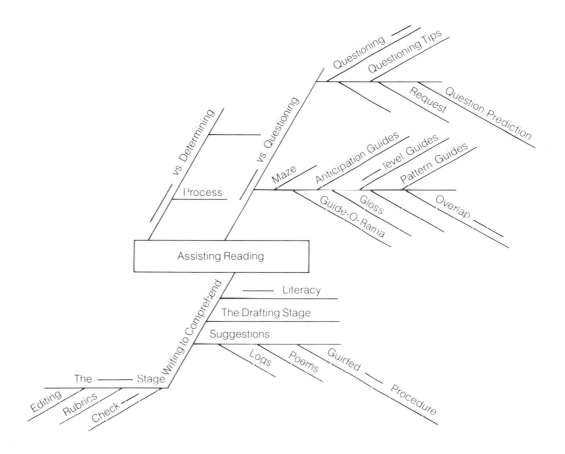

2. After completing the first two assisting activities, do you have any questions about the chapter content? If so, apply the "look-back" strategy by framing your questions and looking back to find the answers.

Reflecting on your Reading

1. Select a chapter from a content textbook. Reflect on what you have learned in this chapter by using the following questions to guide you in discovering what your text offers the teacher in the way of comprehension assistance:

What questioning aids are provided to help the teacher and students develop reading comprehension in this chapter? (e.g., study questions, beginning- or end-of-chapter questions, margin questions, DRTAs, QARs, etc.)

Are these questions specified as comprehension developers rather than as comprehension determiners?

Are the aids sufficient and suitable for your students?

What guiding, or nonquestioning, activities are provided to help develop students' comprehension? (e.g., mapping, pattern guides, three-level guides, etc.)

Are these aids sufficient and suitable for your students?

What new activities to develop comprehension might you want to design to supplement this chapter? Why?

2. Using the following chart, analyze the questions which accompany your textbook:

Question	Is It Fact / Implication / Application?	Is It Recall / Recognition?	Will It Develop / Determine?
#1			
#2			
#3			
.			
.			
.			

3. Identify the three most significant things you learned in this chapter. Jot them down and then draft an explanation of why these three items are important to you. Give specific examples of how you can use this new information in your own teaching. Keep this draft for reference in the next few months.

4. The book *Plain Talk* produced by the Virginia State Department of Education is an excellent resource for using writing to learn in content classrooms. It includes teachers' descriptions of writing activities.

References

Afflerbach, P. (1987). How are main idea statements constructed? Watch the experts. *Journal of Reading, 30*, 512–518.

Alvermann, D. (1987a). Discussion strategies for content area reading. In D. Alvermann, D. R. Dillon, D. G. O'Brien, (Eds.), *Using discussion to promote reading comprehension* (pp. 34–42). Newark, DE: International Reading Association.

Alvermann, D. (1987b). Integrating oral and written language. In D. Alvermann, D. Moore, & M. Conley, (Eds.), *Research within reach: Secondary school reading* (pp. 109–129.) Newark, DE: International Reading Association.

Applebee, A. N. (1981). Writing in the secondary school. Urbana, IL.: National Council of Teachers of English.

Babbs, P. & Moe, A. (1983). Metacognition: A key for independent learning from text. *The Reading Teacher, 36,* 422–426.

Bachman, C. (1989). Reading, Writing and Thinking Math Activities. Presented at the Capital Consortium Reading to Learn Conference, Richmond, VA 4/22/89.

Bader, L. & Pearce, D. (1983). Writing across the curriculum, 7–12. *English Education, 15,* 97–106.

Beyer, B. (1984). Improving thinking skills—defining the problem. *Phi Delta Kappan, 65,* 486–490.

Brown, A. Campione, J. C. & Day, J. (1981). Learning to learn: On training students to learn from texts. *Educational Research, 10,* 14–21.

Brown, A. & Day, J. (1983). Macrorules for summarizing texts: The development of expertise. *Journal of Verbal Learning and Verbal Behavior, 22,* 1–5.

Calkins, L. (1986). *The art of teaching writing.* Portsmouth, NH: Heineman.

Choate, J. S. & Rakes, T. A. (1987). The structured listening activity: A model for improving listening comprehension. *The Reading Teacher, 41,* 194–200.

Cunningham, R. & Shablak, S. (1975). Selective reading guide-o-rama: The content teacher's best friend. *Journal of Reading, 18,* 380–382.

Davison, D. & Pearce, D. (1988). Writing activities in junior high mathematics texts. *School Science and Mathematics, 88,* 493–499.

Dillon, J. T. (1983). *Teaching and the art of questioning.* Bloomington, IN: Phi Beta Kappa Educational Foundation. Fastback # 194.

Durkin, D. (1979). What classroom observations reveal about reading comprehension. *Reading Research Quarterly, 14,* 481–533.

Durkin, D. (1981). Reading comprehension instruction in five basal reading series. *Reading Research Quarterly, 16,* 515–544.

Finley, C. D. & Seaton, M. N. (1987). Using text patterns and question prediction to study for tests. *Journal of Reading, 31,* 124–132.

Gardner, M. K. & Sith, M. M. (1987). Does perspective-taking ability contribute to reading comprehension? *Journal of Reading, 30,* 333–336.

Garner, R., Hare, V. C., Alexander, P., Haynes, J. & Winograd, P. (1984). Inducing use of a text lookback strategy among unsuccessful readers. *American Educational Research Journal, 21,* 789–798.

Gebhard, A. (1983). Teaching writing in reading and the content areas. *Journal of Reading, 27,* 207–211.

Gere, A. (1985). *Roots in the sawdust—Writing to learn across the disciplines.* Urbana, IL: National Council of Teachers of English.

Glaze, B. (1987). Learning logs. In J. Self (Ed.) *Plain talk about learning and writing across the curriculum,* (pp. 149–154). Richmond, VA: Virginia State Department of Education.

Goodlad, J. (1984). *A place called school.* New York: McGraw-Hill.

Gusak, F. J. (1967). Teacher questioning and reading. *The Reading Teacher, 21,* 227–234.

Guthrie, J. T., Burnam, N., Caplan, R. I. & Seifert, M. (1974). The maze technique to assess and monitor reading comprehension. *The Reading Teacher, 28*, 161–168.

Hansen, J. (1981). The effects of inference training and practice on young children's comprehension. *Reading Research Quarterly, 16*, 391–417.

Hansen, J. & Pearson, D. (1983). An instructional study: Improving the inferential comprehension of fourth grade good and poor readers. *Journal of Educational Psychology, 75*, 821–829.

Heimlich, J. E. & Hittleman, S. D. (1985). *Semantic mapping: Classroom applications.* Newark, DE: International Reading Association.

Herber, H. (1978). *Teaching reading in the content areas.* Englewood cliffs, NJ: Prentice-Hall.

Hinchman, R. (1987). The textbook and three content area teachers. *Reading Research and Instruction, 26*, 247–263.

International Reading Association (1988). *New directions in reading instruction.* Newark, DE.

Jacobs, L. (1987). Reading, writing, remembering. *Teaching Pre K-8, 18*, 38.

Manzo, A. V. (1975). The guided reading procedure. *Journal of Reading, 18*, 287–291.

Manzo, A. V. (1969). The request procedure. *Journal of Reading, 11*, 123–126.

Miller, A. (1989). Writing To Learn in Science. Presented at the Capital Consortium Reading to Learn Conference, Richmond, VA. 4/22/89.

Muth, K. D. (1987). Structure strategies for comprehending expository text. *Reading Research and Instruction, 27*, 66–72.

Nessel, D. (1987). Reading comprehension: Asking the right questions. *Phi Delta Kappan, 68*, 442–445.

Novak, J. D. & Gowin, D. B. (1984). *Learning how to learn.* Cambridge, London: Cambridge University Press.

Paris, S. G., Cross, D. R. & Lipson, M. Y. (1984). Informal strategies for learning: A program to improve children's reading awareness and comprehension. *Journal of Educational Psychology, 76*, 1239–1252.

Pearce, D. (1983). Guidelines for the use and evaluation of writing in content classrooms. *Journal of Reading, 17*, 212–218.

Pearce, D. & Bader, L. (1984). Writing in content area classrooms. *Reading World, 23*, 234–241.

Pearce, D. (1987). Group writing activities: a useful strategy for content teachers. *Middle School Journal, 18*, 24–25.

Pearson, P. D. (1985). Changing the face of reading comprehension. *The Reading Teacher, 38*, 724–738.

Pearson, P. D. & Johnson, D. (1978). *Teaching reading comprehension.* New York: Holt, Rinehart & Winston.

Perez, S. A. & Strickland, D. (1987). Teaching children how to discuss what they read. *Reading Horizons, 27*, 89–94.

Raphael, T. (1984). Teaching learners about sources of information for answering comprehension questions. *Journal of Reading, 2*, 303–311.

Raphael, T. (1986). Teaching question answer relationships, revisited. *The Reading Teacher, 39*, 516–522.

Reutzel, D. R. & Daines, D. (1987). The text-relatedness of reading lessons in seven basal reading series. *Reading Research and Instruction, 27*, 26–35.

Santeusanio, R. (1983). *A practical approach to content area reading.* Reading, MA: Addison-Wesley.

Self, J. (1987). Getting the whole picture. In J. Self (Ed.), *Plain talk about learning and writing across the curriculum,* (pp. 1–8). Richmond, VA: Virginia State Department of Education.

Singer, H. and Donlan, D. (1985). *Reading and learning from text.* Hillsdale, NJ: Erlbaum.

Smith, S. & Bean, R. (1980). The guided writing procedure: Integrating content reading and writing improvement. *Reading World, 19,* 290–294.

Teale, W. & Sulzby, E. (1986). *Emergent literacy: Writing and reading.* Norwood, NJ: Ablex.

Vacca, R. & Vacca, J. (1989). *Content area reading.* Glenview, IL: Scott, Foresman.

Vygotsky, L. (1978). A prehistory of written language. In Scribner, et al (Eds.), *Mind in society: The development of higher psychological process.* Cambridge, MA: Harvard University Press.

Walpole, P. (1987). Yes, writing in math. In J. Self (Ed.). *Plain talk about learning and writing across the curriculum.* Richmond, VA: Virginia State Department of Education.

Wasserman, S. (1987). Teaching for thinking. *Phi Delta Kappan, 68,* 460–466.

Wigginton, E. (1986). *Sometimes a Shining Moment: The Foxfire Experience.* NY: Anchor Press/Doubleday.

Williams, J., Taylor, M. B. & Ganger, B. (1981). Text variations at the level of the individual sentence and the comprehension of simple expository paragraphs. *Journal of Educational Psychology, 73,* 851–865.

7 Reflecting on Learning through Critical Thinking

Every now and then a man's mind is stretched by a new idea and never shrinks backs to its former dimensions."

Oliver Wendell Holmes

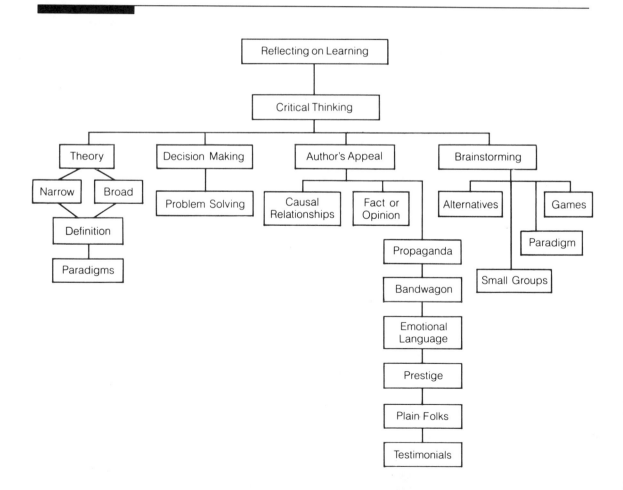

1. Please answer these questions to clarify your previous knowledge about critical thinking.

   What is your definition of critical thinking?

   List reasons why there could be no agreement on the exact nature of critical thinking.

   What systematic steps does a person have to take to solve a problem?

   What propaganda techniques do authors often use to get their ideas across?

2. Below is a list of terms used in this chapter. Some of them may be familiar to you in a general context, but in this chapter they may be used in a different way than you are used to. Rate your knowledge by placing a + in front of those you are sure that you know, a √ in front of those you have some knowledge about, and a 0 in front of those you don't know. Be ready to locate and pay special attention to their meanings when they are presented in the chapter:

   _____ effective thinking   _____ decision making
   _____ paradigm   _____ causal relationship
   _____ propaganda   _____ brainstorming
   _____ testimonial   _____ bandwagon
   _____ prestige   _____ fact
   _____ opinion

Objectives:

As you read this chapter, focus your attention on the following objectives. You will:

1. be able to understand the nature of critical thinking from its most narrow sense to its broadest sense.

2. understand the paradigm for teaching critical thinking as presented in this chapter.

3. be able to teach critical thinking by emphasizing causal relationships, fact and opinion, and propaganda.

4. be able to use brainstorming techniques described in the chapter to teach critical thinking skills to students.

5. be able to use critical thinking games described in the chapter to teach important critical thinking skills.

Peanuts. Reprinted with permission of UFS, Inc./United Media.

Purpose:

Teachers need to expand their repertoire of teaching techniques to include those which assist students in critical thinking. What does it really mean to teach *critical thinking* skills? This is arguably the "hottest" term currently being bandied about at all levels of education. But what exactly does one do when thinking critically? A case could be made that almost every chapter in this book is about critical thinking because the strategies described, when applied, encourage students to think about what they are reading in new and creative ways. It is our job in this chapter to ask you to think critically about the subject of critical thinking. We will analyze critical thinking, define it, and give examples of how it can be emphasized in the Reflection stage of the PAR framework.

Critical Thinking as Reflection

The third step in PAR is Reflection. By this step, the reader can extend the reading experience and begin to think critically about the reading material. As we pointed out earlier, Gray described this process as "reading beyond the lines." Without reflection, a reader may acquire knowledge but does not necessarily learn. Knowledge must be related in a meaningful way to what is already known so that it will be retained and become the base for further learning. Disembodied knowledge is difficult to remember or use. It can be argued that full understanding cannot be achieved until reflection occurs.

Extensions of the reading experience to include reflection can take many forms: further reading about the topic, additional activities from the teachers' manuals, oral presentations, guest speakers, class reports, or group debates. These activities are valuable and important because they can provide a pleasurable association with the content being studied.

One of the most important ways to have students reflect on reading is to ask them to think critically about what they read. Postreading activities designed to improve critical thinking are a crucial part of learning in content area subjects (Clary, 1977). However, recent studies and national reports have indicated that it is also a neglected part of instruction in schools today. As cited in chapter 1 the 1986 National Association of Educational Progress report (Kirsch and Jungeblut, 1986) indicated that today's young adults are literate but have difficulty with the more complex and challenging reading that is required in adult life. The study notes the inability of young people to analyze in order to come to understand more complicated material. Sternberg (1985) laments the lack of correspondence between what is required for critical thinking in adulthood and what is being taught in schools today.

By reinforcing the reading experience through critical thinking, teachers can challenge students to think about content material in new ways. Too often, however, classroom teachers, especially at the elementary level, shy away from teaching critical thinking. The following are some reasons why, we believe, teachers do not emphasize critical thinking:

1. There is confusion over a clear definition of the construct.
2. They have a misguided notion that "critical" means to find fault and emphasize the negative.
3. It is difficult to measure critical reading and thinking skills through tests.
4. Critical thinking skills often are not mandated for minimum competency in a subject.
5. Teachers have a false notion that slow learners and at-risk students are not capable of thinking critically.
6. Teachers perceive that they do not have adequate time to plan instruction in critical thinking.
7. Teachers lack books, materials, and resources to teach critical thinking.

Despite these reservations, the teaching of critical thinking should not be neglected at any K–12 grade level. This important ability will lead to greater success in academic subjects and will be of use to students after graduation. In short, critical thinking is a skill which will aid students in all facets of life, during and beyond the school day (Newton, 1978).

Theoretical Base for Critical Thinking

Critical thinking as an important dimension of learning is currently being promoted in textbooks, in the research literature, and in published programs. Interest in the area is underscored by Unks (1985), who stated, "The ability to think critically is one of the most agreed upon educational objectives" (p. 240). Even though almost everyone agrees that some elements of critical thinking need to be taught across the curriculum, the concept remains so vague that educators are not certain of its meaning, of the best ways for classroom teachers to teach it, and whether it can be taught. After examining a textbook on critical thinking, a reviewer once remarked: "It was a good book but it really didn't contain much critical thinking." This comment underscores the subjective view of the concept—there is no overall accepted definition.

The literature, in fact, supports two interpretations of critical thinking. The first is a narrow definition of critical thinking as the mastery and use of certain skills necessary for the assessment of statements (Beyer, 1983; Ennis, 1962). These skills take the same form as logic or deduction and may include judging the acceptability of authority statements, judging contradictory statements, and judging whether a conclusion follows necessarily from its premises (Ennis, 1962, p. 84). A more encompassing definition includes the skills mentioned above as well as inductive types of skills such as hypothesis testing, proposition generation, and creative argument (Facione, 1984; Ennis, 1981; McPeck, 1981; Sternberg and Baron, 1985). If this definition is accepted, one can agree that the emphasis throughout this text is critical thinking.

We can clarify our view of critical thinking by studying what happens when the skill is put to use. McPeck (1981, p. 13) has identified the following features of critical thinking:

1. Critical thinking cannot be taught in the abstract, in isolation. It is not a distinct subject but is taught in content disciplines. It is critical thinking "about something."
2. While the term may have one correct meaning, the criteria for its correct application vary from discipline to discipline.
3. Critical thinking does not necessarily mean disagreement with, or rejection of, accepted norms.
4. It deals with the student's skill to think in such a way as to suspend or temporarily reject evidence from a discipline when the student feels there is insufficient data to establish truth of some proposition.
5. Critical thinking includes the thought process involved in problem solving and active thinking.
6. Formal and informal logic are not sufficient for thinking critically.
7. Because critical thinking involves knowledge and skill, a critical thinker in one discipline might not be a critical thinker in another discipline.
8. Critical thinking has both a "task" and an "achievement" phase. It does not necessarily imply success.
9. Critical thinking may include the use of methods and strategies as exmplars.
10. Critical thinking does not have the same scope or boundaries as rationality, but it is a dimension of rational thought.

McPeck suggests that at the core of critical thinking is "the propensity and skill to engage in an activity with reflective skepticism" (p. 8). In our complex and rapidly changing society, this ability to be reflective and to be skeptical in weighing evidence before making decisions is of great importance.

Over fifty years ago John Dewey (1933) spoke of the importance of reflective thinking:

> When a situation arises containing a difficulty or perplexity, the person who finds himself in it may take one of a number of courses. He may dodge it, dropping the activity that brought it about, turning to something else. He may indulge in a flight of fancy, imagining himself powerful or wealthy, or in some other way in possession of the means that would enable him to deal with the difficulty. Or, finally, he may face the situation. In this case, he begins to reflect (p. 102).

Students in kindergarten through twelfth grade are seldom taught to reflect, to solve problems by "facing the situation," except in published programs on thinking or in "critical thinking" sections of basal reading materials. The first of McPeck's features calls into question the effectiveness of any published program that teaches critical thinking as a skill, isolated from content. Also, Reyes (1986) in a review of a social studies series, found that "publishers do not deliver material that develops strong critical thinking, even though they have promised it" (p. 153). In another study, researchers (Woodward, Elliott, and Nagel, 1986) found that the critical thinking skills emphasized in elementary basal material were those that could be most readily tested, such as map and globe skills.

Evidence indicates that teachers do not need published "thinking" programs and that they cannot depend upon basal reading materials to teach critical thinking skills. However, they do need to integrate their own critical thinking lessons with those of the textbook. For example, to teach critical thinking, teachers may present a paradigm, then have small groups of students practice the steps of the paradigm with carefully chosen textbook lessons and problem-solving exercises. In this manner, students are taught critical thinking in a concrete context of carefully guided thinking. Studies indicate that, especially at early adolescence, formal reasoning and thinking can best be taught through the teacher's use of guided "prompts" such as paradigms, which enable students to structure their thinking more easily (Danner and Day, 1977; Stone and Day, 1978; Karpus, Karpus, Formisano, and Paulsen, 1977; Shayer, Kuchemann, and Wylam, 1976; Arlin, 1984; Martorano, 1977; Strahan, 1983). In addition to asking teachers to emphasize critical thinking, noted educator Art Costa has called for a school environment where principals and other school leaders encourage teachers "to look carefully at the intelligent behavior of their own students" (Brandt,

1988, p. 13). Further, Costa calls for administrators to model intelligent behavior themselves by:

1. spending time talking about thinking;
2. releasing teachers to engage in critical thinking themselves; and
3. purchasing materials to support critical thinking.

In this text, critical thinking is seen as that multifaceted and complex process alluded to by McPeck which deals with the ability of students to gather data, test hypotheses, and reflect in a skeptical and disciplined manner. The eventual products of this process are life decisions made by persons under pressure to think. Critical thinking, then, is what Moore, McCann, and McCann (1985) call *effective thinking*. The remainder of this chapter presents ways in which teachers at all grade levels can help students use effective thinking to make decisions.

Paradigm for Teaching Critical Thinking

Students will learn more easily and retain information longer when the teacher uses systematic steps—a *paradigm*—to make the class aware of the skill being emphasized. Any critical thinking topic—relevance, propaganda, propositions, or arguments—can be taught in this manner. Teacher should take the following steps to create awareness in the learner:

1. *Explain the skill to be taught.* Explain to students that they will be asked to think in a certain way, to make judgments, and to practice effective thinking. Define the skill and give examples of its use. The definition should be on paper or on the chalkboard so that the skill being taught can be reemphasized at times throughout the lesson.
2. *Introduce the lesson.* When introducing the content lesson, make certain that new information is related to students' prior knowledge.
3. *Develop structured practice using the skill.* Ask students to read the text material or study the problem. Explain how students are to use the critical thinking skill appropriately. Have students practice using the skill for twenty to thirty minutes.
4. *Have students report on their use of the skill.* Students should discuss their observations on how well they acquired the skill or used the skill in a structured practice. They should relate problems and ways to improve in the use of the skill.
5. *Summarize how the skill was used in the content lesson.* Explain again why the skill is important for students to master and how it helped students understand the lesson better.
6. *Review and reinforce the skill.* During the next class period, or certainly within a week, reinforce the skill by asking students to practice using the skill.

A C T I V I T Y   7.1

(Language Arts)

Early Elementary

Skill: **Predicting alternatives**

Step 1. Teacher explains that students need to sometimes find alternatives by thinking about possible events.

Step 2. Teacher reads a story aloud, stopping at crucial points of interest.

Step 3. Teacher asks students to predict as many as four outcomes from what has been read to them. Responses are recorded by teacher on the chalkboard.

Step 4. Students are asked why they chose a particular response.

Step 5. Teacher completes story in this manner and summarizes why it is important to practice this skill.

Elementary

Skill: **Fact or opinion**

Step 1. Teacher explains why it is important for students to differentiate fact from opinion, giving examples of each. She tells students that they will be practicing this skill for several weeks.

Step 2. Teacher has students read silently a newspaper editorial on a current topic of interest. Students discuss what they know about the topic.

Step 3. Teacher has all students underline statements in the article. Students form groups to decide which statements are fact and which are opinion.

Step 4. Groups report back to teacher and discuss why they made particular choices.

Step 5. Teacher summarizes both the lesson and the importance of practicing this skill.

7. *Continue practice with the skill.* It is advisable to go through steps 1 through 5 in at least ten additional lessons. For elementary and middle-school students, this practice should be with different content lessons, to ensure transfer of the skill to other disciplines.

Using this paradigm will help students to acquire skills through guided practice and through repeating the use of the skill a number of times in a structured setting: acquisition of the skill through direct teaching of the skill, internalization of the skill through repeated prac-

A C T I V I T Y 7.2

(Social Studies)

Early Elementary

Skill: **Detecting propaganda techniques**

Step 1. Teacher gives students worksheet listing propaganda techniques: emotional language, generalities, bandwagon effect, plain-folks approach, overuse of endorsements. Teacher explains that these can influence the reader's judgment of the material and relates these techniques to prior knowledge of students.

Step 2. Teacher introduces lesson on political cartoons of World War I and their effect on U.S. citizens.

Step 3. Students form groups to decide techniques used in the cartoons.

Step 4. Groups report back to teacher and discuss findings.

Step 5. Teacher leads discussion, summarizes lesson, and reemphasizes the importance of the skill learned.

Elementary

Skill: **Evaluating consequences of action**

Step 1. Teacher explains that students need to learn to evaluate consequences of possible courses of action. Gives worksheet with 1:3 ratio of occurrence to consequence. "If this happens, then these three consequences could occur . . ."

Step 2. Students read to climax or exciting part of story. Together, students list four or five actions protagonist could take.

Step 3. In groups, students list positive and negative consequences that could occur from each action.

Step 4. Groups report back to teacher and discuss findings.

Step 5. Teacher leads discussion, summarizes lesson by reading what protagonist actually does in story, and reemphasizes the importance of the skill learned.

tice, and transfer of the skill to other learning contexts. This type of teacher intervention is a necessary step in improving cognitive ability. Pearson and Tierney (1983) assess the instructional paradigm most used by teachers at present, which features the use of many practice materials, little explanation of cognitive tasks, little interaction with students about the nature of specific tasks, and strong emphasis on one correct answer, to the extent that teachers supply answers if there is any confusion over a task. Not surprisingly, Pearson and Tierney conclude that such a paradigm is ineffective. We think that the paradigm we describe compares favorably.

Activities 7.1 and 7.2, on pages 251 and 252, illustrate how our critical thinking paradigm can be used by teachers at different grade levels. Only the first five steps are included in these examples.

Critical Thinking To Solve Problems and Make Decisions

Probably one of the most important aspects of critical thinking is that it leads to effective decision making. Figure 7.1 presents a model that illustrates steps in problem solving, all of which lead to effective decision making. The most important by-product of having students use such a model is that they will be more effective thinkers; both their creative and contemplative abilities will improve (Parnes and Noller, 1973).

We offer the following stages in problem solving:

1. *Gathering ideas and information.* Students brainstorm to generate enough information to begin defining the problem. They can play the "reading detective" game or do research to gather information from all possible sources.
2. *Defining the problem.* At this stage, students should recognize the need to resolve a situation that has no apparent solution. Students should also be asked to clarify the nature of the task and completely describe the situation in writing.
3. *Tentative conclusions formed.* This is a creative phase in which possible solutions are suggested from available data.
4. *Testing conclusions.* Students discuss in groups which conclusions work best as solutions to the problem. Poor choices are eliminated

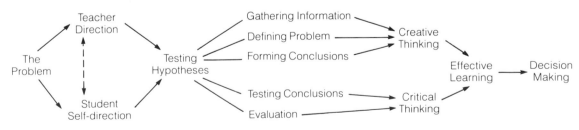

Figure 7.1 Model for Problem Solving

until workable solutions remain. Students may also establish criteria for evaluating outcomes.

5. *Making a decision.* Students give reasons for selecting one of the remaining solutions. They choose from among these alternatives.

Study guides, such as the one in Figure 7.2, can be constructed by teachers as cognitive maps to assist students in using the problem-solving steps detailed in Figure 7.1. Figure 7.3 shows a postgraphic

Figure 7.2 Critical Thinking Guide on Ways to Solve a Problem.

Problem	
Why do we need to solve problem	
Ways to Solving Problem	Reasons for Choosing Method
Method 1	Positive outcomes
	Negative outcomes
Method 2	Positive outcomes
	Negative outcomes
Method 3	Positive outcomes
	Negative outcomes
Best Way to Solve Problem	Reasons for Choosing to Solve Problem in this Manner

Adapted from a decision making model by McTighe, J. and Ryman, F.T., Jr. (1988), Cueing Thinking in the Classroom: The promise of theory-embedded tools, *Educational Leadership*, 45, 7, pp. 18–24.

Figure 7.3 Postgraphic Organizer: Similarity in Themes of Two Stories.

Story Reflection		
Story 1		Story 2
Theme:		Theme:
Event		Event
Event	How themes are similar	Event
Event		Event

A C T I V I T Y   7.3

Decision-Making Model for Mathematics

Mr. and Mrs. Smith wanted to go to Walt Disney World for a week's vacation. They estimated hotels at $75 a night and meals at $50 a day. Plane tickets were $350, round-trip, for each of them. However, through an enterprising travel agent they found a super-saver package for a week's stay at Disney World that included meals, round-trip fare, and lodging for both of them for $210 a day. Which was the least expensive way for the Smiths to take their vacation?

1. *Defining the problem*
   A couple wishes to travel to Walt Disney World in the least expensive way.
2. *Gathering ideas and information*
   First plan: Hotels–$75 a night for 7 nights
   　　　　　　　Meals–$50 a day for 7 days
   　　　　　　　Plane tickets–$350 each for 2 people
   Second plan: Total cost–$210 a day for 7 days
3. *Forming tentative conclusions*
   Determine cost of first plan by multiplying to find total costs for room, food, and air fare.
   Determine super-saver cost by multiplying per diem cost by 7 days.
4. *Testing conclusions*
   Compare costs of first and second plan.
5. *Making a decision*
   First vacation = $1,575
   Second vacation = $1,470
   Super-saver makes sense!

organizer which can be completed by students to discover the analogies between two stories. It is especially important to start this type of activity in early elementary classrooms because unsophisticated learners seldom let their minds journey *across* stories to think about possible similarities of themes. Activity 7.3 shows how the decision-making model can be used in mathematics.

Group decision making can also be taught in consumer mathematics through the use of a "group-and-label" technique. Begin by writing the topic on the board and telling students that they will be reviewing important terminology. Then have students volunteer any terms they can think of that fall under the topic heading. The teacher may

A C T I V I T Y 7.4

Mathematics for the Consumer

unit price	check stub	take-home pay
sales slip	deposit slip	balance
regular time	gross pay	checkbook
cash	sales tax	fractional price
checking account	time card	social security
straight time	withdraw	commission
estimate	net pay	bank statement
overtime	average price	overdrawn
FICA	cancelled check	salary plus commission
outstanding check	piece rate	certified check
reconciliation statement	endorsed	deposit
income	withholding tax	
wage		

Group and Label

Product Purchasing	*Money Records—Banking*	*Wages*
unit price	cash	regular time
sales slip	reconciliation statement	straight time
estimate	outstanding check	overtime
sales tax	certified check	income
average price	endorsed	wage
fractional price	checking account	gross pay
	checkbook	net pay
	deposit slip	take-home pay
	deposit	withholding tax
	withdraw	FICA
	check stub	social security
	balance	piece rate
	bank statement	commission
	overdrawn	salary plus commission
	cancelled check	time card

ask leading questions or even eliminate this step by preparing the list in advance on the board or on a worksheet. Have students reorganize the list into smaller lists of items which have something in common. Each of these sublists should then be given a label. Students may work individually or in small groups to reorganize and label the words. Activity 7.4 provides an example of a group-and-label technique.

Critical Thinking to Analyze Authors' Techniques

Examining the Author

Rarely are students asked to examine the background of an author to determine whether the author is noted for a particular bias. However, as students evaluate textbook information, they should note the source of that information. Most important, they should ask who the writer is and what his or her qualifications are. Baumann and Johnson (1984, p. 78) ask that students read with these questions in mind:

1. What is the source? Is anything known about the author's qualifications, the reputation of the publisher, and the date of publication?
2. What is the primary aim of the author—information, instruction, or persuasion?
3. Are the statements primarily facts, inferences, or opinions?
4. Does the author rely heavily on connotative words that may indicate a bias?
5. Does the author use negative propaganda techniques?

Students can be given these questions to think about and discuss in groups as they read a narrative or expository selection. Also, students can be supplied with multiple-choice items, such as those in Activity 7.5, to aid them in learning to determine an author's qualifications for writing accurate and unbiased statements on a subject. Such an activity can be used to begin class discussion on a reading and to debate after a reading.

Seeing Causal Relationships

Another very important critical thinking skill students need to learn is the ability to distinguish cause and effect when reading text materials, especially in social studies and science. In Chapter 5 this pattern of organization was explained. Simply asking students to search for causes is often not successful; students tend to neglect this critical thinking skill, or worse, misunderstand and misuse it without the teacher's intervention, support, and patience. Moreover, finding causal relationships is difficult because the cause of an event or situation may not be known or may not be traceable. Even so, students should practice distinguishing cause and effect for the practice in thinking it affords regardless of outcome. At the elementary level, this can be achieved through cause-effect story maps which depict the interrelationships in a series of unfolding events. Activity 7.6 provides an example of such a story map.

A C T I V I T Y 7.5

Reliability of Information

Supply students with the following multiple-choice items and others like them. The student checks the source that is most reliable of the three supplied.

1. Japan has the highest per capita income of any country in the world.
    ____ a. Joan Armentrag, salesperson at Bloomingdale's
    ____ b. Bob Hoskins, star golfer
    ____ c. Dr. Alice MacKenzie, economic analyst, the Ford Foundation
2. Mathematics is of no use to anyone.
    ____ a. Bob Brotig, high school dropout
    ____ b. Bill Johnson, editor, *The Mathematics Teacher*
    ____ c. Susan Winnifred, personnel, the Rand Corporation
3. We have proved that honey bees communicate with each other.
    ____ a. John Bowyer, salesman, Sue Ann Honey Co.
    b. Jane Maupin, high-school biology teacher
    ____ c. Martha Daughtry, bank teller
4. Forty-six percent of all married women with children now work outside the home.
    ____ a. Sue Ann Begley, electrician
    ____ b. Carol Radziwell, professional pollster
    ____ c. Joe Blotnik, marriage counselor
5. We must stop polluting our bays and oceans.
    ____ a. Clinton Weststock, president, Save the Bay Foundation
    ____ b. Marjorie Seldon, engineer, Olin Oil Refinery, Gulfport, MI
    ____ c. Carl Kanipe, free-lance writer of human-interest stories

A C T I V I T Y 7.6

Cause-Effect Story Map

List of events:

1. MaLien is a poor peasant boy who lives in a small village in China.
2. MaLien loves to draw.
3. MaLien is given a magic brush by a wizard.
4. MaLien helps the people of his village.
5. The mandarin sees the power of the brush.
6. The mandarin has MaLien put in prison.
7. MaLien escapes with the help of his brush.
8. MaLien helps more people.
9. The mandarin captures MaLien again.
10. The mandarin forces MaLien to use the magic of his brush for selfish reasons.
11. MaLien tricks the mandarin.

These events are depicted by the following story map:

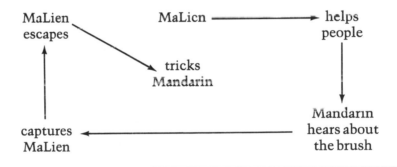

From MaLien and the Magic Brush by Alvin R. Tresselt

For older students, cause-and-effect study guides can be constructed, such as those shown in Activities 7.7 and 7.8.

Cause-Effect Guide

Below is a list of *effects* of the natural laws discovered by Kepler and Newton. Each was *caused* by one of those laws. Match the causes in the second column to the effects listed in the first column and be prepared to explain your choices.

Effects	Causes
____ 1. Mercury, which is the planet closest to the sun, completes one orbit faster (68 days) than the Earth does (365.24 days).	a. Kepler's first law (all planets travel in elliptical orbits).
____ 2. A car moving 50 mph hits a car stopped on the highway. People not wearing seat belts are thrown forward into the windshield.	b. Kepler's second law (the law of areas).
____ 3. A person shoots a shotgun and is knocked backward as the gun fires.	c. Kepler's third law (the size of the ellipse is related to its period).
____ 4. The Earth is closer to the sun during part of its orbit around the sun than at other times.	d. Newton's first law (law of inertia).
____ 5. Halley's comet traveled at a much faster speed as it neared perihelion than when it approached aphelion.	e. Newton's second law (force affects momentum).
____ 6. A baseball pitcher throws the ball, the hitter hits it with the bat, and the ball sails over the center-field fence for a home run!	f. Newton's third law (action-reaction).

Cause-Effect Guide

The Diary of Anne Frank, a play by Frances Goodrich and Albert Hackett.

Match the cause in column A with the effect or result in column B.

A/Causes

_____ 1. Otto Frank is the only survivor of the secret annex.

_____ 2. Miep helps the people in the annex by bringing them food and news from the outside world.

_____ 3. Anne uses her imagination to take a walk in the park.

_____ 4. Mr. Van Daan is caught stealing food.

_____ 5. Anne uses her creativity to make presents for Hanukkah.

_____ 6. Mrs. Van Daan refuses to give up her fur coat.

_____ 7. Peter and Anne grow fond of each other.

_____ 8. Anne is growing up.

_____ 9. Anne is closer to her father than her mother.

_____ 10. The night of Hanukkah, the members of the secret annex hear a thief in the warehouse.

B/Effects

A. Anne achieves a certain freedom while she is in hiding.

B. The inhabitants experience a moment of escape from the reality of war.

C. The members of the annex were able to survive there for over two years.

D. The members of the annex regard Mrs. Van Daan as materialistic.

E. Otto Frank has Anne's diary published.

F. Tension is created between Mrs. Frank and the Van Daans.

G. Anne is continually discovering things about herself.

H. The mothers become worried that their children are becoming too close.

I. The suspense in the play is increased by a new worry that the Green Police will discover their hiding place.

J. Mrs. Frank is hurt when Anne wants her father after her nightmare.

Developed by Linda Love

A C T I V I T Y 7.9

Concept Mapping

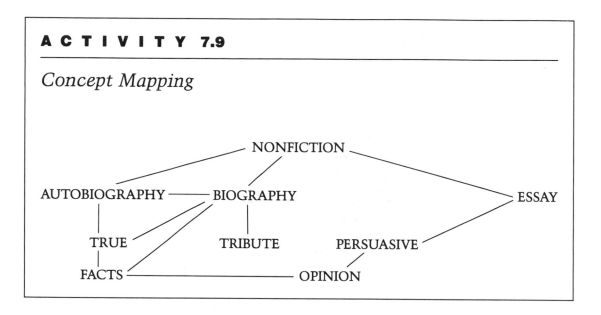

Distinguishing Fact and Opinion

Separating fact from opinion is another higher-level thinking skill that can be taught to students starting in early elementary years. To do so, teachers must train students to see relationships between and among facts, to interpret fact from opinion, to judge subtle inferences of the author, and to interpret the deeper meanings the author had in mind in his writing. Often the reader must bring to bear his past experiences and background to attempt accurate interpretations. With frequent practice, a student can become adept at interpreting the author's point of view and at detecting the biases in the writing. Activities 7.9, 7.10 and 7.11 present ideas for constructing guides and worksheets to illustrate fact and opinion, to help students distinguish one from the other, and to give students practice in writing facts and opinions.

Teachers can also provide practice in distinguishing fact from opinion, explained as mapping in chapter 6, by constructing semantic webbing exercises, with the "webs" partially filled in with facts and opinions. Students are asked to discuss these in groups and to report which descriptions are fact and which are opinion; they are also asked to fill in remaining blanks with *facts only* from the textbook (see Activity 7.12).

A C T I V I T Y 7.10

Worksheet on Fact and Opinion

Place a check by the sentences that state opinions:

_____ 1. Let me tell you about the wild parade.

_____ 2. Young children participating in parades usually look foolish.

_____ 3. Doctors are certified every five years.

_____ 4. According to a recent poll, four out of five doctors feel that their insurance rates are too high.

_____ 5. The sunrise turned the snowy peak a pastel pink.

_____ 6. Van Gogh painted *Starry Night*.

_____ 7. Certain details in *Starry Night* indicate Van Gogh's emotional disturbance.

_____ 8. Last night, every time I bowled the first ball of a frame, I left one pin standing.

_____ 9. The disorder in my room is depressing.

_____ 10. After I drop my books on my desk and throw my clothes on the floor, my room is a mess.

Detecting Propaganda Techniques

Skilled readers know how to absorb important information and throw away what is of no use. They are adept especially at recognizing *propaganda*—persuasive, one-sided statements used to change beliefs or sway opinion. Propaganda can be glaring or extremely subtle, and students need to be made aware, even in the elementary years, of the effects propaganda can have, particularly in the marketplace.

The following are the most often-used forms of propaganda:

1. Appeal to Bandwagon—aimed at the "masses" to join a large group that is satisfied with an idea or product. Readers of this kind of propaganda are made to feel left out if they don't go along with the "prevalent thinking."

2. Emotional Language—plays on the *connotations* of words. Words are carefully chosen to evoke strong feelings in the reader.

3. Appeals to Prestige—a person, product, or concept is associated with something deemed to be important or prestigious by the viewer or reader.

A C T I V I T Y 7.11

Worksheet on Stating Opinions

Directions: Limit the general subjects below and then state a precise opinion about each limited subject.

Example:
General Subject: Traveling

hitchhiking	is/are	dangerous
(limited subject)		(precise opinion)

1. General Subject: Politics

	is/are	
(limited subject)		(precise opinion)

2. General Subject: Medicine

	is/are	
(limited subject)		(precise opinion)

3. General Subject: Television

	is/are	
(limited subject)		(precise opinion)

4. General Subject: Sports

	is/are	
(limited subject)		(precise opinion)

5. General Subject: Education

	is/are	
(limited subject)		(precise opinion)

4. Plain Folks Appeal—the use of persons in an advertisement who seem typical, average, or ordinary (sometimes even dull). This is done to make readers or viewers feel that the people depicted are "regular" folks, like themselves. In this manner, a trust is built.
5. Testimonials—use of famous persons to give heightened credibility to a concept, idea, or product.

Teachers at all grade levels need to prepare students through "awareness" sessions to recognize propaganda techniques. For instance,

A C T I V I T Y 7.12

Semantic Webbing Exercise with Fish

Directions: Below you see the vertebrate FISH listed. Some of the major characteristics have been added. Please complete the characteristics.

Covered with scales

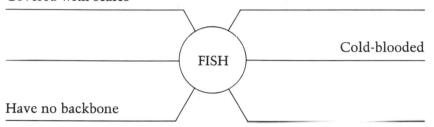

Cold-blooded

Have no backbone

after the techniques listed above are explained, students can be asked to bring in examples of advertisements from newspapers and magazines. In literature classes, students can be asked to discover examples in plays, short stories, and novels. *A Tale of Two Cities*, for example, contains examples of each of these propaganda techniques. Master storytellers like Charles Dickens know how to use such techniques deftly to develop complicated plots.

Activity 7.13, which follows, is an example of an activity to teach students to recognize propaganda. Students are asked to match statements to the propaganda technique they employ.

Critical Thinking through Brainstorming

An activity appropriate to any grade level is brainstorming. Sessions can last from ten minutes to one hour and can be designed to teach any of the techniques discussed in this chapter. An especially productive brainstorming session is one in which small groups of students list as many possible alternatives to a problem as they can. Group captains are chosen to report findings to the entire class. The teacher lists on the chalkboard alternatives deemed worthy by the class. Discussion then centers on how choices can be narrowed to one or two and why the final choices are the best ones. The critical thinking paradigm can

A C T I V I T Y 7.13

Stressing Propaganda

Match each statement with the correct propaganda technique.

a. appeals to bandwagon
b. emotional language
c. appeals to prestige
d. plain folks appeal
e. testimonial

___ 1. Come on down to Charlie Winkler's Auto before every one of these beauties is sold.

___ 2. Larry Bird, star Boston Celtic forward, thinks Reebok shoes are the best.

___ 3. You'll be glowing all over in your new Evening Time gown.

___ 4. Why, people in every walk of life buy our product.

___ 5. Join the American Dining Club today, a way of life for those who enjoy the good life.

___ 6. Already, over 85 percent of our workers have given to this worthy cause.

___ 7. I'll stack our doughnut makers up against any others, as the best in the business!

___ 8. Even butcher Fred Jones likes our new frozen yogurt coolers.

___ 9. One must drink our fine wine to appreciate the truly fine things in life.

___ 10. Lift the weights that Arnold Schwartzenegger lifts—a sure way to a better body.

be emphasized as the framework for the lesson. Another important consideration in these sessions is the size of the brainstorming group. Five-person groups seem to work best; however, three- and four-person groups are also suitable. With groups of over six students, the more vocal students tend to dominate. Brainstorming is creative in nature; it differs from factstorming, introduced in Chapter 3, where prior knowledge about facts already known is being determined.

The "ready reading reference bookmark" (Figure 7.4) developed by Kapinus (1986) can be used to get students ready to brainstorm after reading a passage. In the section "After you read" students can use brainstorming to perform the five thinking operations called for: retelling, summarizing, asking, picturing, and deciding. Students can also

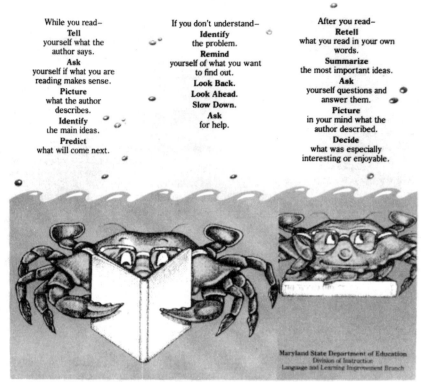

While you read—
Tell
yourself what the
author says.
Ask
yourself if what you are
reading makes sense.
Picture
what the author
describes.
Identify
the main ideas.
Predict
what will come next.

If you don't understand—
Identify
the problem.
Remind
yourself of what you want
to find out.
Look Back.
Look Ahead.
Slow Down.
Ask
for help.

After you read—
Retell
what you read in your own
words.
Summarize
the most important ideas.
Ask
yourself questions and
answer them.
Picture
in your mind what the
author described.
Decide
what was especially
interesting or enjoyable.

Maryland State Department of Education
Division of Instruction
Language and Learning Improvement Branch

Fig. 5. Ready Reading Reference Bookmark

Figure 7.4 Reprinted with permission of Barbara Kapinus, Maryland State
Department of Education.

brainstorm the "While you read" and "If you don't understand" operations at other points in the lesson, before reading, for example, or after reading specific sections.

Think-Reflect in Pairs (TRIP)

For this activity, the teacher divides students into pairs. Students share information on TRIP cards, which list propaganda techniques or situational problems. Answers are printed on the back of cards for immediate reinforcement. Points may be assigned to correct answers, with a designated number of points needed for a good grade in the class. For a different TRIP, students are presented problems from a textbook. They first solve the problem in pairs, then write the problem on the front

A C T I V I T Y 7.14

Think-Reflect in Pairs: TRIP card

Front   *Back*

| A manufacturer gets a World War II hero to make a statement praising his product.

Name the propaganda technique being employed. | testimonial

This correct answer worth 5 points. |

and the answer on the back of a card. In this manner, students create their own TRIP files for reinforcement or future use. Activity 7.14 shows the front and back of a TRIP card.

One-Minute Summary

Critical thinking, a "buzzword" in education, is like the weather: Everyone seems to talk about it, but no one seems to do much about it. Part of the problem is that we do not have an adequate definition of the term. One could take the view that whenever someone reflects or contemplates a fact, an opinion, or a concept, the person has thought critically about learning. To facilitate the teaching of critical thinking, we have presented a paradigm for students to use to practice reflective thinking. We have also suggested activities for brainstorming critical thought and for detecting an author's appeal to bias and propaganda. Closely related to careful and critical thought are decision making and problem solving, extremely important thinking skills. Students who cannot think critically often become poor decision makers or fail to solve problems adequately. It can be argued that no aspect of the curriculum is as important as getting students to think more critically about their own behavior as well as the behavior of people they meet in life and in books. Such thinking may be the very essence of democracy. Reflecting on learning through critical thinking is the third step in PAR.

End-of-Chapter Activities

Preparing the Reader

1. Did the four guide questions, the vocabulary terms, and the graphic overview at the beginning of the chapter adequately prepare you for reading this chapter?

2. Are your thoughts about critical thinking different now than they were at the beginning of the chapter? If so, how?

Assisting Comprehension

1. Choose a chapter in your textbook and decide how you could teach using the critical thinking paradigm described in this chapter. Can a problem be posed for the students to solve?

2. In the chapter you have chosen, is there evidence of the author's use of propaganda techniques?

3. Study the following graphic organizer and, without looking back at the beginning of the chapter, fill in the blocks with correct words that convey key concepts taught in this chapter. You may scan back through the chapter text.

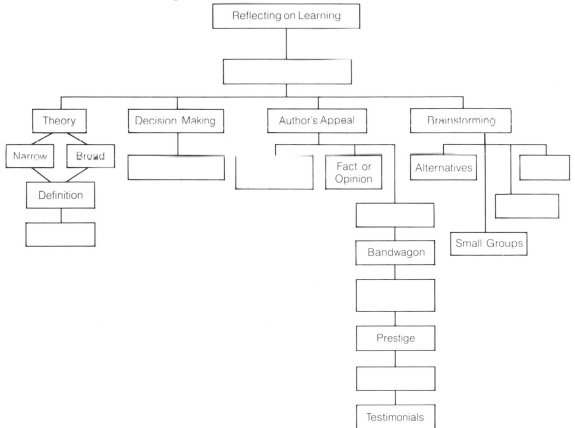

Reflecting on Your Reading

1. Critical thinking is *reflective thinking*. For two days, keep a reflective thinking journal to determine whether you are carefully thinking through problems as they arise or merely reacting intuitively. You can decide whether you are an intuitive or reflective thinker.

2. Can you formulate, from reading this chapter and from your background experience, your own definition of critical thinking? After doing so, check to see whether your definition is closer to the narrow view or the broad view of critical thinking described in this chapter.

References

Arlin, P.K. (1984). *Arlin test of formal reasoning.* East Aurora, NY: Slosson Educational Publications.

Bauman, J.F. & Johnson, D.D. (1984). *Reading instruction and the beginning teacher: A practical guide.* Minneapolis, MN: Burgess.

Beyer, B.K. (1983). Common sense about teaching thinking skills. *Educational Leadership, 41,* 44–49.

Brandt, R. (1988). On teaching thinking: A conversation with Art Costa. *Educational Leadership, 45,* 10–13.

Clary, L.M. (1977). How well do you teach critical thinking? *Reading Teacher, 31,* 142–147.

Danner, F.W., & Day, M.C. (1977). Eliciting formal operations, *Child Development, 48,* 1600–1606.

Dewey, J. (1933). *How we think.* Boston: Heath.

Ennis, R. (1962). A concept of critical thinking. *Harvard Educational Review, 30,* 81–111.

Ennis R. (1981). Rational thinking and educational practice. In J. Soltis (Ed.), *The philosophy of education* (pp. 143–183). Chicago: University of Chicago Press.

Facione, P.A. (1984). Toward a theory of critical thinking. *Liberal Education, 30,* 253–261.

Kapinus, B. (1986). *Ready reading readiness.* Baltimore, MD: Maryland State Department of Education.

Karpus, R., Karpus, E., Formisano, M. & Paulsen, A. (1977). A survey of proportional reasoning and control of variables in seven countries. *Journal of Research in Science Teaching, 14,* 411–417.

Kirsch, I.S. & Jungeblut, A. (1986). *Literacy: Profiles of America's young adults.* Princeton, NJ: National Assessment of Educational Progress.

Martorano, S. (1977). A development analysis of performance on Piaget's formal operations tasks. *Developmental Psychology, 13,* 66–72.

McPeck, J. (1981). *Critical thinking and education.* New York: St. Martin's Press.

McTighe, J. & Lyman, F.T., Jr. (1988). "Cueing thinking in the classroom: The promise of theory-embedded tools," *Educational Leadership, 45,* 7, pp. 18–24.

Moore, W.E., McCann, H., & McCann, J., (1981). *Creative and critical thinking (2nd ed.)* Boston: Houghton Mifflin.

Newton, B.T. (1978). Higher cognitive questioning and critical thinking. *Reading Improvement, 15,* 26–27.

Parnes, S.J., & Noller, R.B. (1973). *Toward supersanity: Channeled freedom.* East Aurora, NY: D.O.K. Publishers, Division of United Educational Services, Inc.

Pearson, P.D. & Tierney, R. (1983). In search of a model of instructional research in reading. In S. Parris, G. Okon, & H. Stevenson (Eds.), *Learning and motivation in the classroom.* Hillsdale, NJ: Erlbaum.

Reyes, D.J. (1986). Critical thinking in elementary social studies text series. *The Social Studies, 77,* 151–157.

Shayer, M., Kuchemann, D.E. & Wylam, H. (1976). The distribution of Piagetian stages of thinking in British middle and secondary school children. *British Journal of Educational Psychology, 46,* 164–173.

Sternberg, R.J. (1985). Teaching critical thinking, Part I. Are we making critical mistakes? *Phi Delta Kappan,* November, 194–198.

Sternberg, R.J., & Baron, J.B. (1985). A statewide apprach to measuring critical thinking skills. *Educational Leadership, 43,* 40–43.

Stone, C., & Day, M. (1978). Levels of ability of a formal operational strategy. *Child Development, 49,* 1054–1065.

Strahan, D.B. (1983). The emergence of formal reasoning during adolescence. *Transescence, 11,* 7–14.

Unks, G. (1985). Critical thinking in the social studies classroom. *Social Education, 44,* 240–246.

Woodward, A., Elliott, D.L. & Carter Nagel, K.C. (1986). Beyond textbooks in elementary social studies. *Social Education, 50,* 50–53.

8 Reading-Study Skills and Study Systems

Our future is as bright as it has ever been,
We have a chance to dream again,
Because of all the time that we've put in."

from "Time In" by The Oak Ridge Boys
1987, MCA Records, Inc.

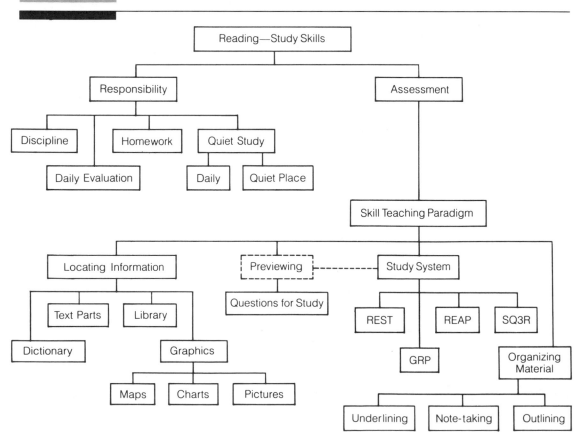

1. Assess yourself by checking whether you perform these skills when study-reading:

   _____ previewing
   _____ skimming
   _____ using a system for study
   _____ outlining
   _____ taking notes while reading
   _____ using table of contents
   _____ using glossary
   _____ using index
   _____ studying charts and graphs
   _____ studying maps and pictures

   How many skills did you check? How often do you share your study strategies with students? Remember that teachers are more willing to teach what they believe in and practice themselves.

2. Below is a list of terms used in this chapter. Some of them may be familiar to you in a general context, but in this chapter they may be used in a different way than you are used to. Rate your knowledge by placing a + in front of those you are sure that you know, a √ in front of those you have some knowledge about, and a 0 in front of those you don't know. Be ready to locate and pay special attention to their meanings when they are presented in the chapter:

   _____ mental set   _____ home reader
   _____ purpose   _____ paradigm
   _____ demand   _____ review/reinforcement
   _____ responsibility   _____ preview
   _____ compulsivity   _____ study system

Objectives: As you read this chapter, focus your attention on the following objectives. You will:

1. be able to understand the importance of training students to be responsible in early elementary classrooms as a precursor to study skills training.

2. be able to understand the importance of assessing students' ability to use study skills at all grade levels.

3. be able, after studying this chapter, to assess students at all grade levels in their use of study skills.

THE FAMILY CIRCUS®   **By Bil Keane**

"Grandma, are your teeth true
or false?"

Family Circus. Reprinted with special permission of Cowles Syndicate, Inc./King
Features Syndicate.

4. understand systems of study described in this chapter and be
   able to use them in your own classroom.
5. be able to instruct students in how to organize materials through
   underlining, note taking, and outlining.
6. be able to teach students how to locate information in textbooks
   and in the library.

Purpose: To be successful in content classrooms, today's students need to have
study skills and to use study systems to improve their
comprehension of assigned text material. Teachers need to be
sensitive to the importance of teaching these skills as they teach
content.

Reading and Study Skills: An Important Combination

In 1917 Thorndike described the process of reading a paragraph. Today,
educators could profit from studying his interpretation for its remark-
able clarity about the nature of the reading process:

Understanding a paragraph is like solving a problem in mathematics. It consists in selecting the right elements of the situation and putting them together in the right relations, and also with the right amount of weight or influence or force for each. The mind is assailed as it were by every word in the paragraph. It must select, repress, soften, emphasize, correlate and organize, all under the influence of the right mental set or purpose or demand. (p. 329)

As Thorndike suggests, reading can be seen as a problem-solving task. This task can be difficult because it requires that readers have a positive attitude toward the purpose for reading, the demands of the text, and their own background experience. Most important, the reader must be in a good frame of mind—have a good mental set—and must have clarity of thought before beginning to read. Reading for study cannot occur unless these conditions are met. In short, the combination of reading and study is a disciplined inquiry which demands much training over many years of schooling.

Although children are taught to read at an early age, often there is no concomitant emphasis on study or study skills (Durkin, 1978–79; Wertsch, 1978; Schallert and Kleiman, 1979). In middle school—or even high school—a teacher may announce that for a period of time students will be trained in how to study and better retain information they have read. We find two problems with this approach: it is isolated from the reading process and transmits the message that study isn't really connected to reading; and this focus on study skills in middle school or high school transmits the message that study skills are pertinent and applicable only late in one's education.

It is because of this hit-or-miss approach toward teaching study and retention strategies, we believe, that so many studies and reports suggest that training in these skills does not guarantee a high level of comprehension (Armbruster and Anderson, 1981; Britton, 1975). This is particularly unfortunate since Elliott and Wendling (1966) substantiated over two decades ago that 75 percent of academic failure is caused by poor study and examination strategies, and Brown and Peterson (1969) found that dropouts often are unable to memorize and retain information. According to Elliott and Wendling, these are teachable skills which 75 percent of high-school dropouts could learn; if they did, they could do passing work.

Responsibility: The Precursor of Study Skills

We maintain that the reason for the cited failure of training in study skills and retention skills is that these skills are not assessed and taught early in the elementary years and that little systematic training takes place from kindergarten through the middle-school years. When a child gets to high school, or even college, it is often too late to break old habits and learn the type of disciplined thinking needed for concentration and study. As we emphasize throughout this text, we believe that study skills need to be taught from kindergarten on, in a systematic program that is understood and practiced by teachers schoolwide. In Table 8.1, we suggest a schedule that might be followed for introducing the skills discussed in this chapter.

Teaching responsibility, from the early elementary grades, will aid students in overcoming two negative factors described by Estes and Vaughan (1986): compulsiveness and distractability. Students will attend to tasks better if they are taught at an early age to concentrate and think about what they are learning, to be responsible for their own learning, to listen carefully to directions, and to have a quiet place and time to study, even if it is for only a short time.

Sybil Stanton (1986) lists these as the basic elements to consider in teaching discipline and responsibility:

1. *Won't power.* Discipline means having to make choices. Letting students know what they *won't do* is as important as deciding what they will do. For instance, students can be told they will have

TABLE 8.1   *Introducing and Teaching Reading-Study Skills: A K–12 Timetable*

	K	1	2	3	4	5	Grade 6	7	8	9	10	11	12
Assess study skills													
Introduce skill-teaching paradigm													
Skill To Be Taught: Responsibility													
Previewing													
Skimming													
System for study													
Outlining													
Note taking													
Locating information													
Interpreting charts and graphs													
Analyzing pictures													
Reading maps													
Formulating the WHY question													

to be able to tell how a graph provides important information but they won't have to reproduce it.

2. *Delayed gratification.* Teachers need to help students in deciding to delay immediate gratification in order to realize long-term or medium-term goals. For instance, students need to be told that they may not have time to watch television before a test in order to spend time on study. After the test, watching television could be a bonus.

3. *Self-development.* Young children can evaluate their own progress in classes and use this self-evaluation to improve. Self-improvement can be a part of each student's grade.

Responsibility can be fostered through daily work routines in the early elementary grades. For example, after students complete assigned seat work, they can be offered a choice of activities. Students whose names are written on a card in green can be allowed to pick from four choices of follow-up activities that the teacher has labeled on charts in the room. Students whose names are written in yellow can select from three choices. Figure 8.1 illustrates this method of allowing students to monitor their own learning and free time.

Figure 8.1. Room chart for student activities.

Homework activities can also be structured to foster responsibility. For example, teachers can send progress reports home with students once a week. The following is an example (developed by Georgette Kavanaugh):

Progress Report

Name: _____   Date: _____

| | | Needs | |
Outstanding	Satisfactory	Improvement	
_____	_____	_____	Pays attention
_____	_____	_____	Follows directions
_____	_____	_____	Participates in class discussions
_____	_____	_____	Cooperates with teacher
_____	_____	_____	Exhibits good behavior
_____	_____	_____	Controls talking

Your child needs the circled supplies replaced as soon as possible.

Glue   Crayons   Scissors   Pencils   Notebook

_____ Your child needs to turn in his/her homework.

Students in kindergarten and first grade can be asked to keep a "home reader" report to record how often they read stories to their parents. Students are asked to read the same book to the teacher after completing the home assignment. The home reader report (developed by Georgette Kavanaugh) looks like this:

HOME READER

Name of Book	Date	Parent's Initial
Farmer in the Dell	9/14	
Run to the Rainbow	9/16	
City Fun	9/21	
Let's Go, Dear Dragon	10/3	
All Upon a Stone	10/10	
Now I Know About Dinosaurs	10/17	

Our most important message is that students can be responsible, even in kindergarten, for monitoring their own homework assignments and completing assignments at home with their parents. The following is a homework assignment sheet (developed by Georgette Kavanaugh) from a kindergarten class:

HOMEWORK—OCTOBER 5–8

Monday	Tuesday	Wednesday	Thursday
Write your name five times on the first page of your notebook. Remember, only the first letter is capitalized. Write your real name, not your nickname.	Think about the things in your class-room. Tell your parent at least 8 things and ask him or her to write them in your book. Can you name more?	Look in a magazine or newspaper. Find a picture that reminds you of fall. Cut it out and paste it in your book.	This week was fire pre-vention week. Draw a pic-ture of your-self in your notebook. Tell your par-ent what you would do if there were a fire in your house. Ask your par-ent to write down what you said beside your picture.

Parents: Notebook *should not* be returned until Friday. All completed assignments will be checked at one time.

Students can also monitor themselves on self-evaluation logs in early elementary school. Figure 8.2 presents a sample log.

By using these suggestions and aids, teachers can begin early in the elementary grades to teach responsibility and discipline. The sense of accomplishment and self-development students feel as a result will be beneficial in helping them establish lasting study and learning patterns.

Study Skills Assessment

Most standardized achievement tests include subtests of study skills. However, these subtests are usually limited in scope, measuring the students knowledge of such "standard" items as reference skills; alphabetization; ability to read maps, charts, and graphs. Often neglected are such important skills as following directions, presenting a report, test taking, note taking, and memory training. To address the need for a broader assessment of study skills, Rogers (1984) divides them into three broad categories: special study-reading comprehension skills, information-location skills, and study and retention strategies. His "study-reading skills checklist," reproduced as Table 8.2, is thorough. Content area teachers can design tests for each of the areas on this checklist or have a reading specialist help question children,

Figure 8.2. Student log: Life in the ocean.

Directions: At the end of each lesson, rate yourself using the number from the code below that best describes how you think you did on that lesson.

Date	Skill	Student Evaluation	Student Comment	Teacher Comment

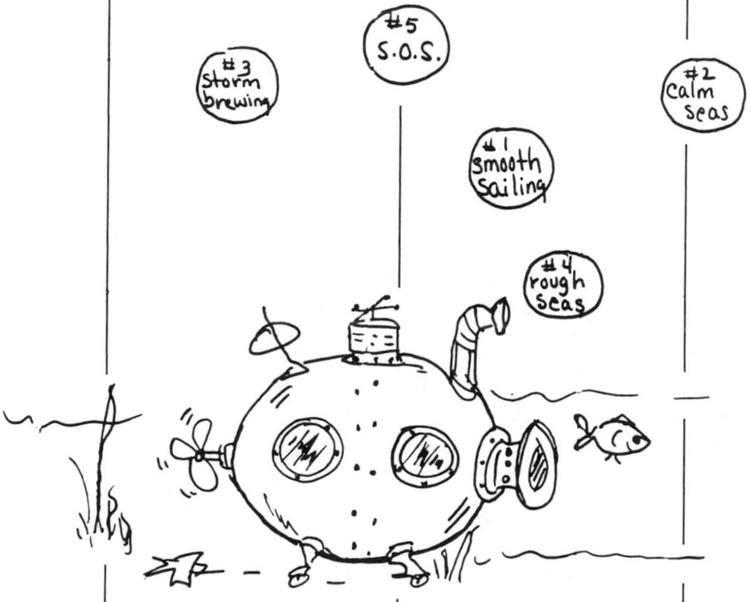

#3 Storm brewing

#5 S.O.S.

#2 Calm seas

#1 smooth Sailing

#4 rough seas

T A B L E 8 . 2   *Study-Reading Skills Checkist*

	Degree of skill		
	Absent	Low	High
I. Special study-reading comprehension skills			
A. Ability to interpret graphic aids			
Can the student interpret these graphic aids?			
1. maps			
2. globes			
3. graphs			
4. charts			
5. tables			
6. cartoons			
7. pictures			
8. diagrams			
9. other organizing or iconic aids			
B. Ability to follow directions			
Can the student follow . . .			
1. simple directions?			
2. a more complex set of directions?			
II. Information location skills			
A. Ability to vary rate of reading			
Can the student do the following?			
1. scan			
2. skim			
3. read at slow rate for difficult materials			
4. read at average rate for reading level			
B. Ability to locate information by use of book parts			
Can the student use book parts to identify the following information?			
1. title			
2. author or editor			
3. publisher			
4. city of publication			
5. name of series			
6. edition			
7. copyright date			
8. date of publication			

Source: Rogers, D. B. Assessing study skills. *Journal of Reading*, January 1984. Reprinted with permission of Douglas B. Rogers and the International Reading Association.

Can the student quickly locate and understand the function of the following parts of a book?

1. preface _____

2. foreword _____

3. introduction _____

4. table of contents _____

5. list of figures _____

6. chapter headings _____

7. subtitles _____

8. footnotes _____

9. bibliography _____

10. glossary _____

11. index _____

12. appendix _____

C. Ability to locate information in reference works

Can the student do the following?

1. locate information in a dictionary _____

   a. using the guide words _____

   b. using a thumb index _____

   c. locating root word _____

   d. locating derivations of root word _____

   e. using the pronunciation key _____

   f. selecting word meaning appropriate to passage under study _____

   g. noting word origin _____

2. locate information in an encyclopedia

   a. using information on spine to locate appropriate volume _____

   b. using guide words to locate section _____

   c. using index volume _____

3. use other reference works such as:

   a. telephone directory _____

   b. newspapers _____

   c. magazines _____

   d. atlases _____

   e. television listings _____

   f. schedules _____

   g. various periodical literature indices _____

   h. others (   ) _____

D. Ability to locate information in the library
   Can the student do the following?
   1. locate material by using the card catalog
      a. by subject _____
      b. by author _____
      c. by title _____
   2. find the materials organized in the library
      a. fiction section _____
      b. reference section _____
      c. periodical section _____
      d. vertical file _____
      e. others (_____) _____

III. Study and retention strategies
A. Ability to study information and remember it
   Can the student do the following?
   1. highlight important information _____
   2. underline important information _____
   3. use oral repetition to increase retention _____
   4. ask and answer questions to increase retention _____
   5. employ a systematic study procedure
      (such as SQ3R) _____
   6. demonstrate effective study habits _____
      a. set a regular study time _____
      b. leave adequate time for test or project
         preparation _____
      c. recognize importance of self-motivation
         in learning _____

B. Ability to organize information
   Can the student do the following?
   1. take notes _____
   2. note source of information _____
   3. write a summary for a paragraph _____
   4. write a summary for a short selection _____
   5. write a summary integrating information
      from more than one source _____
   6. write a summary for a longer selection _____
   7. make graphic aids to summarize information _____
   8. write an outline of a paragraph _____
   9. write an outline of a short selection _____
   10. write an outline for longer selections _____
   11. write an outline integrating information
       from more than one source _____
   12. use the outline to write a report or to make
       an oral report _____

individually or in small groups, on how often and how well they use the skills listed. Teachers may also want to design an assessment of what parents do to help students study and how students evaluate their own study habits. Tables 8.3 and 8.4 reproduce examples of these kinds of assessment.

TABLE 8.3   *Study Skills for Kindergarten and First-Grade Students: Survey of Parents*

Please circle YES or NO in front of each statement.

YES	NO	1.	My child has a special place to study. Where? _____
YES	NO	2.	My child has an independent reading time each night. When? _____
YES	NO	3.	My child watches television while completing homework.
YES	NO	4.	I always supervise my child's homework period.
YES	NO	5.	I sometimes help my child with homework.
YES	NO	6.	I listen to my child read.
YES	NO	7.	My child has a set bedtime. When? _____
YES	NO	8.	I check over my child's homework.
YES	NO	9.	My child has a place to put materials which must be returned to school.
YES	NO	10.	My child eats breakfast daily.
YES	NO	11.	I discuss with my child how he or she does in school each day.
YES	NO	12.	I read to my child often.

TABLE 8.4   *Study Skills for Kindergarten and First-Grade Students: Survey of Students*
Circle the true sentences as I read them.

1. I bring my books to school each day.
2. I listen in class.
3. I read the directions when I begin my work.
4. I ask questions when I don't know what to do.
5. I do my homework every night.
6. I have a special place to do my homework.
7. No one helps me with my homework.
8. I watch TV when I do my homework.
9. I bring my homework to school.
10. I am a good student.

These two surveys (Tables 8.3 and 8.4) were adapted with permission from surveys done by Cornelia Hill.

Using the Skill-Teaching Paradigm

In chapter 7, we presented a paradigm for teaching critical thinking skills. This paradigm can also be used to teach any of the study skills mentioned in this chapter and in chapter 9. Because of the importance of this paradigm, we are reviewing the seven steps:

1. Explain the skill to be taught.
2. Introduce the lesson.
3. Develop structured practice using the skill.
4. Have students report on their use of the skill.
5. Summarize how the skill was used in the content lesson.
6. Review and reinforce the skill.
7. Continue practice with the skill.

The reader might wish to reread the section on this paradigm in chapter 7 for an explanation of each step and for figures illustrating how the paradigm can be used by teachers at different grade levels. Using the paradigm will help ensure that students focus on the skill that is being taught along with the content. To help even more, teachers can distribute to students before the skill lesson the following training outline (Figure 8.3). It explains what skill is to be taught, supplies used,

Figure 8.3. Training outline.

Skill, information, or attitude to be taught: two-column note-taking method
Supplies, information, or equipment: booklet, notebooks, class dictionary

100% Standard: After reading "The United States in Isolation," students will use the two-column system to take notes on the chapter. In pairs, students will exchange papers and grade note taking. Each student must list six major headings or points made by the author.

Major Points (Steps)	Special Points and Materials Used
1. Have students listen to teacher lecture.	Have students work in pairs to check work. Cooperation emphasized. Helping each other.
2. Have students take notes on both lecture and textbook reading material.	
3. Pairs of students exchange papers.	
4. Student must have six major points listed and explained.	
5. Students get to see their own paper again to see where problems occurred.	

the standard students must adhere to to complete the lesson, and steps students will take to complete the training. (The skill itself, two-column notetaking, is explained later in this chapter.) Again, this is a strategy to bring into sharp focus the skill which is to be taught.

Previewing: The Foundation of Study

Chapter 5 describes the DRTA (Stauffer, 1969), which is a technique teachers can use to model correct reading process. The DRTA is also mentioned in chapter 2 as an aid in affective teaching. Fundamental to the DRTA is the previewing stage, which is important for clarifying "cognitive structure" (Ausubel, 1968), or the clarity of student thinking, before students immerse themselves in reading textbook material. In the previewing stages, students select strategies which will match the depth and duration of study needed. To select proper strategies—whether note taking, underlining, or rapid skimming in reading—students must spend time clarifying their thinking about the topic to be read, or *previewing* the material. Students need to ask themselves such questions as these:

How interested am I in this section?
How much do I already know about this topic?
How deeply do I need to think and concentrate to learn this material?
How fast can I read this material?
What do I still need to learn about this topic?

After this previewing stage, students may alter their plan for reading. Teachers might take students step-by-step through the previewing phase, then ask students to write down how they will study the material.

Just as you might size up a piece of clothing and decide it is too big and needs altering, you can size up a reading selection and realize that you need to make "mental alterations." This assessment is the purpose of previewing. Sometimes the preview will yield all the information the reader needs, and, consequently, the material need not be read. In many instances, however, the preview will build anticipation for material which is not familiar to the reader. Chapter 4, on building the reader's background, provides many activities to enhance previewing, which both develops comprehension and encourages good study habits.

During a recent informal study with a group of adults taking a reading improvement course, one randomly selected group of students was asked by one of the authors to read a selection without using a preview strategy and to answer ten questions after reading the selection. Another group was shown a previewing strategy and asked to use the techniques in reading a selection similar in readability and interest to the first selection. The second group was asked to answer ten comprehension questions after the reading. The group without the preview strategy correctly answered 64 percent of the comprehension questions; the group using the preview strategy correctly answered 86 percent of the comprehension questions. Thus, the preview strategy appeared to aid readers in comprehending the selection. Moreover, the 22-percent variance in comprehension scores between the two groups is significant; it can mean the difference between understanding and not understanding the material. A strategy such as previewing, then, if modeled and practiced by teachers from elementary school onward, can enhance student's comprehension of expository and narrative material.

How to Preview

Previewing in order to clarify thinking reduces uncertainty about the reading assignment, allowing students to gain confidence, read in a more relaxed manner, gain interest, and improve attitude toward the material. In addition, previewing strategies enable students to decide how much of the material is in their own background of experience. The result of the previewing strategy is that learners are clearer about what they know and what they need to know. In effect, they have set a purpose for reading before they begin.

When previewing a technical chapter or a report, students should examine and think about the following:

1. Title and subtitle—to discover the overall topic of the chapter or article.
2. Author's name—to see if it is a recognized authority.
3. Copyright—to see if material is current.
4. Introduction—to learn what the author intends to talk about.
5. Headings and subheadings—to identify the topic for the sections to follow. (Forming these headings into questions gives purpose to the reading.)
6. Graphs, charts, maps, tables, pictures—to aid in understanding specific aspects about the chapter or article.
7. Summary—to get an overview of the reading.
8. Questions—to review important topics covered in chapter.

In practicing with a group or class, the teacher assists students in deciding what they already know about the material and what they need to learn. The reader turns those things that are not known into questions, which provide a purpose for reading.

Students reading fiction need to preview the title, illustrations, and introduction in order to make hypotheses about the outcome of the story. This preview heightens suspense and aids in maintaining interest throughout the story. (See DRTA examples in chapter 5.) Most important, predicting story structure gives the reader a purpose for reading, namely, to find out if the predictions are correct. Whether reading fiction or expository material, a very important reason for previewing is that it forces a student to do the more sophisticated kind of thinking required for drawing inferences and developing interpretations. Thus, the student thinks critically about the chapter or story before the reading, operating at times on those higher levels of cognition described by Adler and Van Doren (1952), Bloom (1956), Herber (1970), and Barrett (1972).

We have found that, generally, students on any level will not preview material on their own unless teachers model and provide practice in this important skill. Teachers should first use the skill-teaching paradigm to make students aware that both content and the strategy of previewing are being taught. Second, teachers need to review with students the table of contents of a textbook to aid them in discovering the theme or structure of the course material. In this way, students will get the "gist" or overall idea of what the author is attempting to teach in the textbook. The teacher might ask, for example, why the authors chose to organize a table of contents in a particular manner.

For each new reading or unit of instruction, the teacher can ask students to return to the table of contents to see how this particular segment of learning fits into the overall textbook scheme or pattern. Teachers with a class of poor readers can model the previewing strategy by using preview questions they have constructed and annotated.

Skimming as Central to Previewing

Researchers have reported on the importance of skimming content material for organizing details and making inferences (Sherer, 1975). It is this skill that allows students to preview information. However, students need much practice (and from an early age) to skim material effectively. We recommend skimming-rate drills much like those which will be described in chapter 9. Teachers can ask students to skim rapidly looking for answers to *who, what, when* and *where* questions in the chapter. Students need to be reminded to skim one or two sentences in each paragraph in addition to skimming the title, author, headings, etc., as we described earlier. Also, students need to be assured that they need not worry about what they missed during the preview and skimming phase. They need to be reminded many times that previewing helps to clarify thinking and set a purpose for reading and that they will learn further details in the full reading. In chapter 9 we will discuss how previewing and rapid reading together will enable students to become more efficient.

Developing Study System Strategies Throughout the Grades

Children in first grade, as soon as they are ready, should begin reading stories directed by the teacher using the DRTA technique (Stauffer, 1969). If such guided practice continues, teachers gradually give more and more responsibility for learning to students, as demonstrated by Pearson's (1985) model in Figure 8.4.

If practice in DRTAs is schoolwide and responsibility (as described earlier) is taught, students will receive a firm foundation in study-reading. By fifth or sixth grade, students can be taught a system of study like the SQ3R (Robinson, 1961). In effect, this system is a natural outgrowth of previewing, skimming, and teacher-modeled reading lessons such as the DRTA. SQ3R—which stands for *survey, question, read, recite, review*—should be the first *individual* practice in those concepts already taught in groups and with the entire class.

The following chart summarizes the steps in SQ3R:

Technique	Procedure	Value
1. Survey	Read questions and summary at end of the chapter. Skim-read divisions of material which are usually in boldface type. Read captions under pictures and graphs.	Highlights major ideas and emphases of chapter; helps organize ideas for better understanding later.
2. Question	Turn each heading into a question. (Practice will make this skill automatic.) Write questions in outline form.	Arouses curiosity; increases comprehension; recalls information already known; highlights major points; forces conscious effort in applying the reading process.
3. Read	Read each section of the material to answer questions from headings.	Promotes active search for answers to specific questions; forces concentration for better comprehension; improves memory; aids in lengthening attention span.
4. Recite	After reading entire section, close book and write the answer to your question plus any significant cues; use *own* words; write key examples; make notes brief.	Encourages students to use their own words and not simply copy from book; improves memory and assures greater understanding.
5. Review	Study the topical outline and notes; try to see relationships; check memory by trying to recall main points; cover subpoints and try to recall them from seeing main points.	Clarifies relationships; checks short-term recall; prepares students for class.

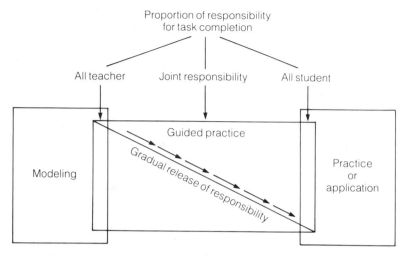

Figure 8.4. The gradual release of responsibility model of instruction.
From Pearson, P. D. "Changing the Face of Reading Instruction," *Journal of Reading,*
April 1985. Reprinted with permission of P. D. Pearson and the International Reading
Association.

Tadlock's (1978) explanation of the success of SQ3R is based on
information-processing theory (Neisser, 1967; Hunt, 1971; Newell and
Simon, 1972). According to Tadlock, we naturally try to reduce uncertainty by (1) processing information through sensory organs; (2) sending
information through memory systems; (3) structuring and categorizing
information in the most meaningful manner, in order to see conceptual
relationships; and (4) storing information for recall at a future time (p.
111). She postulates that SQ3R compensates for any deficiencies in our
information-processing system through the use of a highly structured
study and memory technique. It is important to note that other study
systems similar to SQ3R, such as PQ4R (Preview, Question, Read, Recite,
Review, Rewrite), SQ4R (Survey, Question, Read, Recite, Review,
Rewrite), and SRR (Survey, Read, Review), can work equally well because
all are based on the same premise. Students should be encouraged to
try a study system and adapt it to their own needs. Strict adherence to
the steps is not as important as applying a study strategy that is based
on the four criteria described by Tadlock. An alternative to the SQ3R,
described later in this chapter, is the REAP study system, developed by
Eanet and Manzo (1976) for improving reading, writing, and study skills.
    Study systems such as those described above have not really per-
meated schools across the country. There are probably two reasons for
this. First, teachers themselves did not learn through such a study system; hence, they often give only lip service to the techniques described.

Teachers need to practice previewing and study systems themselves before they can believe in and teach the system to others. Second, study strategies are not systematically introduced throughout educational systems from the early elementary years.

Organizing Information

Students need to understand how reading material is organized and patterned and be able to organize and outline it and take useful notes. The next sections deal with these very important skills.

Outlining

Outlining and note taking are the two most-used study strategies (Annis and Davis, 1978; 1982). There is no agreement, however, on the best way to teach these study skills. Underlining is often cited in the literature as a way to help students organize their thinking enough to begin an outline. Underlining, then, can be a first step to outlining. McAndrew (1983), in a review of the literature on underlining, made several suggestions for teaching this skill.

To begin with teachers should use "preunderlining" reading assignments through handout materials which coincide with the text. Have students mark the text if possible. Teachers need to show students how to underline relevant material. Also, there is a need to demonstrate and teach how to underline higher-level general statements rather than details. Students will be underlining less, but what is underlined will be more important. McAndrew notes that teachers should remind students that, with underlining, less is more. And, he notes, any time saved by underlining can be put to good use in further study of the material. Teachers need to teach students to know when to use techniques other than underlining.

McAndrew also cites research (Fowler and Baker, 1974; Rickards and August, 1975; Cashen and Leicht, 1970) showing that, when these suggestions are followed, significant learning occurs. Even when underlining in textbooks is not possible, preunderlining is an important study strategy for students to learn.

Outlining is an organizational tool, a graphic representation of the chapter that a student wants to understand. Outlines should show the connections of main ideas, supporting details, definitions of terms, and other data to the overall topic. Outlines are valuable because they help students understand difficult texts, take notes, write papers, and give oral presentations.

Teachers should remind students that, when they first begin practicing outlining, they should not concentrate on form (no need for a B for every A). Teachers can help students learn to outline by preparing outlines with key words missing. By replacing the missing words or terms, even younger children can begin to learn outlining. Here is an example of such an outline used in junior high school:

A TIME OF WARS

I. Charlemagne
   A. King of the _____
   B. Crowned head of the _____ Empire
   C. Set up _____
   D. Ruled fairly
II. Vikings
   A. Fierce warriors interested in _____
   B. Traders
III. Crusaders
   A. Pope wanted to free _____ from the Moslem Turks
   B. _____ took the cross as their sign
   C. _____ major crusades
   D. Trade developed
      1. Spices
      2. _____ clothing

The following are some features of successful outlines:

1. The number of headings and subheadings in an outline is determined by the material.
2. Each heading contains one main idea.
3. Ideas are parallel. All ideas recorded with Roman numerals are equally important.
4. All subheadings relate to the major headings.
5. In a formal outline, each category has more than one heading.
6. Each level of heading is indented under the one above it.
7. The first letter of the first word in each heading and subheading is capitalized.

An outline is a type of note taking that enables students to organize material in a hierarchical fashion. This can be accomplished in a graphic pattern as well as in traditional ways. Figure 8.5 presents a graphic representation of material that follows a cause-effect pattern of organization.

Note Taking

Note taking, the second most often-used study skill, has been found to produce good study results. Research which focused on the time students spent on study procedures (isolated from actual study time) showed

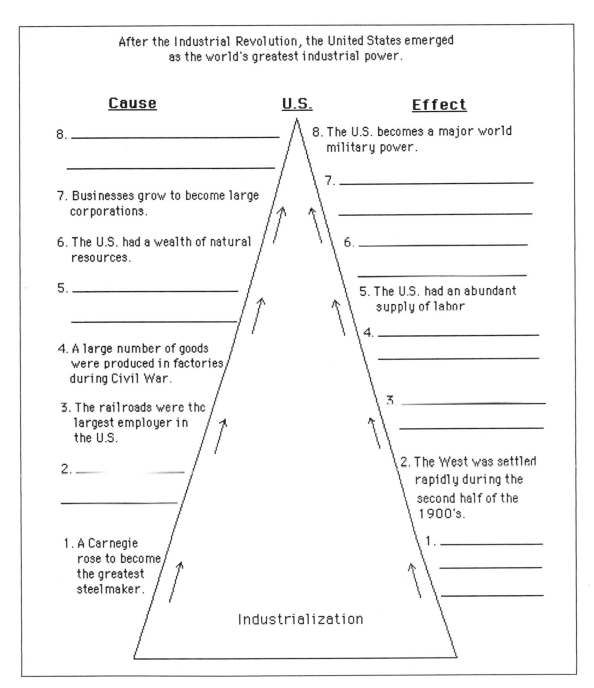

After the Industrial Revolution, the United States emerged
as the world's greatest industrial power.

Cause   **U.S.**   **Effect**

8. _____

8. The U.S. becomes a major world
   military power.

7. Businesses grow to become large
   corporations.

7. _____

6. The U.S. had a wealth of natural
   resources.

6. _____

5. _____

5. The U.S. had an abundant
   supply of labor

4. A large number of goods
   were produced in factories
   during Civil War.

4. _____

3. The railroads were the
   largest employer in
   the U.S.

3. _____

2. _____

2. The West was settled
   rapidly during the
   second half of the
   1900's.

1. A Carnegie
   rose to become
   the greatest
   steelmaker.

1. _____

Industrialization

Figure 8.5. Pattern Guide to Illustrate Note Taking. Social Science: The
Industrial Revolution.
Adapted for classroom use by Patricia Mays Mulherin.

that note taking is more effective than underlining (McAndrew, 1983). McAndrew offers teachers the following suggestions to help their students become effective note takers (p. 107):

1. Be sure students realize that the use of notes to store information is more important than the act of taking the notes.
2. Try to use a spaced lecture format.
3. Insert questions, verbal cues, and nonverbal cues into lectures to highlight structure.
4. Write material on the board to be sure students will record it.
5. When using transparencies or slides, compensate for possible overload of information.
6. Tell students what type of test to expect.
7. Use handouts, especially with poor note takers.
8. Give students handouts that provide space for student notes.

To the students who are taking notes, Morgan et al. (1986) offer some practical advice. First, note taking is a personal matter, i.e., students should develop their own style. To facilitate note taking, students should use a two- or three-ringed notebook with loose-leaf paper to arrange handout material and notes. Also they should write on every other line whenever possible or when it seems logical to separate lines. There will then be room to correct errors or go back and add points that might have been missed. In addition, every-other-line note taking makes for easier reading when reviewing or studying for an exam. In addition, older students should develop their own shorthand system. Abbreviate frequently used words. Morgan offers examples of such abbreviations:

compare	—comp.	data bank	—d.b.
important	—imp.	evaluation	—eval.
advantage	—advan.	developed	—dev.
introduction	—intro.	literature	—lit.
continued	—con't.	definition	—def.
organization	—org.	individual	—ind.
information	—info.	psychology	—psych.
example	—ex.		

Content words should be written in full and spellings checked with a dictionary or textbook. Another good technique is for students to record the next assignment for class as a reminder of where the note taking is heading. Also students should ask questions for better understanding, especially when confused by a concept or when a point has been missed in the lecture. Recognizing what we don't know leads to learning. No one should be embarrassed to ask for clarification; others may need it, too.

Review your notes often and with different purposes in mind. When rereading text assignments, coordinate the chapter with your notes. Be sure to include main ideas from the chapter directly into your lecture notes. For some, rewriting notes is a helpful memory aid. Even though this process is time-consuming, it may well be worth the effort.

REAP: Writing Annotations

Students need frequent chances to practice critical thinking in their reading and writing. One way of providing these opportunities is through an *annotation* system, which will help students think about the understanding they have of the reading and will allow them to get reflections down in writing.

One such system is REAP (read, encode, annotate, ponder), developed by Eanet and Manzo (1976). This procedure is designed to improve comprehension skills by helping students summarize material in their own words and develop writing ability as well as reading ability.

The four steps in REAP are as follows:

R—Reading to discover the author's ideas
E—Encoding into your own language
A—Annotating your interpretation of the author's ideas
P—Pondering whether the article as text information is significant

By creating annotations, students should increase their maturity and independence in reading.

Types of Annotations. There are six different annotation styles that can help a student formulate an understanding of the text.

The *heuristic annotation* is a statement, usually in the author's words, which has two purposes: to suggest the idea of the selection and to provoke a response. To write it, the annotator needs to find the essence of the selection and then to select a quotation that hints at the essence in a stimulating manner. The quote selected must represent the theme or the main idea of the selection.

The *summary annotation* condenses the selection into a concise form. It should be brief, clear, and to the point. It includes no more or less than is necessary to adequately convey the development and relationship of the author's main ideas. In the case of a story, the summary annotation is a synopsis—the main events of the plot.

The *thesis annotation* is an incisive statement of the author's proposition. As the word *incisive* implies, it cuts directly to the heart of the matter. With fiction, it can substitute for a statement of theme. One approach is to ask oneself, "What is the author saying? What one idea or point is being made?" The thesis annotation is best written in precise wording; unnecessary connectives are removed to produce a telegram-like, but unambiguous, statement.

The *question annotation* directs attention to the ideas that the annotator thinks most germane and may or may not be the same as the author's thesis. The annotator must first determine the most significant issue at hand and then express this notation in question form. This annotation answers the question, "What question(s) is the author answering with the narrative?"

The *critical annotation* is the annotator's response to the author's thesis. In general, there are three types of responses a reader may have—agreement, disagreement, or a combination of the two. The first sentence in the annotation should state the author's thesis. In the next sentence, a position should be stated; the remaining sentences are devoted to defending the position.

The *intention annotation* is a statement of the author's intention, plan, or purpose in writing the selection as it is perceived by the student. This is particularly useful with material of a persuasive, ironic, or satirical nature. Determining intention requires that the annotator bring to bear all available clues, both intrinsic, such as tone and use of language, and extrinsic, such as the knowledge of the author.

The *motivation annotation* is a statement which attempts to speculate about the author's probable motive behind the writing. It is an attempt to find the source of the author's belief system and perceptions. The motivation annotation is a high form of criticism. It often requires penetrating psychological insight.

The following exercise will help demonstrate the skill of annotating. After the reading selection, taken from an article by Neil Postman, is a list that includes an example of each type of annotation.

Some time ago, while watching a TV program called "The Vidal Sassoon Show," I came across the quintessential example of what I am talking about. Vidal Sassoon is a famous hairdresser whose TV show is a mixture of beauty hints, diet information, health suggestions, and popular psychology. As he came to the end of one segment of the show in which an attractive woman had demonstrated how to cook vegetables, the theme music came up and Sassoon just had time enough to say, "Don't go away. We'll be back with a marvelous new diet and, then, a quick look at incest." Now, this is more—much more—than demystification. It is even more than revelation of secrets. It is the ultimate trivialization of culture. Television is relentless in both revealing and trivializing all things private and shameful, and therefore it undermines the moral basis of culture. The subject matter of the confessional box and the psychiatrist's office is now in the public domain. I have it on good authority that, shortly, we and our children will have the opportunity to see commercial TV's first experiments with presenting nudity, which will probably not be shocking to anyone, since TV commercials have been offering a form of soft-core pornography for years. And on the subject of commercials—the 700,000 of them that American youths will see in the first 18 years of their lives—they too contribute to opening to youth all the secrets that once were the province of adults—everything from vaginal sprays to life insurance to the causes of marital conflict. And we must not omit the contributions of news shows, those curious entertainments that daily provide the young with vivid images of adult failure and even madness. (From Neil Postman: The Day Our Children Disappear: Predictions of a Media Ecologist. *Phi Delta Kappan*. Bloomington, Indiana: Phi Delta Kappa. 1981. Used with permission of Neil Postman and the *Phi Delta Kappan*.)

Heuristic annotation: (Provocation: intended primarily to stimulate response. Usually employs the author's own words.)
Television represents the ultimate in trivializing all things private and shameful. This trivialization undermines the moral basis of culture.

Summary annotation: (A general sense of the piece, its style and scope; most objective and informative in a nonarousing way.)
Postman describes a Vidal Sassoon television show to demonstrate television's propensity to trivialize all subjects. He says that commercials offer soft-core pornography and news shows show vivid images of adults as failures.

Thesis annotation: (An incisive statement of the basic thesis of a work.)
Television trivializes the culture. It brings everything—the profound, the ordinary, the mundane—to the same level.

Question annotation: (Provides explicit focus to the notion which the annotation writer thought to be most germane.)
What makes television viewing so bad, anyway? Postman thinks he knows, and he explains why in this article.

Critical annotation: (An informative, critical response to a thesis or supporting premise.)
Postman uses emotional language to describe the total destruction that he sees television wreaking on our society; this language is intended to ignite sparks in the reader. His biased thinking ignores the good television does through informational, documentary, and educational programs.

Intention annotation: (Statement of author's intention as students might see it.)
The author intends to strip the mystique of television and expose the negative influences of the medium.

Motivation annotation: (Why the author wrote the passage.)
The author is trying to protect children who are subjected to a steady bombardment of harmful television programs.

While no one would write each type of annotation for each material, writing different annotations with different content materials provides for reflective study.

REST System of Note Taking

The REST system of note taking (Morgan et al., 1986) has been proposed as a way to prepare for note taking before a lecture. This system takes into account the importance of note taking to help integrate the lecture with the textbook. In using the REST system, students should follow these four steps:

RECORD—Write down as much of what the teacher says as possible, excluding repetitions and digressions.

EDIT—Condense notes, editing out irrelevant material.

SYNTHESIZE—Compare condensed notes with related material in text, and jot down important points stressed in the lecture and the text.

THINK—Think and study to insure retention.

To help students practice REST, teachers should distribute handouts for note taking that include space for recording notes on the lecture, for making notes to oneself, and for summarizing main ideas. An example of such a handout, filled out by a junior-high-school student, is shown in Table 8.5.

TABLE 8.5   *Lecture on China: Four Thousand Years of History*

Topics and notes to yourself	Lecture Notes
Check on meaning of term "accoutrements" in Chinese society.	1. Isolated development of Chinese civilization.
egocentric—country means "at center of earth"	2. China's attitude negative toward other areas & civilizations.
	3. Early relations with Western Europe not positive.
Imp.→ know all "barriers" to other civilizations for test.	4. Cut off physically (barriers) from Europe.
	5. Chinese very aware of past.

Summarization and Main Ideas
China has to be studied through viewing it's history. Cycles of Chinese history show "up & down" periods.

Two-Column Note-Taking System

The Cornell system (Pauk, 1974), a practical approach to taking notes, is an alternative to the REST system. Pauk's two-column note-taking system, as it is sometimes called, has an advantage over REST in that it can be used with younger children. To use this system of note taking, students divide the page in the following way:

1/3 page	2/3 page
headings notes to oneself key words	lecture notes

Table 8.6 describes the two-column note-taking system and summarizes its rationale and function (Aaronson, 1975). Figure 8.6 is an example of a note-taking handout teachers can prepare and give to students in elementary grades before a lecture so that they can practice using the Pauk method. This handout employs a modified cloze procedure; students fill in gaps as they listen to the lecture. More and more notes are omitted in subsequent lessons until, eventually, students complete all the note taking themselves.

Guided Reading Procedure

The guided reading procedure (Manzo, 1975) is an excellent activity for teaching students to gather and organize information around main ideas in the reading. According to researchers, (Colwell, Mangano, Childs, and Case, 1986) this technique is very effective as a way for teachers to direct a lesson. The technique uses brainstorming to collect information as accurately as possible and rereading to correct misinformation and fill in conceptual gaps. This method can be used to aid students in becoming more independent in their thinking and studying. These are the steps teachers follow in using the guided reading procedure:

1. Prepare students for the lesson by clarifying key concepts about the reading; assess students' background knowledge. The teacher in this step may ask students to clarify vocabulary terms or make predictions concerning concepts inherent to the reading.
2. Assign the reading selection of appropriate length, and ask students to remember all they can about the reading. Manzo gives these general guidelines for passage length: primary students—90 words—three minutes; intermediate students—500 words—three minutes; junior-high-school students—900 words—seven minutes; high-school students—2,000 words—ten minutes.
3. After the students have completed the assignment, have them close the book and relate everything they know about the material just

read. List statements on the board without editing. As a variation, assign two students to act as class recorders. This enables the teacher to do a better job of monitoring and guiding the class discussion.

4. Direct students to look for inconsistencies and misinformation first through discussion and then through rereading the material.

5. Add new information and help students organize and categorize concepts into a loose outline form. As a variation, students can put information into 2, 3, or 4 categories and title each category.

TABLE 8.6   *Two-Column Notetaking System*

How to organize	Use 8½ × 11 looseleaf paper, sectioned in 2 columns —wide column (2/3 of page) for actual notes —narrow column for headings
Input from lecturer	Right side (record column) (1) main points, flow of ideas (2) use of indentations and numbers or letters for subordinate ideas (3) use of common abbreviations to simplify notetaking
Input from student	Left side (recall column) (1) topics, questions, key phrases, definitions, comments, summarized ideas (2) headings act as recall cues to corresponding information on right side

Rationale for two columns:
  Psychological
	Use of insights from psychology of learning and memory
	(1) process of involvement strengthened:
	    student makes notes, revises, organizes
	(2) use of meaningful association:
	    mass of information consolidated and organized under headings
	(3) emphasis on immediate review:
	    slows forgetting process

Functional	Compartmentalization of functions and goals: (1) input from lecturer: lecture, received (2) input from student: lecture, edified and revised Use of headings (1) helps label and identify notes for easy access (2) can be used to set up possible test questions Sectioning: helps study: input from lecturer covered to test recall

From Shirley Aaronson, "Notetaking Improvement: A Combined Auditory, Functional and Psychological Approach," *Journal of Reading*, October 1975. Reprinted with permission of Shirley Aaronson and the International Reading Association.

6. Have students reread article another time to determine whether the information they listed was accurate.
7. To strengthen short-term recall, test students on the reading.

The results of a guided reading procedure can be seen in Figure 8.7, which is a concept map that students made during step 5 above. (Concept mapping is explained in chapter 10.

Locating Information

Eighteenth-century chronicler James Boswell, in his *Life of Johnson*, said, "Knowledge is of two kinds. We know a subject ourselves, or we know where we can find information upon it." As students progress in school, this second kind of knowledge becomes more important. They need to know how to find information in textbooks, dictionaries, encyclopedias, and trade books. Therefore, instruction in locating information should begin as soon as reading instruction starts. Picture dic-

Figure 8.6. Note Taking.

Grenville's Program (British)	_____
Proclamation of 1763	1. Closed land west of Appalachian Mountains to English settlers.
	2. Passed to please Indians, who
	_____
	3. Settlers _____
	_____
Sugar Act of ___	Passed so colonists _____
	_____
	1. Lowered tax on _____
	2. Set up means for _____
	3. Added taxes to _____
	4. Struck a blow _____
Stamp Act	1. _____
	_____
	2. _____
	_____

Developed by Janice Stuhlmann.

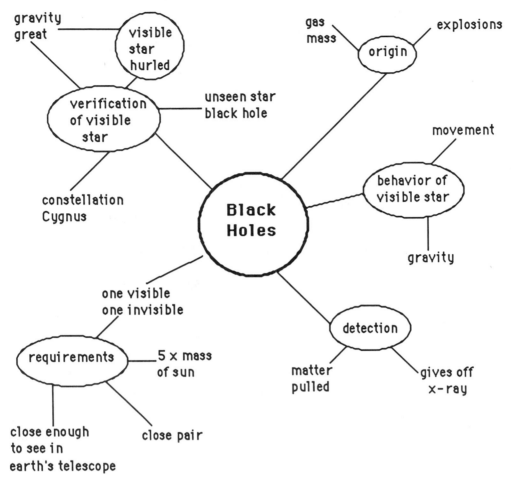

Figure 8.7. Concept map on black holes.
Developed by Holly Corbett.

tionaries, such as *My Little Dictionary* (Scott Foresman, 1964) and the *Storybook Dictionary* (Golden Press, 1966), can provide an introduction to this reference skill. In addition, teachers can create their own picture dictionaries from file cards of words and pictures that students match to each other. As children mature, teachers can introduce alphabetizing through these handmade picture books or they can emphasize alphabetizing more in the published picture dictionaries.

In the intermediate grades, students read well enough to gain from systematic instruction in how to locate information in an encyclopedia. However, even in primary grades students can be taught how to file pictures and materials alphabetically according to key index words such as *farm, city, animal, house,* etc. In this unobtrusive manner, students can be introduced to the telephone book, almanacs, and *Readers' Guide to Periodical Literature.*

Children in the primary grades can also be shown how to use tables of contents and how to scan a textbook for its overall organization. In content reading classes, teachers can discuss tables of contents, glossaries, indexes, headings, picture clues, charts, maps, and graphs. The teacher can introduce all of these skills by asking children to first find the reference (glossary, table of contents) and then locate particular information (a definition in the glossary, a section in the table of contents). Teachers should train students to locate information as students complete daily lessons in their basal readers and content textbooks. In this manner, students at an early age will see the usefulness of this skill.

The ELM's System

Until students have mastered prerequisite skills in alphabetizing, seriation, and classification, they cannot benefit from training in using the library. When these skills are mastered, students can be instructed in use of the card-cataloguing system. Early elementary students can be taught to use the ELM's Classification System, developed for elementary school libraries by Ellen Miller (Barker, 1979). This is an interest-based classification system generally used for those books which have already been designated as "easy" or "primary" (as in the Wilson "E" classification, widely used in children's sections of school libraries). The purpose of the ELM's classification is to organize collections or groups of storybooks around content. It produces, in essence, a permanent display of books categorized by subject. Since children are rarely familiar with authors, they usually seek books by title or subject, such as firemen, giants, witches, etc.

Using this system, children quickly discover that they are capable of locating those books which satisfy their reading tastes. Teachers desiring curriculum-related reading materials find that the system provides easy access to books which were previously scattered throughout the collection. Parents find they can assist very young children in their search for that special book to meet personal interest needs.

ELM is very similar to the Dewey Decimal System. The categories are comparable, but each subject area is identified by a colored band as well as by a two-digit numeral on the book's spine.

The ELM's classification system is organized in the following way:

10 Potpourri (White)
    11   Concepts
    12   Religion—Bible stories
    13   Dictionaries

14 Alphabet books
15 Counting books
16 Reading
17 Picture books (no print)
18 (for future expansion)
19 Thinking skills & creativity development

20 Human Relations (Pink)
21 Home & family life—homes, family members, family activities
22 Friendship—friends, activities, attitudes
23 Economics—money, social implications, etc.
24 Behavior—attitudes, morals, manners, customs, growth, development & safety
25 (for future expansion)
26 Play
27 School life—teachers, attitudes, etc.
28 Community or locality
29 Career education—workers, places of employment, attitudes, etc.

30 Holidays & Occasions (Red)
31 Jewish holidays
32 Parades, circus, fairs, etc.—costumes
33 Birthdays & parties
34 Patriotic occasions & holidays
35 Easter
36 Halloween
37 Thanksgiving
38 Christmas
39 Other

40 Animals (Orange)
41 Prehistoric
42 Insects & spiders
43 Water creatures, amphibians, reptiles
44 Zoo animals
45 Birds
46 House & yard—pets
47 Farm & ranch
48 Field & woods
49 Forest & jungle

50 Science (Green)
51 Mathematics
52 Astronomy—time, calendars, seasons, stars, planets, day & night, etc.
53 Physics—simple machines, gases, sound, light, heat, electricity & electronics, magnetism, nuclear energy, motion, etc.

54 Earth science—structure, properties (air, water, etc.), weather, rocks, minerals, elements, metals, etc.

55 Ecology

56 Food—production, processing, preparation

57 Biology—physical body (care of, parts, functions), etc.

58 Botany—trees, flowers, mold, fungi, algae, etc.

59 Experiments

60 Transportation & Technology (Yellow)

61 Manufacturing—clothing, other goods

62 Water travel & vehicles

63 Rail travel & vehicles

64 Land travel & vehicles—automobiles, trucks, etc.

65 Air & space travel & vehicles—rockets, satellites, etc.

66 Armament—ammunition, weapons, armed forces, etc.

67 Construction—carpentry, tools, machines, machinery, etc.

68 Electrical & electronic equipment

69 Other

70 Activities (Blue)

71 Music—singing, dancing, instruments, etc.

72 Art—types of, color

73 Games, plays, hobbies, crafts

74 Club life & activities

75 Outdoor life—camping, hunting, fishing, woodcraft, etc.

76 Winter sports

77 Water sports

78 Ball games

79 Other

80 Fantasy & Fun (Brown)

81 Mystery & detective stories

82 Humor, jokes, riddles, etc.

83 Legends, myths, tall tales

84 Fairy tales, fables

85 Mother Goose, nonsense verses, rhymes, nursery rhymes & stories

86 Fantasy

87 Ghosts, witches, magic

88 Adventure

89 Collections—short stories, poems

90 Places, People & Happenings (Black)

91 Ancient & Early Times—knights, cavemen, etc.

92 People—biographical fiction

93 Minorities in the United States

94 Europe, Australia

95 Asia

96 Africa
97 North America
98 Frontier life—Indians, pioneers, cowboys, etc.
99 South America, Central America

The ELM's is used with permission of Ellen Miller, the author.

Older students can learn the Dewey Decimal System. They need not memorize this system, but teachers and librarians need to demonstrate how it is organized and why it is helpful.

Dewey Decimal Classification System
000–099   General works
100–199   Philosophy
200–299   Religion
300–399   Social sciences
400–499   Language
500–599   Pure science
600–699   Applied science, or technology
700–799   The arts
800–899   Literature
900–999   History

After becoming familiar with the cataloguing system, students can visit the library in a group or with the whole class. To test students' knowledge of the library, have them fill out "library learner" tickets, which are 3″ × 5″ cards with specific questions to answer. The following is an example:

Library Learner

1. Find a book on a famous American president.
Book name: _____
2. Tell how you found it in the card catalogue.
_____
_____

Information given in card catalogue: _____
_____
_____
_____

Through early training in locating information, students will be ready for the more advanced study techniques already mentioned in this chapter and in chapter 9.

Another technique for locating information is the "library search and seizure" (Sauin, 1978), which helps students become acquainted with reference sources in the school library. In this activity, students locate and record information on a specific subject. Figure 8.8 presents a sample set of questions for a high school English class.

Figure 8.8. Library Search and Seizure for English Classes.

Find the answers to the following questions in our school library. You may ask the teacher or the librarian for help, but remember, you must do the work! All of the answers are in the school library. Happy searching!

1. How many different encyclopedia sets does our library contain?
2. What is the difference between *Dictionary of American Biography* and *Contemporary Authors?*
3. Find a book about Edgar Allen Poe written by Frances Winwar:
   3a. What is the title of the book?
   3b. How long is it?
   3c. Who published it?
4. Find an article about capital punishment written in 1981:
   4a. What magazine published it?
   4b. What is the title of the article?
   4c. How long is it?
   4d. What is the publication month?
   4e. Do we have this magazine in our library?
5. Find a book about *Macbeth* published by Ginn in 1908:
   5a. Who wrote this book?
   5b. What is the title?
6. Find *Reader's Guide to Periodical Literature.* In volumn 40, find a reference of interest to you and complete the following:
   6a. Author _____ Title _____ Journal _____ Date _____ Pages _____ Vol. _____ No. _____
7. Find a resource which will tell you these major facts about Nathaniel Hawthorne on one page. What is it?
   7a. When did Hawthorne live?
   7b. What novels did he write?
   7c. What was the name of his home in Concord, Massachusetts?

Reading Visual Aids

Visual aids and graphics are important to most content textbooks. Yet one of the most common responses of students when questioned about such aids is that they "skip over them." Worse yet, the only time many students get instruction in how to read charts, maps, and graphs is during the infamous "chart, map, and graph week" instituted by many well-meaning but misdirected schools and school systems. Because these skills are taught in isolation, there is little transfer by students into everyday instruction. Teachers need to teach these specialized reading procedures during day-to-day instruction, not just during special weeks.

Charts and Graphs

If students are having particular difficulty reading graphs, teachers can use a modified cloze procedure to teach the skill. For example, Figure 8.9 shows how a modified cloze procedure can be used to teach weather pressure. Figure 8.10 presents a chart detailing the frequency that

HIGHS AND LOWS

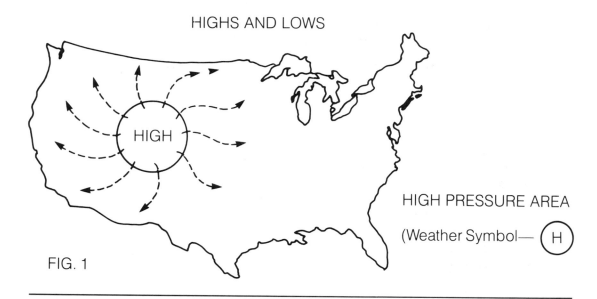

HIGH PRESSURE AREA

(Weather Symbol— H)

FIG. 1

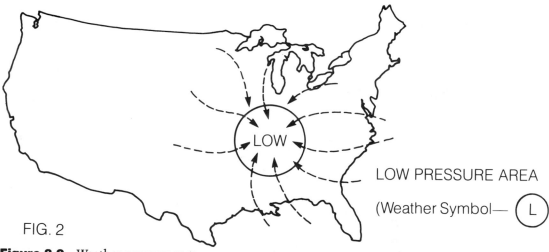

LOW PRESSURE AREA

(Weather Symbol— L)

FIG. 2

Figure 8.9. Weather pressure map.

Directions: In Fig. 1, draw and label a low-pressure area and show its air direction. In Fig. 2, draw and label a high-pressure area and show its air direction. Answer these on the back of the paper: The air in a high-pressure area is spiraling _____ in a _____ direction, with the highest pressure at its _____. The air in a low-pressure area is spiraling _____ in a _____ direction, with the lowest air pressure at its _____ .

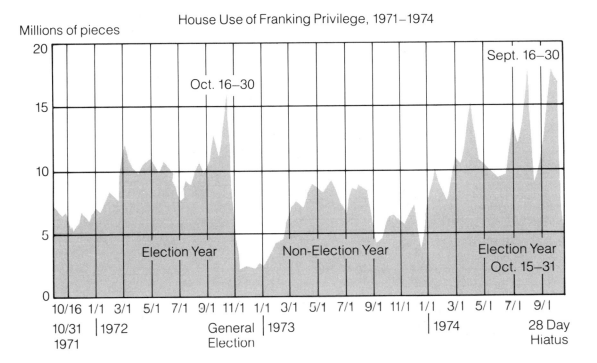

Figure 8.10. House use of franking privilege, 1971–1974.
From Lewinski, M. (1982). *American Government Today*. Glenview, IL: Scott, Foresman, p. 262. Used with permission. Copyright © 1982, 1980 by Scott, Foresman and Company.

1. Which are the years of most franking, election or nonelection years?
2. Which are the months of most franking activity?
3. Is there a clue as to why legislators might be using their franking privileges more at these times?

Figure 8.11. Political cartoon teaching inference.
Cartoon by Roberto Lianez, Norview High School, Norfolk. Used with permission.

1. Describe what is happening in this cartoon.
2. Explain the meaning of each of the three figures.
3. Explain the significance of the decoy, labeled "INF." What is the INF treaty?
4. From your reading of this cartoon, do you feel we should trust the Russians and enter into more and bigger disarmament treaties with them? Why or why not?

franking privileges—writing constituents without paying postage—are used by members of the House of Representatives. While it may seem evident to teachers why the privilege is used by legislators more in election years than in other years, this is an inference many poor readers may not make without explanation or questioning from the teacher. The point is that students need much interpretive skill to read charts and graphs. This skill is improved only through frequent guided practice.

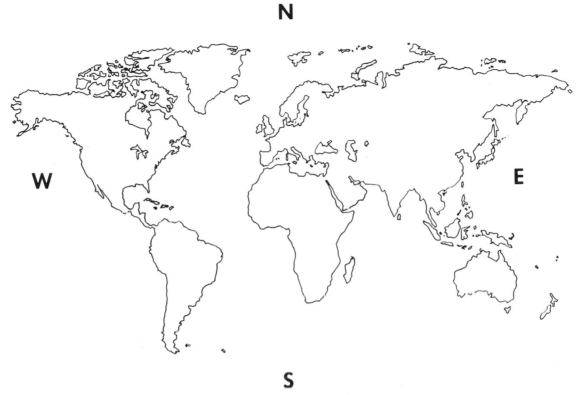

N

W

E

S

Figure 8.12. Map Skills. The World.

I.
Directions: Use the map on p. 158. Find and label:
1. The four oceans
2. The six continents
3. Carlos' home (California)
4. Harald's home (Norway)
5. Your home (Virginia)

II.
Directions: Look at the map on p. 168. Mark and label:
1. (Red) The Gulf Stream current
2. (Red) The North Atlantic Drift current
3. (Blue) The West Wind Drift
4. One other current that you would like to trace
5. Make a dotted line to show the Arctic Circle

Pictures and Maps

Pictures make a textbook interesting and vital. Teachers should frequently ask students to "read" the picture in an effort to clarify thinking about a concept in the chapter. Cartoons are specialized pictures which carry significant messages or propaganda, as our use of cartoons in this text demonstrates. However, students sometimes need considerable background experience to understand cartoons. Therefore, teachers need to question students about the perceptual content of cartoons, as Figure 8.11 demonstrates.

Figure 8.12 and Figure 8.13 demonstrate how teachers can teach students to label maps. Labeling may be done either after students memorize a map or as they consult maps in their textbook. We recommend map labeling as the primary way to get students to learn to use maps and to better remember certain important locations on a map.

The Great Why Question: Assessing Students' WhyQ

As a final reminder in this chapter on reading and study skills, we would like to point out the benefits of the Great Why Question. You have heard that teachers should ask *Who? What? When? Where?* and *Why?* throughout their instruction, but comparing the first four types of questions to the *why* question is like comparing tapioca to chocolate mousse. The first four require factual recall, which students certainly need to have during study periods. The *why* question, however, is much more powerful because it can force a student to immediately use a higher awareness level, another dimension of thought. This type of question literally takes more thought and energy to answer; it takes students from the *how* of an event or circumstance to crucial inferences about the significance and deeper meaning of any event, circumstance, or concept. Through repeated modeling of the question, teachers can aid in making it a habit for students to ask *why?* as they study. Entire homework assignments can be centered around the question "Why do you think _____ did that in the story (chapter)?" Group study sessions can be focused on students writing four reasons why _____ happened in a story or chapter. Finally, teachers can ask, "Why are you feeling that way after reading the story?" or "Why do you think the stock market declined so much yesterday?" or "Why do we need to know about cross-fertilization of plants?" The Great Why Question, if internalized and properly practiced by teachers and students alike, can be a great source of thinking power in reading and study.

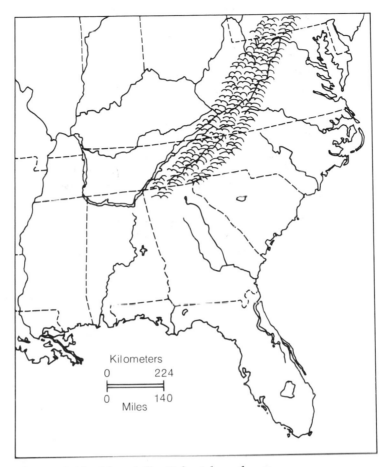

Figure 8.13. Map skills. Colonial southeast.

Complete This Map

Use the map of the Colonial Southeast on page 210 to help you complete this activity.

1. Color the water area BLUE.
2. Color the area covered by the eleven states of the Southeast LIGHT YELLOW.
3. Print the names of the states in the proper places on the map.
4. Print these names in the proper places:
   Mountains: Appalachians, Blue Ridge
   Plains: Atlantic Coastal, Gulf Coastal
   Rivers: Potomac, James, Savannah, Mississippi, St. Johns
   Bays: Chesapeake, Delaware
5. Print these names of early settlements in the proper places on the map.
   Jamestown   St. Mary's
   Charleston   Williamsburg
   Savannah
6. With a BLUE crayon trace over each of the rivers listed above.

One-Minute Summary

Study skills need to be taught systematically, and they need to be emphasized in early elementary grades. Teachers in kindergarten and first grade can teach responsibility by giving students choices in decision making and having them keep records of their work. Also, study skills can be taught by giving students, even at the kindergarten level, small increments of homework for which they are responsible. As students mature and progress through school, more sophisticated study skills can be taught, such as locating information, previewing material, organizing material for study, and using systems of study (REST, GRP, REAP, SQ3R). In junior high school and high school, students can be introduced to a skill-teaching paradigm, which provides opportunities to practice a particular skill. Such a paradigm is valuable because it lets the teacher clearly delineate simultaneously both the content of a lesson and the study skill that will be taught. In this chapter we have also described assessment techniques designed to find out whether students use adequate study skills. The teaching of study skills cannot be left to chance. Students need to be made aware of good study practices at all levels of their schooling and at each step of PAR.

End-of-Chapter Activities

Preparing the Reader

1. Did the authors prepare you well for reading this chapter? What could have been done to make your preparation more complete?

2. How many activities presented for teaching study skills had you already used in your classes? Were there any parts of the chapter that were totally new to you? Were there any aspects of the chapter that interested you because they were new and different?

Assisting Comprehension

1. Pick a reading-study skill to teach and teach it using the seven-step, skill-teaching paradigm. Analyze the process to determine whether students paid more attention to learning the skill when the procedure was used.

2. Use the two-column note taking system to take notes in a class you are presently attending. Evaluate the procedure.

3. Practice the REST system described in this chapter. If you feel it is an aid to learning, use REST with your students in a forthcoming lesson. Ask students whether they enjoyed the REST method of study.

Reflecting on Your Reading

1. Without returning to the chapter, categorize the following terms under the three major categories below. Use a separate sheet of paper.

attitude	daily logs	study-skills assessment
previewing	outlining	graphs
glossary	note taking	cartoons
index	table of contents	pictures
skimming	maps	drafting study questions
charts	setting purpose	compulsivity
home reader	self-discipline	work routines
REST system	REAP system	skill-teaching paradigm
demand		reduction of uncertainty

Responsibility   Using a Study System   Organizing for Study

After completing the exercise, check your work by skimming the chapter again to determine the suitability of your answers.

2. Fill in the postgraphic organizer with the words provided.

charts	assessment	pictures	quiet place
homework	library	dictionary	REAP
responsibility	GRP	daily	note taking
maps	underlining	text parts	

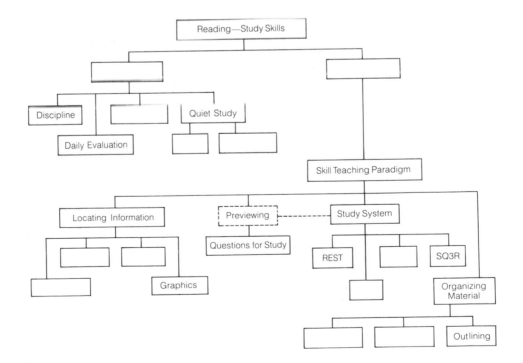

References

Aaronson, S. (1975). Note taking improvement: A combined auditory, functional and psychological approach. *Journal of Reading.* 19, 1, 8–12.

Adler, M. J. & Van Doren, C. (1952). *How To Read a Book.* New York: Simon & Schuster.

Annis, L. & Davis, J. K. (1978). Study techniques—Comparing their effectiveness. *The American Biology Teacher.* (February), 106–110.

Annis, L. & Davis, J. K. (1982). A normative study of students' reported preferred study techniques. *Reading World, 21,* 201–207.

Armbruster, B. B. & Anderson, T. H. (1981). Content area textbooks. Reading Education Report No. 23, Urbana, IL: University of Illinois Center for the Study of Reading.

Ausubel, D. P. (1968). *Educational psychology: A cognitive view.* New York: Holt, Rinehart & Winston.

Barker, D. (1979). "Color It Easy," *School Media Quarterly, 7,* 3, 221–223.

Barrett, T. (1972). Taxonomy of Reading Comprehension. *Reading 360 Monograph.* Lexington, MA: Ginn.

Bloom, B. (1956). *Taxonomy of educational objectives: Cognitive domain.* New York: McKay.

Britton, J., et al. (1975). *The development of writing abilities.* London: Methuen/School Council.

Brown, S. B. & Peterson, T. T. (1969). The rebellious school dropout. *School and Society, 97,* 437–439.

Cashen, V. J. & Leicht, K. L. (1970). Role of the isolation effect in a formal educational setting. *Journal of Educational Psychology, 61,* 900–904.

Colwell, C. G., Mangano, N. G., Childs, D. & Case, D. (1986). Cognitive, affective, and behavioral differences between students receiving instruction using alternative lesson formats. *Proceedings from the National Reading and Language Arts Conference.*

Durkin, D. (1978–1979). What classroom observations reveal about reading comprehension instruction. *Reading Research Quarterly, 14,* 481–533.

Eanet, M. & Manzo, A. V. (1976). REAP—A strategy for improving reading/writing/study skills. *Journal of Reading, 19,* 647–652.

Elliott, D. & Wendling, A. (1966). Capable dropouts and the social milieu of the high school. *Journal of Educational Research, 60,* 180–186.

Estes, T. H. & Vaughan, J. L. (1986). *Reading, writing, and reasoning beyond the primary grades.* Boston: Allyn & Bacon.

Fowler, R. L. & Baker, A. S. (1974). Effectiveness of highlighting for retention of text material. *Journal of Applied Psychology, 59,* 358–364.

Herber, H. L. (1970). *Teaching reading in content areas.* Englewood Cliffs, NJ: Prentice-Hall.

Hunt, E. B. (1971). What kind of computer is man? *Cognitive Psychology, 2,* 57–98.

Manzo, A. V. (1975). Guided reading procedure. *Journal of Reading, 18,* 287–291.

McAndrew, D. A. (1983). Underlining and note taking: Some suggestions from research. *Journal of Reading, 27,* 103–108.

Morgan, R. F., Meeks, J., Schollaert, A., & Paul, J. (1986). *Critical reading/ thinking skills for the college student.* Dubuque, IA: Kendall/Hunt Pub. Co.

Neisser, U. (1967). *Cognitive psychology.* New York: Appleton-Century-Crofts.

Newell, A. & Simon, H. A. (1972). *Human problem solving.* New York: Prentice-Hall.

Pauk, W. (1974). *How to study in college.* Boston: Houghton Mifflin.

Pearson, P. D. (1985). Changing the face of reading comprehension instruction. *The Reading Teacher,* April, 724–737.

Rickards, J. P. & August, G. J. (1975). Generative underlining strategies in prose recall. *Journal of Educational Psychology, 67,* 860–865.

Robinson, F. P. (1961). *Effective Study* (Rev. ed.). New York: Harper & Row.

Rogers, D. B. (1984). Assessing study skills. *Journal of Reading, 27,* 346–354.

Sauin, S. (1978). *Turn-Ons.* Aulander, NC: Fearon Pittman Publishers.

Schallert, D. L. & Kleiman, G. M. (1979). Why the teacher is easier to understand than the textbook. *Reading Education Report, No. 9.* Urbana, IL: University of Illinois, Center for the Study of Reading.

Sherer, P. (1975). Skimming and scanning: De-mything the process with a college student. *Journal of Reading, 19,* 24–27.

Stanton, S. (1986). *The 25 hour woman.* Old Tappan, NJ: F. H. Revell.

Stauffer, R. (1969). *Directing reading maturity as a cognitive process.* New York: Harper & Row.

Tadlock, D. R. (1978). SQ3R—Why it works, based on an information processing theory of learning. *Journal of Reading, 22,* 110–112.

Thorndike, E. L. (1917). Reading on reasoning: A study of mistakes in paragraph reading. *Journal of Educational Psychology, 8,* 823–832.

Wertsch, J. V. (1978). Adult-child interaction and the roots of metacognition. *The Quarterly Newsletter of the Institute of Comparative Human Development, 2,* 15–18.

9 Enhanced Study for Reflection and Retention

It is hard work to fill one's life with meaning."

Chaim Potok,
The Chosen

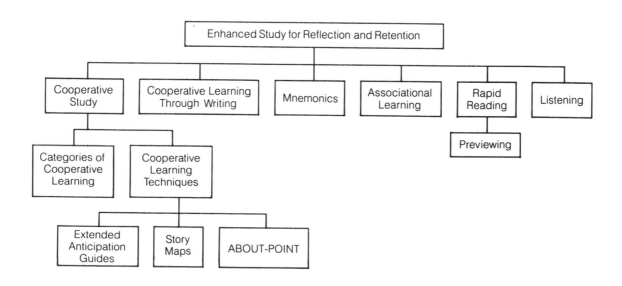

1. Below is a list of terms used in this chapter. Some of them may be familiar to you in a general context, but in this chapter they may be used in a different way than you are used to. Rate your knowledge by placing a + in front of those you are sure that you know, a √ in front of those you have some knowledge about, and a 0 in front of those you don't know. Be ready to locate and pay special attention to their meanings when they are presented in the chapter:

_____ fatigue

_____ cooperative learning

_____ mnemonics

_____ purposive

_____ cybernetic sessions

_____ narrative story guide

_____ visual cooperative study

_____ extended anticipation guide

_____ paired reading

_____ information rush

_____ associational learning

_____ lookbacks

_____ guided writing process

_____ acrostics

_____ acronyms

2. Do you like to study alone or in cooperative study groups? Think about whether you are a "loner" in your study habits or whether you are a "groupie." If you like to study alone, reflect on and list some benefits you might derive from working cooperatively in a study group. If you enjoy cooperative study, reflect on and list the benefits of "going it alone" in studying text material. Whatever your preference, as you read this chapter keep an open mind concerning the flexibility of using both types of study behaviors—quiet, individual study and group study.

Objectives:

As you read this chapter, focus your attention on the following objectives. You will:

1. understand the term *cooperative study*.

2. understand the various categories of cooperative study.

3. be able to use cooperative study techniques such as anticipation guides and story guides.

4. be able to use the ABOUT-POINT technique for enhanced study.

5. understand the importance of cooperative learning through writing.

6. be able to teach the use of mnemonics to students in content area classrooms.

"I want a book on speed-reading and 85 Westerns."

Herman. Copyright 1981 Universal Press Syndicate. All rights reserved. Reprinted with permission of Universal Press Syndicate.

7. be able to use associational learning aids for enhanced study.
8. understand rapid reading and its importance to reading and study.
9. be able to use several rapid-reading drills to improve students' reading rate.
10. understand the importance of teacher-monitored listening strategies to student achievement in all content classes.

Purpose: The teacher's job entails not only training students in traditional study skills but also providing a classroom atmosphere of reflective and cooperative study to help students improve retention of text material. As you read this chapter, remember these "three things you should never forget" from Joan Minninger's book *Total Recall: How to Boost Your Memory Power* (p. 254):

1. People remember what enhances them and gives them pleasure.
2. People forget what cannot be used immediately in their lives.
3. Everyone should be allowed at least a 20 percent margin for error.

Study As Hard Work

The National Bureau of Standards suggests this formula for calculating the temperature of a house's basement:

$$t_b = \frac{A_f U_f t_i - t_0(A_G U_G - A_{w1} U_{w1}) + t_g(A_b U_b + A_{w2} U_{w2})}{A_f U_f + A_g U_g + A_{w1} U_{w1} + A_b U_b - A_{w2} U_{w2}}$$

The world we live in is often complex and genuinely confusing. However, it is hoped that most of it is not as confusing as the above formula. Alfred North Whitehead may have pinpointed the problem when he said, "We think in generalities, we live in detail." Many K–12 students are not good at the detailed thinking Whitehead alluded to. Study and disciplined inquiry of all kinds are, in actuality, attention to detail. Many students refuse to study when the details seem, to them, overwhelming and confusing. For example, a student once said, "My teachers pressure me to study. My parents pressure me to study. You've got to be strong. I just say no to studying." This speaks to how ineffective our posturing, lecturing, and badgering is in getting children to enjoy learning and to study efficiently.

Chapter 1 explains in detail the PAR framework. Almost every technique described in the present chapter emphasizes the importance of Reflection, the R of the acronym, which students should be encouraged to do as part of the learning process. Whereas prereading activities help improve comprehension, postreading reflective study helps guarantee both better comprehension and greater retention of the reading matter. The best place to teach students how to be reflective in studying is in the classroom. Because teachers have little control over study behaviors outside of class, they must provide careful guidance and practice which will then carry over to independent study.

The teaching of reflection and enhanced study can begin when teachers are honest with students, letting them know that learning can sometimes be difficult but that it is always rewarding. The famous Ebbinghaus (1908) studies around the turn of the century described the difficulty of learning. Ebbinghaus postulated that tremendous amounts of information are forgotten in a short period of time—up to 60 or 70 percent in only a few days. He also made these important discoveries which still seem to hold true today:

1. Fatigue is a factor in one's ability to remember.
2. Earlier study and learning tends to get buried by later learning.

Figure 9.1. Ebbinghaus curve of forgetting.

3. Learned images may decay over time and end up changed in meaning from what was originally perceived.
4. Memories erode, and most information (an estimate of 90 percent) is forgotten over prolonged periods of time.

In short, forgetting is natural and remembering is difficult. This fact is graphically illustrated in the Ebbinghaus curve of forgetting, shown in Figure 9.1.

Many students seem to think that remembering is natural and forgetting is difficult, except in their *own* case! Students often feel that everyone else in the class is absorbing and remembering material—that everyone is better at retaining information than they are. Teachers need to allay students' fears by explaining that learning how to study and how to retain information is difficult; these are skills which require the development and practice of prescribed techniques.

Study needn't be equated with "lonely learning," however. In this chapter, we describe cooperative study strategies that both enhance retention and make the arduous task of study more fun and rewarding for students. Also, we will be describing techniques which enhance retention, such as note taking, mnemonic and associational learning aids, and rapid reading with previewing.

Cooperative Study

What Is Cooperative Study?

Almost three decades ago, William Perry (1959) warned of an overemphasis on teaching study skills at the expense of teaching why the skills should be used and when they should be used. He stated that "the mechanics of reading skill are inseparable . . . from the individual's purpose as he reads" (p. 198). Thus, it is as important for teachers to set a purposeful tone and atmosphere for classroom study as it is for them to teach a particular study technique or skill.

There is a growing body of research to indicate that giving students opportunities to learn cooperatively in the classroom can enhance learning (Larson and Dansereau, 1986; Leal, Crays and Moetz, 1985; Palincsar and Brown, 1984; Johnson and Johnson, 1987). Cooperative learning also will aid young children in maintaining and generalizing study skills. Studies show (as is no surprise to the classroom teacher) that without continued practice in a relaxed atmosphere, students discontinue the use of a skill or forget it (Brown and Barclay, 1976; Hagen, Hargrave, and Ross, 1973). One by-product of cooperative learning is that it may lessen stress reactions such as self-deprecation, lack of clear goals, disparagement, immature relationships with teachers, or pervasive depression (Gentile and McMillan, 1987). Most important, students learn the skill of working together as they discuss what and how material can best be learned. Students who work together also appear to have a higher regard for school and for the subjects they are studying and are more confident and self-assured. Rasinski and Nathenson-Mejia (1987) note that the cooperative classroom environment teaches social development, social responsibility (stressed in chapter 8 as an important precursor to study), and concern for one another. Vaughan and Estes (1986), in discussing cooperative learning, note that "an advantage is an increase in the amount of understanding of ideas; with two people studying a text, the chances are that one of them will understand something that confuses the other. Hence, we find again . . . that the object of study is understanding. Rarely, outside of school settings, does one find solitary attempts at understanding; usually people invite others to share in their discoveries and to engage in cooperative learning activities. This is true for erudite scientists and casual readers alike" (p. 147).

Eighty-six years earlier, in 1900, Dewey recognized the worth of cooperative learning with this observation: "When the school introduces and trains each child of society into membership within such a little community, saturating him with the spirit of service and providing him with the instruments of effective self-direction, we shall have the deepest and best guaranty of a larger society which is worthy, lovely, and harmonious" (pp. 27, 28).

Cooperative study means more than telling students to get together in groups and work. Rather, it is a structured experience when students, preferably in groups of two, three, and four, practice learning by using study skills emphasized by the teacher for a particular lesson. Glasser (1986, p. 75) in *Control Theory in the Classroom* gives eight reasons why "small learning-teams" will motivate almost all students. According to Glasser, these teams do the following:

1. Create a sense of belonging
2. Provide initial motivation for students who have not worked previously
3. Provide ego-fulfillment for stronger students to help weaker ones
4. Provide continued motivation for weaker students, who see that team effort brings rewards, whereas their individual efforts were usually not good enough to get rewarded
5. Free students from dependence on the teacher
6. Enable students to get past superficiality to learn in-depth and vital knowledge
7. Teach students how to convince others that they have learned the material (communication skills)
8. Keep students interested and achieving by having teachers change the teams on a regular basis. There is always the chance a student, if not doing well with one team, will be more successful as a member of another cooperative learning team.

Examples of Cooperative Study

Oral Cooperative Study

Karen Wood (1987), in an excellent review of cooperative learning approaches, maintains that verbalizing newly acquired information is the most powerful study technique. Here are some of Wood's suggestions for combining oral and cooperative study:

Group Retelling. Content teachers provide groups of two or three students with different reading material about the same topic. Students read material silently and retell, in their own words, what they have learned to their group. Group members may add to any retelling by sharing similar information from their reading or from their own experiences.

Associational Dialogue. Students work in pairs from an assigned vocabulary list to discuss each word on the list. In this manner, students learn by interacting with others.

Needs Grouping. To determine students' conceptual knowledge of a subject, teachers give pretests (described, with examples, in chapter 3). Students who did not do well on particular areas of the pretest can be grouped together for reflective study over that part of the unit.

Buddy System. Teachers pair weaker students with stronger ones. In this ability grouping, each is asked to take responsibility for the other's learning. Daniel Fader also describes this process in *Hooked on Books.*

Cybernetic Sessions. Wood cites Masztal's (1986) work in describing a technique to summarize lessons through group interaction. After reading a selection, groups brainstorm answers to thought-provoking questions posed by the teacher. Answers are shared in the group and with the whole class.

Research Grouping. During a unit of study, students work in groups to research a topic in the classroom or in the library.

Written Cooperative Study

Writing can be incorporated into cooperative study in several ways. Davey (1987), for example, recommends the following steps as effective in guiding students' writing of research reports:

1. *Topic selection.* Students use factstorming to select a topic or subtopic. (See chapters 3 and 4 for examples of factstorming.)
2. *Planning.* Teams meet to establish a research plan. They generate questions to be answered and a schedule for study.
3. *Researching the topic.* Teams divide questions to be answered and begin taking notes, working in class and in the library. The teacher may help with a library search guide (explained in chapter 8).
4. *Organizing.* Teams meet to share information, organize material in outline form, and decide what information to delete and which questions to research further.
5. *Writing.* Team members work individually or in pairs to write first draft, check initial drafts, and revise and edit the final report.

For early elementary students, Bergenske (1987) suggests that narrative story guides can be a useful cooperative learning technique. Such an activity guides readers to learn the narrative sequence. She recommends that guides be made before story maps or post-graphic organizers. At first, children can work with the teacher to complete a narrative story guide such as the one shown in Figure 9.2. Narrative or general story maps, such as the one in Figure 9.3, may be used by children in creating stories in pairs or in groups of three or more.

Visual Cooperative Study

Bergenske maintains that, after completing narrative story guides, students in early elementary grades will be better able to make and produce postreading concept maps and post-graphic organizers, both valuable aids for cooperative study and learning. In a recent study, Bean et al. (1986) found that a group given instruction in summarizing, generating questions, and creating graphic organizers scored significantly better on text recall than did either a group instructed in graphic organizers only or a group instructed in outlining.

Graphic organizers (explained in chapter 4) allow students to display graphically and visually what they comprehended in a particular reading selection. They also encourage class participation and enable students to interact with each other while involved in the learning process. In this manner, students can take part in a group process to

---

(Title)

Once upon a time in _____ , there lived
(Setting)

_____ and _____
(Character)   (Character)

They had a problem. The problem was that _____

_____
(Problem)

So their goal, or what they wanted to do was _____

_____
(Goal)

In order to accomplish this goal, they did four different things.

They _____

they _____

they _____

and they _____

When they had finished doing these things (episodes) they had solved their problem. So the resolution

was that _____

_____
(Resolution)

This story was created by _____
(author)

Figure 9.2. Narrative story guide.

From Bergenske, M. Dianne. (1987). The missing link in narrative story mapping. *The Reading Teacher*, Vol. 41, no. 3, pp. 333–335. Reprinted with permission of M. Dianne Bergenske and the International Reading Association.

create graphic organizers such as those in Figures 9.4 and 9.5. The first is the product of students' brainstorming after reading a rule book on volleyball in a physical education class. The second was completed by a group after reading a story about the golfer Ben Hogan.

Other Activities for Cooperative Study

Extended Anticipation Guides

Another technique which can be adapted to cooperative learning is the extended anticipation guide (Dufflemeyer, Baum, and Merkley, 1987). As noted in chapter 4, anticipation guides can aid students in predicting outcomes. The extended guide can spark discussion and reinforce or verify information students learned as well as enable students to modify predictions to take into account new insights and information. Figure 9.6 presents two examples: an anticipation guide done individually

Name: _____

1. Title: _____

2. Setting: _____

3. Characters: _____
   _____

4. Problem: _____

5. Goal: _____

6. Episodes: _____
   _____

7. Resolution: _____
   _____

Figure 9.3. General story map.
From Bergenske, M. Dianne. (1987). The missing link in narrative story mapping. *The Reading Teacher*, Vol. 41, no. 3, pp. 333–335. Reprinted with permission of M. Dianne Bergenskc and the International Reading Association.

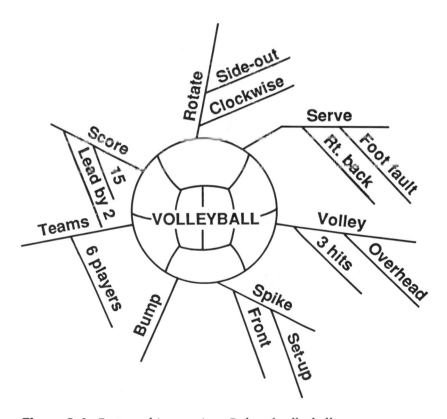

Figure 9.4. Post-graphic organizer: Rules of volleyball.

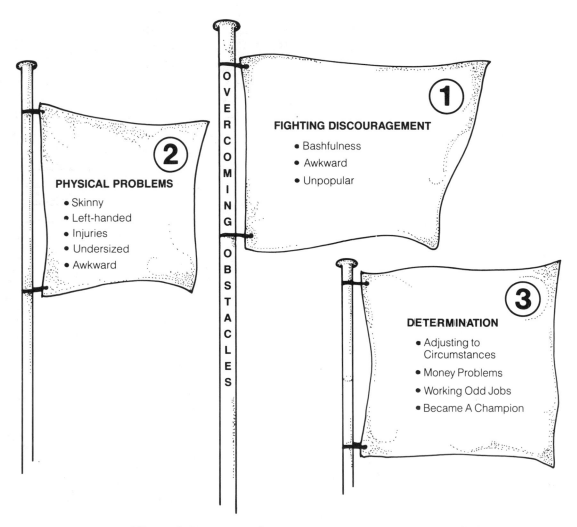

Figure 9.5. Post-graphic organizer on Ben Hogan story called "He Followed the Sun Again.".

by high-school students before reading *The Jungle* and an extended anticipation guide done by students working in groups after reading *The Jungle*.

ABOUT/POINT

The ABOUT/POINT study strategy is a versatile aid for cooperative study (Morgan et al., 1986). In kindergarten and first grade, teachers can use it as a listening and speaking aid after reading a story aloud to students. In upper elementary and junior high school, students can

Figure 9.6. Anticipation Guide and Extended Anticipation Guide.

PART I: ANTICIPATION GUIDE

Instructions: Before you begin reading *The Jungle,* read the statements below. If you agree with a statement, place a check in the "Agree" column in front of it. If you disagree with the statement, place a check in the "Disagree" column. Be ready to explain or defend your choices in class discussion.

Agree	Disagree	Statement
		1. Anyone who works hard can get ahead.
		2. An employer has a responsibility for his employee's safety and welfare.
		3. Companies that process packaged food should be responsible for policing themselves for health violations.
		4. Immigrants were readily accepted into the American system at the turn of the century.
		5. Unions can remedy all labor grievances.

PART II: EXTENDED ANTICIPATION GUIDE

Instructions: Now that you have read *The Jungle* and information related to the statements in Part I, get into groups to complete this section. If you feel that what you read supports your choices in Part I, place a check in the "Support" column below. If the information read does NOT support your choice in Part I, check the "No Support" column and write a reason why the statement cannot be supported in the third column. Keep your reasons brief and in your own words.

Support	No Support	Reason for No Support (in your own words)
1.		
2.		
3.		
4.		
5.		

work in groups to recall information from content material. To use the ABOUT/POINT strategy, teachers ask students to reread a passage then to decide in groups what the passage is "ABOUT" and what details— "POINTS"—support their response. Teachers can provide study sheets which look like this:

This reading is ABOUT _____

_____

and the POINTS are _____

_____

An example of a completed study sheet from a high school business or consumer mathematics class might look like this:

This reading is ABOUT: The high cost, including hidden costs, of automobile ownership.

And the POINTS are:

Few people have cash enough to buy a car outright.

Therefore, they borrow from banks, auto dealers, or small loan agencies.

Costs are affected by the state and region in which the borrower lives.

Few institutions will lend money unless the borrower purchases life insurance.

Paired Reading

Another strategy which works with middle and secondary students is paired reading, developed by Larson and Dansereau (1986). Students begin by reading a short assignment. Then, working in pairs, one partner is designated "recaller" and the other is designated "listener." The recaller retells the passage from memory; the listener interrupts only to ask for clarification. Then the listener corrects ideas summarized incorrectly and adds important ideas from the text material that were not mentioned in the retelling. During the time the listener is clarifying, the recaller can also add clarification. In this manner, the pair works together to reconstruct as much as possible of what they read. The pair can use drawings, pictures, and diagrams to facilitate further understanding of the material. Students alternate roles of reteller and listener after each reading segment, which may number four or five over the course of one class period. Karen Wood notes that paired reading is successful because it is "based on recent research in metacognition which suggests that without sufficient reinforcement and practice, some students have difficulty monitoring their own comprehension" (1987, p. 13). Paired reading is also based on elaboration strategy which, according to Weinstein (1987), helps students learn new concepts by drawing on their prior experiences.

Generative Questions for Cooperative Study

Recent studies have centered on student-generated questions. Davey and McBride (1986) found that children who were trained to develop probing questions after the reading, either individually or in small groups, scored better on a test of comprehension of the material. A similar study by MacDonald (1986) found that groups instructed in methods for asking questions had higher comprehension scores than those groups without this training.

Summarizing in Groups

A number of researchers have addressed the importance of summarization to the study and retention of reading material (Scardamalia and Bereiter, 1984; Garner, 1985). Garner notes that summarization involves

(1) judging ideas deemed important, (2) applying rules for condensing text, and (3) producing a shortened text in oral or written form. Studies consistently show that skilled readers have the ability to make summarizations, whereas unskilled readers almost always lack this ability (Scardamalia and Bereiter, 1984; Garner, 1985; Brown and Smiley, 1977). To learn to write effective summaries, students can be asked to work in groups and use the following six rules suggested by Brown and Day (1983) to write a summary of a text: (1) delete all unnecessary material, (2) delete redundancies, (3) substitute a superordinate term for a list of items, (4) use a superordinate term for a list of actions, (5) select topic sentences from ones provided in the text, and (6) construct topic sentences when not provided explicitly in the text.

Lookbacks

Garner (1985) also discusses the importance of "backtracking" or "text lookback" in overcoming memory difficulties in reading portions of text. There is evidence that both children and adults fail to use such strategies (Garner, Macready, and Wagoner, 1984; Alexander, Hare and Garner, 1984), even though recent research (Amlund, Kardash, and Kulhavy, 1986), as well as earlier research (Samuels, 1979), has shown that repeated readings and reinspection of text makes a significant difference in recall. Ruth Strang, the great reading educator, once said that she was disappointed when she entered a school library and found students reading for long periods of time without looking up to reflect on what they were reading and not glancing back over material during their study.

We recommend that teachers ask students to use the lookback strategy after a reading by working in groups to clarify confusing points. For instance, students in a social studies class can be asked to reinspect a chapter on economic interdependence to find why credit and credit buying are so important to the American economy and to economic growth. Students can then be asked to write a group summary of what the text says about the important concept of credit. For both summaries and text lookback, Garner (1985) stresses the following:

1. Some ideas are more important than others.
2. Some ideas can (and must) be ignored.
3. Students need to be taught how to use titles and topic sentences.
4. Students need to learn that ideas cross boundaries of sentences.
5. "Piecemeal" reading which focuses on comprehending one sentence at a time is not conducive to summarizing or gaining ideas from text.
6. Rules of summarization (such as those presented by Brown and Day) need to be learned and practiced.
7. Students must be taught how and when to apply both the summarization and lookback strategies.

8. These strategies cannot be adequately accomplished in a hurried classroom atmosphere and environment.
9. Students need to practice these strategies in a number of content areas to effect transfer.

Chapter 12 provides information about using lookbacks with at-risk readers.

First-Person Summaries

Students can write first-person summaries and then share them in cooperative learning groups. Often students read an assignment or memorize information without a true understanding of the material. First-person summaries allow students to process information by writing in their own words about a topic. Using the first person forces students to become personally involved in the material. Teachers may be able to recognize and correct any deficiencies in students' understanding by reading their summaries. For instance, when studying photosynthesis in science, students might write a first-person essay in which they take the part of a water molecule. They must explain how they get into a plant, where they journey in the plant, what happens once they reach the chloroplast, etc. In this way, students gain a deeper understanding of the process, and teachers can identify problems in student understanding. This type of assignment also works well with topics such as "a day in the life of a new Irish immigrant in 1835," or "my life as a red blood cell."

Cooperative Learning through Writing

Davey (1987) has suggested that a cooperative learning team for writing research reports "can provide the systematic, guided practice necessary for effective use of many study skills. With this approach, students view their study strategies as functional and relevant to the learning task and are more actively involved because of the teaming component" (p. 705). The example given in chapter 5, Activity 5.7, shows the stages of both writing and group process at work. Konopak, Martin and Martin (1987) suggest teachers follow these steps for producing cooperative writing:

1. Activate prior knowledge of the new topic.
2. Have students share experiences in groups.
3. Have students write on the topic for clarification.
4. Set purpose by introducing new concepts prior to reading.
5. Have students read the passage, relating new information through prior knowledge.
6. Have another writing session to phase in new information.
7. Use whole-class discussion of material centered around the individual writings.

8. Have students meet in small groups to share individual writings and discuss each student's understanding of the topic.
9. Following group discussion, have students rewrite to improve their previous writing.
10. Bring closure by allowing students to use writing in preparing for a test.

The Guided Writing Procedure

The guided writing procedure (Smith and Bean, 1980) is an excellent technique that can be used to enhance learning in the content areas. This technique was explained in detail in chapter 6. We wish to reiterate that the GWP provides an excellent opportunity for students to work cooperatively in groups to accomplish specific objectives. On day one, for instance, students work in groups to list and organize their ideas about a topic. On day 2, students also work in groups to revise earlier drafts.

Why Cooperative Learning Works

In a recent article, Weinstein (1987) has suggested that cooperative learning strategies do work in aiding student comprehension and retention because they fall into one or more of what she calls "categories of learning strategies," i.e., processes and methods useful in acquiring and retrieving information. Weinstein's five categories of learning strategies are:

1. *Rehearsal strategies.* Techniques discussed in this chapter include lookbacks, note taking, and associational dialogue.
2. *Elaboration strategies.* Techniques discussed in this chapter include group retelling, cybernetic sessions, paired reading, student-generated questions, guided writing procedure and listening.
3. *Organizational strategies.* Techniques discussed in this chapter include summarizing, narrative story guides, postgraphic organizer, needs grouping, ABOUT/POINT, research grouping and mapping.
4. *Comprehension monitoring strategies.* Techniques discussed in this chapter include extended anticipation guide and research teams.
5. *Affective strategies.* Techniques discussed in this chapter include paired readings, reduction of anxiety, positive rewards for learning in groups, and buddy system.

Before ending this discussion of cooperative learning, we wish to reemphasize a point made frequently throughout this book: learning is difficult in a hurried, pressured classroom environment. A first grader recently explained, "The teacher never lets me finish. I never have enough time to finish." This is a lament that holds true in all too many classrooms. Jeremy Rifkin (1987), in his new book, *Time Wars*, argues that we appear to be trapped in our own technology. Rifkin maintains that the constant pressure to become more efficient causes Americans to feel that they do not have enough time to get things done. The pressure alluded to by Rifkin, which has permeated even today's classroom, is detrimental because all types of classroom effort have to occur in a calm, unhurried atmosphere where students have freedom to explore ideas, develop creativity, and solve problems.

Mnemonic and Associational Learning

Probably no technique for enhancing memory has been around longer than mnemonics or associational learning. Long before the advent of written symbols, people used rather complex forms of associations in recounting lengthy stories in the oral tradition. It is also known that in eighteenth-century Europe, serious scholarly thought was given to mnemonics. One of the earliest references to the term *mnemonics* is found in an obscure book entitled *A View of the Elementary Principles of Education, Founded on the Study of the Nature of Man*, written in 1833 by a Viennese medical doctor, G. Spurzheim. Even then, the author spent most of his chapter entitled "Mnemonics" trying to convince teachers to use the mnemonic system. It seems that there is a lengthy history of teacher apathy toward memory-training devices. Spurzheim writes:

> The mutual influence of the faculties is the basis of what is called Mnemonics, or of the art of strengthening memory. This art is very ancient, but in consequence of its principles not being sufficiently understood, it has been rejected by some, and extolled to excess by others. The great errors committed in mnemonics, resemble those committed in all branches of education, and in all sorts of institutions. Teachers of every sort look upon themselves as the standard for the whole of mankind, and commonly have recourse to that faculty which is the most active in them, reproduces the most easily its anterior perceptions, and excites other powers with the greatest facility. They err in overlooking the differences of the innate dispositions and talents of different individuals (p. 135).

Over one hundred and fifty years ago Spurzheim related problems that still exist today concerning mnemonics and memory training: some (like the memory-training experts) make too much of its worth, and others (like teachers) reject the notion because they do not understand the benefits. He also speaks to the lack of individualization of instruction long before the term came into use.

Benefits of Mnemonics

There are benefits to memory-training techniques, the chief being that difficult study can be made easier through their use. A recent study by

Peters and Levin (1986) found mnemonics benefited both above- and below-average readers when they read short fictional passages as well as longer content passages. Students instructed in mnemonic strategies remembered significantly more information on names and accomplishments than did those in the control group. Also, Levin, Morrison and McGivern (1986) found that students given instruction in mnemonic techniques scored significantly higher on tests of immediate recall and on recall tests administered three days later than did either a group taught to memorize material or a group that were given motivation talks and then used their usual methods of study. Mnemonics instruction also has been found to be effective for learning new words in foreign language classes (Cohen, 1987). Although a recent study by McDaniel, Pressley, and Dunay (1987) did find that key-word mnemonics did not significantly affect retention of text material, many recent studies have attested to the benefits of mnemonic techniques. Despite these favorable studies, we have observed that teachers still do little memory training with their students, even though it takes only a small effort to get students to try mnemonics. For example, teachers can give vocabulary or chapter terms that need to be memorized and ask students to form groups in which they create their own mnemonics. Teachers can have students share their mnemonics with the whole class and can give rewards for the one judged to be the best. Through such practice, students form the habit of creating mnemonics for themselves. Following are actual mnemonics that were generated and used by students in a number of content areas in third through twelfth grades. To demonstrate that we believe in this technique, the first is an acronym used by one of the authors in a talk frequently given on "total teaching."

Mnemonic	Type	Learned Material
HICCUP	acronym	Total Teaching: Human relations training, Instruction, Classroom management, Content, Use of materials, Preparation
MEAL REPS	acronym	Areas flourishing from 1865–1915: Mass entertainment, Architecture, Literature, Religion, Education, Painting, Sports (grade 11, history)

All eager children must play yet always be happy.	acrostic	Standard United States time zones: Atlantic, Eastern, Central, Mountain, Pacific, Yukon, Alaska, Bering, Hawaii (grade 7, social studies)
Ocie and Alfe Canak in their MG (Two French-Canadian brothers riding in their sports car)	acrostic	Elements of the earth's crust in order of abundance of occurrence: O, Si, Al, Fe, Ca, Na, K, Mg Oxygen, silicon, aluminum, iron, calcium, sodium, potassium, magnesium (high-school chemistry)

Memory-Enhancing Techniques/Associational Learning

Chunking

Chunking, mentioned briefly in chapter 4, refers to grouping large amounts of material into two or three categories to help students remember material more readily and retrieve information more quickly. The following social studies concepts can be hard to remember separately:

labor	machines	drills
trees	computers	water
power plants	wildlife	soil
trucks	oil	buildings
union workers	sunlight	airports

However, chunking information into these categories makes learning the fifteen items much easier:

Natural Resources	Capital Resources	Human Resources
sunlight	airports	union workers
wildlife	buildings	labor
oil	drills	
water	machines	
soil	computers	
trees	trucks	
	power plants	

Chunking information through categorization exercises (which can be used to review for tests) is an excellent way to help poor readers better understand text material. Chunking capitalizes on connecting prior knowledge to new knowledge, thus enhancing learning.

Associations

Students can be taught to memorize words by associating the words with outrageous images. For instance, students can imagine:

dress	. . . dress
car	. . . giant car wearing huge dress
piano	. . . a piano flying over a giant car
computer	. . . a computer coming alive to play the piano

In this manner, one word leads to the next to make a long list of associations.

Method of Loci

This method improves students' ability to remember lists of unrelated objects. It also can be a sequencing task which will enable a student to remember items in a definite order. In this ancient method, used in Roman times by orators, a person mentally "walks through" a house that has very familiar surroundings. By choosing fifteen to twenty distinct loci—familiar places like a stove or closet—a student can place objects to be learned in strategic points throughout the house. Figure 9.7 shows household places used to remember names.

Peg Words

Whereas association deals with linking words together through an outrageous image, peg-word systems associate a target word to a fixed numbered word. Listed below are ten peg words which identify familiar places found at many schools.

1. Computer center	6. Classroom
2. Guidance office	7. Hallway
3. Cafeteria	8. Principal's office
4. Auditorium	9. Nurse's clinic
5. Library	10. Gymnasium

The words to be remembered are linked to the numbered peg word. The peg words do not have to be places. They can also be words that sound similar or rhyme with the word to be learned. An example would be the peg words *commotion* for *commodities* in an economics class or *this criminal* for *discrimination*.

Acronyms

The most time-honored mnemonic, an acronym is a word or phrase made entirely of letters which are cues to words we want to remember. PAR is an acronym for the instructional framework used in this book. In our earlier list of mnemonics, we categorized several as acronyms.

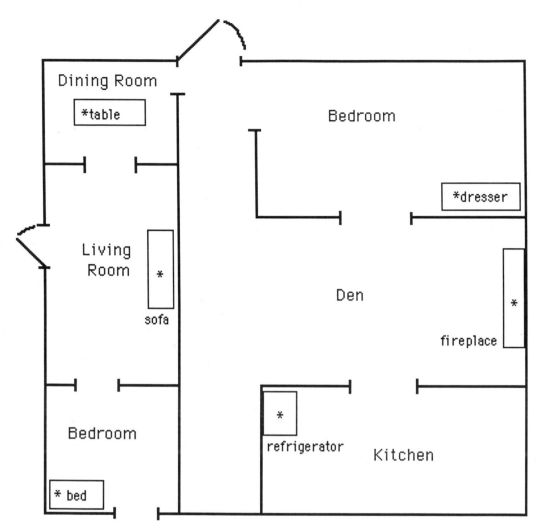

Figure 9.7. A loci map.
*Places with which to associate remembrances.

For example, suppose that we are reviewing musculo-skeletal systems for a test, and among the things we want to remember are the six boundaries of the axilla: Apex, Base, Anterior wall, Posterior wall, Medial wall, and Lateral wall. The initial letters are A B A P M L, which, rearranged, might create an acronym such as A.B. PALM.

Another way of creating an acronym to help us recall part of our information about the axilla would be to take the following list of the six branches of the axillary artery: Supreme thoracic, Thoracromial, Lateral thoracic, Anterior humeral circumflex, Posterior humeral circumflex, and *Subscapular*, and arrange the initial letters S T L A P S into the name of a fictitious patron saint of arteries, St. Laps. Other examples of acronyms include:

HOMES	Names of Great Lakes: Huron, Ontario, Michigan, Erie, Superior
ROY G. BIV	Colors of the spectrum: red, orange, yellow, green, blue, indigo, violet
FACE	The notes represented by the spaces of the G clef

Acrostics

An acrostic is a sentence or rhyme in which the first letter of each word is a cue. Within our mnemonic list, we identified some examples as acrostic. An acrostic to help us remember the boundaries of the axilla could be made using the initial letters *A B A P M L* to create a sentence like

Above, below, and pretty much lost.

An acrostic that might be helpful to us in remembering the planets is the following:

My Very Educated	Mercury, Venus, Earth, Mars,
Mother's Just	Jupiter, Saturn, Uranus, Neptune,
Served Us Nine	Pluto
Pizza pies.	

Mnemonic learning techniques such as those above can be a welcome learning aid especially for poor readers who find that they forget material too quickly (remember Ebbinghaus's studies showing that forgetting is natural). If we could help students to remember ten to fifty items with ease, think how their self-concepts and self-images might be affected. With practice, there seems to be almost no limit to improvement in long-term memory skill. We recommend familiarizing children in primary grades with these memory-enhancing techniques. Then they will possess a skill useful for the rest of their education.

MAD Technique

One way to familiarize primary and upper elementary children with mnemonics is to go MAD—the mnemonic-a-day technique. Have students work in groups to make a mnemonic a day for thirty days. The only stipulation is that each new mnemonic has to be in a different content area than the one created the day before. Children keep MAD logs and periodically refer to the logs to make certain they remember all accumulated mnemonics. By making a game of it, teachers can reward those students or groups of students who can create a MAD example for the most days consecutively. This can be an enjoyable yet purposeful activity.

Rapid Reading with Previewing

Edmund Burke Huey's thirteenth tenet in *The Psychology and Pedagogy of Reading* (1908) was that children should be taught, *from the first of reading instruction,* to read as fast as the nature of the reading material and their purpose would allow. He recommended speed drills to help students get information "efficiently and effectively." In 1925, William S. Gray, in a review of the literature on speed of reading, endorsed speed reading by concluding that such training could result in increased speed without a concurrent drop in comprehension. Many studies followed which addressed the value of speed reading, yet eighty years after Huey's pronouncement, there is probably no area of reading as controversial as that of speed reading. The very mention of "speed reading" carries with it a negative connotation for many teachers at all levels of education. In a recent study of adult readers, Carver (1985) concluded that speed readers he tested could not comprehend more than 75 percent of eighth-grade level material when reading faster than 600 words per minute. He also found that much of what passes as speed reading is really skimming, glossing material at over one thousand words per minute at fairly low comprehension levels. Other studies have questioned the quality of speed-reading research (Collins, 1979; Fleisher, Jenkins and Pany, 1979), the limited utility of eye-movement training (McConkie and Rayner, 1976; Rayner, 1978), and the limits to speed in the act of reading (Carver, 1985; Spache, 1976). Yet there is much more research needed on speed reading, evidenced in a recent study by Just, Carpenter, and Masson (1982) that found fairly positive results for speed readers when they answered higher-level comprehension questions.

Because of the rather suspect nature of speed reading, we recommend rapid reading, or speeding up one's reading, along with an emphasis on previewing the material. Previewing (explained in chapter 8) brings purpose to the reading by having the reader decide what he or she needs and wishes to know. We maintain that students can find answers to their questions more quickly by reading more rapidly after the previewing phase. We also suggest that it is better to read a chapter several times in a more rapid manner than it is to read the chapter one time at a laboriously slow rate. Samuels (1979) found that repeated reading of a material enhanced reader fluency and comprehension. Repeated reading is verification for several rapid readings. We are not advocating reading at 1000 or more words per minute. We do feel some

TABLE 9.1 *Types of Reading and Speed Ranges*

Level of Reading	Example	Purpose	Speed Range
1. Slow-systematic	• Highly technical text • Poetry	Careful analysis and evaluation (when reader has little background information)	100–200 wpm
2. Study-type	• Textbooks	Comprehension and recall of material	200–300 wpm
3. Bold reading	• Novels • Newspapers	Enough comprehension to bring enjoyment	300–600 wpm
4. Rapid reading	• Novels • Newspapers • Magazines • Reference materials	Overviews, skimming, scanning	600–800 wpm

study-reading should be at rates above 200 to 300 words per minute. (See Table 9.1 for types of reading and ranges.)

Study the following comparison.

Typical study-reading

$$200 \text{ wpm} \overline{)4000 \text{ word chapter}}^{\textstyle 20 \text{ minutes reading time}}$$

Rapid reading and previewing

preview phase $1000 \text{ wpm} \overline{)4000 \text{ word chapter}}^{\textstyle 4 \text{ minutes}}$

reading phase $400 \text{ wpm} \overline{)4000 \text{ word chapter}}^{\textstyle 10 \text{ minutes}}$

total time = 4 + 10 = 14

One can see that rapid reading and previewing actually save six minutes of study time over typical study-reading. Therefore, by taking time to preview, students can become more efficient readers. In chapter 4, we noted that, psychologically, previewing is valid because it enables the connection of the new to the known. Previewing also provides a mental "speed-up," which enhances a physical "speed-up."

Remember that reading rate is determined by these factors:

Type of material to be read
Reader's familiarity with contents
Reader's motivation or mood
Reader's purpose
Size of type
Amount of light available
Presence of distractions

Mental Push-ups

There are three reasonably easy exercises teachers can ask students to practice in rapid reading. The first of these is called "mental push-ups"—rate and comprehension drills. At the beginning of class, the teacher asks students to use a 3" × 5" card to "mentally push" themselves down one page of a content chapter or story so fast that they cannot absorb all the information on the page. (Older students who have had practice at the technique and who have better fine motor control can use a finger to pace themselves.) Then students close the book and write down what they learned. After the first reading, the amount retained is usually two to three words. The students repeat the procedure as many times as needed (usually two to four) until there is a "rush" of information, i.e., until they comprehend and can write out or verbalize most of what is on the page. With extended practice, it will take fewer readings for students to comprehend the material. This technique can be used to clarify cognitive structure and increase student attention at the beginning of a class period. With practice, it will help make students more facile and mentally alert in reading short passages.

Rapid-Reading Drills

A second activity in rapid reading is a variation on the idea explained above. Rapid-reading drills of three minutes can be conducted by teachers at the beginning of classes. Students are asked to read as fast as possible, in a straightforward, rapid-reading drill. Again, young children can use a 3" × 5" card as a pacer; they can later use the finger-pacing technique. The teacher can conduct one or two three-minute drills without taking away too much time from the day's lesson. In rapid-reading drills, students are not asked to write out what they learned. As a variation, however, they could be asked to form groups and discuss what each remembered from the reading.

Preview and Rapid-Reading Drill

A third exercise, the preview and rapid-reading drill, can be used when the teacher is directing the reading of a content chapter. Here the teacher monitors the previewing phase, culminating with students writing specific questions they wish to have answered in the reading (see DRTA, chapter 6). The previewing phase can be done as a whole class, in groups, or individually. Then the teacher asks that students read more rapidly than usual to find the answers to their preview questions. It should be noted that the three activities can be accomplished in any content area and can be started with better readers at a second-grade level.

Listening

Listening is a study skill which can enhance learning in any classroom. Gold (1981) describes the directed listening technique as a strategy for motivating and guiding students to improve listening. Teachers motivate students before the lesson by asking them to listen for certain information in the lecture or in the oral reading. In this prelistening discussion phase, students brainstorm areas of interest and questions to be answered. Teachers then deliver a lecture or read to the students portions of a chapter from a textbook. Thus, students are trained to know why they must listen and what they are expected to learn from listening.

As a variation, listening guides, similar to the extended anticipation guides explained earlier in this chapter, can be constructed to point to parts of the lecture or oral reading that need to be emphasized. In this manner, students are taught to listen more carefully for details and key points. Through such an *active listening* strategy, even primary students can be trained to be better listeners. To provide additional assistance for at-risk students, who often fail to pay attention to directions and who are often poor listeners, chapter 12 has a section on active listening with tips for better listening and examples of listening guides we have mentioned.

Time Line

The enhanced study and retention skills described in this chapter need to be emphasized from the early elementary years through high school in a systematic program that is understood and practiced by all teachers at all grades throughout a school. Table 9.2 presents strategies explained in this chapter within a time frame for introducing and emphasizing such skills.

Keep in mind that Table 9.2 is not meant to pinpoint the exact time each technique should be started; rather the table is meant to give a rough idea of when these strategies can be emphasized. Individual teachers may find that, in their particular class and content area, a technique may be adapted to work earlier than suggested. Also, this time line does not preclude teachers from using the techniques with students for the first time in senior high school. Better late than never!

T A B L E   9 . 2   *A Time Frame for Introducing and Teaching Strategies for Reflection and Retention*

Skill	K	1	2	3	4	5	6	7	8	9	10	11	12
Cooperative study													
group retellings			─	─	─	─	─	─	─	─	─	─	─
associational dialogue				─	─	─	─	─	─	─	─	─	─
needs grouping		─	─	─	─	─	─	─	─	─	─	─	─
buddy system				─	─	─	─	─	─	─	─	─	─
cybernetic sessions				─	─	─	─	─	─	─	─	─	─
research grouping			─	─	─	─	─	─	─	─	─	─	─
narrative story guides	─	─	─	─	─	─	─	─	─	─	─	─	─
general story maps	─	─	─	─	─	─	─	─	─	─	─	─	─
postgraphic organizers	─	─	─	─	─	─	─	─	─	─	─	─	─
extended anticipation guides				─	─	─	─	─	─	─	─	─	─
ABOUT/POINT						─	─	─	─	─	─	─	─
paired readings	─	─	─	─	─	─	─	─	─	─	─	─	─
student-generated questions	─	─	─	─	─	─	─	─	─	─	─	─	─
summarizations			─	─	─	─	─	─	─	─	─	─	─
look-backs	─	─	─	─	─	─	─	─	─	─	─	─	─
first-person summaries						─	─	─	─	─	─	─	─
Guided writing procedure			─	─	─	─	─	─	─	─	─	─	─
Mnemonics			─	─	─	─	─	─	─	─	─	─	─
Associational learning	─	─	─	─	─	─	─	─	─	─	─	─	─
MAD techniques			─	─	─	─	─	─	─	─	─	─	─
Rapid reading			─	─	─	─	─	─	─	─	─	─	─
Listening	─	─	─	─	─	─	─	─	─	─	─	─	─

One-Minute Summary

In chapters 8 and 9, we have explained study skills and study systems which will enhance students' ability to think and learn. By explaining and modeling study methods, teachers can show students how to obtain the most from their study. In addition, cooperative learning, mnemonics, associational learning, note taking, rapid reading with previewing, and listening have been identified as strategies which enhance retention of content because they provide an opportunity for students to practice, under a teacher's guidance, five important categories of learning and memory training—rehearsal, elaboration, organizational thinking, comprehension monitoring, and affective thinking.

Techniques described in this chapter work best when students have learned to be relaxed and to incorporate the PAR framework described in earlier chapters. Cooperative study requires an atmosphere of seriousness of purpose, confidence and assistance, and, above all, commitment to disciplined inquiry and study. Jacob Bronowski (1973), one of the great thinkers of the twentieth century, said this concerning the importance of commitment in human endeavor:

> We are all afraid—for our confidence, for the future, for the world. That is the nature of human imagination. Yet every man, every civilization, has gone forward because of its engagement with what it has set itself to do. The personal commitment of a man to his skill, the intellectual commitment and the emotional commitment working together as one, has made the Ascent of Man. (p. 438)

End-of-Chapter Activities

Preparing the Reader

Did the authors prepare you to read this chapter? How many of the selected vocabulary terms did you know before reading the chapter? Has your understanding of those terms improved after reading the chapter? For additional reflections, we recommend a writing exercise using the new terms.

Assisting Comprehension

1. What does the Bronowski quotation which ended this chapter mean to you? What relevance does it have to this chapter?

2. Study and complete the following graphic organizer:

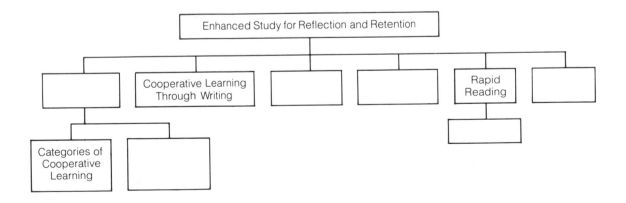

Reflecting on Your Reading

1. Think back over what you have learned in this chapter. Do you think about study skills in a new way after completing this chapter? What is new to you?

2. Think about and list ways you might change the day-to-day operations of your class to incorporate some or all of the techniques described in this chapter.

References

Aaronson, S. (1975). Notetaking improvement: A combined auditory, functional, and psychological approach. *Journal of Reading, 19,* 8–12.

Alexander, P. A., Hare, V. C., & Garner, R. (1984). The effects of time, access, and question type on response accuracy and frequency of lookbacks in older, proficient readers. *Journal of Reading Behavior, 16,* 119–130.

Amlund, J. T., Kardash, C. A. M., & Kulhavy, R. W. (1986). Repetitive reading and recall of expository text. *Reading Research Quarterly, 21,* 49–53.

Bean, T. W., et al. (1986). The effect of metacognitive instruction in outlining and graphic organizer construction on students' comprehension in a tenth-grade world history class. *Journal of Reading Behavior, 18,* 153–169.

Bergenske, M. D. (1987). The missing link in narrative story mapping. *The Reading Teacher, 41,* 333–335.

Britton, J. et al. (1975). *The development of writing abilities.* London: Methuen/Schools Council.

Bronowski, J. (1973). *The ascent of man.* Boston: Little, Brown

Brown, A. L. & Barclay, C. R. (1976). The effects of training specific mnemonics on the meta mnemonic efficiency of retarded children. *Child Development, 47,* 71–80.

Brown, A. L. & Smiley, S. S. (1977). Rating the importance of structural units of prose passages: A problem of metacognitive development. *Child Development, 48,* 1–8.

Brown, A. L. & Day, J. D. (1983). Macrorules for summarizing texts: The development of expertise. *Journal of Verbal Learning and Verbal Behavior, 22,* 1–14.

Brown, R. & Bass, H. (1985). *One flag, one land.* Morristown, NJ: Silver Burdette.

Carver, R. (1985). How good are some of the world's best readers? *Reading Research Quarterly, 20,* 389–419.

Cohen, A. D. (1987). The use of verbal and imagery mnemonics in second-language vocabulary learning. *Studies in Second Language Acquisition, 9,* 43–61.

Collins, C. (1979). Speedway: The action way to speed read to increase reading rate for adults. *Reading Improvement, 16,* 225–29.

Davey, B. (1987). Team for success: Guided practice in study skills through cooperative research reports. *Journal of Reading, 30,* 701–705.

Davey, B. & McBride, S. (1986). Effects of question-generation training on reading comprehension. *Journal of Educational Psychology, 78,* 256–62.

Dewey, J. (1900). *The School and Society*. Chicago, IL: University of Chicago Press.

Dufflemeyer, F. A., Baum, D. D. & Merkley, D. J. (1987). Maximizing reader-text confrontation with an extended anticipation guide. *Journal of Reading, 31* (2), 146–49.

Ebbinghaus, H. (1908). *Abriss der Psychologie*. (Trans. and Ed. Max Meyer.) New York: Arno Press, 1973.

Fleisher, L. S., Jenkins, J. R. & Pany, D. (1979). Effects on poor readers' comprehension of training in rapid decoding. *Reading Research Quarterly, 15,* 30–48.

Garner, R. (1985). Text summarization deficiencies among older students: Awareness or production ability? *American Educational Research Journal, 22,* 549–560.

Garner, R., Macready, G. B. & Wagoner, S. (1985). Reader's acquisition of the components of the text-lookback strategy. *Journal of Educational Psychology, 76,* 300–309.

Gentile, L. & McMillan, M. (1987). Stress and reading difficulties: Teaching students self-regulating skills. *The Reading Teacher. 41,* 170–78.

Glasser, W. (1986). *Control theory in the classroom*. New York: Harper & Row.

Gold, P. C. (1981). The directed listening-language experience approach. *Journal of Reading, 25,* 138–141.

Gray, W. S. (1925). *Summary of investigations related to reading*. Supplementary Educational Monographs, No. 28, Chicago, IL: The University of Chicago Press.

Hagen, J. W., Hargrave, S. & Ross, W. (1973). Prompting and rehearsal in short-term memory. *Child Development, 44,* 201–204.

Huey, E. B. (1908). *The psychology and pedagogy of reading*. New York: Macmillan.

Johnson, D. W. & Johnson R. T. (1987). *Learning together and alone: Cooperative, conjunctive, and individualistic learning*. Englewood Cliffs, NJ: Prentice-Hall.

Just, M. A., Carpenter, P. A. & Masson, M. E. J. (1982). *What eye fixations tell us about speed reading and skimming*. (Technical report.) Pittsburgh, PA: Carnegie-Mellon University.

Konopak, B. C., Martin, M. A. & Martin, S. H. (1987). Reading and writing: Aids to learning in the content areas. *Journal of Reading, 31,* 109–115.

Larson, C. & Dansereau, D. (1986). Cooperative learning in dyads. *Journal of Reading, 29,* 516–520.

Leal, L., Crays, N. & Moetz, B. (1985). Training children to use a self-monitoring study strategy in preparation for recall: Maintenance and generalization effects. *Child Development, 56,* 643–653.

Levin, J. R., Morrison, C. R. & McGivern, J. E. (1986). Mnemonic facilitation of text-embedded science facts. *American Educational Research Journal, 23,* 489–506.

MacDonald, J. (1986). Self-generated questions and reading recall: Does training help? *Contemporary Educational Psychology, 11,* 290–304.

Masztal, N. B. (1986). Cybernetic sessions: A high involvement teaching technique. *Reading Research and Instruction, 25,* 131–138.

McConkie, G. W. & Rayner, K. (1976). Asymmetry of the perceptual span in reading. *Bulletin of the Psychometric Society, 8,* 365–368.

McDaniel, M. A., Pressley, M. & Dunay, P. K. (1987). Long-term effect of vocabulary after keyword and context learning. *Journal of Educational Psychology, 79,* 87–89.

Minninger, J. (1984). *Total recall: How to boost your memory power.* Emmaus, PA: Rodale Press.

Morgan, R., Meeks, J., Schollaert, A. & Paul, J. (1986). *Critical reading/thinking skills for the college student.* Dubuque, IA: Kendall-Hunt Pub. Co.

Otto, W. (1985). In search of the world's greatest speed readers. *Journal of Reading, 29,* 284–287.

Palincsar, A. S. & Brown, A. L. (1984). Reciprocal teaching of comprehension-fostering and comprehension-monitoring activities. *Cognition and Instruction, 1,* 117–175.

Perry, W. (1959). Students' use and misuse of reading skills. *Harvard Educational Review, 29,* 193–200.

Peters, E. E. & Levin, J. R. (1986). Effects of a mnemonic imagery strategy on good and poor readers' prose recall. *Reading Research Quarterly, 21,* 179–192.

Rasinski, T. & Nathenson-Mejia, S. (1987). Learning to read, learning community: consideration of the social contexts for literacy instruction. *The Reading Teacher, 41,* 260–265.

Rayner, K. (1978). Eye movements in reading and information processing. *Psychological Bulletin, 85,* 616–660.

Rifkin, J. (1987). *Time wars.* New York: Henry Holt & Company.

Samuels, S. J. (1979). The method of repeated readings. *The Reading Teacher, 32,* 403–408.

Scardamalia, M. and Bereiter, C. (1984). Development of strategies in text processing. In H. Mandl, N. L. Stein, and T. Trabasson (Eds.), *Learning and comprehension of text,* Hillsdale, NJ: Erlbaum, 379–406.

Smith, C. C. & Bean, T. W. (1980). The guided writing procedure: Integrating content reading and writing improvement. *Reading World, 29,* 220–294.

Spache, G. D. (1976). *Investigating the issues of reading disabilities.* Boston, MA: Allyn and Bacon.

Spurzheim, G. (1833). *A view of the elementary principles of education, founded on the study of the nature of man, 2nd ed.* Boston: MA, Capen and Lyon.

Vaughan, J. & Estes, T. (1986). *Reading and reasoning beyond the primary grades.* Boston: Allyn and Bacon.

Weinstein, C. E. (1987). Fostering learning autonomy through the use of learning strategies. *Journal of Reading, 30,* 590–595.

Wood, K. (1987). Fostering cooperative learning in middle and secondary level classrooms. *Journal of Reading, 31,* 10–18.

10 Teaching Vocabulary through PAR

Our knowledge is like a smoking torch of pine giving light one step at a time."

Santayana

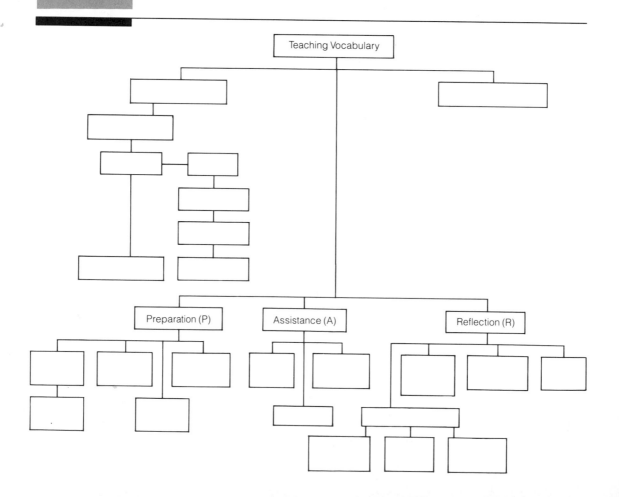

1. Departing from our custom in previous chapters, we ask the reader to construct a graphic organizer rather than review one that has been constructed or anticipate words from the chapter. First study the words below and use the graphic skeleton as a guide to make your own graphic organizer for this chapter. Feel free to adapt your graphic organizer to your goals and objectives.

word analogies	simple	semantic feature
word knowledge	concept	analysis
comprehension	interactive cloze	structural analysis
disjunctive	structured	modified cloze
enrichment	overview	magic squares
cinquain	concept mapping	context clues
teaching	conjunctive	network diagram
techniques	dictionary	
semantic mapping	relational	
knowing word	word puzzles	

2. After you finish constructing your graphic organizer, study the relationships among key concepts and ask yourself the following questions:

   a. What is the relationship between vocabulary knowledge and concept development?

   b. How do students' background experiences in a subject influence their conceptual thinking and word knowledge of the subject?

   c. Can students learn strategies that will help them figure out words in the context of reading? Are these strategies always sufficient to determine the meaning of a word?

   d. Are there ways to get students more interested in finding out the meanings of unfamiliar words through the context of passages, the structure of words, or the dictionary? In general, how can content teachers create more enthusiasm for word study?

3. Background knowledge is important to understanding the nuances of meaning of words. Consider these three sentences:

   The man stuffed the basket.
   The man wove the basket.
   The man emptied the basket.

   Describe the mental image you have of what is happening in each of the three sentences. Would differences in background experiences create different mental images? Can you describe a second mental image for each sentence?

Funky Winkerbean. Reprinted with permission of NAS, Inc./King Features Syndicate.

Objectives:

As you read this chapter, focus your attention on the following objectives. You will:

1. understand the relationship of vocabulary knowledge to reading comprehension.
2. realize that, as students mature, they can add depth to their understanding of words.
3. understand the four types of concepts in teaching vocabulary.
4. realize that a student's lack of understanding of concepts and vocabulary can contribute significantly to school failure.
5. use teaching strategies to increase a student's conceptual understanding of words.
6. identify strategies for teaching vocabulary before reading.
7. identify strategies for teaching vocabulary during reading.
8. identify strategies for teaching vocabulary after reading.

Purpose:

Vocabulary knowledge is the key to understanding concepts in all content classes. Vocabulary instruction should be provided in a systematic manner prior to reading, during reading, and after reading.

The Importance of Vocabulary Instruction

How students learn will significantly determine whether they learn concepts and develop understandings. Vocabulary instruction, which is one of the most important facets of reading in any discipline, should be taught through the PAR framework—there are times when students need Preparation (P) in vocabulary before reading a chapter or lesson; often students need Assistance (A) with vocabulary during or immediately after the reading; and there are occasions when students need longer periods of Reflection (R) on vocabulary, to determine how terms convey meaning and relationships. Vocabulary development, then, should take place prior to the reading, during the reading, and after the reading.

Misplaced accuracy is often a problem in vocabulary knowledge. This situation is analogous to that of car owners who regularly take their cars to the local car wash but forget to take them to a mechanic for important maintenance, such as lubrications, oil and filter changes, and tune-ups. In short, they take more care with the cosmetics than with the substance of the automobile—the engine, drive train, and chassis. Similarly, teachers who always have students read grandly through chapters without concentrating on the vocabulary—especially the vocabulary which carries the major concept load of the chapter—are also guilty of emphasizing form over substance. Meaning in a reading passage is conveyed in words, which are the essence of the chapter, much like the engine and chassis are the underpinnings or the foundation of the automobile. Attention to detail is the foundation of understanding. Words, technical vocabulary, and key concepts are the details of a chapter or passage that must be understood for the "big picture" of the chapter to be brought into focus.

Vocabulary development needs to take place in all classrooms. It has been said that war is too important to leave to the generals. Likewise, vocabulary development is too important to leave to the English and reading teachers. Each content field has unique terms and specialized vocabulary whose meanings, if known, lead the reader to the core of conceptual understanding of the text. For instance, in a mathematics lesson on addition and subtraction of fractions, consider the importance of the term *common denominator*. Little else can make sense to the student who does not know this important concept. If teachers in all content areas concentrate on effectively teaching the understanding of terms and concepts within a unit of instruction, students will develop better speaking, listening, reading, and writing vocabularies.

Vocabulary Knowledge and Comprehension

Over four decades ago, Davis (1944) and Thurstone (1946) said that knowledge of word meanings is one of the most important factors in reading comprehension. It is also important to understand nuances of words, or their "shades of meaning." Important concepts are often conveyed through subtle distinctions in meaning. To illustrate, the columnist George Will once said that anyone who doesn't know the difference between *disinterested* (impartial) and *uninterested* (not interested) should have to be tried in court by an uninterested judge.

When students do not understand the nuances of meaning of words such as these, they will often have trouble comprehending text. However, when less difficult words are inserted to simplify the readability of passages, studies show that readers have improved comprehension of the passage (Chall, 1958; Wittrock, Marks, & Doctorow, 1975).

How Vocabulary Is Related to Comprehension

Anderson and Freebody (1981) describe three views that explain the relationship between vocabulary knowledge and reading comprehension. The first, the *instrumentalist* view, assumes that the whole is the sum of its parts, i.e., that knowing the individual words of a passage is a prerequisite for knowing what the entire passage means. Teachers who follow the instrumentalist view would preteach the vocabulary in the Preparation phase of the PAR framework.

The *aptitude* view assumes that students have different aptitudes for learning vocabulary and especially for learning new words easily. Teachers who believe in this view will provide Assistance and Reflection on word strategies to help students unlock meanings of language. For instance, a teacher holding such a view might work on word analogies, context clues, and structural word cues.

The third view emphasizes *general knowledge* as the most important aspect of vocabulary and comprehension development. According to this view, readers' background knowledge is very important in determining how much of the vocabulary they will understand and absorb. Those students with broad background and understanding of the world will have an easier time learning vocabulary because of their broader background experience. This view has been substantiated in the research literature for at least two decades (Ausubel, 1968; Henry, 1974; Graves, 1985). For instance, those students who have toured historic Philadelphia could relate to a passage about the influence of the Constitution more easily than those who have not had such first-hand experience. Teachers who follow this view would emphasize building on background knowledge in all phases of the PAR framework. For example, a teacher might ask students what they know about small-loan agencies in a business mathematics lesson on small loans. She might carefully present new vocabulary such as *collateral, passbook savings, debt, consolidation loans*. At each phase of the lesson, she would try to identify how much students already know about the topic. In this manner, the teacher would be practicing the general knowledge view of teaching vocabulary and concepts.

Another aspect of the general knowledge view is that students can develop a generalized understanding of a word only through seeing words in different contexts (Beck, McCaslin and McKeown, 1980; Mezynski, 1983; Stahl, 1983). For instance, a student could first encounter the word *metamorphosis* in a geography textbook in a specific reference to the change that occurs when igneous or sedimentary rocks are exposed to intense heat and pressure. Later, the student might encounter the word in a science textbook and in class discussions of the changes that insects pass through from zygote to adult. As a less technical, scientific word for change, *metamorphosis* may also surface in a student's literature textbook to describe the changes in a character's development. This exposure to *metamorphosis* in several settings will enable the student to develop a generalized understanding of the word in a variety of contexts and settings. Figure 10.1, which follows, illustrates how the concept of metamorphosis in insects might be taught in the early elementary grades.

All three of these views can and should be applied at appropriate times in teaching vocabulary in content subjects. In each phase of the PAR framework, teachers can stress words as concepts necessary for student understanding, teach strategies for learning and enriching language, and develop the background knowledge students need for adequate vocabulary development. No one view is sacrosanct. Taken as a whole, the three views explain why vocabulary knowledge is important for reading comprehension.

Understanding Words

It is generally agreed that readers can "know" a word and that each may relate it to a different experience. The sentence "John took a *plane,*" for example, could be interpreted in different ways. A young child reading it might imagine playing with a toy; a high-school student would imagine a scene in an airport; and an adult who is a carpenter might imagine a carpenter's tool. Recently, Simpson (1987) has stated that "word knowledge is not a static product but a fluid quality that takes on additional characteristics and attributes as the learner experiences more" (p. 21). Dale (1965) has described the following continuum of word knowledge:

1. Student has seen the word.
2. Student has heard the word but doesn't know what it means.
3. Student recognizes the word and knows vaguely what it means.
4. Student knows one or several meanings of the word.

Students can sometimes be successful at stage 2 or 3 of this continuum, but obviously a teacher's goal should be that students learn fully the key words of a discipline of study. Full concept learning of vocabulary, according to Simpson (1987), requires that one recognize and generate critical attributes—both examples and nonexamples—of a concept, see relationships between concepts to be learned and what is already known, apply the concept to a variety of contexts, and generate new contexts for the learned concept.

Part I

    A. Check the sentences that the author *said* in your reading. Check 4.

_____ 1. Metamorphosis occurs in four stages.

_____ 2. A caterpillar stores food in its body.

_____ 3. Caterpillars eat pizza.

_____ 4. Butterflies and moths undergo complete metamorphosis.

_____ 5. Butterflies go for walks.

_____ 6. Caterpillars drink cokes.

_____ 7. A cocoon is a protective shell around the caterpillar.

    B. Check the sentences that tell what the author *meant*. Check 3.

_____ 1. While in the cocoon, a caterpillar changes into a butterfly or moth.

_____ 2. Butterflies are pretty.

_____ 3. A caterpillar eats at McDonald's.

_____ 4. Puppies change into caterpillars.

_____ 5. Caterpillars eat a lot for a small creature.

_____ 6. Metamorphosis means change.

Part II.

Color the stages as directed.

Metamorphosis of a Butterfly

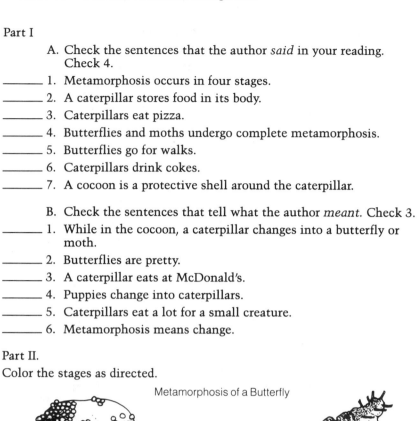

Stage 1—The Egg
The Egg
Color Me Lightly

Stage 2—The Larva
The Caterpillar
Color Me Green

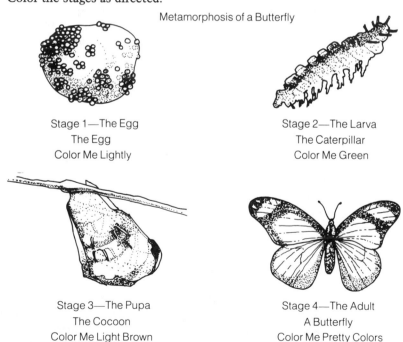

Stage 3—The Pupa
The Cocoon
Color Me Light Brown

Stage 4—The Adult
A Butterfly
Color Me Pretty Colors

Figure 10.1. Reading assignment: "Metamorphosis" (handout).
Information obtained from *Accent on Science* (teacher's edition).

Simpson suggests teachers develop the first suggestion above by asking students to exclude concepts from a list such as this one for elementary mathematics:

1. order
2. grouping
3. fraction
4. properties
Concepts excluded _____
Relationship of remaining concepts _____

Students in a world history class could be asked to use the textbook to brainstorm both attributes and nonattributes of a certain concept, such as *nationalism*.

Nationalism

Attributes   *Nonattributes*
honor   maturity
pride   democracy
superiority   cooperation
wealth   isolationism
power   equality
imperialism
prestige
force
racism

Operation 2 can be implemented by having students brainstorm targeted vocabulary concepts, then write definitions. Also, classification exercises such as the one in Table 10.1 can be completed by students *prior* to reading to determine their knowledge.

For mental operation 3, students can apply what they know about a vocabulary concept most readily by being exposed to the word in different contexts (as in our earlier example of *metamorphosis*). Stahl (1983) has called this teaching comprehension through developing *contextual knowledge.*

Mental operation 4, generating new contexts for a learned vocabulary term, can be developed by having students generate new sentences from previously learned concepts (Stahl, 1986). Teachers will want to encourage frequent practice in this task. To facilitate such thinking, Simpson recommends a technique called *paired-word sentence generation:* two words are given, and students are asked to write a sentence demonstrating their knowledge of the relationship between the chosen words. Here are several examples:

> transcendentalists——intuition
> abolitionist——indictment
> genes——environment
> graph——plot
> juvenile delinquency——recession

Understanding Concepts

Bruner, Goodnow, and Austin (1956) identified four types of concepts: (1) simple, (2) conjunctive, (3) disjunctive, and (4) relational. In a *simple concept*, classification is based on one common element, such as that shared by a geometric figure (squares, circles, triangles). When a student can choose a square from among other figures, that student demonstrates knowledge of the concept *square*. In a *conjunctive concept*, classification is based on the inclusion of all attributes. The conjunctive concept operates in distinguishing a baseball team, which has nine players, from a football team, which has eleven. A *disjunctive concept* is one that embraces different items that need not have all the attributes of the category. The legal term *felony* includes rape, arson, and murder. (Though they seem very different, they are examples of disjunctive concepts.) *Relational concepts* represent relative circumstance, such as direction (north, south, etc.), size (larger, smaller, etc.), and degree (hot, cold, etc.). In understanding relational concepts, students organize

TABLE 10.1 *Classification Exercise (Elementary Level)*

Directions: Below are three categories to describe animals—those who have fur, those who have feathers, and those with smooth skin.

Fur	Feathers	Smooth Skin

Place each of the following animal names under the category to which it belongs.

duck	goose	monkey	parrot	horse	seal
tiger	whale	bear	chicken	robin	frog
fox	dolphin	turkey	snake		

experiences and background knowledge into conceptual hierarchies according to *class, example,* and *attribute* relations (Vacca & Vacca, 1989). For example, *vertebrates* represent a classification in the *animal kingdom. Mammal,* an example of a vertebrate, can further be classified by attributes such as *warm-blooded* and *nurturing* of their young. Another example, one that might be used when discussing alcohol abuse, is the following:

class: alcohol
example: methyl (wood)
            isopropyl (rubbing)
            ethyl (drinking)
attributes: methyl—preservative; a cleaning solvent
            isopropyl—muscle relaxant
            ethyl—effects: intoxicant; depressant properties:
                colorless, clear; flammable products:
                mustard gas

All four types of concepts should be taught in content subjects if students are to learn vocabulary. That is, students must make simple classifications, be able to combine attributes, be able to understand subtle differences in very similar concepts, and learn conceptual relationships. Teachers should also remember that "big words" do not always carry as big a conceptual load as smaller ones. Size alone is not always the best criteria for how important a word is. (It is an old saying, for instance, that *if* is the biggest word in the English language, and it has only two letters.)

Concepts, Vocabulary, and School Failure

Many times there is a mismatch between school expectations and students' achievement, especially in the case of "at-risk" students (discussed more fully in chapter 12). This is true despite a plethora of compensatory educational programs designed to reduce the conceptual and language deficits of culturally disadvantaged and minority children (Lindfors, 1980). These children are often taught vocabulary through rote exercises that require dictionary definitions of extensive numbers of technical and specialized terms. This method of teaching vocabulary and concepts is product oriented; the rote production of the written word is the product (Abrahams, 1976). These vocabulary exercises are used despite the fact that most disadvantaged students, at-risk populations, and generally poor readers use action words in much of their communication ("he gone," for example); they use *process* to facilitate information rather than memorization of an extensive written vocabulary. Because the vocabulary exercises described present words and terms too often in the abstract, these students seem unable to grasp either their surface or their underlying meaning.

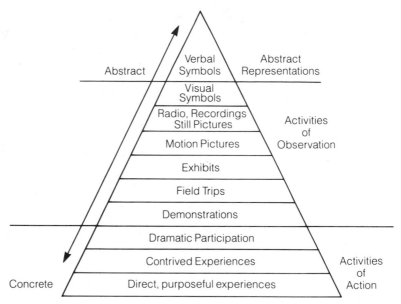

Figure 10.2. Adapting Dale's Cone of Experience model for vocabulary building.
From Edgar Dale, *Audio Visual Methods in Teaching*, 3rd ed. Copyright © 1969 by Holt, Rinehart and Winston, Inc. Used with permission of the publisher.

To help these students, who seem to be operating at Piaget's pre-operational or early concrete operational level of cognitive functioning (the thinking level of three- to seven-year olds), teachers need to present concepts in a very concrete manner, through direct and purposeful experiences (Piaget and Inhelder, 1969). Edgar Dale's classic cone of experience (Figure 10.2) demonstrates the importance of what are called "activities of action," through which students learn concepts through direct experience whenever possible. When hands-on experiences are not possible, students need "activities of observation," such as field trips, demonstrations, graphics, and visuals. Dale maintains that learning concepts by starting with written language (the "products" alluded to earlier by Abrahams) is very difficult for poor readers.

Sinatra recommends that teachers structure learning activities to include the physical involvement of students in establishing a "conceptual base" for language development. For example, in a unit on the Old West, the word *pemmican* might be encountered. Teachers might bring beef jerky for students to feel, touch, discuss, and taste. Later, students could study the meaning of *pemmican* within the context of the unit. To check retention, Sinatra recommends cloze passages. (The interactive cloze procedure will be described later in this chapter.) Sinatra cites his own work with one thousand black students in grades one through eight in an outdoor camping program. Those students were highly successful at learning vocabulary words associated with the camping experience (Sinatra, 1975). Sinatra's interpretation (1977) of the relationship between the visual and the verbal in learning vocabulary and comprehension is depicted in Figure 10.3, which follows.

In the remainder of this chapter, we will describe several strategies for developing vocabulary. They can be used before reading, during reading, or shortly after reading. They can also be used as follow-up activities (usually the next day) to reading. In keeping with the tenets of Dale and Sinatra, we will describe how teachers can use the strategies whenever possible to teach vocabulary in concrete ways.

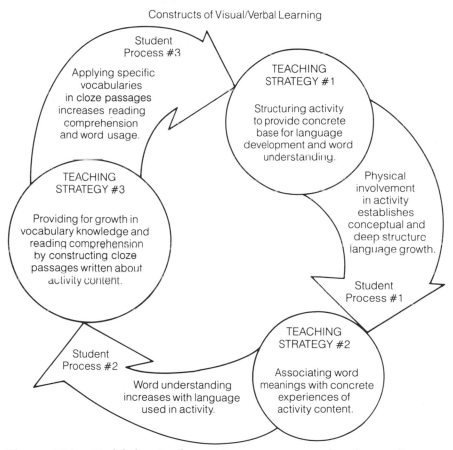

Constructs of Visual/Verbal Learning

Student Process #3

Applying specific vocabularies in cloze passages increases reading comprehension and word usage.

TEACHING STRATEGY #1

Structuring activity to provide concrete base for language development and word understanding.

Physical involvement in activity establishes conceptual and deep structure language growth.

TEACHING STRATEGY #3

Providing for growth in vocabulary knowledge and reading comprehension by constructing cloze passages written about activity content.

Student Process #1

Student Process #2

TEACHING STRATEGY #2

Associating word meanings with concrete experiences of activity content.

Word understanding increases with language used in activity.

Figure 10.3. Model showing how to increase conceptual understanding through the structuring of experiential activities.

From Richard Sinatra: The cloze technique for reading comprehension and vocabulary development. *Reading Improvement*, 1977, *14*, 80–92. Courtesy of Project Innovation, Chula Vista, Calif.

Preparing Students to Read through Vocabulary Instruction

The teaching of vocabulary terms *before* reading is the teacher "teaching" the terms as much as the student exploring and attempting to make sense of the terms before beginning the reading. Learning is something that must be accomplished by the student; the teacher cannot learn for the student. Therefore, any vocabulary work before reading should be an effort to apply the new terminology to the student's background of experience. Douglas Barnes, in his book *From Communication to Curriculum*, has said that

> children are not "little vessels . . . reading to have imperial gallons of facts poured into them until they were full to the brim," as Dickens put it. They have a personal history outside the school and its curriculum. In order to arrive at school they have mastered many complex systems of knowledge; otherwise they could not cope with everyday life. School for every child is a confrontation between what he "knows" already and what the school offers; this is true both of social learning and of the kinds of learning which constitute the manifest curriculum. Whenever school learning has gone beyond meaningless rote, we can take it that a child has made some kind of relationship between what he knows already and what the school has presented. (1976, p. 22)

Four strategies—graphic organizer, concept mapping, modified cloze, and network diagram—can be used before reading to solidify, as Barnes puts it, "the relationship between what the student knows already and what the school has presented."

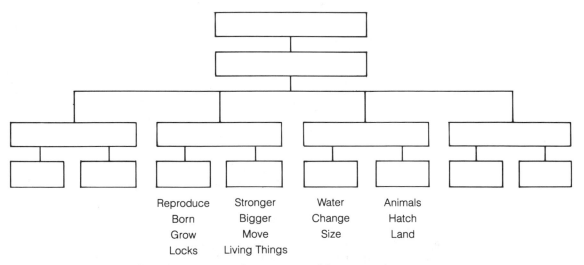

Figure 10.4. Graphic organizer (elementary).

Graphic Organizers

The structured overview (Barron, 1969), which was presented as the graphic organizer and described in chapter 4 primarily as a motivation technique, has been found to improve comprehension (Williams, 1973). It is also an effective strategy for getting students on the same "wave length" as the teacher in understanding the direction a lesson is taking. The teacher interacts with students by displaying the diagram and discussing why it is arranged in a particular way. Students can also arrange the graphic organizer into a meaningful pattern, possibly working in small groups.

Figures 10.4, 10.5, and 10.6 illustrate how graphic organizers can be used to develop vocabulary. In Figure 10.4, the vocabulary terms students use to complete the diagram are listed at the bottom. If students have not had practice in this activity, the teacher may wish to place the words next to the part of the diagram where they belong, as in Figure 10.5. The diagram in Figure 10.6 (answers in Figure 10.7) presents a technique for a high-school biology class. In each case, the objective is to have students, working in pairs or small groups, arrange the words or terms conceptually. Teachers should ask students to share answers with the class in order to discuss definitions.

Modified Cloze Exercises

Cloze as a means of determining background is presented in chapter 3. Cloze passages can be constructed to teach technical or general vocabulary. Passages used in this manner are modified for instructional pur-

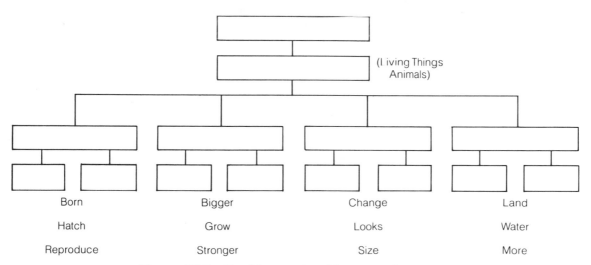

Figure 10.5. Graphic organizer (elementary).

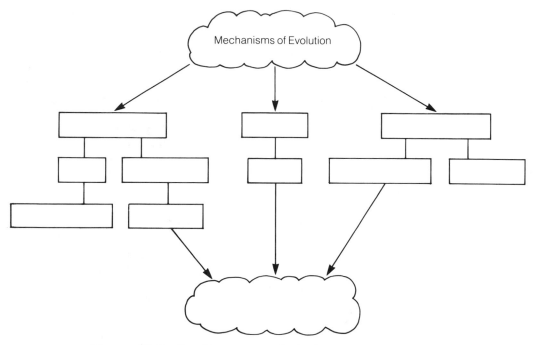

Figure 10.6. Graphic organizer for biology.

Word Bank
vocabulary

mutation	polyploidy	speciation	barrier	gene pools
gene	chromosome	isolation	migration	natural selection (2)

poses. Instead of deleting words at predetermined intervals, as when measuring readability and checking students' reading ability, teachers select a very important passage from the text and delete key words. Teachers may also create their own cloze passage of 50 to 100 words to assess students' knowledge of vocabulary and concepts on a certain topic. Activity 10.7 presents a passage of approximately 70 words to

---

A C T I V I T Y 10.7 Crocodiles

This article is about crocodiles, who live mainly in _____ . Crocodiles eat _____ and are ferocious, sometimes reaching a length of over _____ feet and a weight of _____ . A full-grown crocodile can _____ a man while the poor fellow _____ . There are probably about _____ crocodiles alive today. They believe in _____ their young and often have fun _____ with other crocodiles. Crocodiles are known for their _____ and _____ .

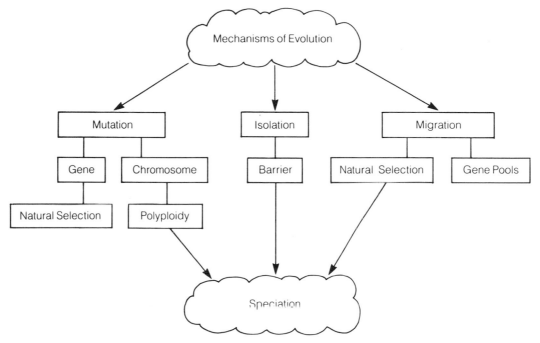

Figure 10.7. Answers for Biology Graphic Organizer (Figure 10.6).

assess students' knowledge of crocodiles. Students can fill in the blanks individually, then discuss their answers in small groups. The best, or most unusual, answers can eventually be shared with the entire class.

Semantic Mapping

A semantic map (Johnson and Pearson, 1984) is a diagram depicting the interrelationships and hierarchies of concepts in a lesson. Mapping was introduced in chapter 6 as a way to develop comprehension. This activity can be used as a prereading or postreading exercise. To use semantic mapping before reading, follow these steps:

1. Select an important word from the reading assignment. (In the two examples which follow, the words are *animals* and *rivers*.)
2. Ask students to think of as many related words and key concepts as possible that will help to understand the key word.
3. List these words on the board as they are identified.
4. As an extension of this activity, have students rank the words or categorize them into "most important" and "least important." This activity might help students begin to see that all words in the lesson are not equally important and that information needs to be categorized.

5. Organize the words into a diagram similar to the one in Figure 10.8.

Novak and Gowin (1986) describe a similar technique they call "concept mapping." The biggest difference between their concept map and Johnson and Pearson's semantic map is in the former's heavy emphasis on *linking* words to connect words or concepts. Figure 10.9

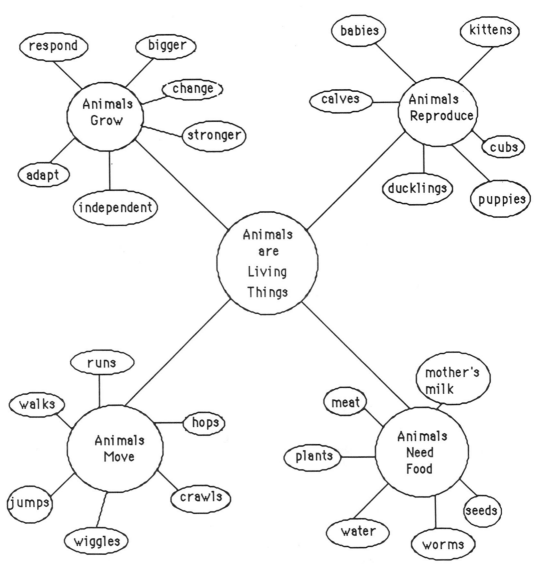

Figure 10.8. Semantic map.

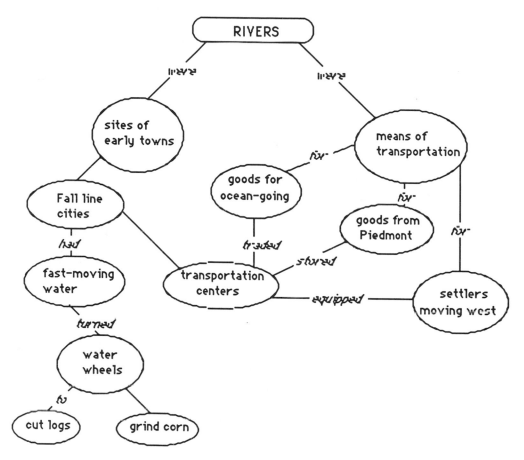

Figure 10.9. Concept map: Junior high school.
Developed by Diane Buchanan.

shows a concept map of *rivers*. Both semantic maps and concept maps are excellent at getting students to clarify this thinking before reading the assignment.

Network Diagrams

Network diagrams can stimulate students to recall what they know about a topic. These diagrams help students organize their thoughts, and they involve them in anticipating the reading assignment. The diagram can be constructed either as a handout or on the board. Sometimes students will be able to only partially complete the diagram before reading; they should be encouraged to return to finish the diagram after the reading or to revise some of their entries.

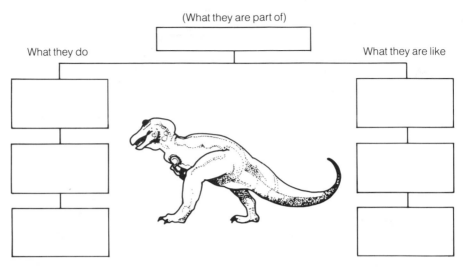

Figure 10.10. Network diagram of dinosaur.

After students complete the diagram, teachers can discuss new vocabulary terms and explain how they fit into the diagram. For instance in the dinosaur diagram in Figure 10.10, the teacher may ask students what these terms have to do with the diagram: environment, characteristics, reptile, folklore, physical features, herbivorous. In this way, teachers ask students to relate new vocabulary to concepts they already know and have recorded on their network diagrams.

Assisting Students in Vocabulary Development

Students need strategies at their disposal in all content areas and at every grade level which will provide assistance *as they read* in interpreting unfamiliar words. Teachers cannot "protect" students from words by teaching prior to reading every difficult vocabulary term they will encounter. McMurray, Laffey and Morgan (1979) found that students skipped over unfamiliar words when they had no strategy for learning vocabulary. Four excellent techniques for assisting readers are: context clue discovery, structural analysis, dictionary verification, and vocabulary lists.

Context Clue Discovery

To begin to understand the importance of "concepts in context," think of any word in isolation; then try to define it. For instance, let's examine the word *run*. It is not difficult to give a synonym for the word, but it does not have a clear meaning until it is placed in a context. You may have immediately thought of the most common definition "to move with haste," but anyone who would define run as "to be or campaign as a candidate for election" or "to publish, print, or make copies," or even "to cause the stitches in a garment to unravel" would have been equally accurate. A precise meaning cannot be determined until the word is seen in context.

Students often use context clues to help determine the meaning of a word (Konopak, 1988; Drum and Konopak, 1987). Sometimes, however, students aren't successful at making use of context clues because they lack a systematic strategy for figuring out the unknown word (Hafner, 1967). To help students develop the ability to use context as a way of discovering the meaning of unfamiliar words, teachers can discuss the many clues in the text they should look for:

Definition

Authors often define a word in the same sentence in which it appears. This technique is used frequently in textbooks when an author introduces terminology. Note the following examples:

> The *marginal revenue product* of the input is the change in total revenue associated with using one more unit of the variable input. The *peltier effect* is the production of heat at the junction of two metals on the passage of a current.

Signal Words

Words or phrases may be used to signal the reader that a word or term is about to be explained or that an example will be presented. Some of the most frequently used signal words are listed below, followed by two sentences using signal words.

the way	especially	such
this	in that	in the way that
for example	these (synonym)	like
such as		

> Americans do need to fear *hyperinflation,* especially as it involves prices rising at a very rapid rate.
> There was a large *extended family,* in that many relatives were living in close proximity.

Direct Explanations

Often authors provide an explanation of an unfamiliar term that is being introduced. This is a technique used frequently in difficult technical writing.

> Joe was a *social being,* whose thoughts and behaviors were strongly influenced by the people and things around him and whose thoughts and behaviors strongly influenced the people he was around.

Pemmican, concentrated dried buffalo or venison meat, pounded flat, was a staple in the diet of the American Indian.

Mead emphasized that the mind is a social product; indeed, one of the most important achievements of socialization is the development of *cognitive abilities*—intellectual capacities such as perceiving, remembering, reasoning, calculating, believing.

Synonyms

A complex term may be followed by a simpler, more commonly understood word, even though the words may not be perfect synonyms. Again, the author is attempting to provide the reader with an explanation or definition, in this instance by using a comparison. In the following example, *obscure* is explained in the sentence by comparison to the word *unintelligible.* In the second sentence *attacks* helps explain *audacious comments.*

The lecture was so *obscure* that the students labeled it unintelligible. There were *audacious comments* and attacks on prominent leaders of the opposition.

Antonyms

Here the author presents a contrast within the sentence.

The young swimmer did not have the *perseverance* of her older teammates and quit at the halfway point in the race. All this is rather *optimistic,* though it is better to err on the side of hope than in favor of despair.

Inferences

Students can infer the meaning of an unfamiliar word from the mood and tone of the selection. In this case, meaning must be deduced through a combination of the author's use of mood, tone, and imagery and the reader's background knowledge and experience. The author thus paints a picture of meaning rather than concretely defining or explaining the word within the text.

In the passage below, the meaning of *opaque* is not made clear. The reader must infer the meaning from the mood and tone of the paragraph and from personal experience with a substance such as black asphalt.

This is it, this is it, right now, the present, this empty gas station, here, this western wind, this tang of coffee on the tongue, and I am patting the puppy, I am watching the mountain. And the second I verbalize this awareness in my brain, I cease to see the mountain or feel the puppy. I am *opaque,* so much black asphalt. But at the same second, the second I know I've lost it, I also realize that the puppy is still squirming on his back under my hand. Nothing has changed for him. He draws his legs down to stretch the skin out so he feels every fingertip's stroke along his furred and arching side, his flank, his flung-back throat. (From *Pilgrim at Tinker Creek*, Annie Dillard, New York: Harper's Magazine Press, 1975.)

Research suggests that students can use context clue strategies to unlock the meaning of unfamiliar terms (Quealy, 1969). Therefore, it is a good idea to have these six steps (with explanations and sample sentences) posted at points around the classroom or on a handout to be kept in the student's work folder.

Structural Analysis

Even if students practice and remember the strategy, there are times when context clues are not going to be of much help in decoding unfamiliar words (Schatz, 1984). For example, readers would probably have trouble guessing the meaning of the following underlined terms from clues in the context:

Nations impose burdens that violate the laws of *equity*.
A very important finding about the effects of mass media relates to *latency*.
We all felt there was a better way than this of studying *ornithology*.

Using context clues in these sentences would probably give readers a vague idea of the meaning or no idea of the meaning; they might find themselves spending a great deal of time and energy trying to derive the meaning of the unknown words. In these cases, it may be faster to use structural analysis to derive the meaning.

Consider the following passage concerning "sexual dimorphism."

An interesting relationship between sexual dimorphism and domestic duties exists among some species. Consider an example from birds. The sexes of song sparrows look very much alike. The males have no conspicuous qualities which immediately serve to release reproductive behavior in females. Thus courtship in this species may be a rather extended process as pair-bonding (mating) is established. Once a pair has formed, both sexes enter into the nest building, feeding and defense of the young. The male may only mate once in a season but he helps to maximize the number of young which reach adulthood carrying his genes. He is rather inconspicuous, so whereas he doesn't turn on females very easily, he also doesn't attract predators to the nest.

The peacock, on the other hand, is raucous and garish. When he displays to a drab peahen, he must present a veritable barrage of releasers to her reproductive IRMs. In any case, he displays madly and frequently and is successful indeed. Once having seduced an awed peahen, he doesn't stay to help with the mundane chores of child rearing, but instead disappears into the sunset looking for new conquests. (From R.A. Wallace: *Biology: The World of Life*. Copyright 1975 by Goodyear Publishing Co., Santa Monica, California.)

After reading this passage we know that

> a relationship exists between sexual dimorphism and some species,
> sparrows share domestic duties,
> peafowl do not share domestic duties, and
> mating and pair-bonding are different for sparrows and peafowl.

What is the cause of the difference? Your response should be "sexual dimorphism." If you know *di* means "two" and *morph* means "form or shape," then you can figure out the term *sexual dimorphism*. (See the Appendix for a list of prefixes, suffixes, and roots of words with meanings and examples.)

Dictionary Use

Students should use a dictionary when neither the context in which the word appears nor the structure of the word itself provides the information necessary for full comprehension of a word. Since using the dictionary can be time-consuming, this should be done only when absolutely necessary for full understanding. Also, teachers should not assume that students know how to properly use the dictionary but should construct practice exercises to make certain students have internalized this important skill. First, give students a dictionary entry such as the following (from Funk & Wagnall's *Standard College Dictionary*, New York: Harcourt, Brace and World, 1963, p. 492):

> **fet·ter** (fet'ər)   *n.* **1.** A chain or other bond put about the ankles to restrain movement or prevent escape; shackle. **2.** *Usually pl.* Anything checking freedom of movement or expression. —*v.t.* **1.** To put fetters upon; shackle; bind. **2.** To prevent the free movement or expression of; hold in check; confine; restrain. [OE *feter, fetor.* Cf. Du. *veter* lace. Related to FOOT.]

Then get the students to answer questions such as the following:

1. How do you pronounce this word? _____
2. What does *n* mean? _____
3. What does *OE* mean? How would you find out what it means? _____
4. What is the first meaning given for the word? _____
5. What is the second meaning given for the word? _____
6. Down through the ages, what has this word related to? (etymology) _____
7. Where could you find more information about this word? _____

Students could also be encouraged to make lists of new vocabulary, with dictionary definitions, and keep them in notebooks or on file cards. Using file cards, students can write the word and its dictionary pronunciation on the front side and record on the back side the sentence in which it was found and the dictionary definition. Periodically, students can exchange the notebooks (in elementary grades) or file cards (in junior-high and secondary grades) to call the vocabulary terms to each other as they often do with spelling words: one student calls the term and his partner gives the definition and uses the word in a sentence. In this manner, students make a habit of working daily and weekly with words to expand their content vocabulary.

Reflecting on Vocabulary for Increased Comprehension and Retention

An intriguing finding consistently emerging from reading research is that it is beneficial to spend time reinforcing the lesson after the reading. The more students are asked to discuss, brainstorm, and think about what they have learned, the more they comprehend and retain the material. Probably, then, the reflection phase of vocabulary development holds the most promise in teaching students to thoroughly grasp the meaning of difficult terms in their reading. In this section, we offer a number of strategies for reflection which are best carried out by students working in small groups.

Interactive Cloze Procedure

Meeks and Morgan (1978) describe a strategy called the interactive cloze procedure, which was designed to encourage students to pay close attention to words in print and to actively seek the meaning of passages by studying vocabulary terms. They offer the following paradigm for using the interactive cloze:

1. Select a passage of 100 to 150 words from a textbook. It should be a passage that students have had difficulty comprehending or one that the instructor feels is important to fully comprehend.
2. Make appropriate deletions of nouns, verbs, adjectives, or adverbs. The teacher can vary the form and number of deletions depending on the purpose of the exercise.
3. Tell students to complete the cloze passage individually, filling in as many blanks as possible. Set a time limit based on the difficulty of the passage.
4. Divide students into small groups, three to four students per group. Instruct them to compare answers and come to a joint decision as to the best response for each blank.
5. Reassemble the class in a large group. Read the selection intact from the text. Give students opportunities to express opinions on

the suitability of the author's choice of terms compared to their choices.

6. Strengthen short-term recall by testing over cloze passages.

Meeks and Morgan described using the technique to teach imagery by omitting words that produce vivid images. The following passage from H.G. Well's *The Red Room* (1896) could be used in this manner:

> . . . I saw the candle in the right sconce of one of the mirrors _____ and go right out, and almost immediately its companion followed it. There was no mistake about it. The flame vanished, as if the wicks had been suddenly _____ between a _____ and a thumb, leaving the wick neither _____ nor smoking, but _____ . While I stood _____ , the candle at the _____ of the bed went out, and the _____ seemed to take another step towards me.

Vocabulary words:

finger	gaping	wink	black
shadows	foot	glowing	nipped

The interactive cloze can also be used to have students reflect on difficult concepts, as the following exercise illustrates:

> ### Nature vs. Nurture
> Is man's behavior an outgrowth of his _____ , that is the genetic factors, . . . or is it a result of _____ , that is, the totality of the environmental events that he _____ ? . . . It is in this relatively new field of _____ genetics that we see _____ , the _____ , and the importance of their interaction taken seriously.

[From G. Kimble, N. Garmezy, & E. Zigler: *Principles of General Psychology* (4th Ed.) Copyright 1968 by John Wiley & Sons, Inc., New York, NY.]

Words deleted from passage:

behavior	environment	heredity
nature	nurture	experiences

Semantic Feature Analysis

Semantic feature analysis (Baldwin, Ford, and Readance, 1981; Johnson and Pearson, 1984) is a technique for helping students understand deeper meanings and nuances of language. To accomplish the analysis, first the teacher lists terms vertically on the chalkboard and asks students

TABLE 10.2   *Semantic Feature Analysis*

Concepts: The natural resources of each region influence industries and how the people of the region live.

Directions: Check all the columns that can describe the word in the list. Use your text to help you.

	Natural Resource	Agriculture	Mining	Lumbering	Manufacturing
1. Minerals	+		+		+
2. Coal	+		+		
3. Forests	+			+	+
4. Orchards		+			
5. Ship-building					+
6. Peanuts		+			
7. Soil	+	+			
8. Chemicals			+	+	+
9. Paper				+	+
10. Tobacco		+			
11. Climate	+	+			

to help choose the features that will be written across the top of the chalkboard. (Teachers can also choose the features beforehand.) Students then complete the matrix by marking a (+) for features that apply to each word. In certain situations, students can be asked to make finer discriminations: always (+), sometimes (0), and never (−) categories. We recommend students do this analysis having read the lesson using a technique such as the guided reading procedure (see chapter 7) or the directed reading-thinking activity (chapter 6). Table 10.2 presents a semantic feature analysis of natural resources and industry for elementary grades.

Word Puzzles

Word puzzles are enjoyed by almost all students and, with computer programs, they are now easier to construct (see Appendix for examples of such computer programs). The teacher enters the vocabulary terms and definitions, and the computer program constructs the puzzle. If a computer is unavailable, teachers can construct their own puzzles by graphically displaying the terms across and down and drawing boxes around the words. The boxes are numbered both across and down, and definitions are placed beside this grid. Figure 10.11 presents a word puzzle constructed for a social studies class of learning-disabled students.

Postgraphic Organizers

Earlier in this chapter, we discussed how students could construct their own graphic organizers before reading to learn new vocabulary terms and to attempt to construct a hierarchical pattern of organization. To enhance concept development, students can return to the organizers after reading. If the teacher uses a DRTA, students can construct a postgraphic organizer (Barron and Stone, 1973) directly after the reading. Figure 10.12 presents a postgraphic organizer in mathematics.

List-Group-Label

Taba (1967) devised a categorization technique that has withstood the test of time as an excellent reflective activity. This word-relationship activity begins with the teacher suggesting a topic and asking students to supply words they know which describe the topic. The teacher may supplement the words given by the students, or she may ask students to skim the text to find more words. With students whose abilities or backgrounds are limited, the teacher can provide the list. This list, from a chapter on the history of India, was developed by a teacher:

People of India: Past and Present

Dravidians	Marco Polo	Buddhists
Mauruas	British East India Company	Jawaharlal Nehru
French	Siddhartha Gautama	Vasco da Gama
Hindus	Buddha	Mohandas K. Gandhi
rajah	Mongols	British government
Akbar	Vedas	Alexander the Great
Aryans	Guptas	English
Ashka		

Next, students organize the list of words into smaller lists of items that have something in common. It is best during this phase for students to work in small groups to categorize and label the words. Here are the words listed above, grouped and labeled.

Religion	*Invaders*	*Explorers*
Siddhartha Gautama	Dravidians	Marco Polo
Buddha	Aryans	Vasco da Gama
Hindus	Alexander the Great	English
Buddhists	Mauruas	French
Vedas	Mongols	

Across Clues:
4. The way things are
7. The first one or ones
8. Carried off against one's wishes
9. Regions; parts of a country
10. A person who is the property of another
12. Grew or became larger
14. Opposite of low
15. Work; workers as a group
17. ——— and manufacturing were both important in the North.
18. Coin; ten cents
20. If you do not get to class on time, you are ———.
22. Pay; money paid for work done
24. Animal that barks; sometimes chases cats
25. Steamboats and ——— were important means of transportation in the 1830s.

26. Not the South; the ———
27. Opposite of yes
28. Crop grown in the South used in making cigarettes
29. It is dark; turn on a ———.

Down Clues
1. Connected with government
2. Not skilled; not trained in a certain job
3. Get a living for; arrange food, clothing, shelter for
5. Rocky ——— Intermediate School
6. Free time after work is done
9. Not the North but the ———
11. The Atlantic ———
13. Small, poorly built shelters generally made of wood
16. The color of a valentine heart
19. One of the main crops in the South; used to make cloth
21. Teacher of this class: Mrs. ———
23. The United States of ———

Word List:
AMERICA
CONDITIONS
COTTON
DIME
DOG
FARMING
HIGH
INCREASED
KIDNAPPED
LABOR
LATE
LEISURE
LIGHT
NORTH
NO
OCEAN
ORIGINAL
POLITICAL
RED
RUN
SECTIONS
SHACKS
SLAVE
SOUTH
SUPPORT
TAPSCOTT
TOBACCO
TRAINS
UNSKILLED
WAGES

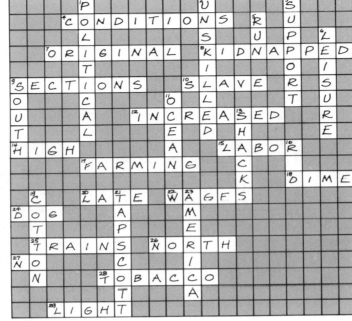

Figure 10.11. Crossword puzzle in social studies.

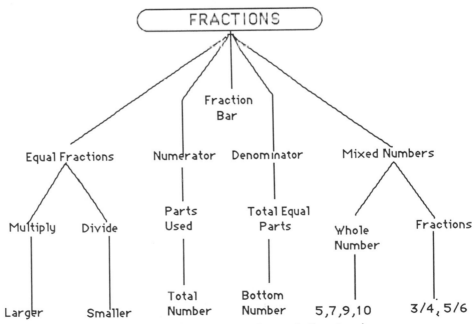

Figure 10.12. Post-graphic organizer for math (fractions).

Ruled India	*Worked for India's Freedom*
rajah	Mohandas K. Gandhi
Ashka	
Guptas	
Akbar	
British East India Company	
British government	
Jawaharlal Nehru	

Finally, groups explain their categories and labels to the entire class; then the whole class tries to reach a consensus on what the correct labels are and where the particular words belong. The teacher needs to act as guide during this final phase to make certain that discussion and labeling are being channeled in the proper direction. It is also essential that students are allowed to provide a rationale for their decisions. The focus on explanation and discussion in this activity makes it an excellent strategy for teaching difficult vocabulary, concept development, and critical thinking, especially since all learning depends on students' ability to create meaningful categories of information. This activity, practiced in a relaxed and purposeful atmosphere, can be a powerful tool for helping students to develop concepts, improve comprehension, and retain information.

Reflection through Language Enrichment

Many of the activities explained immediately prior to this section and earlier in this chapter are so enjoyable for students that interest in words will be heightened. The following section, emphasizing word play, will provide additional techniques which help students experience the pleasure of working with words. Specifically, four techniques will be discussed: word analogies, magic squares, cinquains, and vocabulary bingo.

Word Analogies

Word analogies are enjoyable activities that are excellent for structuring higher-level thinking. To do word analogies, students must be able to perceive relationships between what amounts to two sides of an equation. This may be critical thinking at its best, in that the student is often forced to attempt various combinations of possible answers in solving the problem. Students may have difficulty initially with this concept; therefore, the teacher should practice with students and explain the equation used in analogies:

_____ is to _____ as _____ is to _____.

Where, is to = :
           as = ::

For elementary students, teachers initially would spell out "is to" rather than use symbols. In addition, students say that analogies are easier when the blank is always given in the fourth position, as in the following analogies, which are appropriate for an elementary class:

1. Colt is to horse as child is to _____.
   brother   mother   sister
2. Chick is to hatched as cub is to _____.
   born   old   young
3. Animal is to living as chair is to _____.
   nonliving   moving   running
4. Young is to cub as old is to _____.
   puppy   chick   bear
5. Hot is to cold as day is to _____.
   up   night   long

More difficult analogies can be constructed by varying the position of the blank, as in the following examples (elementary level):

6. _____ is to pretty as like is to different.
   handsome   ugly   cute
7. Day is to night as _____ is to city.
   suburbs   trash   country
8. Puppy is to _____ as young is to old.
   playful   dog   kitten
9. Tadpole is to frog as _____ is to butterfly.
   caterpillar   cocoon   moth
10. _____ is to little as cow is to calf.
    long   wet   big

Analogies can also present a very sophisticated challenge for older students, as the following high-school level activity emphasizing technical vocabulary demonstrates:

High-School Biology
Word Analogies

1. _____ : tissue :: organ : system
   arm   *cell*   chlorophyll   nucleus
2. _____ : photosynthesis :: root : absorption
   vein   plant   *leaf*   flower
3. photosynthesis : glucose :: respiration : _____
   lungs   pollution   breath   *energy*
4. reptiles : _____ :: mammals : hair
   gills   claws   skin   *scales*

5. gymnosperm : cone :: angiosperm : _____
   mosses   ferns   *flowers*   liverworts
6. pseudopod : _____ :: cilia : paramecium
   euglena   bacteria   *amoeba*   fungi
7. spicules : sponges :: exoskeleton : _____
   cockroach   jelly fish   tapeworm   human

Magic Squares

Any vocabulary activity can come alive through the use of magic squares, a process which can be applied at all levels—elementary, junior high, and high school. Magic squares are special arrangements of numbers which when added across, down, or diagonally always equal the same sum. The following is an example from China which is several thousand years old:

4	9	2
3	5	7
8	1	6

magic number = 15

Teachers can construct vocabulary exercises by having students match a lettered column of words to a numbered column of definitions. Letters on each square of the grid match the lettered words. Students try to find the magic number by matching the correct word and definition and entering the number in the appropriate square on the grid. Figures 10.13 and 10.14 illustrate this activity, the first for an elementary lesson on crabs and the second for a French lesson.

Directions: Select from the numbered statements the best match for each vocabulary word. Put the number in the proper space. The total of the numbers will be the same across each row and down each column. Find the magic number.

A. blue crab
B. hermit crab
C. calico crab
D. fiddler crab
E. microscopic
F. larval stage
G. zoeae
H. megalopa
I. adult
J.
K. abdomen
L. apron
M. paddles
N. molt
O. arthropod
P. hibernate

1. to pass the winter in a dormant state
2. lives alone in the shell of a sea snail
3. lady crab with red spots
4. swimming aids; legs to help swimming
5. too small to be seen by unaided eye
6. posterior part of body of arthropod
7.
8. 2nd stage of crab's growth
9. fully grown, mature crab
10. larval stage of crab's growth
11. newly hatched, earliest stage
12. protective shield of under shell
13. burrowing animals which live on sandy beaches
14. to shed outer covering (shell)
15. invertebrate organism having horny covering and jointed limbs
16. a crustacean with blue claws

A	B	C	D
E	F	G	H
I	J 7	K	L
M	N	O	P

Figure 10.13. Crab squares.
Developed by Marcie Mansfield.

Directions: Select from the numbered responses the answer which best completes the sentence. Put the number in the proper space in the ile magique box. The total of the numbers will be the same across each row and down each column.

A. La Martinique est située dans l'océan _____ .
B. Les gens qui habitent la Martinique sont _____ .
C. Les Martiniquais parlent _____ .
D. Le climat de la Martinique est _____ .
E. La Martinique est dans la mer _____ .
F. _____ sont des produits importants de la Martinique.
G. La Martinique et la Guadeloupe sont des _____ d'outre-mer.
H. Beaucoup de Martiniquais sont d'origine _____ .
I. La ville principale de la Martinique est _____ .

1. colonie française
2. tropical
3. le tourisme
4. 1946
5. Fort-de-France
6. français
7. africaine
8. des Martiniquais
9. des Caraïbes
10. Atlantique
11. Joséphine de Beauharnais
12. départements
13. le café, le sucre

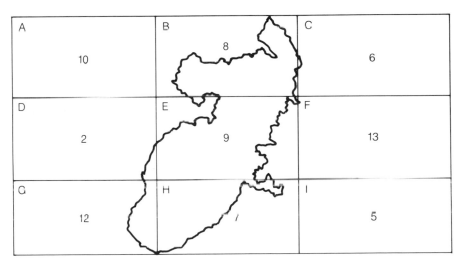

Figure 10.14. Une ile magique.
Developed by Billie Anne Baker.

Using what you already know about Martinique and the information you have put together from *une ile magique*, write a paragraph of at least seven sentences. Include in your paragraph the answers to the following questions: Qu'est-ce que c'est que la Martinique? Où est la Martinique? Qui sont les habitants de la Martinique? Quelle langue parlent-ils? Quel est le climat de la Martinique? Quels sont des produits importants de la Martinique?

Cinquains

A cinquain (pronounced sĭng-kān') is a five-line poem with the following pattern: the first line is a noun or the subject of the poem; the second line consists of two words that describe the first line (adjectives); the third line is three action words (verbs); the fourth line contains four words that convey a feeling; and the fifth line is a single word that refers back to the first line. Students at all educational levels will be pleased to participate in this language-enrichment activity. Cinquains require thought and concentration and can be tried in any content area. Following are examples completed by students in elementary school, junior high school, and high school.

Elementary

Clouds
dark, heavy
Billowing, gliding, creeping
Soft pillows of rain
Thunderheads

Jon
happy, aware
jumping, darting, asking
has to be challenged
creative

Junior High School

(After reading *Johnny Tremain*.)

The Sons of Liberty
brave, aggressive
daring, risk taking, rebelling
they detested British taxes
Whigs

Johnny Tremain
apprentice, brave
hardworking, riding, daring
true to the Whigs
silversmith

Boston
busy, beautiful
shipping, helping, inviting
people in a revolt
trade city

Boston Tea Party
aggressive, risky
planning, breaking, entering
done for American independence
risk taking

Minute Men
courageous, unselfish
daring, caring, believing
work on moment's notice
commoners

Rab
attractive, sensitive
loving, caring, giving
died for his country
brave

(Junior high school *Johnny Tremain* cinquains developed in Anne Forrester's class.)

High School

(Biology.)

viruses
subcellular, deadly
invading, threatening, killing
can attack almost anybody
poison

viruses
subcellular, microscopic
threatening, invading, devastating
deadly bombs awaiting victims
poisons

(English, on studying composer Richard Wagner.)

monster
conceited, talented
haranguing, groveling, unloving
unscrupulous in every way
genius

composer
brilliant, devoted
compelling, annoying, troubling
beauty and the beast
Janus

man
trapped, alone
writing, composing, manipulating
in his own world
genius

(High school biology and English cinquains developed in Sharon Sidone's class.)

Vocabulary Bingo

Bingo is one of the most popular of all games. Teachers can work with words in a relaxed atmosphere by playing vocabulary bingo. Steps in playing vocabulary bingo are:

1. Students make a "bingo" card with a list of vocabulary words. (The game works best with at least twenty words.) They should be encouraged to select words at random to fill each square.
2. The teacher (or student reader) reads definitions of the words aloud, and the students cover the word that they believe matches the definition. (It's handy to have the definitions on 3″×5″ cards and to shuffle them between games.) The winner is the first to cover a vertical, horizontal, or diagonal row.
3. Check the winner by rereading the definitions used. This step not only keeps everyone honest but serves as reinforcement and provides an opportunity for students to ask questions.

A bingo game on glaciers can be constructed using the following words and definitions.

glacier	A moving river of ice
meltwater	Water flowing from a melting glacier
esker	Ridge or hill of sand and gravel deposited within a stream channel of a decaying glacier
valley	Glaciers that form in high mountains
Ice Age	A period of colder than normal weather when a continental glacier covered most of North America
kettle lakes	Depressions gouged out by receding continental glaciers and filled by the meltwater of those glaciers
abrade	To rub or wear away by friction
continental	Glacier covering large areas of flat land
Cape Cod	An area of Massachusetts deposited by the last continental glacier
snow line	The point on a glacier where melting matches snowfall

cirque	Bowl-shaped recess of hollow in a mountain caused by glacial erosion
piedmont	Glaciers that form at the foot of mountains where valley glaciers extend onto plains
iceberg	A large chunk of a continental glacier that has broken off and floated out to sea
drift	Pile of boulders, sand, and clay left by a melting glacier
Greenland	An island in the North Atlantic covered by a continental glacier
Alps	Mountains in Switzerland with many horned peaks
plucking	The combination of freezing and pulling that is a major force of erosion by valley glaciers
horn	A three-sided peak eroded by glacier action
moraine	Deposit of unlayered gravel, sand, clay, and boulders left by the melting of a glacier

Bingo card:

meltwater	esker	Piedmont	abrade
continental	Cape Cod	snow line	cirque
iceberg	free	drift	Greenland
plucking	horn	moraine	ice age
kettle lakes	Alps	valley	glacier

(Developed by Patricia Russell.)

Suggestions for Variations

1. Periodic table bingo—Students make bingo cards with symbols of elements. The names of the elements are called out, or, for a higher level of difficulty, the caller could use other characteristics of elements like atomic number or a description, e.g., "a silvery liquid at room temperature, used to fill balloons."

2. Math—geometric shapes. Student bingo cards could be completed using the names of shapes—triangle, octagon, trapezoid, etc. Caller uses definitions.

Bingo is an excellent game to play as a review. Most students enjoy the competition and participate enthusiastically. The constant repetition of the definitions is a good reinforcer for the aural learner.

One-Minute Summary

This chapter has emphasized that concept development—the main reason for vocabulary study—is enhanced when teachers (1) take more time to prepare carefully for the reading lesson by having students study difficult vocabulary terms, (2) assist students with certain long-term aids and strategies to figure out unfamiliar words, and (3) ask students to reflect over concepts they have learned and had clarified. Numerous vocabulary strategies were presented with the idea that students will learn and grow intellectually when teachers spend considerable time preparing, assisting, and reflecting over key concepts which are transmitted through words and vocabulary terms.

End-of-Chapter Activities

Preparing the Reader

The following represents one way to graph the overview using the terms listed at the beginning of the chapter.

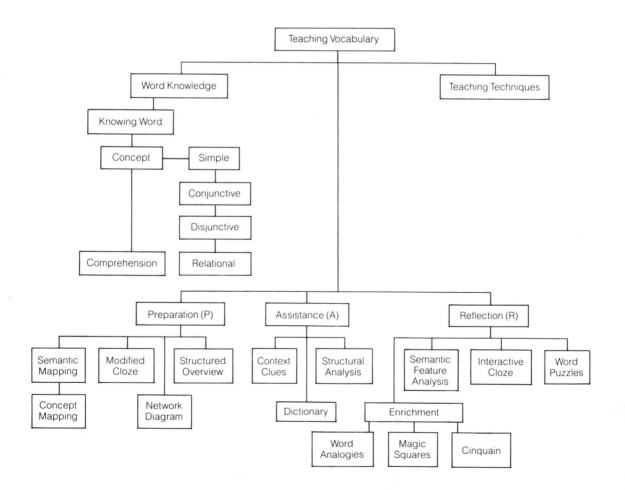

Chances are your graphic organizer was not exactly like this one. It would have been extremely difficult to anticipate exactly the relationship of concepts in the chapter. If your graph looked somewhat different, think about why yours was different and what your rationale was for placing terms where you did. By juxtaposing your framework for teaching vocabulary with that of the authors, it is hoped that you will gain a better sense of the chapter.

Assisting Comprehension

1. See how well you remember the following specific techniques by recalling what they are and how you would use them. If the activity is done in stages or steps, jot down what you remember about those stages.

structured overview
word analogies
interactive cloze
semantic feature analysis
context clue teaching
concept mapping
network diagrams

2. Why is it important to follow the PAR framework when deciding how, where, and when to teach vocabulary terms?

Reflecting on Your Reading

1. Has reading this chapter changed your thinking in any way on the importance of teaching vocabulary and concepts to your students?

2. Since a knowledge of the nuances of meaning can be important to comprehension, reflect on your reading of this chapter and recall words whose nuances of meaning made them difficult for you to comprehend. Can you name specific words which you knew in other contexts but which were subtly different in the context of this chapter?

References

Abrahams, R.D. (1976). *Talking black*. Rowley, MA: Newbury House.

Anderson, R.C. & Freebody, P. (1981). Vocabulary knowledge. In J.T. Guthrie (Ed.), *Comprehension and teaching: Research perspectives*. Newark, DE: International Reading Association.

Ausubel, D.P. (1968). *Educational psychology: A cognitive view*. New York: Holt, Rinehart & Winston.

Baldwin, R.S., Ford, J.C. & Readance, J.E. (1981). Teaching word connotations: An alternative strategy. *Reading World, 21*, 103–108.

Barnes, D. (1976). *From communication to curriculum*. New York: Penguin Books.

Barron, R. (1969). The use of vocabulary as an advance organizer. In H.L. Herber and P.L. Sanders (Eds.), *Research in reading in the content areas: First year report.* Syracuse, NY: Syracuse University Reading and Language Arts Center.

Barron, R. & Stone, F. (1973). The effect of student constructed graphic post organizers upon learning of vocabulary relationships from a passage of social studies content. Paper presented at the meeting of the National Reading Conference, Houston, TX.

Beck, I., McCaslin, E. & McKeown, M. (1980). *The rationale and design of a program to teach vocabulary to fourth-grade students.* Pittsburgh, PA: University of Pittsburgh, Learning Research and Development Center.

Bruner, J.S., Goodnow, S.J. & Austin, G.A. (1956). *A study of thinking.* New York: Wiley.

Chall, J.S. (1958). *Readability: An appraisal of research and application.* Columbus, OH: Ohio State University, Bureau of Educational Research.

Dale, E. (1965). Vocabulary measurement: Techniques and major findings. *Elementary English, 42,* 895–901.

Davis, F.B. (1944). Fundamental factors of comprehension in reading. *Psychometrika, 9,* 185–197.

Drum, P. & Konopak, B. (1987). Learning word meanings from written context. In M. McKeown and M. Curtis (Eds.), *The nature of vocabulary development.* Hillsdale, NJ: Lawrence Erlbaum.

Graves, M.F. (1985). *A word is a word . . . or is it?* New York: Scholastic.

Hafner, L. (1967). Using context to determine meanings in high school and college. *Journal of Reading, 10,* 491–498.

Henry, G.H. (1974). *Teach reading as concept development: Emphasis on affective thinking.* Newark, DE: International Reading Association.

Johnson, D. & Pearson, P.D. (1984). *Teaching reading vocabulary* (2nd ed.). New York: Holt, Rinehart & Winston.

Konopak, B.C. (1988). Using contextual information for word learning. *Journal of Reading, 31,* 334–338.

Lindfors, J.W. (1980). *Children's language and learning.* Englewood Cliffs, NJ: Prentice-Hall.

McMurray, M., Laffey, J. & Morgan, R. (1979). College students' word identification strategies. *Twenty-eighth Yearbook of the National Reading Conference.*

Meeks, J. & Morgan, R. (1978). New use for the cloze procedure: Interaction in imagery. *Reading Horizons, 18,* 261–264.

Mezynski, K. (1983). Issues concerning the acquisition of knowledge: Effects of vocabulary training on reading comprehension. *Review of Educational Research, 53,* 253–279.

Novak, J.D. & Gowin, D.B. (1986). *Learning how to learn.* Cambridge, England: Cambridge University Press.

Piaget, J. & Inhelder, B. (1969). *The psychology of the child.* New York: Basic Books.

Quealy, R. (1969). Senior high schools students' use of contextual aids in reading. *Reading Research Quarterly, 4,* 512–533.

Schatz, E.K. (1984). The influence of context clues on determining the meaning of low frequency words in naturally occurring prose. Unpublished doctoral dissertation, University of Miami.

Simpson, M.L. (1987). Alternative formats for evaluating content area vocabulary understanding. *Journal of Reading, 30,* 20–27.

Sinatra, R. (1975). Language experience in Title I summer camping problems. *Reading Improvement, 12,* 148–156.

Sinatra, R. (1977). The cloze technique for reading comprehension and vocabulary development. *Reading Improvement, 14,* 80–92.

Stahl, S. (1983). Differential word knowledge and reading comprehension. *Journal of Reading Behavior, 15,* 33–50.

Stahl, S. (1986). Three principles of effective vocabulary instruction. *Journal of Reading, 29,* 662–668.

Taba, H. (1967). *Teacher's handbook for elementary social studies.* Reading, MA: Addison-Wesley.

Thurstone, L.L. (1946). A note on a re-analysis of Davis' reading tests. *Psychometrika, 11,* 185–188.

Vacca, R.T. & Vacca, J.L. (1989). *Content area reading.* Boston: Little, Brown.

Williams, C.K. (1973). The differential effects of structured overviews, level guides, and organizational pattern guides upon the reading comprehension of twelfth-grade students. Unpublished doctoral dissertation, State University of New York at Buffalo.

Wittrock, M.D., Marks, C. & Doctorow, M. (1975). Reading as a generative process. *Journal of Educational Psychology, 67,* 481–489.

11 Designing Classroom Tests Which Elicit Critical Reading and Thinking

The test of a first rate intelligence is the ability to hold two opposed ideas in mind at the same time."

F. Scott Fitzgerald

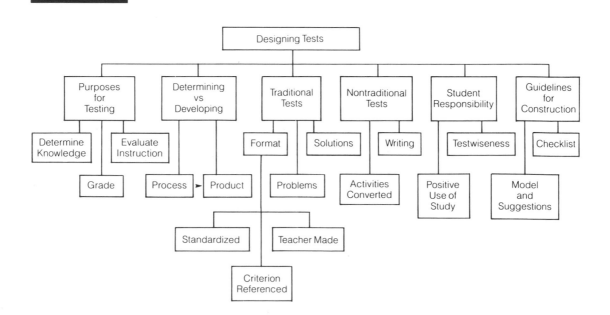

1. What procedures do you follow when you design classroom
tests? Do you make the test before you teach the content?
jot down possible questions as you are teaching the content?
make the test the night before you administer it?

2. What suggestions about test design do you have for other
teachers? Jot down at least three tips that you can explain to
others.

3. What was your worst experience ever in designing and
administering a classroom test? What was your best? (If you
haven't taught yet, what experiences do you remember from your
student days?) What qualities made these experiences the worst
and best?

4. Below is a list of terms used in this chapter. Some of them may
be familiar to you in a general context, but in this chapter they
may be used in a different way than you are used to. Rate your
knowledge by placing a + in front of those you are sure that you
know, a √ in front of those you have some knowledge about, and
a 0 in front of those you don't know. Be ready to locate and pay
special attention to their meanings when they are presented in
the chapter:

_____ testwise   _____ curving
_____ nontraditional test   _____ SCORER

5. Refresh yourself on the roles of process and product in reading
comprehension and on the difference between developing and
determining comprehension. The diagram below will help you to
review. These issues were discussed in chapter 6.

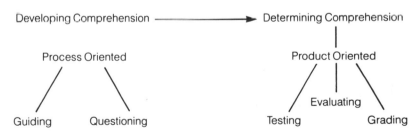

Developing Comprehension ⟶ Determining Comprehension

Process Oriented   Product Oriented

Guiding   Questioning   Testing   Evaluating   Grading

Objectives:

As you read this chapter, focus your attention on the following
objectives. You will:

1. understand how to apply PAR in designing classroom tests.
2. explain the relationship of reading comprehension as a product
to testing.

Shoe. Reprinted with permission of Tribune Media Services.

3. learn a way to administer "pop quizzes" fairly.
4. describe traditional tests, including standardized, criterion-referenced, and teacher-made tests.
5. enumerate three problems and several suggestions for improving traditional tests.
6. learn how to develop nontraditional tests.
7. understand the role of testwiseness in student performance on tests.

Purpose: Have you ever taught what you thought was an excellent unit, only to test your students and be disappointed by their grades? What happened? Didn't they pay attention? Didn't they study? Perhaps the answer is more complicated than these questions would indicate. In reading this chapter, you may discover new ways to look at old testing procedures.

Putting PAR to Work for Determining Comprehension

This chapter capitalizes on the previous ten chapters. We assume that you have read those chapters and are incorporating some of the suggestions into your teaching plans. By teaching with an affective/cognitive emphasis and by applying the PAR framework, you should already be reaping the results of improved student understanding. At the stage of reflection, preparation and assistance have taken place. Vocabulary and study skills are being used. Students should be actively thinking and learning your content material. You should be seeing this happen right before your eyes. However, although seeing is believing, grading is also a necessary component of teaching. And testing is one major way that grades are derived.

Why design and use all of the new activities and suggestions introduced in the previous chapters and then determine student comprehension with the same old test procedures? Other than the fact that this alternative won't work too well anyhow, it just doesn't "fit" anymore. Tests should match the learning, not vice-versa. As Beyer (1984) writes, "Much so-called teaching of thinking skills consists largely of giving students practice in answering old test questions, a procedure that probably focuses students' attention more on question-answering techniques than on the specific cognitive skills that are the intended outcomes of such activities." Rather than giving practice with stale questions, teachers will want to discover ways to introduce "zest" into their tests as well as into their teaching strategies, thus eliciting the cognitive skills which are the ultimate goal of instruction.

Why Test, Anyhow?

Tests are the culmination of periods of study about a content topic. Tests come in many forms, from informal observations of student learning to formal and final exams. Students' ages and the topics covered will make a difference in the type of assessment to be made. Teachers do need to test in some way; that is part of their instruction.

Purposes of Testing

Teachers must have a way to determine what their students learned. The main purpose for giving a test is to determine comprehension by assessing student-generated products which demonstrate their learning. The usual format is that teachers ask questions about what they have taught and students answer them. These answers are then evaluated by the teachers to determine how well the material was learned. A secondary reason for testing is that tests provide teachers with grades. Test grades are a form of progress report to students, parents, and administrators.

In addition, test responses give teachers material they can study to evaluate their presentation of material. Although sometimes overlooked, this purpose for testing has the greatest potential for creating an optimal reading-thinking-learning environment in classrooms. If several students can produce fine responses to questions, teachers might assume not only that students are confident with the topic but also that they as teachers are presenting the content in ways which assist comprehension effectively. If several students cannot produce satisfactory answers, it is very possible that the material should be retaught using different instructional strategies. When teachers consider tests as a way to evaluate their instruction as well as to determine students' current knowledge levels and to assign grades, they will find that they often alter their instruction and revise their tests. The effect is that both teachers and students begin to improve at their respective jobs.

The Ideal Student Reaction to Testing

Students who have received preparation, assistance, and opportunities for reflection before they demonstrate their comprehension are sometimes even appreciative about showing what they have learned. Teachers do sometimes hear comments like, "Boy, that was a good test," or "I'm glad you asked that," or "That test really gave me a chance to express what I learned." Consider this student's critique of his chemistry test:

> The chemistry test this afternoon was the best exam that I have ever taken! The exam was fair . . . comprehensive, and challenging. . . . After finishing problem number six, I . . . wrote EXCELLENT QUESTION! It dealt with the rate of a chemical reaction. It presented information, asked us to determine one value, then gave more information and asked us to determine another value. So that covered the "take the information and plug it into a formula" type question. Then we were asked if, by varying the initial conditions, we could still determine a reaction rate equation; if so, we were to write it, and if not, we were to design an experiment that would give us the necessary information. This covered the "What do you know? What do you need to know in order to figure out the unknown? And how would you propose to find out the information?" WOW! I was impressed with that question in particular. (From *The Teaching Professor*, 1988)

Tests as Products of Reading Comprehension

Product versus Process

In chapter 6, we discussed the role of process and product in reading comprehension. When teachers administer tests, they are focusing on the product of comprehension. They expect that students have already processed the material and are ready to demonstrate their knowledge.

The Role of Process, Revisited

What goes on *as* the reader reads and thinks about the material is the process. The reader may stumble over unfamiliar words or word uses, may struggle to relate what is already known to new information, may analyze the material to identify patterns of organization, and may engage in many other mental activities to facilitate ultimate understanding. *While* the reader is learning the content material, the teacher is employing strategies to assist reading comprehension. This is the time for discussion, cooperative group work, interactive listening-speaking-writing, and exploration of thoughts.

The Role of Product, Revisited

As was stated in chapter 6, "A product results from understanding." Tests are the major way in which this product is derived. There comes a time when the readers *have* read and thought about the material. The words have been learned now, the relationships have been built, patterns of organization have been identified, and activities have facilitated a satisfactory understanding. *After* the understanding has been assisted, then, it is time to measure the learning achieved. What is measured is the product of comprehension.

Finding out what students have learned is an essential part of content reading instruction. What is important for teachers to realize is that determining the product of comprehension does have a very important place in instruction, but not before a PAR foundation is built. Process comes first; products result. When accomplished in this order, student reactions and performance are surprisingly gratifying.

Determining versus Developing Comprehension

When they construct tests, teachers are focusing on determining comprehension. They expect to elicit from students the product of their comprehension. They expect that students have already developed comprehension because of the assistance they have had in processing the material. All of us recognize that the thinking and learning about a topic may never be complete, but we also know that, practically speaking, we must provide closure on a topic and proceed to the next one. Determining comprehension is a closing step in instruction.

The Role of Developing Comprehension, Revisited

Developing comprehension is a process-oriented activity. It is the means to the end. Many of the guiding activities presented in previous chapters are excellent vehicles to achieve comprehension. For example, when questioning is used as an activity to facilitate the process of learning, it develops comprehension. In this case, assessing student knowledge is not the object, nor is grading. Students are assisted, not quizzed. Question-and-answer sessions during content lessons should foster understanding, not determine it. Readers should be encouraged to generate their own questions before and during their reading, so they can become independent in assisting their own learning. Such is the intent of activities like the DRTA, SQ3R, and previewing.

The Role of Determining Comprehension, Revisited

Determining comprehension is a product-oriented activity. It is the end to the means. When the object of instruction is to decide if readers have learned the material, then some product of comprehension which demonstrates this learning is necessary. Remember that Durkin (1979) discovered how questions function in many classrooms as a way of *assessing* rather than *promoting* comprehension. If a true exchange of ideas is not occurring, then development of comprehension is probably not occurring either, but testing of a thinly disguised nature might be! Teachers need to distinguish between developing and determining comprehension, then accomplish each in its proper time. Determining comprehension is a necessary component of instruction, but it is not the only component. Determining comprehension belongs at the product stage of learning.

The Role of Pop Quizzes in Comprehension

The use of pop quizzes underscores the dilemma between developing and determining comprehension. The objective of pop quizzes is probably to find out if students read the assignment. But suppose students *attempted* to read the assignment and experienced difficulty? In this case, students may be penalized for not understanding rather than not reading the material. Instead, pop quizzes should be used to test for a product which teachers can be reasonably sure has been achieved. For instance, rather than "popping" at students questions which will be graded, a teacher could check to see if students followed instructions for reading an assignment. A teacher could also use a writing activity such as those described in chapter 6 to make sure homework was attempted. If understanding the homework was the problem, the students' written comments will show the teacher that an attempt was made. If students do this, they demonstrate that they have tried to read for the assigned purpose. This demonstration will accomplish the same purpose as a pop quiz. The homework comprehension sheet designed by a middle school social studies teacher (Activity 11.1) is an example of how a teacher can tell if students attempted their homework. This example will also help the teacher to focus the lesson. This teacher has already taught SQ3R as a means of study. Students surveyed and wrote three questions they expected to answer about pages 192–194 before the homework to read those pages was assigned. When students arrive in his class the following day, he distributes this exercise.

The teacher can rapidly review responses to a homework comprehension sheet to find out who has completed the assignment. Areas of student confusion as well as student interests can be ascertained. This activity serves as a check of homework and also as a way to determine student background for the rest of the lesson.

ACTIVITY 11.1

Homework Comprehension Sheet

On this paper and back side I want you to answer the following questions as completely as you can.

1. How did you study pages 192–194 in Social Studies?
2. What did you learn from these pages?
3. Do you see any similarities between your life and the life of the people mentioned?
4. Were there any passages, terms, or concepts you found difficult to understand?
5. What part of this reading did you find most interesting?
6. How do you feel you answered these questions?
7. Why do you feel the way you do?

Developed by Charles Carroll.

Most quizzes should be given after students have received assistance in developing their comprehension. Suppose a mathematics teacher assigns problems for homework. During the next period, the teacher answers any questions students have about their computations. Students will have time to correct their homework and to place it into their notebooks. They will not have the time during class to complete the assignment if they have not done it before class, nor will they benefit much from the explanations if they have not completed the homework. So, they will need to spend extra time that evening, hoping that they can reconstruct the day's discussion. On the second day after the homework assignment, the teacher gives a "pop" quiz: Students have five minutes to correctly reproduce three problems from the previous day's homework. They may use their notebooks. Five minutes is not enough time to compute those problems, but it is enough time to copy them from a notebook. In this way, the teacher has determined who did the homework as well as who has good study habits and pays attention. A few pop quizzes of this nature will most likely accomplish what a teacher desires: that students try to do their homework and arrive in class with questions which will help them develop their comprehension before they are tested.

When teachers question and quiz with the objective being to give grades, they are focusing on the product of comprehension. But, as was noted earlier, in all fairness, the product can only be measured after comprehension has already occurred. The product, a response, is a demonstration of understanding. First, teachers must be sure that students know how to read the material with understanding. It is not fair to ask students to demonstrate a pattern of organization or to articulate a main idea until they are aware of what the pattern is and what the ideas are. Thus, the teacher's first objective is assisting comprehension; grades come later.

We encourage teachers to think carefully about why they plan to administer a pop quiz, then design that quiz according to their objectives. If the objective is to promote student independence and responsibility, then the math teacher's solution works very well. If it is to "catch" students, we ask teachers to please think again about developing versus determining comprehension.

Traditional Tests

Most of us can describe tests. We have taken many of them and, if we are practicing teachers, have administered a few. Test items are usually phrased as objective questions, essay questions, or a combination. Objective tests include multiple choice, true-false, matching, and completion questions. Teachers find such items easy to grade but more difficult to phrase. Students sometimes label objective items as "tricky," "confusing," or even "too easy." Essay tests require students to write about a given topic. The parameters of the expected response are provided by the teacher within the question. Essay formats are also labeled "subjective" to indicate that teachers must spend time considering responses carefully when grading. Students sometimes label essay questions as "confusing," "too hard," or "not fair." In this chapter, we hope to convince you that essay questions are not subjective when questions are written carefully, nor are they difficult to grade when they are carefully constructed. Furthermore, essay questions are a viable solution to testing critical thinking and the applied level of comprehension.

Standardized Tests

Standardized tests were introduced briefly in chapter 3 as a source of information about students' background knowledge in the content to be studied. Of course, the major purpose of standardized tests is to test information known about a subject; therefore, standardized tests are the ultimate traditional test. They consist usually of multiple choice or closure questions, which are readily and quickly scored by hand or by computerized scan sheets. One correct answer is expected per item. Many classroom teachers follow standardized test formats as they construct classroom tests.

A major purpose for using standardized tests is to compare the performance of groups, such as the results from one school compared with those of a school system, or a system to the state, or the state to the nation. The test is designed with care by a group of experts and piloted on a representative sample of students. The results are studied, the test is modified, and a set of norms is developed. These norms become the basis for comparing results; hence the term "norm-referenced" is often used to describe standardized tests. Scores on a standardized test are rendered according to consistent measures, such as percentiles, stanines, standard score equivalents, grade equivalents, or normal curve equivalents.

Not all standardized tests are equally satisfactory to all users. Perhaps the norming group is not representative of the particular population to be tested. Perhaps the items on the test do not reflect the content taught to the students tested. Perhaps the test purports to test content that it, in fact, does not really test. However, standardized tests are subject to a system of checks which help users make appropriate selections. These measurement concepts include validity—the "truthfulness" of the test—and reliability, the "consistency" of the test. Validity is a check of whether the standardized test does measure what it claims. Reliability is a check of whether the standardized test will produce roughly the same results if administered more than once to the same group in the same time period. In other words, reliability is a check of how dependable the test is.

Because the main purpose of a standardized test is to compare the performance of groups rather than to provide a measure of individual student performance and a grade, teachers do not usually rely on these tests in their classroom testing. If such a use were pertinent, the teacher would select the standardized test that was best suited to classroom use by asking:

1. Does this test measure what I have taught?
2. Can I depend on it to give about the same results if I administered it today and tomorrow?
3. Is the norming group similar to my group of students?

Criterion-Referenced Tests

Criterion-referenced tests are less formal than standardized tests. Their format is much like that of standardized tests, usually multiple choice or closure. Because they are less formal, short answer, true-false and other objective type items might be included. The purpose of criterion-referenced tests is to measure whether a student can perform a specific task or knows a specific body of knowledge. Thus, their purpose is closer to that of classroom tests.

The criterion is the level of performance necessary to indicate that a student "knows" the task. This criterion is decided by the educators using the test; therefore, two schools could use the same test but set a different criterion. As a result, the test would relay different information to each school. One group might set 85 percent as a passing score, and the other might set 90 percent as passing. The level of performance on the task is the score: A score of 85 percent means that the student responded correctly to 85 percent of the items. Whether that is acceptable is decided by the test user. No grade-equivalent score, stanines, or other scores are determined.

Because criterion-referenced tests indicate mastery of a task, they should be based on specific objectives. For example, the objective might be stated: "The student will demonstrate mastery by correctly identifying forty-eight of fifty states and their capitals." If a student was taught fifty states and capitals and could identify forty-eight on the test, that student demonstrates mastery of the criterion.

When criterion-referenced tests are designed by educators to test a general body of content and are disseminated for testing and scoring from a central base, such as a publishing company or a state department of education, they become more like standardized tests in that they are now uniform in item construction, administration, and use. If teachers elect to use a criterion-referenced test developed by an outside source, they should select the best one by asking:

1. Do the objectives and criteria match my objectives in this content?
2. Are there enough items included to give me a good indication that my students have met the criteria?
3. Do the test items reflect the way in which I taught the information?

Criterion-referenced tests are not new; only their evolution into more uniform, formalized tests is. In fact, the concept of criterion mastery is what teachers rely on as they design classroom tests. Thus, most of our discussion in this chapter is based on tests that are criterion referenced but designed by individual teachers for individual classroom use.

Problems with Traditional Tests

The single greatest problem with traditional tests is that the grades students receive on them are very often disappointing to teachers. We think that the single best solution to this problem is that teachers stop "jumping the gun" by giving tests before students are ready to take them. Yet, even allowing for this solution, many other problems with traditional tests have been identified.

What Research Indicates

Captrends (1984) reports a study of 342 teacher-made tests in a Cleveland, Ohio, school district. Tests from all grade levels were reviewed by administrators, supervisors, and teachers representing all subject areas. The format these reviewers found throughout the tests was similar to that described by us. Teachers had designed objective, short-answer tests. Only 2 percent of all items in the 342 tests were essay-type.

The researchers found many problems with the presentation of the test items. Directions were often unclear, sometimes nonexistent. Poor legibility, incorrect grammar, and weak writing skills made some items difficult to read. Point values for test items and sections were noticeably absent. Ambiguity in questions led to the possibility of more than one correct response or student confusion about choices to make in responding to items.

In addition, the type of questions asked were predominately literal. Almost 80 percent of all items concentrated on knowledge of facts, terms, and rules. The middle-school tests used literal questions even more than the elementary or high-school tests did. Questions at the application level of comprehension accounted for only 3 percent of all questions asked. (Hathaway (1983) provides a more complete description of this project.)

What Teachers Indicate

After studying content area reading instruction, many of the authors' students take a hard look at tests they have been giving to their own students. One eighth-grade English teacher found that, on one of her original tests, "the primary comprehension focus was a mixture of all three levels, but more literal and inferential than application . . . comprehension was dependent on recall more than real learning . . . the test was too long and *looked* hard . . . I neglected to give point values or the weight of the test in the final grade" (Baxter, 1985). This teacher revised her test and summarized her satisfaction with the new version in this way:

> All in all, I feel that the best feature of my redesigned test is that it captures many concepts and is in a more appealing form. In relation to the original test, I feel this test allows the student to demonstrate more of his/her knowledge of the material covered in the unit by giving specific responses, especially in the discussion section. I feel this test will net better student response because it appears shorter, looks more appealing and is different from usual tests I would have given in similar teaching situations before. (Baxter, 1985)

A tenth-grade science teacher (Vess, 1985) concluded that her test was cluttered, with fifty objective items crowded on one and one-half pages. In addition, her test was based on literal comprehension, with reward being given to memory rather than to critical thinking. She realized that she had paid little attention to concepts or a progression from the factual to the applied. Another teacher (Givler, 1986) labeled her original test "Exhibit #1—The Stone Age." Her second attempt became "Exhibit #2—The Bronze Age," and her third attempt "Exhibit #3—The Silver Age." She felt that she had not yet progressed to "The Golden Age!"

Summarizing the Problems

We see three problems with teacher-designed classroom tests. First, teachers seem to rely on the objective format, with factual questions dominating. We infer that teachers find such items easier to construct and more important to test. Whatever the underlying reasoning, a major problem with this format is that students *will* learn what we model; if we send the message through our tests that the factual level is much more important than the interpretive or applied levels, then that is what students will learn. Even if our instruction emphasizes interpretation and application of content, the message inherent in the test questions will supercede the instructional intent. Students won't learn how to think critically if we don't require that they demonstrate such thinking on tests.

Second, teachers seem to have problems expressing themselves clearly when they write questions and construct tests. This problem may imply that teachers need more practice in writing and in expressing themselves clearly. However, it may indicate most clearly that teachers need practice in constructing good questions, a topic covered in chapter 6 of this text.

Third, students may not be ready for a test because they have not developed enough understanding of the topic. This problem might occur because teachers need to provide more assistance or because students have not achieved enough responsibility for their own learning.

Suggestions for Improving Test Design

The situation is far from hopeless, as the student's comments about his excellent chemistry exam and the teacher's analysis of her improved test indicate. In the remainder of this chapter, we will suggest several strategies which can help teachers to present improved alternatives to the tests they are now using.

Improvements in Traditional Test Formats

Many teachers prefer the traditional test. There is great value in what is known and experienced. By reviewing the questioning traps and tips presented in chapter 6 and then applying them to constructing test items, traditional tests can be improved immensely. In constructing traditional tests teachers will want to remember that:

1. Questions on a test should reflect a balance between the three basic comprehension levels.

2. The difficulty of questions should be related to the task required. Recall is harder than recognition; production is harder than recall. Questions with several parts are more difficult than questions with one part. Selecting is easier than generating. Teachers will want to vary their use of difficult and easier questions within a test.

3. Sometimes the answer a student gives is unanticipated but better than the expected response. Teachers will want to write questions carefully to avoid ambiguity but still encourage spontaneous critical thinking.

4. The best-worded test items do not provide secondary clues to the correct answer. Carter (1986) found that teachers often give inadvertent clues to students, who are very facile at discerning this giveaway. For instance, students learn that correct answers on a multiple choice test are often keyed to choice C; the longest choice is more likely to be the correct answer; the stem will often have one obvious match among the multiple choices. Students realize that, for both multiple choice and true-false items, positive statements are more likely to be correct choices than negative statements. Teachers sometimes give answers away with grammatical clues. With Carter's study in mind, teachers will want to express themselves very carefully!

5. When wording test items, teachers need to consider their students' language proficiency. A well-worded test which does not match the students' knowledge of language will result in poor comprehension, even though the students' learning may be excellent. Drum, Calfee, and Cook (1981) caution that "the abilities needed for successful test performance on a comprehension test include the following:

Accurate and fluent word recognition;

Knowledge of specific word meanings;

Knowledge of syntactic/semantic clause and sentence relationships;

Recognition of the superordinate/subordinate idea structure of passages;

Identification of the specific information requested in questions; and

Evaluation of the alternate choices in order to select the one that best fits" (pp. 488–489).

Improvements in Preparing and Assisting Students with Traditional Tests

By using PAR, teachers will have fulfilled much of their instruction role in readying students to take tests. We have found that certain other techniques also prepare and assist students in test performance.

First, teachers who encourage students to use study questions find this technique very helpful. Study questions can be used in a variety of ways. Initially, the teacher might prepare a list of questions to be included on the test. This list could be distributed at the beginning of a unit, for handy reference throughout the unit. Or the teacher could suggest possible questions while the information is being presented, and then collate all of the questions after the unit is completed. With essay questions, this list can become the pool for test items. The teacher might tell students that only questions from this list will be found on the test. Such a technique has merit for two reasons: A test bank is acquired as the unit progresses, thus eliminating last-minute test construction; and students have a study guide which is familiar and non-threatening but very thorough. If the teacher has created questions which follow the question-construction guidelines and has covered representative content with these questions, the technique works well.

Some teachers advise students before testing what the specific test questions will be. This technique would work better with essay questions than with objective questions. Although many teachers are hesitant about providing questions in advance, fearing that students will then not study everything, this can be a wise way to prepare and assist students. The fact is that students cannot study everything anyhow, and they certainly cannot remember everything for a long period of time. If the essential information is covered in the proposed questions, then a question list can be very effective.

Having students create the questions for a test is sometimes a good technique. This option requires that students understand the content thoroughly and also understand how to write good questions. An alternative for younger students and those not as proficient at question construction is to have students use brainstorming to predict possible test topics and then informally generate questions. A first grader could speculate: "I think you might ask me to explain about how fish breathe." Students can construct possible items for an objective as well as an essay test, or they can review items from sample tests the teacher provides. If teachers encourage students to create possible test questions, they should also include some version of the students' questions on the actual test.

Any variation on student construction of the test questions will provide them with practice in the art of questioning and answering, provoke critical thinking, and promote the students' responsibility for their own learning. A further bonus is that when students are familiar with the teacher's way of designing a test, they will be less anxious about being tested. Test anxiety accounts for much poor test response.

Second, teachers have also found that allowing students to use open books or open notes—or both—enables students to concentrate on producing the best responses on a test and assists them in the actual test-taking process. Such a technique encourages good note-taking strategies and clear organization of information by promoting recognition and production rather than recall. All of these practices contribute to the likelihood of a desirable product.

Improvements for Grading Traditional Tests

One of the reasons that teachers rely so much on objective, factual tests is that grading tests is a time-consuming job. When test items are ambiguous or unclear, grading is even more time-consuming because the teacher will have to consider many unanticipated responses. So the simplest improvement is to write clear, unambiguous items the first time.

Some teachers find that their grading is streamlined when they read all students' responses to a test question before going on to the next question, rather than reading each student's test completely before proceeding to the next test. In this way, teachers can grade not only for what they expect students to have learned, but also for what students, as a group, demonstrate that they have learned. Often a teacher will discover that an expected piece of information or a hoped-for insight is not apparent on any student's paper; such a discovery indicates to the teacher that more instruction may be necessary. The teacher might not count the omission incorrect in the grading because no student produced the information.

If results of a test are disappointing and there is time left in the grading period to allow for it, a teacher may want to have students retake the test after some review is done. In this way, the old test becomes the assistance for learning, and the new test is graded. Or the old and new test grades can be averaged. Such a grading technique demonstrates the value of learning over the grade itself. However, this technique still provides the necessary grade.

If results of a test are disappointing but there is no time in the current grading period to reteach and retest, some teachers prefer to *curve* the grades, or rank students according to their standing in the test group. Grades are then based on a theoretical frequency distribution. By using a curve, the teacher indicates that, although the grade is important, it is not truly reflective of what the teacher knows these students can do. Reteaching should occur during a later grading period, but the curving procedure will meet immediate requirements.

One major disadvantage to curving is that, once a teacher uses this technique, students expect the teacher to curve whenever students do poorly. Therefore, a teacher should resort to a curve only *if* these conditions are met: 1) the test was difficult and the teacher could see that expectations were too demanding; 2) the average of all the students who took the test was significantly lower than a C; and 3) those who failed did so not because of a lack of study but because of a lack of understanding.

Nontraditional Tests

Everyone appreciates variety. Teachers may be pleasantly surprised that students increase productivity when the measurement device looks more like the strategies that have been used to instruct than the same old test format. "Conventional policy-based testing . . . is the wrong kind of tool for thoughtfulness. It makes people accountable only for the development of very low levels of knowledge and skill" (Brown, 1987). While Brown's comments refer mostly to standardized tests, we think that they are applicable to teacher-made tests as well. Novak and Gowin (1984) encourage teachers to use new strategies for testing because they argue that even when poorly made objective tests are redesigned, they don't correlate with the type of achievement required in a world where concepts are more important than facts. "Practicable alternatives to objective testing have not been available" (Novak and Gowin, p. 94). These authors believe that it is necessary to alter our testing procedures if we want to produce critical, thoughtful readers. They also argue that creative thinkers often perform much better on tests which are nontraditional and reflect nontraditional instructional activities.

By employing some of the strategies we have presented in this text, it is very possible to construct tests which contain few traditional items. The most nontraditional test would eliminate questioning altogether. While teachers might not wish to design an entire test with no questions, some nontraditional items might spark interest. As mentioned earlier, primary teachers are especially attracted by nontraditional tests, and intermediate and secondary teachers may prefer adding some nontraditional items to a more traditional test. We think that the possibilities are as numerous as the types of activities we have presented in this text.

The following activities can be used as nontraditional test items. Teachers who have designed tests using such items say that they elicit more critical thinking from their students. Although only a few examples can be presented, we are sure that teachers will see the possibilities for designing many activities as nontraditional test items.

PAR Activities as Test Items

Graphic Organizers

At the beginning and ends of most of the chapters in this text, the reader has encountered graphic organizers. At the start of the chapter, the organizer is presented in full, and at the end of the chapter the organizer is shown with gaps; the reader is asked to try to identify what is missing and recall where it should be placed within the organizer. The activity is developed to encourage our readers to make sure they understand what they have read. Similarly, a teacher can instruct using a graphic organizer, map, structured overview, jot chart, or any such visual aid and then present this organizer with blanks on a test. It then becomes a nontraditional test item for eliciting responses which demonstrate knowledge of facts. Such is the case with the example in Activity 11.2, designed by an eleventh-grade teacher.

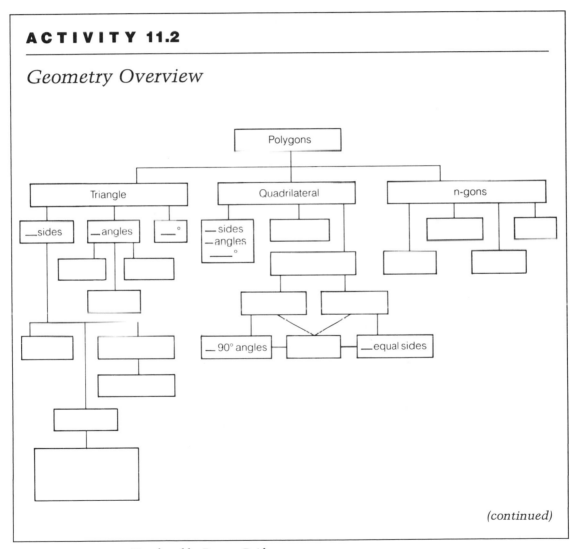

ACTIVITY 11.2

Geometry Overview

(continued)

Developed by Frances Reid.

ACTIVITY 11.2 Continued

Key

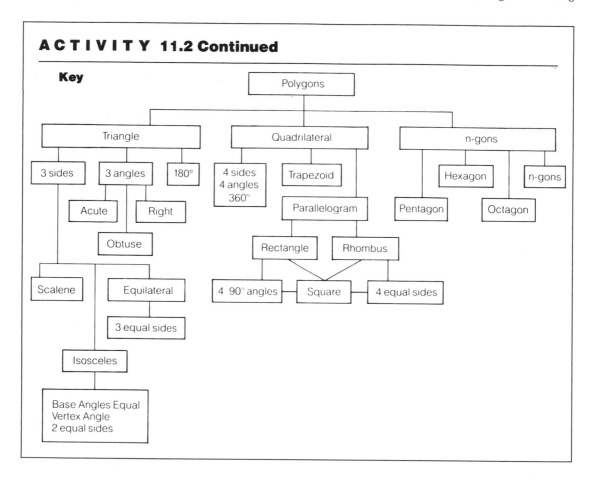

If the teacher provides a list of terms which could complete the organizer, then recognition of facts is tested. Such is the case for the example in Activity 11.3, designed by a second-grade teacher.

If a teacher asks students to *explain* why they have positioned words at certain points, then the interpretive level of comprehension is being tested. If the teacher asks that students *create* an organizer using terms they have learned during the lesson and describe how they learned, the applied level of comprehension is demonstrated. No traditional questions have been asked, yet comprehension can be determined and a product can be graded.

The test item might read this way:

Study the organizer I have drawn for you. It is like the one we studied in class, but in this one there are several blank spaces. Using the list of terms attached, fill in the term that fits best in each space (1 point each). Now, write one sentence beside each term listed; this sentence should explain why you think the term belongs where you put it on the organizer (2 points

ACTIVITY 11.3

Social Studies Organizer—Test Item

Description of Activity: The students would fill in a graphic organizer to determine comprehension. The overview would have previously been introduced on an overhead projector to help build background of key concepts in the unit. The students would have received a copy of the organizer to take home and study. The graphic organizer would be presented to the Chapter 1 students as a posttest at the conclusion of the unit. Since Chapter 1 students might have a difficult time remembering the concept names, an answer key would have to be included with the organizer.

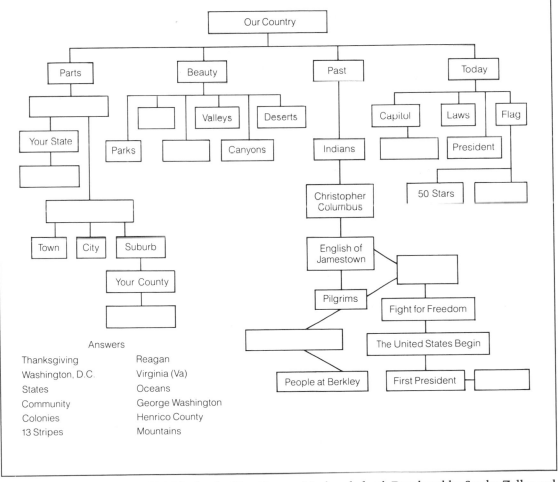

Answers

Thanksgiving	Reagan
Washington, D.C.	Virginia (Va)
States	Oceans
Community	George Washington
Colonies	Henrico County
13 Stripes	Mountains

From *Neighborhoods*, "Our Country," 2nd-grade level. Developed by Sandra Zeller and Brenda Winston.

each). Next, write an essay which includes the information on this organizer. Your first paragraph should talk about the main idea; your second paragraph should provide four (4) details; your third paragraph should summarize by telling what new information you have learned by reading this chapter (25 points).

Notice that the directions are specific and that point values are given for each procedure. A visual aid would be provided as well as the list of terms. Factual knowledge is tested, but some interpretation and application are also required. Writing an essay is also a part of this question. Because the components of the essay are defined, grading it should be simplified.

Factstorming Revisited

Factstorming is a good preparation activity because students identify familiar terms about a topic before they study further. If a teacher takes a factstormed list and asks students to add to that list *after* the study has been completed, the additions become a measure of new learning. If students are asked to explain each addition, they are demonstrating interpretation of information. If students categorize the already-known and new information and then write an essay about this categorization, application is demonstrated. Using factstorming as a test item is similar to the third step in a "What-I-Know" activity, but it is now to be graded.

Guides as Nontraditional Test Items

Anticipation guides ask students to think about what they already know and connect it to new information as they read. Similarly, pattern guides and three-level guides require that students think and organize as they read. When guides were described earlier in this text, the possibilities for extending their use as writing activities were introduced. These opportunities can be incorporated into a test. For example, students can be asked to consider a statement which has been discussed in class. They could, on the test item, write what they think the statement means, whether the author would agree or not, and whether reading the material changed their opinion about the statement. Advanced students, or those who have used guiding statements often, can be required to produce new statements which could apply to this material. Again, an essay is used to measure learning.

Cubing Revisited

After having used cubing before and during reading about a topic, students should be able to write an essay based on cubing. Such an essay would include paragraphs which answer each cube question. The cubing format contains its own organization, so writing the test question and grading the response is simplified.

Writing as a Product

Writing activities have been described throughout this text. The emphasis has been on the process of writing to assist reading and reflection about reading (see chapter 6). Writing as a product that demonstrates one's learning, for a grade, is appropriate for testing if the writing is judged for content, not for functional errors, and if students have developed writing skills.

Since we have described writing essays as a traditional component of testing, why do we discuss writing as a nontraditional test item? Precisely because we think that writing as a traditional item has been misused and underused. Since only 2 percent of test items in the Cleveland study cited earlier were essay questions, we surmise that teachers don't consider writing to be a traditional test component. We speculate that this is the case because teachers think that grading essays is too subjective and time-consuming and that students can't express their knowledge effectively in writing. We wish to rebut this logic.

First of all, if students write regularly on content subjects, they will receive plenty of practice in using writing as a thinking activity. Since practice makes perfect, the more writing that students engage in, the more effective their writing will become. Writing to demonstrate learning will evolve very naturally. A plan for process writing tailored to the learning-disabled and high-risk student is discussed by Zaragoza (1987), who developed a writing program for her students and published the "books" they produced. When teachers engage students in writing about topics they are studying, teachers will see improvements and realize that assisting through writing is not difficult. Ways to grade final products will become apparent. What is most important to realize is that the product of writing—a test essay, perhaps—is the culmination of the process of writing. The stages of writing presented in chapter 6 identify product as the last expectation. So, writing an essay is an excellent nontraditional test item in the sense that it is the result of writing opportunities to assist the reader.

Second, grading writing is not subjective if the criteria a teacher has identified for the expected product are clear and follow from the instruction. The example question presented for a graphic organizer test item asks for a written product; the criteria are clear and point values are given. By stating and then using such criteria, especially along with such techniques as grading all responses to one essay at one time, teachers will find that subjectivity is minimized.

Third, yes, grading essay portions of tests is probably more time-consuming than grading objective portions. The grading time can be reduced by following suggestions we have made, but an element of time is involved. Instruction takes time; grading tests takes time. If the ultimate goal for teachers is students who understand the material and can demonstrate that understanding, then teachers must spend the time to arrive at that goal. Isn't this worth the time spent? Isn't this part of the job?

Encouraging Student Responsibility

Tests can be designed that encourage students to take responsibility for their own learning. Coleman (1969) has stated that students need to perceive themselves as having a significant influence over their own educational destinies. Negative perceptions are often the result of a passive learning situation when children accept control by others as their fate. Ideally, students should view tests as opportunities to express what they have learned rather than as exercises in futility. How can such an active view of tests be designed?

Promoting the Use of Positive Study Skills

Chapters 8 and 9 present several activities which teachers can use to promote students' use of study strategies. Before presenting a test to students, teachers will want to incorporate many of these study activities into their instruction. Test items then can be phrased to include reference to a study strategy, such as: "By employing SQ3R, state three questions you had about this chapter before reading it and what answers you found to those questions after you finished reading and studying the chapter."

A Test PAR

Teachers can design tests with a self-rating included on the test. Hoffman (1983) originated this rating technique to be used in journal entries. We have created a version for tests. The first questions on a test might be: How did you study for this test? How much did you study? How well do you think you will do? The answers show how the students prepared. Before the test is returned, a second set of questions should be asked: Now that you have taken the test, and before it is returned, was this test what you expected and prepared for? What grade do you think you will receive? This question can assist the student in taking responsibility for studying and producing a good test response. The third set of questions promotes reflection. It is answered after the teacher has returned and reviewed the test with students: Now that you have gone over your test, would you say that you studied adequately? Was your grade representative of your learning? Why or why not? What have you learned about taking tests?

Such a three-step process built into the testing procedure will send the message that the student is ultimately responsible for producing a demonstration of learning. If teachers use the procedure often on tests, the student should begin to take a more and more active role. Teachers will also be enlightened by students' views of studying and taking tests. This information can aid teachers in instruction and in constructing tests. The student responses to each question foster writing opportunities also.

For this test PAR to work, teachers should grade and return tests promptly. The answers should be reviewed, through written comments on the tests, in class discussion, or both, so that students can use the test as a learning experience for the next test. Only under these conditions can an environment for reflection be assured. One of the requirements for designing good tests is to use previous tests as the base for constructing new tests. Students certainly learn how to take an individual teacher's tests by learning that teacher's style. Teachers should learn how to design tests by learning the students' styles as well. Did students need clearer directions? Did they use appropriate study procedures? Do they need reminders about certain test procedures?

SCORER

SCORER (Carmen and Adams, 1972; Lee and Allen, 1981) is a test-taking strategy. High SCORERs *schedule* their time; identify the *clue* words to help answer the questions (the directions should contain them); *omit* the hardest items, at least at first; *read* carefully to be sure they understand and fully answer the question; *estimate* what should be included in the response, perhaps by jotting down some notes or an outline; and *review* their responses before turning in the test. Teachers might teach SCORER to students and then insert the acronym into test directions or include it as a reminder on tests. Students could even be asked to account for how they used SCORER while completing their test. This strategy places responsibility on students to take a test wisely, in an organized and comprehensive manner. SCORER could become part of any test design.

Testwiseness

Students should be *testwise*. This does not mean that they should know the test items and answers before a test, although we do advocate that guiding questions and open notes are sometimes very acceptable ways to give tests. Testwiseness means that students have a plan of attack, regardless of the specific test content. They are used to taking tests. They are confident because they understand how tests are designed and can capitalize on that knowledge in demonstrating their learning. Testwiseness is knowing the program, to use Hart's terminology, or, in other words, the system. When they know how to take a test, students can concentrate their energy on answering the items. Testwiseness helps to alleviate test anxiety. Panic—the "blank mind" syndrome—can be avoided. The older mammalian brain can send encouraging messages to the newer mammalian brain, and the student can then apply thinking skills to show knowledge.

Carter's study indicated that students do discern the inadvertent clues teachers give in designing test items. This discernment is testwiseness. Teachers want to devise clues which are deliberate, not inadvertent. In designing tests, for instance, many teachers will provide a bit of information in one question which can help students to answer another question. Students who watch for these clues are SCORERs.

Studies (Scruggs, White and Bennion, 1986; Ritter and Idol-Mastas, 1986) have indicated that instruction in testwiseness can help students to perform better on tests. An instructional session which reviews a list of testwiseness tips is helpful, particularly with older students, in improving results on standardized tests. When a teacher wants students to improve performance on classroom tests, such testwiseness instruction is best done in the content teacher's classroom with application to that particular test.

Testwiseness Tips

The following list of testwiseness tips is representative, but not exhaustive, of the suggestions which teachers can draw upon in helping students become proficient test takers. We encourage teachers to study the list of tips with the goal of designing tests which provide intended clues to students. Inadvertent clues should be avoided. Students should be taught to use the intended clues to advantage. Crist and Czarnecki (1979) in *The Care and Feeding of Your Grade Point Average* provide an entertaining way to learn testwiseness tips. Their photographs, quotations and concise advice can help teachers at any level to teach testwiseness.

1. Be calm.
2. Read through the entire test before answering any items. Look for questions which might provide clues to other answers.
3. Plan your time. If one question is worth several points and others are worth much less, spend the majority of the time where the greatest number of points can be made.
4. Answer first the questions you are most confident of answers for.
5. For objective tests:
   Remember to be logical and reason. Consider your possible answers carefully.

Look for "giveaway" words which often indicate extremes and should be avoided in selecting the correct answer: *all, none, never, always.*

For multiple choice items, think what the answer should be, then look at the choices. Also, eliminate implausible responses by thinking carefully about each choice.

6. For essays:

Jot down an outline of what you intend to write before you start writing.

Be sure you understand the teacher's terms: *list* means to state a series, but *describe* means to explain about the items. *Compare* means to show similarities; *contrast* means to show differences.

Make sure you answer all parts of the question.

Testwiseness Tests

Parrish (1982) has even developed a test of testwiseness! Teachers may find such a test to be an effective way to instruct in testwiseness. Items would be designed to fit the students. A sample item from Parrish's test reads:

In order to read directions effectively, one should: a) Question as one reads b) Read and do one step at a time c) Read the directions in their entirety first d) Read them aloud. (p. 673)

Guidelines for Test Construction

A Model for Constructing Tests, with Mainstreamed Students in Mind

Wood and Miederhoff (1988) point out that, if tests are a "necessary nuisance" for the majority of students, they are a symbol of failure for mildly handicapped students, who are often provided with some special instruction but spend much of their time in the regular classroom. They are expected to perform in the "main stream" academically but usually encounter more learning problems than the average learner. They suggest that minor changes in test construction can "mean the difference between success and failure for mainstreamed students" (p. 2). In most cases, the adaptations will be minor, and they will often be useful for all the students. Figure 11.1 shows their model for adapting a teacher-made test. Using their model, Wood and Miederhoff (1978) present the following suggestions for constructing tests for all students in general and for mainstreamed students in particular.

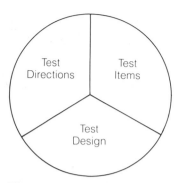

Figure 11.1. Model for adaptations when constructing the teacher-made test.
From Wood, J. W. (1987). A model for adapting the teacher made test. *Statewide Institutes for Adapting Instruction for Regular Educators (Project TRAIN).* Richmond, Va.: VCU. Reprinted with permission.

Test Directions

Suggestions for all students

1. Keep directions simple; avoid unnecessary words.
2. State directions in sequential order or place them at the beginning of each separate test section.
3. State only one direction in each sentence.
4. Underline the word *Directions* to focus the students' attention.
5. Avoid using words such as *never, not, always.* If you must use these, underline and capitalize.
6. List directions vertically if there is more than one statement. (pp. 4–5)

Suggestions for mainstreamed students:

1. Define any unfamiliar or abstract words.
2. Provide an example of how the student is to respond. (This suggestion, and others which deal with giving visual prompts, is to be used at the discretion of the teacher. Some educators feel that providing an example invalidates a test designed to measure memory of specific facts or processes. However, some handicapped students may never be able to remember material without visual prompts. For them failure is an almost certainty without modifications.)
3. Avoid oral direction as the only means of making the purpose of the test known to students. Read directions orally as well as having them clearly written on the test. (p. 5)

Multiple Choice

Suggestions for all students

1. Avoid using unnecessary words which do not help the student in selecting the correct answer.
2. State the question and the responses for the item simply.
3. Be sure that all choices are grammatically correct. (p. 6)

Suggestions for mainstreamed students

1. Avoid frequent use of choice responses which may distract from the actual question: such as *either, or; all of the above; none of the above.*
2. Let the student circle the correct answer rather than select a letter from a group of possible responses. This reduces the possibility of copying errors when transferring letters to the blanks.
3. Arrange answer and distractors vertically on the page. (pp. 6−7)

Matching

Suggestions for all students

1. Place all matching items and choice selections on the same page.
2. Place a blank next to each item for the letter of the correct answer. Blanks should all be arranged on the same side of the questions. (p. 7)

Suggestions for mainstreamed students

1. Use no more than ten items in the matching lists. If you have more than ten items, group them by concepts in clusters of ten.
2. Have only one correct answer for each item.
3. Avoid having students draw lines to the correct answer. This is visually confusing.
4. Keep all matching items brief. The student who has comprehension and/or reading problems may not be able to process long, wordy items.
5. Keep items in a logical order. Alphabetize one column of matching items and/or place numbers in sequence. (pp. 7−8)

True-False

Suggestions for all students

1. Avoid stating questions in the negative.
2. Avoid tricky items.
3. Avoid long, wordy sentences.
4. Avoid trivial statements or ones which are not assessing student knowledge. (p. 8)

Suggestions for mainstreamed students

1. Avoid using *never, not, always* in statements. If you must use them, underline and capitalize.
2. Be specific and give examples for answering.
3. Avoid using too many true-false questions at one time. No more than ten per test is suggested. (p. 9)

Completion

Suggestions for all students

1. Write simple and clear test items.
2. Avoid the use of statements taken directly from the textbook. Taken out of context, these are frequently too general and ambiguous to be used as questions. (p. 9)

Suggestions for mainstreamed students

1. Provide large blanks for students with handwriting and/or motor control problems.
2. Place possible answers immediately under the blank to reduce memory load. (pp. 9–10)

Essay

Suggestions for all students

1. Define any unclear terms.
2. Select questions which correspond to the domain level of the student. For example, *define* is on the knowledge level, *predict* is on the interpretive level. (p. 10)

Suggestions for mainstreamed students

1. Use items which can be answered briefly.
2. Be sure students know the meaning of clue words, such as *discuss, contrast, compare, criticize, define, describe, list.* Underline clue words.
3. Provide an answer check sheet which lists the components expected in the response.
4. Allow students to outline answers or provide an outline for them.
5. Make sure the question is written on the students' reading levels.
6. Use a limited number of essay questions on each test. Allow the student extra time to write the answers.
7. Allow the student to orally record answers rather than writing them. (p. 11)

Test Design

Suggestions for all students

1. If possible, test, teach, and retest for a final grade.
2. Construct the test in logical sequential order: from simple to complex problems.
3. Use test items which reflect the technique used to teach.
4. Type or print legibly. Use large print when available. If hand writing the test, be sure items are listed clearly, concisely, and neatly.
5. Prepare a study guide for the test which matches the design of the actual test. (p. 12)

Suggestions for mainstreamed students

1. Design the test to reflect the students' knowledge rather than elements such as the ability to follow complicated directions, use of elaborate vocabulary, or ability to work under time constraints.
2. Adjust readability level of the test to meet the students' needs.
3. Prepare the test in short sections which can be administered individually if necessary.
4. Place one type of question per page: one page for multiple choice questions and one page for essays.
5. Review individually with the student or allow a peer tutor or the resource teacher to review with the student prior to the test.
6. After consulting the student privately concerning personal testing preferences, design the test to meet those needs.
7. If using the chalkboard for tests, clear other material from the board, then print or write in large, legible letters. Avoid lengthy tests for students with copying difficulties.
8. Avoid oral tests and quizzes.
9. Plan to allow handicapped students to take tests in the special classroom if time, reading ability, or embarrassment are problems.
10. Clearly duplicate using *black ink* if available. Avoid using faded purple dittos with all students, but especially for those students with visual acuity and visual perception difficulties.
11. Use a large sheet of dark construction paper under the test to act as a border. Provide a sheet of paper with a "window frame" cut in it to help the student read the test. This helps those students with visual acuity and visual perception problems.
12. If the student has difficulty finishing on time, administer an adapted, shortened version of the test. Another option is "split-halves" testing, where one section of the test is administered one day and one section the next day.

13. If a modified test is necessary for a mainstreamed student, design it to resemble the regular test to avoid embarrassing the mainstreamed student. (pp. 12–14)

(List of suggestions adapted from Wood and Miederhoff (1978) with permission of the authors.)

A Checklist for Designing a Test

The following list of questions summarizes the information presented in this chapter and provides a checklist for test construction. The checklist is useful to teachers who want to review previously designed tests which produced unsatisfactory results.

1. How have you prepared students to study for this test?

If you suggested certain study strategies, have you asked questions which will capitalize on these strategies? For instance, if you suggested that students study causes and effects by using a pattern guide, are you designing test items which will call for demonstration of causes and effects?

2. Have you included SCORER, a self-assessment of test preparedness, or another way of reminding the students about their responsibilities as test takers?

3. Do the items on your test reflect your goals and objectives in teaching this content?

Test items should test what was taught. If a major objective is that students be able to name states and their capitals, how can this test measure that objective?

4. What is your primary comprehension focus? Why?

If you think that factual knowledge is more important on this test than interpretation or application, can you justify this? Remember that too many tests rely too much on factual questions at the expense of other levels. Be sure that this level is the most important in this test.

5. Do you require comprehension at each taxonomic level?

What proportion of your questions address each level? What is your reasoning for this division? Remember that tests imply the thinking teachers expect of their students. Have you asked your students to think broadly and deeply?

6. What types of responses are you asking of students? Will they need to recognize, recall, or produce information?

A good balance of responses is usually preferable to only recognition, recall, or production. More thinking is required of students when production is requested.

7. Have you phrased your test items so that comprehension is dependent on the learned material rather than on experience or verbatim recall?

    Remember that, although the preparation stage often calls for students to identify what they already know before a topic is taught, your test should find out what they have learned since then.

8. Is the weight of the test in the final grade clear to students? Is the weight of each item on the test clear? Is the weight of parts of an item clear within that item?

9. Did you consider alternatives to traditional test items, such as statements (instead of questions), organizers, or cubing? Is writing an important part of your test? Why or why not?

10. For objective tests, what format have you selected and why (multiple choice, true-false, incomplete, short answer)? How many of each type do you include? Why?

11. For essay tests, have you carefully asked for all of the aspects of the answer that you are looking for? Are descriptive words (describe, compare, etc.) clear?

12. Is the wording on this test clear? Is the test uncluttered, with items well-spaced? Does the test look appealing?

13. Have you been considerate of the needs of mainstreamed students in your test design?

One-Minute Summary

The focus of this chapter has been on how teachers can test as they have taught. We have presented evidence that teacher made tests are often not as well constructed as is desirable to facilitate the best student results. Traditional tests, including standardized, criterion-referenced, and teacher-made tests, have been described. Suggestions for constructing traditional tests have been provided.

We have shown how PAR can be applied to designing tests, and we have discussed how many of the activities presented in this text can be adapted for use on teacher-made tests. We have promoted the construction of nontraditional tests because we think such tests can most readily reflect PAR.

We have also made suggestions for teachers to consider when testing mainstreamed students, so that special students will be able to demonstrate the product of their comprehension. Finally, we have asked thirteen questions to guide the teacher in designing classroom tests in content areas. To understand how these questions can help a teacher in constructing a test, we have included in the appendix one teacher's description of a poetry test she designed as well as a copy of her test.

End-of-Chapter Activities

Preparing the Reader

1. As you read this chapter, were you able to rely on your background knowledge from reading the previous ten chapters?

2. Rethink your response to question 2 under Determining and Building Background. Would your suggestions be different now?

Assisting Comprehension

1. Study the following organizer, and without looking at the beginning of the chapter, fill in the blank spots. You may look back through the chapter for clues.

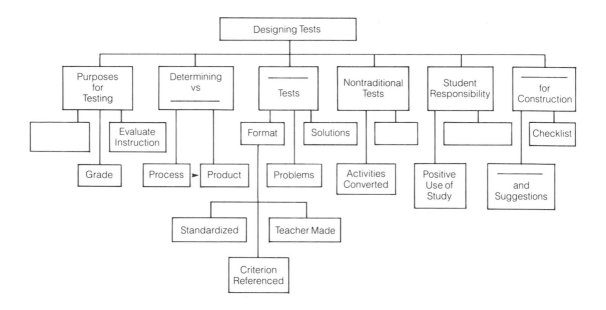

2. What activities that you have learned about in this text could you use to construct nontraditional test items? How would you adapt them for test items?

3. Think of some reasons for constructing at least a rough draft of your unit test *before* you begin teaching the unit. How could knowing what your test will be like aid you and your students during the preparing, assisting, and reflecting processes?

4. How can you use some of the testwiseness tips included in this chapter as you design your tests?

Reflecting on Your Reading

1. You might want to extend your own learning about test design by reading some of the following books:
Banesh Hoffman's *Tyranny of Testing*, Crowell-Collier, 1962.
Stephen Gould's *The Mismeasure of Man*, Norton, 1981.
Walter Hathaway's *Testing in the Schools*, Jossey-Bass, 1983.
Crist and Czarnecki's *Your Study Skills or the Care and Feeding of Your Grade Point Average*, Shippensburg Collegiate Press, 1976.

2. For more information about standardized and formal, criterion-referenced testing, readers will find that Gipe's text, *Corrective Reading Techniques*, published by Gorsuch Scarisbrick in 1987, will be helpful.

3. By using the guidelines which end this chapter, analyze a test that you have given and determine if it should be redesigned.

4. Select a chapter from a content textbook. Using the questions below, find out what the chapter provides to aid you in testing students and how adequate the aid is.

What questioning aids are provided to help the teacher *determine* comprehension of this chapter? (Aids might include chapter tests or suggestions for designing a test.) Are these aids specified to determine rather than to develop comprehension?

Fill in the chart below as a way to analyze these questions.

Question	Is it Literal/Interpretive/Applied	Is it Recall/Recognition	Will it Develop/Determine
#1			
#2			
#3 . . .			

What nontraditional activities are suggested or provided to help you determine a student's comprehension? (These might include mapping, pattern guides, three-level guides, graphic organizers, etc.)

How closely do the testing measures match the chapter objectives?

What suggestions are given to students to prepare them for the test?

Have suggestions been provided for testing different types of learners (learning disabled, gifted, etc.)?

What testing might you want to design to supplement what is provided in this chapter? Why?

References

Baxter, J. (1985). Designing a test. Unpublished paper from a course assignment, Virginia Commonwealth University.

Beyer, B. (1984). Improving thinking skills—defining the problem. *Phi Delta Kappan, 65,* 486–490.

Brown, R. (1987). Who is accountable for thoughtfulness? *Phi Delta Kappan, 69,* 49–52.

Carmen, R. & Adams, W. (1972). *Study skills: A student's guide to survival.* New York: Wiley.

Carter, K. (1986). Test-wiseness for teachers and students. *Educational Measurement: Issues and Practices, 5,* 20–23.

Coleman, J.C. et al. (1969). *Equality of educational opportunity.* Washington, D.C.: Superintendent of Documents.

Crist & Czarnecki. (1978). *Your study skills or the care and feeding of your grade point average.* Shippensburg, PA: Shippensburg State Press.

Drum, P., Calfee, R. & Cook, L. (1981). The effects of surface structure variables on performance in reading comprehension tests. *Reading Research Quarterly, 16,* 486–514.

Durkin, D. (1979). What classroom observations reveal about reading comprehension instruction. *Reading Research Quarterly, 14,* 481–533.

Exams: Students know a good one when they see one. (1988). *The Teaching Professor, 2,* 2.

Givler, J. (1986). Designing a test. Unpublished paper from a course assignment, Virginia Commonwealth University.

Hathaway, W. (Ed.) (1983). *Testing in the schools.* Chicago: Jossey-Bass.

Hoffman, S. (1983). Using student journals to teach study skills. *Journal of Reading 26,* 344–347.

Koenke, C. (1988). Testwiseness: Programs and problems. *Journal of Reading, 31,* 480–483.

Lee, P. & Allen, G. (1981). Training junior high LD students to use a test-taking strategy. ED 217 649.

cNovak, J.D. & Gowin, D.B. (1984). *Learning how to learn.* London: Cambridge University Press.

Parrish, B. (1982). A test to test test-wiseness. *Journal of Reading, 25,* 672–675.

Ritter, S. & Idol-Mastas, L. (1986). Teaching middle school students to use a test-taking strategy. *Journal of Educational Research, 79,* 350–357.

Scruggs, T., White, K. & Bennion, K. (1986). Teaching test-taking skills to elementary-grade students: A meta-analysis. *Elementary School Journal, 87,* 69–82.

Vess, L. (1985). Designing a test. Unpublished paper from a course assignment, Virginia Commonwealth University.

Window on the classroom: A look at teachers' tests (1984). *Captrends, 10,* 1–3.

Wood, J. (1987). A model for adapting the teacher made test. *Statewide Institutes for Adapting Instruction for Regular Educators (Project Train).* Richmond, VA: Virginia Commonwealth University.

Wood, J. & Miederhoff, J. (1988). Adapting test construction for mainstreamed language arts students. Unpublished paper, Virginia Commonwealth University.

Zaragoza, N. (1987). Process writing for high-risk and learning disabled students. *Reading Research and Instruction, 26,* 290–301.

12 At-Risk Readers

Do we have a chance to find the girl?" asked Dawson. "There is always a chance, my dear Dawson, as long as one can think."

> Detective Basil of Baker Street
> *The Great Mouse Detective*, © Walt Disney Productions, 1986

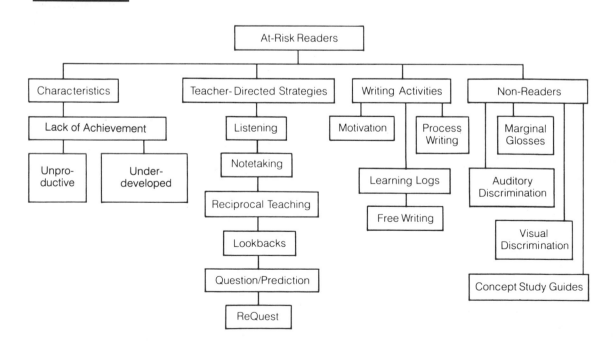

1. With deference to all who have ever used stream-of-consciousness, from Laurence Sterne in the eighteenth century to present-day authors, these random thoughts of "at-risk" students are offered:

   . . . I was in line at Hardee's today with my friend, Jim, and he yelled that he deserved to go first because he was five levels higher in reading than I was. Everybody heard it.

   . . . The teacher talked to the whole class on "present participles"—I'm still not sure what they mean.

   . . . I gave the teacher a poem I made up just for her and she told me it was nice but I needed to work harder on my handwriting. My printing wasn't neat and clear enough.

   . . . I'm never going to get anywhere in school. I'm a failure. I know I'll never be what my parents want me to be. Maybe I should just give up.

   Practice an imaging exercise in which you try to think as a poor reader or failing student might, as the examples above illustrate. The rationale for this exercise is, of course, to have you experience in some small way the frustrations felt every day by children who are bewildered by constant failure and lack of respect. Try imagining how these students would feel in the following circumstances:
   (a) Being berated by a teacher;
   (b) Getting a fifth consecutive failing grade on the weekly spelling test; and
   (c) Being threatened by Dad after receiving a poor report card.

2. Below is a list of terms used in this chapter. Some of them may be familiar to you in a general context, but in this chapter they may be used in a different way than you are used to. Rate your knowledge by placing a + in front of those you are sure that you know, a √ in front of those you have some knowledge about, and a 0 in front of those you don't know. Be ready to locate and pay special attention to their meanings when they are presented in the chapter:

_____ locus of control	_____ substandard
_____ legitimate	_____ lookbacks
_____ visual-motor perception	_____ reciprocal
_____ kinesthetic	_____ fluency
_____ style	_____ visual discrimination
_____ auditory discrimination	

Shoe. Reprinted with permission of Tribune Media Services.

Objectives: As you read this chapter, focus your attention on the following objectives. You will:

1. understand and identify characteristics of "at-risk" students.
2. understand why teachers have to discourage passive approaches to reading.
3. identify a number of teacher-directed strategies for aiding at-risk learners in reading.

Purpose: At-risk learners, who constitute a sizeable portion of the school population, have special needs which must be addressed by classroom teachers to reverse the growing failure and dropout rate in our nation's schools.

Characteristics of At-Risk Students

In the second chapter we discussed the four psychological needs of power, love, freedom, and fun described by Glasser (1986) in *Control Theory in the Classroom*. At-risk learners are desperate, yet unfulfilled, in search of these four important affective needs. Often their lives are governed by fear, threat, and negative thinking. They feel helpless and powerless and exhibit an external locus of control (discussed in chapter 2), feeling out of control of their own destiny.

Pellicano (1987) defines at-risk students as "uncommitted to deferred gratification and to school training that correlates with competition, and its reward, achieved status (p. 47)." Thus Pellicano sees at-risk students as "becoming unproductive, underdeveloped, and noncompetitive" (p. 87) in our necessarily technological and complex world. He sees at-risk youngsters as not so much "socially disadvantaged" (the label of the 1960s) but, rather, economically disadvantaged. Pellicano cites a litany of dropouts, school failures, alcohol and drug abusers, handicapped and poverty-stricken children—all making America "at-risk" of becoming a third-rate world power unable to respond to economic world market forces. He calls for a national policy agenda that "legitimates the school as a mediating structure for those who are powerless to develop their own potential" (p. 49).

Zaragoza (1987) has defined at-risk first graders as children from a low socioeconomic background who often do not speak English, have poor standardized test scores, and perform unsatisfactorily on reading and writing exercises. Many of these students come from the inner city. The students alluded to by Pellicano and Zaragoza manifest the poorest reading behaviors and are so fearful and negative that they often cannot be motivated, especially by threats (see our chapter 2). Psychologists tell us that when an organism is threatened, its perception narrows to the source of the threat. This may be why so many poor students "take it out" on the teacher. Feeling threatened, they don't pay attention to course work, to commands, to anything but how to repay the teacher for all the failure and frustration they feel. Like children who have not matured, at-risk students tend to focus entirely too much on the teacher, thus developing an external locus of control. Remember that in chapter 2 we stated that students are more likely to read because of feelings they have for a teacher rather than because of a specific reading activity. Therefore, it can be that a teacher's attitude toward students and learning is powerful; in fact, it appears to be a major factor in promoting interested readers (Wigfield and Asher, 1984).

How do we develop the potential of this type of student? First and foremost, teachers need to be positive and caring enough to realize that these students are not going to change overnight. They have acquired bad study habits and negative thinking over an entire lifetime. As Mark Twain once said, "A habit cannot be tossed out the window. It must be coaxed down the stairs a step at a time." Bad behavior and poor reading habits are difficult to break. However, through modeling and guided practice in using techniques such as those listed for good readers in Table 12.1, even the poorest students can change their reading patterns.

We do not claim that simply using the strategies described in this chapter will solve our nation's problem with at-risk students. The task is arduous and often frustrating for teachers, and no one set of strategies will solve such an overwhelming problem. We do say, however, that using the PAR system and the strategies explained in this chapter and text, along with much attention to the affective domain of teaching, will be a step in the right direction. We must begin now to enable this sizable failing group of students to become successful participants in the educational process.

TABLE 12.1. *Contrasting good and poor readers*

Good Readers	Poor Readers
Before Reading	
Build up their background knowledge on the subject.	Start reading without thinking about the subject.
Know their purpose for reading.	Do not know why they are reading.
Focus their complete attention on reading.	
During Reading	
Give their complete attention to the reading task.	Do not know whether they understand or do not understand.
Keep a constant check on their own understanding.	Do not monitor their own comprehension.
Monitor their reading comprehension and do it so often that it becomes automatic.	Seldom use any of the fix-up strategies.
Stop only to use a fix-up strategy when they do not understand.	
After Reading	
Decide if they have achieved their goal for reading.	Do not know what they have read.
Evaluate comprehension of what was read.	Do not follow reading with comprehension self-check.
Summarize the major ideas in a graphic organizer.	
Seek additional information from outside sources.	
A dramatic improvement for poor readers results when they are taught to apply intervention strategies to content text.	

Orange County Public Schools, 1986. Used with permission.

Teacher-Directed Strategies Which Work Well with At-Risk Learners

Listening Strategies

Activities designed to teach content material *and* listening are important for at-risk students and poor readers. One of these activities is *listen-read-discuss,* or *LRD* (Alvermann, 1987). With this technique, the teacher first lectures on a selected portion of material. Students then read that portion with the purpose of comparing lecture and written content. Afterwards, students and teacher discuss the lecture and reading. LRD works best to promote discussion if the material is well organized.

The *student listening activity,* or *SLA* (Choate and Rakes, 1987) is another technique for improving listening skills. In using this strategy, the teacher first discusses concepts in the material. She sets a clear purpose for listening, then reads aloud, interspersing several prediction cues with the reading. Finally, the teacher questions students about what they heard using these levels of questions: factual, inferential, and applied.

First step to note taking also promotes listening and purpose setting. One incidental result of this technique is that it offers practice in group note-taking strategies. The activity can be modified for teacher-based instruction or for an independent student learning experience, depending on the ages of students. First step to note taking includes five steps:

1. A listening purpose is set by either the teacher or a student. If, for instance, the student is completing the activity for independent practice, perhaps he or she will listen to the evening news with the purpose of identifying the major news stories and two significant details of each story.

2. Listening with a purpose commences. Students might listen to the teacher read, listen to the news on television, or listen to a tape recording, for example. No writing is allowed during the listening.

3. The students react by listing what they heard in relationship to the stated purpose. Responses are now recorded, but no modification is made.

4. Students listen to the material again, with the list in sight. No writing is allowed during the listening. (If students listened to the evening news, then either a recording of that news broadcast or a late evening news show would provide an appropriate second listening.)

1*	2
shrimp	*fairy* shrimp
salamander	wood beetle
mole cricket	*other* mole crickets
sow bug	spider
lizard	sponge
ants	lichens
fireflies	
centipede	
snail	
mosquito	
butterfly	
jellyfish	

*Listening Purpose: Listen to identify all of the creatures you hear about.

After you edit these lists, creatures can be grouped by similar characteristics, or put into sequence as they are mentioned in the story.

Figure 12.1. First and second responses to listening to *All Upon a Stone.*

5. The list is now edited by students individually or in small groups to add, delete, or modify information. The list will then be organized in a logical pattern. Notes for study have been generated.

Figure 12.1 shows the list generated by students after listening to *All Upon a Stone* by Jean Craighead George a first and second time.

Teacher-Directed Strategies for At-Risk Learners

ReQuest

Manzo (1969) describes ReQuest, a procedure for questioning which encourages students to ask informed questions. This procedure is included in this chapter rather than chapter 5 or 6 (on comprehension) because it seems to work especially well in a remedial situation or with very poor readers. The key to this technique is that it requires students to "open up" their thinking, to question and think critically. Also, a very short selection is involved, usually a paragraph, which doesn't overwhelm the slow reader.

With this technique, the teacher and students first read silently a selected portion of the text (usually one or two paragraphs). The students then ask the teacher questions about what they read. The teacher must keep the book closed during this phase. When the students exhaust their questions, the teacher begins asking questions. During this phase, the students must also keep their books closed. The activity can be repeated with other paragraphs, as time allows. The teacher then sets purposes for reading the remainder of the lesson, referring to the questions asked and information received during the ReQuest.

Since Manzo had remedial readers and small groups in mind when designing ReQuest, some modifications for the content class are in order. The teacher should probably select a small but representative portion of text and not try to use ReQuest for a long period of time. The teacher might also want to limit the questioning time. It is likely that students' questions will be mainly literal; the teacher can then concentrate on inferences and applications. If ReQuest is used often, students will readily adapt to asking more sophisticated questions. After focusing on listening, speaking, and reading in this activity, teachers can follow the steps in using written rather than oral questions. Written questions tend to be more intricate than oral questions and will thus enhance students' levels of sophistication with writing as well.

Text Lookbacks

Often students think that they must recall information to answer questions. They do not realize that readers must frequently go back to the text to find information which helps to answer a question. Text lookbacks (Garner, Hare, Alexander, Haynes, Winograd, 1984), originally designed for remedial readers participating in a study (see chapters 6 and 9), feature strategies used by successful readers. Readers should be taught the following: *why* to use them (because a reader can't remember everything); *when* to use them (when the question asked calls for information from the text); and *where* to use them (where skimming or scanning will help one to find the portion of text which should be read carefully). Next, readers should practice looking back for answers to questions asked after the reading is completed. Lookbacks are necessary when readers realize that they didn't understand all of what they read. Good readers know how to evaluate their reading and to decide whether they should look back. But poorer readers don't have this skill, so text lookbacks will give them practice and reinforcement.

In the authors' classes, we encourage college students to write down their own questions about material which is confusing them. They submit these questions at the start of class, and we look over the assigned reading from the students' perspectives during class discussion time. This procedure requires writing, reading, listening, and speaking.

Reciprocal Teaching

Palinscar and Brown (1986) have described a strategy to promote independent learning from a text. In this strategy, students and teachers establish a dialogue and work together in comprehending text. Reciprocal teaching, as it is called, has at the heart of its structure four shared goals: prediction, summarization, questioning, and clarification. First, the teacher assigns a paragraph. Next, the teacher summarizes the paragraph and asks students several questions about the paragraph. The teacher then clarifies any misconceptions or difficult concepts. Finally, the students predict what will be discussed in the next paragraph or segment. When the next cycle begins, roles are reversed and students become the modelers.

We recommend this strategy because, like the ReQuest procedure, reciprocal teaching uses small segments of reading; thus, the poor reader is not overwhelmed by too much reading. Like ReQuest, it is a highly structured method which attempts to make use of all the language arts—listening, writing, reading, and speaking. Palinscar and Brown (1986) explain that this technique has been proven successful with small and large groups, in peer tutoring, in science instruction, and in teaching listening comprehension.

Toward School Responsibility for Learning: From Dependence to Independence in Purpose Setting

Although teachers must help readers set purposes initially, readers must begin to set their own purposes for reading as soon as possible. Hawkes and Schell (1987) caution that teacher-set reasons to read may encourage dependence and a passive approach to reading. Self-set reasons to read promote readers who are active and ultimately independent. To wean readers from dependence, teachers could use many of the activities mentioned throughout this book until students are familiar with them and understand what purpose setting involves. Then teachers could ask readers to create their own versions of these activities. Eventually, readers will be setting their own purposes as a result of this intermediate step. That is, what students can initially accomplish only with the aid of the teacher, they are eventually able to perform alone (Gavelek, 1986). The goal is that the teacher gradually release purpose-setting responsibility to the students, enabling them to become independent learners. This goal is especially difficult to meet with at-risk students, but it is just as important.

Writing Activities for At-Risk Learners

Motivating At-Risk Students to Write

Poor readers require techniques to motivate them to engage in both practical writing and creative writing. First of all, students need to be given adequate time to write. A homework assignment in writing usually is not successful with at-risk students. In the primary and intermediate grades, students will be motivated by pictures which the class can discuss and then use as a basis for a story. The class can discuss characters in a picture, and students can be asked what is happening in the picture, what may be about to happen, and what may have happened in the past. To accompany the picture, the teacher may construct sentences such as the following, which the students can complete. For example, for a picture showing the signing of the Declaration of Independence:

1. The man in the picture is _____.
2. He is signing _____.
3. If I were at the signing, I would _____.
4. The men in the picture look _____.
5. There are no women in the picture because _____.
6. The men will soon be _____.

In addition to practicing with closure as above, students can be motivated to write by being given a beginning to a story, such as the following:

> The man knew it was not wise to refuse the "mugger," who was young and strong and mean looking. But he wanted to save his pocket watch. That watch was so special; it had a long history in his family. Should he refuse to give it to the thief?

By explaining why they would or would not surrender their pocket watch, students practice composing their own paragraphs. For exceptionally reluctant learners, however, the teacher might scramble paragraphs and ask students to reassemble the sentences into a coherent paragraph. Here is an example from high school business math:

Directions: Put these sentences in the proper order, making a coherent paragraph. Use these transition words: also, unfortunately, however (if you wish to use another, please justify).

_____ State laws governing unemployment insurance differ widely.
_____ People are afraid of being unemployed.
_____ There is no uniform method by which benefits are computed.
_____ People are scared of having no income to support their families.
_____ Every state has some form of unemployment insurance.

The purpose of using writing as a means of learning is to help at-risk students read and think better through awareness of their own ability to write. From an emphasis on paragraphs, teachers can eventually move to an emphasis on research and writing about ever-bigger amounts of information. Calkins (1986) suggests the following cycle for content area research writing:

1. Choose the research area and focus on a specific writing topic.
2. Take notes to learn about the topic.
3. Focus in depth on the topic by analyzing information.
4. Do more research on the topic.

5. Get ready to write by rehearsing for writing.
6. Make drafts, revise, have teacher-student conferences.
7. Edit and publish material.
8. Cycle back for more research with perhaps a new focus.

Calkins's point 7 is very important in getting any students to write. Whenever possible, students should write for an audience, even if "publishing" means merely taking completed writing products home to parents and/or kin.

The most important factor in motivating the writing of slow learners, perhaps, is making certain we don't emphasize mechanics too early in learning the writing process. Such students have been discouraged by teachers who find fault and dwell on their inadequacies. Remember that many failing students have poor handwriting skills and are often weak in spelling and grammar. In grading, teachers should inform students that they will be graded on the sincerity and fluency of their efforts. Later teachers can ask for more clarity in student writing. Finally, the goal is to produce students who write correctly and with some style. Remember that motivation comes from following this progression in grading student writing:

Fluency → Clarity → Correctness → Eloquence & Style

Also, remember that research suggests that semiliterate students may have a vocabulary not exceeding 500 words (Pei, 1965; Tonjes and Zintz, 1981). Patience is the key when teaching students with these limitations.

At-risk students are generally characterized as passive learners who lack ability to produce and monitor adequate reading behaviors (Harris & Graham, 1985; Torgensen and Licht, 1983). Yet Adler (1982) has said that "genuine learning is active, not passive. It involves the use of mind, not just the memory. It is a process of discovery, in which the student is the main agent, not the teacher" (p. 50). Writing that stresses discovery and active learning alluded to by Adler represents an excellent way for passive students to become active learners who are responsible for "building" their own concepts as they write. Such techniques can aid even children with severely limited capacity to learn. Over four decades ago, Strauss and Lehtinen (1947) successfully used writing in helping to teach brain-injured children to read. They saw writing as valuable in developing the visual-motor perception and the kinesthetic abilities of these children. Researchers since that time, such as Myklebust (1965), Chomsky (1971), Graves (1983), and Moffett (1979), have advocated that writing programs be adopted in the schools. Recent research has also documented the benefits of teaching the writing process to learning-disabled students and other students with special needs (Barenbaum, 1983; Douglass, 1984; Kerchner and Kistinger, 1984; Harris and Graham, 1985; Radencich, 1985; Roit and McKenzie, 1985).

Writing-to-learn activities have been discussed in a number of earlier chapters in this text. In this chapter, we describe writing activities which are excellent for at-risk learners. These strategies act as catalysts to aid learning-disabled and at-risk children to gain control and become much more active and involved in their learning. Self (1987) has suggested a number of writing-to-learn strategies, which are listed in Table 12.2. These are excellent general writing strategies for at-risk learners.

Process Writing

The four generally accepted stages of writing were discussed in previous chapters. For at-risk learners, considering writing in several more phases is advisable. Teachers need to be aware that the writing process occurs in stages. Denny Wolfe and Robert Reising, in their book, *Writing for Learning in the Content Areas* (1983), describe these ten phases of the process writing approach.

1. *Prevision Experience.* This is the struggling initial stage when students are formulating thoughts about some experience they have had or thinking about a stimulus the teacher has shared with them. Students cannot simply sit down and write without careful thought about the sense of the piece of writing to be crafted.
2. *Reflection.* Here students should begin to focus their thinking about a topic by utilizing individual "think time" or discussing the topic in a small-group brainstorming session.
3. *Selection.* In this phase, the topic or topics and subtopics begin to emerge. Students choose the topic after careful study throughout phases 1 and 2.
4. *Zero Draft.* Through free writing, games, graphic visuals, student(s) begin to build a conceptual framework which the authors call a "bank." The bank provides a collection of raw data for the first draft.
5. *First Draft.* The student completes a first rendering, with little editing or revising.
6. *Peer Inquiry.* Teacher divides students into groups of two to five to exchange ideas about first drafts and deal with student perceptions about the topic. Each student should get at least one response to his or her own writing. If time permits, all papers are read and critiqued by all students.
7. *Revision.* With the results of phase 6, the student begins to make changes, to revise, and to edit. Here the student is truly becoming a writer, growing and learning through crafting the piece of writing.
8. *Teacher Inquiry.* Here the teacher reads, not as a grader, but as a reviewer of the student's work. The teacher gives as much feedback as possible about ways to further improve the draft.
9. *Revision.* The student makes another revision based on the teacher's comments. Here also the student is asked by the teacher to reconsider every phase, possibly going back to the prevision stage.

T A B L E 1 2 . 2 . *Some Writing-to-Learn Strategies*

Writing To:	Suggested Teacher Instructions
1. Discover what one does or doesn't already know	Write down what you already know about the process of photosynthesis.
2. Assemble information by taking notes and making notes about subject matter	Draw a line down the center of your paper. On the left side, take notes on the important concepts you read in Chapter 12. On the right side, make a personal note about each recorded note. (React to, rephrase, respond to, question, or associate the ideas with something you know.)
3. Predict what will happen next in the text	Now that you have read about lungs, what do you need to know next? What do you think will come next in the chapter?
4. Paraphrase, translate, or rephrase the text	There are ten sections in Chapter 12. After receiving a number from one to ten, rephrase your respective section in your own words. Tomorrow we will read our own version of Chapter 12.
5. Associate images, events, ideas, or personal experiences with subject matter	When you think about the Declaration of Independence, what do you see (images, events, ideas, or even a personal experience that reminds you of that time in our history)?
6. Define concepts or ideas about subject matter	In your own words, define the terms in bold print found in the second section of Chapter 12.
7. React or respond to texts or discussions	Take the last five minutes of class to write down the most important ideas for you in our discussion.

Reprinted from Judy Self, "The Picture of Writing to Learn" in *Plain Talk About Learning and Writing Across the Curriculum*, Virginia Department of Education, Spring, 1987. Used with permission.

10. *Evaluation/Publication.* The student's writing is evaluated by the teacher and "published" in the sense that the teacher, other students, family, and friends read the work. In special cases, writing may be published outside the classroom as letters to the editor, articles in the school newspaper, etc.

Zaragoza (1987) lists several fundamental elements different from Wolfe and Reising's. In the "time to write" stage, she describes how students need a thirty minute block of time each day devoted expressly to writing so that they will acquire the habit of writing. Zaragoza also calls for children to have considerable freedom in choosing the topic, in order to build the self-confidence that what they say is important.

Writing To:	Suggested Teacher Instructions
8. Create problems to be solved with subject matter	Make up a word problem that reflects a real-life situation in which the solver would have to use the formula for finding the area of a rectangle.
9. Apply the subject matter to one's own life	After reading about the concept of supply and demand, choose one product that you frequently use and tell how your life would change if its balance of supply and demand were interrupted.
10. Sketch or narrate observations and/or one's responses or reactions to them	Sketch out or tell in story form what happened on your field trip. For some of the events, give your personal reactions to what happened.
11. Summarize concepts and ideas from texts or discussions	Write a summary of Chapter 12. *Or* summarize the ideas we discussed in class today.
12. Question what the text or lecture means or how the parts of the topic relate	List at least three things in Chapter 12 that aren't clear to you. *Or* write down two questions you would like to ask the author of this.
13. Talk on paper with the teacher or another student about a topic or idea	Choose a friend and write your understanding of and your questions about photosynthesis.
14. Invent a role or language that characterizes the subject matter or person under study	Having now studied the Middle East, write a statement you think our State Department might release about the recent kidnappings of Americans in Beirut.
15. Analyze a topic, or one's reactions to it	List the images you see in this poem and try to figure out how they relate to one another or to the message of the poem.
16. Solve problems with the subject matter	How and where in this story is Hemingway's philosophy of death apparent?

The entire idea of process writing is to establish a feeling of control by the student, to "learn that the influence of their choices extends beyond their work to the larger classroom environment" (Zaragoza, p. 292). She also recommends that after the first draft a revision be done and teachers edit this version. Later, children "publish" their work in the form of student-made books. The critical element in the writing process, according to Zaragoza, is the teacher-student conference. These conferences, which can take place during any phase of the program, allow for one-on-one advising, editing, and sharing. The researcher feels that emphasizing writing process can help develop in children "traits that will perhaps save them from being labeled LD" (p. 298).

Children who are very reluctant can be taught to write stories through "prompter" cards that name several characters, traits, problems to write about, and locations for the story. These attributes can be changed to encourage the child to write fresh stories. An example:

Character	*Trait*	*Problem*	*Location*
cannibals	mean	shipwrecked	in a tent
coward	nasty	horrified	in a spaceship
champion	miserable	no way to leave cave	at a movie
hero	elegant	scared by a ghost	at school
giant	impudent	soaked with rain	on a deserted island
soldier	nice	lights went out	in a crowded city
prince	ungrateful	car was out of control	on a boat
baby	lonely	teetering on the brink	on Mars

Summarizing

Research shows that poor readers have trouble identifying important ideas in a passage and have trouble using the rules for summarizing (Winograd, 1984). Summary writing can help at-risk students by allowing them to reduce their thinking about the reading passage. That is, the teacher can get these students to concentrate on the "big picture," or gist of the reading, while not getting caught up in minutiae. A practical way to get students to concentrate on the gist of the reading is to start them with the ABOUT/POINT technique such as the following (discussed in chapter 9):

> **This article on cumulus clouds is about _____ and the points are _____, _____, and _____.**

A number of reading professionals and researchers have formulated rules for condensing major ideas in a text (Kintch and Van Dijk, 1978; Brown, Campione, and Day, 1981). Here are the rules students should generally follow:

1. *Delete unnecessary detail.* With practice, students will become adept at separating important text information from minor facts and trivial statements.
2. *Delete redundant information.* Students make lists and collapse information into broader categories of information as they notice redundancies occurring.
3. *Use blanket terms.* Students should replace lists of smaller items of information with more encompassing terms.
4. *Summarize paragraphs, select topic sentences.* Often paragraphs have easily identifiable topic sentences. Sometimes there is no discernible topic sentence, however, and students have to create their own topic sentence for the summary. This can be very difficult for poor readers. Much practice is needed for these students to feel successful at this difficult stage.

5. *Write first draft of summary.* Here students need to integrate information by making more general certain topic sentences, key words, and phrases already compiled in steps 1–4. The first four stages prepare students to write the first draft of the summary.

6. *Revise summary.* In this phase, students can, with the help of the teacher or of other students, rework the summary to make it more readable. By doing so, students will get a clearer idea of the major points covered in the material.

Hare and Borchardt (1984) used similar rules in an experimental study with minority high school students. Compared to a control group which made little progress, the experimental group improved in summary-writing ability as well as the ability to use the rules to write summaries. It would appear from the results of this study and from our observation in the classroom that summary writing can be used to help the at-risk student.

Learning Logs and Journals

Learning logs are a relatively simple yet always effective way to get all students to write in content area classes. Sometimes called journals, logs are used to stimulate thinking. Normally students write in their logs every day, either as an in-class activity or an out-of-class assignment. Students can be asked to write entries that persuade, that tell of personal experiences and responses to stimuli, that give information, or that are creative and spontaneous. Figure 12.2 shows how teachers can motivate students by providing a number of learning-log assignments.

Figure 12.3 gives an example of how a content area learning log might look if the teacher structures columns to get students thinking and reacting to what is being learned. This structure especially helps the at-risk student to focus on a task and come to closure.

Once students have practiced keeping a log, the teacher can ask them to respond in a more open-ended, less structured fashion. For instance, Page (1987) got the following response from a student, Carla, in exploring *Antigone* in a high-school English class:

> I get Sophocles and Socrates mixed up. Socrates is a philosopher. Athens is talked about a great deal in mythology. Wow, they had dramatic competitions. I wonder if he had the record for the most wins at the competition. I bet if Polyneices were alive, he would be very proud of his sister. I would! The chorus seems similar to today's narrator.

Page notes also that students are more motivated to learn when they keep a journal or log. She cites positive comments of three students about such writing:

> I love the writing journals. Having to keep a writing journal is the extra push I need to expand my ideas, when, otherwise I would not. My journal

Read _____, and in your learning log write: (teacher chooses one from below)

1. any passage or item that puzzles you.
2. any items that intrigue you.
3. three things you agree (disagree) with.
4. how it makes you feel.
5. what you think will happen next.
6. three new concepts and your definition of them.
7. how this reading relates to your life.
8. two things this reading has in common with _____.
9. what you think the author was like.
10. why you think _____ acted like (he/she) did.
11. what you think it would be like to live in   _(setting)_ .
12. a summary of this   (chapter, section, book) .
13. your reaction to _____.
14. three things you'd like the class to discuss.
15. a cause-effect flowchart.
16. how you can use this knowledge in your own life.
17. something the reading reminds you of.
18. what you think it means, and why you think that.
19. what you would do if you were   _(character)_ .
20. why _____ is important.

Figure 12.2. Sample learning log assignments to follow a text reading.
From Glaze, B. "Learning Logs," *Plain Talk About Learning and Writing Across the Curriculum*, 1987. Richmond, VA: Virginia Department of Education, Commonwealth of Virginia, p. 151. Used with permission.

		Name _____ Class (Subject) _____		
Date	Prediction: What's going to happen?	Facts: What have I learned?	Question: What don't I understand yet?	My Opinion: How do I feel about this reading?

Figure 12.3. Learning log.

has brought to life many ideas that may have died if I had not been required to keep a journal. I am somewhat proud of it.—*Carla*

Writing journals are my favorite. I like having a place to write down important events in my life and literary ideas, poems, stories, etc.—*Allison*

I feel that the writing journal by far is the most expressive and open writing that we have done in class. I always try to come up with original and creative entries. I feel that the journal has sparked some new creativity in me—and my essays (product paper) reflect it. They seem to be more imaginative than before.—*Betsy*

(1987, p. 39–40)

Learning-log entries like those above are examples of what is sometimes called *free writing*, an attempt to motivate students by getting them to write of their perceptions of certain events or classroom operations. These are attempts at getting students to think and write without the encumbrance of worry over mechanics and correctness. It may be just the prescription for students who, at all grade levels, are "turned off" to learning.

Additional Strategies for Very Poor Readers and Nonreaders

What can the content area teacher do with the student who can barely read or who is a nonreader? The teacher can (a) pretend such a student is really not that bad a reader and do nothing, (b) get help from a reading specialist, or (c) assign extra work to help students in this situation. Ideally, content area teachers will do both (b) and (c). The reading specialist can help with basic skills while aiding the content teacher in adapting assignments for this type of student. While most of the techniques described in this book will help the very poor reader or nonreader, two techniques which are especially important for the success of such students are presented here. They are auditory and visual discrimination exercises, and concept-formation study guides.

Auditory and Visual Discrimination Exercises

Cruickshank (Cruickshank et al., 1961) lists the following prerequisites for reading readiness:

1. Mental age of six or more
2. Adequate language development
3. Sentence memory
4. Visual memory and visual discrimination
5. Auditory memory and auditory discrimination

6. Correct enunciation and pronunciation
7. Motor ability
8. Visual maturity
9. Motivation

As children mature and develop, they master most of these readiness factors. However, auditory and visual discrimination problems may continue for many children into middle school and even high school. Weaknesses in these two important areas may mean that students will be severely hindered in learning to read. We suggest that content area teachers ask reading specialists to evaluate nonreaders in regard to these two important factors. Nonreaders weak in these areas can be helped through auditory and visual discrimination games and worksheets. For instance, words similar or alike in beginning, middle, and ending sounds to selected words in the unit can be called to the nonreader by the teacher or by another student. It can be done in this manner:

> Are the beginning (middle, ending) sounds of these two words alike or different? (word in unit) zygoma   xylophone

Teachers can also construct auditory discrimination games in which students get points for correct answers or move a space across a racetrack for each correct answer.

Herber (1970) proposed visual discrimination exercises, or what he called "word recognition exercises." These are lists, twenty-five lines long, of words of similar configuration. Students are asked to pick the word that is the same as the first word or to find two words anywhere on the line that are the same. Herber advocated that students in need of visual discrimination training keep records of speed and accuracy. Figure 12.4 is an example of this activity for a high-school science class.

With much practice in auditory and visual discrimination over one semester, the very poor reader or nonreader should master these skills and begin to make real progress in reading. Once these readiness skills are mastered by students in upper elementary grades and above, these students can often "hurdle" a number of grade levels in reading because of their age and the benefit of their prior knowledge.

Concept-Formation Study Guides

Concept-formation study guides (Thompson and Morgan, 1976) are excellent motivational tools for reluctant readers. Such guides make use of a fundamental learning operation: the categorization of facts—(lower-order concepts)—under more inclusive, higher-order concepts.

1. weather   wealthy   weapon   weather   whether
2. atmosphere   atmospheric   atmosphere   atomic   almost
3. temperature   temperament   temperance   tepid   temperature
4. meteorologists   meteor   meteorologists   metallic   meteorological
5. humidity   humility   humidity   humorous   humanity
6. predict   predict   predestined   predicament   predicate
7. observation   observe   preservation   observation   obtain
8. hygrometer   hydrogen   hygrometer   hyperactivity   hibiscus
9. dew   due   dues   dew   do
10. frost   foster   frown   fawn   forest   frost
11. clouds   clouds   clout   closure   clown
12. cirrus   circus   serious   cirrus   circumference
13. cumulus   accumulate   calcium   cumulative   cumulus
14. stratum   stride   status   stratum   straight
15. precipitation   prescription   precipitous   precipitation   precipitate
16. forecast   forecast   overcast   forehead   forewarn
17. barometer   bargain   barometer   bartender   baron
18. mercury   merchant   merry   mercury   mercurial
19. anemometer   anemone   anemometer   meter   antimatter
20. front   fond   frown   front   from
21. tornado   torrent   tornado   torture   torn
22. radar   raiding   radiant   radar   radio
23. satellites   satiate   satisfy   static   satellites
24. hurricane   hurry   hurricane   hurried   hamper
25. wind   wand   wind   wane   windy

Figure 12.4. Science word recognition exercise.

Thompson and Morgan note that "once a key concept has been acquired, we use it at different levels of abstraction, complexity, and generality, depending upon our stage of motivation" (p. 132). It is the function of this type of study guide to teach the key concepts of a passage and to provide practice in applying those concepts to more complex and more general situations. Again, creating higher-level generalities of concepts is a skill often completely lacking in reluctant readers and at-risk learners. Figures 12.5 and 12.6 present two examples of concept-formation study guides, the first for elementary and the second for high-school levels.

Please read "Pick a Pack of Perfect Pets," pp. 1–3.

I. Directions: Read the story. Put an (X) before each statement you think is true.
———— 1. A person should find out how the neighborhood feels about pets.
———— 2. Some small pets grow into large pets.
———— 3. Someone must care for your pet if you are sick.
———— 4. A kangaroo will not make a good pet.
———— 5. Do not read about a pet before you buy it.
———— 6. It is hard to keep a pet in a small apartment in the city.

II. Put true statements from part I where they fit below.

Choosing a pet depends on:

Size   Care   Space

III. When you are finished, get together with a classmate and discuss your answers.

Figure 12.5. Concept formation study guide: Elementary.

One-Minute Summary

There is an old saying in education that we, as teachers, must work with:

the haves,
the halves, and
the have nots.

The reader would probably agree that one does not have to be a great teacher to teach the "haves": those with the motivation to learn and the skills to do work above their grade level. The true art of teaching is in relating to the "halves" and the "have nots." The halves are those who have marginal skills to learn a subject but are not motivated to do so. The have nots are usually not motivated to learn, and they do not have the necessary thinking, reading, and study skills to be successful. This chapter has presented unique strategies for unique individuals, those at-risk students who, more than ever in our nation's history, need teacher assistance and empathy to help them become productive citizens in a technological society. With such students, the challenge for teachers is great, and the rewards may be few. But these special students can and must be reached if our society is to prosper.

The Move to Winter Grasslands

Key Concept: Social transience

Main Idea: Interaction between a people and the physical and social environment which surrounds them influences the way the basic needs of life are met.

PART I

Directions: Think of a family that you know who recently moved. What reasons did this family have for moving? In the chart below complete a listing of reasons our families and Al'Azab families have for moving from one place to another.

Reasons for Moving

American Families	Bedouin Al'Azab Clan
1. Dad's new job	1. Good grasslands
2.	2.
3.	3.
4.	4.
5.	5.
6.	6.
7.	7.
8.	8.
9.	9.
10.	10.

PART II

From your list above, answer the following questions:

1. Select those items under the "our" list that are related to making a living. Do the same thing for the Al'Azabs. How are the reasons different? Alike?

2. Based on the information you have organized above, make a list of the Al'Azab basic needs of life. Are they different from our family's basic needs?

3. Based on the information you have organized above, define in your own words what you think "social transience" is.

Figure 12.6. Concept formation study guide: High school social studies.

End-of-Chapter Activities

Preparing the Reader

How well did the authors prepare you to read this chapter? How did their preparation techniques help clarify your thinking about the chapter?

Assisting Comprehension

1. What are the characteristics of at-risk learners described in this chapter?

2. Fill in parts of the following postgraphic organizer.

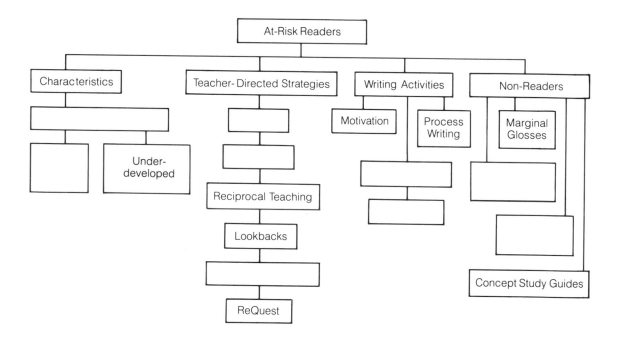

Word List:

free writing	listening	visual discrimination
note taking	learning logs	auditory discrimination
unproductive	question/prediction	lack of achievement

Reflecting on Your Reading

1. How has this chapter helped you better deal with that sizable segment of the school population identified as at-risk readers?

2. Write specific plans you have for improving instruction for at-risk students in your classes.

References

Adler, M. J. (1982). *The paideia proposal.* New York: MacMillan.

Alvermann, D. (1987). Discussion strategies for content area reading. In D. Alvermann, D. R. Dillon, D. G. O'Brien (Eds.), *Using discussion to promote reading comprehension* (pp. 34–42). Newark, DE: International Reading Association.

Barenbaum, E. (1983). Writing in the special class. *Topics in Learning and Learning Disabilities, 3,* 12–20.

Brown, A. L., Campione, J. & Day, J. D. (1981). Learning to learn: On training students to learn from texts. *Educational Researcher, 10,* 14–24.

Brown, A. L., Day, J. D. & Jones, R. (1983). The development of plans for summarizing texts. *Child Development, 54,* 968–979.

Calkins, L. M. (1986). *The art of teaching writing.* Portsmouth, NH: Heinemann.

Choate, J. S. & Rakes, T. A. (1987). The structured listening activity: A model for improving listening comprehension. *The Reading Teacher, 41,* 194–200.

Chomsky, C. (1971). Write first, read later. *Childhood Education, 47,* 296–299.

Cruickshank, W., Bentzen, F. A., Ratzeburg, F. H., & Tannhauser, M. (1961). *A teaching method for brain-injured and hyperactive children.* New York: Syracuse University Press.

Douglass, B. (1984). Variations on a theme: Writing with the LD adolescent. *Academic Therapy, 19,* 361–362.

Garner, R., Hare, V. C., Alexander, P., Haynes, J. & Winograd, P. (1984). Inducing use of a text lookback strategy among unsuccessful readers. *American Educational Research Journal, 21,* 789–798.

Gavelek, J. R. (1986). The social contexts of literacy and schooling: A developmental perspective. In T. Raphael (Ed.), *The contexts of school-based literacy* (pp. 3–26). New York: Random House.

Glasser, W. (1986). *Control theory in the classroom.* New York: Harper & Row.

Glaze, B. (1987). *Learning logs.* Richmond, VA: Virginia Department of Education, Commonwealth of Virginia.

Graves, D. (1983). *Writing: Teachers and children at work.* Portsmouth, Heinemann.

Hare, V. C. & Borchardt, K. M. (1984). Direct instruction of summarization skills. *Reading Research Quarterly, 20,* 62–78.

Harris, K. & Graham, S. (1985). Improving learning disabled students' composition skills: Self-control strategy training. *Learning Disability Quarterly, 8,* 27–36.

Hawkes, K. S. & Schell, L. M. (1987). Teacher-set prereading purposes and comprehension. *Reading Horizons, 27,* 164–169.

Kerchner, L. & Kistinger, B. (1984). Language processing/word processing: Written expression, computers and learning disabled students. *Learning Disability Quarterly, 7,* 329–335.

Kintch, W. & Van Dijk, T. (1978). Toward a model of text comprehension and production. *Psychological Review, 85,* 363–394.

Manzo, A. V. (1969). The request procedure. *Journal of Reading, 11,* 123–126.

Middle school curriculum planning guide for reading. (1986). Orlando, FL: Orange County Public Schools.

Moffett, J. (1979). Integrity in the teaching of writing. *Phi Delta Kappan, 61,* 276–279.

Myklebust, H. (1965). *Development and disorders of written language.* New York: Grune & Stratton.

Page, B. (1987). From passive receivers to active learners in English. *Plain talk about learning and writing across the curriculum.* Richmond, VA: Virginia Department of Education, Commonwealth of Virginia.

Palinscar, A. S. & Brown, A. L. (1986). Interactive teaching to promote independent learning from text. *The Reading Teacher, 39,* 771–777.

Pei, M. (1965). *The story of language.* Rev. ed. New York: Mentor Books.

Pellicano, R. (1987). At-risk: A view of "social advantage." *Educational Leadership, 44,* 47–50.

Radencich, M. (1985). Writing a class novel: A strategy for LD students? *Academic Therapy, 20,* 599–603.

Roit, M. & McKenzie, R. (1985). Disorders of written communication: An instructional priority for LD students. *Journal of Learning Disabilities, 18,* 258–260.

Self, J. (1987). The picture of writing to learn. *Plain talk about learning and writing across the curriculum.* Richmond, VA: Virginia Department of Education, Commonwealth of Virginia.

Singer, H. & Doulan, D. (1980). *Reading and learning from text.* Boston: Little, Brown.

Strauss, A. A. & Lehtinen, L. (1947). *Psychopathology and education in the brain-injured child.* (Vol. 1). New York: Grune & Stratton.

Thompson, G. & Morgan, R. (1976). The use of concept formation study guides for social studies reading materials. *Reading Horizons, 17,* 132–136.

Tonjes, M. J. & Zintz, M. V. (1981). *Teaching reading/thinking study skills in content classrooms.* Dubuque, IA: Brown.

Torgensen, J. & Licht, B. (1983). The learning disabled child as an inactive learner: Retrospect and prospects. In J. McKinney & L. Fergans (Eds.), *Topics in learning disabilities* (Vol. 1). Norwood, NJ: Ablex.

Wigfield, A. & Asher, S. (1984). Social and motivational influences on reading. In P. D. Pearson (Ed.), *Handbook of reading research.* New York: Longman.

Winograd, P. N. (1984). Strategic difficulties in summarizing texts. *Reading Research Quarterly, 19,* 404–425.

Wolfe, D. & Reising, R. (1983). *Writing for learning in the content areas.* Portland, ME: J. Weston Walch.

Zaragoza, N. (1987). Process writing for high-risk learning disabled students. *Reading Research and Instruction, 26,* 290–301.

Appendices

Appendix I

Remarks Made at the Reading Across the Curriculum Conference, VCU, April 3, 1984, by Brian Kane

Introduction

Several years ago I was jolted by a *National Geographic* article on attempts to teach language to a chimpanzee. Having spent twenty years teaching in public high school, I felt threatened by this prospect. Fortunately, in spite of some premature claims of success, it is generally accepted that the monkey has not really assimilated language.

I, however, am of the opinion that a high school student *can* assimilate language. This has led me to the conclusion that the way to improve the reading and writing skills of human beings is by requiring that they read and write. Allow me to repeat. I believe that if you require students to read and write, they will improve in their ability to read and write.

This startling observation is the apex of my comments. However, I do want to comment on four additional areas:

I. Reading and the content areas
II. High School as a place where students avoid responsibility
III. Practice and reality
IV. Real reading

I. Reading and the Content Areas

Education is premised upon language. Language involves reading, writing and speaking. You cannot separate language from education. Language not only conveys, it shapes. If you increase or refine the ability of a human being to use language, you literally affect his mind. You cannot deal with any subject on any level without language. Indeed, how you use language affects the subject matter. Subject matter and language are fused. They cannot be separated.

The bulk of what we know as education is built upon the ability to read. Reading has different levels. Skimming the phone book, reading *People* magazine, or a poem, or *Moby Dick*, or a tax book are all forms of reading but they are all different. To assume that students who read a paragraph out loud in class understand or can learn that material can be fallacious.

It is easier to explain to students than it is to require that they read, understand and assume responsibility for what they have read. It may be easier to explain, *but it is not as effective in terms of what the student learns.* The proper type of reading is, at its best, individualized instruction. It is one-on-one: the student's intellect attempts to decipher the meaning of printed symbols. Confronting, deciphering, understanding the information contained in the

453

written word is, in the jargon of our trade, a learning experience. Having deciphered and understood the written word, the student is then in a position, with additional effort, to learn.

It is important to note that I am speaking of learning and not "covering the material." In my judgement, if you are serious about having students learn, you have to be serious about reading and writing. A student who can read, understand and explain the *Declaration of Independence* has learned.

II. High School as a Place Where Students Avoid Responsibility

The game. The basis for the game is that the school is responsible for the student. Somehow the student never becomes responsible for himself. As students move through the grades they become more adult, more aware, and more cynical about the system that treats them as children and they respond in kind. "I can't, I don't have a pencil." "My book is in my locker." "I did my homework, but my dog ate it." "I had to work last night." "My sister didn't bring my textbook home." The school perpetuates the idea that the student isn't responsible for himself with passes, excused absences, make-up policies, notes from parents that are often forged or lies. When a student asks a teacher, "May I be excused from class?" he is asking for the teacher to accept responsibility for the student's absence.

Learning, however, *is* a student's responsibility. You can't push a string, and if a student doesn't or won't accept responsibility for learning, he won't learn. The student must at some point, for some reason, elect to learn.

In the same manner, a student must elect to read in an attempt to understand. He must engage the printed symbols on the page in an attempt to fathom the intent. As a teacher, I can prepare, or assist, or clarify, or answer questions, but I cannot read for the student. Nor can I, in the last analysis, make him read. Therefore, teachers must conduct their classes such that the student *elects* to read and attempts to understand in lieu of a slow and painful death. Not only is it okay to give the student unfair choices, I urge you to do so, just so long as he reads.

III. Practice and Reality

Too often we engage in practices that promote the avoidance of the responsibility for reading and learning while at the same time reward the student for *not* reading and learning. Students know that in spite of all the talk, they are in school to get grades, earn credits, move on to graduation. Learning is not an important consideration. This has been described as the vaccination theory of education: a course is something you take and having taken it, you have had it. Having had it, you need not take it again. Thus my government students cry out "but this is government class and we shouldn't be graded on English." What they mean is they passed English, and therefore it is unfair of me to expect them to use English. I try to point out that it is difficult to explain what you know about "how a bill becomes a law" in an essay without using English. But logic never convinces them.

Book reports, "read chapter 23," "read chapter 23 and do the questions at the end" are examples of practices that allow the student to avoid the responsibility of reading while earning grades.

Book reports are a time-honored tradition in school. Everyone has made book reports, and a few have even read the books. Students don't read books because they get graded on the *report*, not on reading books. (Am I telling anybody anything new?) Yet, year in and year out, we require, with full knowledge that books are not being read, that book reports be done. Book reports are assigned, generated, grades are produced, recorded and averaged. Students then graduate reading on an eighth-grade level having made twelve book reports.

Teacher assigns chapter 23 to be read for homework. While students avoid learning whatever it is we are teaching, they do learn. They know that the day chapter 23 is due, the teacher will explain chapter 23 and therefore they don't read chapter 23. It is my guess that most of the chapters assigned for reading in American public high schools are not read; don't have to be read; all you have to do is pass the unit test.

"Read chapter 23 and do the questions at the end." Provided the student does his own work and doesn't copy the homework in homeroom, he will more than likely first turn to the end of the chapter and read the first question. Then he will turn to the start of the chapter and skim until he finds the answer, which is often in italics. Having recorded the correct answer, he moves on to the second question and will complete the assignment and again receive a grade which will be averaged with his book report grade. Thus the assignment is completed, grades are obtained, and reading is avoided.

IV. Real Reading

Real reading, or reading as a means to understanding and learning, is a relatively slow and often ponderous chore. Real reading involves encountering new words, information, concepts or views. It requires that I utilize my intellect, that I have a dialogue with the printed symbols. The words must talk to me, and I must respond. Real reading can be trying to understand an IRS tax book, or *Moby Dick*, or a poem, or the Gettysburg Address, or a theorem in geometry. It is *not* reading a Harlequin romance, or the comics, or *Hot Rod* magazine. This process of attempting to understand or learn by reading is hard work and is thus avoided by most human beings, including students. Thus we, as teachers, *must* require it if it is to be utilized and developed. And if we are successful and students do this sort of reading, then two things occur: first, students learn and second, students learn *how* to learn so that they gain the potential of controlling their education and can elect to learn what is important or interesting to them in the course of their life.

Thank you.—*Brian Kane, Teacher*

Reprinted with permission of Brian Kane.

Resources Developed by Teachers

A social studies unit for third graders:

A. "Virginia Beach in a Box," *Barbara Teuscher*
B. PAR chapter analysis and suggested complementary activities for a high school English textbook, *Bonnie McLaughlin*
C. Three completed Bader Textbook Analyses, *Adrienne Gillis, Pat Bossler, and Todd Barnes*

A. *A Social Studies Unit for Third Graders*

Virginia Beach in a Box
Unit length: 2 weeks
Grade Level: 3rd Grade

Developed by Barbara Teuscher

Diagnostic Instruments

Interest Inventory

Name of student: _____

1. After school I usually like to _____.
2. In the evening I usually like to _____.
3. On the weekends I like to _____.
4. I like to play _____.
5. My family and like to _____.
6. I belong to _____.
7. When I am grown _____.
8. I think my father and mother want me _____.
9. I think museums are _____.
10. I enjoy school most _____.

Attitude Inventory

Directions: Write 1—I agree. 2—I disagree. 3—I am undecided.

_____ 1. Virginia Beach is a great place for a vacation.
_____ 2. There is a lot to do in Virginia Beach.
_____ 3. It would be more fun to live in the mountains than in Virginia Beach.
_____ 4. Virginia Beach is a safe city in which to live.
_____ 5. Museums are boring.

_____ 6. It would be interesting to learn about Virginia Beach.
_____ 7. Citizens should know about the city in which they live.
_____ 8. It would be more fun to live on a farm than in Virginia Beach.
_____ 9. Virginia Beach is unattractive.
_____ 10. Cities should have lots of parks for families.

A Cloze Passage: Christmas at Adam Thoroughgood's House

It was the night before Christmas at Capt. Adam Thoroughgood's plantation on the Lynnhaven River. Great logs burned in the _____ and bread baked in _____ brick oven which got _____ warmth from the fire.

_____ and his wife Frances _____ talking together in their _____ story-and-a-half _____ house. The busy mother _____ the family had worked _____ weeks cooking and preparing _____ the great Christmas party _____ take place next day. _____ year was 1675.

Upstairs, _____ in their trundle beds _____ deep feather mattresses, were _____ sons: Argoll, John, Adam, Francis, _____ Robert. Baby Rose slumbered _____ a wooden cradle which _____ Thoroughgood now and then _____ with her foot.

"Adam," _____ Frances Thoroughgood. "The ship _____ England is overdue. I _____ worried about the young _____, Master Lovitt, whom we _____ to educate the boys. _____ also long for the _____ we have ordered from _____. I had so hoped _____ would be here in _____ for the children's Christmas.

"_____ bother your pretty head," _____ comforted his wife. "Didn't _____ old carol you were _____ to baby Rose have _____ about 'I saw three _____ come sailing in, on _____ Day, on Christmas Day'?"

"_____ have hummed for _____, and prayed too," replied _____, "and looked long down _____ river, but never a _____ in sight.

"Well, _____ time for you to _____. I have told young Moses _____ can wake the boys _____ soon as it is _____. Caleb will build the _____ up and Sukey has _____ breakfast started. Merry Christmas, _____ Thoroughgood. The clock points _____ twelve."

The winter sunrise colored the eastern sky and was reflected in the waters of the Lynnhaven.

Answer sheet for cloze test

1. fireplace	8. of	15. five
2. the	9. for	16. and
3. its	10. for	17. in
4. Adam	11. to	18. Madam
5. sat	12. the	19. rocked
6. snug	13. asleep	20. said
7. brick	14. on	21. from

22. am	32. the	42. it's
23. teacher	33. humming	43. dream
24. engaged	34. words	44. he
25. I	35. ships	45. as
26. things	36. Christmas	46. light
27. London	37. I	47. fire
28. they	38. weeks	48. the
29. time	39. Frances	49. Madam
30. Don't	40. the	50. to
31. Adam	41. sail	

Philosophy

It is the responsibility of today's schools to educate our students to be active thinkers and problem solvers. We cannot accomplish this goal if we continue to have teacher-directed instructional strategies. Progressive theorists have suggested that the role of teachers will have to change dramatically. Teachers would not teach; they would become facilitators. The goal of teaching in the content area would be to encourage the students to be active in discovering and structuring reality for themselves, to become assertive inquirers and managers of their environment, and to encourage students to develop their own understanding, and to draw inferences, rather than be given information. These rather lofty goals can be accomplished through such student-oriented strategies as this unit plan.

Concepts to Be Taught

1. To have students acquire some knowledge of the historical background of Virginia Beach.
2. To have students acquire some knowledge of the geography of Virginia Beach.
3. To have students acquire some understanding of how the city government operates.
4. To have students develop skills in collecting, evaluating, and organizing information from a variety of sources.
5. To have students develop skills in interpreting data from maps, charts, and graphs.
6. To encourage inductive thinking.

Materials

Maps

1. Bicentennial Map
2. Chamber of Commerce, Ocean Front
3. Historical Map of Virginia Beach
4. 1930 Map at Princess Anne Court House
5. Planning Dept. Map of Virginia Beach

6. Revolutionary War Map
7. Virginia Beach

Miscellaneous

8. Flow Chart—Government
9. Virginia Seal

Pamphlets and Brochures

10. The Battle of the Virginia Capes
11. Council-Manager Plan—Answers to Your Questions
12. Virginia Beach, Va., Municipal Government: An Outline
13. Virginia Beach—A Self-Guided Motor Tour
14. Annotated Pictures of Historical Sites in Virginia Beach
15. Brochures of Francis Land House, Lynnhaven House, and Rose Hall

A-V Materials

16. Virginia Beach, An Emerging City (Film)
17. Video Tape of Virginia Beach

Books

18. Kyle, L. V. *The Witch of Pungo.* 1973. JCP Corp. of Virginia Beach
19. *A Country Woman's Scrapbook.* 1980. JCP Corp. of Virginia Beach
20. *Virginia Beach: A Pictorial History.* 1974. Richmond, Va.: Hale Publishing Co.

Concept Key for Materials

Materials	Concepts					
	1	2	3	4	5	6
1.	x	x			x	x
2.		x			x	x
3.	x	x			x	x
4.	x	x			x	x
5.			x	x	x	x
6.	x				x	x
7.		x			x	x
8.		x		x	x	x
9.				x		
10.	x	x				
11.			x	x		
12.			x	x		
13.					x	
14.	x			x		
15.	x			x		
16.	x	x	x	x		

17.	x	x	x	x
18.	x	x		
19.	x	x		
20.	x	x		x

Activities

1. Show film, *Virginia Beach: An Emerging City.*
2. Play tape, *Virginia Beach.*
3. Administer Interest Inventory.
4. Administer Attitude Scale.
5. Begin reading *The Witch of Pungo* aloud to the class.
6. Visit City Hall chambers.
7. Assign individuals or groups to visit places of interest and report to classroom—either oral or written, with displays and posters. Places might be:
   Lynnhaven House, Mt. Trashmore, Seashore State Park, Back Bay, Fort Story
8. Take field trip to Cape Henry Lighthouse and Cross.
9. Take walking field trip to old Coast Guard Station, and the Norwegian Lady.
10. Construct a lighthouse using pattern.
11. Interview a longtime resident of the city concerning changes which have taken place and the city history.
12. Structured Overview of Virginia Beach
13. Cloze Procedure
14. DRTA
15. Three-Level Study Guide
16. Concept Guide
17. Make a time line of events in the city.
18. Locate on the outline map the community in which they live.
19. Identify a problem in the city. Research the problem and detail some possible solutions.
20. Identify the characteristics of a good leader.
21. Design a mural showing the most important events in the development of the city.
22. Plan a model city.
23. Design a bumper sticker.
24. Make charts showing the amount of local tax money spent for various services in the community.
25. Make a graph showing the number of qualified voters in the city and the percentage who voted in the last five elections.
26. Maintain bulletin board of current Virginia Beach news.
27. Have a "Virginia Beach Historic Fair" as a culminating activity—students wear old costumes, cook old-style food, display homemade crafts, play old games, hold contests, etc.
28. End of unit evaluation

Concept Key for Activities

Activities	Concepts 1	2	3	4	5	6
1.	x	x	x	x		
2.	x	x	x	x		
3.	–	–	–	–	–	–
4.	–	–	–	–	–	–
5.	x	x	x	x	x	x
6.			x	x		x
7.	x	x	x	x		x
8.	x			x		
9.	x			x		
10.				x	x	x
11.	x	x	x	x		x
12.	x	x	x	x	x	x
13.						x
14.						x
15.	x	x			x	
16.	x	x				
17.	x	x	x	x	x	x
18.		x			x	x
19.				x		x
20.				x		x
21.	x			x		x
22.				x		x
23.						x
24.			x	x	x	x
25.			x	x	x	x
26.	x	x	x	x	x	x
27.	x	x	x	x	x	x
28.	x	x	x	x	x	x

Fry's Readability Formula for *The Witch of Pungo*. Kyle, L. V., 1973, JCP Corp. of Virginia Beach.

Paragraph I
   Sentences: 6.50
   Syllables: 129
Paragraph II
   Sentences: 6.25
   Syllables: 123
Paragraph III
   Sentences: 6
   Syllables: 128
Grade level: 6th grade

DRTA Synopsis

Title: *The Witch of Pungo.* Kyle, L. V. 1973, Four O'Clock Farms Pub. Co., Virginia Beach.

Discussion: Joey looked at the title and the few pictures. He said he had been to Pungo. He described it as being neat, pretty and having lots of farms. Then we discussed witches—his perception was the stereotyped appearance of a tall black hat, black dress, red eyes, wart on the end of her nose, and long fingers with warts on her hands. They did evil magic on people. They don't live today, but did long ago.

Prediction: The story is about a witch that lived in Pungo a long time ago who did evil things to people.

Evaluation: I fully endorse this teaching technique as a guided reading process. It teaches the correct reading process, develops self-worth in the students and provides a vehicle for students to go from the concrete level of thinking to the more formal and abstract.

Structured Overview

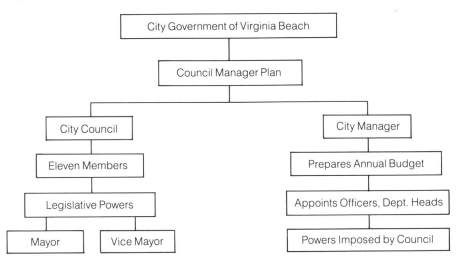

Three-Level Study Guide—*Blackbeard's Treasure*

Part I: Getting the facts.

Directions: Read each statement below. Check each true statement about the story.

_____ 1. While boating, Lem discovered a trunk buried in the sand.
_____ 2. Lem built a lookout where Blackbeard was supposed to have his.
_____ 3. Blackbeard was a famous pirate operating off Cape Henry.
_____ 4. Blackbeard's lookout was in Chesapeake Bay.
_____ 5. Edward Teach was Blackbeard's real name.

_____ 6. Blackbeard's head was cut off and placed on the bowsprit of a ship.

_____ 7. It is said that Blackbeard's headless body swam seven times around his ship and then sank from sight.

_____ 8. The chest that Lem found was about 300 years old.

_____ 9. The buried gold allowed Lem to go to college in England.

_____ 10. There was not enough gold to take care of Lem's family and plantation.

Part II: What did the author mean? (Check three statements.)

_____ 1. Everyone liked Blackbeard.

_____ 2. Pirates were thieves and murderers.

_____ 3. Lem actually found a buried treasure.

_____ 4. Lem liked learning and school.

_____ 5. Lem was just a pleasure seeker.

Part III: How can we use these meanings? Check those which apply.

_____ 1. Where there's smoke, there's fire.

_____ 2. Silence is golden.

_____ 3. You can't judge a book by its cover.

_____ 4. The early bird catches the worm.

_____ 2. Every cloud has a silver lining.

_____ 6. Leave no stone unturned.

Concept Guide—*The Witch of Pungo*

Check the following statements if they are true from your reading.

_____ 1. Women that sold their souls to the Devil were witches.

_____ 2. In return they received magical powers from the evil spirit.

_____ 3. In some parts of the world there are people who practice witchcraft.

_____ 4. If her neighbors did not like her, they could say a woman was a witch.

_____ 5. If a witch was ducked and drowned, she was innocent.

_____ 6. If she untied herself, and was able to swim, she was called a witch.

_____ 7. Grace Sherwood was an ugly woman with long black hair and a wart on the end of her nose.

_____ 8. It was said Grace Sherwood had come through the keyhole into a lady's bedroom and changed her into a big black cat and rode away on her.

_____ 9. Grace Sherwood danced around cows in the pasture and made them give sour milk.

_____ 10. Grace Sherwood drowned, therefore she was not a witch.

Place the above sentences under the correct categories.

Do Witches Exist?   *Traits of Witches*   *Fate of Witches*

Virginia Beach in a Box Unit Test

Answer these items True or False. 2 points each.

_____ 1. Two council members are elected from each borough.
_____ 2. Virginia Beach ranks third in population in comparison with other cities in Virginia.
_____ 3. The Mennonites are leaving Virginia Beach because it is becoming too heavily populated.
_____ 4. Agriculture and tourism are two industries in Virginia Beach.
_____ 5. Oceana is one of the largest submarine bases in the world.
_____ 6. Camp Pendleton is located at Cape Henry.
_____ 7. Tunis was the first name of Oceana.
_____ 8. Virginia Beach ranks third in land size in comparison with other cities in Virginia.
_____ 9. Four council members are elected at-large.
_____ 10. Walking was the main way of travel in early Princess Anne County.

Fill in the blank with the correct answer. 20 points.

1. We have _____ council members in Virginia Beach.
2. The _____ connects Virginia Beach with the Eastern shore.
3. The _____ and the _____ are two historic houses in Virginia Beach.
4. The president of the city council is called the _____.
5. Chesapeake Bay means "_____."
6. _____ and _____ are two churches of early Princess Anne County which are still in use today.
7. _____ and _____ are two colleges in Virginia Beach.

Match Section A to Section B: 20 points.

Section A
a. Adam Thoroughgood
b. Fisherman
c. Council-manager
d. Kempsville
e. Neptune

f. a witch
g. Norwegian Lady
h. George Washington
i. City manager
j. Cape Henry

Section B

_____ 1. He was responsible for the first lighthouse at Cape Henry.
_____ 2. The form of government we have in Virginia Beach.
_____ 3. The name of the festival held in the fall in Virginia Beach.
_____ 4. He renamed the Chesopean River the Lynnhaven River.
_____ 5. The place where the first permanent settler set foot.
_____ 6. Grace Sherwood was one of these.
_____ 7. Title of the head of the city government.
_____ 8. Erected to the memory of people lost in a shipwreck off the beach.
_____ 9. The first settlers in Virginia Beach after the Indians.
_____ 10. The name of the town at Kemps Landing.

Identify. 16 points.

1. Name two capes at the entrance to the Chesapeake Bay.
2. Name two military bases located in Virginia Beach.
3. Name the four boundaries of Virginia Beach.

Answer the following questions in one to two sentences. 7 points each.

1. Early Indians used the area around present day Pungo for what reason?
2. In 1824 the Court House was built at Princess Anne. Why was it felt this was a good location?
3. Name four of the seven boroughs in Virginia Beach.
4. Describe early schools in Virginia Beach.

You may use the back of your test to complete these answers.

Answer Sheet to Unit Test

True—False

1. False	6. False
2. True	7. True
3. True	8. True
4. True	9. True
5. False	10. False

Fill in the Blank

1. Eleven
2. Chesapeake Bay Bridge Tunnel
3. Adam Thoroughgood House, John B. Dey Home, the Huggins House, the Hermitage
4. Mayor
5. Mother of waters
6. Old Donation, Eastern Shore Chapel, Nimmo Church, and Oak Grove Church
7. Tidewater Community College, Virginia Wesleyan College

Matching

1. h
2. c
3. e
4. a
5. j
6. f
7. i
8. g
9. b
10. d

Identify

1. Cape Henry and Cape Charles
2. Fort Story, Little Creek, Oceana,
3. North—Chesapeake Bay
   East—Atlantic Ocean
   South—North Carolina
   West—Norfolk

Short-Answer Essay

1. Hunting
2. Well-populated area

3. Kempsville, Pungo, Blackwater, Va. Beach, Lynnhaven, Princess Anne, and Bayside
4. Small one-room school houses

Student Daily Log Sheet

Name _____

Activity	I learned a lot	I learned some	I didn't learn	I liked it	I didn't like it	I needed help
1.	x			x		x
2.	x			x		
26.	x			x		
23.		x		x		x
11.	x			x		
10.			x			x

Teacher's Activity Roll

Name	Day 1	Day 2	Day 3	Day 4	Day 5	Day 6	Day 7
John	1,2	26,4,15	10	16	18,25	11,23	5,7
Nan	1,2	26,4,15	10	16	18,25	11,23	5,7
Joe	1,2	26,4,15	10	16	18,25	11,23	5,7
Tom	1,2	25,4	15	10	18,16	11,23	5,7
Sue	1,2	25,4	15	10	18,16	11,23	5,7
Sally	1,2	25,4	15	10	18,16	11,23	5,7

B. *A PAR Chapter Analysis and Suggested Complementary Activities for a High School English Textbook*

Developed by Bonnie McLaughlin

Content Area—English, secondary level

Chapter Selected for Revision: "First Harvest"

Text Bibliography:

Hodgins, Francis and Kenneth Silverman, eds. "First Harvest." *Adventures in American Literature.* Heritage Edition Revised. Orlando: Harcourt Brace Jovanovich, 1985. 95–163.

Silverman, Kenneth and John Kuehl. "First Harvest." *Teacher's Manual, Adventures in American Literature.* Heritage Edition Revised. Orlando: Harcourt Brace Jovanovich, 1985. 53–70.

Chapter Evaluation

I. *Overview*

The "First Harvest" unit covers the literary period following the American Revolution up to approximately the middle of the nineteenth century and includes the early Romantic writers, Washington Irving, James Fenimore Cooper, William Cullen Bryant and Edgar Allan Poe. I chose this particular unit because my students' reaction to the chapter introduction included comments like, "Let's skip this period and get on to something good," and, "This is going to be worse than Benjamin Franklin's 'Moral Perfection' stuff!" The introduction had a deadly effect on both my eleventh grade average ability and high ability classes, the intended audience for the text. I found that the chapter introduced too many difficult abstract concepts without adequate concrete examples and explanations, so what was meant to arouse their interest had actually confused and bored them. All the "ism" words—nationalism, classicism, romanticism— had "blown their minds." Student interest improved as we began reading the selections by Irving and Cooper, but the majority of students experienced comprehension problems with Bryant's poetry and Poe's short story, "The Fall of the House of Usher." This was particularly frustrating to many of them because they had anticipated enjoying a titillating horror story. I was not surprised when the average readability level of this unit turned out to be grade 13 on the Fry Readability Graph.

The text is "inconsiderate" in other aspects besides readability. For instance, the introduction does not set up clear and coherent relationships to the reading selections within the unit. Moreover, the editors seem to assume that the reader has more prior knowledge than the average 11th grader actually has. I had the general impression that the unit introduction was difficult, but I thought that this was a function of the subject matter. A closer look at the style and organization of the writing revealed a weak pattern of organization and transition, problems with coherence within certain paragraphs, and an abundance of abstract terminology. The concluding comments of the unit presented a topic for an essay in which the student was asked to relate the ideas in the introduction with the text selections of the unit. I considered this to be one of the most "inconsiderate" portions of the unit because the relationships were vague and in some cases nonexistent for the material provided within the unit.

My experience with this chapter of our new textbook was even more disappointing to me because in the past my students had enjoyed studying this literary period, and I had expected a similar response. The assigned material in the introduction did nothing to interest and motivate the students to learn, and I had to reinspire them to begin reading the authors' selections. At this point I had to work with a group that no longer had a positive or even neutral attitude toward the new unit; the prevailing attitude was decidedly negative. I was able to revive and maintain their interest once we began reading text selections and supplementary short stories by Irving and Poe, but I had the feeling that this could have been a much more enjoyable learning experience for them if we had had a better beginning.

II. *Analysis of Chapter*

    A. Preparation for Learning

        1) Determining Background

        This area is a weakness in both the text and the teacher's manual. The textbook does nothing either before the introduction or within the unit to determine the student's background knowledge. In defense of the text, the units are meant to be studied in chronological order, and I imagine the editors logically assume that the previous units would have been completed before beginning the "First Harvest" unit. The teacher should be generally aware of what the students know up to that period in time, but nothing is in the text to determine what they know about the historical influences, events, authors, and types of literature written in the "First Harvest" unit. However, I did find a few suggestions in the manual under "Introducing the Selection" located before the material on Washington Irving. The manual advises the teacher to ask, "What pieces by Irving have they read? What characteristics do they associate with him?" These suggestions were the only evidence I found of strategies to determine background.

        2) Building Background

        In quantity of material and usability of material this is a definite strength in both the textbook and teacher's manual; however, understanding the information is a problem, especially with average ability students. The introduction to the unit accompanied by a two page time line feature presents abundant historical background. The time line is framed by appropriate small pictures related to events and literary figures of the time period and with dates captioned by significant events and literary publication data. The dates are very hard to see because they are white against a yellow background, but I see this as a minor annoyance, since I do not teach date memorization. The manual also presents the teacher with an "Overview" that contains supplementary ideas to be used in conjunction with the text introduction. Several of the points made in the "Overview" are more relevant than the points brought out in the textbook. Neither the text nor the manual provides any vocabulary, study skills, or comprehension guided features for the introduction. The only highlighted subheading within 7 pages of printed text after the title (which only appears on the page preceding the printed text) is "CLASSICISM AND ROMANTICISM." The printed text is broken up by three color pictures, an engraving of a bank in Philadelphia and two landscapes. There is nothing to indicate to the teacher or the student what purpose these illustrations serve. Because I have pored over these pages for many days now, I have surmised that the purpose is to illustrate Classical architecture—the bank—and Romantic art—the landscapes. I wish the editors had not inconsiderately assumed that my students and I would have readily guessed this relationship!

The textbook builds background on each author with a one or two page biographical sketch including paragraphs which focus on a critical evaluation of his works. These "biographies" are usually accompanied by a portrait of the author and are printed in very small type. Again, there are no vocabulary, study skills, or comprehension guided features that accompany the text anywhere. The teacher's manual builds knowledge of the authors and their works through the "Introducing the Selection" and the "Presentation" features that are given for each text selection in the unit. These features contain what are supposed to be additional tidbits of information that will arouse interest and stimulate motivation. They are sprinkled with comments like, "Your class may be intrigued to know that Cooper's descriptions of a buffalo stampede, a prairie fire, and an Indian council were not drawn from life. . . ." and, "The class may be interested in knowing that this story first appeared in Irving's *Tales of a Traveler* . . ." (pp. 57, 55). Unfortunately, the editors have not met my classes. Some of these ideas are useful, but most of them seem directed toward a collegiate level student. For building background for each author's selection, the manual provides a vocabulary list with as few words as 14 and as many words as 74. The only guidance the teacher is given for the use of these lists is that the words are for previewing and studying and they are defined in the textbook glossary. In general, the text and manual supply an extraordinary amount of background information, but little direction in effective strategies to use that information and less direction for the student to comprehend that information.

    B. Assisted Reading and Study
        1) Reading with a Purpose

Nothing in the textbook explicitly directs the student to read for a purpose, but the division of reading by author and samples of his work implicitly directs the student to read for understanding of each author's contribution to literature. The teacher's manual suggests only five objectives for the entire unit within the "Overview" section. Also under the heading of "Objectives of the Unit" the manual provides a list of literary terms and techniques and composition skills covered in the unit. This is useful only as a table of contents. A "Suggested Time Requirements" feature that approximates the number of days to be spent on each author is useful in preplanning the unit and dividing the reading into segments. The "Presentation" feature of the manual "includes suggestions on handling the selection in class, with emphasis on significant elements, techniques, and meanings" (p. 1). These suggestions are sometimes useful to the teacher in planning objectives for high ability students.

        2) Developing Comprehension

The text selections are footnoted to define difficult words, to translate foreign words, to explain allusions, and to define archaic words. This is the only aid to developing comprehension within the reading assignments. Most of the selections are followed by small print explanations of literary terms or techniques that define the term, point out examples in the text, and ask the student to discover further examples of its use. These explanations are intended for extension activities, but with high ability students the discussion of a literary term could be used before the assigned reading and then serve to aid in comprehension and/or to provide a purpose for reading. Three selections are followed by small print commentaries that could be used to develop comprehension of very difficult selections that may justify a second reading.

C. Reflection of Learning
   1) Determining Comprehension

For each prose selection in the unit the teacher's manual provides a "Reading Check," a ten statement true-false quiz, for occasional use to determine whether or not the student has read his assignment. These determine only literal comprehension and the questions are sometimes so tricky that those students who have read the assignment do no better than the ones who just guess at the answers. For instance, one statement is, "The devil offers Tom money that was buried by the pirate Blackbeard." The statement is true up to the point of naming the pirate, who was Kidd not Blackbeard. But remembering the name of the pirate is an insignificant detail. These questions can be useful if the teacher rewords the statements to eliminate trickiness and ambiguity. The best feature for determining comprehension is the "For Study and Discussion" section that follows each text selection. Suggested answers are provided in the teacher's manual. These questions are both the "Right There" and the "Think and Search" varieties. They require the students to interpret what they have read or to focus on how the author used a certain literary technique to create a desired effect. The questions prompt the student to pay close attention to relevant detail and direct the student's search for meaning by citing quotations or giving page and paragraph locations for easy reference. The questions are well constructed, but the drawbacks to using them are the small type print and the apparent length, sometimes eleven lines long, which "turns off" an average ability student, even though the length of the question is justified for the answer being sought. For this reason the question format is more suitable for high ability students. These questions seldom determine the applied level of comprehension, but the composition assignments that follow most of the selections do ask the "On Your Own" questions that require applied levels of comprehension.

   2) Extension

There are three categories of extension activities that follow each text selection. One category is the "Language and Vocabulary" activity. These activities are built upon some vocabulary introduced in the text but extend to a more refined and intensive word study. These activities are often geared to the high ability student. The second category is discussion of a literary term or technique. These are closely related to the text selections and therefore reinforce comprehension of the text as well as extend their understanding of literary style. These discussions have great potential, but in this particular unit the terms covered are for the poetry selections and they become overly technical for the average student. The third category is the "Composition" assignment that follows most of the selections. These assignments generally bear a close relationship to the text selection, establish a clear purpose for writing, and require applied levels of comprehension, such as analysis, synthesis, and evaluation. These are challenging and useful assignments for high ability students, but often too difficult for average students and sometimes uninteresting to students and teachers alike. The culminating extension activity for the entire unit is a section headed "Critical Reading and Writing." This section briefly summarizes the unit and provides an essay question meant to determine the students' comprehension on applied levels. However, I chose not to use this question because the text had not clearly established the points the text editors were asking the students to discuss. An additional extension feature is given in the manual under the heading "For Student's Leisure Reading." This suggests extended reading projects by listing novels, short stories, and poems by unit authors. This list is useful in supplementing whole class reading as well as independent reading.

III. *Summary*

A. Strengths

The "First Harvest" unit of the textbook and manual is very strong in offering an abundance of usable information to build background. Another strength is the section "For Study and Discussion," which offers questions that both develop and determine comprehension for each text selection. The critical commentaries also increase understanding. The text selections "The Devil and Tom Walker" and "The Raven" have a high degree of interest for 11th grade students. There are ample extension activities geared to the high ability student.

B. Weaknesses

The unit neglects strategies to determine background and lacks comprehension guided features such as providing a purpose for reading. The absence of these strategies compounds the problem of readability which is already too high (grade 13) for average ability students.

C. Anticipating Difficulties

One of the most significant difficulties in working with this text will be in using the introduction as an overview for the unit. Some important questions to address are:

How can I capitalize on what the students already know?
How can I make the information comprehensible to the average student?
How can I maintain the student's awareness of the relationship between concepts in the introduction and ideas expressed in the individual text selections?
How can I make the student aware of the relevance of this unit to his or her own life?

Because the density of new abstract concepts is high, I will need to divide the reading assignment into manageable and logical segments. For each text selection I should plan methods to determine background and establish purposes for reading. I will need to be selective in using the wealth of information available to teach. If I attempted to use all the information, I could produce a dangerous "cognitive overload" that could "black out" student brain power for weeks. I will need to supplement the text with less difficult and more interesting selections better suited to average students. I must adapt the composition assignments for average students and plan effective approaches to developing comprehension with vocabulary study.

IV. Strategies for Change

A. Strategies for Revision of the Introduction to "First Harvest"

Summary: The following activities were devised for average ability students to facilitate their comprehension of the difficult concepts in the unit introduction. I plan to use these strategies in numerical sequence as presented. The first activity was developed to determine student background and then to use that information as a preview of the first two paragraphs of the assignment. I have decided to break down the reading assignment into more manageable segments which follow the organizational pattern of the author. In a sense I have imposed subheadings for the material where none exist. I will also try to explicitly demonstrate the relevance of studying our heritage by having the students make connections between our past and our present. Because the text does not incorporate comprehension guided features and neglects purposeful reading instruction, I have developed several directed study aids. The extended reading activity proposes to further emphasize the link between the values, attitudes, and concerns of Americans of the past and of Americans of the modern world.

1) Activity One is meant primarily to determine student background. My specific objectives are to introduce the phrase *American nationality*, to explain the meaning of this concept as it is used within the context of the introduction, to stimulate discussion of this concept, and to find out student impressions of what this means in order to link prior knowledge to new knowledge. The model for the format of this activity is an adaptation of an advance organizer with related factstorming.

Activity One

Teacher's introduction: The "First Harvest" unit introduction begins with a discussion of the American nationality. (Put on board.) Within your reading assignment the author uses the word *nationality* to mean the distinguishing traits of a nation, much like the word *personality* is used in reference to the character traits of an individual. Before reading the opening paragraphs of the introduction, I would like to hear what you think are some of the traits that make up the American nationality. We will first break into small (5 member) groups to examine 3 excerpts from passages that are closely related to American nationality. These are to serve as a starting point. After evaluating the traits implied in the excerpts, each member of the group should add at least one more trait that he or she thinks is characteristic of the American nationality. You will have ten minutes to discuss and record your impressions. Then we will come together as a whole class and share our findings. Select one group member as a reporter. (Divide into groups and distribute the following as a handout. Circulate and observe groups. Put accumulated findings on the board when groups rejoin whole class.)

Handout:

These three excerpts give clues to some of the traits of the American nationality. Read each one, and if you can, identify the source of the excerpt. Discuss as a group what traits you think these excerpts represent. Record your ideas under Part A below.

1. ". . . one Nation under God, indivisible, with liberty and justice for all."
2. "Four score and seven years ago our fathers brought forth on this continent a new nation, conceived in liberty, and dedicated to the proposition that all men are created equal."
3. "Give me your tired, your poor,
   Your huddled masses yearning to breathe free,
   The wretched refuse of your teeming shore.
   Send these, the homeless, tempest-tossed to me,
   I lift my lamp beside the golden door."

Part A: Record below your group's ideas about the above excerpts.

Part B: Each group member should add another trait that he or she believes is a characteristic of the American nationality. List your group's five ideas in the space below.

2) Activity Two is a directed study strategy to be used immediately following the culminating class discussion of Activity One. This is an adaptation of a Directed Reading-Thinking Activity, modified because the independent reading assignment is very brief. My objectives are to highlight the main idea of what is to be learned, to preview the pattern of organization, to stimulate the student to make a prediction about what he or she will learn, and to establish a purpose for reading. This strategy is also similar to a brief selective reading guide.

Activity Two

Handout to accompany independent reading assignment:

Silent Reading Assignment: The first and second paragraph of the "First Harvest" introduction, page 96.

Read the following before you read your assignment.

The first paragraph of the introduction describes Michel Crevecoeur's impression of the American nationality in the decade before the American Revolution. Crevecoeur was a Frenchman who immigrated to America and became a citizen of New York in 1765. Do you think any of his ideas will be the same as those we listed in our class discussion? If so, which ones? Read the paragraph to discover any similarities between his ideas and our list.

The second paragraph points out the differences between Crevecoeur's vision of how the American nationality would develop in time and the reality of what actually occurred in America. What do you think some of those differences were? Read to find out what these differences were.

Use the space below to make notes for discussion.

Paragraph One:
Your predictions:

Your actual findings in reading the text:

Paragraph Two:
Your predictions:

Your actual findings in reading the text:

3) Activity Three has been chosen as an extension activity and would follow the discussion of the first two paragraphs of the unit introduction. My objectives are to reinforce what has already been learned, to guide my students in connecting past situations to contemporary life in America, and to evaluate a brief written response to their reading to determine if they can apply their learning to a new reading encounter.

Activity Three

Introduction: I would like you to read an article about the Statue of Liberty celebration that was printed in the *Richmond Times-Dispatch* on Sunday, July 6, 1986. The article is entitled, "Celebration of Liberty Doesn't Reach Everybody." What do you think the article will be about? (Spend only a few minutes discussing their predictions.) Let's read to find out exactly what the title means. (Distribute copies of the article.)

Read the article independently and then answer the following questions in concise paragraphs.

1. Which of the two paragraphs in the "First Harvest" introduction seems more related to the ideas expressed in the newspaper article? Explain the reason for your answer by giving two specific similarities that you found.
2. Do you agree or disagree with the following statement?

   In modern America too many differences still exist between the ideals our country stands for and the realities of American life.

In a paragraph tell whether or not you agree with this statement and explain why by giving three reasons for your answer.

4) Activity Four is a strategy to develop comprehension for the next segment of reading. It is an elaboration of the analogy established in Activity One—that nationality is to country as personality is to individual. This analogy will be used to preface pages 96–99, which include a time line. The questions stem from the analogy but also reflect the pattern of organization and main ideas in the text. My objective is to strengthen and emphasize the coherence within the first four pages of the introduction to enhance understandability.

Activity Four

Analogy to be used as teacher's oral presentation:

We have already discussed general characteristics of the American nationality. Today we will read more about the early formation of national traits. To understand the importance of those early years of development, it will be useful to recall the connection we made between the word *personality* and the word *nationality*. What factors influence the development of someone's personality? In studies of human development, many authorities say that the early childhood years are critical in the formation of an individual's personality. A child grows rapidly, physically and mentally, in those early years of development. A child is eager to explore his world and test his limits, and in doing so he learns from his mistakes as well as his successes. Heredity and environment are also factors that influence his evolving personality. Eventually a young person's unique identity emerges, and with increasing maturity, he or she is able to contribute to his community as a responsible young adult.

What factors influenced the building of the American nationality? If we think of our country as an infant born on July 4, 1776, we can also think of the time period after the Revolution, which our text calls the "First Harvest" years, as those important formative years of our then young nation. Our country grew rapidly in those years, and the desire for exploration was strong among our people. We tested our limits and extended our boundaries. We sometimes made serious mistakes but learned valuable lessons and continued to progress. Our nationality was also molded by heredity—the traditions and beliefs of our ancestors—and by environment—America's geographic features and its position in the Western hemisphere. Eventually our young nation gained the respect of Europeans as a country capable of making its own worthy contributions to the world, and our nationality was becoming firmly established.

Student Assignment:

Read pages 96 (begin with 3rd paragraph) through 99. DO NOT NEGLECT A CLOSE EXAMINATION OF THE PICTURES AND CAPTIONS OF THE TIME-LINE. Look for and take notes on the following points as you read:

1. specific examples of how our nation grew economically and industrially
2. the ways our country expanded geographically
3. the issue that was becoming more and more a source of regional conflict
4. the purpose of a specifically national literature
5. the names of important authors whose works were published in this time period
6. the approximate time span this unit covers

5) Activity Five is an anticipation guide to be used primarily to build background for the ideas that will be introduced under the heading, "Classicism and Romanticism," pages 100–104. My objective is to preview the classical versus Romantic view of relationships among man, nature and the universe, to preview the pattern of organization which is comparison-contrast, and to dispel the common misconception that Romanticism is the same as romantic love. (The latter has proven to be a source of confusion to many of my students in the past.)

Activity Five

Anticipation Guide for "Classicism and Romanticism"

Do you think you are more likely to have attitudes that would make you a classicist or a Romantic? Read each of the statements below and put a check in the appropriate blank space to indicate whether or not you agree or disagree with the statement. After reading the text, you will be able to decide whether your attitude is Romantic or classic.

Agree   Disagree

1. The order of the universe is like a ladder with God at the top, angels under Him, then men like kings and presidents down to thieves and bums; next on the ladder are the animals, under them are the plants, and at the very bottom are rocks and minerals.

2. You are a part of the universe, "no less than the trees and the stars, you have a right to be here, and whether or not it is clear to you, there is no doubt the universe is unfolding as it should."

3. Nature operates by a set of unchangeable laws and can be fully understood if we logically study those laws.

4. Nature is full of wonder and mysteries that even scientists cannot explain.

5. When I am faced with a problem, I most often rely on my instincts to help me solve it.

6. When I am faced with a problem, I most often use logic and reason to help me solve it.

7. Romanticism is not the same as romantic love.

6) Activity Six is a partial guide to be completed for a grade. It is designed to determine comprehension of the contrast in attitudes between classicism and Romanticism. The answers will have been provided during a notetaking session following the reading of this section, so students will have a study guide to prepare for this test.

Activity Six

Test on Classicism and Romanticism

Name:
Date:
Period:

Directions: Fill in the spaces with statements that show the contrast in attitudes between eighteenth-century classicism and nineteenth-century Romanticism. This is the key; it contains the answers.

18th-Century Classicism	vs.	19th-Century Romanticism
1. Topic: The essential guide to truth and knowledge—		
Logic and reason are the surest guides to truth.		To discover truth, man can rely on his intuitions.
2. Topic: The view of nature—		
Nature is like a machine and is governed by unchanging laws.		Nature is mysterious, beautiful, and in a state of constant change.
3. Topic: The function of literature—		
Literature should illustrate the common values of humanity and the rational laws of human existence.		Literature should express the writer's own emotional and intuitive experience.

4. Topic: The style of literature—

| Literature should exhibit clarity, order and balance. | The style of literature should reflect the writer's creativity. |

5. Topic: The value of the individual—

| The common good is more important than the individual. | The dignity, worth, and freedom of the individual is of central importance. |

6. Topic: The value of imagination—

| Imagination must be restrained by reason and common sense. | Imagination is a boundless resource for understanding human nature. |

7. Topic: The importance of tradition—

| Tradition has established valid, reliable standards for living. | Tradition gives us insight into the past, but innovative change and reform should be encouraged for better living. |

B. Strategies for Revision of Text Selections within "First Harvest"

Summary: Activities 7 through 10 were developed to supplement selections by unit authors. They include a prereading vocabulary exercise to build background and to provide practice in using context clues as a study skill. The activities designed for "The Raven" are meant to be used to develop and determine comprehension through the use of a three-level guide and follow-up writing assignment. The jot chart will be given to the students after the introductory material has been read and studied. In this way the jot chart can serve as an overview which will be filled in during the progressive study of each author. Categories on the chart will help maintain the connection between the authors and two main ideas in the introduction—that these authors were influential in establishing a national literature and that their works exhibit characteristics of the emerging 19th-century Romantic movement. The completed jot chart can then be used as a study guide for a unit test.

7) Activity Seven is a vocabulary exercise to prepare the student for reading "The Devil and Tom Walker." It is designed to build background and to reinforce vocabulary study skills.

Activity Seven

You should always attempt to discover the meaning of unfamiliar words that you encounter in your reading. We have discussed that clues to the meaning of a word can come from the context in which the word is used. Some of the context clues we learned were:

Restatement (signaled by the words *which is, in other words, or,* etc.)
Example (signaled by the words *like, such as, these include,* etc.)
Comparison (signaled by the words *as, similarly, in the same way,* etc.)
Contrast (signaled by the words *however, unlike, different,* etc.)

We also know that sometimes we have to read between the lines to find context clues and infer meaning from.

The main idea and supporting detail
Cause and effect relationships
Implied comparison and contrast

The following sentences are from Washington Irving's "The Devil and Tom Walker." Read each sentence carefully and see if you can determine the meaning of the underlined word from the context of the passage. Write your prediction of the definition in the space provided. (After the students have completed this exercise, we will discuss and verify their predictions and discuss the context clues used.)

1. "A few miles from Boston in Massachusetts, there is a deep inlet, winding several miles into the interior of the country from Charles Bay, and terminating in a thickly wooded swamp or <u>morass</u>."

Predicted meaning:

2. "Tom's wife was a tall <u>termagant</u>, fierce of temper, loud of tongue, and strong of arm."

Predicted meaning:

3. "They lived alone in a <u>forlorn</u> looking house that stood alone and had an air of starvation."

Predicted meaning:

4. "Tom had long been picking his way cautiously through this treacherous forest, stepping from tuft to tuft of rushes and roots, which afforded <u>precarious</u> footholds among the deep sloughs;"

Predicted meaning:

5. The devil "insisted that the money found through his means should be employed in his service. He proposed, therefore, that Tom should employ it in the <u>black traffic</u>; that is to say, that he should fit out a slave ship. This, however, Tom <u>resolutely</u> refused: he was bad enough in all conscience; but the devil himself could not tempt him to turn slave trader."

Predicted meanings:

6. Then the devil proposed that Tom should become a <u>usurer</u>.
   "To this no objections were made, for it was just to Tom's taste.
   "'You shall open a broker's shop in Boston next month, . . . You shall extort bonds, foreclose mortgages, drive the merchants to bankruptcy—'
   "'I'll drive them to the devil,' cried Tom Walker."

Predicted meaning:

7. "In this way he made money hand over hand and became a rich and mighty man. He built himself, as usual, a vast house, out of <u>ostentation</u>; but left the greater part of it unfinished and unfurnished, out of <u>parsimony</u>."

Predicted meanings:

8) Activity Eight is a three-level guide for "The Raven" designed to develop comprehension of the poem using literal, interpretive, and applied-level statements.

Activity Eight

Directions: Check the statements that can be found within the lines of Edgar Allan Poe's poem "The Raven," and note the number of the line or lines where you found the words.

_____ 1. On a dreary midnight the speaker was weak and weary.
_____ 2. He had hoped that reading his books would stop the sorrow he felt about the lost Lenore.
_____ 3. In the silence that followed the tapping on his door, he whispered, "Lenore?"
_____ 4. The speaker positioned himself in a cushioned seat in front of the bird.
_____ 5. The speaker asked the Raven to tell him if his soul would clasp the sainted maiden, Lenore, in heaven.
_____ 6. The speaker says the eyes of the Raven seem like the eyes of a demon that is dreaming.

Directions: Check each statement that is a reasonable interpretation of what Poe meant to say in this poem.

_____ 1. The speaker of the poem was physically and mentally drained by his grief over his lost love, Lenore.

_____ 2. The speaker begins to believe that the Raven is actually talking to him when he says, "Nevermore."

_____ 3. The speaker imagines that the Raven can tell him about what lies beyond death.

_____ 4. The speaker loses all hope of recovering from his grief.

_____ 5. The speaker's grief has driven him to insanity.

Directions: Check the statements below that you think are true by your own experience or study and can also be supported by your interpretation of "The Raven."

_____ 1. The imagination is a powerful force.

_____ 2. If a person allows his imagination to take full control of his mind, he could lose the ability to perceive reality.

_____ 3. An abnormally strong fear of death can cause mental illness.

_____ 4. Excessive, prolonged grief can result in insanity.

_____ 5. A person's emotional state can affect the way he perceives reality.

_____ 6. A guilty conscience can become an unbearable burden.

9) Activity Nine is a writing assignment to be used to determine comprehension of "The Raven." It is an extension of the three-level guide used in Activity Eight and would follow class discussion of the guide.

Activity Nine

It would be possible to find supporting evidence in the text of the poem for any of the following statements:

1. The imagination is a powerful force.

2. If a person allows his imagination to take full control of his mind, he could lose the ability to perceive reality.

3. An abnormally strong fear of death can cause mental illness.

4. Excessive, prolonged grief can result in insanity.

5. A person's emotional state can affect the way he perceives reality.

Choose one of the statements with which you most agree. This will become the topic for your essay on the theme of "The Raven." Put the statement in your own words to use as a thesis sentence for the essay. Read the poem again and take notes on specific details that would support your thesis. This is the gathering evidence stage. Next review and organize the evidence you have found. It may be best to present your evidence in a time order sequence as it appears in the poem, or you may want to move from least to most important details. Once you have decided on a pattern of organization, write your first draft to bring to class tomorrow. We will work on revision in writing groups tomorrow and the final draft will be due the next day. Remember that the purpose of this assignment is to describe your interpretation of the theme of the poem and give supporting evidence from specific details in the poem.

10) Activity Ten is a jot chart to be used to develop comprehension of how unit authors contributed to the growth of our national literature and how they exhibited Romantic characteristics in their writing. The chart will be distributed to students before we actually begin the text selections and will serve as an outline of important points to be considered in the study of each author. The student will gradually fill in the chart throughout the progressive study of each author. The completed chart can be used for review and as a study guide for a unit test. A sample of this jot chart follows.

Activity 10

"First Harvest" author	"First" in what? Contribution to our national literature	Title of selection we read by this author	Distinctive characteristics of author's style	Characteristics that connect this author to the Romantic movement
Washington Irving	1st American writer to gain world-wide reputation His tales reflect American values, traditions, and superstitions	"The Devil and Tom Walker" "The Legend of Sleepy Hollow"	folktale style satire (caricatures, irony, stereotypes, exaggeration) deliberate use of American scene as setting	—wrote imaginative fiction —linked the natural world with supernatural mystery —showed a direct interest in the past
James Fenimore Cooper	America's 1st major novelist created our 1st national literary hero	excerpts from *The Prairie* and *The Deerslayer*	sobriquets artificial vocabulary and dialogue deliberate use of American scene as setting	—created an American Romantic hero, Natty Bumppo —showed a direct interest in the past —wrote about relationship between man and nature and the vast American wilderness
William Cullen Bryant	1st major American Romantic poet	"Thanatopsis" "To a Waterfowl"	archaic words lofty diction poetic inversion	—was a national spokesman for a new "religion of nature"
Edgar Allan Poe	1st to write detective stories 1st to present "single effect" theory of short story form	"The Bells" "The Raven" "Fall of the House of Usher" "Cask of Amontillado"	musicality in verse arabesque and grotesque elements "single effect"	—explored the inner world of human nature —emphasized the role of imagination

C. *Three Completed Bader Textbook Analyses*

Developed by Adrienne Gillis, Pat Bossler, and Todd Barnes

TEXT BOOK ANALYSIS CHART

Book Title *Types of Literature*
Publisher *Ginn and Company*
Grade Level *Tenth*
Content Area *English*

+ Excellent/ Evident Throughout	✓ Average/ Somewhat Evident	– Poor/ Not Evident		Comments

LINGUISTIC FACTORS:

Checklist — Comments

Expository Passages used 8th grade level for 10th graders. Expository Passages used on or below grade level

	✓		Generally appropriate to intended grade level(s) according to ___Fry___ formula
	✓		Linguistic patterns suitable to most populations and fit intended level(s)
✓			Vocabulary choice and control suitable
✓			New vocabulary highlighted, italicized, in boldface or underlined
	✓		New vocabulary, defined in context
✓			New vocabulary defined in margin guides, glossary, beginning or end of chapter

Vocab choice consistent. In boldface and caps. Explained in context of expository passages. As footnotes and in glossary. Good resource

CONCEPTUAL FACTORS:

Concepts at or below grade level. Most concepts are defined and explained. Lack of inductive presentation. Boldfaced and repeated.

✓			Conceptual level generally appropriate to intended grade level(s)
✓			Concepts presented deductively
		✓	Concepts presented inductively
✓			Major ideas are highlighted, italicized, in boldface type or underlined
	✓		Appropriate assumptions made regarding prior level of concepts
✓			Sufficient development of new concepts through examples, illustrations, analogies, redundancy
✓			No evidence of sexual, racial, economic, cultural, or political bias

Sometimes too many assumptions. Good use of examples, illustrations etc. No bias - culturally diverse selections - good!!

ORGANIZATIONAL FACTORS:

✓			Units, chapters, table of contents, index present clear, logical development of subject
✓			Chapters of instructional segments contain headings and sub-headings that aid comprehension of subject
✓			Introductory, definitional, illustrative, summary paragraphs/sections used as necessary
	✓		Topic sentences of paragraphs clearly identifiable or easily inferred
✓			Each chapter/section/unit contains a well-written summary and/or overview

All are present - well presented. Very well done. Introductory paragraphs appear as well as passages. For expository material. Summary exercises and overviews for units appear.

WRITING STYLE:

✓			Ideas are expressed clearly and directly
✓			Word choice is appropriate
✓			Tone and manner of expression are appealing to intended readers
✓			Mechanics are correct

Yes - clearly explained. Interesting - well chosen. Interesting for all readers. No mechanical errors found.

+ Excellent/ Evident Throughout	✓ Average/ Somewhat Evident	− Poor/ Not Evident	Checklist	Comments

LEARNING AIDS:

✓			Questions/tasks appropriate to conceptual development of intended age/grade level(s)	*Questions and tasks well stated*
	✓		Questions/tasks span levels of reasoning: literal, interpretive, critical, values clarification, problem-solving	*Less emphasis on values and problem solving*
✓			Questions/tasks can be used as reading guides	*Discussion questions are purposeful*
	✓		Suitable supplementary readings suggested	*Not listed besides authors other works*

TEACHING AIDS:

	✓		Clear, convenient to use	*Teacher handbook used*
	✓		Helpful ideas for conceptual development	*Could be more motivational*
		✓	Alternative instructional suggestions given for poor readers, slow learning students, advanced students	*No suggestions given. Teaching Tests satisfactory*
✓			Contains objectives, management plans, evaluation guidelines, tests of satisfactory quality	*Objectives clearly stated*
	✓		Supplementary aids available	*Listed in handbook are addresses to write to*

BINDING/PRINTING/FORMAT/ILLUSTRATIONS:

✓			Size of book is appropriate	*Appropriate for 10th grade*
✓			Cover, binding, and paper are appropriate	*All are of good quality*
✓			Type-face is appropriate	*Very readable print*
✓			Format is appropriate	*Many helpful features*
✓			Pictures, charts, graphs are appealing	*Very colorful prints*
	✓		Illustrations aid comprehension of text	*Most are designed for this*
✓			Illustrations are free of sexual, social, cultural bias	*No bias whatsoever*

SUMMARY:

25	11	2	Totals	*It is clear that this textbook has many good qualities; but there is room for improvement*

The strengths are:
This text has more strengths than weaknesses. The strengths are good reinforcement in vocabulary with appropriate activities; good textbook format with many helpful features; a culturally diverse choice of authors and illustrations; clear word choice and explanation of ideas; and a higher level of thinking skills are required to answer discussion questions and to do activities in text

The weaknesses are:
There are a few weaknesses, but they include a lack of preparatory information given before the literary selections; a lack of activities requiring inductive thinking skills; a lack of suggested supplementary reading in bibliographical form and no instructional suggestions are given in the handbook for slower or advanced students.

As a teacher, I will need to:
1. Prepare students beforehand for reading by relating content to their background and providing supplementary instructional materials.
2. Create possible activities that would require inductive thinking skills.
3. Suggest possible sources for outside reading that are related to content.
4. Aid comprehension of selections for slower students and challenge advanced students with supplementary activities and assignments that are also interesting.

*Original TEXT ANALYSIS CHART by: Dr. Lois Bader, Michigan State University

+ Excellent/ Evident Throughout	✓ Average/ Somewhat Evident	— Poor/ Not Evident

TEXT BOOK ANALYSIS CHART

This text is used as a primary source in independent study course for high school students who have previously failed this course. Teacher is primarily a tutor.

Book Title _Rise of the American Nation_

Publisher _Harcourt Brace Jovanovich_

Grade Level _11_

Content Area _U.S History_

LINGUISTIC FACTORS:

Checklist — Comments

+	✓	—	Checklist	Comments
		—	Generally appropriate to intended grade level(s) according to ___SMOG___ formula	Readability is inappropriate for independent study by weak students
	✓		Linguistic patterns suitable to most populations and fit intended level(s)	Reasonable sentence length + frequency of subordination.
+			Vocabulary choice and control suitable	Not dumbed down nor intellectual.
+			New vocabulary highlighted, italicized, in boldface or underlined	Use of italics good to bring words to students attention
+			New vocabulary, defined in context	
		—	New vocabulary defined in margin guides, glossary, beginning or end of chapter	No margin guides - no glossary. Definite weakness for students reviewing for tests.

CONCEPTUAL FACTORS:

+	✓	—	Checklist	Comments
	✓		Conceptual level generally appropriate to intended grade level(s)	Without teacher explanation, concepts not evident -
		—	Concepts presented deductively	Concepts drawn for students little student critical thinking
	✓		Concepts presented inductively	Weakness in study situation
+			Major ideas are highlighted, italicized, in boldface type or underlined	Boldface headings assist pre-reading Text for stronger students
	✓		Appropriate assumptions made regarding prior level of concepts	Not for independent study. Accomplished by accompanying independent study syllabus
	✓		Sufficient development of new concepts through examples, illustrations, analogies, redundancy	Effort made to include minorities who played a part in U.S History
+			No evidence of sexual, racial, economic, cultural, or political bias	

ORGANIZATIONAL FACTORS:

+	✓	—	Checklist	Comments
+			Units, chapters, table of contents, index present clear, logical development of subject	Overall time order, subdivided into thematic subject areas using cause-effect or problem-solution.
+			Chapters of instructional segments contain headings and sub-headings that aid comprehension of subject	Boldface and brightly colored - helpful for pre-reading + review
	✓		Introductory, definitional, illustrative, summary paragraphs/sections used as necessary	No summary sections a weakness. All others included.
+			Topic sentences of paragraphs clearly identifiable or easily inferred	Many inferred easily by teacher, but not by students.
+			Each chapter/section/unit contains a well-written summary and/or overview	Each chapter has overview and outline, but no summary.

WRITING STYLE:

+	✓	—	Checklist	Comments
+			Ideas are expressed clearly and directly	Text is well written.
+			Word choice is appropriate	Not dumbed down; not too intellectual
	✓		Tone and manner of expression are appealing to intended readers	Factual, not involving.
+			Mechanics are correct	No problem; well written.

+ Excellent/ Evident Throughout	✓ Average/ Somewhat Evident	— Poor/ Not Evident	Checklist	Comments
			LEARNING AIDS:	Few very challenging questions
	✓		Questions/tasks appropriate to conceptual development of intended age/grade level(s)	Focus on recall of interrelationships. Almost totally literal and
	✓		Questions/tasks span levels of reasoning: literal, interpretive, critical, values clarification, problem-solving	inferential questions in syllabus
+			Questions/tasks can be used as reading guides	Accompanying syllabus questions very good for this purpose.
		—	Suitable supplementary readings suggested	None suggested.

TEACHING AIDS: None available

				Teacher uses independent study
		—	Clear, convenient to use	syllabus as study guide for
		—	Helpful ideas for conceptual development	students by using end of
		—	Alternative instructional suggestions given for poor readers, slow learning students, advanced students	chapter questions for pre-reading activities and student
		—	Contains objectives, management plans, evaluation guidelines, tests of satisfactory quality	self-monitoring of comprehension. Course not designed to be
		—	Supplementary aids available	teacher assisted.

BINDING/PRINTING/FORMAT/ILLUSTRATIONS:

				Too much text to cover independently
	✓		Size of book is appropriate	Sturdy, good quality.
+			Cover, binding, and paper are appropriate	Type style alternates every
+	✓		Type-face is appropriate	few units. I don't know why.
+			Format is appropriate	Colorful maps, "period photos"
+			Pictures, charts, graphs are appealing	Few needed because many photos
+	✓		Illustrations aid comprehension of text	Accurate to historical period.
			Illustrations are free of sexual, social, cultural bias	

SUMMARY:

17	12	9	Totals	Appropriate in classroom, lacks learning aids for independent study

The strengths are: This text is well organized, has a clear writing style, and is accompanied by excellent illustrations and maps. New vocabulary is defined in context, which is helpful to weaker readers who do not use glossaries. Accompanying course syllabus for independent study complements text by providing learning objectives, discussion (overview) and review

The weaknesses are: Lack of teaching aids make adaptation of this course to individual differences difficult. Syllabus questions do not challenge higher level thinking skills (even though end-of-chapter questions in text do, they are not assigned as part of course.) Text may be too difficult for independent reading. Text long and too detailed.

As a teacher, I will need to:
Continue to adapt the activities in the accompanying syllabus to individual student needs. Students need a lot of help with reading comprehension strategies since the majority of learning relies on each student's reading ability. Addition or substitution of more questions at the evaluative or critical thinking levels.

*Original TEXT ANALYSIS CHART by: Dr. Lois Bader, Michigan State University

+ Excellent/ Evident Throughout	✓ Average/ Somewhat Evident	− Poor/ Not Evident

TEXT BOOK ANALYSIS CHART

Book Title *Silver Burdett Music* *Centennial Edition*

Publisher *Silver Burdett*

Grade Level *2*

Content Area *Music*

LINGUISTIC FACTORS:

Checklist — Comments

+	✓	−	Checklist	Comments
___	___	✓	Generally appropriate to intended grade level(s) according to __modified Fry__ formula	*According to Fry, the text was too easy. I have taught from it for 3 yrs. and I disagree. I find it very appropriate.*
✓	___	___	Linguistic patterns suitable to most populations and fit intended level(s)	*Suitable to all population. I have taught.*
___	✓	___	Vocabulary choice and control suitable	*Sometimes hard for slow readers.*
✓	___	___	New vocabulary highlighted, italicized, in boldface or underlined	*Italicised in boldface or colored*
___	✓	___	New vocabulary, defined in context	*New vocabulary introduced + defined + illustrated w/songs.*
___	___	✓	New vocabulary defined in margin guides, glossary, beginning or end of chapter	*Book is not organized by chapters. No margin guides or glossary. New vocab. defined in con xt.*

CONCEPTUAL FACTORS:

+	✓	−	Checklist	Comments
✓	___	___	Conceptual level generally appropriate to intended grade level(s)	*All musical concepts are appropriate for 2nd grade introduction and paced well*
___	✓	___	Concepts presented deductively	*Presented this way a sufficient no. of times*
✓	___	___	Concepts presented inductively	*Major way concepts are presented*
✓	___	___	Major ideas are highlighted, italicized, in boldface type or underlined	*Italicized in boldface or colored.*
✓	___	___	Appropriate assumptions made regarding prior level of concepts	*For use by K-9, but can stand alone, so concepts are appropriately introduced.*
___	✓	___	Sufficient development of new concepts through examples, illustrations, analogies, redundancy	*Book cannot stand alone. Student needs teacher guidance + records. Concepts repeated*
✓	___	___	No evidence of sexual, racial, economic, cultural, or political bias	*Pictures include children of many races + cultures and both sexes.*

ORGANIZATIONAL FACTORS:

+	✓	−	Checklist	Comments
✓	___	___	Units, chapters, table of contents, index present clear, logical development of subject	*Organized into units built around concepts. Clearly presented with an index + table of contents.*
___	___	✓	Chapters of instructional segments contain headings and sub-headings that aid comprehension of subject	*No chapters.*
✓	___	___	Introductory, definitional, illustrative, summary paragraphs/sections used as necessary	*Few paragraphs, mostly songs. Illustrative sections used as needed.*
___	✓	___	Topic sentences of paragraphs clearly identifiable or easily inferred	*Few paragraphs; many single sentences, but topics are clear.*
___	___	✓	Each chapter/section/unit contains a well-written summary and/or overview	*Presented in teacher's guide.*

WRITING STYLE:

+	✓	−	Checklist	Comments
✓	___	___	Ideas are expressed clearly and directly	*Text is brief and clear.*
✓	___	___	Word choice is appropriate	*Readable for majority of 2nd graders.*
✓	___	___	Tone and manner of expression are appealing to intended readers	*Direct "no frills" expression.*
✓	___	___	Mechanics are correct	*Did not find any incorrectness.*

+ Excellent/ Evident Throughout	✓ Average/ Somewhat Evident	— Poor/ Not Evident	

Checklist   **Comments**

LEARNING AIDS:

| ✓ | ___ | ___ | Questions/tasks appropriate to conceptual development of intended age/grade level(s) |

Most 2nd level students will have developed necessary coordination + concepts.

| ___ | ✓ | ___ | Questions/tasks span levels of reasoning: literal, interpretive, critical, values clarification, problem-solving |

Seem to center most often on literal interpretive + critical.

| ___ | ✓ | ___ | Questions/tasks can be used as reading guides |
| ___ | ___ | ✓ | Suitable supplementary readings suggested |

Questions are guides for songs.
None mentioned but supplementary listening material is suggested in teacher's edition.

TEACHING AIDS:

✓	___	___	Clear, convenient to use
✓	___	___	Helpful ideas for conceptual development
✓	___	___	Alternative instructional suggestions given for poor readers, slow learning students, advanced students
✓	___	___	Contains objectives, management plans, evaluation guidelines, tests of satisfactory quality
✓	___	___	Supplementary aids available

Very helpful, easy to use.
Many suggestions in teacher's ed.
Instructions for phys. handicapped in teacher's edition.
Listed in teacher's edition.
Spirit masters, records, instruments, competency tests, teachers guide.

BINDING/PRINTING/FORMAT/ILLUSTRATIONS:

✓	___	___	Size of book is appropriate
✓	___	___	Cover, binding, and paper are appropriate
✓	___	___	Type-face is appropriate
✓	___	___	Format is appropriate
✓	___	___	Pictures, charts, graphs are appealing
✓	___	___	Illustrations aid comprehension of text
✓	___	___	Illustrations are free of sexual, social, cultural bias

Easy to hold for second grade
Durable and eye-catching.
Large and easy to read
Easy to follow and appealing
Colorful varied, clear
Very much interrelated
Show many cultures + both sexes.

SUMMARY:

| 26 | 7 | 4 | Totals |

This book seems very strong, and I agree, after teaching it

The strengths are: *Eye catching illustrations, easy-to-read print, clear concept organization, and clear directions for students. The book provides for gradual, consistent progress and may be complete in itself or used as a part of the 9-year program.*

The weaknesses are: *① In a few songs, all verses are used on the record, but only two are printed in the student text. ② Text not organized into clear chapters.*

As a teacher, I will need to: *give a large amount of help and reinforcement to slow readers as they try to keep up with the words on fast songs. The teaching pace may need to be slower and charts, etc., may need to be used. I will also need to give much guidance on instrument-playing activities and demonstrations to reinforce directions given in their book.*

*Original TEXT ANALYSIS CHART by: Dr. Lois Bader, Michigan State University

Readability Resources

A. The Raygor Readability Estimate
B. Computer programs for readability assessment and related information

A. *The Raygor Readability Estimate*

Alton L. Raygor—University of Minnesota

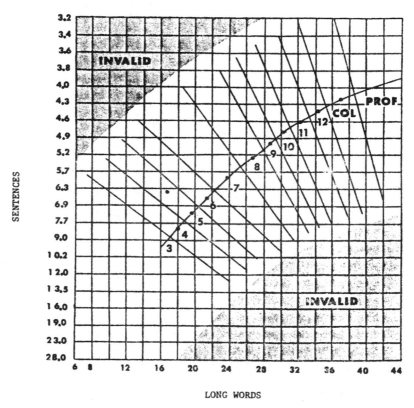

LONG WORDS

Directions: Count out three 100-word passages near the beginning, middle, and end of a selection or book. Count proper nouns, but not numerals.

1. Count sentences in each passage, estimating to nearest tenth.
2. Count words with six or more letters.
3. Average the sentence length and word length over the three samples and plot the average on the graph.

Example	Sentences	6 + Words
A	6.0	15
B	6.8	19
C	6.4	17
Total	19.2	51
Average	6.4	17

Note mark on graph. Grade level is about 5.

No copyright, reproduction permitted.

B. *Computer Programs for Readability Assessment and Related Information*

Commercial Programs

Prices range from $50 to $80 at time of this printing.

1. *Readability* is available from: Micro Power and Light at 12820 Hillcrest Road, Suite 224, Dallas, TX, 75230. This program requires that the user enter a sample of text material; no minimum amount is specified. Information is provided about the difficult words in the material, as well as number of syllables and sentences. The program computes nine readability formulas: Dale-Chall, Flesch, Flesch-Kincaid, Fog, ARI, Coleman, Powers, Holmquist, and Fry. A composite chart can be viewed; a Fry graph can be viewed. For Apple.
2. *Readability Analysis Program* is available from: Random House at 201 E. 50th Street, New York, NY, 10022. This program requires that the user enter at least one 100-word sample of text and suggests nine 100-word samples. Information is given about the number of syllables, words, and characters in a sample. The program computes six readability formulas. Flesch, Fog, Dale-Chall, SMOG, Wheeler-Smith, and Spache. For Apple and IBM. A review can be found in *Educational Technology*, April 1982.
3. *Reading Level Analysis* is available from: Bertamax at 311 W. McGraw, Seattle, WA, 98119. This program requires that at least one 100-word sample be entered. Information is given about the number of words, syllables, and sentences in a sample. The program computes the Wheeler-Smith and Spache indexes for grades 1–3 materials; it computes the Dale-Chall, Flesch, Fog, and SMOG for fourth grade and above. For Apple.

Public Domain Programs

These programs can be copied with no penalty and at no cost.

1. The Virginia State Reading Association provides a series of public domain computer programs for Apple and IBM users. Some of the disks

include simple readability programs as written by teachers. The disks are available for the price of copying and postage. Write to Ron Magin, VSRA Computer Literacy Committee, Wild Turkey Drive, Rappahannock, VA for more information.

2. A listing of the Fog readability program is available in P. Grose and K. Sadowski (1985), "FOG Index—a readability program for microcomputers," *Journal of Reading, 28*, 614–618. The reader can copy the listing and enter the program to disk at no charge but personal time.

Professional Books Which Discuss Computers and Readability

Computer Applications in Reading by Blanchard, Mason, and Daniel is available from International Reading Association, Barksdale Road, Newark, DE, 19714. Third edition (1987).

Computers and Reading Instruction by Geoffrion and Geoffrion is available from Addison-Wesley Publishing Company, Reading, MA (1983).

Teaching Reading Using Microcomputers by Rude is available from Prentice-Hall, Inc., Englewood Cliffs, NJ, 07632 (1986).

Resources on Critical Thinking: "Teaching for Thinking—A Selected Bibliography"

Prepared by Gloria K. Barber, Jane C. Koontz, Division of Instructional Media and Technology—Virginia Department of Education, 1987

Much has been written on how children must be taught to evaluate their thinking and apply the results to their everyday behavior. This bibliography includes only a fraction of what has been written and is limited to journal articles published in the last five years. Only those references are cited which provide examples of techniques for teaching thinking skills. The reader is encouraged to consult texts on subjects such as: *thought and thinking, creative thinking,* and *critical thinking,* for in-depth coverage on teaching thinking.

Adams, Dennis, "Teaching Students Critical Viewing Skills." *Curriculum Review,* Vol. 26, no. 3 (January–February 1987), pp. 29–31. Focusing on video technology, this discussion of integrating new electronic media into the classroom suggests ways to help students critique and use new visual technologies effectively and to develop visual literacy.

Brown, Jerry. "On Teaching Thinking Skills in the Elementary and Middle School." *Phi Delta Kappan,* Vol. 64 (June 1983), pp. 707–14.

Carney, Cathy. "Teacher Computer More Learning." *Computing Teacher,* Vol. 13, no. 6 (March 1986), pp. 12–15. Describes a project in which middle school teachers turned over keyboarding instruction to a computer assisted instruction (CAI) program which enabled them to focus their efforts during the CAI on teaching higher level thinking skills.

De Bono, Edward. "The Direct Teaching of Thinking As A Skill." *Phi Delta Kappan,* Vol. 64 (June 1983), pp. 703–08.

"Direct Instruction" and "Teaching for Thinking." *Educational Leadership,* Vol. 42 (May 1985), entire issue.

Ennis, Robert. "A Logical Basis for Measuring Critical Thinking Skills." *Educational Leadership,* Vol. 43, no. 44 (October 1985), pp. 44–48. Proposes an expanded definition of critical thinking and discusses its components. Includes an outline of goals and objectives for thinking skills curriculum.

Erickson, Bonnie, "Increasing Critical Reading in Junior High Classrooms." *Journal of Reading,* Vol. 30, no. 5 (February 1987), pp. 430–39. Describes these content area reading strategies, anticipation-reaction guides, text previews, and three-level study guides, that emphasize cooperative small group learning and higher order critical thinking.

"Framework for Teaching Thinking." *Educational Leadership,* Vol. 43 (May 1986), entire issue.

Hughes, Carolyn. "Teaching Strategies for Developing Student Thinking." *School*

Library Media Quarterly, Vol. 15, no. 1 (Fall 1986), pp. 33–36. Describes 10 key elements of generic teaching strategies for developing student thinking.

Jay, Ellen. "The Elementary School Media Teacher's Role in Educating Students To Think." *School Library Media Quarterly*, Vol. 15, no. 1 (Fall 1986), pp. 28–32. Suggests activities for use by school library media specialists who wish to foster the development of thinking skills by elementary students.

Karras, Ray. "A Realistic Approach to Thinking Skills: Reform Multiple Choice Questions." *Social Science Record*, Vol. 22, no. 2 (Fall 1985), pp. 38–43. Multiple-choice tests are here to stay. They should do more than test for rote memory. Suggestions to help teachers prepare test questions are made.

Mancall, Jacqueline. "Educating Students To Think. The Role of The School Library Media Program." *School Library Media Quarterly*, Vol. 15, no. 1 (Fall 1986), pp. 18–27. Areas covered include helping students develop thinking skills and how children process information.

Moses, Monti. "Teaching Students To Think— What Can Principals Do?" *NASSP Bulletin*, Vol. 70, no. 488 (March 1986), pp. 16–20. Outlines leadership capabilities that principals can exert to improve the teaching of higher level thinking skills to students.

Murray, Ann. "A Collaborative Approach to the Teaching of Thinking." *Journal of Staff Development*, Vol. 6, no. 2 (October 1985), pp. 133–37. Improve staff development by providing multi-district graduate-credit programs. Outlines of a course teaching thinking are described.

Reahm, Douglas. "Developing Critical Thinking Through Rehearsal Techniques." *Music Educators Journal*, Vol. 72, no. 7 (March 1986), pp. 29–31. How secondary students can be taught to think critically about the music they are performing.

Reyes, Donald. "Critical Thinking in Elementary Social Studies Text Series." *Social Studies*, Vol. 77, no. 4 (July–August 1986), pp. 151–154. Applys a review of literature on critical thinking of five widely used elementary social studies textbook series (Holt, Laidlaw, McGraw-Hill, Silver Burdett and Scott Foresman).

Rhoades, Lynn. "Using the Daily Newspaper to Teach Cognitive and Affective Skills." *Clearing House*, Vol. 59, no. 4 (December 1985), pp. 162–164. Provides a number of ways teachers can use newspapers to teach comprehension and critical thinking.

Rosenbaum, Roberta. "Teaching Critical Thinking in the Business Mathematics Course." *Journal of Education for Business*, Vol. 62, no. 2 (November 1986), pp. 66–69. Appropriate strategies for teaching a student to interpret and understand quantitative data in marketing management, accounting and data processing as described.

Rothen, Kathleen. "Hazel, Fiver, Odysseus, and You: An Odyssey into Critical Thinking." *English Journal*, Vol. 76, no. 3 (March 1987), pp. 56–59. Compares Richard Adams' "Watership Down" to "The Odyssey" and offers a selection of classroom activities for students that use Adams' novel to study classic literature.

Sadler, William. "A Holistic Approach To Improving Thinking Skills." *Phi Delta Kappan*, Vol. 67, No. 3 (March 1987), pp. 56–59. Six principles to follow when teaching students to think.

Scenters-Zapica. "From Oral Communication Skills to Research Skills." *English Journal*, Vol. 76, no. 1 (January 1987), pp. 69–70. Outlines some strategies that students can follow when beginning a research assignment, especially useful when they are new to the process of research.

Sternburg, Robert. "Teaching Critical Thinking, Part 1: Are We Making Critical Mistakes?" *Phi Delta Kappan*, Vol. 67, no. 3 (November 1985), pp. 194–98. Describes the significance between the kinds of problems that adults really face and the problems that students are taught to resolve in critical thinking problems.

_____. "Teaching Critical Thinking, Part 2: Possible Solutions." *Phi Delta Kappan*, Vol. 67, no. 4 (December 1985), pp. 277–80. Covers techniques for everyday application and methods for countering emotional and motivational blocks.

Strahan, David. "Guides Thinking: A Strategy for Encouraging Excellence at the Middle Level." *NASSP Bulletin*, Vol. 70, no. 487 (February 1986), pp. 75–80. Middle-level teachers can avoid passive seatwork and encourage students to think using a "guided thinking" approach, designed to help adolescents develop more sophisticated thinking and reasoning skills.

Sullivan, David. "Using a Textbook for Critical Thinking: An Introductory Lesson for Identifying Point of View." *New England Social Studies Bulletin*, Vol. 43, no. 2 (Winter 1985–86), pp. 31–33. Shows how teachers can teach students to recognize different points of view.

"Teaching Thinking Skills." *Educational Leadership*, Vol. 39 (October 1981), entire issue.

"Thinking Skills in the Curriculum." *Educational Leadership*, Vol. 42 (September 1984), entire issue.

Thurmond, Vera. "Analytical Reading: A Course That Stresses Thinking Aloud." *Journal of Reading*, Vol. 29, no. 8 (May 1986), pp. 729–32. Describes a course which used the special techniques to teach verbal reasoning and vocabulary skills to minority high school students.

Tralter, Gwendolyn. "I Thought What?" *Clearing House*, Vol. 60, no. 2 (October 1986), pp. 76–78. Links thinking to intellectual, moral and emotional responsibility.

Vandergrift, Kay. "Critical Thinking Misfired: Implications of Student Responses to "The Shooting Gallery." *School Library Media Quarterly*, Vol. 15, no. 2 (Winter 1987), pp. 86–91. Cites limited meanings derived from a film "The Shooting Gallery," by eighth grade students to support argument that students are not using critical analysis in responding to works of art.

"When Teachers Tackle Thinking Skills." *Educational Leadership*, Vol. 42, (November 1984), entire issue.

Appendix V Vocabulary List of Prefixes, Suffixes, Roots

Commonly used prefixes:

Prefix	Example	Meaning
a-, an-	amoral	not, without, lacking
ab-, a-, abs-	abhor	away from
ad-, ac-, af-, ag-, al-, an-, ap-, ar-, as-, at-	adhere	toward
ambi-	ambivalence	both
amphi-	amphitheater	on both sides, around
ante-	antebellum	before
anti-	antibiotic	against
auto-	automatic	self
bi-	bisect	two
centi-	century	hundred
circum-	circumstance	around
con-, com-, co-, col-, cor-	correlate	with, in association, together
contra-	contradiction	against
de-	descend	away from, out of, separation
dec-, deca-	decade	ten
di-	dicotyledon	two, twice, double
dia-	diameter	through, between, across
dis-	dissatisfied	not
ex-, e-, ef-	evict	out of, from
for-	forehand	away, off, wrong
fore-	forefront	before, front, superior
hepta-	heptagon	seven
hexa-	hexagon	six
hyper-	hypersensitive	over, above
hemi-	hemisphere	half
in-, il-, ir-, im-	invisible, invade	not, also means in and is used as an intensifier
inter-	interact	between, among
intra-, intro-	introvert	within
kilo-	kilocycle	thousand
milli-	millennium	thousand
mis-	misspell	wrong, not

Prefix	Example	Meaning
mono-	monopoly	one
multi-	multitude	many
non-	nonsense	not
nona-	nonagon	nine
ob-, oc-, of-	obstruct	toward, to, on, over, against
oct-	octagon	eight
omni-	omnipotent	all
pan-	pantheist	all
per-	perceive	through, thoroughly, very
pro-	promote	in favor of, advancing
quadr-	quadrupled	four
quin-	quintuplet	five
re-	reorganize	backward, again
retro-	retrograde	backward
se-	select	apart
semi-	semiannual	half
sex-	sextant	six
sub-, suc-, suf-, sur-, sug-, sus-	supplant	under, below, slightly
super-	supercede	above, beyond
syn-, sym-	synchronize	with, together
sept-	September	seven
tele-	telegraph	distance
tetra-	tetrameter	four
trans-, tra-	traverse	across, beyond, through
tri-	triple	three
un-	unnatural	not
uni-	unilateral	one
ultra-	ultramodern	beyond, farther

Commonly used suffixes:

Suffix	Example	Meaning
-able, -ible	durable, visible	able
-acy	piracy, privacy	quality, state, office
-age	breakage, orphanage	pertaining to; also, a noun-forming suffix
-al	rental, abdominal	adjective or noun-forming suffix
-ance, -ence	insurance, competence	adjective or noun-forming suffix
-ant	reliant, servant	adjective or noun-forming suffix
-arium, -orium	aquarium, auditorium	place, instrument

Suffix	Example	Meaning
-ary	dictionary, elementary	pertaining to, connected with
-ate	activate, animate	verb-forming suffix used with English nouns
-ation, -ition	creation, condition	combination of -ate, and -ion used for forming nouns
-esque	picturesque	style, manner, distinctive character
-cle, -icle	corpuscle, denticle	small, diminutive
-ferous	coniferous	bearing
-ful	colorful	full of
-ic	democratic, phonic	suffix forming adjectives from nouns
-fy, -ify	fortify, magnify	to make, to cause to be
-hood	childhood, statehood	station, condition, nature
-ism	conservatism, Marxism	used to form nouns denoting action, practice, principles, doctrines
-ity	acidity, familiarity	used to form nouns expressing state or condition
-itis	appendicitis	inflammation, abnormal states or conditions
-ive	creative, suggestive	suffix of adjectives expressing tendency, disposition, function
-ize	memorize, modernize	verb suffix
-ment	statement	denotes an action, resulting state, product
-mony	testimony, parsimony	result or condition, denotes action or condition
-or	conqueror, generator	one who does something
-ose, -ous	verbose, porous	full of
-oid	avoid, ellipsoid	resembling, like
-osis	hypnosis	denotes action, state, process or condition
-tude	solitude, altitude	indicates nouns formed from adjectives

Here are some roots or bases of words with examples:

Root or base	Examples	Meaning
ag, act	activate, enact, agile, agency	to do
ambi	ambivalent, ambidextrous	both
anthrop	anthropology, anthropomorphic, misanthrope	man
aqua	aquifer, aquatic, aqueous	water
aud	audible, audition, auditorium, audience	hear
auto	automatic, automation, automaton	self
bene	benefit, benevolent, benign	good
cap, capt, chap	decapitate, capture, captain, chapter	head
ceed, cede, cess	proceed, precedent, cease	go, yield
chrom	chromatic, chromosome	color
chron	synchronize, chronology, chronic	time
cogn	cognition, recognize, cognitive	know
corp	corporate, corpulent, corporation	body
cred	credit, incredible, credulous	belief
don, donat	donate, donor, condone, pardon	to give
dent, dont	orthodontist, dental, dentifrice	tooth
derm	dermatology, epidermis, dermatitis	skin
dic, dict	dictionary, dictate, predict, indict	say
dox	doxology, paradox	belief
duc	duct, reduce, produce, conduct	lead in
fac, fic, fy	manufacture, factory, verify	make, do

Root or base	Examples	Meaning
fer	transfer, ferry, confer, defer, suffer	bear
fie	confident, infidel, confide	faith
fluc, flux	fluctuate, fluxion	flow
gress	transgress, congress, egress	step
graph	graphite, telegraph, phonograph	write
ject	deject, rejection, conjecture, trajectory	throw
loc	local, locate, location, dislocate	place
loq, loc	eloquent, elocution, interlocutor	speak
mal	malevolent, malapropism, malefactor	bad
manu	manufacture, manuscript, manacle, manual	hand
neb	nebulous, nebula	cloudy
mit, mis	emit, permit, dismissal, omit, missile	send
miso, misa	misanthrope, misogamy	bad
mort	mortician, mortuary, mortify	dead
morph	morphology, endomorph, metamorphosis	shape
mov, mot, mob	motivate, motion, motile, remove	move
omni	omnipresent, omniscient, omnipotent	all
phil	philosophy, philanthropy, philharmonic	love
path	sympathy, empathic, pathetic	suffering, disease, feeling
ped	pedestrian, pedometer, pedicure	foot
pod	podiatrist, pseudopod	foot
scrib, script	transcript, prescribe, description	write

Literature in the Content Curriculum

A. A PAR approach to using tradebooks with second-grade science study: "Plants and Animals Extended Reading," *Sara Gallant*
B. History bibliography: Books on blacks, immigrants, and indians to be used with social studies chapters on slavery, immigration and settlement of the Western United States, *Sue Jewell*
C. Geometry trade books for fifth grade, *Paula Mitchell*
D. The *Hamlet* puzzle, *Linda Tabor*

A. *A PAR approach to using tradebooks with second-grade science study:* "Plants and Animals Extended Reading." Developed by Sara Gallant. Seven books will be read relating to Unit 11, "Plants and Animals of Long Ago."

For each of the books, a review will be made including a note to the teacher detailing

— why the book was selected
— the readability level determined by using the SMOG formula—if the book contains 20 sentences or more (if book contains less than 20 sentences, the Fry short-form formula will be used)
— what are the possibilities for its use in relation to the chapter and PAR
— a purpose to the child (for why he or she might want to read this selection)

1. Aliki. (1981). *Digging Up Dinosaurs.* New York: Thomas Y. Crowell.

NOTE TO THE TEACHER: *Digging Up Dinosaurs*

Why this book was selected and its relation to the unit:

Unit 11 has two chapters devoted to fossils—as keys to the past; and the role of the scientist, as he learns about the many kinds of animals of long ago, by studying these artifacts.

SMOG readability level: 5.9—This book would need to be shared by the teacher to her student audience.

What are the possibilities for use in relation to Unit 11 and the PAR framework? After reading Chapters 1 and 3, one of the extension suggestions is to have a science-resource person speak to the boys and girls about how scientists find the fossils; and what it is like to assemble the bones to make dinosaur skeletons.

This is a fine PAR extension suggestion, but—after the text has been read and before the resource person visits, *Digging Up Dinosaurs* should be read to the class by the teacher. Aliki combines humorous drawings and interesting text, showing the kinds of things a paleontologist does. With this information in place—plus having read the Heath text, the children *will be ready* to extend their experience even further by being ready for the visit by the resource person.

A CHILD'S PURPOSE FOR READING: *Digging Up Dinosaurs*

(The child does not read this book, because of its readability level. What the child will do here is to apply the information in an activity.)

Now that we've used three ways to get information about people who work with fossils to learn about the past, (i.e., the Heath Science Book, *Digging Up Dinosaurs*, and the paleontologist), I want you to write down—with your partner—at least 16 words which could be used to describe:

A person who works with trees   *A person who works with animals*
                                                    of long ago

The class will discuss (factstorm) after all the groups have finished to see who came up with the best collection of words. Maybe all of us together can think of some more.

2. Amos, William H. (1982). *Life in Ponds and Streams*. Washington: Books for Young Explorers, National Geographic Society.

NOTE TO THE TEACHER: *Life in Ponds and Streams*

Why this book was selected and its relation to the unit:

Life in Ponds and Streams, a National Geographic Publication, is filled with text and beautiful pond/stream photographs. The photographs alone would cause the child to select this book from the library shelf. (This book relates to Chapter 5, "Endangered Plants and Animals.")

SMOG readability level: 3.1

What are the possibilities for use in relation to Unit 11 and the PAR framework?

This book would possibly need to be shared by the teacher with her student audience, using the study skill of categorization (in conjunction with the Preparation Phase Building Background). The teacher, in order to build background before starting Chapter 5, "Endangered Plants and Animals," will factstorm, discuss with class where animals live (ponds, zoos, swamps, jungles). Then, she will ask children about the kinds of pond animals and to try to think of a way they can classify them as she reads aloud *Life in Ponds and Streams*. After the book has been read, the children factstorm, recalling various animals living in the pond/stream community (deer, raccoons, beavers, salamanders). While looking at their list (on overhead), the boys and girls work out a strategy for classifying (by grouping animals according to where in pond environment their "space" is). In groups of two or three, the children make categories (air birds, bees; land raccoons, deer; water beavers, otters; air herons, robins, owls). When the groups have finished classifying, the classifications will be discussed by the entire class.

A CHILD'S PURPOSE FOR READING: *Life in Ponds and Streams*

Did you enjoy hearing about those ponds and stream animals when I read *Life in Ponds and Streams* to you on Monday? Wasn't it wonderful that when we just put the (classification) "headings" on the board, you and your classmates could come up with so many of the pond-community animals from the book?

With your across-the-aisle partner I would like for you to make a jot chart and "plug-in" the animals under the right headings. (Remember how we did "jot" charts last week.)

Sample	beaver	deer
Lived in water		
Lives on land		

The other children will be interested in seeing the "jot chart" (study skills) when you have finished. If you want to look at the book again, get it off the shelf.

3. Berman, Sam. (1969). *Dinosaur Joke Book.* New York: Grosset & Dunlap.

NOTE TO THE TEACHER: *Dinosaur Joke Book*

Why this book was selected and its relation to the unit:

This is a fun book appealing to second-graders, simply because it's a joke book—about dinosaurs (Chapters 1, 2, 3).

SMOG readability level: 4.8

This is not a true prediction, as most of the 3- and 4-syllable words are dinosaur names.

What are the possibilities for use in relation to Unit 11 and the PAR framework?

Since the children are well into the dinosaur information from Health Science, they would enjoy working with jokes, especially dinosaur jokes. Using a "post-graphic organizer" strategy will *extend the reader's experience* (Reflection Phase).

The teacher/class will discuss possible replies to the jokes before the answers are read from the book. (Why does Stegasaurus hum all the time? Answer: He doesn't know any words to the songs.) Then, the children will listen to several more jokes read; but, now, no answers will be supplied. Working in small groups, the boys and girls will come up with appropriate answers—and illustrate them, too. All replies will be shared when the group has finished.

A CHILD'S PURPOSE FOR READING: *Dinosaur Joke Book*

Did you enjoy our dinosaur joke time today? Weren't the picture-answers neat that everyone did? How would you like to check this book out for tonight, read the riddles to your fourth-grade brother, and see what he has to say for "answers," before you read the ones from the book? Be sure, as the two of you read and create new replies, to write them down. I want you to share them with the group tomorrow. Have a good time!

4. Brown, Marc and Krensky, S. (1982). *Dinosaurs, Beware!—A Safety Guide.* Boston: Little, Brown and Company.

NOTE TO THE TEACHER: *Dinosaurs, Beware!—A Safety Guide*

Why the book was selected: This book builds a relationship between practicing safety (a tie-in with Health) and staying alive. If you aren't careful, warns author Marc Brown, "you, too," can become "extinct" just like the dinosaurs. (This book is dedicated to "endangered species everywhere.") The teacher can assist the children in "Building Background" with other understandings detailed in this beautifully illustrated volume: that it is not wise to eat strange plants (like those pictured in chapter 5, "Endangered Plants and Animals"), as they might be poisonous.

SMOG readability level: 3.6

What are the possibilities for its use in relation to the chapter and PAR?

An ABOUT/POINT strategy could be used in the PAR Reflection phase. Here the teacher reads *Dinosaurs, Beware!—A Safety Guide* to her class-audience. Then, in small groups, she has the boys and girls recall as many of the facts as they can. (The children also recall two Chapter 11 vocabulary words—extinct, endangered—used in Brown's book.) Then, as a class they must say what an endangered person would do so he wouldn't become extinct: "During a thunderstorm, stay out of water and away from trees. Lightning strikes both places."

A CHILD'S PURPOSE FOR READING: *Dinosaurs, Beware!—A Safety Guide*

I want you to look at the pictures and read about some modern 1988 dinosaurs. (Remember, I read this to you last week.) These dinosaur children seem to dress just about the same way you do.

When you finish, I want you to write down

       "In Case of Fire," (p. 12)   "With Animals," (p. 14)

and see how many things that you can recall about these two subjects. Do this with your partner. Good luck!

5. Ipcar, Dahlov. (1958). *The Wonderful Egg.* New York: Doubleday & Co., Inc.

NOTE TO THE TEACHER: *The Wonderful Egg*

Why this book was selected and its relation to the unit:

The Wonderful Egg is a "mystery" story devoted to looking at all of the dinosaurs (in beautiful pictures/reading descriptions of each) to decide whose egg it is that we see on the first page of the book. Along with the story thread, you are given great information on the types of dinosaurs and the earth as it was then.

SMOG readability level: 5.2

What are the possibilities for use in relation to Unit 11 and the PAR framework?

In order to determine which dinosaurs children are familiar with, before the teacher reads this book, she will have a class discussion, followed by having boys and girls do a "Discriminative Self-Inventory."

After reading, she will:

(1) Discuss "whose egg" it was.
(2) Examine the inventory again, having youngsters put plus signs by the names they know now.
(3) Have the class divide into groups and compile a few sentences about their favorite dinosaur, to be shared later.

A CHILD'S PURPOSE FOR READING: *The Wonderful Egg*

Now that you have heard *The Wonderful Egg*, and you have seen all of the most important dinosaurs of 65 million years ago, I want you to cut-and-paste to make your favorite dinosaur from those we talked about in our discussion.

You may want to look at *The Wonderful Egg* to find your "creature." See what really "stands-out" on him. Think! Whichever dinosaur you make, try to put in his special features. When everyone has finished, we will share with the class.

6. Clark, Ann Nolan. (1969). *Along Sandy Trails*. New York: The Viking Press, Inc.

NOTE TO THE TEACHER: *Along Sandy Trails*

Why this book was selected and its relation to the unit:

Along Sandy Trails, filled with pages of beautiful photographs and almost-poetic descriptions of the Arizona desert, is written as though the seven-year-old Indian child in the story was giving you a guided tour of her individual special spot on earth—her environment.

There is a strong relationship between Ann Nolan Clark's book and Chapter 5 "Endangered Plants and Animals."

SMOG readability level: 3.6

What are the possibilities for use in relation to Unit 11 and the PAR framework?

Along Sandy Trails—the first time it's used—needs to be shared by the teacher with her student audience. With their prior knowledge in place (own background, the Chapter 5 text), the boys and girls will be able to identify with Ann Nolan Clark's Indian child as she takes a walk with her grandmother. After reading, the teacher, using a study-skills classification strategy (extension of reading experience—Reflection), will have the children discuss/recall the animals/plants the "story child" described (quails, bird eggs, cactus flower). Inspired by the child in the story, the children will discuss their own "earth beauty spots" (Maymont's animal farm, the James River). An elaborate contrast/compare fact-storming list will grow out of this discussion.

7. Cortesi, Wendy. (1978). *Explore a Spooky Swamp*. Washington: Books for Young Readers, National Geographic Society.

NOTE TO THE TEACHER: *Explore a Spooky Swamp*

Why this book was selected and its relation to the unit:

Explore a Spooky Swamp, a National Geographic publication, is related to Chapter 5, "Endangered Plants and Animals." This book, full of beautiful photographs, covers the adventures two children have on a boat trip through the Okefenokee Swamp.

SMOG readability level: 4.2

What are the possibilities for use in relation to Unit 11 and the PAR framework?

This book could be used for DRTA strategy (Preparation Phase Preparing the Reader) to give a feeling-flavor for Chapter 5, "Endangered Plants and Animals". The teacher would "factstorm," discussing animals, plants, and feelings one might have on a boat trip into a mysterious swamp, home for animals only.

The teacher then shows children the exciting-looking book, *Explore a Spooky Swamp*. Children speculate about what might be seen on this boat trip (alligators, snapping turtles, water lilies, frogs). As the pages are read, pauses are made to justify predictions, to anticipate what animal-creature might appear next. As a result, this DRTA preparation strategy has the children ready to read "Endangered Plant/Animals" (Health Science), and has encouraged listening and speaking.

A CHILD'S PURPOSE FOR READING: *Explore a Spooky Swamp*

Would you like to look at *Explore a Spooky Swamp* when you have finished your morning work? You will enjoy looking at the pictures again. Try to imagine how the animals might have felt when they saw the little red boat and the strange two-legged animals approaching. Surely the swamp community wondered *why* the visitors had come. Pretend that you are the alligator; write a few sentences giving your version of the reasons for the visit. Plan to share your story at reading-group time (First-Person-Interview Extending Reading Experience).

B. *History Bibliography: Books on Blacks, Immigrants, and Indians to Be Used with Social Studies Chapters on Slavery, Immigration, and Settlement of the Western United States*

Developed by Sue Jewell

Books for Children on Black History

Angelou, Maya. *I Know Why the Caged Bird Sings.* New York: Random House, 1972, 248 pp. The story of the author's childhood growing up in Mississippi in the early 1900s.

Angelou, Maya. *Gather Together in My Name.* New York: Random House, 1974, 270 pp. The second book about Maya Angelou's life includes selections from *The Autobiography of Malcolm X*, Claude Brown's *Manchild in the Promised Land*, and Ernest Gaines's *The Autobiography of Miss Jane Pittman.*

Angelou, Maya. *Singin' and Swingin' and Gettin' Merry Like Christmas.* New York: Random House, 1976, 269 pp. This is the third segment of her autobiography, and she is an adult with a small son to care for. She is very suspicious of kindness shown her. She moves into the white world, enters show business and tours Europe and Africa. Her writing reflects a magnificent sense of life and love and celebration of just being human which has won her such a large following.

Bernard, Jacqueline. *Journey Toward Freedom: The Story of Sojourner Truth.* New York: Grosset & Dunlap, 1967, 253 pp. The story of a powerful personality with strong-minded opinions and no-nonsense behavior who began her life as a slave torn from her family and beaten by a cruel master. She was an obedient slave. As she became a woman she tried to separate truth from falsehoods. She gained her freedom and then tried to help others become free.

Brownmiller, Susan. *Shirley Chisholm.* New York: Archway Books, 1968, 118 pp. The biography of the first black woman ever to be elected to Congress (1968) tells of her childhood in Barbados through her first year as Representative of Brooklyn's 12th Congressional District. The author especially notes the people, both historic and contemporary, who influenced Chisholm's life.

Bryan, Ashley (selected and illustrated). *I'm Going to Sing.* New York: Atheneum, 1982, 53 pp. (vol. 2) These spirituals are American, rooted deeply in the sorrows of slavery and the rhythms of Black Africa. There is humor, piety, sorrow, anger, weariness, and wonder in them. Because they are so rich and beautiful, so melodic and rhythmic, they are loved throughout the world and have had great influence on composers of all kinds of music.

Felton, Harold William, *James Weldon Johnson.* New York: Dodd, Mead, 1971, 91 pp. An ambitious Afro-American in the 1880s takes advantage of what Florida has to offer in education and then moves on with his friend, Ricardo Rodrigues, to Atlantic University. On the train, the conductor orders them to the "colored people's car." When they start speaking Spanish and are thought to be foreign instead of black, they are allowed to remain in the first-class car.

Gilroy, Tom. *In Bikole.* Westminster, MD: Alfred A. Knopf, 1978, 82 pp. Eight modern stories of life in a west African village offer insight into daily joys and sorrows. They are based on real events, revealing a blend of ancient tradition and modern influence.

Goodman, Walter. *Black Bondage: The Life of Slaves in the South.* New York: Farrar, Straus & Giroux, 1969, 144 pp. "Why am I a slave? Why are some people slaves and others masters? Was there ever a time when this was not so? How did the relation commence?" These were questions which puzzled Frederick Douglass when he was only eight years old. He was born into slavery but escaped when he was twenty-one. He devoted his life to fighting for his people's rights.

Hamilton, Virginia. Illustrator Eros Keith. *The House of Dries Drear.* New York: Macmillan, 1968, 246 pp. A black professor and his family move from North Carolina to Ohio into a large old home near the university where he has taken a teaching position. The family is warned of evil forces which surround the house and have to do with slavery and the underground railroad. However, the family moves in anyway. Even though fiction, there's much information about the underground railroad.

Hamilton, Virginia. *Junius Over Far.* New York: Harper & Row, 1985, 277 pp. Junius decides to follow his grandfather in search of his lost heritage though he knows the situation on grandfather's home island is dangerous.

Hamilton, Virginia. *Zeely.* New York. Macmillan, 1967, 122 pp. Elizabeth Perry and her younger brother John, who are black, spend the summer with Uncle Ross on his farm in the southern United States. This story brings out many interesting details of black history. In the story Zeely tells Geeder (Elizabeth), the most important thing anyone can do is accept oneself.

Hermence, Belinda. *Tancy.* Boston, MA: Houghton Mifflin, 1984, 201 pp. The story begins with the sudden death of Tancy's kind master, Will Gaither, from a ruptured appendix. It is then that Tancy realizes

what life could be like without her master and mistress. Information about the blacks is good, and so I am including this selection, even though it may be beyond an average reader. This is geared to the above-average student.

Kaufman, Mervyn D. *Jesse Owens.* New York: Thomas Y. Crowell, 1973, 33 pp. Jesse Owens is one of seven children of an Afro-American family. Though as a child he is sickly and underweight, it is discovered by a coach he has a talent as a runner. When he is in his early twenties, he competes in the 1936 Olympics and his success proves beneficial to all of his family.

Meltzer, Milton. *The Black Americans: A History in Their Own Words.* New York: Thomas Y. Crowell, 1982, 291 pp. Included are selections from letters, speeches, memoirs, and testimonials of black Americans which record their experiences from 1619 to the present. Other books by Milton Meltzer: *All Times, All Peoples: A World of Slavery; A Picture History of Black Americans* (with Langston Hughes and C. Eric Lincoln); *The Human Rights Book.*

Ojigbo, A. Okion (compiler and editor). *Young and Black in Africa.* New York: Random House, 1965, 106 pp. Eight stories by young Africans from Kenya, Nigeria, Ghana, South Africa, Guiana, and Malawi convey warmth, pride, humor, and sometimes heartbreak of growing up in Africa.

Robeson, Susan. *The Whole World in His Hands: A Pictorial History of Paul Robeson.* Secaucus, NJ: Citadel Press, 1981. Paul Robeson was one of the world's great interpretative artists. He was an athlete, scholar, orator, and linguist, fluent in more than twenty languages. He was a star in theater, film, and concert stage. He was also controversial. He was outspoken and persecuted for it.

Sterling, Dorothy. *Freedom Train,* New York: Scholastic Book Services, 1971, 191 pp. Harriet Tubman was born a slave and her goal in life was to gain her freedom. She devoted her life to bringing others out of slavery by way of the underground railroad.

Taylor, Mildred. *Roll of Thunder Hear My Cry.* New York: Bantam Books, 1984, 210 pp. This book is based on the author's childhood and is set in the 1930s. It is told from the point of view of Cassie, the only daughter in a family of four children. Because she is surrounded by love and is protected by her family, she doesn't realize just how cruel prejudice can be until she goes on her first trip to town.

Vlakos, Olivia. Illustrator George Ford. *African Beginnings.* New York: Viking Press, 1967, 264 pp. The searcher, in the absence of written records, has turned to the archaeological record for cultural beginning, and to the ethnographers, who have lived with and studied living African people. So, from these, a "shadowy" outline of Africa's past emerges.

Webb, Sheyann and Rachel West Nelson. *Selma, Lord, Selma.* Tuscaloosa, AL: University of Alabama Press, 1980, 146 pp. This is the dramatic story of two young girls caught up in the civil rights demonstrations in Selma, Alabama. It is the recollection of some memorable events (told to Frank Sikora) in their lives. A significant contribution to the history of the Civil Rights Movement.

Books for Teachers on Black History

Berlin, Ira and Ronald Hoffman. *Slavery and Freedom in the Age of the American Revolution.* Charlottesville, VA: University of Virginia Press, 1984. A history of slavery and freedom of the black man and woman during the period of the American Revolution.

Blassingame, John (editor). *Slave Testimony.* Baton Rouge, LA: Louisiana State University Press, 1977, 745 pp. A compilation of blacks' experiences in slavery told through letters, interviews, speeches, and autobiographies. The central theme is that the blacks valued freedom and they wanted to keep their families together. Throughout many of their lives, they were deprived of both.

Brodie, Fawn. *Thomas Jefferson: An Intimate History.* New York: Bantam Books, 1974, 676 pp. Most of the books written about Jefferson have been about his intellect and its impact on society. This book is about Jefferson and the life of the heart, rather than the mind. It discusses the relationship of Thomas Jefferson and Sally Hemmings, his slave. The evidence does seem strong that they had a long affair, and that Jefferson truly loved Sally Hemmings.

Buckley, Gail Lumet. *The Hornes: An American Family.* Westminster, MD: Alfred A. Knopf, 1986, 262 pp. Gail Buckley is Lena Horne's daughter who traces her family back six generations to its antebellum roots in Georgia. She blends memoir (Civil Rights Movement) with the family saga, based on voluminous papers kept by the family since the nineteenth century, which has produced a social history. She shows us 100 years from Emancipation to Civil Rights Movement.

Chase-Riboud, Barbara. *Sally Hemmings.* New York: Viking Press, 1979, 344 pp. A novel about Sally Hemmings and Thomas Jefferson. Though there is speculation about a relationship between the two, there are documents which present strong evidence and they are included in this book. Well written and researched.

Clark, Barbara Smith. *After the Revolution.* Westminster, MD: Pantheon Books, 1982, 186 pp. This book is about four lives of ordinary people after the American Revolution: a farmer, a merchant, a small planter of Tidewater, Virginia, and a freedman of Philadelphia. Of special interest is Richard Allen, freedman. Though he was free, his life was more limited than whites. He did not have a part in the creation of a new nation. He had been born a slave, but when he obtained his hard-fought freedom, he wondered, "Would it be possible to get off the bottom rungs of the social ladder?" Richard Allen spent his life looking for answers to questions like that. He was a significant leader in the black community of Philadelphia and as successful as a black person of his times could be.

Dixon, Melvin. *Change of Territory.* Charlottesville, VA: University of Virginia Press, 1983, 62 pp. A book of poetry which commemorates the drama of black history, the age of slavery, and displacement from Africa. It covers much ground in historical and personal experiences.

Farish, Hunter. *Journal and Letters of Phillip Vickers Fithian 1773–1774: A Plantation Tutor of the Old Dominion.* Charlottesville, VA: University of Virginia Press, 1984. Insight into the lives of all those living on a plantation, including the slave population.

Maddex, Jack P. Jr. *The Virginia Conservatives.* Chapel Hill, NC: University of North Carolina Press, 1970, 296 pp. This study in Reconstruction Politics from 1867–1879 is concerned with what happens to people defeated by revolutionary war; some withdraw, some just drift, some fume at being deprived of their social base, and others adapt and even find leadership positions by conforming. The slavery system in antebellum Virginia put the state solidly with the Confederacy.

Mallial, William. *Slave.* New York: W. W. Norton, 1986, 280 pp. A literary autobiography told to William Mallial by Hadi Abbabba Guwah about his life as an African slave captured by Moslem slave traders from his Nigerian village. He retraces the misfortunes and horrors of his life and emerges as a man intelligent enough to grab every opportunity to better himself.

Martin, Waldo E. *The Mind of Frederick Douglass.* Chapel Hill, NC: University of North Carolina Press, 1982, 333 pp. Frederick Douglass was the foremost black American of the 19th century and, so, many biographies have been written about him. But what makes this one special is that it reaches beyond the facts to the intellectual workings that made the man. The author in the second half of the book shows how 19th-century Afro-American intellectual history drew from sources in Protestant Christianity, the Enlightenment, and romanticism to find a basis for commitments to abolition and the elevation of free blacks.

Morgan, Edward S. *American Slavery—American Freedom: The Ordeal of Colonial Virginia.* New York: W. W. Norton, 1984. An extensive study of slavery as it existed in the Colonial period.

Roark, James L. *Masters without Slaves.* New York: W. W. Norton, 1977, 209 pp. Southern plantation owners were so attached to the institution of slavery that when it was ended by the Emancipation Proclamation, they were devastated. In the south after the Civil War, the land was worth little and cotton prices could not be overcome. Planters generally found gradual decline and poverty. Being poor was something the affluent had not experienced. This book looks from the masters' view of the loss of slavery. Many went to South America, leaving all business to their sons. Some even took their own lives.

Rosengarten, Thomas. *Tombee: Portrait of a Cotton Planter.* West Caldwell, NJ: William Morrow, 1985, 750 pp. A portrait of the life and times of a southern slaveholder, Thomas B. Chaplin (1822–1890), heir to a fortune in land and slaves. The plantation journal kept by Chaplin for 15 years while trying to make sense of his losses is what gives body to this project. From the slaveholder's perspective, he says he must deal with tricky slaves.

Smith, Page. *Trial by Fire.* New York: McGraw-Hill, 1982, 995 pp. A general American history book beginning just before the Civil War which has much information about slaves—from abolitionist views to the effect of emancipation to "psychological environment" to wartime changes in attitude toward slavery. Diaries, journals, and letters are widely used. There are revealing descriptions of the wartime lives of black Americans.

Sweet, Leonard. *Black Images of America.* New York: W. W. Norton, 1984. A history of blacks during the period of 1784–1870.

Tate, Thad W. *The Negro in 18th Century Williamsburg.* Charlottesville, VA: University of Virginia Press, 1984, 141 pp. The focus is on the black population in Williamsburg in colonial Virginia. Topics examined are actual number of slaves at that time, the distribution of ownership, the work the slaves performed, their living conditions, and the potential impact on Christianity. The topics permit some conclusions about the degree of independence and sense of community that life in Williamsburg gave blacks. Especially interesting is the evolution of the blacks' legal status from ordinary indentured servant to servant for life to slave, which led to the development of a separate legal code for blacks. This helps a teacher explain to children how slavery evolved.

Williamson, Joel. *After Slavery.* Chapel Hill, NC: University of North Carolina Press, 1970. A study of the Negro in North Carolina during reconstruction, 1861–1877, using primary source material and careful analysis of that material. It is the state in which the slave played the most important and controversial role during reconstruction.

Woodward, C. Van. (editor). *Mary Chestnut's Civil War.* New Haven, CT: Yale University Press, 1981, 863 pp. The diary of a woman who was close to the action during the Civil War because her husband was a high-ranking member of the Confederate government. Aristocratic and patriarchal, she had a horror of slavery and called herself an abolitionist, although she herself was a slaveholder.

Books for Teachers and Children on American Indians

Anderson, Bernice, *Indian Sleepman Tales.* New York: Bromhall House, 1940, 145 pp. Legends of the Otoe Tribe, who settled in what is now Nebraska.

Baker, Olaf. Illustrator Stephen Gammell. *Where the Buffaloes Begin.* New York: Frederick Warne, 1981, 40 pp. The story of Little Wolf, who longs to find the lake where the buffaloes begin. The book is rich in images as it evokes the Plains Indians' feelings of reverence for the buffalo. The full and double-page drawings are magnificent.

Balch, Glenn. *Brave Riders.* New York: Thomas Y. Crowell, 1959, 192 pp. When his father is killed trying to recover Pawnee horses stolen in a Sioux raid, Little Elk is hurt and confused. He is fifteen years old and does not want to follow in his father's footsteps as a warrior and leader of his people. Several incidents occur, however, which make him change his mind. An accurate look at Indian culture.

Bierhorst, John (editor). *Indian Poetry: The Sacred Path.* New York: William Morrow, 1983, 191 pp. A collection of spells, prayers, and power songs of the American Indians.

Bonham, Frank. *Chief.* New York: E. P. Dutton, 1971, 215 pp. Henry Crowfoot, known as Chief, is a high school senior who has his tribe's interests at heart when he develops a science project he believes will lead to the tribe's development of a glue factory. He accidentally sets fire to the school lab after breaking into the school, so he is arrested. As a result of his arrest, his public defender looks at some documents passed down to Chief from his grandfather. It seems the Indians own one half of the downtown area of Harbor City! This story reveals the pride and disappointments of many Native Americans.

Brain, Jeffrey. "Eyewitness Documents Gain New Authority from Records of

Archaeology." *Clues to America's Past.*
Washington, D.C.: National Geographic
Society, 1976, pp. 75–104. Brain goes back
to Hernando De Soto, 1539, Mississippi
Valley, and draws from four sources to tell
the story of his encounter with Indians,
then in the aboriginal state: 1) A brief
report from the King of Spain by an official
named Luys Hernandez de Biedma;
2) a narrative by Grugalo Fernandez
de Ovieda y Valdes based on a diary kept
by De Soto's secretary, Rodrigo Ranjel; 3) a
longer one by a Portuguese known as the
Gentleman of Elvas; 4) a history compiled
by Garcilaso de la Vega. (teacher
and above-average students)

Brink, Carol Ryrie. *Caddie Woodlawn: A
Frontier Story.* New York: Macmillan,
1935, 270 pp. Caddie is a strong-willed,
tomboyish girl, according to people in the
Wisconsin farming community in the
1860s. She has a strong belief in freedom
and justice and she puts them into
practice when she overhears the men in
the community plotting an attack on the
Indians.

Clifford, Ethel Rosenberg. Illustrator Richard
Cuffari. *The Year of the Three-Legged
Deer.* Boston, MA: Houghton Mifflin,
1972, 164 pp. Fourteen-year-old Takawsu
and his sister Chilili live with their white
father and Indian mother on the Indian
frontier in 1819. (above-average reader)

Corcoran, Barbara. Illustrator Richard Cuffari.
This Is a Recording. New York:
Atheneum, 1971, 168 pp. Marianne,
fourteen, travels from Boston to Montana
to visit her grandmother, whom she hasn't
seen in twelve years. She will be there
while her parents are in Europe. She isn't
at all sure she will enjoy the visit until she
meets Oliver, a Native American boy who
works for her grandmother.

Crompton, Anne Eliot. *The Ice Trail.* New
York: Methuen, 1980, 89 pp. The story of a
white boy captured by the Avenaki Indians
and raised as an Indian. Formerly, he was
Danial Abbott, but he became known as
Tanial. After an Indian attack on his
people, he was saved by Awaos. One day

when he does not return with the other
braves, and they bring back a pair of ice
skates not knowing what they are, Tanial
sees his chance to return to his other life.
Based on a New Hampshire legend which
may be true.

Distad, Audree. Illustrator Tony Chen. *Dakota
Sons.* New York: Harper and Row, 1972,
159 pp. The story is about a boy named
Tad whose best friend moves away, leaving
him no one to play with. He thinks his
summer is going to be dull until he meets
Ronnie, who lives at the nearby Indian
school. Tad has never had to deal with
prejudice and does not know what to do.
Both boys develop an appreciation of
Indian culture.

Flores, Dan L. (editor and introduction by).
*Jefferson and Southwestern Exploration:
The Freeman and Curtis Accounts of the
Red River Expedition of 1806.* Oklahoma
City, OK: University of Oklahoma Press,
1984, 386 pp. Surveyor/astronomer
Thomas Freeman and naturalist Peter
Curtis left Natchez, Mississippi in the
spring of 1806, planning to explore the
recently acquired Louisiana Purchase, but
they only completed half of their planned
trip. They were turned back by the
Spanish army. But from what is contained
in their diary, Flores makes a fascinating
adventure retelling going past Indian
villages deep into the natural environment
west of the Mississippi.

Farquhar, Margaret C. Illustrator Brinton
Turkle. *Indian Children of America.* New
York: Holt, Rhinehart & Winston, 1964,
48 pp. Introduces the origins, customs, and
cultures of the American Indians.

Hilton, Suzanne. *Getting There: Frontier
Travel Without Power.* Philadelphia, PA:
Westminster Press, 1980, 180 pp. This
book uses personal accounts to describe
events. The one with the Indians is
particularly interesting. One woman wrote
of "how handsome—for an Indian." A few
interesting points for the short number of
pages devoted to Indians.

Hofsinde, Robert. *Indian Medicine Man.* New
York. William Morrow, 1966, 94 pp.

Describes the medical practices or "lore" of different Indian tribes.

Jones, Weyman B. *Edge of Two Worlds.* New York: Dial Press, 1968, 143 pp. In 1842, fifteen-year-old Calvin Harper is traveling by wagon train from Texas to law school in Boston when the group is attacked by Comanches. Calvin is thrown from the wagon seat and lands in a clump of weeds where he lies unnoticed. He wanders for days until he finally finds water. As he bends to take a drink, he comes face to face with a shotgun held by a very old, wrinkled indian. It is Sequoyah. Based on a true story.

Lampman, Evelyn Sibley. *Half-Breed.* Garden City, NY: Doubleday, 1967, 263 pp. During the 1840s, twelve-year-old Pale Eyes' mother, Muskrat-Hiding, separates herself from her white husband who has been gone for six years and marries an Indian in her clan. Pale Eyes feels his mother has disgraced the family and decides to leave the Crow tribe and find his father.

Lyback, Johanna R. M. Illustrator Dick West. *Indian Legends of Eastern America.* Chicago, IL: Lyons & Carnahan, 1963, 180 pp. Tales from the oral tradition of the Indian tribes of the East.

Miles, Miska. Illustrator Peter Parnall. *Annie and the Old One.* Boston, MA: Little, Brown, 1971, 44 pp. The story of a Navaho Indian family. The grandmother is elderly and knows her death will come soon. She tries to get her granddaughter to understand the cycle of life and to be ready to accept it. The weaving is symbolic of the cycle. Grandmother is ready to teach Annie to weave, but she says she is not ready. Many Indian terms and cultural aspects of the Navahos are included.

Manjo, F. N. Illustrator Anita Lobel. *Indian Summer.* New York: Harper & Row, 1968, 62 pp. A frontier woman struggles to save her cabin and four children from the Indians.

Moulton, Gary. *John Ross, Cherokee Chief.* Athens, GA: University of Georgia Press, 1986, 296 pp. The author examines the life of the man who led the Cherokee people during the most trying and tragic period of their history. He was the principal negotiator with the whites during the Georgia gold rush, he guided the tribe through the treacherous years of the Civil War, and he struggled to preserve unity among his people during their removal westward along "the trail of tears." (Good book for teachers.)

National Geographic. *The World of the American Indian.* Washington, D.C.: National Geographic Society, 1974, 384 pp. This book is intended to show the Indian as he was—his beliefs, his customs, his appearance—and provide an understanding of the way he is today. Includes a rich array of cultural detail.

National Geographic. *Trails West.* Washington, D.C.: National Geographic Society, 1974. In the words of one of the authors, Wallace Stegner, "The reasons for heading to the lands beyond sundown" were as varied as the men and women the West attracted. Sheer adventure drew some. Hostile Indians were a continuing threat on the Gila and Bozeman Trails. The authors delved into letters and journals to see through the eyes of those who had been there. Writers and photographers alike joined wagon train reenactments to "travel back themselves."

O'Dell, Scott. *Sing Down the Moon.* Boston, MA: Houghton Mifflin, 1970, 137 pp. Told in first person about the narrator's family and his tribe, the Navahos. Much information about their customs and culture.

Richter, Daniel K. *Rediscovered Links in the Covenant Chain.* Charlottesville, VA: University of Virginia Press, 1984. A collection of previously unpublished transcripts of New York Indian Treaty Minutes from 1677–1691.

Raskin, Joseph. *Indian Tales.* New York: Random House, 1969, 63 pp. Ten Iroquois Indian tales, including, "How the Bear Lost Its Tail," "How the Chipmunk Got Its Stripes," and "Why Animals Do Not Talk."

Steele, William O. *Flaming Arrows.* New York: Harcourt Brace & Jovanovich, 1957, 178 pp. One night in 1784, a neighbor of eleven-year-old Chad Rabun and his family warns them Indians have been spotted crossing the Cumberland River and heading their way. So they load their belongings onto their horses and head for the stockade. This book is about the Indians and more.

Tamany, Irene R. Illustrator L. F. Cary. *Indian Tales*. Columbus, OH: C. E. Merrill, 1968, 128 pp. A young Indian boy tries several ways to earn an eagle feather.

Books for Children on Immigration and Settlement of the Western United States

Friedman, Russell. *Immigrant Kids*. New York: E. P. Dutton, 1980, 72 pp. Chronicles the lives of immigrant children at home, school, work, and play in the late 1800s and early 1900s.

Gay, Kathryn. *The Germans Helped Build America*. New York: Messner, 1971, 96 pp. Traces reasons for and the history of German immigration to the United States and discusses the contributions of German-Americans to various aspects in their new life.

Hautzig, Esther. *The Endless Steppe: A Girl in Exile*. New York: Scholastic Book Services, 1974, 240 pp. A true account of Esther Hautzig as a young Jewish girl and what happened to her between the time she was forced by the Nazis to leave her lovely town of Velna, Poland, and her immigration to America. Helps one understand why America was such a haven to someone like Esther Hautzig.

Haviland, Virginia (editor). Illustrator Ann Strugnell. *North American Legends*. New York: Philomel Books, 1979, 209 pp. An anthology of myths, legends, and tales of North American Indians; stories of American Indians and Eskimos; tales brought by European Immigrants and Black Americans. Some show how black and Indian folklore are interwoven. Another, "A Stepchild That Was Treated Mighty Bad," shows how European

immigrants retain their roots but adapted to ways of American culture.

Holland, Ruth. Pictures by H. B. Vestal. *The German Immigrants in America*. New York: Grosset & Dunlap, 1969, 61 pp. Traces the history of German immigrants from the 17th century to the present day and describes their contributions to social, industrial, and cultural life in the United States.

Johnson, James. *The Irish in America*. Minneapolis, MN: Lerner Publications, 1966, 78 pp. Covers life in Ireland in the 19th century and the life of the Irish in the United States before, during, and after the Civil War. Also tells about famous Americans of Irish ancestry and the Irish in politics in America.

Kunz, Virginia. *The Germans in America*. Minneapolis, MN: Lerner Publications, 1966, 86 pp. Tells about the life of the Germans in the United States and how they adapted.

Lasky, Kathryn. *Irish Immigrants*. New York: Macmillan, 1984, 171 pp. Birdie Flynn, a gifted Irish Catholic teenager in East Boston, struggles with the consequences of her brother's part in vandalizing a synagogue.

Madison, Winifred. *Maria Luisa*. Philadelphia, PA: J. B. Lippincott, 1971, 187 pp. Maria Luisa, a Mexican-American, experiences prejudice for the first time when she and her brother Juan go from Arizona to California to live with Uncle Emilio and his family. His daughter makes fun of Luisa's clothes and manners. When she starts school she finds everyone speaks English so fast, she cannot understand and is too shy to ask for help.

Marzollo, Jean. *Half Way Down Paddy Lane*. New York: Dial Press, 1981, 178 pp. An Irish girl living in Massachusetts finds herself transported back in time to the 1850s in her Massachusetts town. She must adjust to the prejudices against the Irish.

Norris, Gunilla Brodde. *A Feast of Light*. Westminster, MD: Alfred A. Knopf, 1967,

126 pp. Ulla is a nine-year-old who has just moved from Sweden to America and finds adjustment very difficult. When she enters the American school, she doesn't understand English. She feels awkward about her clothes and lack of understanding the other children. She feels she is being laughed at. The author has drawn from personal experience.

Robbins, Albert. *Coming to America: Immigrants from Northern Europe.* New York: Dell, 1981, 189 pp. Immigrants naturally have mixed feelings about leaving their native land to settle in America. They have hope for a better life, religious freedom, and a chance to earn a decent living. This author relates first-person accounts from the immigrants about the contrast of their old country and their new country. He also relates their stories about the attacks they faced at the hands of the Indians.

Trapp, Maria Augusta. *The Sound of Music.* New York: Dell, 1969, 352 pp. The true story of one family's immigration from Austria to America. The story was the basis for the play and movie "The Sound of Music," though this book was published after the productions of both. In July 1938, on the pretense of going mountain climbing in Italy, the family left the country by a carefully planned escape and made it safely to America. Fortunately for them, they had chosen the day before the Austrian border was closed by the Nazis.

Books for Teachers on Immigrants

Barringer, Felicity. *Flight from Sorrow.* New York: Atheneum, 1984, 280 pp. A book about a woman whose portrait renews the meaning of the word *survivor.* Born in 1932, Tamara Wall with her mother and brothers were forced by the Nazis to go to Siberia. Their treatment was brutal and her family perished. Through a stranger, Millie Lifschitz, who had lost track of her own family and wanted to help Tamara, she was able eventually to emigrate to the United States. This is the story of how she got here and what she did with her life. The true heroine of the story is Millie Lifschitz, and you find out why by reading the story.

Catton, Bruce and William C. Catton. *The Bold and Magnificent Dream: America's Founding Years, 1492–1815.* Garden City, NY: Doubleday, 1978, 463 pp. The story of the shaping of America told by well-known historian Bruce Catton with his son William. It includes information about specific Indian tribes, immigrants, and slavery. An extraordinary historical narrative and analysis.

Flexnor, James Thomas. *An American Saga.* New York: Little, Brown, 1984, 494 pp. This is the story of James Flexnor's family beginning in the 1820s—the night an explosion occurred at his great-grandfather's brewery in what is now Czechoslovakia. With that, the Flexnor fortunes went up in smoke. This led eventually to Morris, James's grandfather, coming to America and settling in Kentucky.

Gilbert, Martin. *Scharansky: Hero of Our Time.* New York: Viking Press, 1986, 467 pp. The story of someone who refuses to accept the Russian way that people do not have a right to stand up and speak of their beliefs politically. He has spent eight years in soviet prisons and labor camps. He is working for the right of the Jews to emigrate.

Ivinskaya, Olga. *A Captive of Time: My Years with Pasternak.* Garden City, NY: Doubleday, 1978, 412 pp. A story of love in Russia in the late 1940s and early 1950s. It is the love affair on which Boris Pasternak's book, Dr. Zhivago, is based. It gives the view of Russia that one pays so dearly for decisions not in keeping with the Russian ideals of the government. Pasternak is brilliant, but he is controversial and his novel was banned there. For her association with him, Olga Ivinskaya spent twelve years in prison and labor camps.

Jordan, Terry. *German Seed in Texas Soil.* Austin, TX: University of Texas Press, 1966, 206 pp. This is about the large number of Germans who moved into Texas and the influence they had on agricultural life and the economy there. They were in turn affected by the culture and physical environment.

Riley, Edward. *The Journal of John Harrower: An Indentured Servant in the Colony of Virginia, 1773–1776.* Charlottesville, VA: University of Virginia Press, 1984. John Harrower came from Scotland to Fredericksburg, Virginia, where he was hired by Col. William Daingerfield of "Belvidera" Plantation, now located on U.S. 17 and the Rappahannock River about seven miles below Fredericksburg. He was a tutor to the children of Col. Daingerfield. He kept a record of his daily life and dreamed of bringing his wife and children to America, but died just before his four-year term of service ended.

Rosenfeld, Harvey. *Raoul Wallenberg: Angel of Rescue.* Buffalo, NY: Prometheus Books, 1982, 220 pp. A Swedish diplomat tells of his mission to save as many Jews as possible from death at the hand of Adolph Hitler. He saved thousands, and many of them eventually emigrated to America and Canada. Wallenberg was imprisoned by the Russians and his fate is still unknown.

Rugoff, Milton. *The Beechers: An American Family in the 19th Century.* New York: Harper and Row. 1981, 800 pp. This biography of an enormously influential family actually covers an entire era of American history. It offers information on slaves, immigrants, and Indians. Included is Harriet Beecher Stowe, one of the most successful and influential writers in American History.

Schector, Leona and Jerrold. *An American Family in Moscow.* Boston, MA: Little Brown, 1975, 402 pp. Jerrold Schector spent 1968–1970 stationed with *Time* magazine's Moscow Bureau and took his family with him. They made every attempt to blend themselves into life in the Russian capital. Schector struggled daily with problems of reporting critical events of the day such as the invasion of Czechoslovakia, the harassment of Aleksandr Solzhenitsyn, and the States' crackdown on Jewish emigration.

Shevchenko, Arkady. *Breaking with Moscow.* Westminster, MD: Alfred A. Knopf, 1985, 378 pp. Arkady Shevchenko was the highest-ranking Soviet official ever to defect. In April 1978, he shocked the world diplomatic community by seeking refuge in the United States. He was even willing to give up his family, including his adored daughter. He had been Under Secretary General of the United Nations and former advisor to Soviet Foreign Minister Andrei Gromyko. He was an intelligent man and had long known the price of not being able to think for himself. He wasn't willing to pay that price.

Singer, Isaac Bashevis. *A Man in Search of Love.* Garden City, NY: Doubleday, 1985. This is about Singer's immigration to America from Poland. Also published with Singer's *A Little Boy in Search of God* and *Lost in America* in the single volume *Love and Exile.* In *Lost in America* he examines his love of both America and Poland.

Smith, Hedrick. *The Russians.* New York: Ballantine Books, 1976, 682 pp. Hedrick Smith, journalist with the *New York Times,* spent a year in Moscow as correspondent. He writes of his impressions. For the poor, life is very depressing; living in small quarters, spending so much time waiting in lines just to buy food, having to walk everywhere, and then having someone always watching and listening.

Stratton, Joanna L. *Pioneer Women: Voices from the Kansas Frontier.* New York: Simon & Schuster, 1981, 267 pp. This book contains reminiscences of pioneer women of the Midwest in the 1850s. It is written using manuscripts of women who actually lived there. They tell of hardships and what they liked about their land, discussing slaves, immigrants, and Indians.

Wallace, Amy. *Genius, The Prodigy: A Biography of William James Sides, America's Great Child Prodigy.* New York: E. M. Dutton, 1986, 297 pp. A product of the immigrant's drive for success, William James Sides suffers at the hands of his father, a brilliant Russian immigrant and psychologist associated with William James who pushes his son to be the epitome of the "superbaby" of the early 1900s, but with tragic consequences.

C. *Geometry Trade Books for Fifth Graders*

Developed by Paula Mitchell

Text: Angles Are Easy as Pie

Author: Robert Froman

Publisher: Thomas Y. Crowell Company, New York, 1975

Reader Rating: Easy

Summary: Part of a series of books called Young Math Books, this short volume explores angles, triangles, and quadrangles. It uses a humorous approach with an alligator guide throughout the book. It provides explanations, illustrations, and activities. (33 pages)

Possible Uses:
Activity source.
Good basic explanation of concepts.
Practical applications and analogies.

Text: Circles

Authors: Mindel and Harry Sitomer

Publisher: Thomas Y. Crowell Company, New York, 1971

Reader Rating: Medium

Summary: Part of a series of books called Young Math Books, this short volume explores circles. It includes a good explanation on using a protractor. It provides activities to help explain concepts. The illustrations are large and colorful. (33 pages)

Possible Uses:
Activity source
Good explanation of circle diameter and radius.
Possible project.

Text: Directions and Angles
The Reason Why Books

Authors: Irving and Ruth Adler

Publisher: The John Day Company, New York, 1969

Reader Rating: Medium

Summary: This book tells about both directions and angles and how they are related. It covers the sizes of angles and the use of a protractor. Parallel and intersecting lines are discussed as well as quadrilaterals. Practical applications of geometry are shown as flag signals, map directions and latitude and longitude are discussed. Illustrations are used to help explain concepts. Several activities are provided. (47 pages)

Possible Uses:
Examples of practical applications.
Good explanations of geometric concepts.

Text: Exploring Triangles
Paper-Folding Geometry

Author: Jo Phillips

Publisher: Thomas Y. Crowell Company, New York, 1975.

Reader Rating: Easy

Summary: Another in the Young Math Books series, this book presents having fun with triangles through the use of paper folding. Vocabulary such as angle, side, vertex, and equilateral are used to explore different aspects of triangles. Readers are also given directions on using a compass to complete several different activities. Drawings are large and detailed to aid comprehension. (34 pages)

Possible Uses:
Source of several good activities.
Extensions of concepts dealing with triangles and using a compass.

Text: Fun with Figures

Authors: Mae and Ira Freeman

Publisher: Random House, New York, 1946

Reader Ratings: Hard

Summary: Though somewhat dated in appearance, this book of easy experiments for young people provides some good activities for hands on experimentation. It is well-illustrated and easy to follow. (60 pages)

Possible Uses:
Source of activities to explore in geometry.

Text: Math for Smarty Pants

Author: Marilyn Burns

Publisher: Little, Brown and Company, Boston, 1982

Reader Rating: Medium

Summary: An excellent book written in an upbeat style for students. It is full of practical explanations, activities, diagrams, and puzzles which are informative and entertaining. Many areas of math are covered. (128 pages)

Possible Uses:
Source for activities.
Contains good geometry game.
Good problem-solving activity.

Text: Mathematics Encyclopedia

Author: Leslie Foster

Publisher: Rand McNally and Company, New York, 1986

Reader Rating: Medium

Summary: This colorful and attractive math encyclopedia covers many aspects of numbers in an entertaining fashion. Eight different pages are devoted to geometry and includes information on triangles, quadrilaterals, use of a protractor, and much more. Diagrams and photographs are detailed and interesting. An index is provided for easy location of subjects. Excellent source book for the classroom. (137 pages)

Possible Uses:
Source for activities.
Contains good directions for drawing certain shapes, using a compass, etc.
Provides practical application of geometry.

Text: Mathematics
The World of Science

Authors: Irene Fekete and Jasmine Denyer

Publisher: Facts on File Publications, New York, 1984

Reader Rating: Hard

Summary: This book is part of a twenty-five volume set of encyclopedias on scientific subjects designed for eight- to twelve-year-olds. Pages 16 to 23 and pages 32, 33, and 38 deal with geometric concepts. The book contains colorful illustrations and photographs. There is a glossary in the back as well as an index that comes in handy. (64 pages)

Possible Uses:
Information source book.
Could spark interest in other areas.

Text: Right Angles
Paper-Folding Geometry

Author: Jo Phillips

Publisher: Thomas Y. Crowell Company, New York, 1972

Reader Rating: Easy

Summary: Another book in the Young Math Books series, this book allows the reader to quickly learn to fold an accurate model of a right angle by following the clear instructions provided. The book shows how to test angles in a room, and explore the meaning of more mathematical terms such as congruent and similar. (33 pages)

Possible Uses:
Simple and clear explanations of geometric terms.
Source for activities dealing with right angles.
Extension of concepts dealing with angles, rectangles, and quadrilaterals.

Text: Science Experiences: Shapes

Author: Jeanne Bendick

Publisher: Franklin Watts, Inc., New York, 1968

Reader Rating: Easy

Summary: A simply written book that discusses shapes and the names of specific shapes such as sphere, right angle, square, circle, etc. The book discusses different aspects of shapes and poses questions to the reader to consider as he or she continues. There are numerous activities suggested. The print in the book makes it appear more simple than the concepts that it presents, which could affect student appeal. An index is provided. (70 pages)

Possible Uses:
Source for activities.
Source for analogies.

Text: Straight Lines, Parallel Lines, Perpendicular Lines

Author: Mannis Charosh

Publisher: Thomas Y. Crowell Company, New York, 1970

Reader Rating: Medium

Summary: In this interesting book, the reader explores the world of straight, parallel, and perpendicular lines. There are many experiments and activities that will help the reader recognize different types of lines. (33 pages)

Possible Uses:
Source of simple, clear explanations of terms.
Activity source.
Problem-solving examples.

Text: String, Straight Edge, and Shadow
The Story of Geometry

Author: Julia E. Diggins

Publisher: The Viking Press, New York, 1965.

Reader Rating: Hard

Summary: Told in story-like fashion, this history of geometry is both informative and entertaining. It explains how geometry was used in ancient times and how it could be used today. Illustrations on almost every page help students develop comprehension of the material. (160 pages)

Possible Uses:
Read aloud a chapter to spark interest.
Source book for practical applications of geometry.
Source of historical information on geometry.

Text: The Wonderful World of Mathematics

Author: Lancelot Hogben

Publisher: Doubleday and Company, Inc., New York, 1968

Reader Rating: Hard

Summary: This interesting book gives information on many aspects of mathematics, from ancient times to modern day. It contains much useful information about geometry and includes illustrations and diagrams. There is an illustrated "Glossary of Arithmetical Terms" in the back which is very helpful. An index is provided to assist the reader. (96 pages)

Possible Uses:

Good source of historical information.
Shows practical uses of geometry.
Helpful illustrations.

D. The Hamlet Puzzle

HAMLET
T H E M E S

His inability to make decisions		His treatment of Ophelia		His madness, real or feigned	
Appearance/ Reality	Corruption/Guilt	Depression/ Suicide	Revenge	The Supernatural	Love/Relationship
The Catcher in the Rye	The Catcher in the Rye	The Catcher in the Rye	Killing Mr. Griffin	Demian	The Catcher in the Rye
To Kill a Mockingbird	To Kill a Mockingbird	Very Far Away From Anywhere Else	Demian	Down a Dark Hall	Jacob I Have Loved
Mary Done: a Love Story	Demian	I Am The Cheese	The Outsiders	Interstellar Pig	The Outsiders
The Dancing Madness	The Outsiders	Demian		Christine	Mary Done: a Love Story
Demian		The Outsiders		Pet Sematary	Demian

CLASS STUDY

GROUP STUDY

INDIVIDUAL STUDY AND PROJECTS

Developed by Linda Tabor

A Poetry Test with Explication

Developed by Meredith Randall

Introduction

Throughout the poetry unit, my students have many opportunities to accumulate study material. I incorporate activities that not only are useful in their assigned purpose but will also be useful as study aids. These include jot charts, structured overviews, poetry logs, and writing assignments.

I explain the testing procedure to my students in advance of the test and make sure they understand what they will be expected to do. Also in advance, I give them the criteria I will use to grade the tests. We also go over test-taking skills and study skills so my students can get maximum benefit from the materials they possess: This review includes reading directions, strategies for objective questions, and the writing steps, including the use of short outlines, for essay questions.

Since the desired outcome of my testing is to determine what knowledge of the material a student has gained, it is only fair to eliminate as much as possible the non-content items that may distract or cause the student to be unable to demonstrate his or her knowledge of poetry.

I include non-traditional testing measures in my determination of comprehension as this is the way I teach the unit. One of my assignments is a jot chart on the elements of poetry found in various poems, and thus one method of testing is to have the students complete a partially filled chart. My students will have been instructed in two methods of writing essays on poetry, cubing, and keying, and I use one of these on the tests. I include the method of the activity and the poems but expect the students to be able to create or recreate a written answer in association with the steps.

My primary level is applied. I feel that a student has not truly learned a poem until he can associate to his own experiences and make the poem meaningful for himself. My test includes all levels of comprehension, but has opportunities for the student to express his own opinion of the poems. I require my students to recognize, recall, and produce information. The test has a matching section which calls for the student to recognize associations in lists, a partially completed jot chart which requires a recall of the missing items, main idea statements which require the students to recognize a portion of a poem and be able to recall the main idea of the fragment, and a writing section that allows the student to apply his personal feelings to a poem. The writing assignment carries the most point value. I instruct my students in the point values assigned to each section and help them to designate their time appropriately. I phrase the test items in a manner that allows the students to show me what they remember about the unit, not what they have forgotten. The items have stem clues that help in recognition, and I instruct my students in how to effectively read the question so that they may use the clues to their advantage.

The test consists of four parts. The first three sections should not take more than twenty minutes. The fourth part, the essay, will take more time.

The first part of the test is a matching section. This section contains ten items from the poems which are to be matched to ten ideas. Most of the matches are literal, but some require an interpretive level of comprehension. This section of the test is worth twenty points, two points per item, and should not take much more than five minutes.

The second section of the test is a partially completed jot chart which the student completes. The chart has ten missing items. The students will have completed this chart as an activity and will have had it to study by. Therefore, this mostly requires recall, but the nature of the chart allows other areas of use as well. The chart itself contains and provides clues to help the student remember some of the answers. This section is worth twenty points, two points per item, and should take only about five minutes.

The third section is the main idea statement. This section presents short passages from some of the poems. The student needs to recognize the poem and tell what main idea is expressed by the passage. There are seven passages presented, and the student is responsible for choosing and completing five. Each answer is worth four points for a total of twenty for the section. This section should take about ten to fifteen minutes.

The last part of the test has the student prepare a short essay in response to directions. The student has a choice of two activities. One is a cubing activity and the other involves the keys to poetry. I provide the students with the formats for both. The student is given a choice of three poems to write about. Only one will be done. I provide the student with a copy of the poems. This section requires more time and effort than the others and is worth forty points. I tell the students that this item will require more time, and that they should plan accordingly. I instruct my students to write down ideas or a short outline to help them organize their thoughts. I will be able to determine their understanding of the idea of the poem from the outlines even if they do not complete the entire essay.

I provide space on the test sheets for answers and the essay, and I also let the students use additional paper if they need it. The work done prior to the test provides my students with ample study material. If the students have worked on the poems and kept up with the assignments, they have little or no trouble with the test. I provide additional time outside of the class for my students who may need additional time to come in and complete the test. I am available for clarification of directions and test items. I discuss the test format before the day of the test to make sure that my students are not distracted from doing their best content work due to any items in the test situation. Taking these measures allows me to determine the level of comprehension of my students.

Test for Poetry Chapter

Part 1

Match the items in the first column to their corresponding item in the second column. Write the letter of the response next to the item in the first column.

Each item is worth two points. This section is worth twenty points. This section should only take approximately five to ten minutes of your time.

1. Optileast	*e*	a.	squander
2. fame	*f*	b.	hair
3. troubled woman	*h*	c.	waste more time
4. sow	*c*	d.	dream
5. medicine	*b*	e.	cheerful beast
6. words	*a*	f.	frog
7. wild horse	*d*	g.	bigly mean
8. Pessimost	*g*	h.	autumn flower
9. nobody	*i*	ı.	banishment
10. heartbreak	*j*	j.	hoard

Part 2

Fill in the blanks on the jot chart. There are ten blanks to complete. Each answer is worth two points. This section of the test is worth twenty points. This section should not take you more than five to ten minutes.

Title	Author	Speaker	Mood	Theme	Devices
I'm Nobody! Who Are You?	Emily Dickenson		melancholy satirical		similes; somebody, frog structure constrasting stanzas
The Optileast and the Pessimost	Eve Merriam	author	mostly cheerful	people have different moods our moods change	
Medicine	Alice Walker		loving caring	medicine does not always come in a bottle love is important	
Troubled Woman	Langston Hughes	author			simile: woman, autumn flowers imagery dark, gray autumn
Driving to Town to Mail a Letter	Robert Bly	author		you can find peace in unusual places also in yourself	imagery: quiet, snowy night assonance: repeated vowel "o"
Words	Pauli Murray	author	displeased but hopeful	people use some words too quickly and others not enough	
Ride a Wild Horse	Hannah Kahn	author	confident adventurous		imagery: wild horse structure: no planning, irregular

Title	Author	Speaker	Mood	Theme	Devices
I'm Nobody! Who Are You?	Emily Dickenson	A nobody person	melancholy satirical	fame, publicity can be overrated being unknown can be just fine	similes; somebody, frog structure constrasting stanzas
The Optileast and the Pessimost	Eve Merriam	author	mostly cheerful	people have different moods our moods change	sound rhyme
Medicine	Alice Walker	granddaughter	loving caring	medicine does not always come in a bottle love is important	shape: unabraided hair lack of punctuation
Troubled Woman	Langston Hughes	author	sad despairing	pain can affect the way we are despair can take away your spirit	simile: woman, autumn flowers imagery dark, gray autumn
Driving to Town to Mail a Letter	Robert Bly	author	peaceful emphasizes solitude	you can find peace in unusual places also in yourself	imagery: quiet, snowy night assonance: repeated vowel "o"
Words	Pauli Murray	author	displeased but hopeful	people use some words too quickly and others not enough	simile: word, pennies personification of words
Ride a Wild Horse	Hannah Kahn	author	confident adventurous	we should have dreams and go after at least one of them	imagery: wild horse structure: no planning, irregular

Part 3

This section contains seven passages from poems we have studied. You are to choose *five* of the passages and write underneath the passage what you think is the main idea expressed by the passage. Each answer is worth four points. This section is worth twenty points. This section should take approximately ten to fifteen minutes.

1. Queer as can be, although they're not kin.
   They dwell within the very same skin.

   from "The Optileast and the Pessimost."
   People have different moods.
   and their moods change quickly.
   If one mood is showing, another is
   waiting to pop up and take its place.

2. The medicine is all in her long unbraided hair.

   "Medicine"
   Medicine, what helps you feel better, does not
   always come from a doctor.
   the love of another person may be as
   necessary as regular medicine.

3. There is a privacy I love in this snowy night.
   Driving around, I will waste more time.

   "Driving to Town to Mail a Letter"
   You can find peace and happiness in
   solitude and may waste time to
   remain in the mood.

4. This troubled woman bowed by weariness and pain
   Like an autumn flower...

   "Troubled Woman"
   A woman (or person) troubled by years of
   misery, pain or despair is like an autumn flower.
   The environment is dark and dreary and
   she is withered and unable to embrace life.

5. But the slowly wrought words of love And the thunderous words of heartbreak—These we hoard.

"Words"
We often fail to speak the words of love and comfort as freely as we should.

6. Before you die, Whatever else you leave undone—
Ride a wild horse, Into the sun.

"Ride a Wild Horse"
Have a dream(s) and at least once do something to satisfy your dream.

7. How dreary to be somebody!
How public, like a frog.

"I'm Nobody! Who Are You?"
Being famous is like being a frog—you must stay out in public and croak your story to stay that way.

Part 4

In this section you will write an essay. Choose *one* of the three poems to write about. The choices are "Ride A Wild Horse," "The Optileast and the Pessimost," and "Medicine." The poems are attached.

Choose to *either* follow the key guide or the cubing guide. (Both guides are included.) Answer each section of the guide. Use your answer to write a short essay on the theme of the poem.

Your essay should have a minimum of three paragraphs. Be sure to include the title and author of the poem, the theme expressed in your own words, how the author establishes the theme (literal and interpretive reading), an applied association (either to your life or the world in general), and a conclusion.

This section is worth forty points and should take about thirty minutes. If you do not finish in class, you may come back after school to complete the essay. I will also consider your answers to the guide items in determining your comprehension.

6 Keys to Unlocking a Poem

1. Read Title

The first step in unlocking a poem is in the title. Read the title. Make associations between the title and your own life. What kind of mood does the title put you in? What do you anticipate the poem will be about? What does the title make you think of?

2. Overview the Poem

Read the entire poem over to yourself. Get a feel for the overall feeling the poem gives you. Does the poem present any type of picture to you? How does the poem affect you? How does it make you feel?

3. Associate

Associate your overview feelings to the title. What does the poem say about the title? What does the title have in relation to the poem?

4. Hunt

Reread the poem looking for key words or phrases that express or intensify the feeling the poem gave you. What are the literal meanings of the words or phrases?

5. Interpret

How does the author use the phrases found in number 4 to establish his or her theme? What interpretive or symbolic meaning do the words or phrases have?

6. Unlock Yourself

Think of other things that could bring up the same mood. What type of things could cause you to be in that mood? Try to think of experiences that you have had that are similar to the ideas of the poem.

Guide to Cubing

Follow the steps in order in relation to the poem.

1. Describe: Describe the main idea of the poem. What do you think the author is trying to say?

2. Compare: Does this idea remind you of any similar idea or issues? Does the author provide any other issues or ideas for comparisons?

3. Associate: Associate the idea to your life. What does it make you think of? What kind of feeling does it give you? Does it make you think of any specific incidents in your life?

4. Analyze: What are the points the author makes? How does the author establish or reinforce his or her ideas? Look for examples in the poem.

5. Apply: Apply this idea to your world. How is it relevant in today's society? Does the poem have meaning for today's reader?

6. Argue: Tell how the idea can be used in life. Either support the author's idea or argue against its relevance. What importance does the idea have?

What I Look for in the Essay

General:

Composition technique as it would be discussed in class. This includes grammar, spelling, syntax, word choice, and clarity. The students will have already been over (several times) the composition evaluation format.

Each essay should have an introduction which gives the title and author, and the theme. The body should reflect how the theme is established through both literal and interpretive means.

There should also be an applied section showing associations the student has made. The essay should also have a conclusion that ties the essay together.

"Ride A Wild Horse"

Theme: We should all, at some time, break free of our routine, safe world, and work to follow a dream or reach a special goal.

Literal: Colored horse: not the usual type ride across the sky into the sun: not something that can really be done. Not normal way of thinking.

Interpretive: We should break free of the normalness of our worlds. We should risk trying something we think can't be done. We should try to reach a dream or goal we may not ordinarily go after.

Applied: Mention a personal goal or dream and why it is a "wild horse."

"The Optileast and the Pessimost"

Theme: People are different and have different moods. A variety of items can change or trigger moods. Our moods can change rapidly.

Literal: Two types of "mood-beasts" live inside each person. They are not active together but work to complement each other. One is cheerful and the other is more serious or, at times, sad.

Interpretive: Each beast is a mood or feeling. Although two are shown for contrast, people possess the ability to experience many moods. These moods change often and may be triggered by almost anything.

Applied: Mention a time when the student has been generally happy but maybe one thing was bothering him or her (or vice-versa).

"Medicine"

Theme: Medicine, that which heals, is not always from a doctor. Sometimes love is the best medicine.

Literal: Grandma wakes to give grandpa the medicine. She is old and withered, with long, unbraided hair.

Interpretive: Waking and bringing the grandfather his needed "medical" medicine is an act of love performed by the grandmother. The love is also a medicine in that it helps the grandfather feel better. The long hair and the word "withered" present a picture of an aged woman. The two have probably been together for quite a long time. The love has had a chance to grow deep and strong. This strength can also be medicinal.

Applied: The student should associate a time when someone provided a loving act or gesture to help him or her feel better, or perhaps a time he or she has done this for someone else.

Activity Contributors

PAR Diagram, p. 21, Dawn Bubb, Walter Richards, Chesterfield County Schools

Bader Textbook Analysis Chart, pp. 82–83, Lois Bader, Michigan State University

Prior Knowledge Telegram, p. 86, Grace Hamlin, Surry County Schools

Science Clozure, p. 89, Carole Baughan, Goochland County Schools

Science Recognition Pretest, p. 93, *Three-level Guide*, p. 203, *Science Map*, p. 212, *Science Concept Map*, p. 302, Holly Corbett, Henrico County Schools

Art Self-inventory, p. 94, *Art Anticipation Guide*, p. 144, Joan Phipps, Richmond City Schools

Health Self-inventory, p. 94, *Health Analog*, p. 136, Kathy Feltus, Chesterfield County Schools

English Self-inventory, p. 95, *Graphic Organizer*, p. 140, *QAR Overview*, p. 219, Rebecca McSweeney

Math PreP, p. 96, Nancy Campbell, Hanover County Schools

Science What-I-Know, p. 97, *Science Crab Squares*, p. 381, Marcelle Mansfield, Henrico County Schools

Modified What-I-Know Sheet, p. 98, *Geometry Tradebooks*, pp. 507–508, Paula Mitchell, Henrico County Schools

Math Inventory of Skills, p. 101, Dana Walker, Hanover County Schools

Social Studies Inventory of Skills, p. 104, Margaret McKenzie, Hanover County Schools

Music Anticipation Guide, p. 120, Todd Barnes, Northumberland County Schools

Math Multiple Text, p. 127, *Math Graphic Organizer*, pp. 138, 407, Frances Reid, King William County Schools

Social Studies Graphic Organizer, p. 139, Charles Sicola, Hanover County Schools

Science Graphic Organizer, p. 141, *Science Prewriting*, pp. 188–189, Kathryn Davis, The Riverside School

Social Studies Anticipation Guide, p. 142, Helen Lipscomb, Henrico County Schools

Social Studies Anticipation Guide, p. 143, Diana Gordon, Goochland County Schools

English Anticipation Guide, p. 145, Robert Witherow, Hopewell City Schools

Anticipation Guide Acrostic, p. 144, *English Jot Chart*, p. 230, Linda Cobb, Richmond City Schools

Math Cubing, p. 165, Debbie Prout, Henrico County Schools

Social Studies Flat Cube, p. 167, Mary Jane McKay, Hopewell City Schools

Social Studies Factstorming, p. 173, Helen Byrd, Chesterfield County Schools

Social Studies DRTA, p. 174, Faye Freeman, Virginia Beach Public Schools

English DRTA, p. 177, *English Guided Writing*, p. 233, Frances Lively, Henrico County Schools

Math Anticipation Guide, p. 180, Dawn Bubb, Chesterfield County Schools

English Clue Game, pp. 182–183, *English Map*, p. 211, Vicki Ford, Henrico County Schools

Social Studies Clue Game, pp. 184–185, Debra Sims Fleischer, Henrico County Schools

Home Economics Three-Level Guide, p. 206, Ava Brendle

Social Studies Pattern Guide, p. 208, Vicki Douglas, Henrico County Schools

Math QAR, pp. 220–221, Mary Frances Siewert, Henrico County Schools

Math Top It Off, p. 228, Connie Bachman, Henrico County Schools

Modified Bio Poem, p. 229, M.J. Weatherford, Henrico County Schools

Home Economics Jot Chart, p. 231, Lila Mait, Hanover County Schools

Science What-I-Learned, p. 229, Anne Miller, Goochland County Schools

Cause-Effect Study Guide, p. 261, Linda Love, Virginia Beach Public Schools

Homework Activities for Kindergarten, pp. 278–279, Georgette Cavanaugh, Norfolk Public Schools

Study Skills Survey, p. 284, Cornelia Hill, West Point Schools

Cause-Effect Pattern Guide, p. 293, Patricia Mays Mulherin, Chesterfield County Schools

Note-taking Guide, p. 301, Janice Stuhlmann, Norfolk City Schools

ELM'S Classification System, pp. 303–306, Ellen Miller, Retired assistant professor, Old Dominion University

Political Cartoon, p. 310, Roberto Lianez, Norview High School, Norfolk

Social Studies Concept Map, p. 367, Diane Buchanan, Norfolk City Schools

French Magic Square, p. 381, Billie Anne Baker, Henrico County Schools

Social Studies Cinquains, p. 383, Anne Forrester, Chesapeake City Schools

Biology and English Cinquains, p. 384, Sharon Sidone, Virginia Beach City Schools

Social Studies Bingo, pp. 384–385, Patricia Russell, Department of Defense (DOD) Schools

Homework Comprehension Sheet, p. 397, Charles Carroll, Chesterfield County Schools

Comments About Tests, pp. 401–402, Jane Baxter, Linda Vess, Chesterfield County Schools, Julie Givler, Hanover County Schools

Social Studies Graphic Organizer, p. 409, Sandra Zeller, Brenda Winston, Henrico County Schools

Remarks, pp. 453–455, Brain Kane, Chesterfield County Schools

Social Studies Unit, pp. 456-466, Barbara Teuscher, Virginia Beach Public Schools

PAR Chapter Analysis, pp. 467–483, Bonnie McLaughlin, Hanover County Schools

Resources on Critical Thinking, pp. 493–495, Gloria Barber, Jane Koontz, Virginia State Department of Education

Primary Science Tradebooks, pp. 501–507, Sara Gallant, Henrico County Schools

History Tradebooks, pp. 507–517, Sue Jewell

Hamlet Puzzle, p. 522, Linda Tabor

Poetry Test, pp. 523–532, Meredith Randall

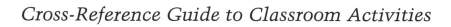

Cross-Reference Guide to Classroom Activities

Grade Level	Science	Math
Primary	PAR Example (pp. 27–29) Activity 3.8 What-I-Know Sheet (p. 97) Activity 4.12 Anticipation Guide (p. 143) Activity 5.6 Jot Chart (p. 186) Activity 5.9 Prewriting (pp. 188–89) Figure 10.13 Magic Squares (p. 381) Figure 12.1 Listening (p. 432) Figure 12.5 Concept Formation (p. 446) PAR Approach to Tradebooks (pp. 501–7)	Activity 3.10 Wiebe-Cox Inventory (p. 100) Activity 5.1 Cubing (p. 165)
Intermediate	Gator Example (pp. 60–61) Activity 4.1 Graphic Organizer (p. 141) Cubing (p. 164) Figure 8.2 Student Log (p. 280) Figure 10.1 Three-Level Guide (p. 356) Table 10.1 Classification Exercise (p. 358) Figures 10.4, 10.5 Graphic Organizer (pp. 362–63) Figure 10.8 Map (p. 366)	Activity 3.7 PreP (p. 96) Activity 4.4 Math Preview (p. 133) Activity 7.3 Decision-Making Model (p. 255) Figure 10.12 Post-graphic Organizer (p. 377) Geometry Tradebooks (pp. 517–21)
Middle	Example of Affective Questions (p. 58) Activity 3.1 Clozure (pp. 90–91) Activity 3.3 Recognition Activity (p. 93) Activity 6.2 Three-Level Guide (pp. 203–4) Activity 6.3 Map (p. 212) What I Learned (p. 229) Figure 8.7 Concept Map (p. 302) Figure 10.10 Network Diagram (p. 368)	Example of Math Book Inventory (p. 101) Activity 5.5 Anticipation Guide (p. 180) Activity 6.12 QAR (pp. 220–21) Top It Off! (p. 228) Writing Activity (p. 439)

High School	Activity 4.15 Preguiding Questions (p. 146)
	Activity 6.11 Mapping (p. 215)
	Activity 7.7 Cause-Effect Guide (p. 260)
	Figure 10.6 Graphic Organizer (p. 364)
	Biology Analogies (p. 379)
	Figure 12.4 Word Recognition Exercise
	  (p. 445)
		Activity 4.3 Multiple Text Example (p. 127)
		Activity 4.6 Graphic Organizer (p. 138)
		Activity 6.1 Three-Level Guide (p. 202)
		Activity 7.4 Consumer Math-Group Label
		  (p. 256)
		Activity 11.2 Geometry Overview (p. 407)

Social Studies	English/Language Arts	Other
Activity 4.10 Anticipation Guide (p. 142) Example of Factstorming (p. 173) Activity 6.6 Pattern Guide (p. 208) Activity 7.2 Propaganda (p. 252) Activity 11.3 Graphic Organizer (p. 409) Social Studies Unit (pp. 456–66)		**Health** Activity 3.5 Self-Inventory (p. 94) Activity 4.5 Analogy (p. 136)
Activity 3.12 Maze (p. 92) Activity 3.12 Chapter Inventory (p. 104) Activity 4.11 Anticipation Guide (p. 143) Comprehension Levels (p. 166) Biopoem (p. 229) Activity 7.2 Evaluating Consequences (p. 252) Figure 8.6 Note Taking (p. 301) Chunking (p. 336) Activity 11.1 Homework Comprehension (p. 397) Writing Activity (p. 440) Social Studies Unit (pp. 456–66)	Activity 3.11 Textbook Treasure Hunt (p. 102) Clozed Parts of Speech (p. 127) Activity 7.1 Fact-Opinion Guide (p. 251) Activity 7.6 Cause-Effect Story Guide (p. 259) Figures 9.2, 9.3 Narrative Story Guides (pp. 326–27)	**Music** Activity 4.1 Anticipation Guide (p. 120) Music Text Checklist (pp. 488–89)
Activity 5.3 DRTA (pp. 175–76) Activity 5.7 Mystery Clue Game (pp. 184–85) Cinquains (p. 382) Figure 8.3 Training Outline (p. 285) Outlining (p. 292) Figure 8.5 Cause-Effect Guide (p. 293) Figures 8.12, 8.13 Map Reading (pp. 311, 313) Figure 10.9 Concept Map (p. 367) Vocabulary Bingo (pp. 384–85) Social Studies Tradebooks (pp. 507–17)	Example of Affective Questions (p. 60) Activity 3.6 Self-Inventory (p. 95) Activity 5.4 DRTA (p. 177) Activity 6.15 Guided Writing Procedure (p. 233) Activity 7.8 Cause-Effect Guide (p. 261) Cinquains (p. 382) English Text Checklist (pp. 484–85) Poetry Test (pp. 523–32)	**Art** Activity 3.4 Self-Inventory (p. 94) Activity 4.13 Anticipation Guide (p. 144)
PAR Example (pp. 22–26) Analogy (p. 134) Activity 4.7 Graphic Organizer (p. 139) Activity 5.2 Flat Cube (p. 167) Activity 6.5 Three-Level Guide (p. 207) Activity 6.9 Overlap Map (p. 213) Activity 7.14 TRIP (p. 268) Table 8.5 REST Notetaking (p. 298) List-Group-Label (p. 376) Figure 10.11 Crossword (p. 377) Figure 12.6 Concept Formation (p. 447) Social Studies Text Checklist (pp. 486–87)	Activity 3.6 Self-Inventory (p. 95) Activity 4.2 Rewrite (p. 124) Activity 4.8 Graphic Organizer (p. 140) Activity 4.14 Anticipation Guide (p. 145) Activity 5.6 Mystery Clue Game (pp. 182–3) Activity 6.3 Three-Level Guide (p. 205) Activity 6.7 Map (p. 211) Activity 6.13 Jot Chart (p. 230) Figure 8.8 Library Exercise (p. 307) Figure 9.6 Anticipation Guide (p. 329) Interactive Cloze (p. 374) Learning Log (p. 441) Hamlet Puzzle (p. 522)	**Latin** Activity 6.10 Overlap Map (p. 214) **French** Figure 10.14 Magic Square (p. 381) **Psychology** Interactive Cloze (p. 374) **Home Economics** Activity 6.4 Three-Level Guide (p. 206) Activity 6.14 Jot Chart (p. 231)

Index